STREET ATLAS
Edinburgh
and East Central Scotland

Contents

III Key to map symbols

IV-V Key to map pages

VI-VII Route planning

VIII Administrative and post code boundaries

1 Street maps

232 Extra-large-scale map of Edinburgh town centre

234 Index of hospitals, industrial estates, railway stations, schools, shopping centres, street names and universities

PHILIP'S

First edition published 1995
First colour edition published 1999 by

Ordnance Survey® and	George Philip Ltd., a division of
Romsey Road	Octopus Publishing Group Ltd
Maybush	2-4 Heron Quays
Southampton	London
SO16 4GU	E14 4JB

ISBN 0-540-07656-2 (pocket)

**The mapping between pages 1 and 233 (inclusive) in this
atlas is derived from Ordnance Survey® OSCAR® and Land-
Line® data and Landranger® mapping.**

Ordnance Survey, OSCAR, Land-line and Landranger are
registered trade marks of Ordnance Survey, the national
mapping agency of Great Britain.

Printed and bound in Spain by Cayfosa

Digital Data

The exceptionally high-quality
mapping found in this book is
available as digital data in TIFF
format, which is easily convertible
to other bit-mapped (raster) image
formats.

The index is also available in digital
form as a standard database table.
It contains all the details found in
the printed index together with the
National Grid reference for the map
square in which each entry is
named and feature codes for places
of interest in eight categories such
as education and health.

For further information and to
discuss your requirements, please
contact the Ordnance Survey
Solutions Centre on 01703 792929.

Motorway (with junction number)	**Railway station** Walsall
Primary route (dual carriageway and single)	**Glasgow Underground station**
A road (dual carriageway and single)	**Midland Metro**
B road (dual carriageway and single)	**Metrolink station**
Minor road (dual carriageway and single)	**London Underground station**
Other minor road (dual carriageway and single)	**Docklands Light Railway station**
Road under construction	**Tyne and Wear Metro**
Pedestrianised area	**Private railway station**
Postcode boundaries DY7	**Bus, coach station**
County and Unitary Authority boundaries	**Ambulance station**
Railway	**Coastguard station**
Tramway, miniature railway	**Fire station**
Rural track, private road or narrow road in urban area	**Police station**
Gate or obstruction to traffic (restrictions may not apply at all times or to all vehicles)	**Accident and Emergency entrance to hospital**
Path, bridleway, byway open to all traffic, road used as a public path	**Hospital**
The representation in this atlas of a road, track or path is no evidence of the existence of a right of way	**Church, place of worship**
Adjoining page indicators	**Information Centre** (open all year)
	Parking, Park and Ride P P&R
	Post Office PO
The map area within the pink band is shown at a larger scale on the page indicated by the red block and arrow	**Important buildings, schools, colleges, universities and hospitals** Prim Sch
	Water name River Medway
	Stream

Acad	**Academy**	Meml	**Memorial**
Crem	**Crematorium**	Mon	**Monument**
Cemy	**Cemetery**	Mus	**Museum**
C Ctr	**Civic Centre**	Obsy	**Observatory**
CH	**Club House**	Pal	**Royal Palace**
Coll	**College**	PH	**Public House**
Ent	**Enterprise**	Recn Gd	**Recreation Ground**
Ex H	**Exhibition Hall**	Resr	**Reservoir**
Ind Est	**Industrial Estate**	Ret Pk	**Retail Park**
Inst	**Institute**	Sch	**School**
Ct	**Law Court**	Sh Ctr	**Shopping Centre**
L Ctr	**Leisure Centre**	TH	**Town Hall/House**
LC	**Level Crossing**	Trad Est	**Trading Estate**
Liby	**Library**	Univ	**University**
Mkt	**Market**	YH	**Youth Hostel**

River or canal (minor and major)
Water
Tidal water
Woods
Houses
Non-Roman antiquity *House*
Roman antiquity VILLA

■ The dark grey border on the inside edge of some pages indicates that the mapping does not continue onto the adjacent page ■ The small numbers around the edges of the maps identify the 1 kilometre National Grid lines

The scale of the maps is 3.92 cm to 1 km (2½ inches to 1 mile)

0   ¼   ½   ¾   1 mile
0 250m 500m 750m 1 kilometre

The scale of the maps on pages numbered in red is 7.84 cm to 1 km (5 inches to 1 mile)

0   220 yards   440 yards   660 yards   ½ mile
0 125m 250m 375m ½ kilometre

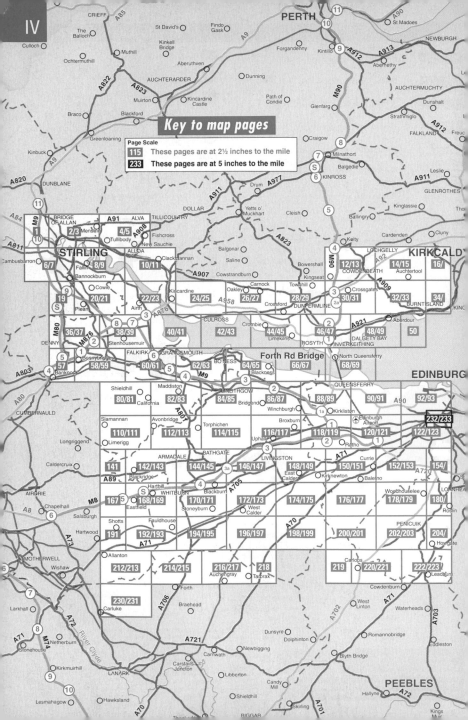

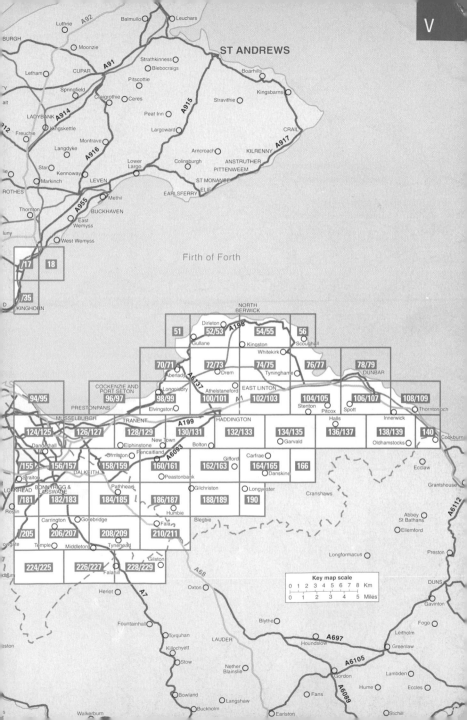

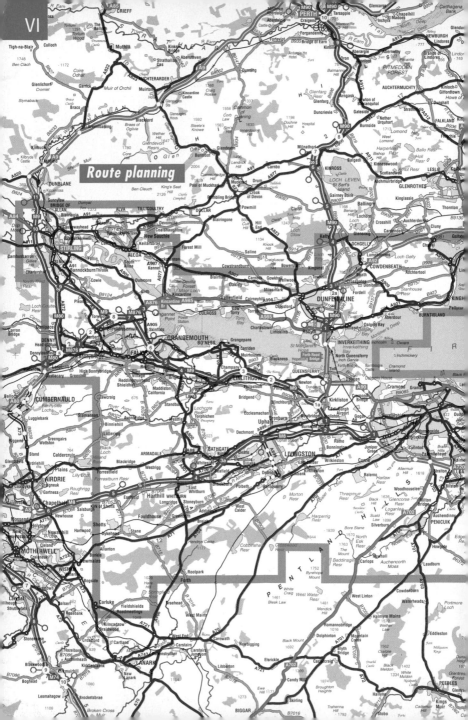

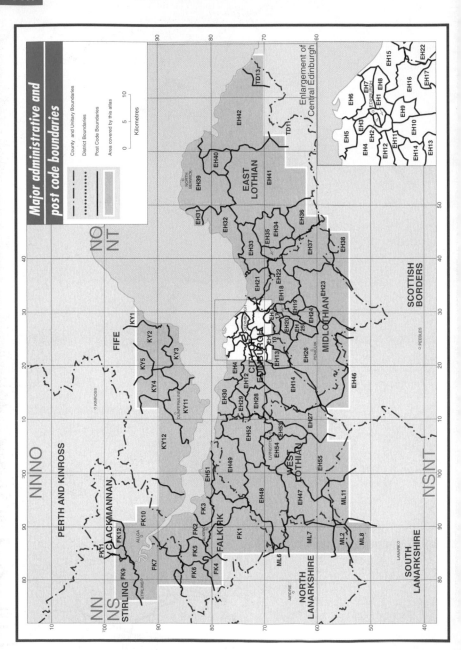

Major administrative and post code boundaries

County and Unitary Boundaries
District Boundaries
Post Code Boundaries
Area covered by this atlas

0   5   10
Kilometres

Enlargement of Central Edinburgh

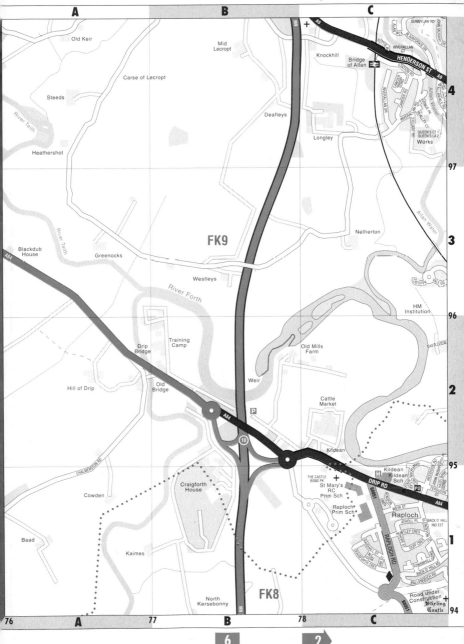

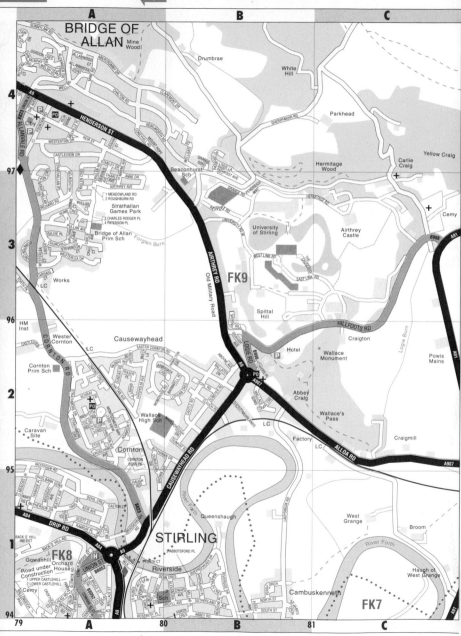

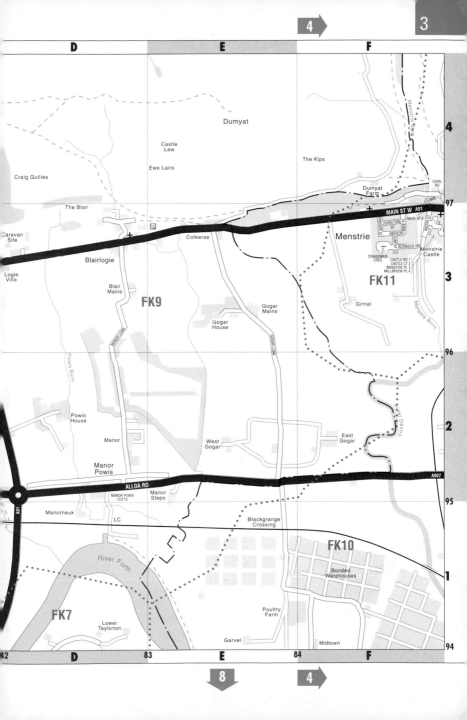

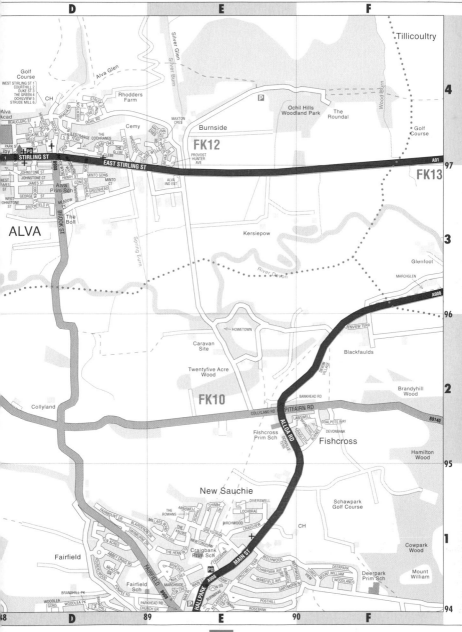

D   E   F

Tillicoultry

Golf Course

WEST STIRLING ST 1
COURTHILL 2
DUKE ST 3
THE GREEN 4
OCHILVIEW 5
STRUDE MILL 6

Alva Glen

Silver Glen

Silver Burn

Rhodders Farm

CH

P

Ochil Hills
Woodland Park

The Roundal

Wood Burn

4

Golf Course

Alva
Acad

Cemy

Burnside

MAXTON
CRES

FK12

PROVOST
HUNTER
AVE

STIRLING ST

EAST STIRLING ST

A91

97

FK13

Alva
Prim Sch

MINTO GDNS
MINTO CT

MEADOW

GREENHEAD

BROOK ST

The Bo'll

ALVA

Kersiepow

3

Glenfoot

MARCHGLEN

Spring Burn

River Devon

A908

96

HOWETOWN

Caravan Site

BENVIEW TERR

Blackfaulds

2

Twentyfive Acre Wood

FK10

Brandyhill Wood

Collyland

COLLYLAND RD

PITFAIRN RD

BANKHEAD RD

BROOK HILL SQ

ALLOA RD

B9140

LAWSWELL

COALPOTS WAY

DEVONBANK

Fishcross
Prim Sch

Hamilton
Wood

Fishcross

95

New Sauchie

DIVERSWELL

LOCHBRAE

Schawpark
Golf Course

CH

Cowpark
Wood

THE ROWANS

ARROWSWELL

CHINEW

BIRCHWOOD

CRAIGVIEW

FAIRMOUNT DR

BLAIRDENON RD

MILLARS WD

THE KNOWE

NEWTONSHAW

Craigbank
Prim Sch

MAIN ST

BEECHWOOD

DEERPARK

MOUNT WILLIAM

WOODLANDS

Deerpark
Prim Sch

Mount
William

Fairfield

ABBEY CRAIG RD

MEADOW
GR

FAIRFIELD

BRAEMAR
CRES

HALLPARK

A908

CHAMPARK AVE

MANSFIELD AVE

GARTMORN

POSTHILL

ROSEBANK

Fairfield
Sch

BRANSHILL PK

WOODLEA
GDNS

WOODLEA PK

PARKHEAD RD

CHURCH GR

SPROTWELL TER

P

P

D   E   F

88   89   90   94

1

FK9

FK8

River Forth

Falleninch

DUMBARTON RD

King's Knot

A811

King's Park Farm

4

Polrogan Bridge

Bankend

White House

South Kersebonny

Golf Course

CH

BALMORAL PL

QUEENS RD

B8051

Hollandbush

Hayford House

ST THOMAS'S WELL

Cemy

HOMESTEADS

King's Park

93

Johnny's Bridge

Hillhead

Raploch Burn

Dr BROOMHILL

DOUGLAS TERR

SNOWDON PLACE LA 1
SNOWDON PL 2

PARK PL

TOUCH RD

Cambusbarron

THOMSON PL

MAIN ST

PO

Liby

DALMORGLEN PK

Batterflatts

BATTERFLATS GDNS

Torbrex

3

Johnny's Burn

QUARRY RD

FINTRY TERR

CARSE DYKE DRES

THE YETTS

OLD DROVE RD

WOODSIDE

UNDERWOOD RD

Polmaise Farm

Kings Park

FK8

Gartur

Cambusbarron Prim Sch

WALLACE PL

ROSE TERR

PLEASANCE RD

SYCAMORE PL

BIRCH AVE

92

Cambusbarron Quarry

Murray's Wood

FK7

Gillies Hill

Polmaise Castle

Bearside

Coxet Hill

CULTENHOVE CRES

FK8

2

Touchadam Craig

Murrayshall Quarry

Fir Park

Haggs Wood

TOWN BURN

CULTENHOVE PL

GRAYSTALE RD

Castlehill

Murrayshall Farm

91

Graystale

Sauchie Craig

Moor Burn

Wallstale

Bannock Burn

1

Middlethird Wood

Chartershall House

Chartershall Farm

CHARTERSHALL RD

90

Cultenhove

76

A

77

B

78

C

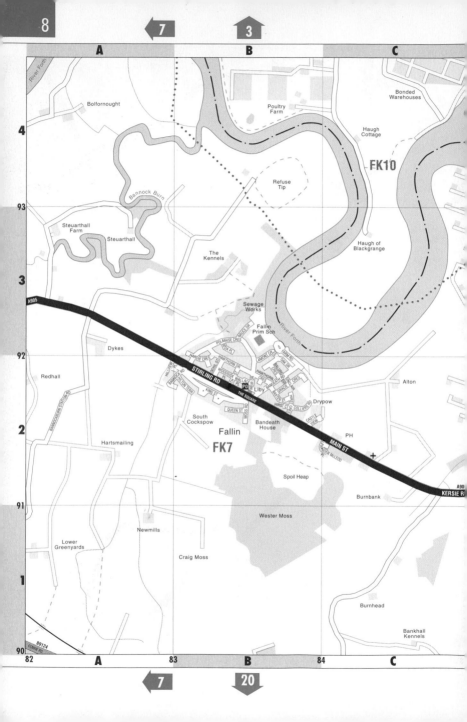

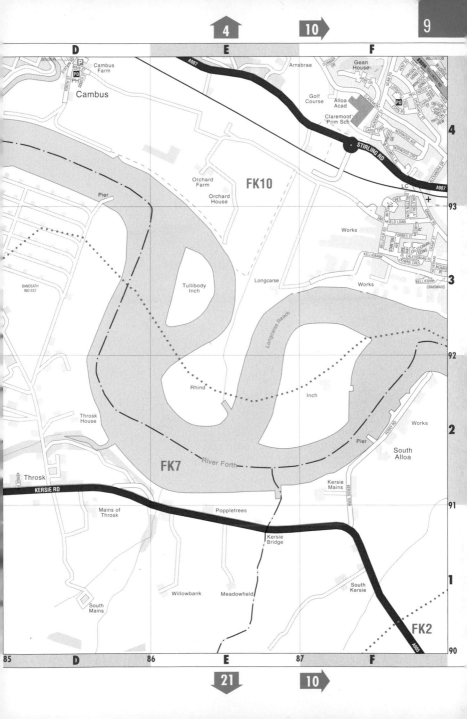

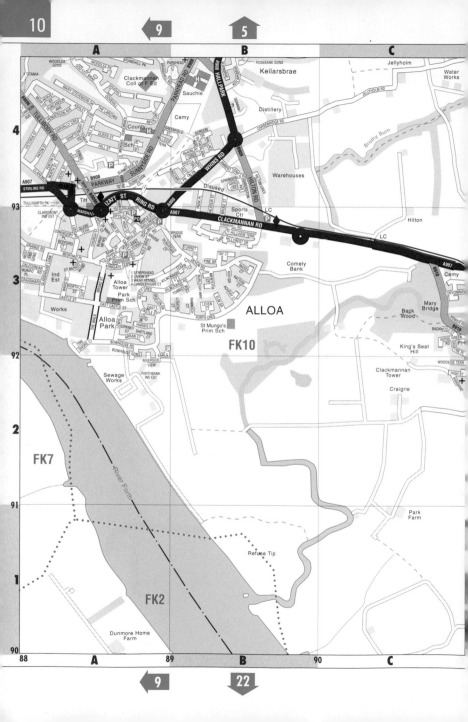

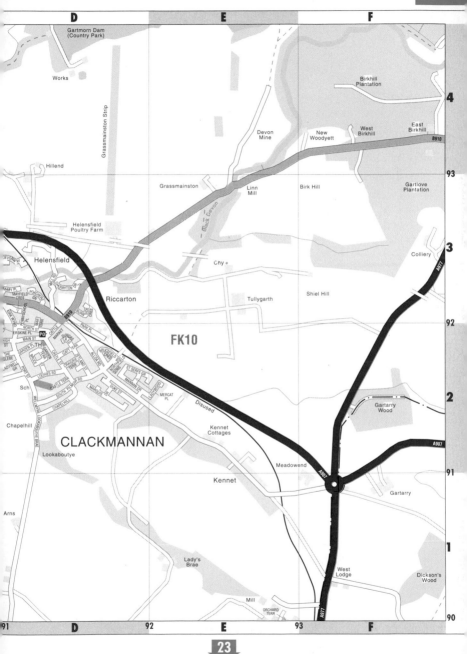

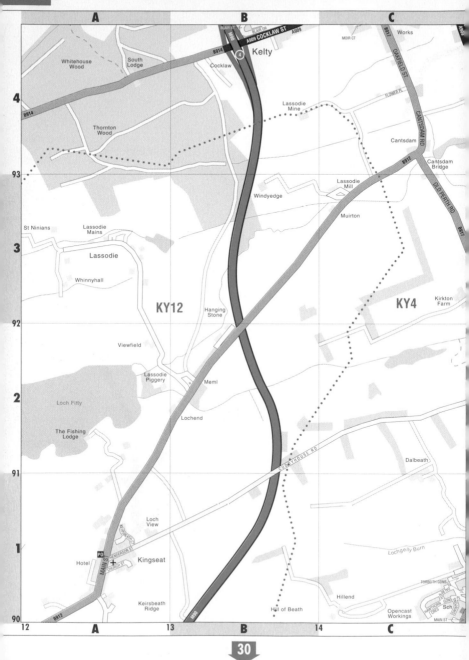

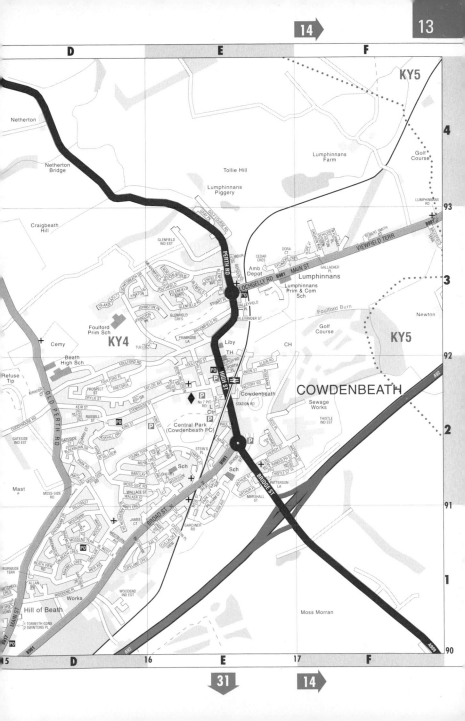

LOCHGELLY

1 FORRESTER CT
2 BOLAN SQ
3 DRYBURGH PL
4 KNOCKHILL CL
5 THE CROSS

Golf Course

CH

Sir James Black Gait

Drummond

Station Rd

Auchterderran Rd

B981

B9149

B920

Page St

Loughgelly Ind Pk

Works
Mast

Mast

A92

B9149

CH

Powguild

Lochend

Melgund Lodge

Westerton

Brucefield Terr

Dickson Ct

Lumphinnans Rd

B981

The Avenue

Mackenzie Cres

Watters Cres

KY5

Loch Gelly

Colvin's Knowe

Lochside Plantation

Little Raith

Easter Lochhead

Wester Lochhead

KY4

Dronachy Burn

Walton East Strip

Walton East Clump

KY2

Walton

Raith Hill

Chemical Works

Cemy

Manse

B925

B925

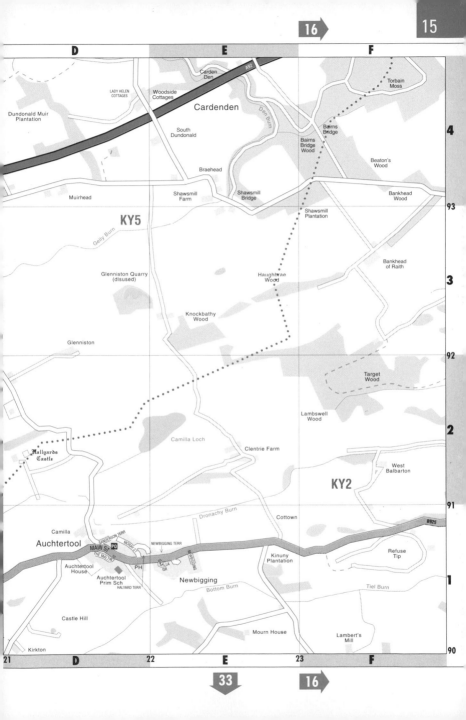

33

16 ▶

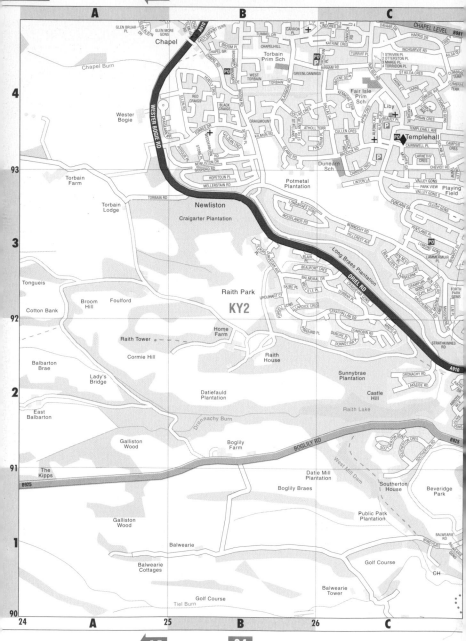

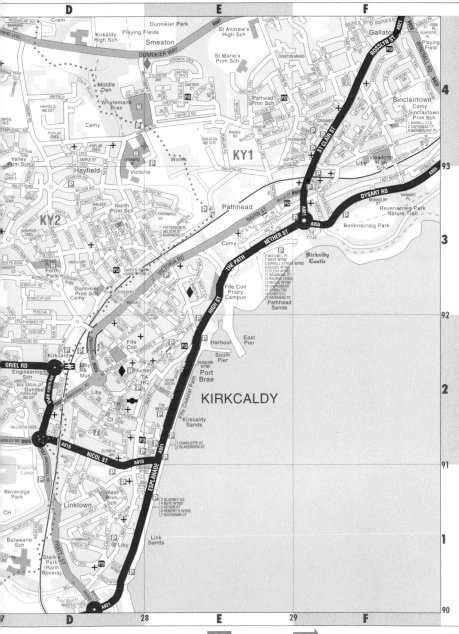

KIRKCALDY

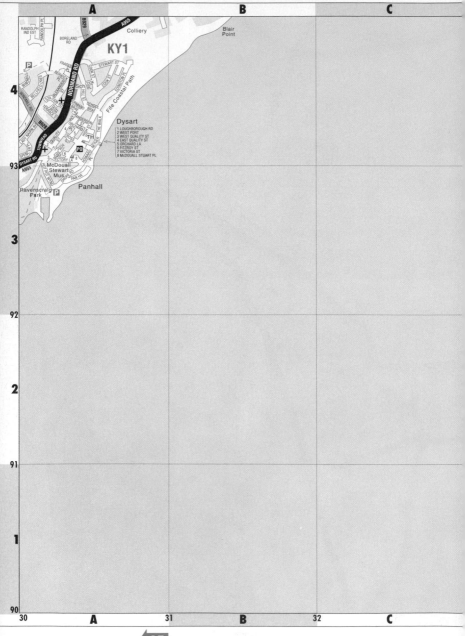

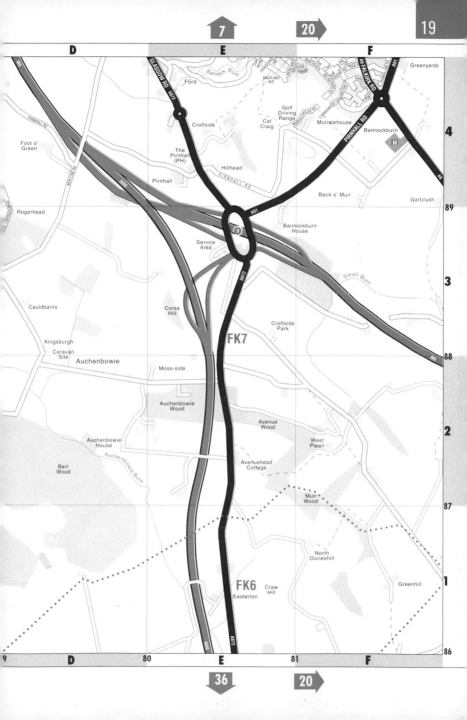

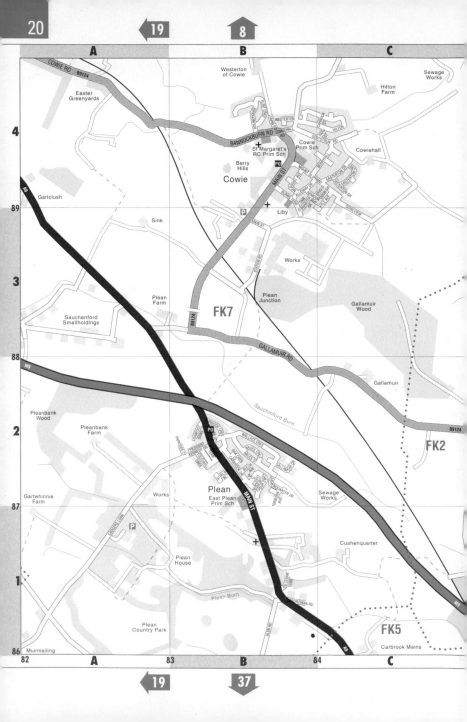

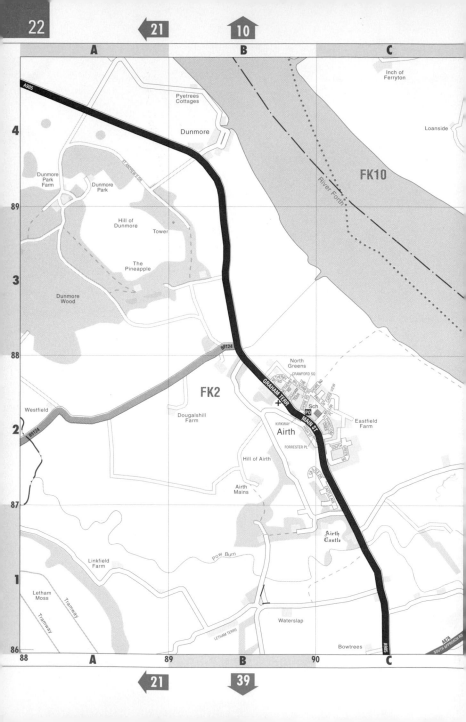

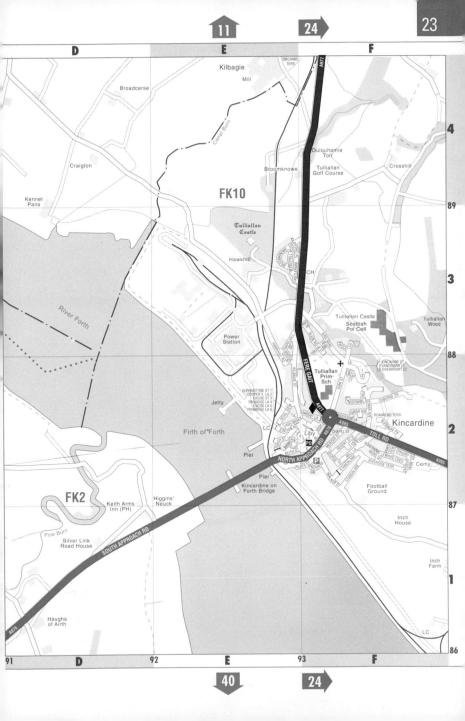

D
E
F

Kilbagie
Mill
ORCHARD TERR.
A977

Broadcarse

Canal Burn

Dulquhamie Toll

Craigton
Broomknowe
Tulliallan Golf Course
Crosshill

Kennet Pans
FK10
4

89

Tulliallan Castle

Hawkhill
CH

3

Tulliallan Castle
Tulliallan Wood

River Forth
Scottish Pol Coll

88

Power Station
FERE GAIT
Tulliallan Prim-Sch

1 KINCAIRNE CT
2 SANDEMAN CT
3 SIVEWRIGHT CT

Jetty
ELPHINSTONE ST 1
COOPER'S LA 2
EXCISE ST 3
PARADISE LA 4
EXCISE LA 5
PRIMROSE LA 6

Kincardine
TOLL RD

A985

Firth of Forth
WAR AVE
ROANHEAD TERR

LC
Libry
PO
Kincardine
2

Pier
CHAPEL ST
NORTH APPROACH RD
RIVERSIDE TERR
Cemy.

Pier
Kincardine on Forth Bridge
Football Ground

FK2
87

Keith Arms Inn (PH)
Higgins' Neuck
SOUTH APPROACH RD
Inch House

Pow Burn

Silver Link Road House
Inch Farm

1

Haughs of Airth
A876
LC

86

91
D
92
E
93
F

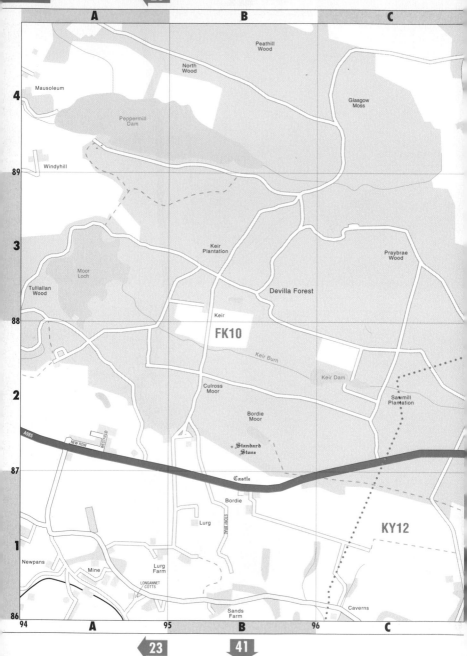

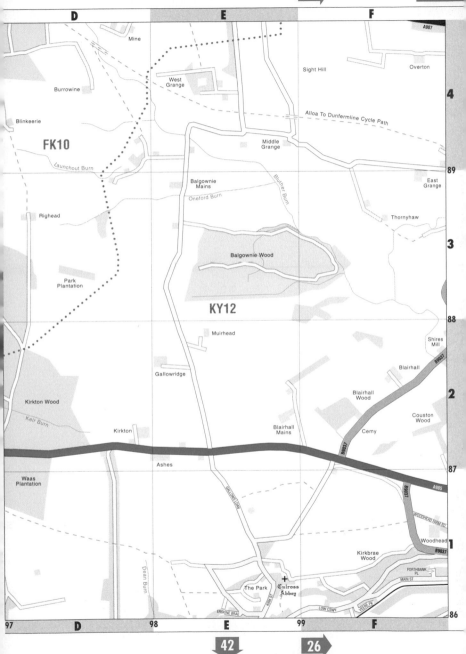

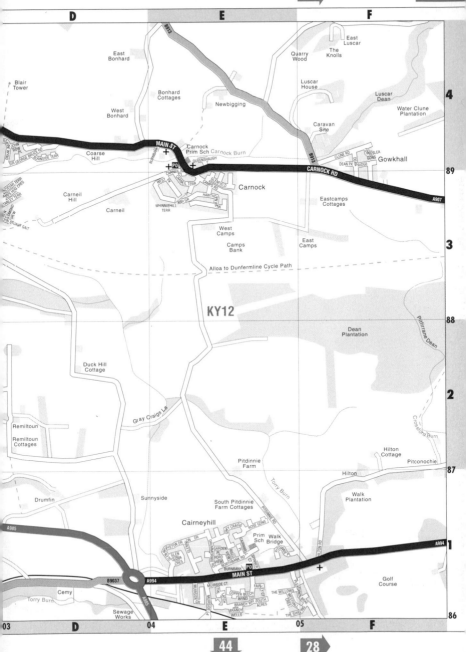

D
E
F

B973

East
Bonhard

Blair
Tower

Bonhard
Cottages

Newbigging

East
Luscar

The
Knolls

Quarry
Wood

Luscar
House

Luscar
Dean

Water Clune
Plantation

West
Bonhard

Caravan
Site

4

Coarse
Hill

MAIN ST

Carnock
Prim Sch Carnock Burn

CARNOCK RD

CLINE RD

CHESLEA
GDNS

Gowkhall

DEAN PK BRIDGE

89

QUEENSHAUGH

Carnock

A907

Carneil
Hill

WEST GR

CARNEIL TERR

ASH GR

GLENEIFFY

CAMBUS

HAWTHORN

PINE

Eastcamps
Cottages

Carneil

WHINNYHILL
TERR

West
Camps

Camps
Bank

East
Camps

3

Alloa to Dunfermline Cycle Path

KY12

88

Dean
Plantation

Pitfirrane Dean

Duck Hill
Cottage

2

Gray Craigs La

Crossford Burn

Remilton

Remilton
Cottages

Hilton
Cottage

Pitconochie

Pitdinnie
Farm

Hilton

87

Torry Burn

Walk
Plantation

Drumfin

Sunnyside

South Pitdinnie
Farm Cottages

PITDINNIE RD

A985

Cairneyhill

MORISTON DR

JADE DR

GLEN
VIEW

ST CRAIGS

ROSE GDNS

Prim
Sch

Walk
Bridge

A994

GARDEN

BURNBANK

SPINNERS

1

Cemy

B9037

MAIN ST

A994

PD

Golf
Course

Torry Burn

Sewage
Works

MUIRSIDE CT

COPPER BEECH

BRANDY
WELLS

FAIR...

THE WILLOWS

86

03
D
04
E
05
F

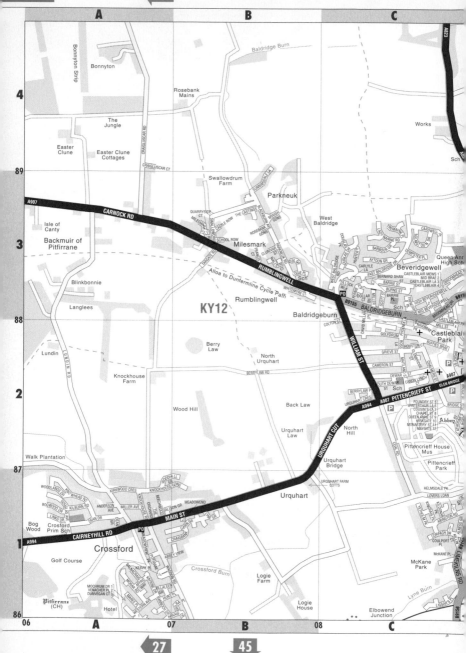

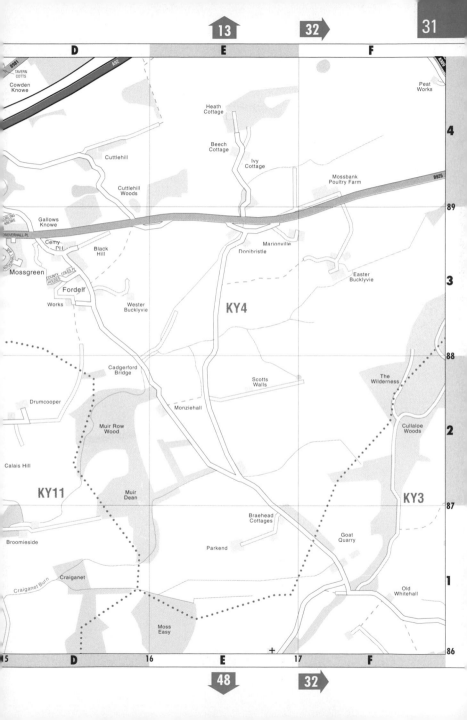

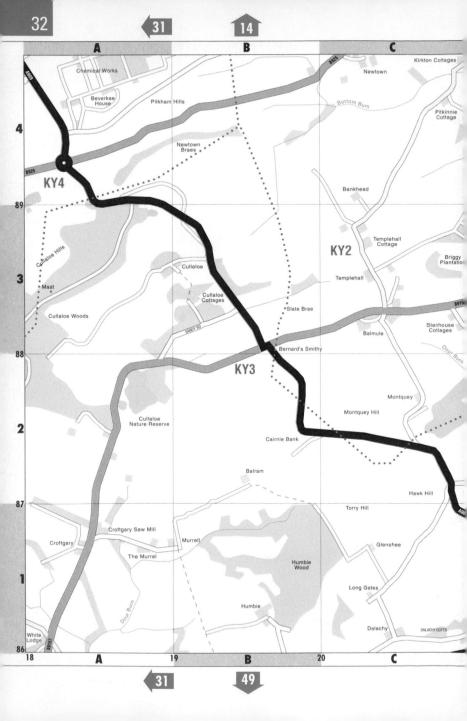

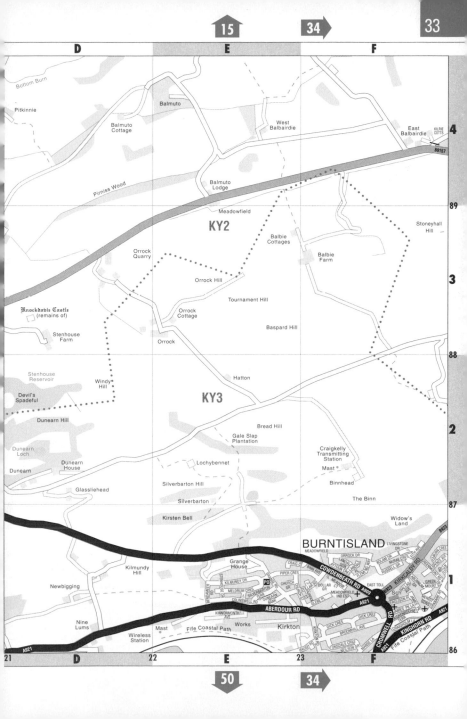

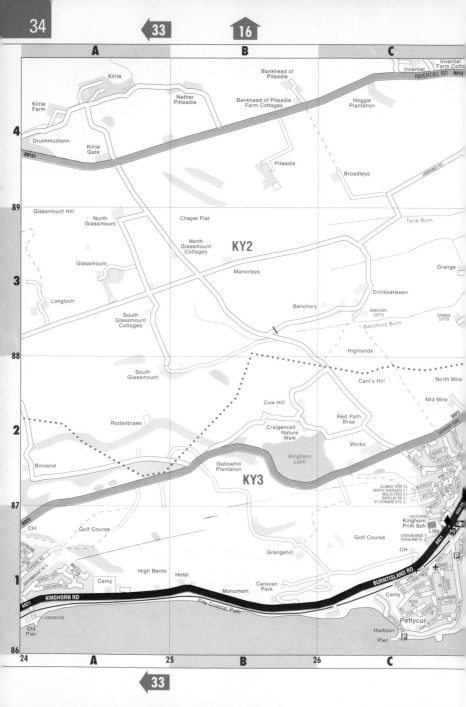

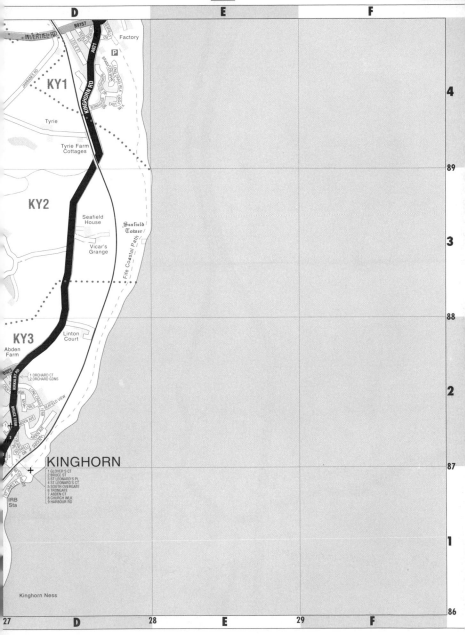

KY1

KY2

KY3

KINGHORN

Factory

Tyrie

Tyrie Farm
Cottages

Seafield
House

Vicar's
Grange

Seafield
Tower

Fife Coastal Path

Linton
Court

Abden
Farm

1 ORCHARD CT
2 ORCHARD GDNS

1 GLOVER'S CT
2 BRUCE ST
3 ST LEONARD'S PL
4 ST LEONARD'S CT
5 SOUTH OVERGATE
6 TRONGATE
7 ARDEN CT
8 CHURCH WLK
9 HARBOUR RD

IRB
Sta

Kinghorn Ness

INVERTIEL RD

KINGHORN RD

D   E   F

4

89

3

88

2

87

1

86

27   D   28   E   29   F

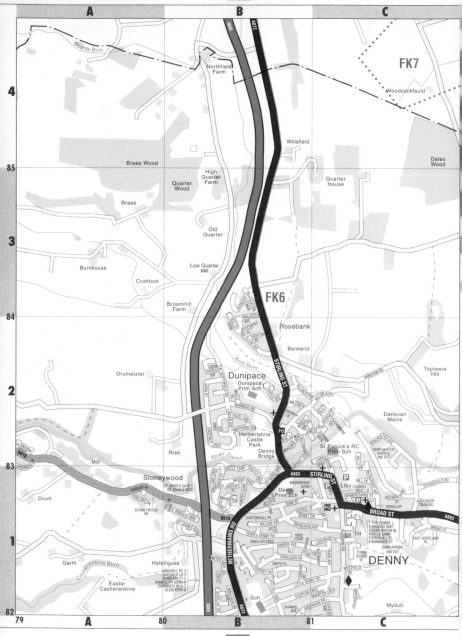

FK7

Woodcockfauld

Northfield Farm

Boards Burn

Willisfield

Braes Wood

Dales Wood

High Quarter Farm

Quarter Wood

Quarter House

Braes

Old Quarter

Burnhouse

Croftfoot

Low Quarter Mill

FK6

Broomhill Farm

Rosebank

Bankend

Drumelzier

Avon Burn

Dunipace

Dunipace Prim Sch

Toptowie Hill

BARNEGO RD

Denovan Mains

Risk

Herbertshire Castle Park

Denny Bridge

St Patrick's RC Prim Sch

WINCHESTER AVENUE IND EST

River Carron

STIRLING ST

Mill

Stoneywood

A883 STIRLING ST

Liby CHURCH

Gill PK

HERBER

Denny Prim Sch

BROOMPARK GDNS

HERBERTSHIRE ST

ANDERSON PARK RD

KIRKSLAP

Drum

ST JOHN'S GATE 1
ST JOHN'S GR 2

BROAD ST

A883

BROAD ST

TH

EAST BORELAND PL

STONEYWOOD PK

KNIGHTS WAY

B818 NETHERMAINS RD

CUSTONHALL PL

1 THE VENNEL
2 HARLAWS WAY
3 DUNCARRON PL
4 VILLA BANK
5 KIRKHALL PL
6 BANKSIDE CT

DUNCARRON IND EST

WILSON AVE

ST JOHN'S LANE

TEMPLE DENNY RD

ROSE TERR

DENNY

Garth

SINCLAIR CRES

SAWERS AVE

FERGUSON DR

WESTFIELD

Castlerankine Burn

Holehouse

LANGHILL PL 3
GARVALD LA 4
DUNCAN CT 5
RANDOLPH GDNS 6
CARNOCH WLK 7
GLEN TERR 8

GRANGE AVE

SMITH PL

Easter Castlerankine

Sch

OVERTON CRES

SHANKS AVE

Mydub

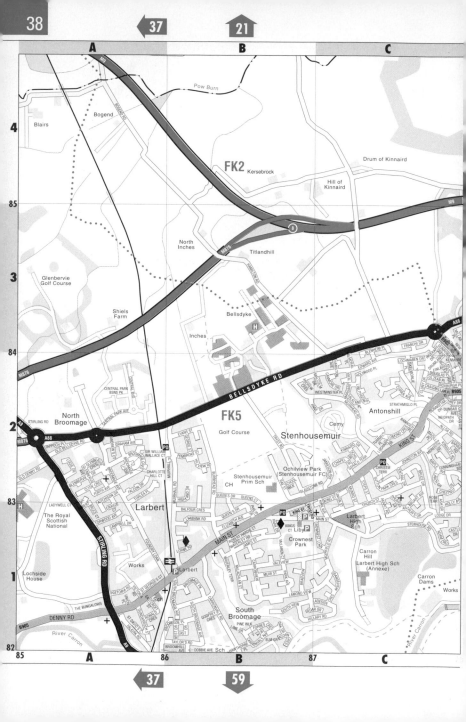

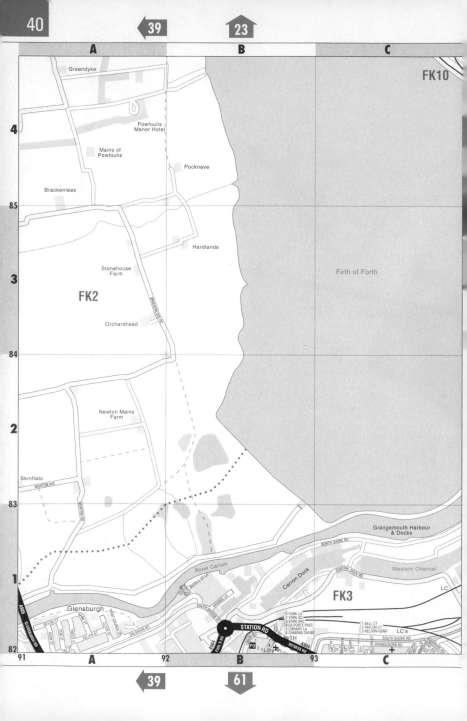

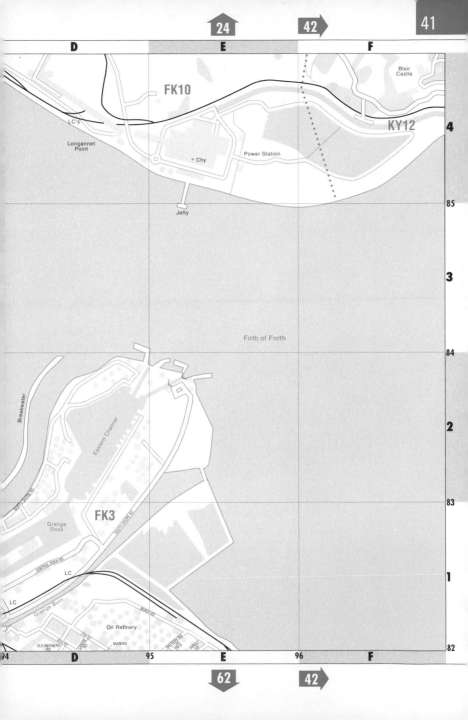

D
E
F

FK10

Blair
Castle

LC's

KY12

4

Longannet
Point

Chy

Power Station

85

Jetty

3

84

Firth of Forth

Breakwater

Eastern Channel

2

83

FK3

Grange
Dock

SOUTH DOCK RD

CENTRAL DOCK RD

LC

1

LC

Grange Burn

BEACH RD

82

Oil Refinery

OLD REFINERY
RD

MAIN RD

94

D

95

E

96

F

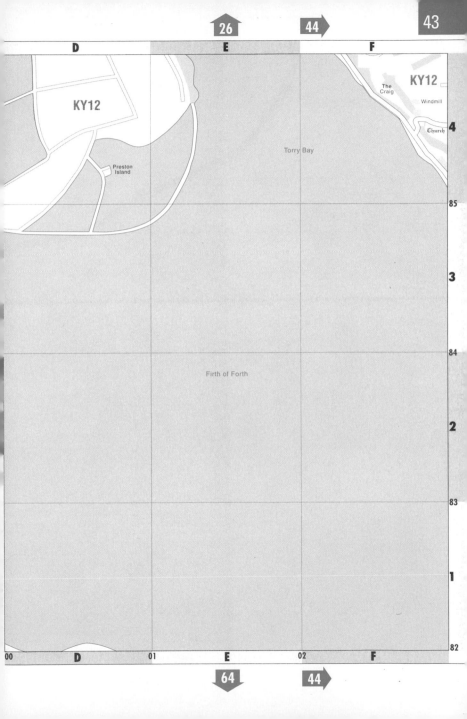

D

E

F

KY12

The
Craig

KY12

Windmill

4

Church

Torry Bay

Preston
Island

85

3

84

Firth of Forth

2

83

1

82

00

D

01

E

02

F

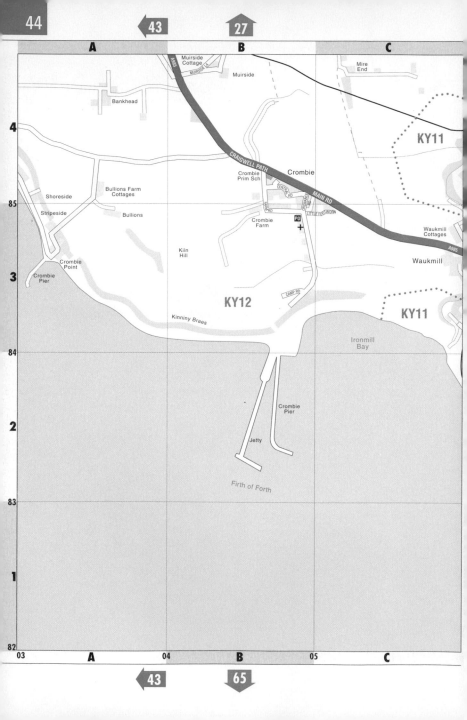

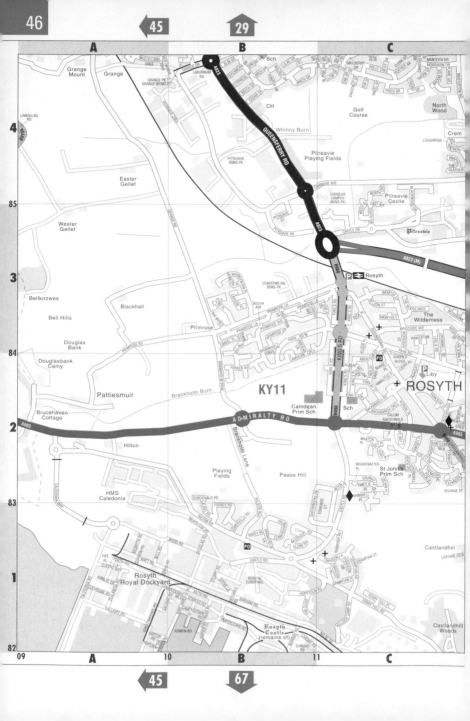

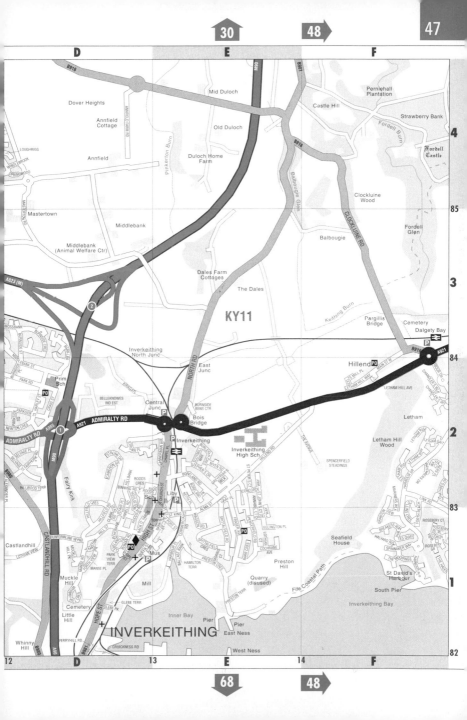

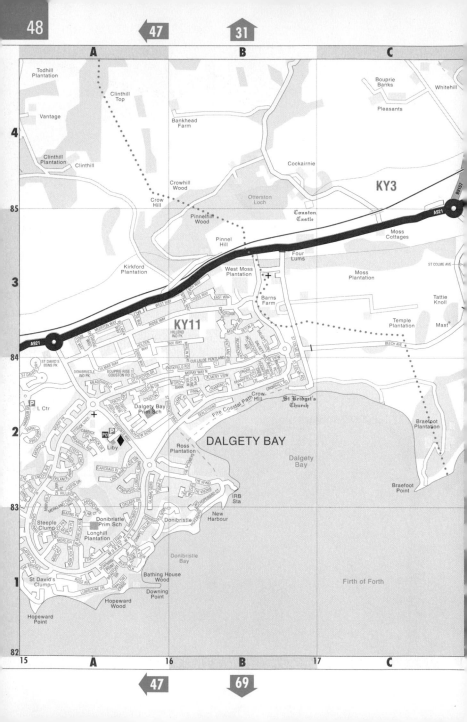

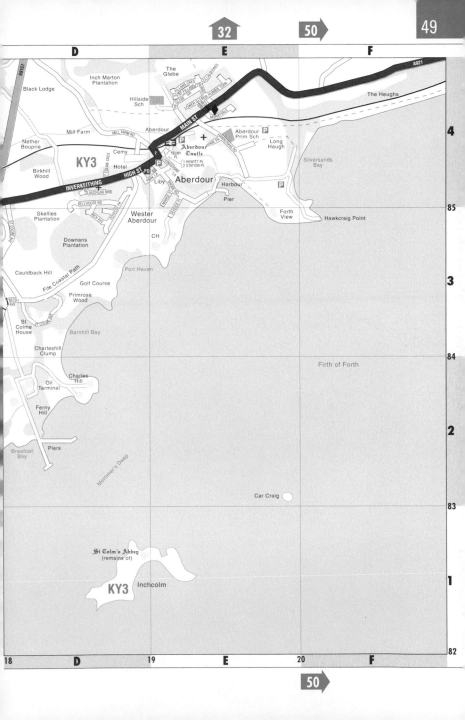

D
E
F

B9157

Black Lodge

Inch Marton
Plantation

The
Glebe

VILLARS CRES
ST FILLANS
PL
DR
M.O.CRES

A921

The Heughs

Hillside
Sch

LOWER DR
LUMSDAINE DR
HAWKCRAIG TERR

MONTVALE

MAIN ST

Mill Farm

MILL FARM RD

Aberdour

Aberdour
Prim Sch

P

Long
Haugh

4

Nether
Bouprie

KY3

Cemy

COLME CRES

Aberdour
Castle

P

HAWKCRAIG RD

Silversands
Bay

Birkhill
Wood

Hotel

HIGH ST

INVERKEITHING

2

TELNY
PL

MANSE LA
SHORE RD

PAGE

1 HEWITT PL
2 STATION PL

85

Skellies
Plantation

BELL HOUSE RD
INCH AVE
CORVINE
BLAUCHLAN RISE

P

Libv

Aberdour

MANSE ST
MAINS LA
TERRACE LA

Harbour

Pier

P

Forth
View

Hawkcraig Point

Downans
Plantation

Wester
Aberdour

CH

ST COLME AVE

Cauldback Hill

Fife Coastal Path

Port Haven

3

Golf Course

Primrose
Wood

ST COLME
AVE

ST COLME
DR

St
Colme
House

Barnhill Bay

Firth of Forth

84

Charleshill
Clump

Oil
Terminal

Charles
Hill

Ferny
Hill

2

Braefoot
Bay

Piers

Mortimer's Deep

Car Craig

83

St Colm's Abbey
(remains of)

KY3

Inchcolm

1

82

18
D
19
E
20
F

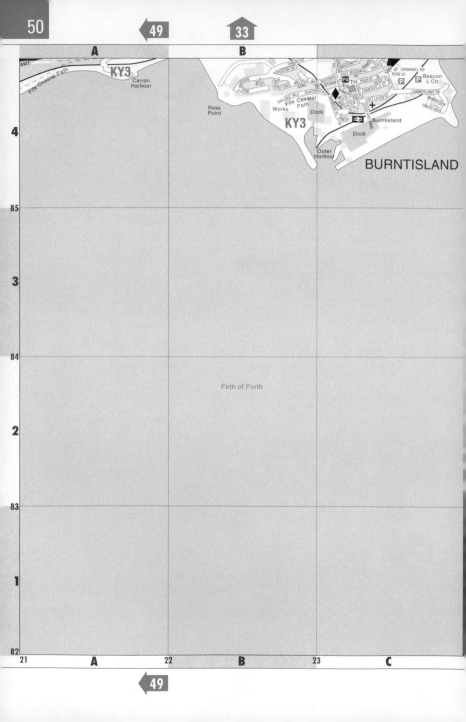

49
33

A　　　　　　**B**

A921

Fife Coastal Path

KY3

Carron
Harbour

Ross
Point

Fife Coastal
Path

Works

KY3

Dock

Outer
Harbour

Dock

TOLLGN RD
WINDOW OPT
WEST BROOMHILL
2ND CRES
MELVILLE
GDNS
RD
SYMAN
SEAFORTH A

SAILORS WLK

EAST BROOMHILL
EAST CRES
RD
RD
CROMWELL RD
ROSE ST
HIGH ST
SOMERVILLE ST
EAST LEVEN ST
WEST LEVEN ST
KIRKGATE
LAMMERLAWS RD
NORTH VIEW
SOUTH VIEW

PO
TH
Liby

P
P
Beacon
L Ctr

Burntisland

BURNTISLAND

Firth of Forth

4

85

3

84

2

83

1

82

21　　　　　**A**　　　　22　　　　**B**　　　　23　　　　**C**

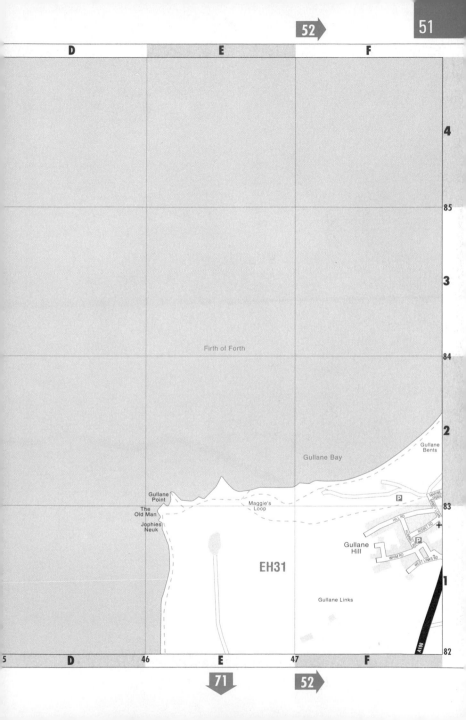

D
E
F

4

85

3

84

Firth of Forth

2

Gullane Bay
Gullane Bents

Gullane Point
Maggie's Loop
P
MARINE TERRACE

The Old Man
83

Jophies Neuk
HILL RD
NISBET RD

+

Gullane Hill
P

WHIM RD
WEST LINKS RD

EH31

1

Gullane Links

A198

5
D
46
E
47
F
82

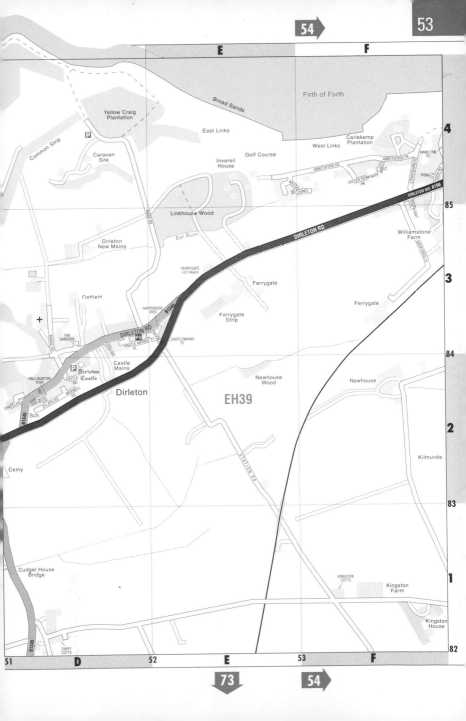

53

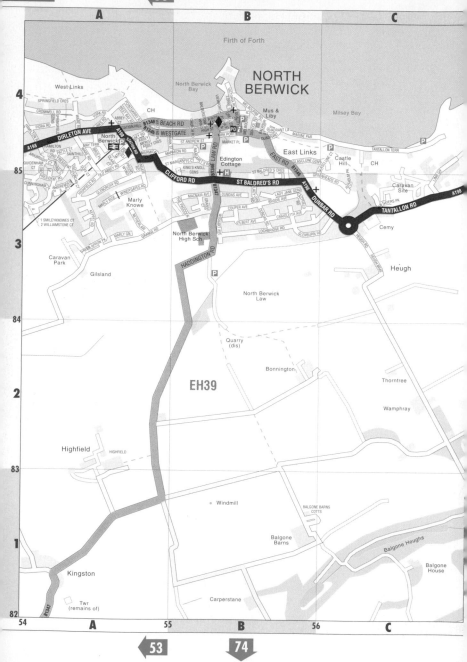

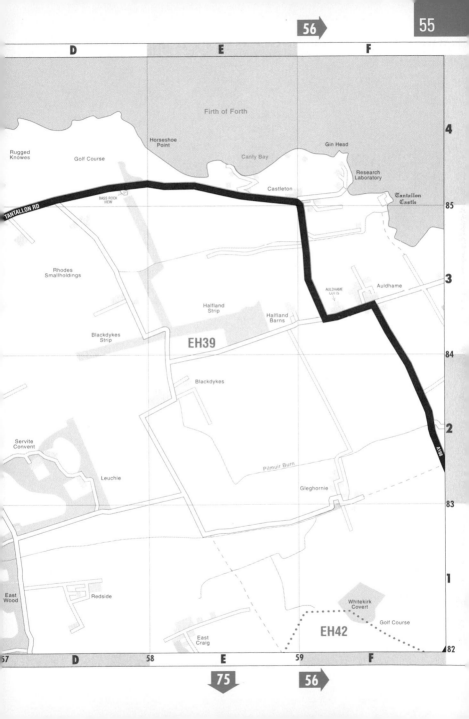

D   E   F

Firth of Forth

4

Rugged
Knowes

Golf Course

Horseshoe
Point

Canty Bay

Gin Head

Research
Laboratory

Castleton

Tantallon
Castle

TANTALLON RD

BASS ROCK
VIEW

85

Rhodes
Smallholdings

3

AULDHAME
COTTS

Auldhame

Halfland
Strip

Halfland
Barns

Blackdykes
Strip

EH39

84

Blackdykes

Servite
Convent

2

Leuchie

Pilmuir Burn

A198

Gleghornie

83

East
Wood

Redside

1

Whitekirk
Covert

Golf Course

East
Craig

EH42

82

A　　　　　　B　　　　　　C

4

85

3　Cave

SEACLIFF →

Seacliff

84　　　　　　Chapel Brae

Crow Wood

2

EH39

Pilmuir Burn

Scoughall

83　　　　　　Coastguard Lookout

New Mains

Scoughall Links

1　　　　　Peffer Burn　　　　　Peffer Sands

Pefferside

A198

EH42

A198

82
60　　　A　　61　　　B　　62　　　C

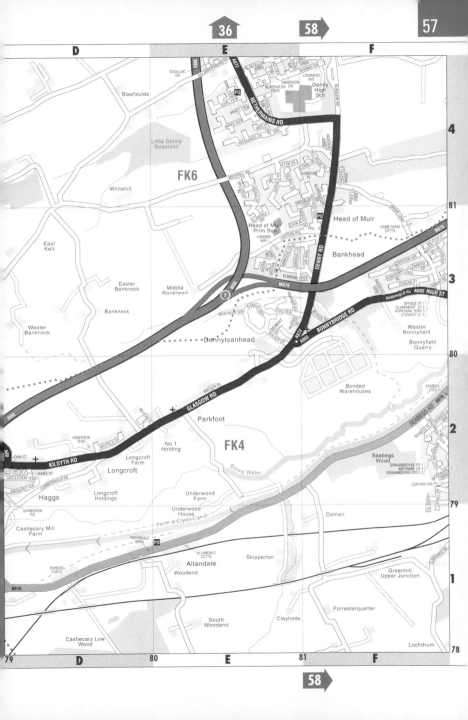

57
37

A   B   C

Cuthelton

FK6

Cemy

Nursery

Hills of
Dunipace

FK5

B905

A883

4   Chacefield
Wood

Weir

River Carron

Bogton

A883

Bonnybridge
Golf Course

A88

M876

CH

PRIMROSE
ST

NORWOOD
PL

NORWOOD
CT

81

Sewage
Works

Bonny Water

Works

Wester
Carmuirs

A80

PO

St Bonnybridge
Prim Sch

LAKESIDE AVE

GATESIDE AVE

THORNTON AVE

FALKIRK RD

Bonnybridge

Rowan Tree Burn

WEST CARMUIRS LMM

3   THORNTON AVE

H

Park

HIGH ST

MAIN ST

PRINCESS ST

Forth and Clyde Canal

A803

Bonnybridge

P P

Cowden Hill

Liby

BONNYSIDE RD

Bonnyside
Farm

CHATTAN
IND EST

80

SEABEGS RD

Antonine
Prim Sch

MURNIN
ROAD
IND EST

BROOMHILL RD

FK4

FK1

Works

B816

MANNFIELD
AVE

ROMAN RD

St Joseph's
Prim Sch

B816

2

Milnquarter

1 GRAHAMSDYKE CRES
2 LEAPARK DR
3 BANTON PL
4 LAURELBANK AVE

HILLEW RD

Works

BONNYHILL RD

High
Bonnybridge

BROOMSIDE RD

79

Greenhill

Margreta

Bonnyhill
Farm

Howierig

GLENTARGIE RD

GREENHILL CT

1

Drum

Drum
Wood

FK1

Greenrig

78

82   A   83   B   84   C

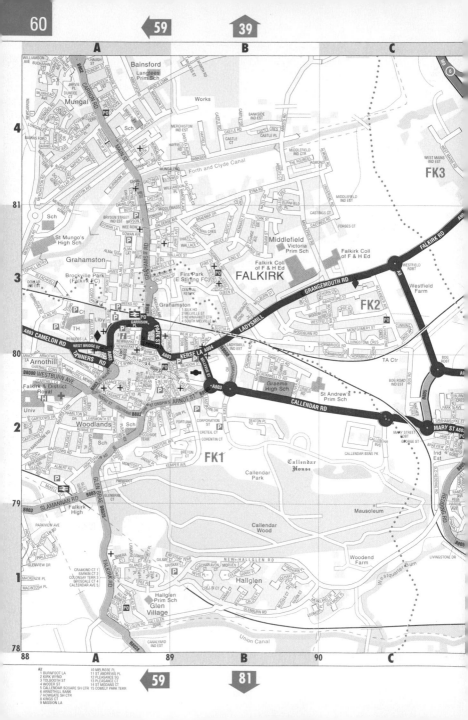

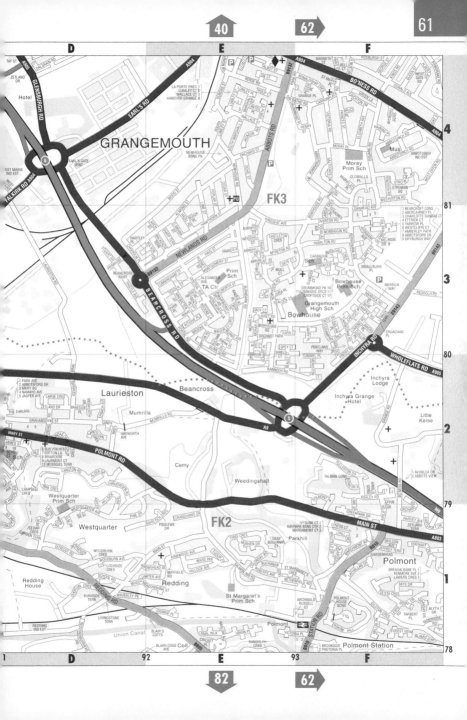

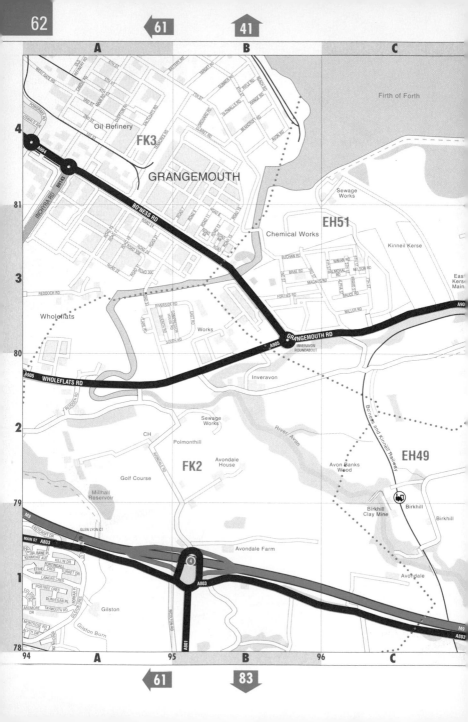

D
E
F

4

81

Firth of Forth

Carras
Gate

The
Fishery

Shore
Woods

3

Stacks
Cottages

EH51

Black Ness

Blackness
Bay

Blackness
Castle

Stacks

Pier

80

Hotel
PO
Blackness

B903

Blackness
House

Hope Park
Lodge

Burnshot

Blackness
Prim Sch

Old Burnshot

Black Burn

2

B9109

Dyland
Cottages

EH49

79

Champany
Holdings

A904

Cauldcoats
Holdings

Mannerston
Holdings

Mannerston

Binns Hill
Twr

1

Paddockhall

The Binns

The Binns

M9

Garden
House

Merrylees

West Lodge

A904

78

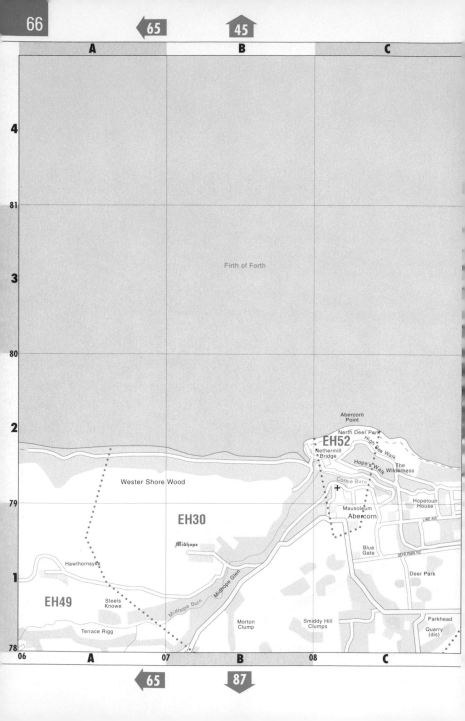

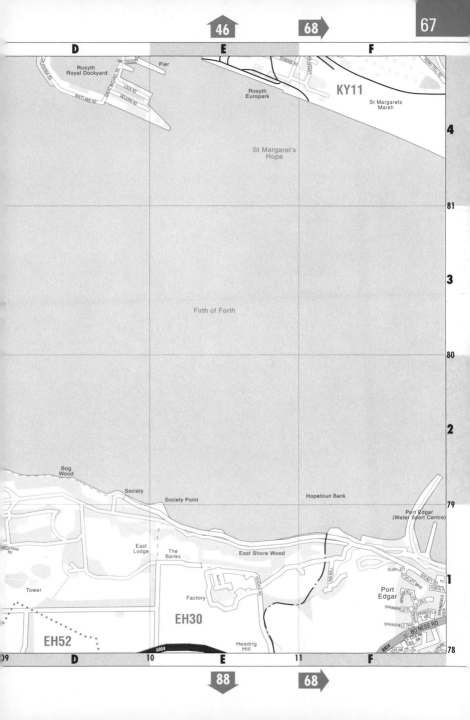

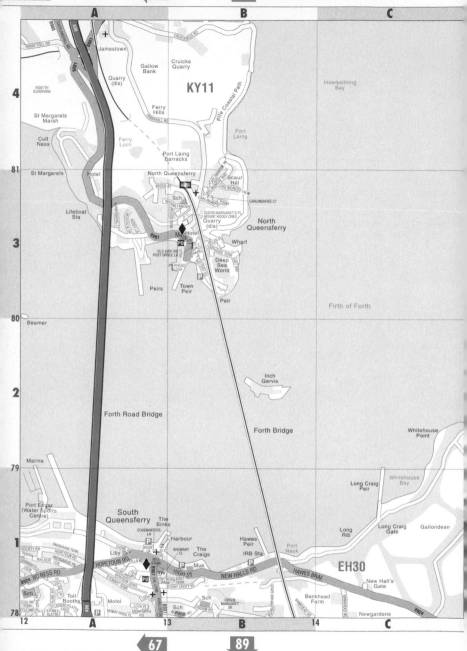

BB80
CASTLANDHILL RD
FERRY TOLL RD
B981

Jamestown

Gallow Bank

Cruicks Quarry

Quarry (dis)

KY11

Inverkeithing Bay

ROSYTH EUROPARK

St Margarets Marsh

Cult Ness

Ferry Hills

FERRYHILL RD

Port Laing

Fife Coastal Path

Ferry Loch

St Margarets

Port Laing Barracks

North Queensferry

Hotel

BROCK

Sch

Scaur Hill

CARLINGNOSE POINT

Lifeboat Sta

B981

HELEN PL

Queen Margaret's PL

Mount Hooly Cres

Quarry (dis)

North Queensferry

MAIN ST

Hotel

CHAPEL PL

Wharf

Old Kirk Rd
Post Office La

CORTLEIDE TERR

Deep Sea World

PIERHEAD BLDGS

Peirs

Town Peir

Peir

Firth of Forth

Beamer

Inch Garvie

Forth Road Bridge

Forth Bridge

Whitehouse Point

Marina

Whitehouse Bay

Port Edgar (Water Sports Centre)

Long Craig Peir

Long Craig Gate

Gailondean

Long Rib

South Queensferry

The Binks

COVENANTERS LA

Harbour

Hawes Peir

Port Neuk

EH30

SOCIETY RD

FARQUHAR TERR

FORTH WALKER

Liby

SHORE RD

ROSE ST

BREWERY CL

The Craigs

Mus

IRB Sta

BB924

BO'NESS RD

HOPETOUN RD

VILLA RD

HIGH ST

NEW HALLS RD

HAWES BRAE

New Hall's Gate

Sch

Toll Booths

Motel

HENRY ROSS PL

LOCH PL

VIEWFORTH

Sch

QUEEN MARGARET DR

Bankhead Farm

BANKHEAD RD

BB924

Newgardens

D	E	F

4

81

3

Firth of Forth

80

2

Hound
Point

Peatdraught
Bay

The
Warrens

Fishery
Cottage

EH30

79

Leuchold

Leuchold Wood

Castle Craig
Clump

Castle
Craig

Midlothian
Clump

Barnbougle
Castle

Crow
Thickets

Mons Hill

1

Dalmeny Park

New England

Peacock Ride

Livingston
Clump

Dalmeny
House

78

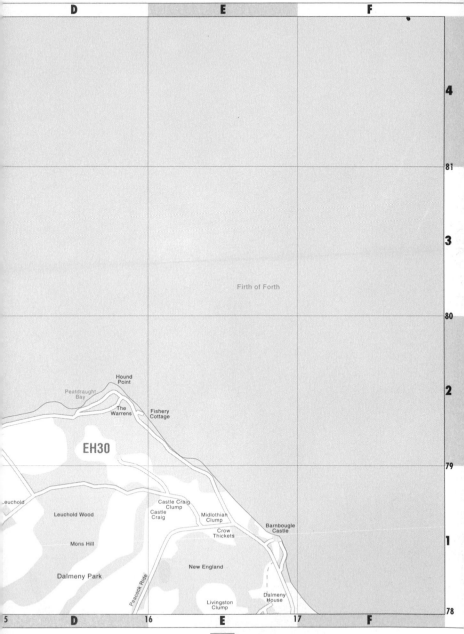

A **B** **C**

4

81

3

80

Firth of Forth

Craigielaw Point

Golf
Course

Green
Craig

EH32

Green Craig
(Hotel)

2

Harestanes
Wood

79

Gosford Bay

1

78

42 **A** 43 **B** 44 **C**

A198

Tollbar Strip

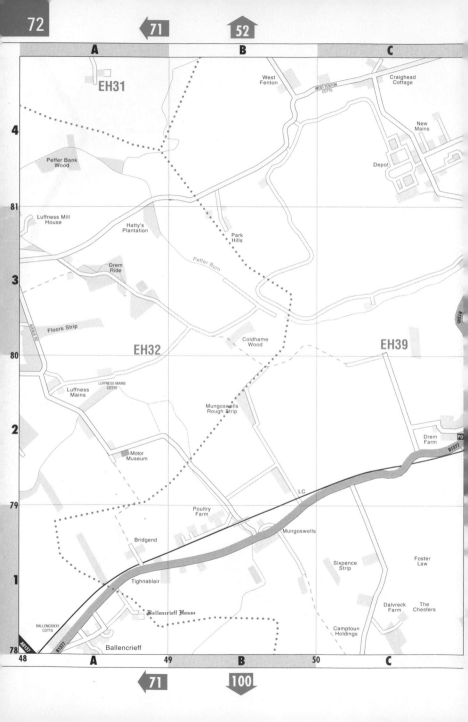

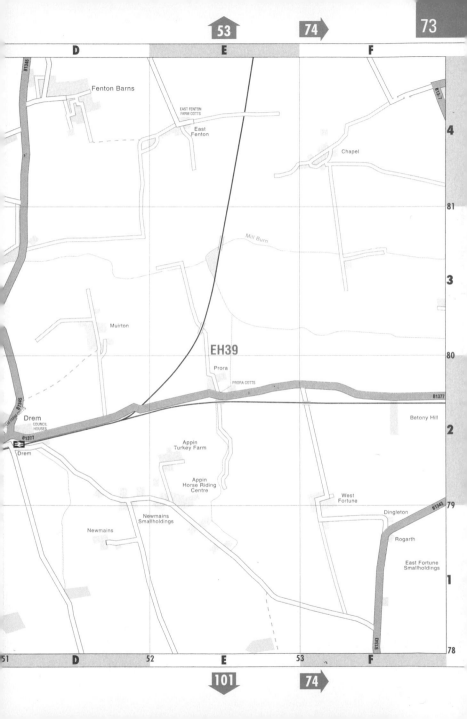

D **E** **F**

B7345

Fenton Barns

EAST FENTON
FARM COTTS

East
Fenton

Chapel

4

81

Mill Burn

3

Muirton

EH39

80

Prora

PRORA COTTS

B1377

Drem
COUNCIL
HOUSES

Betony Hill

2

B1377

E3

Drem

Appin
Turkey Farm

Appin
Horse Riding
Centre

West
Fortune

Dingleton

B1343

79

Newmains
Smallholdings

Rogarth

Newmains

East Fortune
Smallholdings

1

B1343

78

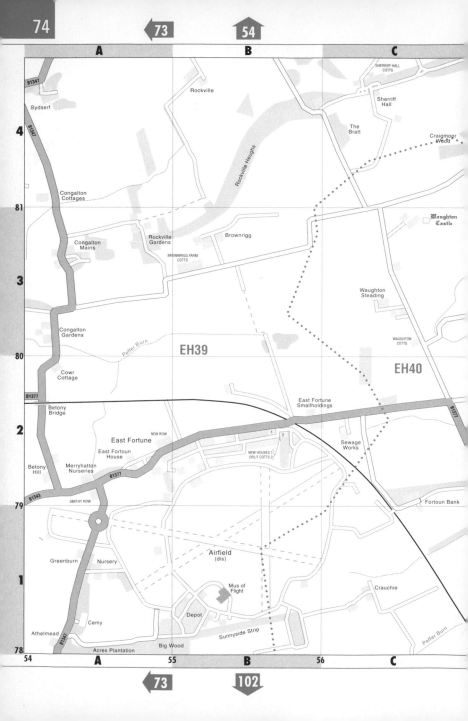

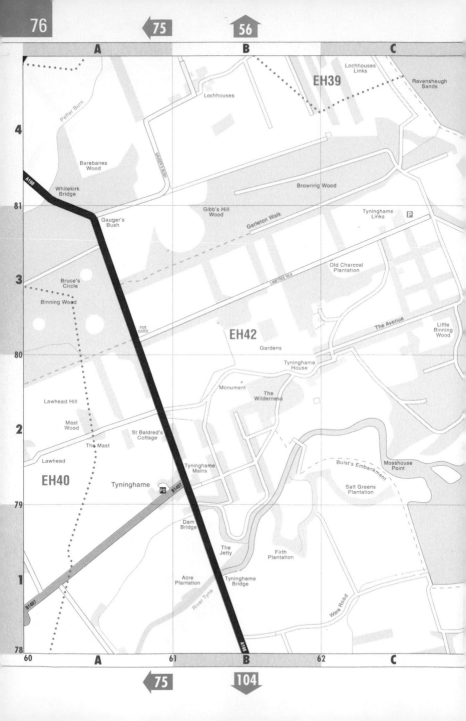

75
56

A   B   C

4

EH39

Lochhouses Links

Ravensheugh Sands

Peffer Burn

Lochhouses

Barebanes Wood

Brownrig Wood

Whitekirk Bridge

81

Gauger's Bush

Gibb's Hill Wood

Garleton Walk

Tyninghame Links

Old Charcoal Plantation

3

Bruce's Circle

Binning Wood

FIVE GATES

LAMBTREE WALK

EH42

The Avenue

Little Binning Wood

Gardens

80

Tyninghame House

Lawhead Hill

Monument

The Wilderness

Mast Wood

2

St Baldred's Cottage

The Mast

Lawhead

Bulst's Embankment

Mosshouse Point

EH40

Tyninghame

Tyninghame Mains

Salt Greens Plantation

79

Dam Bridge

The Jetty

Firth Plantation

1

Acre Plantation

Tyninghame Bridge

River Tyne

Ware Road

78

60   A   61   B   62   C

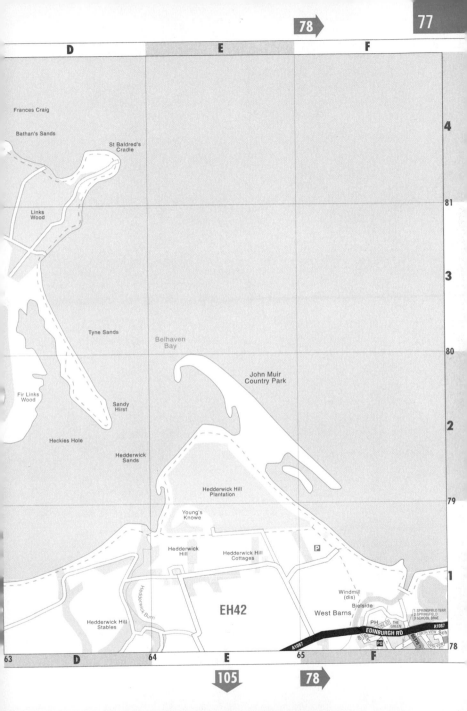

Frances Craig

Bathan's Sands

St Baldred's
Cradle

Links
Wood

Tyne Sands

Belhaven
Bay

John Muir
Country Park

Fir Links
Wood

Sandy
Hirst

Heckies Hole

Hedderwick
Sands

Hedderwick Hill
Plantation

Young's
Knowe

Hedderwick
Hill

Hedderwick Hill
Cottages

Hedderwick
Burn

EH42

Windmill
(dis)

Bjelside

West Barns

1 SPRINGFIELD TERR
2 SPRINGFIELD
3 SCHOOL BRAE

Hedderwick Hill
Stables

PH

THE
GREEN

FORTH VIEW Sch

EDINBURGH RD

A1087

A1087

77

A   B   C

4

81

3

80

2

Long Craigs

The Gripes

Victoria Harbour

Meikle Spiker

CUSTOM HOUSE SQ

Old Harbour

Caravan Site

BAYSWELL PK

BAYSWELL RD

MAYVILLE

CASTELLAU COTTS

Lifeboat Sta

St Margarets

CH

Golf Course

NORTH RD

LAUDERDALE CRES

LETHAM RD

LETHAM

Liby

1 COLVIN ST
2 THE VENNEL

79

Winterfield Mains

BACK RD

BELHAVEN RD

A1087

HIGH ST

FRIAR'S CROFT

3 WOODBUSH PL
4 WOODBUSH CT

WINTERFIELD PL

MANOR GDNS

Belhaven Hill (Boys Sch)

GALA GN

Dunbar Grammar Sch

LAMMERMUIR CRES

DOUN RD

Dunbar Prim Sch

COUNTY CL

COSSARS WYND

PO

BEAUMONT TERR

1

SEAFIELD CRES

A1087 EDINBURGH RD

HIGH ST

DUKE ST

BREWERY LA

Belhaven

ASH DR

POPLAR ST

HAZEL

ELM RD

COUNTESS RD

DUNBAR

EH42

Retreat

Dunbar

QUEEN'S RD

ROXBURGHE TERR
ROXBURGHE PK

CH

H Belhaven

Rosebank House

Lochend Kennels

Lochend Cottages

Hallhill Cottages

Lochend Gardens

BRUNT CT

LATCH RD

LOCHEND AVE

BRAESMOOR

A1087

78

Sch

66   A   67   B   68   C

77
106

107

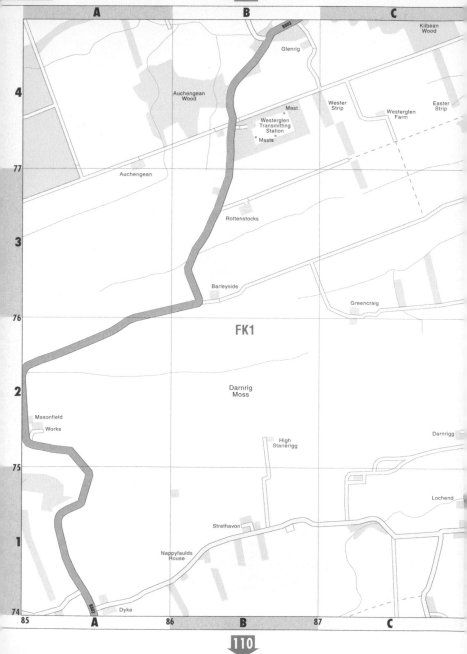

A
B
C

Kilbean
Wood

Glenrig

4

Auchengean
Wood

Mast

Wester
Strip

Easter
Strip

Westerglen
Transmitting
Station

Westerglen
Farm

Masts

77

Auchengean

Rottenstocks

3

Barleyside

Greencraig

76

FK1

2

Darnrig
Moss

Masonfield

Works

High
Stanerigg

Darnrigg

75

Lochend

Strathavon

1

Nappyfaulds
House

74

Dyke

85
A
86
B
87
C

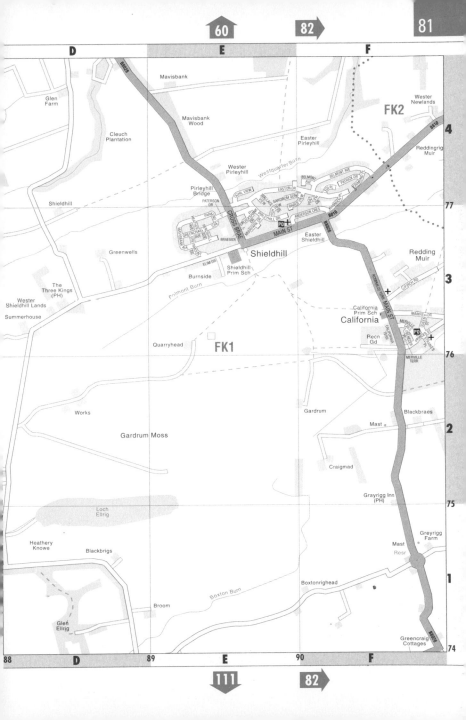

D
E
F

Mavisbank

Glen
Farm

Cleuch
Plantation

Mavisbank
Wood

Wester
Newlands

FK2

4

BB18

Easter
Pirleyhill

Reddingrig
Muir

Shieldhill

Wester
Pirleyhill

Westquarter Burn

Pirleyhill
Bridge

SCHL VIEW

EASTON DR

BELMONT AVE

PATRICK DR

BELMONT
AVE

77

PATERSON
DR

GARDRUM GDNS

BRAES

ANDERSON CRES

CROSS BRAE

Greenwells

PAPA

HEATHER DR

GREENOAKE
AVE

MUIRSIDE

ELM DR

BRAESIDE

MAIN ST

PD

Easter
Shieldhill

Redding
Muir

BB10

Shieldhill

The
Three Kings
(PH)

Wester
Shieldhill Lands

Summerhouse

Burnside

Polmont Burn

Shieldhill
Prim Sch

Shieldhill

CHURCH RD

Redding
Muir

California
Prim Sch

California

MAIN ST

MANSFIELD DR

MERVILLE
TERR

NORMAN TERR

+

+

3

Recn
Gd

+

MERVILLE
TERR

76

Quarryhead

FK1

Gardrum

Blackbraes

Works

Mast

2

Gardrum Moss

Craigmad

Grayrigg Inn
(PH)

75

Loch
Ellrig

Heathery
Knowe

Blackbrigs

Mast

Resr

Greyrigg
Farm

1

Glen
Ellrig

Broom

Boxton Burn

Boxtonrighead

Greencraig
Cottages

BB28

74

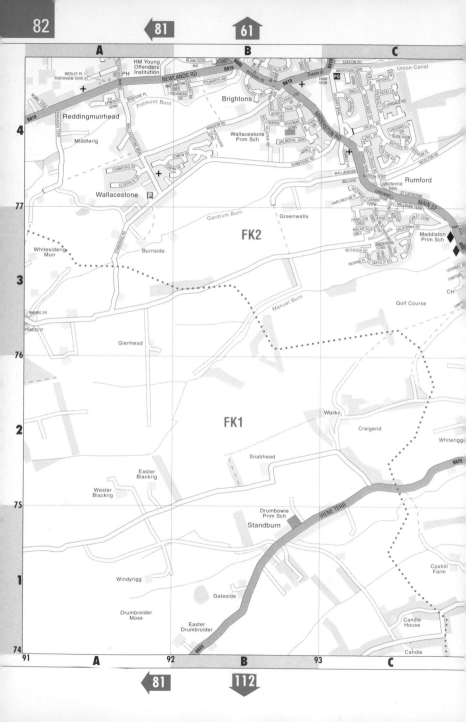

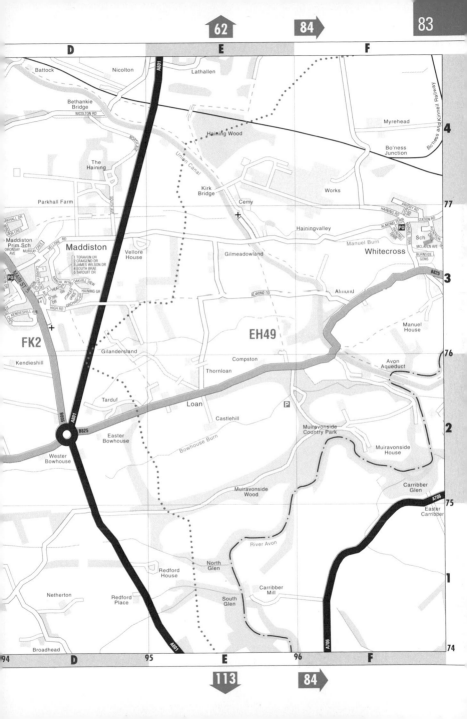

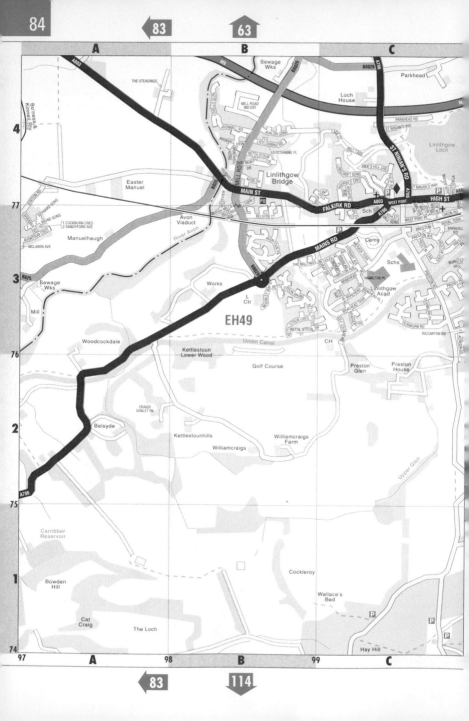

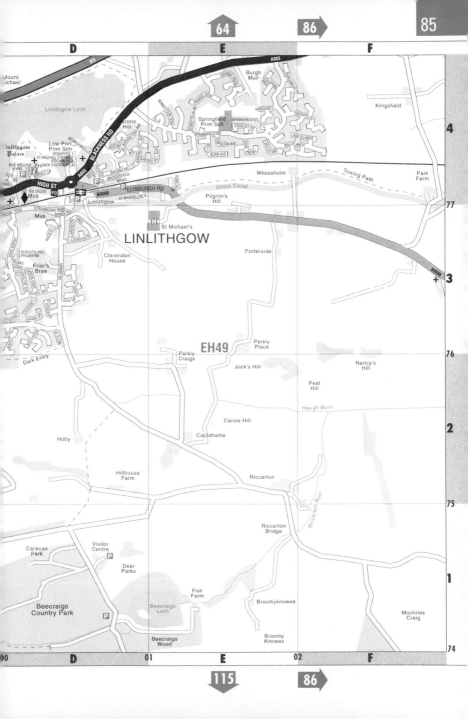

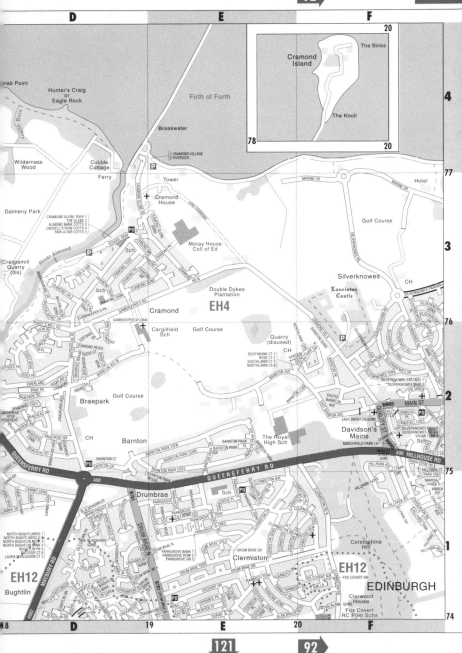

D · E · F

20

Cramond Island

The Binks

Firth of Forth

Breakwater

The Knoll

78

20

4

Inab Point

Hunter's Craig or Eagle Rock

1 CRAMOND VILLAGE
2 RIVERSIDE

MARINE DR

MARINE DR

Hotel

77

Wilderness Wood

Couble Cottage

Ferry

Tower

Cramond House

Golf Course

Dalmeny Park

CRAMOND GLEBE TERR 1
THE GLEBE 2
ALMOND BANK COTTS 3
CADDELL'S ROW COTTS 4
FAIR-A-FAR COTTS 5

Moray House Coll of Ed

Silverknowes

CH

3

Craigiemill Quarry (dis)

River Almond

Sch

Double Dykes Plantation

Lauriston Castle

EH4

Cramond

Cargilfield Sch

Golf Course

Quarry (disused)

CH

76

SOUTHBANK CT 1
ROSE CT 2
SOUTHLAWN CT 3
NORTHLAWN CT 4

Braepark

Golf Course

Barnton

CH

South Barnton Ave

Davidson's Mains

MAIN ST

B9085

EAST BARNTON GDNS

2

The Royal High Sch

Marchfield Park La

A90

HILLHOUSE RD

Barnton Park

Drumbrae

QUEENSFERRY RD

A90

75

QUEENSFERRY RD

Sch

Corstorphine Hill

Clermiston

EH12

FOX COVERT GR

EH12

EDINBURGH

EH12

Bughtlin

DRUM BRAE N

MAYBURY RD

NORTH BUGHTLIN 1
NORTH BUGHTLIN NEUK 2
NORTH BUGHTLIN BANK 3
BOGHALL PK 5
BALFOUR CT 7
LAURA FERGUSSON CT 7

PARKGROVE BANK 1
PARKGROVE ROW 2
PARKGROVE GN 3

Clerwood House

Fox Covert RC Prim Schs

A902

74

8 · D · **19** · E · **20** · F

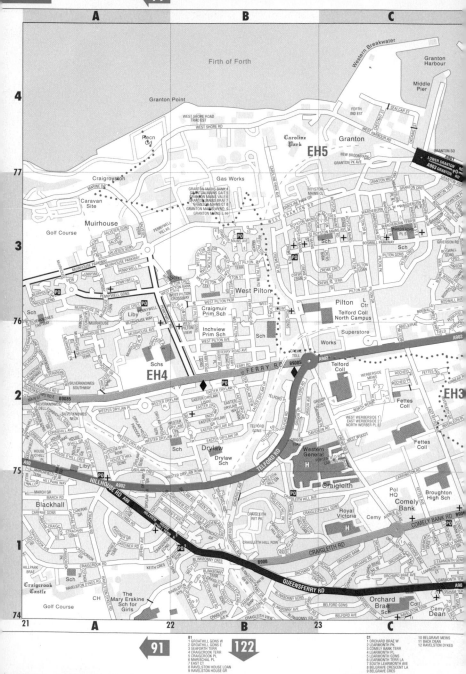

B1
1 GROATHILL GDNS W
2 GROATHILL GDNS E
3 SEAFORTH TERR
4 CRAIGCROOK TERR
5 CRAIGCROOK PL
6 MARISCHAL PL
7 EAST CT
8 RAVELSTON HOUSE LOAN
9 RAVELSTON HOUSE GR

C1
1 ORCHARD BRAE W
2 LEARMONTH PK
3 COMELY BANK TERR
4 LEARMONTH PL
5 LEARMONTH GDNS
6 LEARMONTH TERR LA
7 SOUTH LEARMONTH AVE
8 BELGRAVE CRESCENT LA
9 BELGRAVE CRES
10 BELGRAVE MEWS
11 BACK DEAN
12 RAVELSTON DYKES

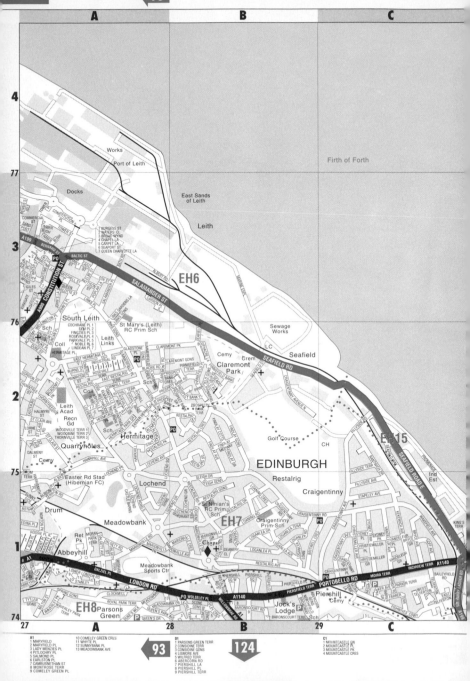

A B C

4

Works
Port of Leith

77 Docks East Sands of Leith

Leith

Firth of Forth

COMMERCIAL ST
SAND PORT
TIMBER BUSH
TOWER ST

1 BURGESS ST
2 WATERS CL
3 BROAD WYND
4 CHAPEL LA
5 CARPET LA
6 SEAPORT ST
7 QUEEN CHARLOTTE LA

3 A199 BALTIC ST SALAMANDER ST EH6 ALBERT RD MARINE ESP

PO CONSTITUTION ST CABLES WYND

76 South Leith St Mary's (Leith) RC Prim Sch Sewage Works

Sch COCHRANE PL 1 EXM PL 2 FINGZIES PL 3 ROSEVALE PL 4 NORVALE PL 5 NOBLE PL 6 LINDEAN PL 7 Leith Links GLADSTONE PL LC Seafield Seafield
Coll HERMITAGE PL EAST HERMITAGE PL CLAREMONT PK Cemy Crem SEAFIELD RD
Cemy CLAREMONT GDNS Claremont Park
BLACKIE RD PIRNIEFIELD Claremont Park

2 Leith Acad Recn Gd RESTALRIG BANK CRES S BANK ST CRAIGENTINNY AVENUE N
WOODVILLE TERR 1 WOODBINE TERR 2 THORNVILLE TERR 3 Sch Coll Hermitage PO
Golf Course CH EH15

DALMENY ST HALMYRE ST ST CLAIR AVE LORNE ST Quarryholes Cemy HARKMILLE AVE

75 Cemy Easter Rd Stad (Hibernian FC) Lochend EDINBURGH Restalrig Craigentinny HILLSIDE TERR Ind Est
DRUM TERR SLEIGH DR SLEIGH GDNS FILLYSIDE AVE STAPELEY AVE

1 BOTHWELL ST Drum Meadowbank St Ninian's RC Prim Sch CRAIGENTINNY RD PO INCHVIEW TERR A1140
EDINA PL ROSSIE PL Ret Pk Park Abbeyhill EH7 Craigentinny Prim Sch Chapel KING'S TERR
Meadowbank Sports Ctr Deanery LOGANLEA PL LOGANLEA AVE RESTALRIG AVE MOIRA TERR

74 EH8 Parsons Green LONDON RD Piershill Piershill PORTOBELLO RD Piershill Terr Piershill Cemy
TYLER'S Sch QUEEN'S DR PO WOLSELEY PL A1140 WILLOWBRAE RD Jock's Lodge BARONSCOURT TERR Sch

27 A 28 B 29 C
93 124

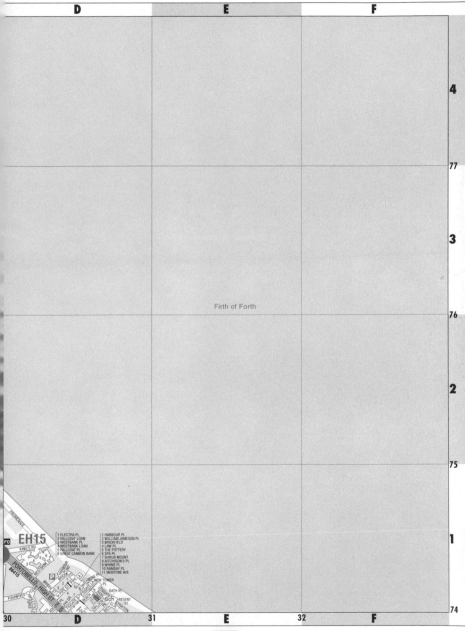

Firth of Forth

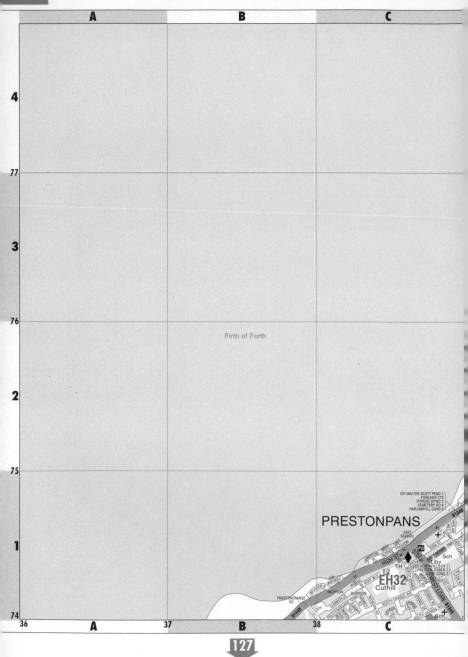

A B C

4

77

3

76

Firth of Forth

2

75

SIR WALTER SCOTT PEND 1
FOWLERS CT 2
PYPERS WYND 3
CEMETERY RD 4
HARLAWHILL GDNS 5

PRESTONPANS

EAST
SEASIDE

1

HIGH ST

EH32
Cuthill

GILES NORTHFIELD CT 1
PRESTON TOWER 2
GLEB GDNS 3

THE
POTTERY

PRESTONGRANGE
RD
INGVIEW
BURNSIDE

NORTH GRANGE AVE

74
36 37 38
A B C

D E F

4

77

Firth of Forth

3

76

COCKENZIE AND PORT SETON

Harbour

Cockenzie Harbour

Pier

LINKS RD

B1348

Seton Sands Caravan Park

GOSFORD RD

Power Station

EDINBURGH RD

Sch

EH32

Seton Chapel formerly (Collegiate Church)

Seton House

75

Coal Store

Rowanhill Cl

Seton East

Seton

A198

HIGH ST

Cemy

Seton West Mains

EH33

Preston

Preston Lodge High Sch

PO

Works

A198

1

Tower PRESTON TOWER

Meadowmill

B1361

A198

74

D E F

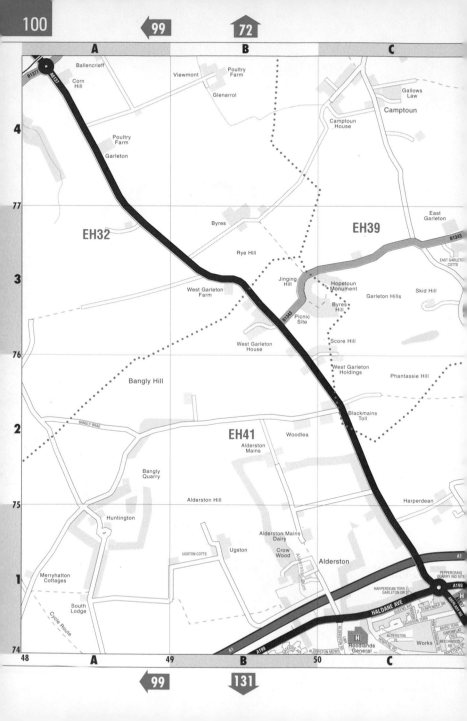

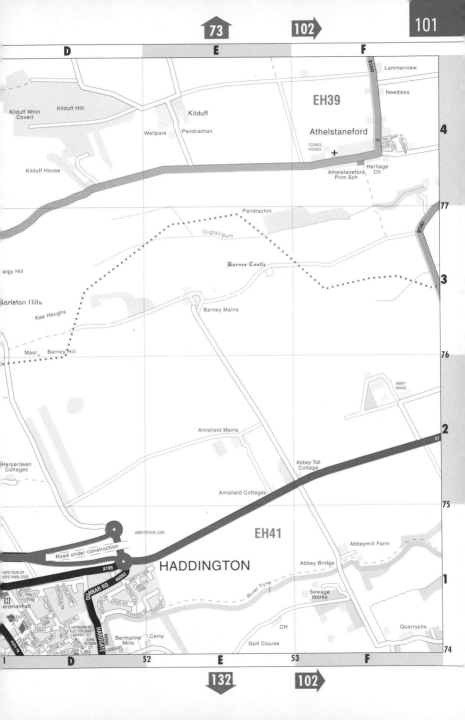

D E F

Lammerview

EH39

Needless

Kilduff Whin Covert

Kilduff Hill

Kilduff

Athelstaneford

Wellpark

Pendrachan

4

Kilduff House

COUNCIL HOUSES

+

Athelstaneford Prim Sch

Heritage Ctr

77

Pendrachin

Cogtail Burn

Barnes Castle

aigy Hill

3

Garleton Hills

Kae Heughs

Barney Mains

Mast

Barney Hill

76

ABBEY MAINS

Amisfield Mains

2

Abbey Toll Cottage

Harperdean Cottages

Amisfield Cottages

75

ABBOTSVIEW JUNC

EH41

Abbeymill Farm

Road under construction

HOPETOUN DR
HOPE PARK CRES

A199

HADDINGTON

Abbey Bridge

erdmanflatt

DUNBAR RD

A6093

ABBOT'S VIEW
CAREY'S VIEW

River Tyne

Sewage Works

1

H

CRAIG AVE

RIVERSIDE DR

CH

Bermaline Mills

Cemy

Quarrypits

Golf Course

74

D E F

52 53

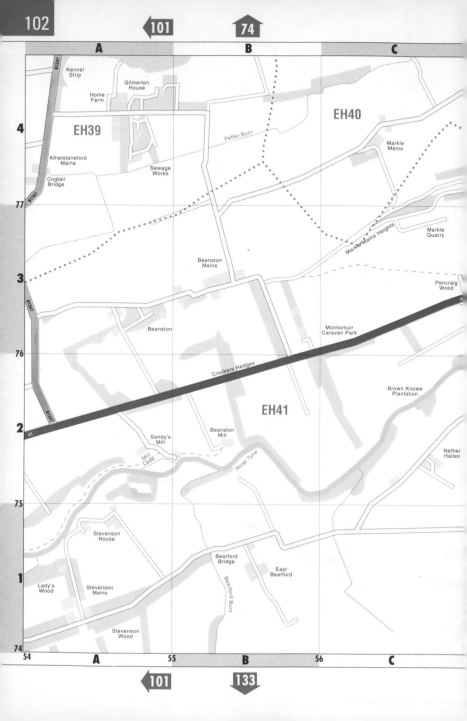

101
74

A　　　　　　　　　B　　　　　　　　　C

Kennel
Strip

Gilmerton
House

Home
Farm

EH39

EH40

4

Markle
Mains

Athelstaneford
Mains

Peffer Burn

Sewage
Works

Cogtail
Bridge

77

Markle Mains Heights

Markle
Quarry

Beanston
Mains

3

Pencraig
Wood

Beanston

Monksmuir
Caravan Park

76

Crockers Hedges

EH41

Brown Knowe
Plantation

2

A1

Sandy's
Mill

Beanston
Mill

Mill Cade

River Tyne

Nether
Hailes

75

Stevenson
House

Bearford
Bridge

East
Bearford

1

Lady's
Wood

Stevenson
Mains

Bearford Burn

Stevenson
Wood

74

54　　　　　A　　　　　55　　　　　B　　　　　56　　　　　C

101
133

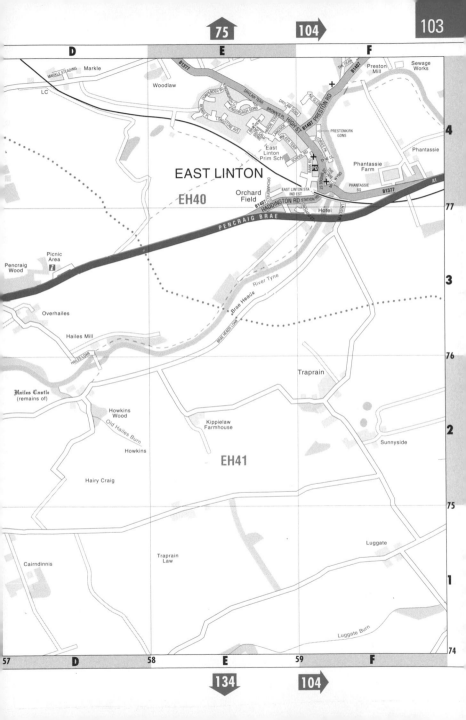

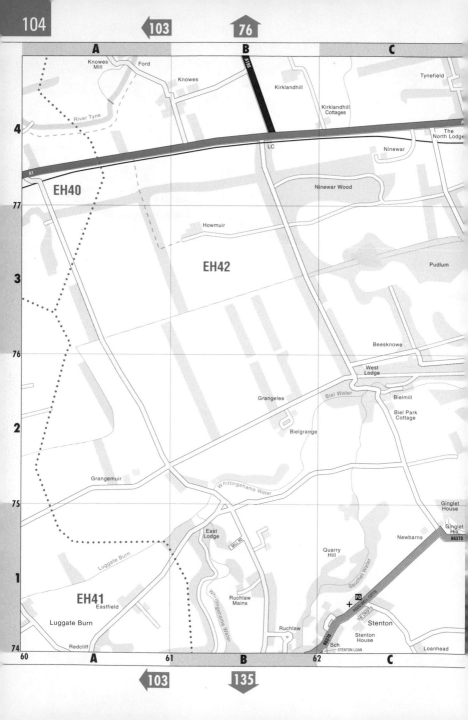

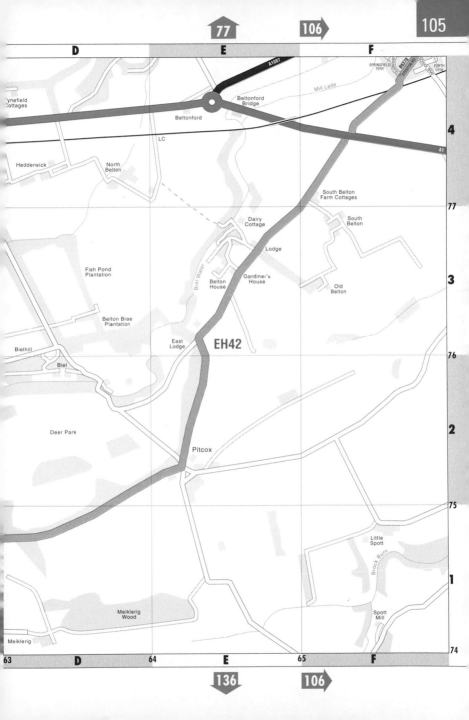

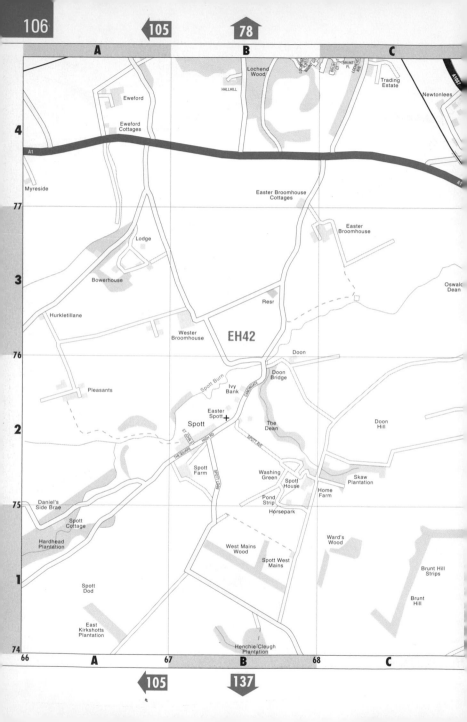

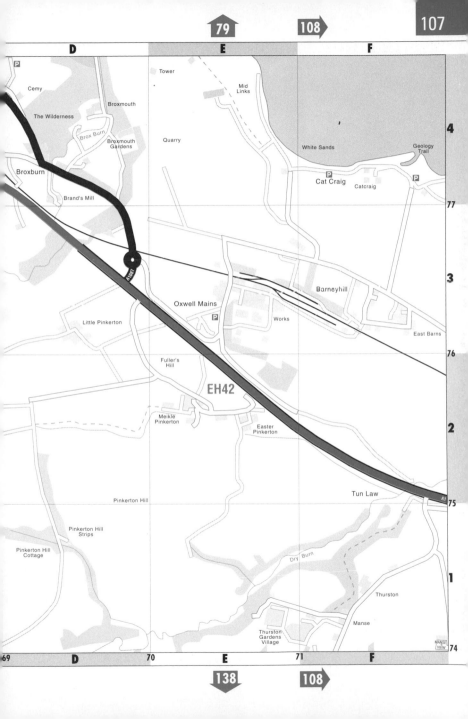

D E F

P
Cemy
Broxmouth
The Wilderness
Brox Burn
Broxmouth Gardens
Broxburn
Brand's Mill

Tower
Quarry

Mid Links
White Sands
Cat Craig
Catcraig
Geology Trail
P
P

4
77

A1087

Oxwell Mains
Little Pinkerton
P
Works
Barneyhill
East Barns

3
76

Fuller's Hill
EH42
Meikle Pinkerton
Easter Pinkerton

2

Pinkerton Hill
Pinkerton Hill Strips
Pinkerton Hill Cottage
Dry Burn
Tun Law
A1
75

Thurston
Manse
Thurston Gardens Village

1

MANSE VIEW
74

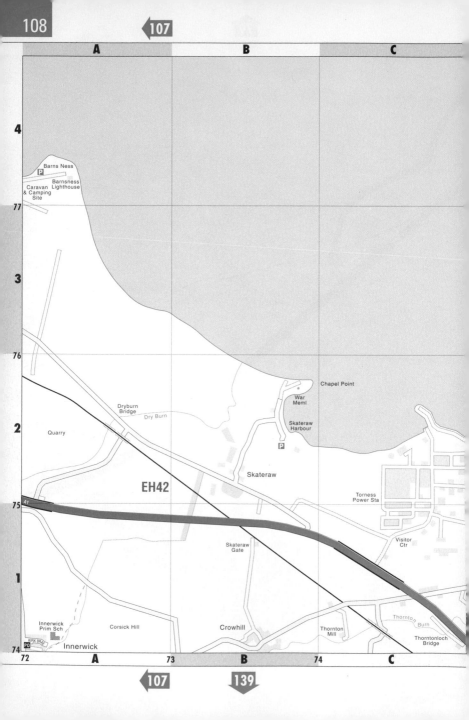

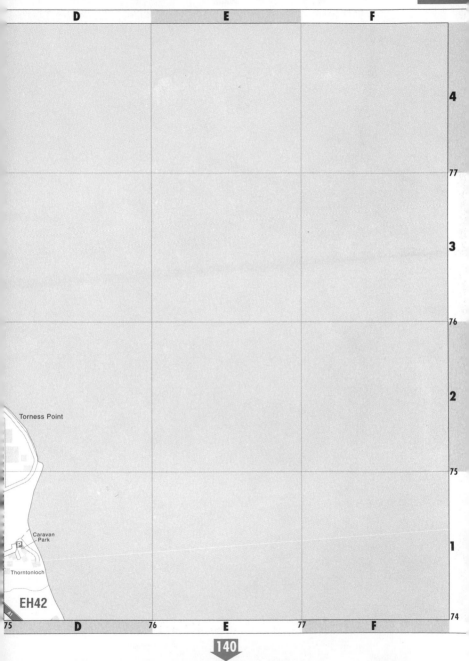

Torness Point

Caravan Park

Thorntonloch

EH42

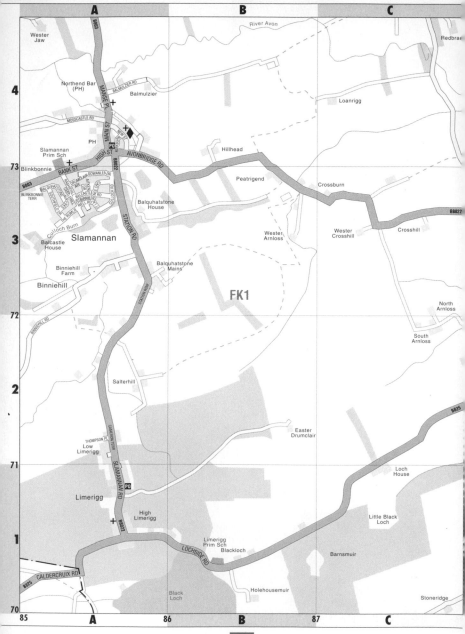

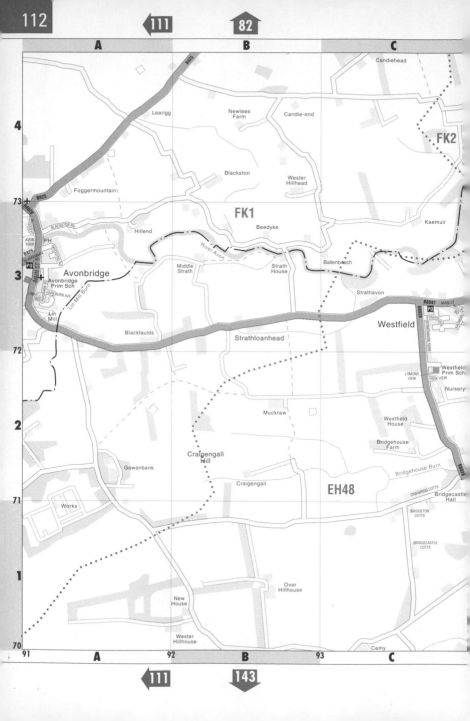

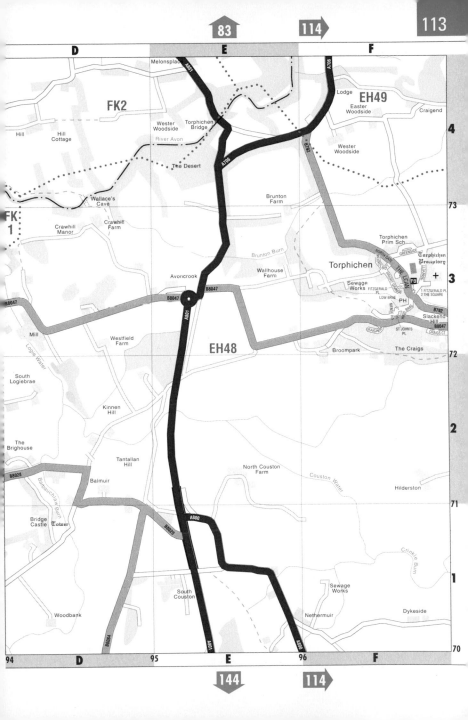

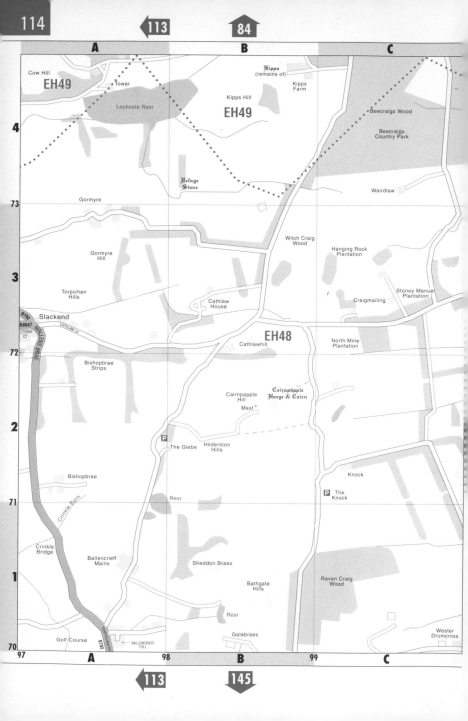

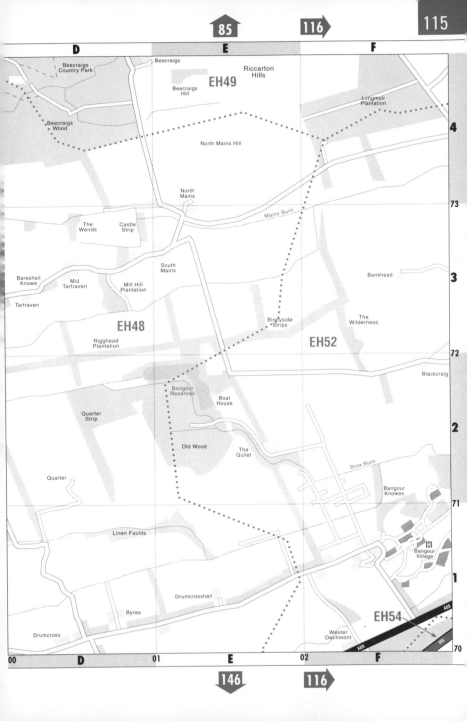

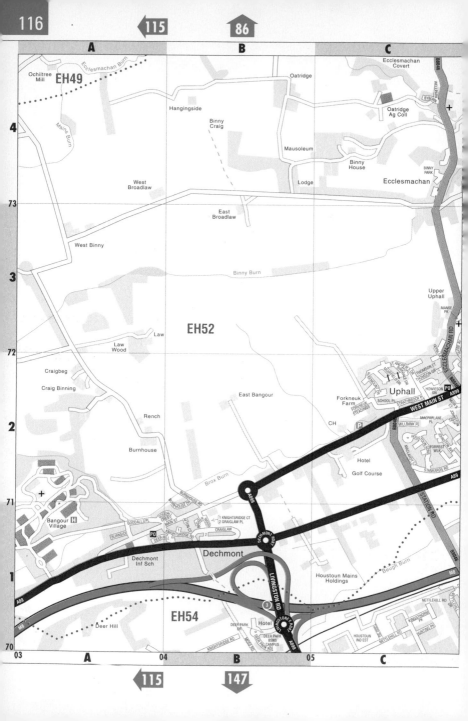

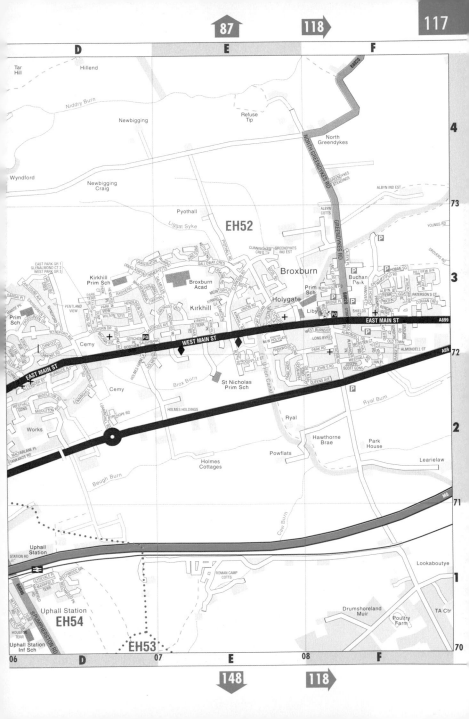

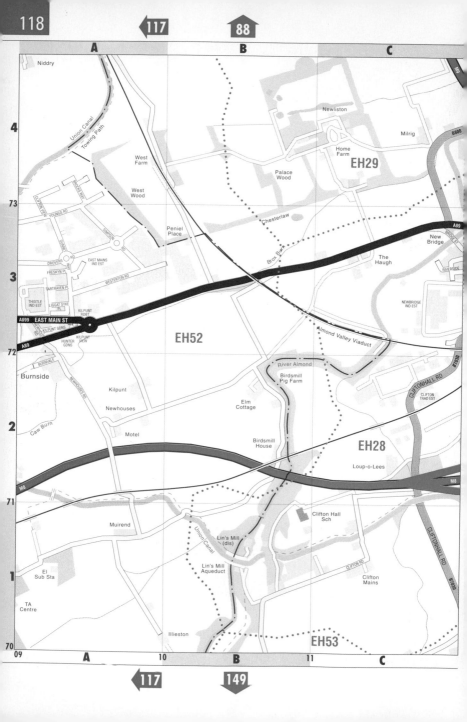

D
E
F

MAITLAND HOO LA
Breastmill
Maitland Bridge
Hallyards
River Almond
EH29
Edinburgh Airport
EH12
4
P
P
73
Sewage Works
Lochend
Ingliston Market
PH
East Mains of Ingliston (Smallholdings)
Royal Highland Showground
Mus
A89
EDINBURGH RD
PH
BRIDGE ST
PO
RIVERSIDE
PARKSIDE
A8
West Ingliston
GLASGOW RD
A8
3
Newbridge
NEWBRIDGE IND EST
NEWBRIDGE RDBT
QUEEN ANNE DR
LOCHEND IND EST
QUEEN ANNE PK
HARVEST DR
LUMBSDEN RD
Ratho Station
Hillwood Prim Sch
HILLWOOD GDNS
HILLWOOD RD
HILLWOOD VIEW
HILLWOOD CRES
HILLWOOD AVE
L'WOOD RISE
Middle Norton
CLIFTONHALL RD
ALEXANDRA BSNS PK
PH
Norton House Hotel
Norton Mains
72
Hillwood Cottage
EH28
Hillwood Quarry
Hillwood
M8
Claylands Farm
2
Hillend
Ratho Byres
Freelands Cottage
Works
Cemy
FREELANDS RD
Freelands
Ratho Hall
Manse
P
Towing Path
71
Union Canal
HALLCROFT NEUK
HALLCROFT CRES
HALLCROFT GDNS
HALLCROFT Gth
HALLCROFT PK
HALLCROFT RISE
CRAIGPARK AVE
Ratho Prim Sch
North St
WEST CROFT
EAS CROFT
RATHO PK RD
CH
Ratho Park Gardens
Golf Course
WILKIESTON RD
CRAIGPARK CRES
LUMSDEN CT
MAIN ST
PO
VOGRIE SKY
HILLVIEW COTTS
BYPASS
CLIFTONHALL RD
EH27
Ratho
1
Ratho Mains
Ransfield
Ransfield Cottages
EH27
70

12
D
13
E
14
F

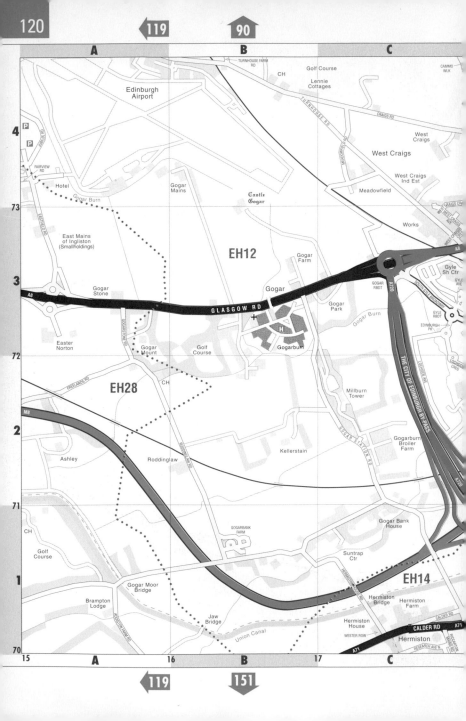

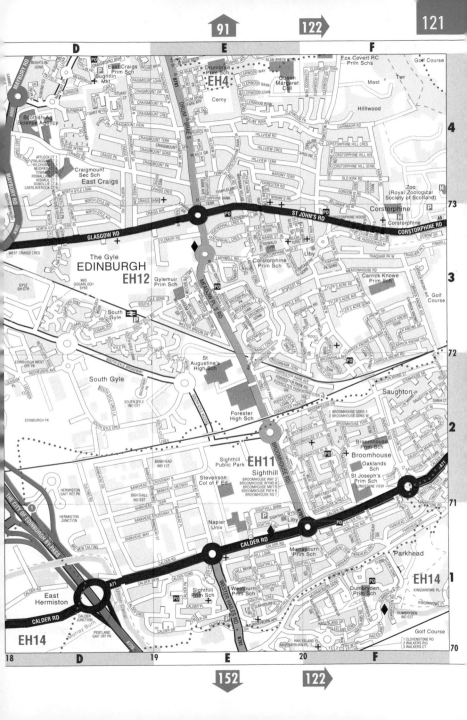

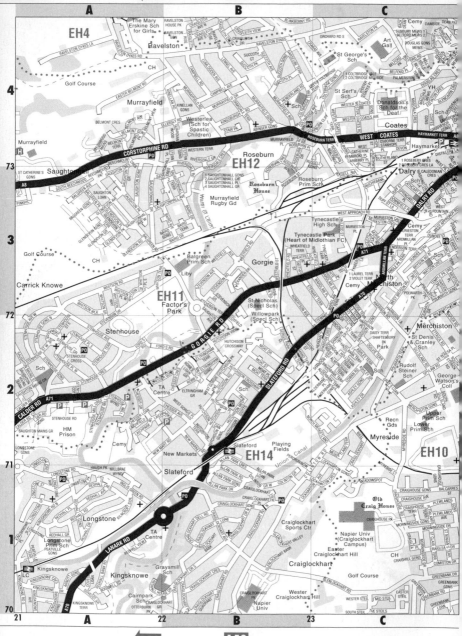

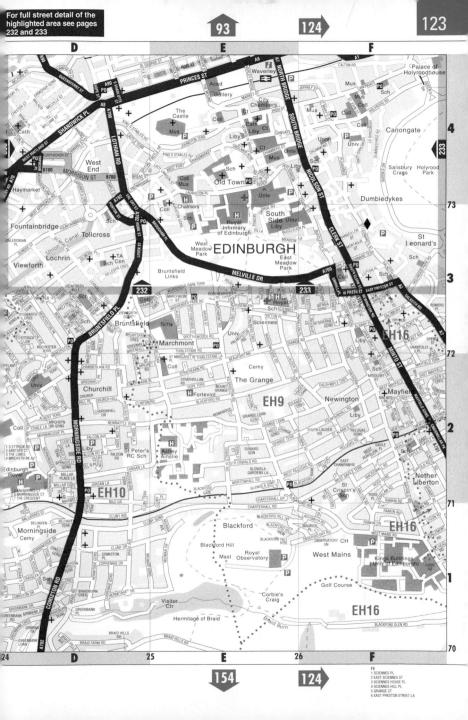

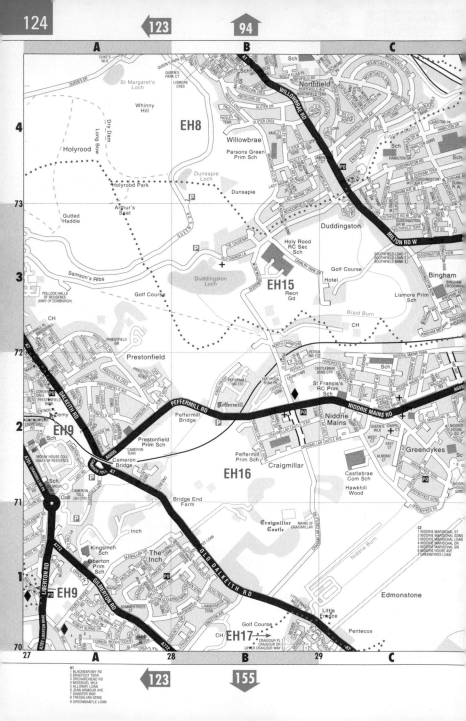

← 123
94

A   B   C

4

DUKE'S WLK

QUEEN'S DR

QUEEN'S PARK CT

St Margaret's Loch

LISMORE CRES

Northfield

WILLOWBRAE RD

MOUNTCASTLE DR

Sch

Whinny Hill

Dry Dam

Long Bow

EH8

Holyrood

Willowbrae

Parsons Green Prim Sch

Dunsapie Loch

73

Holyrood Park

Dunsapie

Duddingston

Gutted Haddie

Arthur's Seat

THE CAUSEWAY

OLD CHURCH LA

Holy Rood RC Sec Sch

MILTON RD W

Bingham

3

Samson's Ribs

POLLOCK HALLS OF RESIDENCE (UNIV OF EDINBURGH)

Golf Course

Duddingston Loch

EH15

Recn Gd

Hotel

Golf Course

SOUTHFIELD LOAN 2
SOUTHFIELD BANK 3

DUDDINGSTON VIEW

Lismore Prim Sch

BINGHAM CROSSWAY

Braid Burn

CH

BINGHAM MEDWAY

BINGHAM BROADW

CH

72

A7

Prestonfield

PRIESTFIELD GR

NORTH CRAIGOUR

PEFFER PL

HAREWOOD RD

CASTLEBRAE BSNS CTR

NIDDRIE MAINS TERR

Sch

PEFFERMILL RD

Peffermill

PEFFERMILL IND EST

HOLYROOD BSNS PK

St Francis's RC Prim Sch

NIDDRIE MAINS RD

A6095

2

CORDEN CRES
PRESTONFIELD CRES

DALKEITH RD

A7

Peffermill Bridge

Prestonfield Prim Sch

EH9

Sch

MORAY HOUSE COLL HALLES OF RESIDENCE

A6095

CAMERON TERR

Cameron Bridge

Peffermill Prim Sch

CRAIGMILLAR CASTLE TERR

CRAIGMILLAR CASTLE AVE

EH16

Niddrie Mains

Craigmillar

Castlebrae Com Sch

Hawkhill Wood

Greendykes

71

A772

CAMERON TOLL (SH CTR)

Coll

Bridge End Farm

Inch

Craigmillar Castle

MAINS OF CRAIGMILLAR

OLD DALKEITH RD

Niddrie Burn

GREENDYKES RD

C2
1 NIDDRIE MARISCHAL ST
2 NIDDRIE MARISCHAL GDNS
3 NIDDRIE MARISCHAL LOAN
4 NIDDRIE MARISCHAL DR
5 NIDDRIE MARISCHAL GN
6 NIDDRIE HOUSE AVE
7 GREENDYKES LOAN

1

A701 LIBERTON BRAE

LIBERTON RD

GILMERTON RD

EH9

Kingsinch Sch

Liberton Prim Sch

The Inch

SUMMERTREES CT

LAMMERMOOR TERR

KINGSTON AVE

Little Fragroe

Edmonstone

Golf Course

Pentecox

70

A772

WOODSTOCKS

GLENMARNOCK

Sch

CH **EH17** → CRAIGOUR PL 1
CRAIGOUR DR 2
UPPER CRAIGOUR WAY 3

27   A   28   A   29   C

A1
1 BLACKBARONY RD
2 BRAEFOOT TERR
3 ORCHARDHEAD RD
4 MOSSGIEL WLK
5 ALLOWAY LOAN
6 JEAN ARMOUR AVE
7 SHANTER WAY
8 TRESSILIAN GDNS
9 GREENMANTLE LOAN

← 123
155

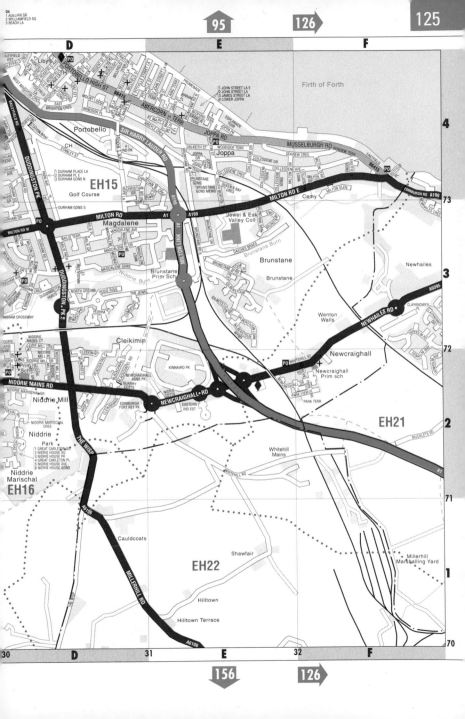

125

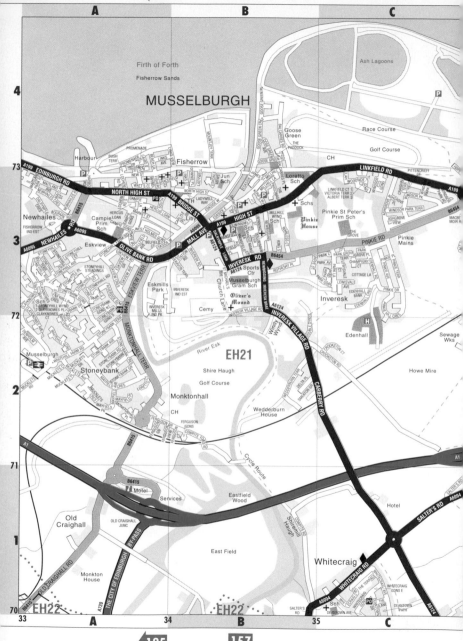

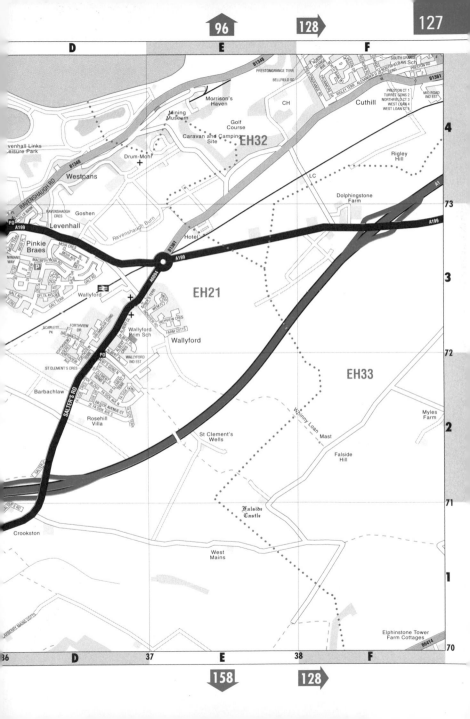

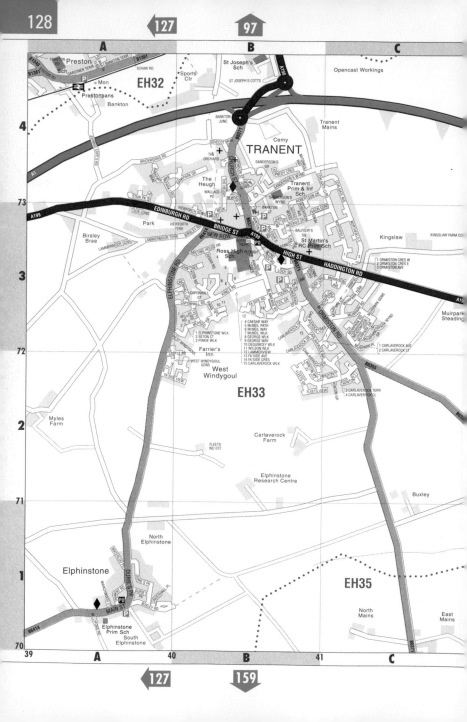

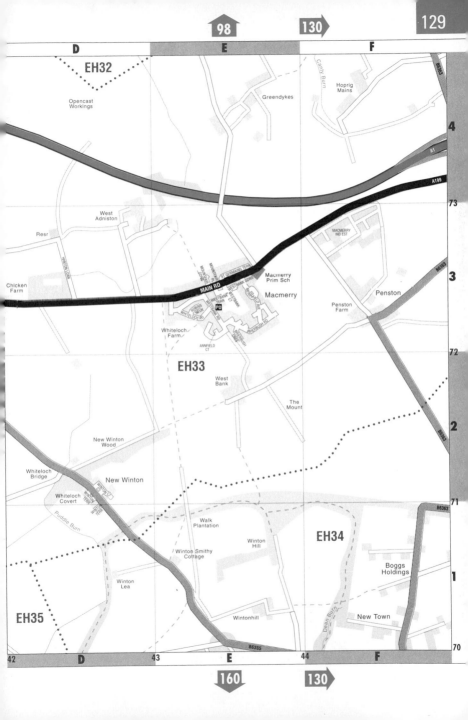

D
E
F

EH32

Opencast
Workings

Greendykes

Catty Burn

Hoprig
Mains

B6363

4

A1

A199

73

West
Adniston

Resr

MACMERRY
IND EST

B6363

3

Chicken
Farm

MORRIS PL
MCLEOD DR
ST GERMAINS TERR

Macmerry
Prim Sch

Penston

WESTBANK GDNS
WESTBANK
TERR
MONCRIEFF CT

MAIN RD

Macmerry

Penston
Farm

PO

ROSS DR

Whiteloch
Farm

MUIRPARK
NEUK
WHITELOCH RD

OVERLEIGH CT

BRITON DR
OVERLEIGH DR

ANNFIELD
CT

72

EH33

West
Bank

The
Mount

B6363

2

New Winton
Wood

New Winton

B6363

71

Whiteloch
Bridge

Whiteloch
Covert

WINTON WALK
WINTON WYND

Walk
Plantation

B6363

Puddle Burn

Winton
Hill

EH34

Boggs
Holdings

1

Winton Smithy
Cottage

Winton
Lea

Dean Burn

New Town

EH35

Wintonhill

B6355

70

42
D
43
E
44
F

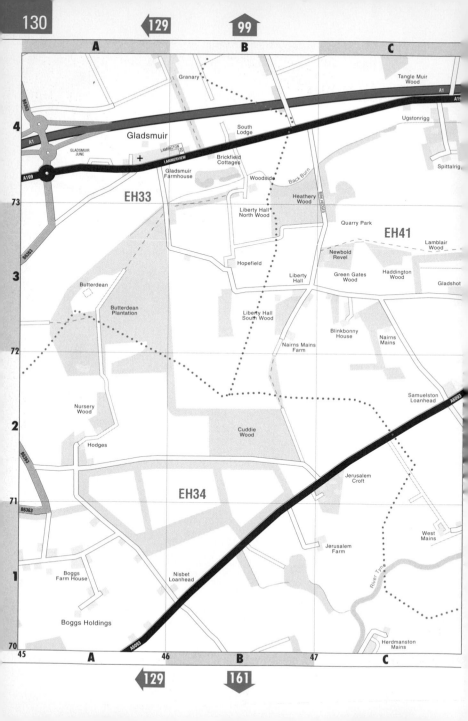

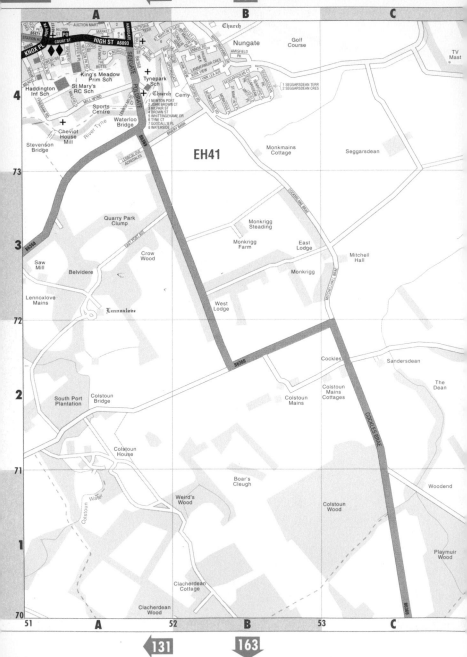

EH41

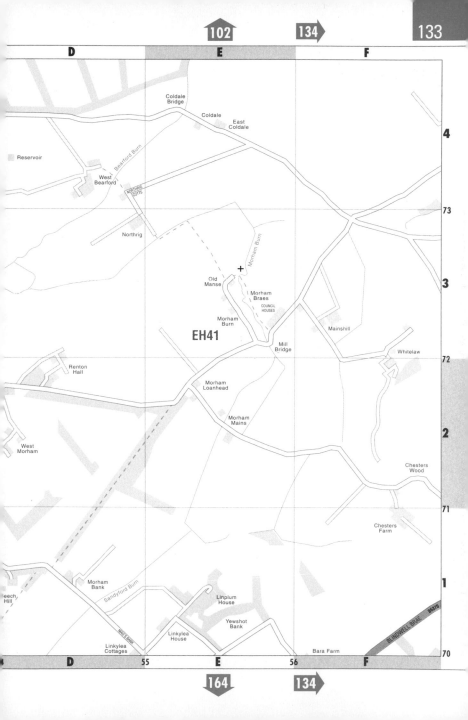

Coldale
Bridge

Coldale

East
Coldale

4

Reservoir

West
Bearford

NORTHRIG
COTTS

Bearford Burn

73

Northrig

Morham Burn

3

Old
Manse

Morham
Braes

COUNCIL
HOUSES

Mainshill

Morham
Burn

EH41

Mill
Bridge

Whitelaw

72

Renton
Hall

Morham
Loanhead

Morham
Mains

2

West
Morham

Chesters
Wood

71

Chesters
Farm

Morham
Bank

Sandyford Burn

1

Beech
Hill

Linplum
House

Yewshot
Bank

BLINDWELL BRAE

B6370

MACO'S BARNS

Linkylea
House

Linkylea
Cottages

Bara Farm

70

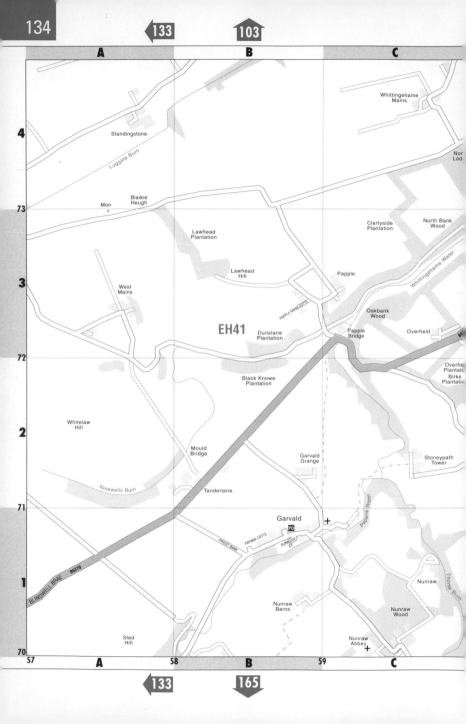

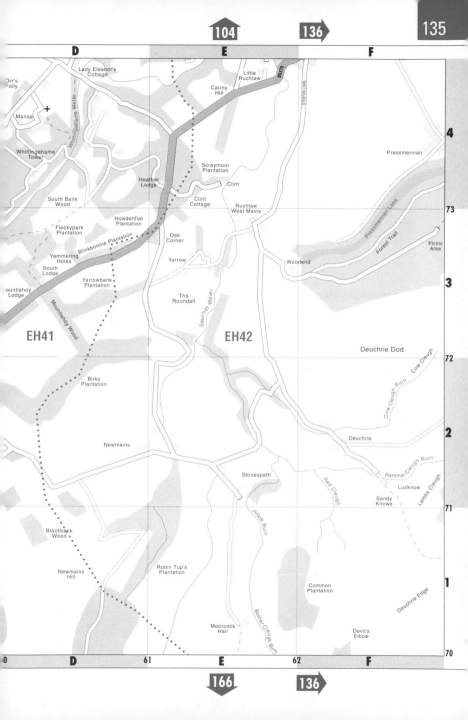

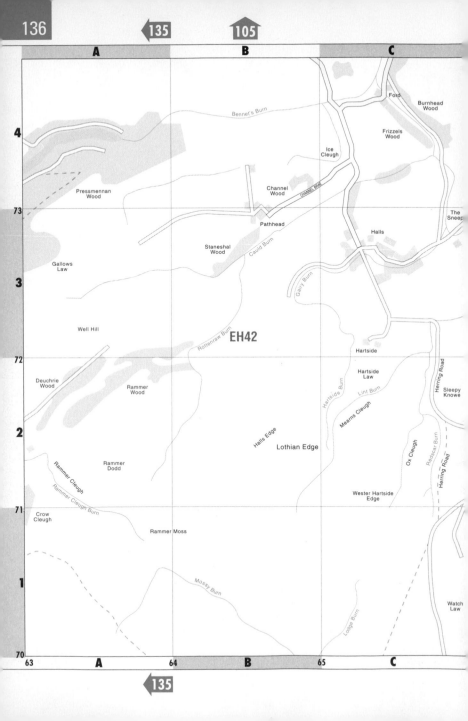

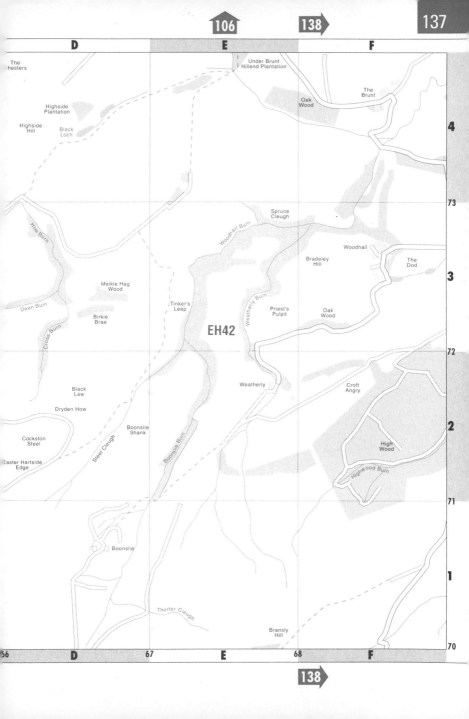

106
138

D
E
F

The Chesters

Under Brunt
Hilend Plantation

Oak
Wood

The
Brunt

Highside
Plantation

Highside
Hill

Black
Loch

4

Spruce
Cleugh

73

How Burn

Woodhall Burn

Woodhall

The
Dod

Bradeley
Hill

3

Meikle Hag
Wood

Tinker's
Leap

Weatherly Burn

Priest's
Pulpit

Oak
Wood

Dean Burn

Birkie
Brae

EH42

Cross Burn

72

Black
Law

Weatherly

Croft
Angry

2

Dryden How

Boonslie
Shank

High
Wood

Cockston
Steel

Steel Cleugh

Boonslie Burn

Easter Hartside
Edge

Highwood Burn

71

Boonslie

1

Thorter Cleugh

Bransly
Hill

70

56
D
67
E
68
F

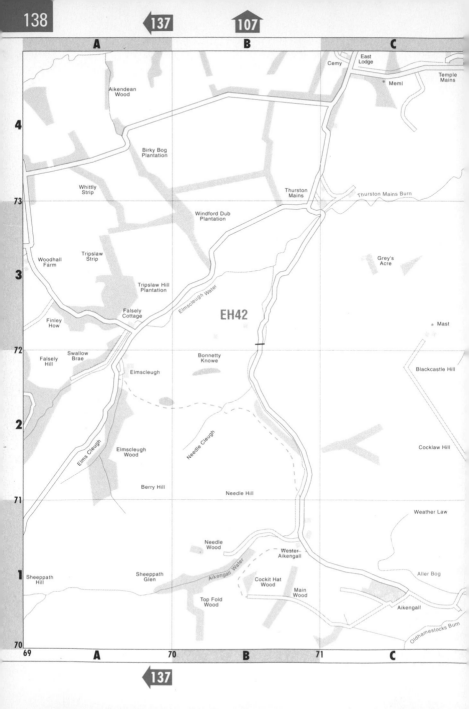

A
B
C

Cemy
East
Lodge

Meml
Temple
Mains

Aikendean
Wood

4

Birky Bog
Plantation

Whittly
Strip

Thurston
Mains

Thurston Mains Burn

73

Windford Dub
Plantation

Grey's
Acre

Tripslaw
Strip

Woodhall
Farm

3

Tripslaw Hill
Plantation

Elmscleugh Water

EH42

Finley
How

Falsely
Cottage

Mast

72

Falsely
Hill

Swallow
Brae

Bonnetty
Knowe

Blackcastle Hill

Elmscleugh

2

Elms Cleugh

Elmscleugh
Wood

Needle Cleugh

Cocklaw Hill

Berry Hill

Needle Hill

71

Weather Law

Needle
Wood

Wester-
Aikengall

Aikengall Water

Aller Bog

1

Sheeppath
Hill

Sheeppath
Glen

Cockit Hat
Wood

Main
Wood

Aikengall

Top Fold
Wood

Oldhamestocks Burn

70

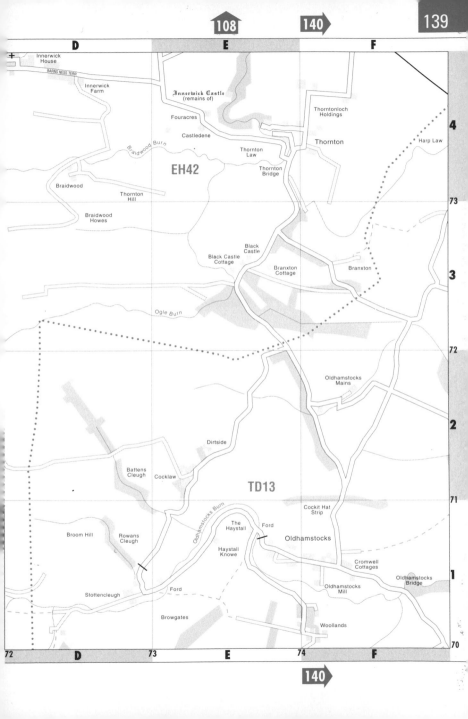

D
E
F

+ Innerwick
House

BARNS NESS TERR

Innerwick
Farm

Innerwick Castle
(remains of)

Fouracres

Castledene

Braidwood Burn

Thornton
Law

EH42

Thornton
Bridge

Thorntonloch
Holdings

Thornton

Harp Law

4

Braidwood

Thornton
Hill

73

Braidwood
Howes

Black
Castle

Black Castle
Cottage

Branxton
Cottage

Branxton

3

Ogle Burn

72

Oldhamstocks
Mains

2

Dirtside

Battens
Cleugh

Cocklaw

TD13

Cockit Hat
Strip

71

Broom Hill

Rowans
Cleugh

Oldhamstocks Burn

The
Haystall

Ford

Oldhamstocks

Haystall
Knowe

Cromwell
Cottages

Oldhamstocks
Bridge

1

Stottencleugh

Ford

Oldhamstocks
Mill

Browgates

Woollands

70

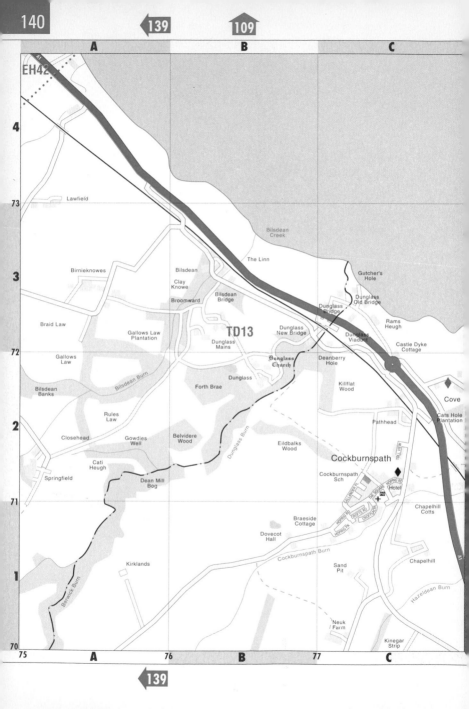

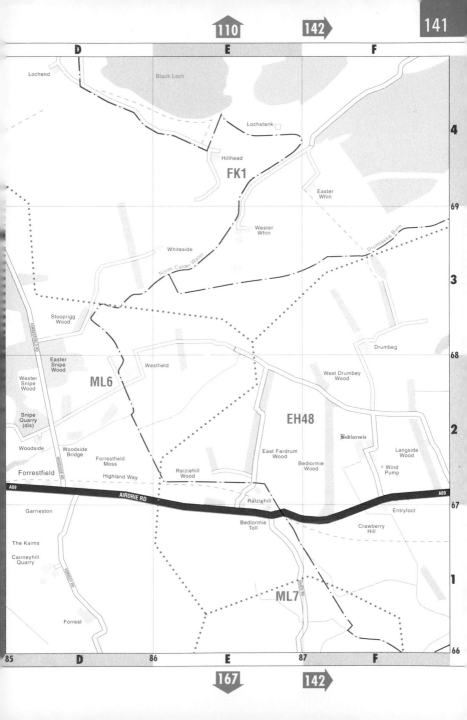

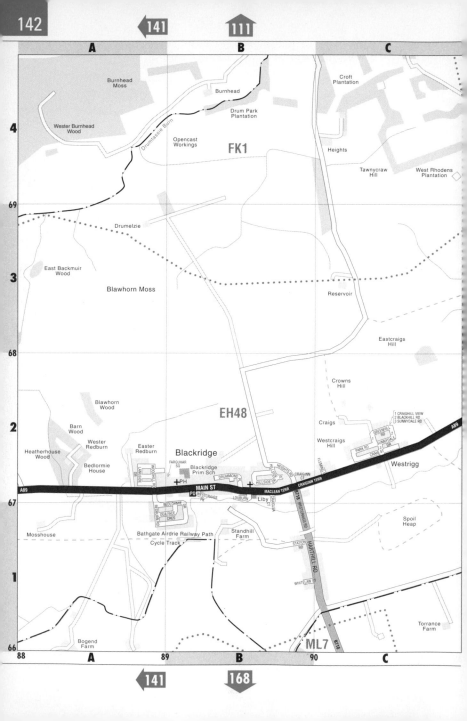

A   B   C

4

Burnhead
Moss

Wester Burnhead
Wood

Burnhead

Drum Park
Plantation

Croft
Plantation

Drumtassie Burn

Opencast
Workings

FK1

Heights

Tawnycraw
Hill

West Rhodens
Plantation

69

Drumelzie

3

East Backmuir
Wood

Blawhorn Moss

Reservoir

Eastcraigs
Hill

68

Crowns
Hill

2

Blawhorn
Wood

Barn
Wood

Wester
Redburn

Heatherhouse
Wood

Bedlormie
House

Easter
Redburn

FARQUHAR
SQ

Blackridge

Blackridge
Prim Sch

DRUMMOND

EH48

Craigs

Westcraigs
Hill

PARK RD

GREENHILL
RD

1 CRAIGHILL VIEW
2 BLACKHILL RD
3 SUNNYDALE RD

SUNNYDALE
DR

CRAIG ST

A89

Westrigg

HEIGHT RD

CRAIGINN TERR

FLEMINGT

67

A89

+ PH

MAIN ST

HILLSIDE DR

+

Liby

MACLEAN TERR

CRAIGINN TERR

B718

WESTCRAIGS RD

Spoil
Heap

Mosshouse

Bathgate Airdrie Railway Path
Cycle Track

Standhill
Farm

STATION
RD

HARTHILL RD

1

WHITE LAW ST

Bogend
Farm

66

ML7

B718

Torrance
Farm

88   A   89   B   90   C

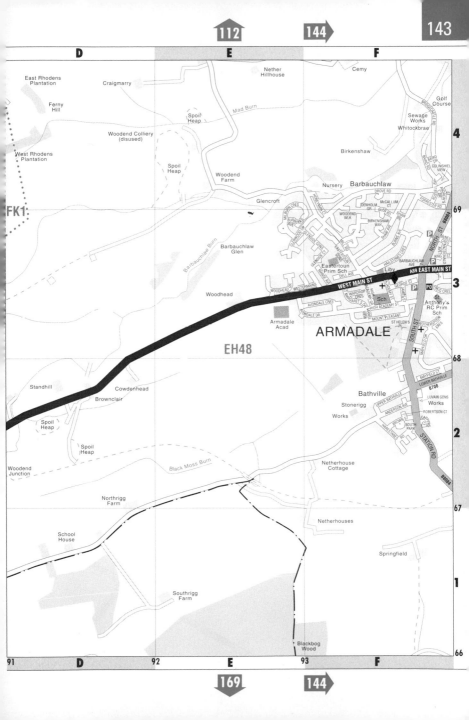

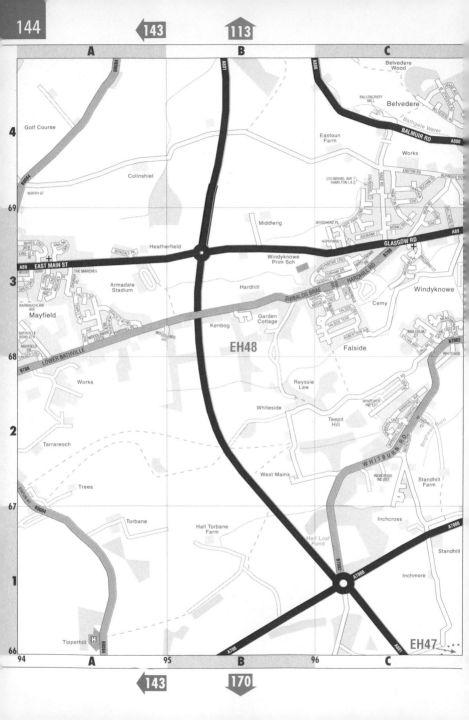

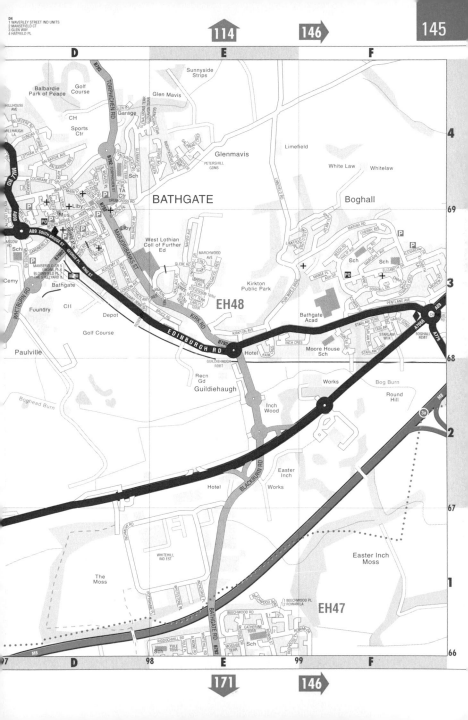

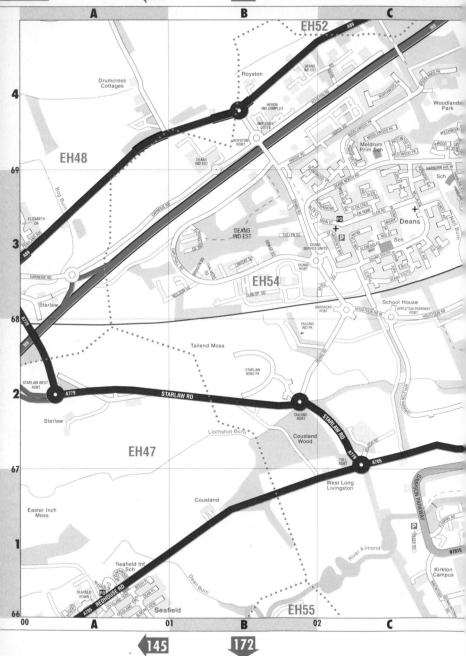
145

115

EH52

A89

M8

Drumcross
Cottages

Royston

DEANS
IND EST

HERON
IND COMPLEX

Woodlands
Park

WOODLANDS PK

4

EH48

MUSSELBEE
COTTS

ROYSTON RD

ROYSTON RD

NORTHWOOD PK

BEECHWOOD

HARDIE RD

MIDDLEWOOD PK

WESTWOOD PK

NAIL BURN

Meldrum
Prim Sch

WESTWOOD PK

ROYSTON
RDBT

HARBURN AVE W

Sch

69

Bog Burn

CARNEGIE RD

HARDIE RD

DEANS NORTH RD

OAKKNOWE

GLEN CRES

GLEN TERR

SMD'Y

Deans

A89

CAPITAL RD

DEANS
IND EST

PO

MAIN ST

P

GLEN RD

SMD'Y

MID ST

Sch

3

Starlaw

CARNEGIE RD

TEVIOTDALE TIG AV

BRANDON SQ

CHAMBERS SQ

LINDSAY SQ

CULLEN SQ

DEANS
SERVICE UNITS

DEANS SOUTH

GLENEAGLES WAY

DEANS SOUTH

DUTC

BUTE

NEILSTON SQ

DEANS
RDBT

DEANS SOUTH

M8

A779

DEANS
IND EST

DUNLOP SQ

EH54

School House

APPLETON PARKWAY
RDBT

68

BARRACKS
RDBT

HOUSTOUN RD W

HOUSTOUN RD

TAILEND
IND PK

Tailend Moss

STARLAW
BSNS PK

STARLAW WEST
RDBT

A779

STARLAW RD

Tailend
RDBT

STARLAW RD

2

Starlaw

Lochshot Burn

Cousland
Wood

A779

TOLL
RDBT

A705

67

West Long
Livingston

SIMPSON PARKWAY

EH47

Easter Inch
Moss

Cousland

River Almond

P

B7015

1

Kirkton
Campus

Seafield Inf
Sch

REDHOUSE RD

SEAFIELD
ROWS

Dean Burn

A705

Seafield

EH55

66

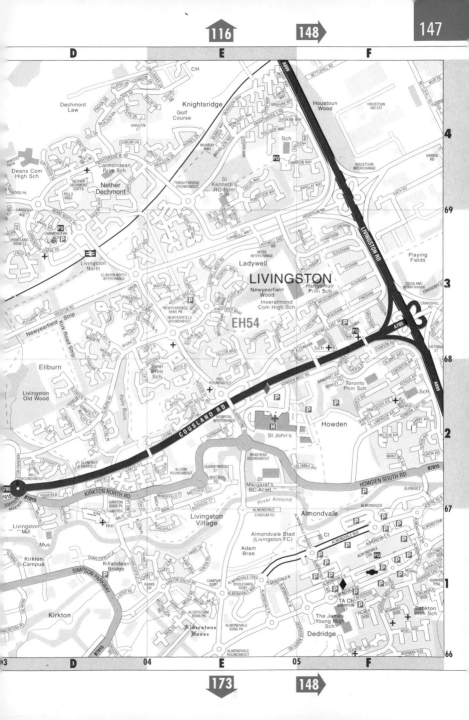

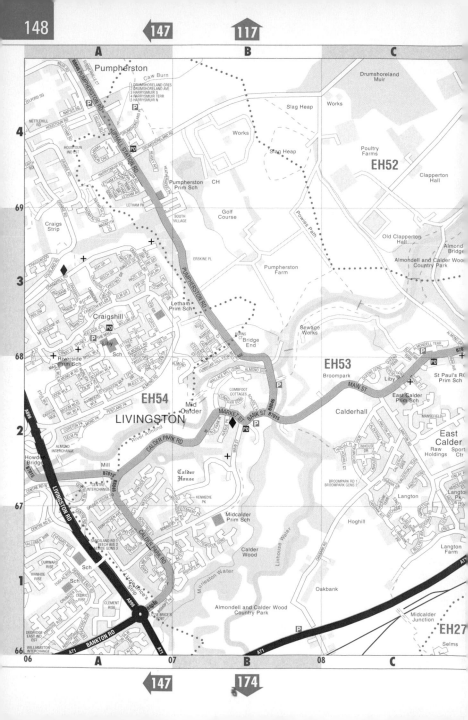

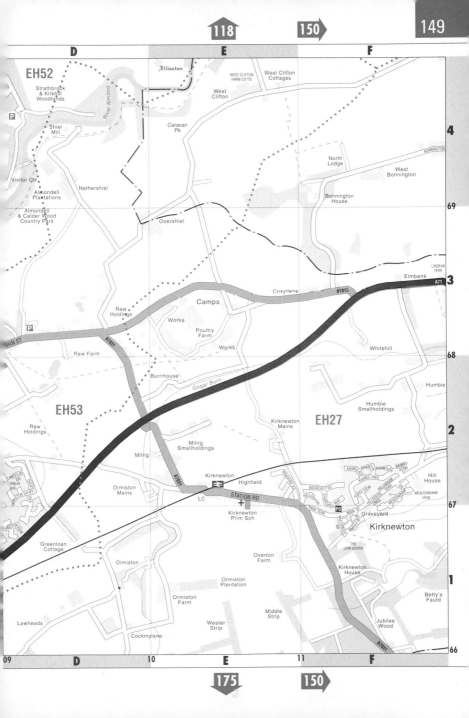

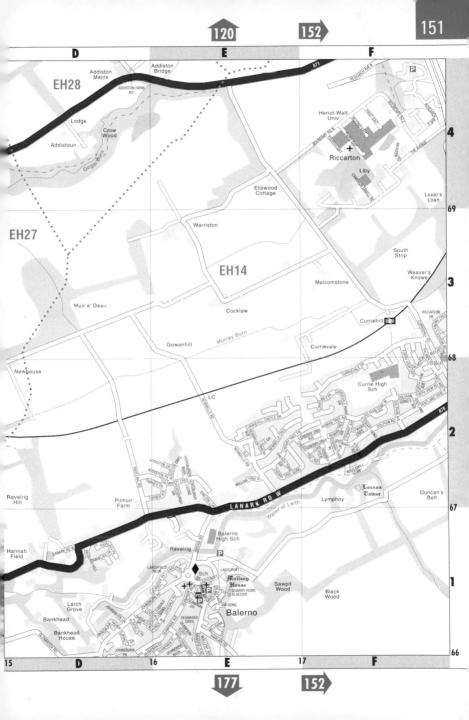

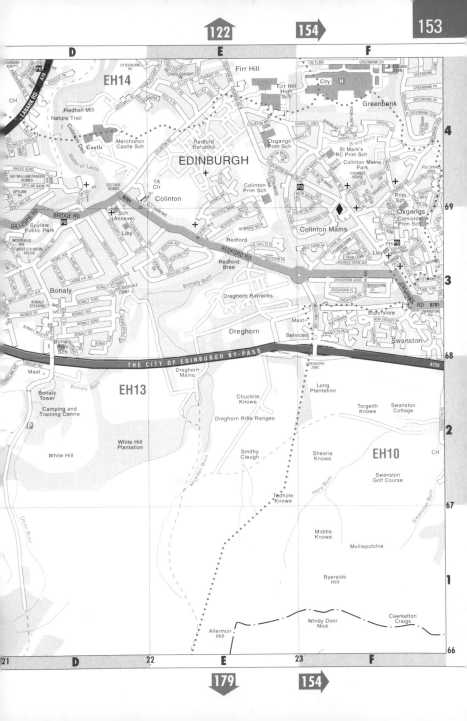

153
123

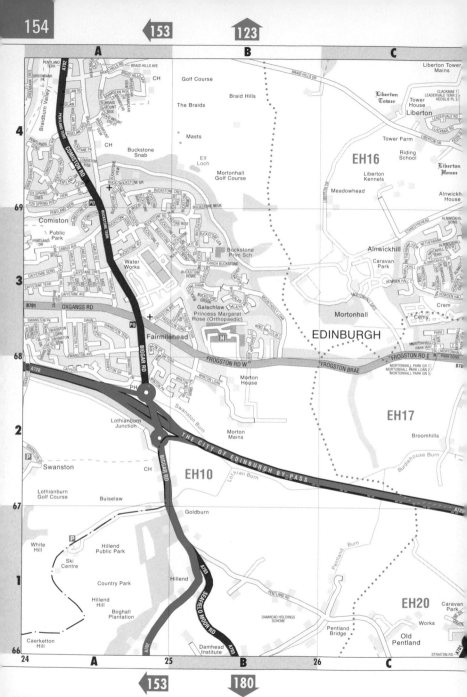

153
180

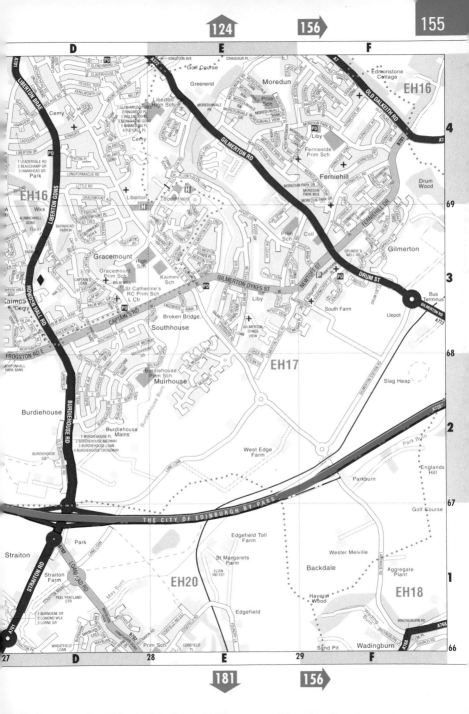

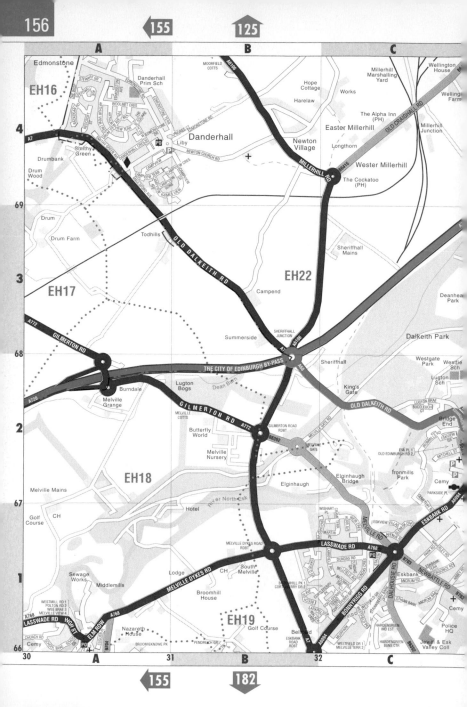

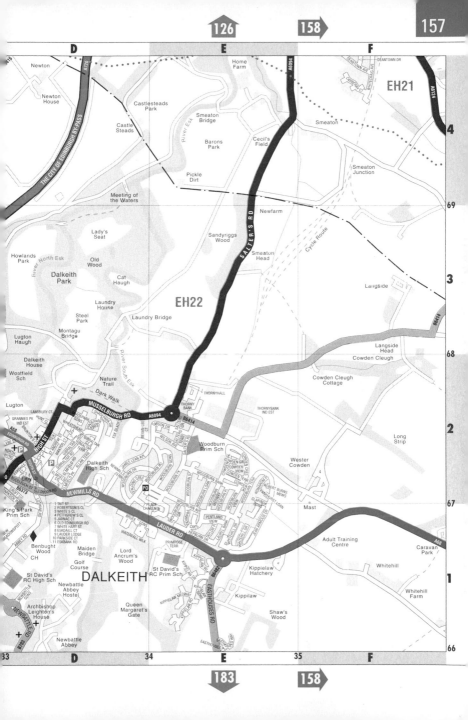

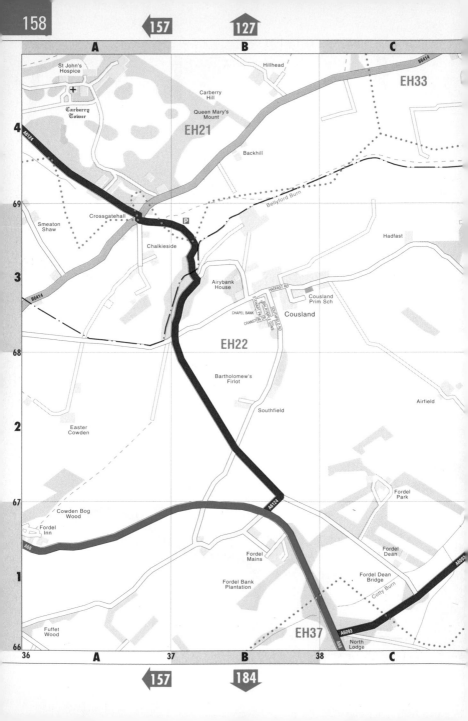

157
127

A B C

St John's Hospice

Carberry Tower

B6414

EH33

Hillhead

Carberry Hill

Queen Mary's Mount

EH21

Backhill

4

A6124

69

Bellyford Burn

Crossgatehall

Smeaton Shaw

P

Chalkieside

Hadfast

3

B6414

Airybank House

HADFAST RD

Cousland Prim Sch

CHAPEL BANK

Cousland

SMEATON RD

BLACKSMITH'S CLOSE

CRANSTON DR

68

EH22

Bartholomew's Firlot

Southfield

Airfield

2

Easter Cowden

Fordel Park

67

Cowden Bog Wood

A6124

Fordel Inn

A68

Fordel Dean

Fordel Mains

Fordel Dean Bridge

A6093

1

Fordel Bank Plantation

Cotty Burn

Fuffet Wood

EH37

A6093

A68

North Lodge

66

36

A

37

B

38

C

157
184

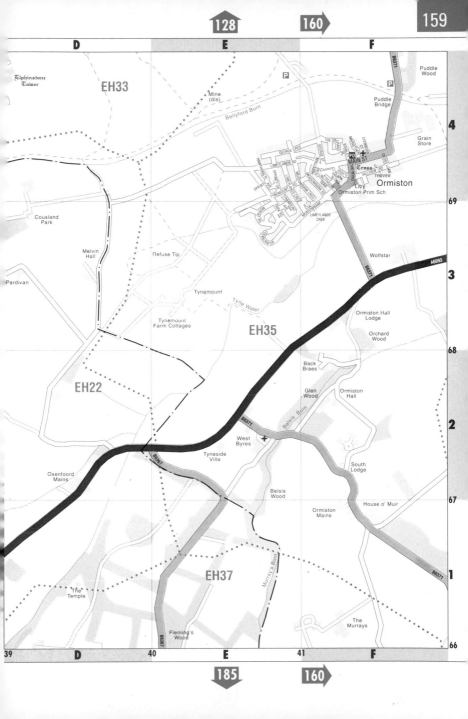

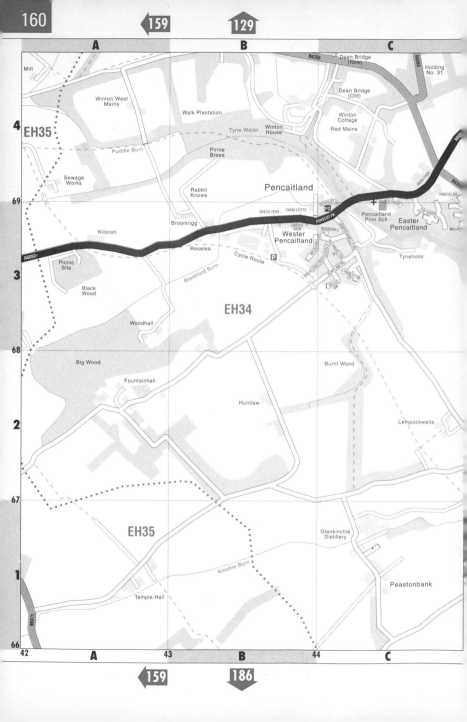

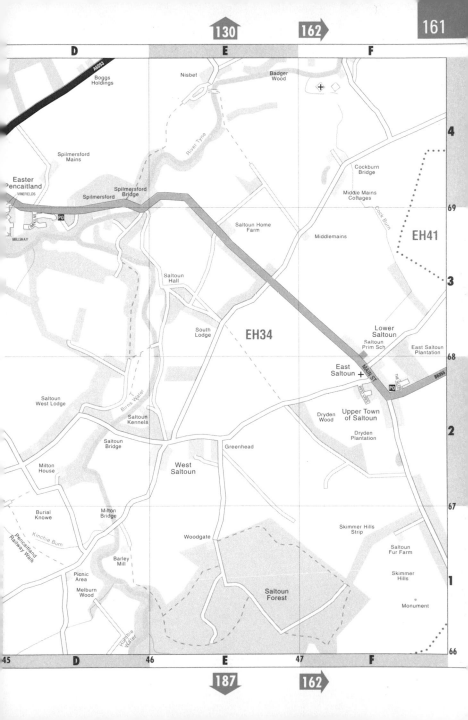

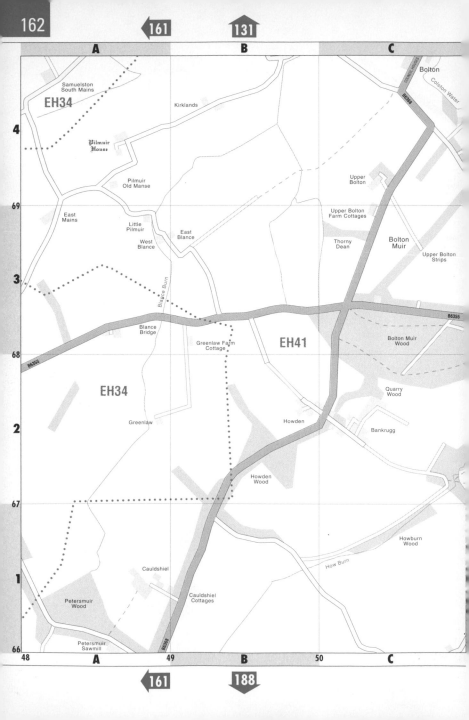

A B C

Bolton
Colston Water

Samuelston
South Mains

EH34

Kirklands

4

Pilmuir
House

Upper
Bolton

Pilmuir
Old Manse

69

Upper Bolton
Farm Cottages

East
Mains

Little
Pilmuir

East
Blance

Thorny
Dean

Bolton
Muir

West
Blance

Upper Bolton
Strips

3

Blance Burn

B6355

Blance
Bridge

Bolton Muir
Wood

68

Greenlaw Farm
Cottage

EH41

B6355

EH34

Quarry
Wood

Greenlaw

Howden

Bankrugg

2

Howden
Wood

67

Howburn
Wood

How Burn

Cauldshiel

1

Cauldshiel
Cottages

Petersmuir
Wood

B6368

Petersmuir
Sawmill

66

48 A 49 B 50 C

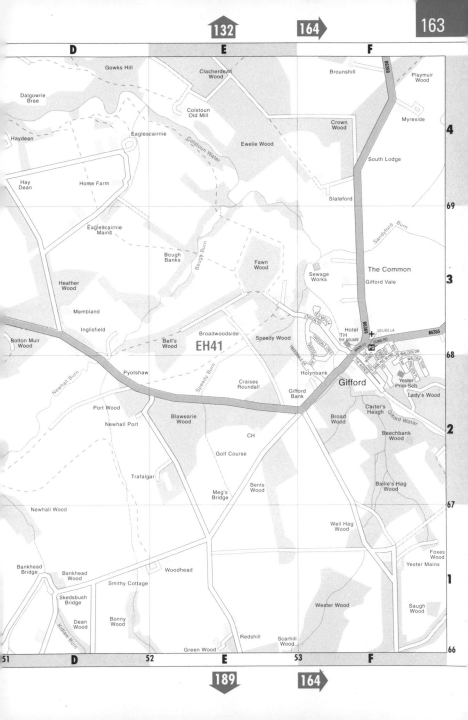

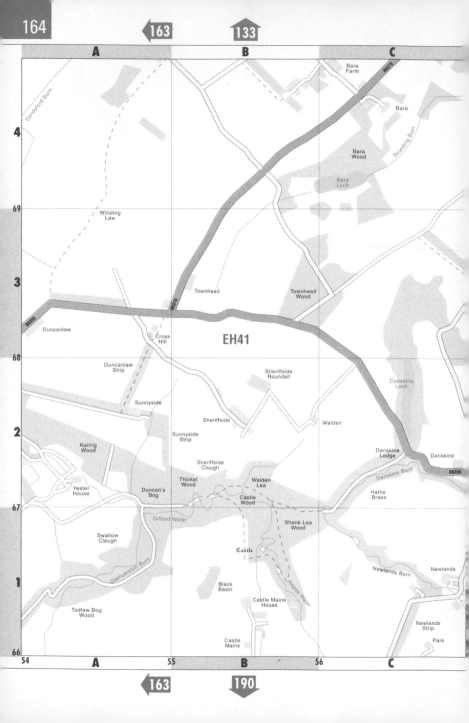

163
133

A **B** **C**

Sandyford Burn

Bara Farm

B6370

Bara

4

Bara Wood

Sounding Burn

Bara Loch

Winding Law

69

3

B6370

Townhead

Townhead Wood

B6355

Duncanlaw

Cross Hill

EH41

Danskine Loch

68

Duncanlaw Strip

Sheriffside Roundall

Sunnyside

Sheriffside

Walden

2

Kailrig Wood

Sunnyside Strip

Danskine Lodge

Danskine

Sheriffside Clough

Danskine Burn

B6355

Yester House

Duncan's Bog

Thicket Wood

Walden Lea

Hattie Braes

67

Castle Wood

Gifford Water

Shank Lea Wood

Swallow Cleugh

Castle

Newlands Burn

Newlands

Gamuelston Burn

Black Basin

Hopes Water

1

Castle Mains House

Newlands Strip

Todlaw Bog Wood

Park

Castle Mains

66

54 **A** 55 **B** 56 **C**

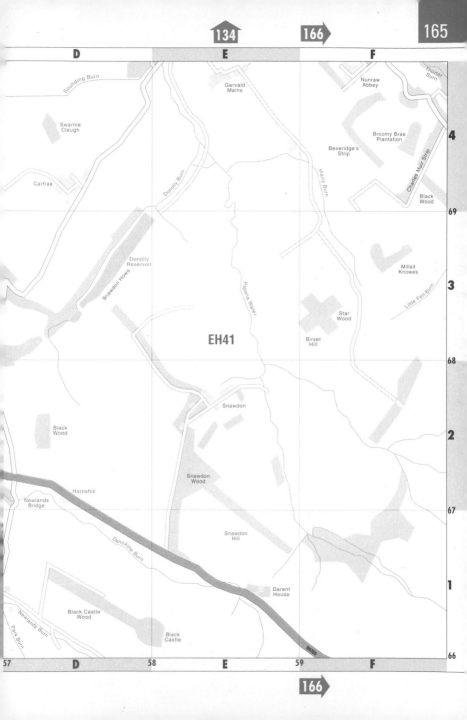

D
E
F

Sounding Burn

Garvald
Mains

Nunraw
Abbey

Thorter
Burn

Swarnie
Cleugh

Broomy Brae
Plantation

4

Beveridge's
Strip

Charlie Muir Strip

Carfrae

Donolly Burn

Hairy Burn

Black
Wood

69

Donolly
Reservoir

Papana Water

Millsit
Knowes

Little Fen Burn

3

Snawdon Howe

Star
Wood

68

EH41

Birset
Hill

Snawdon

Black
Wood

2

Snawdon
Wood

Hornshill

Newlands
Bridge

Snawdon
Hill

67

Danskine Burn

Darent
House

1

Newlands Burn

Black Castle
Wood

Park Burn

Black
Castle

B6355

66

57
D
58
E
59
F

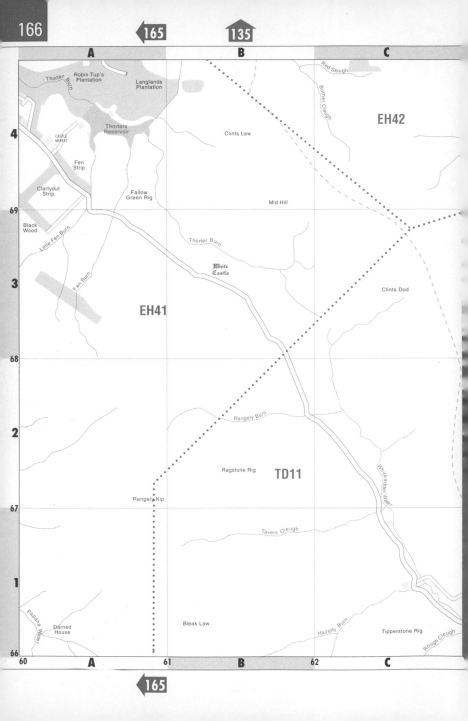

A   B   C

Thorter Burn

Robin Tup's
Plantation

Langlands
Plantation

4

Clints Law

EH42

CASTLE
MOFFAT

Thorters
Reservoir

Fen
Strip

Clartydut
Strip

Fallow
Green Rig

69

Mid Hill

Black
Wood

Little Fen Burn

Thorter Burn

Fen Burn

White Castle

3

EH41

Clints Dod

68

Rangely Burn

2

Ragstone Rig

TD11

White Adder Water

Rangely Kip

67

Tavers Cleugh

1

Papana Valley

Darned
House

Bleak Law

Hazely Burn

Tipperstone Rig

Rough Cleugh

66

60   A   61   B   62   C

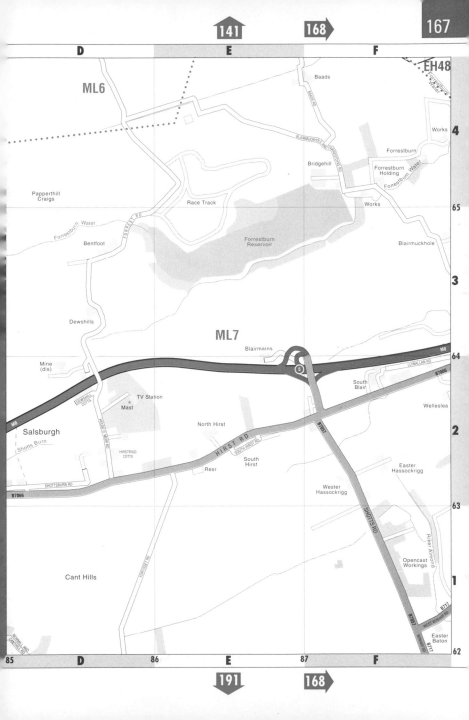

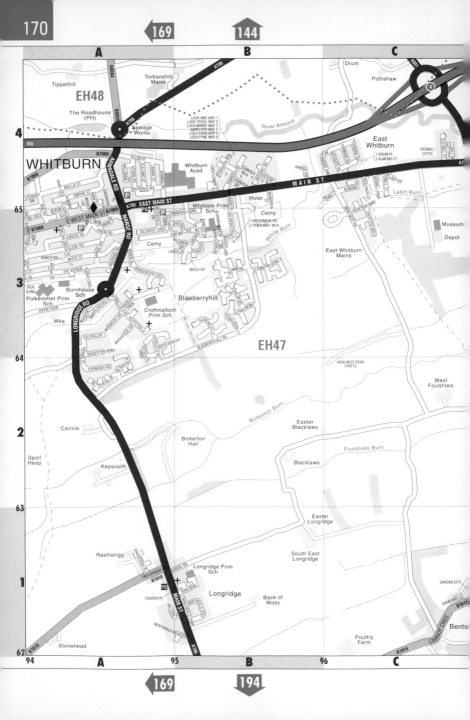

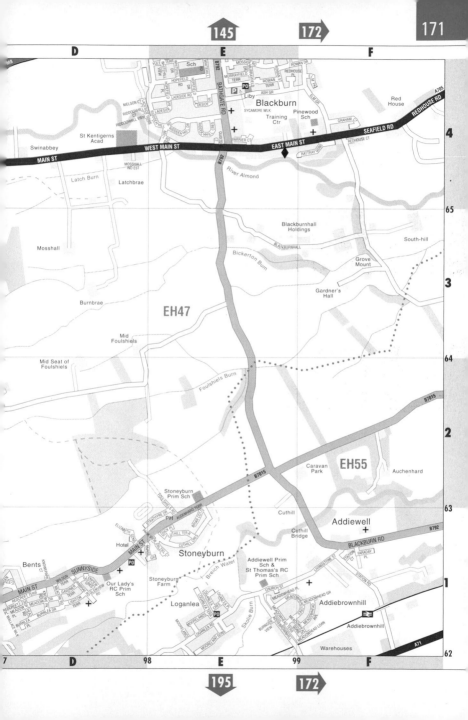

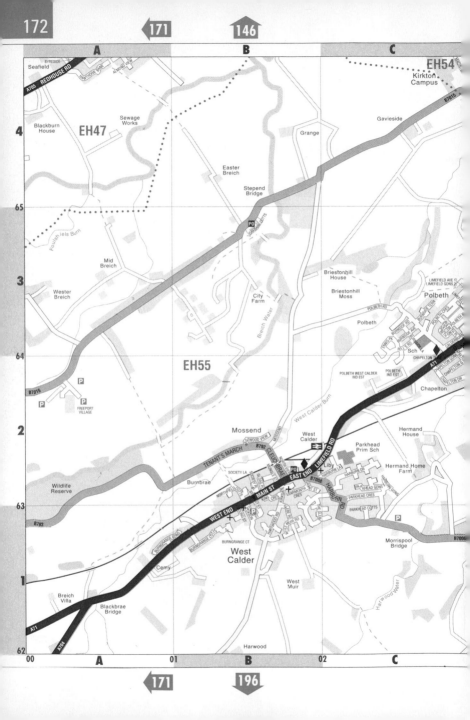

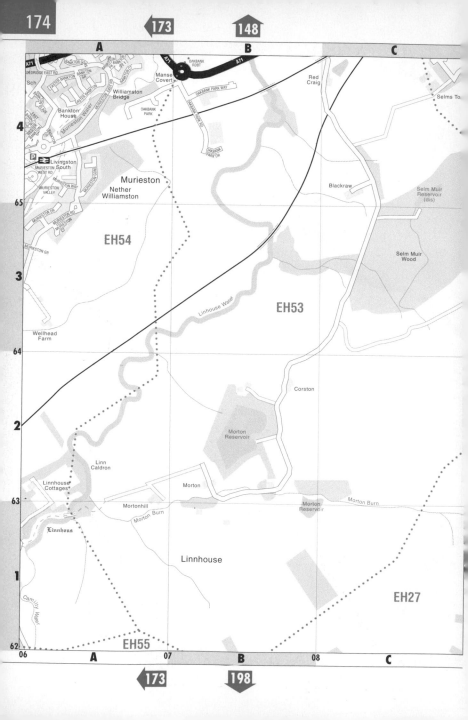

173
148

A   **B**   **C**

A71

OAKBANK RDBT

Manse Covert

Oakbank Park

A71

Red Craig

Selms To

Sch

DEDRIDGE EAST RD

CASTLE BANKTON

Williamston Bridge

OAKBANK PARK WAY

OAKBANK PARK RD

Bankton House

OAKBANK PARK DR

4

Livingston South

Blackraw

Selm Muir Reservoir (dis)

MURIESTON WEST RD

Murieston

Nether Williamston

65

MURIESTON VALLEY

Selm Muir Wood

MURIESTON RD

EH54

MURIESTON GR

3

EH53

Linhouse Walk

64

Wellhead Farm

Corston

2

Morton Reservoir

Linn Caldron

Linnhouse Cottages

Morton

63

Mortonhill

Morton Burn

Morton Reservoir

Morton Burn

Linnhous

Morton Burn

Linnhouse

1

EH27

Camilty Water

EH55

62

06   **A**   07   **B**   08   **C**

173
198

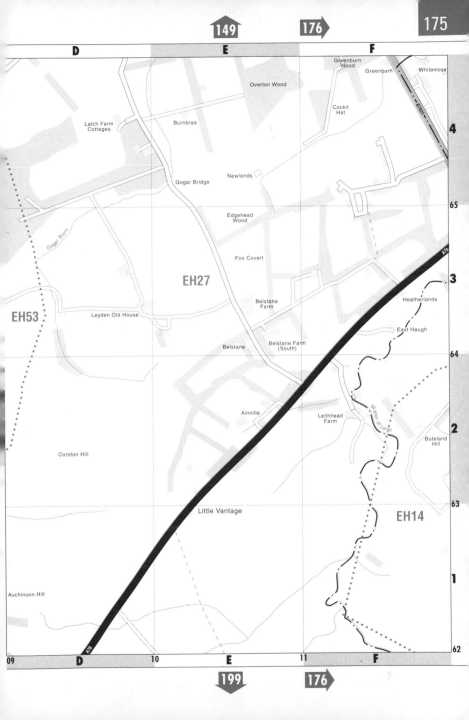

D E F

Greenburn
Wood
Greenburn
Whitemoss

Overton Wood

Cockit
Hat

Latch Farm
Cottages

Burnbrae

4

Gogar Bridge

Newlands

65

Edgehead
Wood

Gogar Burn

Fox Covert

EH27

Heatherlands

3

EH53

Belstane
Farm

East Haugh

Leyden Old House

Belstane Farm
(South)

64

Belstane

Ainville

Water of Leith

Leithhead
Farm

2

Buteland
Hill

Corston Hill

Little Vantage

63

EH14

Auchinoon Hill

1

62

09 D 10 E 11 F

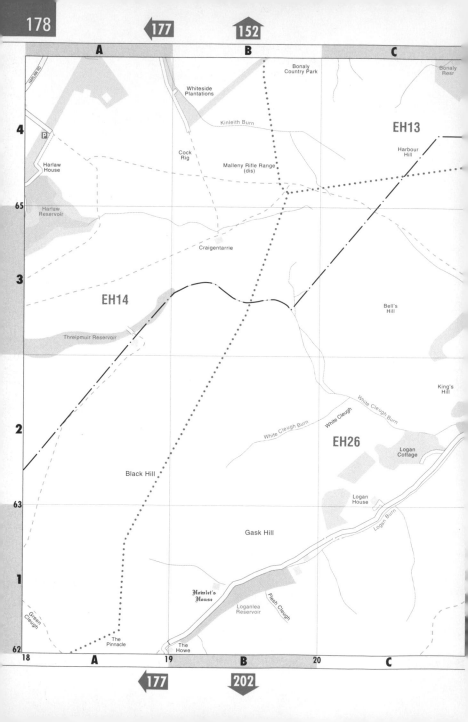

177
152

A

B

C

Bonaly
Country Park

Bonaly
Resr

Whiteside
Plantations

Kinleith Burn

4

EH13

Cock
Rig

Harbour
Hill

Malleny Rifle Range
(dis)

Harlaw
House

65

Harlaw
Reservoir

Craigentarrie

3

EH14

Bell's
Hill

Threipmuir Reservoir

King's
Hill

White Cleugh Burn

White Cleugh Burn

White Cleugh

2

White Cleugh Burn

EH26

Logan
Cottage

Black Hill

63

Logan
House

Logan Burn

Gask Hill

1

Howlet's
House

Green
Cleugh

Flesh Cleugh

Loganlea
Reservoir

The
Pinnacle

62

The
Howe

A

B

C

A B C

4

Caerketton Hill

Boghall Plantation

Boghall

Boghall Burn

EH10

Damhead Institute
DAMHEAD HOLDINGS SCHEME

Tigh-na-Geat House

Pentland House

A703

EH20

Pentland Pk

Pentland Mains

New Pentlan

S STRAITON RD
PENTLAND RD

Nursery

A768 Niven's Knowe Rd A7

Niven's Knowe

DRYDEN GLEN

65

Fulford

SEAFIELD MOOR RD

Woodfield Cottage

Pentland Grove

Seafield

Pentlandfield

Roslin Prim Sch (annexe)

BROOKFIELD TERR

SEAFIELD RD

PH

PO

Bilston Burn

Bilston Wood

Dryden Towe

3

Easter Howgate

Woodside Cottages

Easter Bush

SNOWDROP VIEW

Bilston

Black Wood

Langhill Farm

A703

64

A702

Kill Burn

A703

Moat Cottage

EH25

EH26

Gowkley Moss

Bush

Lodge

PH

Roslin

B7006 MAIN ST

2

Glencorse House

Loganbank

Glencorse Burn

Pentlands Science Pk

Cemy

Lodge

B7003

PENICUIK RD

ST CLAIR CRES

Roslin Prim Sch

B7006

63

New Milton Farm

Milton Cottages

Milton Mill

B7026

Sand Pit

Roslin Glen

B7003

1

Training Centre

Milton Bridge

CH

PO

Milton Bridge

Golf Course

Whinny Brae

THE BRAE

EVELYN TERR

The Glencorse Centre

Auchendinny

Eskhill

Oatslie

Picnic Area

Roslin Glen Ctry Pk

River North Esk

Lea Farm

62

Glencorse Prim Sch

EDINBURGH RD

A701

Barracks

HAWKINS TERR

B7026

PH

24 A 25 B 26 C

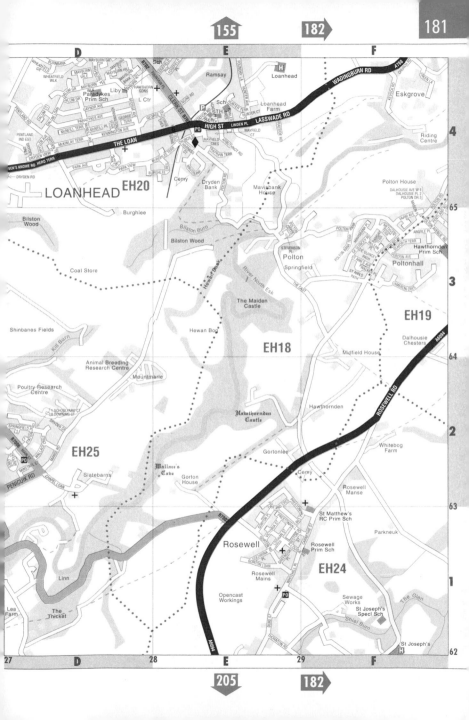

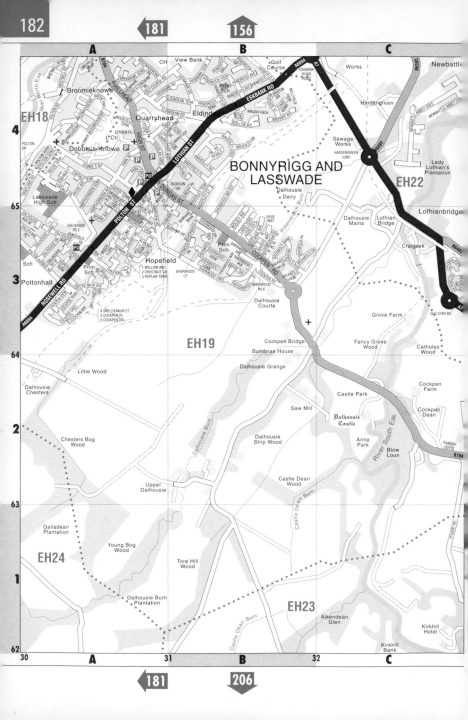

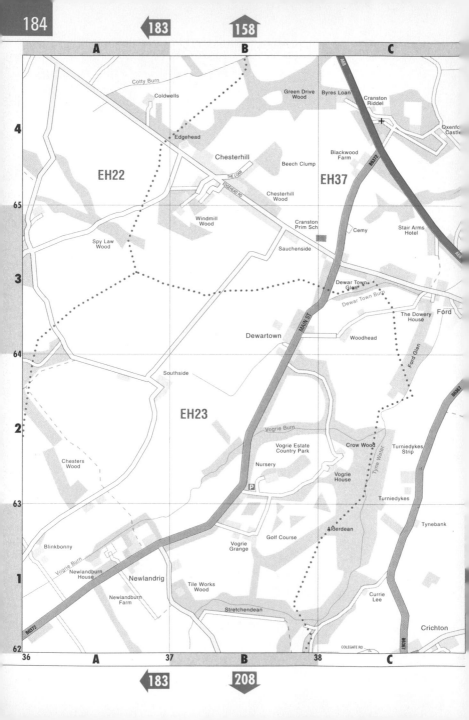

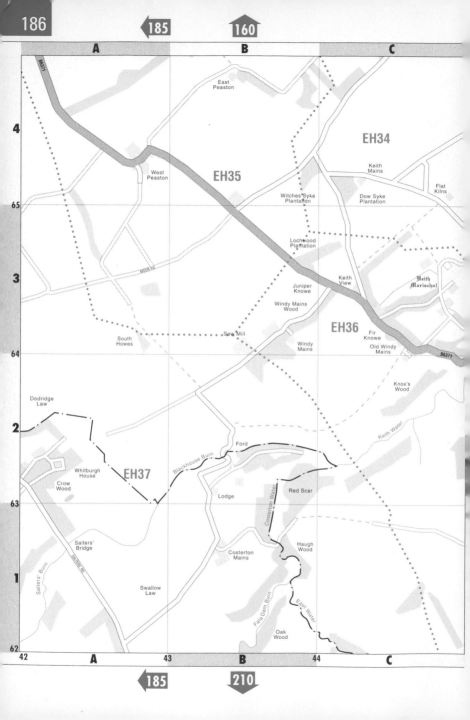

A   B   C

B6371

East
Peaston

4

EH34

Keith
Mains

West
Peaston

EH35

Flat
Kilns

65

Witches Syke
Plantation

Dow Syke
Plantation

Lochwood
Plantation

MOOR RD

3

Keith
Marischal

Juniper
Knowe

Keith
View

Windy Mains
Wood

EH36

Fir
Knowe

Saw Mill

South
Howes

Windy
Mains

Old Windy
Mains

64

B6371

Knox's
Wood

Dodridge
Law

Keith Water

2

Blackhouse Burn

Ford

Whitburgh
House

EH37

Crow
Wood

Lodge

Red Scar

Costerton Water

63

Salters'
Bridge

Haugh
Wood

Costerton
Mains

Salters' Burn

SALTERS RD

1

Swallow
Law

Fala Dam Burn

East Water

Oak
Wood

62

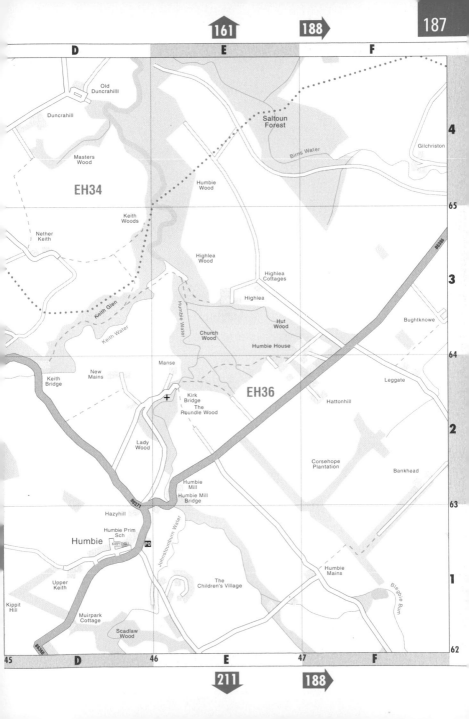

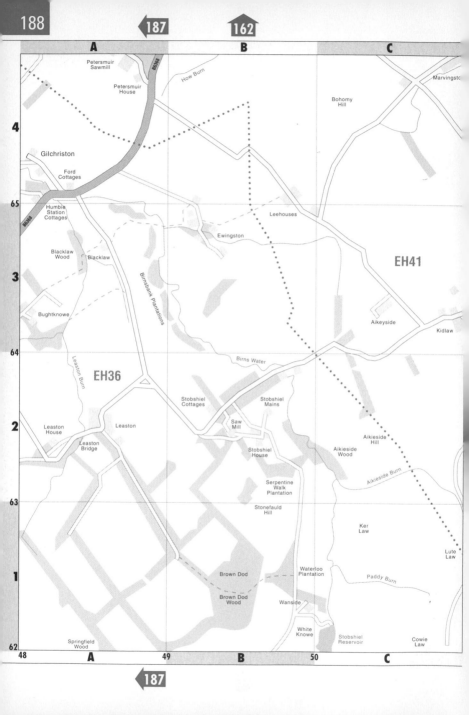

187
162

A   B   C

4

Petersmuir
Sawmill

How Burn

Petersmuir
House

Marvingsto

Bohomy
Hill

Gilchriston

Ford
Cottages

65

Humbie
Station
Cottages

Leehouses

EH41

Blacklaw
Wood   Blacklaw

Ewingston

3

Bughtknowe

Birnsbank Plantations

Aikeyside

Kidlaw

64

Birns Water

Leaston Burn

EH36

Stobshiel
Cottages

Stobshiel
Mains

2

Leaston
House

Leaston

Saw
Mill

Aikieside
Hill

Leaston
Bridge

Stobshiel
House

Aikieside
Wood

Aikieside Burn

Serpentine
Walk
Plantation

63

Stonefauld
Hill

Ker
Law

Brown Dod

Waterloo
Plantation

Paddy Burn

Lute
Law

1

Brown Dod
Wood

Wanside

White
Knowe

Stobshiel
Reservoir

Cowie
Law

Springfield
Wood

62

48   A   49   B   50   C

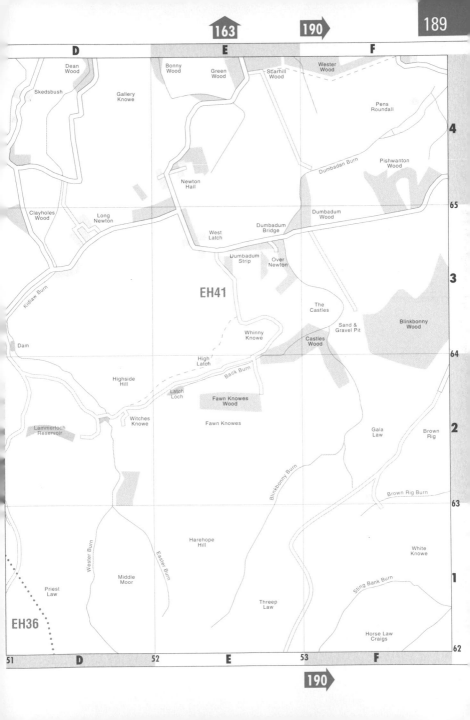

A

B

C

Little Todlaw
Wood

Baxtersyke

Quarryford

QUARRYFORD
FARM COTTS

The Forge

Holly
Cottage

4

Park
Strips

Longyester

65

Dod
Law

Blinkbonny
Wood

Smiddy
Wood

3

Stell
Wood

Hopes Water

Brookside Burn

Fawn's
Wood

Bentyhall

EH41

64

Harelaw Burn

East
Hopes

Beech
Wood

Hopes

Nipper
Knowes

Knock
Hill

Soon Hope Burn

Knockhill
Wood

Mid Burn

2

Soon
Hope

Fennie
Law

Kingside
Rig

63

Fennie Burn

Hare
Law

West
Hopes

Pyatshaw
Plantation

Sting Bank

Crow
Cairn

1

Harestone
Hill

Whitstone
Cairn

Hopes
Reservoir

Long Grain

Fall Burn

The
Fall

62

54

A

55

B

56

C

191

168

A   B   C

B717

4

BENHAR RD

61

CH

Golf Course

Starryshaw Farm

South Calder Water

B717

3

Spoil Heap

Stanebent

Cairneyhead

ML7

Stane

STABLE RD

Torbothie

GRAY ST

HIGH ST

60

CEDAR WYND

HAZEL ST

CEDAR ST

ELM ST

THRIFTIE RD

KEITH DR

CALDER DR

Northfield

Stane Prim Sch

SOUTH BELLSIDE

SOUTH BELLSIDE

Torbothie

CEMETERY RD

MAUSE RD

CHARLOTTE ST

NEVIS PL

GARTEN DR

Cemy

1 ETIVE WLK
2 ULG WAY
3 GAIP WYND
4 BOWMORE WLK
5 TORRIN LOAN
6 SPRINGHILL VIEW
7 DORNIE WYND
8 MORAR WAY
9 COIRE LOAN
10 SUNA PATH
11 SALEN LOAN

EH47

2

B7010

MAIN ST

SANDYVALE PL

LOCHRIGE CRES

TULLOCH RD

APPIN TERR

LANSDOWNE CRES

LAGGAN AVE

Stane

BRIDGE

KNUT CRES

BLINNY CT 1
TARBRAX PATH 2

SPRINGHILL RD

Springhill

B7010

59

BELMONT DRIVE

LARCHFIELD LA

NORTHFIELD AVE

FELLWOOD RD

B715

HEADLESROSS RD B715

Works

Springhill

Knowton Farm

SPRINGHILL AND LEADLOCH RD

A71

1

Works

Lingore Line

A71

58

88   A   89   B   90   C

191

213

D
E
F

Spoil Heap

Fauldhouse Moor

Jubilee Cottage

4

Moss

Tippet Knowe

ML KINNON RD
NORTH VIEW
EAST WOOD
EASTFIELD VIEW
SOUTH VIEW
EAST VIEW
VICTORIA PK
LANRIGG RD

St John the Baptist RC Sch

Sports Ground
61
CROFTFOOT DR

Fauldhouse Hills

Spoil Heap

Spoil Heap

Benhar Junction

EH47

THORNTON PL

Warehouse

Leadloch

Braehead

Meadowfoot

Fauldhouse

SHOTTS RD

CALEDONIAN TERR

Liby
SCOTT PL
BARTON RD
VICTORIA RD
CHURCH
GREENHILL
B7015
KIRKHILL CT
SHEEPHOUSEHILL
BELLONA TERR
Falla Hill Prim Sch
MAIN ST
PO
KNOWLAN
TALLANT
ELDRICK VIEW
CLARICK CRES
ELDRICK RD
BLACKFAULDS CT
GARDEN SQUARE
DUNN
HILLVIEW
Greenburn
CH
LINN RD

Cemy
Fauldhouse
60

Golf Course

Bridge-end

Wayside
A71

2

SPRINGHILL AND LEADLOCH RD

East Badallan

Meikle Eldrick

Breich Water

Works

Lingore Linn

West Badallan

59

Wee Eldrick

Muldron Bridge

Headlesscross

Muldron

Shafts (dis)

Risland Knowes

1

B715

58

91
D
92
E
93
F

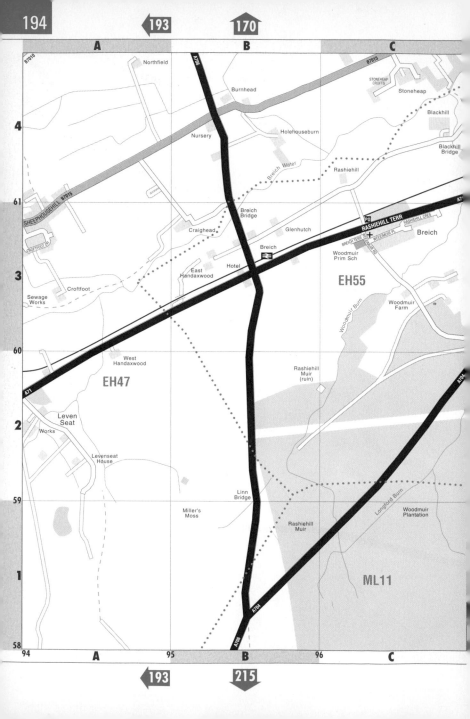

D
E
F

EH47

MOORELAND
GDNS

Hotel

Nether
Longford

A71

West Mains
Cottages

East
White Sykes

Newhouse

4

Nether Longford Moss

61

Longford Burn

Spoil
Heap

Longford

Rusha

Poultry
Farm

Longhill Burn

Longford
Bridge

3

Pateshill Cottage

EH55

60

2

Works

Pate's Hill

Woodmuir Plantation

59

Harwood Water

1

ML11

58

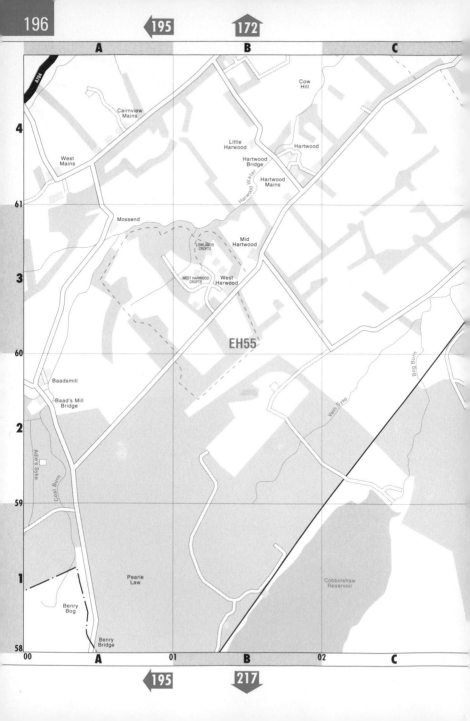

D E F

West Broomhill

Tor Whitie

B7008

Torphin Bridge

Harburn

Lodge

4

Coalheughead Farm

Bog Burn

CH

Bents Burn

Over Williamston

Whistle Lodge

East Torphin

Broadmeadow

Haymains

West Torphin

LC

61

Dog Bush Knowe

Harburn House

Golf Course

3

Black Burn

Harburnhead

EH55

Camp Wood

Camilty Moss

60

Tip

Camilty Plantation

Camilty Hill

EH27

2

Castle Greg ROMAN FORTLET

59

Crosswood Burn

A70

P

Harburnhead Hill

Crosswood Bridge

Shear Bridge

B7008

1

Otter Burn

A70

58

03 D 04 E 05 F

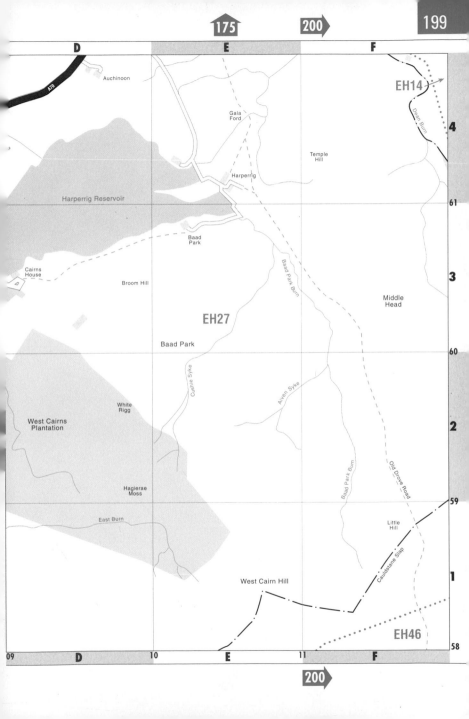

D E F

Auchinoon

A70

Gala Ford

Temple Hill

4

Harperrig

61

Harperrig Reservoir

Baad Park

Cairns House

3

Broom Hill

Middle Head

Baad Park Burn

EH27

Baad Park

60

Cushie Syke

White Rigg

West Cairns Plantation

2

Aven Syke

EH14

Dean Burn

Hagierae Moss

Baad Park Burn

Old Drove Road

East Burn

59

Little Hill

West Cairn Hill

1

Cauldstane Slap

EH46

58

09 D 10 E 11 F

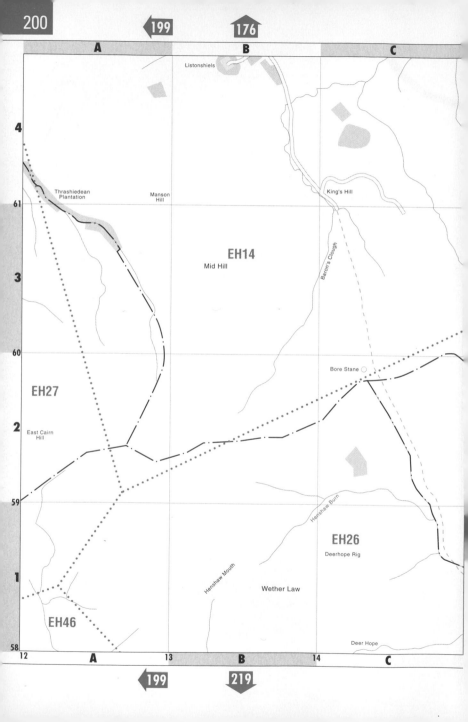

Listonshiels

4

Thrashiedean
Plantation

Manson
Hill

King's Hill

61

EH14

Mid Hill

3

Baron's Clough

60

Bore Stane ○

EH27

East Cairn
Hill

2

EH26

Henshaw Burn

59

Deerhope Rig

1

Henshaw Mouth

Wether Law

EH46

Deer Hope

58

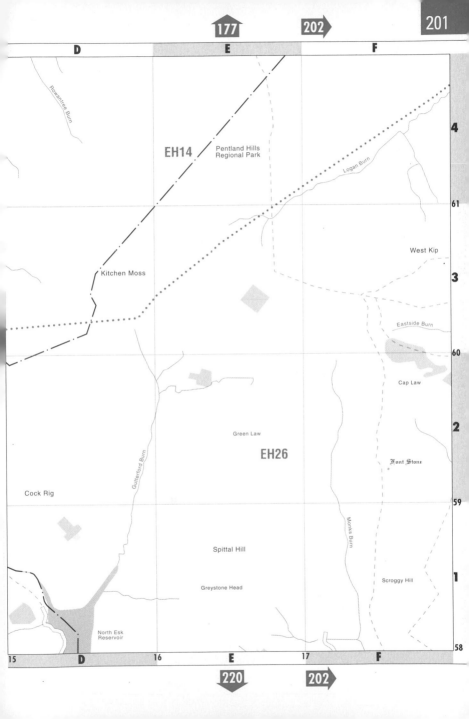

D
E
F

4

61

Rowantree Burn

EH14

Pentland Hills
Regional Park

Logan Burn

West Kip

3

Kitchen Moss

Eastside Burn

60

Cap Law

2

Green Law

EH26

Font Stane

Gutterford Burn

Cock Rig

59

Monks Burn

Spittal Hill

1

Greystone Head

Scroggy Hill

North Esk
Reservoir

58

15
D
16
E
17
F

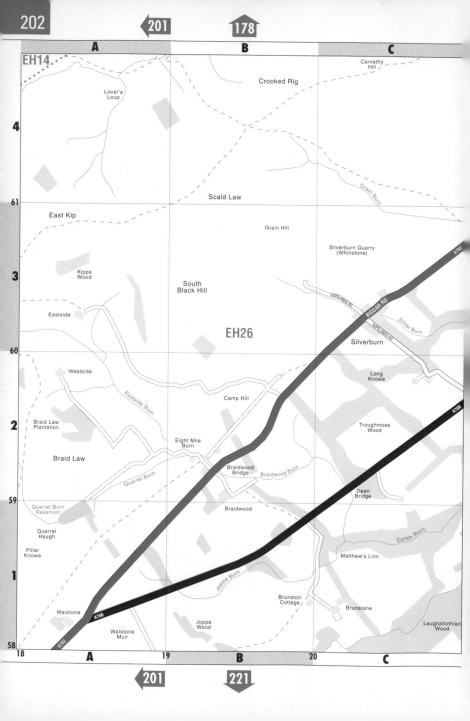

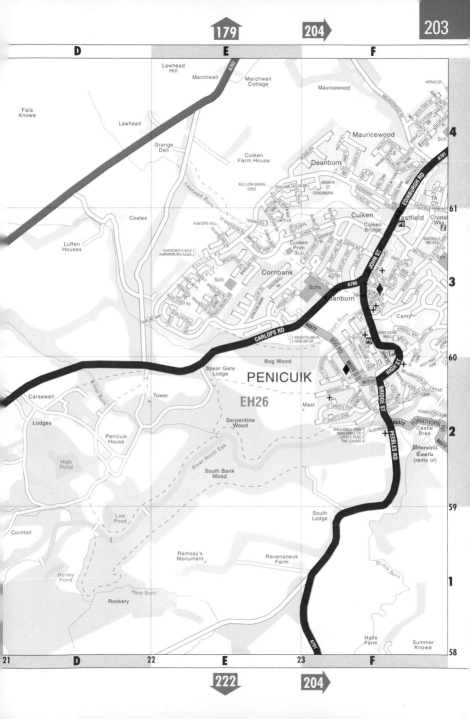

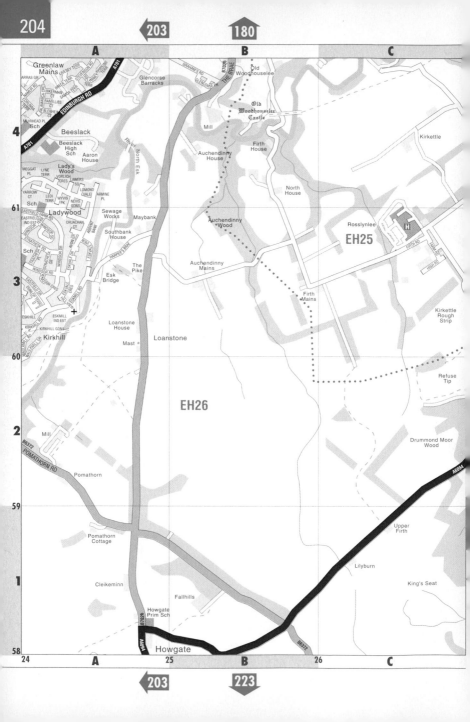

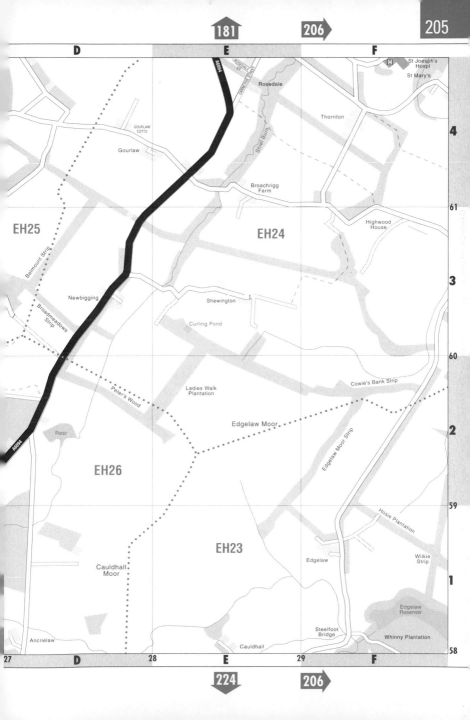

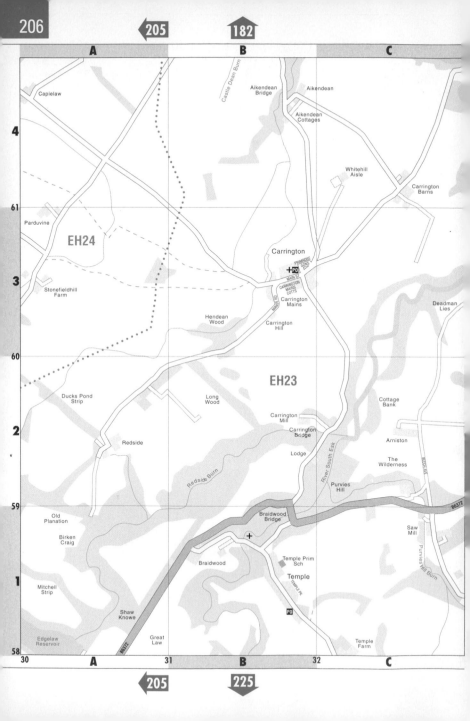

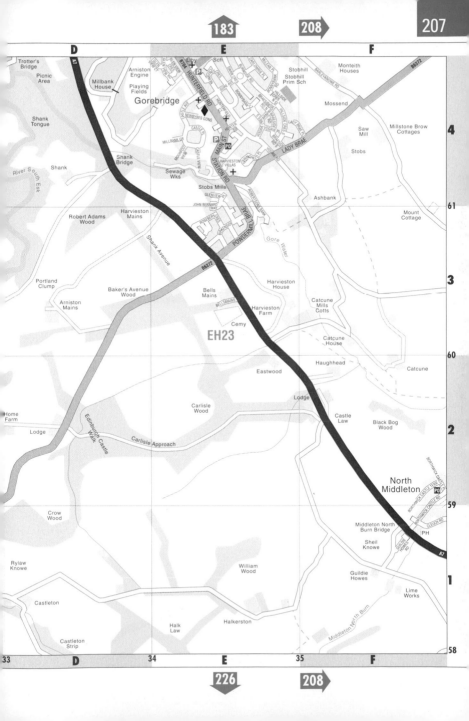

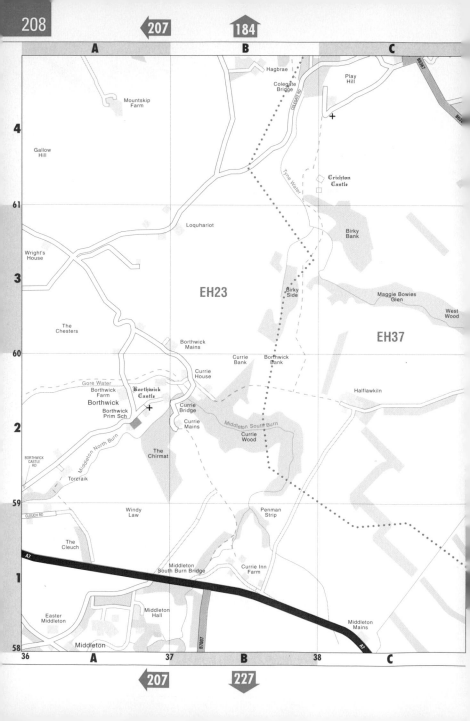

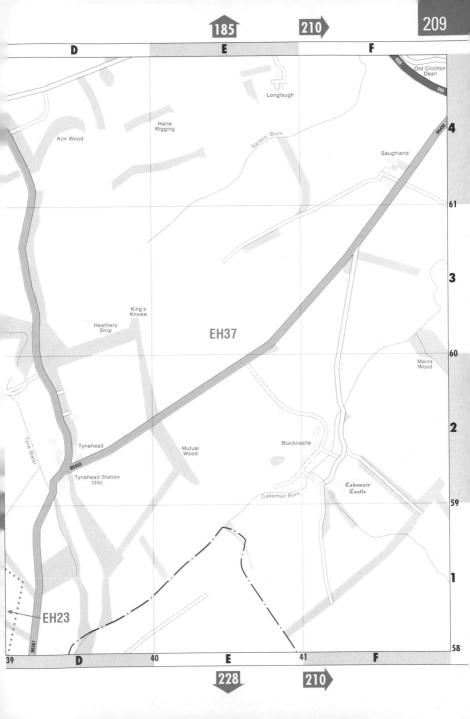

D
E
F

Old Crichton
Dean

A68

Longfaugh

Harle
Rigging

B6458

4

Kiln Wood

Salters' Burn

Saughland

61

King's
Knowe

3

Heathery
Strip

EH37

60

Mains
Wood

Tyne Water

Tynehead

B6458

Mutual
Wood

Blackcastle

2

Tynehead Station
(dis)

Cakemuir
Castle

Cakemuir Burn

59

1

EH23

B6367

58

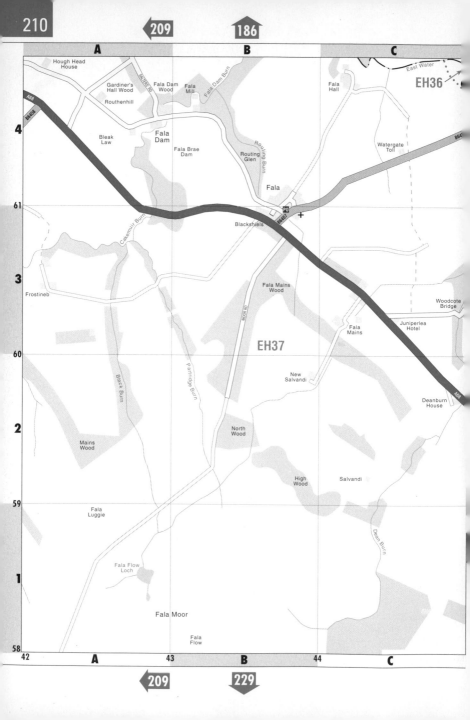

D E F

4

B6368

Johnstounburn Water

Johnstounburn

Boarland
Cottage

East Water

B6457

East Water
Bridge

Chesterhill
House

Saw
Mill

Boarland
Wood

Keith
Hill

61

Dean Burn

Mavishall

Harehope
Wood

Meikle
Law

Woodcote
Mains

Woodcote
Mill

EH36

Little
Law

Linn Dean Water

Pogbie

3

Keith
Hill

Woodcote
Park

Pogbie Burn

60

Millar
Wood

Kate's
Cauldron

Round
Hill

Pogbie
Hill

Taipenny
Knowe

2

B6368

Soutra
Mains

King's Road

B6368

EH37

Soutra
Hill

59

Soutra
Mains
Wood

Huntershall

Carfrae
Common

1

Soutra Aisle

Hen
Moss

Armel Water

B6368

A68

58

45 D 46 E 47 F

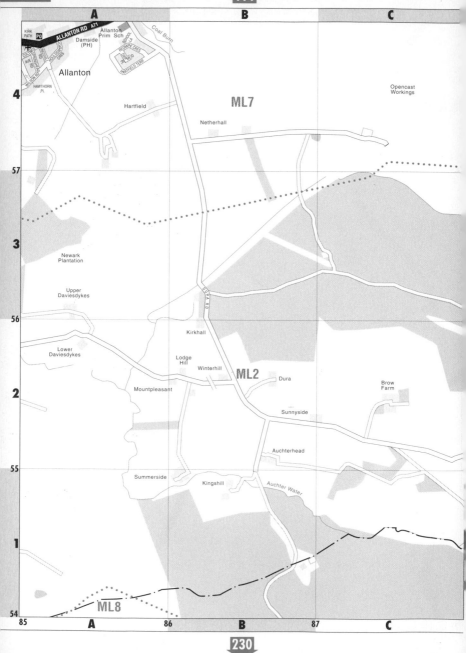

ML7

ML2

ML8

Allanton

KIRK
PATH
PO
ALLANTON RD A71
Damside
(PH)
Allanton
Prim Sch
SCHOOL
REDPARK CRES
HARTFIELD TERR
Coal Burn

Hartfield

Netherhall

Opencast
Workings

Newark
Plantation

Upper
Daviesdykes

Lower
Daviesdykes

Kirkhall

DYKE RD

Lodge
Hill
Winterhill

Mountpleasant

Dura

Brow
Farm

Sunnyside

Auchterhead

Summerside

Kingshill

Auchter Water

D
E
F

4

ML7
EH47

Opencast Workings

Causeyhill

57

3

ML11

Lark Law

56

ML2

Spoutcross

2

Cairney
DURA RD

Mon

55

Auchterhead Muir

Auchterhead

1

ML8

54

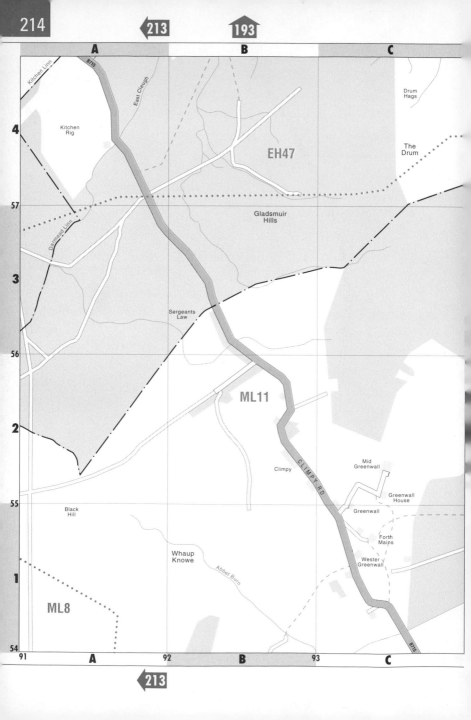

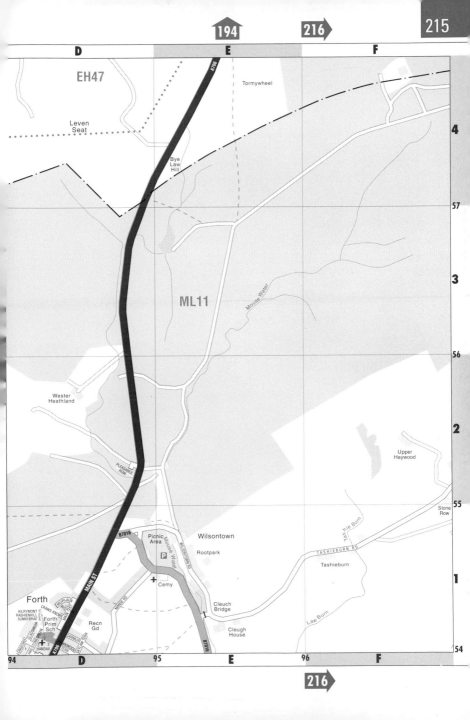

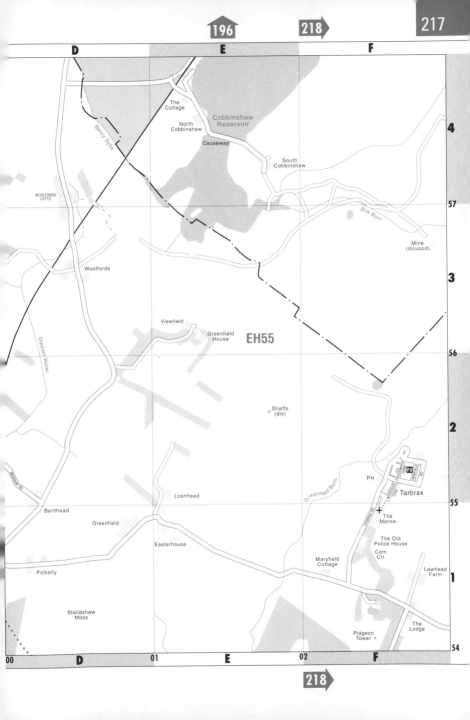

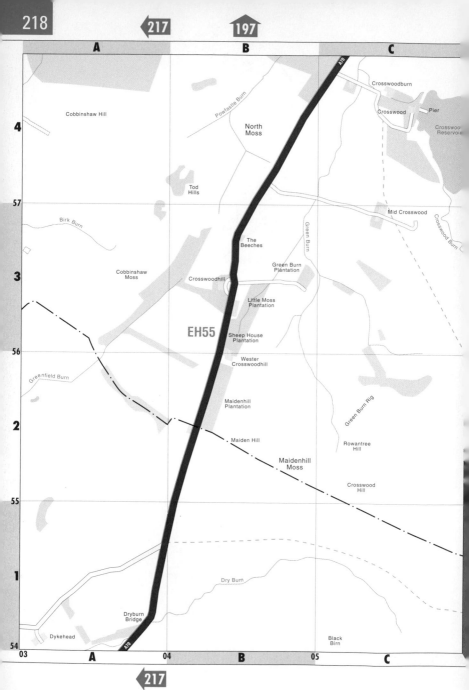

217
197

A

B

C

Crosswoodburn

Crosswood · Pier

Cobbinshaw Hill

North
Moss

Crosswoo
Reservoir

4

Powfastle Burn

Crosswood Burn

57

Tod
Hills

Mid Crosswood

Birk Burn

The
Beeches

Green Burn

3

Cobbinshaw
Moss

Crosswoodhill

Green Burn
Plantation

Little Moss
Plantation

EH55

Sheep House
Plantation

56

Wester
Crosswoodhill

Greenfield Burn

Maidenhill
Plantation

Green Burn Rig

2

· Maiden Hill

Rowantree
Hill

Maidenhill
Moss

Crosswood
Hill

55

1

Dry Burn

Dryburn
Bridge

A70

Dykehead

Black
Birn

54

03

A

04

B

05

C

217

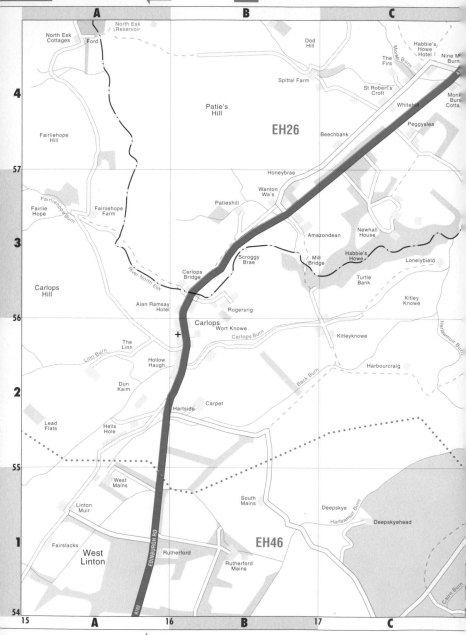

A   B   C

North Esk Cottages
Ford
North Esk Reservoir

Dod Hill

Habbie's Howe Hotel
The Firs
Mone Burn
Nine M Burn

Spittal Farm

St Robert's Croft

Whitehill

Moni Burn Cotta

4

Patie's Hill

EH26

Beechbank

Peggyslea

Fairliehope Hill

57

Honeybrae

Fairliehope Burn

Fairlie Hope

Fairliehope Farm

Patieshill

Wanton Wa's

Amazondean

Newhall House

3

River North Esk

Scroggy Brae

Mill Bridge

Habbie's Howe

Lonelybield

Carlops Bridge

Turtle Bank

Carlops Hill

Alan Ramsay Hotel

Rogersrig

Kitley Knowe

56

Carlops

Wort Knowe

Kitleyknowe

Harkawmuir Burn

The Linn

Carlops Burn

Linn Burn

Hollow Haugh

Back Burn

Harbourcraig

2

Dun Kaim

Carpet

Hartside

Lead Flats

Hells Hole

55

West Mains

South Mains

Deepskye

Harlawmuir Burn

Deepskyehead

Linton Muir

Fairslacks

1

EDINBURGH RD

West Linton

Rutherford

EH46

Rutherford Mains

Cairn Burn

A702

54

15   A   16   B   17   C

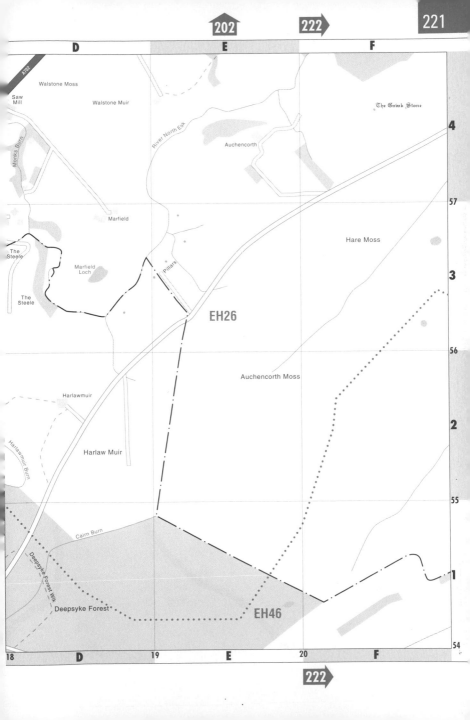

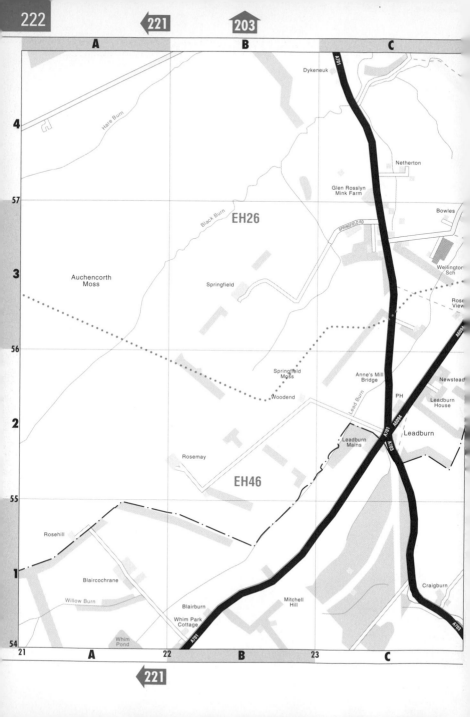

A B C

4

Dykeneuk

Netherton

Glen Rosslyn
Mink Farm

57

Hare Burn

Black Burn

EH26

Bowles

SPRINGFIELD RD

Wellington
Sch

3

Auchencorth
Moss

Springfield

Rose
View

56

Springfield
Moss

Anne's Mill
Bridge

Newstead

Woodend

Lead Burn

PH

Leadburn
House

2

Rosemay

Leadburn
Mains

Leadburn

EH46

55

Rosehill

1

Blaircochrane

Craigburn

Willow Burn

Mitchell
Hill

Blairburn

Whim Park
Cottage

54

Whim
Pond

21 A 22 B 23 C

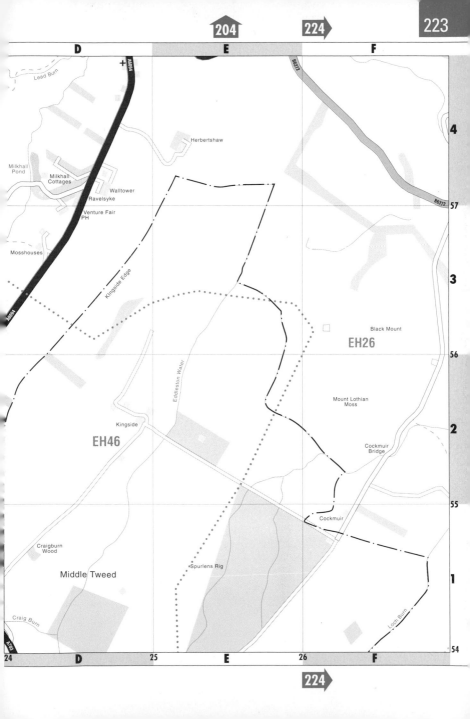

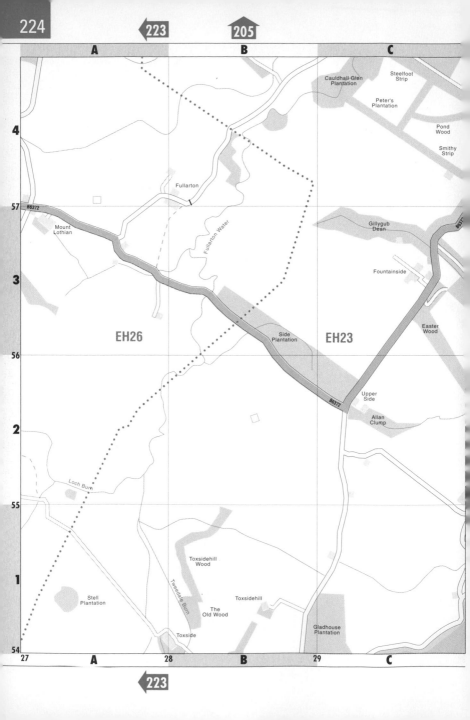

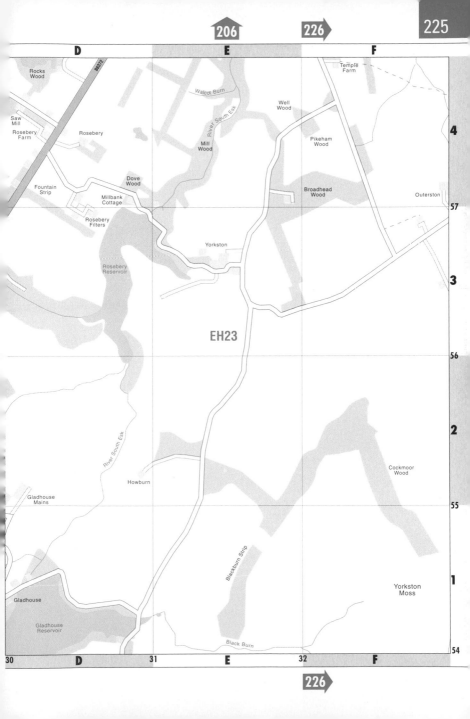

206
226

D
E
F

Rocks
Wood

Saw
Mill

Rosebery
Farm

Rosebery

Walcot Burn

Well
Wood

Temple
Farm

Pikeham
Wood

4

Mill
Wood

Fountain
Strip

Dove
Wood

Broadhead
Wood

Outerston

57

Millbank
Cottage

Rosebery
Filters

Yorkston

Rosebery
Reservoir

3

56

EH23

River South Esk

2

Cockmoor
Wood

Howburn

Gladhouse
Mains

55

Blackburn Strip

Gladhouse

Yorkston
Moss

1

Gladhouse
Reservoir

Black Burn

54

30
D
31
E
32
F

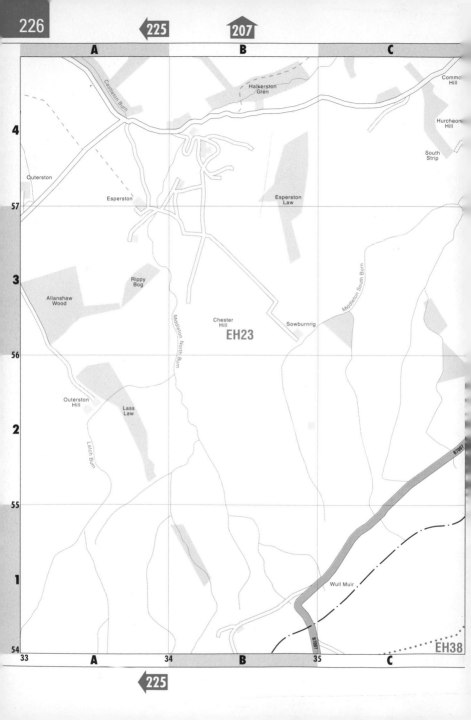

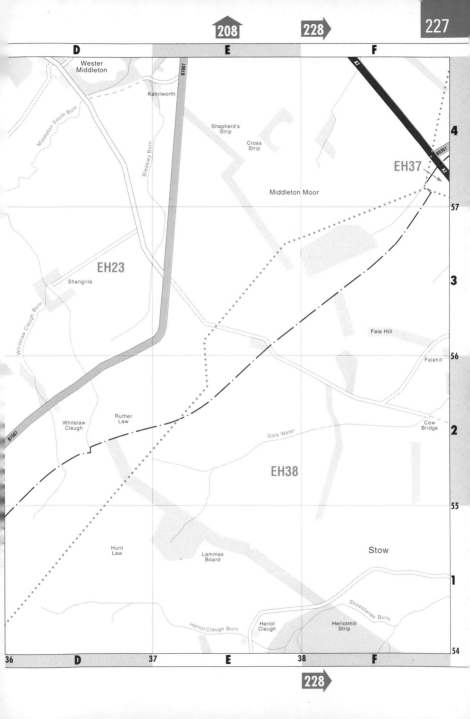

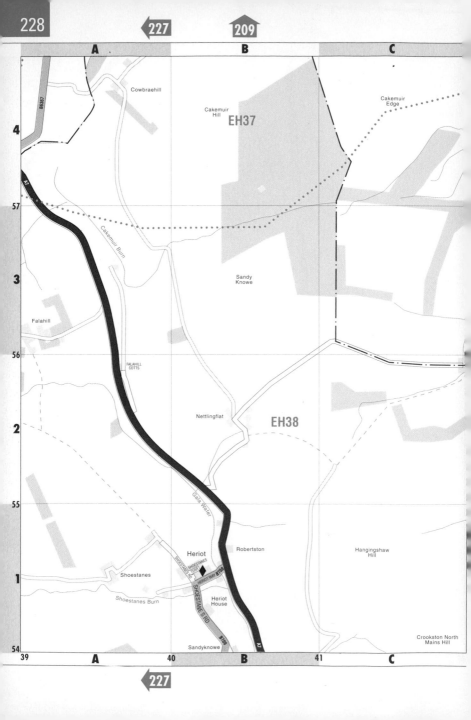

D E F

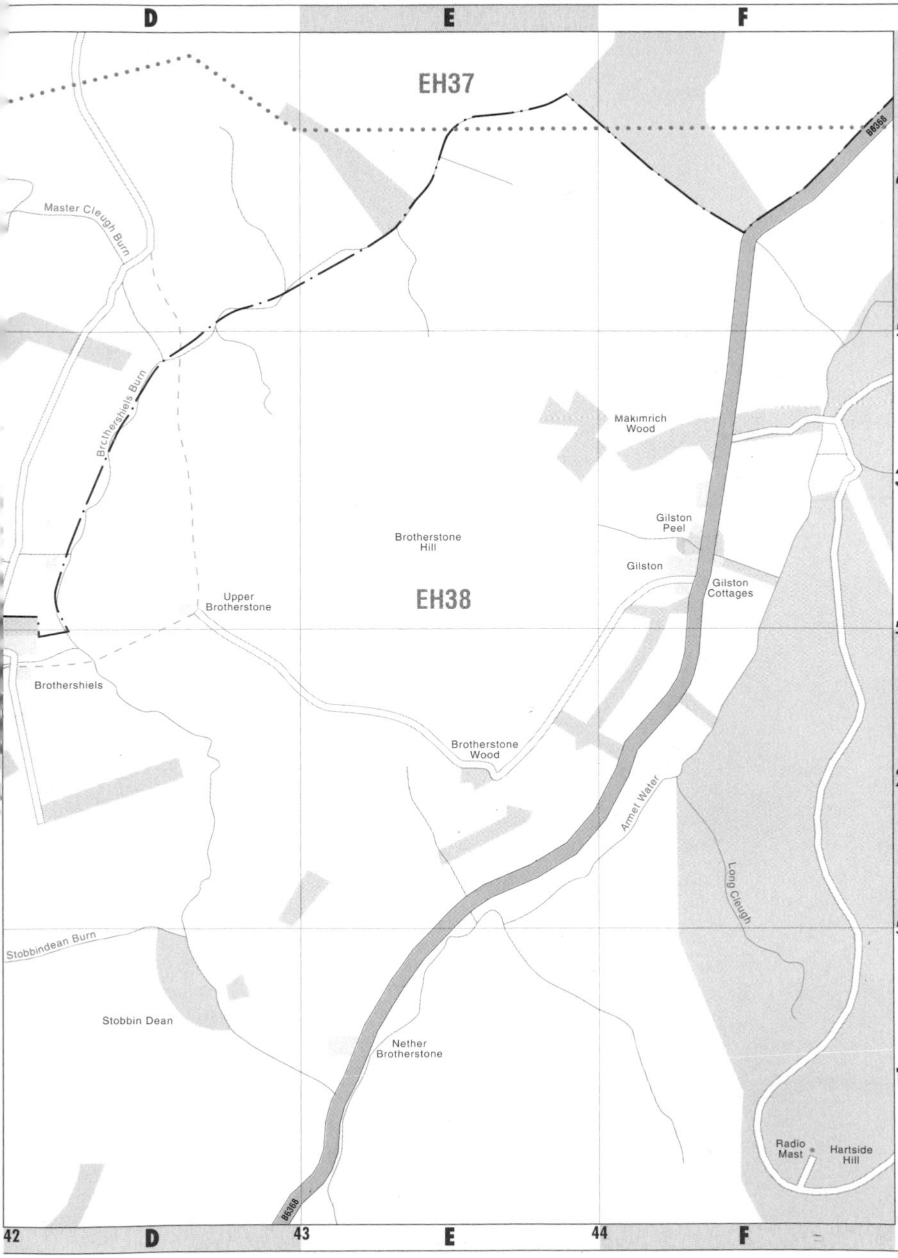

EH37

Master Cleugh Burn

Brotherdhiels Burn

EH38

Makimrich Wood

Gilston Peel

Brotherstone Hill

Gilston

Gilston Cottages

Upper Brotherstone

Brothershiels

Brotherstone Wood

Armet Water

Long Cleugh

Stobbindean Burn

Stobbin Dean

Nether Brotherstone

Radio Mast

Hartside Hill

42 D 43 E 44 F

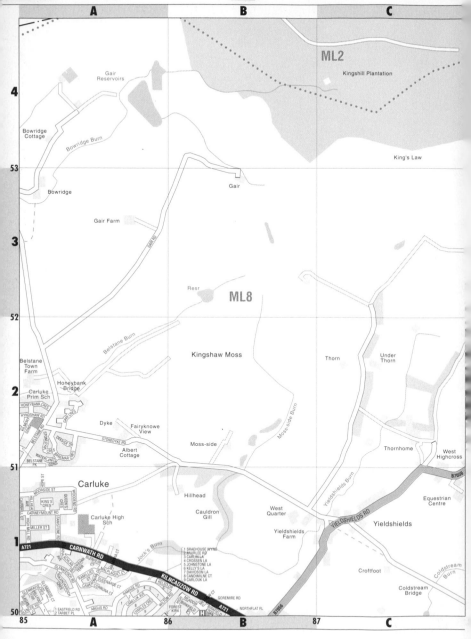

A   **B**   **C**

ML2

Kingshill Plantation

4

Gair Reservoirs

Bowridge Cottage

Bowridge Burn

King's Law

53

Bowridge

Gair

Gair Farm

GAIR RD

3

Resr

ML8

52

Belstane Burn

Kingshaw Moss

Thorn

Under Thorn

Belstane Town Farm

Honeybank Bridge

Carluke Prim Sch

2

HONEYBANK CRES

HYNDSHAW RD

GAIR CRES

DRESS DYKE RD

STONEDYKE RD

Dyke

Fairyknowe View

Moss-side

Moss-side Burn

Thornhome

West Highcross

Albert Cottage

51

Yieldshields Burn

B7056

Carluke

MOORSIDE ST

KING'S CRES

WOODEND RD

Hillhead

Cauldron Gill

West Quarter

YIELDSHIELDS RD

Yieldshields

Equestrian Centre

CARNIEYMOUNT RD

Carluke High Sch

MILLER ST

TANSTONE CRES

Jock's Burn

Yieldshields Farm

1

A721

CARNWATH RD

BLENHEIM

KILNCADZOW RD

KELSO DR

1 SRAEHOUSE WYND
2 MUIRLEE RD
3 CARLIN LA
4 CROSSEN LA
5 JOHNSTONE LA
6 KELLY'S LA
7 DAVIDSON LA
8 CANDMILNE CT
9 CARLOUK LA

Croftfoot

Coldstream Burn

GLENAFFRIC

RAMBLES

MACLAGGAN

CORRUNA CT

RAMSAY RD

ANGUS RD

CAMELUKE AVE

CHARLES CRES

MILTON RD

GOREMIRE RD

FOREST KIRK

BIRKENSHILL

MENDOCK

A721

NORTHFLAT PL

Coldstream Bridge

1 EASTFIELD RD
2 TARBET PL

50

85   **A**   **86**   **B**   **87**   **C**

D E F

ML2

Black Law

4

53

Birniehall

Netherton Burn

3

Thornmuir

ML8

Springfield
Reservoir

52

Hill of
Westerhouse

Middlehope
Farm

Easterseat

Springfield

2

B7056

Knowehead

Middlehouse

YIELDSHIELDS RD

Netherton Burn

Westerhouse

Damhead

East
Highcross

51

Coldstream Burn

Candymill Burn

1

ML11

Mid
Coldstream

Craigend

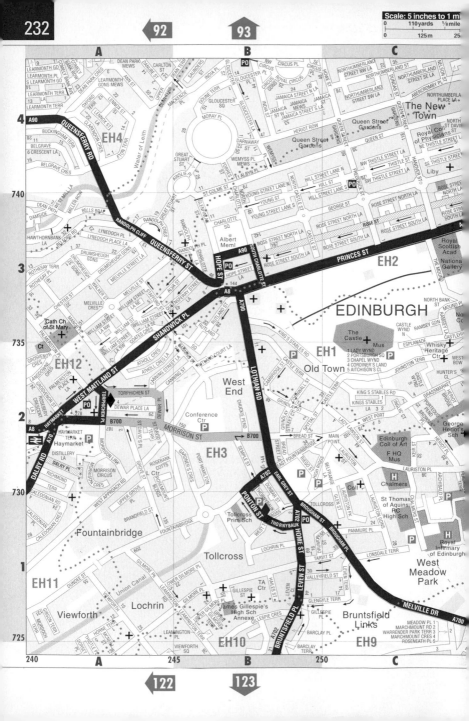

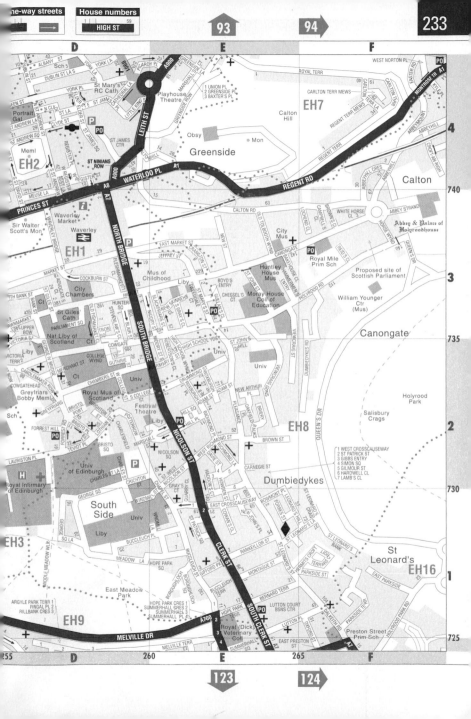

Index

Street names are listed alphabetically and show the locality, the Postcode District, the page number and a reference to the square in which the name falls on the map page

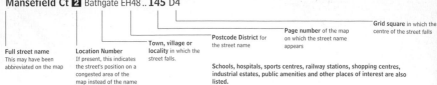

Mansefield Ct **2** Bathgate EH48 .. **145** D4

Full street name
This may have been abbreviated on the map

Location Number
If present, this indicates the street's position on a congested area of the map instead of the name

Town, village or locality in which the street falls.

Postcode District for the street name

Page number of the map on which the street name appears

Grid square in which the centre of the street falls

Schools, hospitals, sports centres, railway stations, shopping centres, industrial estates, public amenities and other places of interest are also listed.

Abbreviations used in the index

App	Approach	Cl	Close	Espl	Esplanade	Mdw	Meadows
Arc	Arcade	Comm	Common	Est	Estate	N	North
Ave	Avenue	Cnr	Corner	Gdns	Gardens	Orch	Orchard
Bvd	Boulevard	Cotts	Cottages	Gn	Green	Par	Parade
Bldgs	Buildings	Ct	Court	Gr	Grove	Pk	Park
Bsns Pk	Business Park	Ctyd	Courtyard	Hts	Heights	Pas	Passage
Bsns Ctr	Business Centre	Cres	Crescent	Ho	House	Pl	Place
Bglws	Bungalows	Dr	Drive	Ind Est	Industrial Estate	Prec	Precinct
Cswy	Causeway	Dro	Drove	Intc	Interchange	Prom	Promenade
Ctr	Centre	E	East	Junc	Junction	Ret Pk	Retail Park
Circ	Circle	Emb	Embankment	La	Lane	Rd	Road
Cir	Circus	Ent	Enterprise	Mans	Mansions	Rdbt	Roundabout

S	South
Sq	Square
Strs	Stairs
Stps	Steps
St	Street, Saint
Terr	Terrace
Tk	Track
Trad Est	Trading Estate
Wlk	Walk
W	West
Yd	Yard

Town and village index

Abercorn 66 C1
Aberdour 49 E4
Aberlady 71 E2
Addiewell 171 F1
Airth 22 B2
Allandale 57 E1
Alloa 10 B3
Alva 5 D3
Armadale 143 F3
Athelstaneford 101 F4
Auchendinny 180 B1
Auchengray 216 C1
Auchtertool 15 D1
Avonbridge 112 A3
Balerno 151 E1
Bankhead 57 F3
Bannockburn 7 F1
Bathgate 145 E4
Bilston 180 C3
Blackburn 171 E4
Blackness 65 F2
Blackridge 142 B2
Blairhall 26 A4
Bo'ness 63 F4
Bolton 162 C4
Bonnybridge 58 A3
Bonnyrigg and
Lasswade 182 B4
Borthwick 208 A2
Breich 194 C3
Bridge of Allan 2 A4
Bridgend 86 B2
Brightons 82 B4
Broxburn 117 E3
Burntisland 50 C4
Cairneyhill 27 E1
California 81 F3
Cambus 9 D4
Cambusbarron 6 B3
Cardenden 15 E4
Carluke 230 A1

Carnock 27 E3
Carrington 206 B3
Charlestown 45 D2
Clackmannan 11 D2
Cockburnspath 140 C2
Cockenzie and
Port Seton 97 E3
Comrie 26 B4
Cousland 158 B3
Cowdenbeath 13 F2
Cowie 20 B4
Craigiehall 90 B2
Crombie 44 B4
Crossford 28 A1
Crossgates 30 C3
Culross 42 B4
Currie 152 A2
Dalgety Bay 48 B2
Dalkeith 157 D1
Dalmeny 89 F4
Danderhall 156 B4
Dechmont 116 B1
Denny 36 C1
Dennyloanhead 57 E3
Dirleton 53 D2
Drem 73 D2
Dunbar 78 B1
Dunfermline 29 E3
Dysart 18 A4
East Calder 148 C2
East Fortune 74 A2
East Linton 103 E4
East Saltoun 161 F2
East Whitburn 170 C4
Easthouses 183 E4
Ecclesmachan 116 C4
Edinburgh 123 E3
Edinburgh 232 C3
Elphinstone 128 A1
Fala 210 B4
Falkirk 60 B3

Fallin 8 B2
Fauldhouse 193 F3
Fishcross 5 F2
Fordell 31 D3
Forrestfield 141 D2
Forth 215 D1
Garvald 134 B1
Gifford 163 F2
Gladsmuir 130 A4
Gorebridge 207 E4
Gowkhall 27 F4
Grangemouth 61 E4
Gullane 52 A1
Haddington 101 E1
Haggs 57 D2
Halbeath 30 A3
Harthill 168 C3
Hartwood 191 D1
Heriot 228 B1
High Bonnybridge 58 B2
High Valleyfield 26 A1
Hillend 47 F2
Howgate 204 A1
Humbie 187 D1
Innerwick 108 A1
Inverkeithing 47 D1
Kelty 12 B4
Kincardine 23 F2
Kinghorn 35 D2
Kingseat 12 A1
Kirkcaldy 17 E2
Kirkliston 89 D1
Kirknewton 149 F1
Larbert 38 A1
Laurieston 61 D2
Letham 39 E4
Limekilns 45 F2
Linlithgow 85 D3
Livingston 147 E3
Loanhead 181 D4
Lochgelly 14 B4

Longcroft 57 D2
Longniddry 98 C3
Longridge 170 B1
Macmerry 129 E3
Maddiston 83 D3
Manor Powis 3 D2
Mayfield 183 F3
Menstrie 3 F3
Mid Calder 148 B2
Musselburgh 126 B4
New Winton 129 D2
Newbridge 119 D3
Newcraighall 125 F2
Newmills 26 B1
Newton 88 A4
Newtongrange 183 D3
North Berwick 54 B4
North Middleton 207 F2
North Queensferry 68 B3
Oakley 26 C4
Ormiston 159 F4
Pathhead 185 D3
Pencaitland 160 B4
Penicuik 203 E2
Philpstoun 86 B3
Plean 20 B2
Polbeth 172 C3
Polmont 61 F1
Prestonpans 96 C1
Pumpherston 148 A4
Queensferry 89 D4
Ratho 119 E1
Ratho Station 119 E3
Redding 61 E1
Reddingmuirhead 82 A4
Rosewell 181 E1
Roslin 180 C2
Rosyth 46 C2
Saline 167 D2
Seafield 146 A1
Shieldhill 81 E3

Shotts 191 F3
Silverburn 202 C3
Skinflats 39 F2
Slamannan 110 A3
South Alloa 9 F2
Spittal 99 E4
Spott 106 B2
Standburn 82 B1
Stenhousemuir 38 B2
Stenton 104 C1
Stirling 7 E4
Stoneyburn 171 E1
Straiton 155 D1
Tarbrax 217 F2
Temple 206 B1
Threemiletown 86 C2
Throsk 9 D2
Torphichen 113 F3
Torryburn 26 C1
Torwood 37 F3
Townhill 29 E4
Tranent 128 B4
Tullibody 4 B2
Tyninghame 76 A2
Uphall 116 C2
Uphall Station 117 D4
Wallacestone 82 A4
Wallyford 127 E3
Wellwood 29 D4
West Barns 77 F1
West Calder 172 B1
West Linton 220 A1
Westfield 112 C3
Westquarter 61 D1
Whitburn 170 A4
Whitecraig 126 C1
Whitecross 83 F3
Whitekirk 75 F4
Wilkieston 150 A3
Winchburgh 87 F1

1st St FK3 ... 62 A4
2nd St
Grangemouth, Chemical Works
EH51 ... 62 B3
Grangemouth, Oil Refinery
FK3 ... 62 A4
3rd St
Grangemouth, Chemical Works
EH51 ... 62 B3
Grangemouth, Oil Refinery
FK3 ... 62 A4
4th St
Grangemouth, Chemical Works
EH51 ... 62 C3
Grangemouth, Oil Refinery
FK3 ... 62 A4
5th St
Grangemouth, Chemical Works
EH51 ... 62 C3
Grangemouth, Oil Refinery
FK3 ... 62 A4
6th St
Grangemouth, Oil Refinery
FK9 ... 41 D1
Grangemouth, Chemical Works
EH51 ... 62 C3
7th St
Grangemouth, Chemical Works
EH51 ... 62 C3
Grangemouth, Oil Refinery
FK3 ... 62 B4
8th St FK3 ... 62 B4
A1 Ind Pk EH15 ... 125 D4
Abbey Craig Rd FK10 ... 5 D1
Abbey Cres EH39 ... 54 A4
Abbey Ct EH39 ... 54 A4
Abbey La EH8 ... 94 A1
Abbey Mains EH41 ... 101 F2
Abbey Mews EH39 ... 54 A4
Abbey Mill FK8 ... 7 E4
Abbey & Palace of
Holyroodhouse EH8 ... 233 F3
Abbey Park Pl KY12 ... 29 D2
Abbey Rd Dalkeith EH22 ... 157 D1
Dunbar EH42 ... 78 B1
North Berwick EH39 ... 54 A4
Stirling FK8 ... 2 B1
Abbey Rd Pl FK8 ... 7 E4
Abbey St Edinburgh EH7 ... 94 A1
High Valleyfield KY12 ... 26 A1
Abbey View
Crossford KY12 ... 28 B1
Dunfermline KY11 ... 29 F1
Abbeygrange EH22 ... 183 D3
Abbeyhill EH8 ... 233 F4
Abbeyhill Cres EH8 ... 233 F4
Abbeyhill Prim Sch EH7 ... 94 A1
Abbeymount EH8 ... 233 F4
Abbot Rd FK7 ... 7 E2
Abbot St KY12 ... 29 D2
Abbot's View EH41 ... 101 D1
Abbots Cl EH39 ... 53 F4
Abbots Ct FK2 ... 60 B4
Abbots Mill KY2 ... 17 D2
Abbots Moss Dr FK1 ... 59 F1
Abbots Rd Falkirk FK2 ... 60 B4
Grangemouth FK3 ... 61 E4
Abbots View FK2 ... 61 E4
Abbots Wlk KY2 ... 16 C2
Abbotsford Cres
Edinburgh EH10 ... 123 D2
Shotts ML7 ... 191 F3
Abbotsford Ct EH10 ... 123 D2
Abbotsford Dr
Grangemouth FK3 ... 61 F3
Laurieston EH22 ... 61 D2
Abbotsford Dr S ... 61 F3
Abbotsford Pk
Edinburgh EH10 ... 123 D2
North Berwick EH39 ... 53 F4
Abbotsford Pl FK8 ... 2 B1
Abbotsford Rise EH54 ... 148 A1
Abbotsford St FK2 ... 60 A4
Abbotsgrange Rd FK3 ... 61 F4
Abbotshall Rd KY2, KY1 ... 17 D1
Abbotsinch Ind Est FK3 ... 61 F4
Abbotsinch Rd FK3 ... 61 F4
Abbotsview Junc EH41 ... 101 D1
Abden Ave KY3 ... 35 D2
Abden Ct KY3 ... 35 D2
Abden Pl KY3 ... 35 D2
Abel Pl KY11 ... 29 F2
Abercairny Cres FK1 ... 82 C3
Abercairney Pl FK3 ... 61 F4
Abercorn Ave EH8 ... 124 B4
Abercorn Cres EH8 ... 124 B4
Abercorn Ct EH8 ... 124 B4
Abercorn Dr EH8 ... 124 B4
Abercorn Gdns EH8 ... 94 B1
Abercorn Gr EH8 ... 124 B4
Abercorn Pl EH52 ... 87 E4
Abercorn Prim Sch
EH52 ... 87 E4
Abercorn Rd EH8 ... 124 B4
Abercorn Terr EH15 ... 125 E4
Abercrombie Pl FK11 ... 3 F3
Abercromby Dr FK9 ... 2 A4
Abercromby Pl
Edinburgh EH3 ... 232 C4
Stirling FK8 ... 7 D4
Tullibody FK10 ... 4 A1
Aberdour Castle KY3 ... 49 E4
Aberdour Cres KY11 ... 29 E1
Aberdour Pl KY11 ... 29 E1
Aberdour Prim Sch KY3 ... 49 E4

Aberdour Rd
Burntisland KY3 ... 33 E1
Dunfermline KY11 ... 29 F1
Aberdour Sta KY3 ... 49 E4
Aberlady Prim Sch EH32 ... 71 E2
Aberlady Rd EH41 ... 100 C1
Aberlour St KY11 ... 46 C2
Abinger Gdns EH12 ... 122 B4
Abington Rd KY12 ... 28 C1
Aboyne Ave FK9 ... 2 B2
Aboyne Gdns FK9 ... 16 C4
Academy La EH20 ... 181 E4
Academy Pk EH6 ... 94 A2
Academy Pl FK7 ... 7 F1
Academy Rd
Bo'ness EH51 ... 64 A4
Stirling FK8 ... 7 D4
Academy Sq KY11 ... 45 E2
Academy St Alloa FK10 ... 9 F4
Armadale EH48 ... 143 F3
Bathgate EH48 ... 145 D3
Edinburgh EH6 ... 94 A2
Academy The EH51 ... 64 A4
Acheson Dr EH32 ... 127 F4
Achray Ct KY10 ... 10 B3
Achray Dr FK9 ... 2 A2
Ackam Path EH20 ... 181 E4
Acorn Cres EH54 ... 38 B1
Acre Rd EH51 ... 64 B3
Acredale Bathgate EH48 ... 145 D3
Linlithgow EH49 ... 85 D3
Acredales EH41 ... 131 F4
Acredales Wlk EH41 ... 131 F4
Adam Cres FK5 ... 38 C1
Adam Pl KY5 ... 14 A4
Adam Smith Ct KY1 ... 17 E2
Adam Smith Ct KY1 ... 17 E2
Adam Sq EH54 ... 173 E3
Adambrae Rd EH54 ... 173 E4
Adambrae Rdbt EH54 ... 173 E4
Adams Loan FK2 ... 39 D1
Adams Well EH13 ... 153 E4
Adamson Ave KY12 ... 17 D3
Adamson Cres KY12 ... 29 E3
Adamson Pl FK9 ... 2 A2
Adamson Rd KY5 ... 14 A4
Addiebrownhill EH55 ... 171 E1
Addiebrownhill Sta
EH55 ... 171 F1
Addiewell Prim Sch &
St Thomas's RC Prim Sch
EH55 ... 171 E1
Addiston Cres EH14 ... 151 E2
Addiston Farm Rd
EH28 ... 120 A1
Addiston Gr EH14 ... 151 E2
Addiston Pk EH14 ... 151 E2
Adelaide St EH54 ... 148 A3
Adelphi Gr [1] EH15 ... 125 D4
Adelphi Pl EH15 ... 125 D4
Admiral Terr EH10 ... 123 D3
Admiralty Rd
Inverkeithing KY11 ... 47 E2
Rosyth KY11 ... 46 B2
Admiralty St EH6 ... 93 F3
Advocate's Cl EH1 ... 233 D3
Affleck Ct EH12 ... 121 D4
Affric Dr FK2 ... 39 E1
Affric Loan ML7 ... 191 F3
Affric Way EH54 ... 146 C3
Afton Ct Dechmont EH52 ... 116 B1
Stirling FK7 ... 7 E3
Afton Dr FK6 ... 57 E4
Afton Gr KY11 ... 29 F3
Afton Pl EH5 ... 93 D3
Afton Terr EH5 ... 93 D3
Agnew Terr EH6 ... 93 E3
Ailsa Gr KY2 ... 16 C4
Ainslie Gdns FK2 ... 61 F2
Ainslie Pl EH3 ... 232 B4
Airdrie Rd ML6 ... 141 D2
Airlie Dr FK2 ... 61 A3
Airth Dr FK2 ... 7 E2
Airth Prim Sch FK2 ... 22 C2
Airthrey Ave FK9 ... 2 A3
Airthrey Dr FK5 ... 39 D2
Airthrey Rd FK9 ... 2 B3
Aitchison Dr FK5 ... 38 A2
Aitchison's Cl EH1 ... 232 C2
Aitchison's Pl EH15 ... 95 D1
Aitken Cres FK7 ... 7 D1
Aitken Ct KY1 ... 17 D1
Aitken Dr Slamannan FK1 ... 110 A1
Whitburn EH47 ... 170 A4
Aitken Gdns FK1 ... 59 F3
Aitken Orr Dr EH52 ... 117 F3
Aitken St KY1 ... 17 D4
Aitken Terr FK1 ... 59 E3
Akarit Rd FK5 ... 38 C1
Alan Breck Gdns EH4 ... 91 E1
Alan Wlk FK9 ... 1 C4
Alany Ind Est KY12 ... 29 D2
Albany La EH1 ... 93 E1
Albany St
Dunfermline KY12 ... 29 D2
Edinburgh EH1 ... 233 D4
Albert Ave EH6 ... 61 F4
Albert Cl EH21 ... 127 D3
Albert Cres EH21 ... 127 D3
Albert Rd Edinburgh EH6 ... 94 A3
Falkirk FK1 ... 60 A2
Harthill ML7 ... 168 C3
Albert St Edinburgh EH7 ... 93 F2
Rosyth KY11 ... 46 C2

Albert Terr
Edinburgh EH10 ... 123 D2
Musselburgh EH21 ... 126 C3
Alberta Ave EH54 ... 147 F2
Albion Pl EH7 ... 94 A1
Albion Rd EH7 ... 94 A1
Albion Terr EH7 ... 94 A1
Albyn Cotts EH52 ... 117 F3
Albyn Dr EH54 ... 173 F3
Albyn Ind Est EH52 ... 117 F4
Albyn Pl Broxburn EH52 ... 117 F3
Alcorn Rigg EH14 ... 152 C4
Alcorn Sq EH14 ... 152 C4
Alder Gr Dunfermline KY11 ... 29 E1
Westquarter FK2 ... 61 D2
Alderbank
Livingston EH54 ... 147 F3
Penicuik EH26 ... 203 F2
Alderbank Gdns EH11 ... 122 C2
Alderbank Pl EH11 ... 122 C2
Alderbank Terr EH11 ... 122 C2
Alderston Dr KY12 ... 29 E3
Alderston Mdws EH41 ... 100 C1
Alderston Pl EH41 ... 100 C1
Alderston Rd EH41 ... 131 F4
Alderstone Bsns Pk
EH54 ... 147 E1
Alderstone Rd
Livingston, Adambrae EH54 ... 173 E4
Livingston, Howden EH54 ... 147 E2
Alemoor Cres EH7 ... 94 A2
Alemoor Pk EH7 ... 94 A2
Alexander Ave
Falkirk FK2 ... 60 C3
Grangemouth FK3 ... 61 E3
Alexander Dr
Bridge of A FK9 ... 2 A4
Edinburgh EH11 ... 122 B3
Prestonpans EH32 ... 127 F4
Alexander McLeod Pl
FK7 ... 8 C2
Alexander Pk EH52 ... 117 F2
Alexander Pl KY11 ... 46 C2
Alexander Rd ML7 ... 191 E3
Alexander St
Cowdenbeath KY4 ... 13 E3
Dysart KY1 ... 18 A4
Uphall EH52 ... 117 D2
Alexander The Third St
KY3 ... 34 C1
Alexandra Bsns Pk
EH28 ... 119 D3
Alexandra Dr Alloa FK10 ... 9 F4
Bathgate EH48 ... 145 F3
Alexandra Pl FK8 ... 2 B1
Alexandra St
Dunfermline KY12 ... 29 D3
Kirkcaldy KY1 ... 17 E3
Alford Ave KY2 ... 16 C4
Alfred Pl EH9 ... 123 F2
Alice Cox Wlk KY11 ... 29 E1
Alice Gr KY4 ... 30 C3
Aline Ct KY11 ... 48 A1
Alison Gr KY12 ... 28 A1
Alison St KY1 ... 17 D1
Allan Barr Ct FK1 ... 60 A1
Allan Cres Denny FK6 ... 36 B2
Dunfermline KY11 ... 29 F1
Allan Ct FK3 ... 40 C1
Allan Park Cres EH14 ... 122 B2
Allan Park Dr EH14 ... 122 B1
Allan Park Gdns EH14 ... 122 B1
Allan Park Loan EH14 ... 122 B1
Allan Park Rd EH14 ... 122 B1
Allan Pk
Cowdenbeath KY4 ... 13 D1
Kirkliston EH29 ... 89 D1
Stirling FK8 ... 7 D4
Allan Rd EH47 ... 169 F3
Allan St EH42 ... 93 D1
Allan Terr EH22 ... 157 D2
Allan's Prim Sch FK8 ... 7 D4
Allanbank Rd FK1 ... 38 B1
Allandale Cotts FK4 ... 57 E1
Allanfield EH7 ... 93 F1
Allanton Prim Sch
ML7 ... 212 A4
Allanton Rd ML7 ... 191 E1
Allanvale Rd FK9 ... 1 C4
Allanwater Gdns FK9 ... 2 A4
Allanwood Ct FK9 ... 2 A4
Allardice Cres KY4 ... 14 B3
Aller Ct KY12 ... 26 C4
Aller Pl EH54 ... 147 D2
Allermuir Ave EH25 ... 180 C3
Allermuir Rd EH13 ... 153 D3
Allison Pl EH29 ... 89 D1
Alloa Acad FK10 ... 9 F4
Alloa Rd
Clackmannan FK10 ... 11 D2
Falkirk FK2 ... 39 D2
Fishcross FK10 ... 5 E4
Manor Powis FK9 ... 3 D2
Stenhousemuir FK5 ... 38 C2
Tullibody FK10 ... 4 B2
Alloa Twr FK10 ... 10 A3
Alloway Cres FK1 ... 59 F1
Alloway Dr KY2 ... 20 B4
Alloway Loan [5] EH16 ... 124 A1
Alma La FK2 ... 60 A3
Alma St Falkirk FK2 ... 60 A3
Inverkeithing KY11 ... 47 E2
Alma Terr FK2 ... 60 A3
Almond Ave EH52 ... 119 F4
Almond Bank Cotts EH4 ... 91 D3
Almond Cres EH19 ... 182 A3

Almond Ct
East Whitburn EH47 ... 170 C4
Edinburgh EH16 ... 124 C2
Falkirk FK2 ... 60 C4
Livingston EH54 ... 148 B2
Stirling FK7 ... 7 E2
Almond East Rd EH54 ... 148 A3
Almond Gn EH12 ... 121 D4
Almond Gr
East Calder EH53 ... 148 C3
Queensferry EH30 ... 89 E4
Almond Intc EH54 ... 148 A2
Almond Prk EH54 ... 148 A2
Almond Pl KY1 ... 17 E4
Almond Rd
Blackburn EH47 ... 145 E1
Dunfermline KY11 ... 29 F1
Falkirk FK2 ... 60 C4
Livingston EH54 ... 148 A2
Maddiston FK2 ... 83 E3
Newbridge HE12 ... 119 F4
Almond S EH53 ... 148 B3
Almond Side EH53 ... 148 B2
Almond Sq
East Whitburn EH47 ... 170 C4
Edinburgh EH12 ... 121 D4
Almond St
Grangemouth FK3 ... 61 E3
Whitburn EH47 ... 170 A4
Almond Terr
Harthill ML7 ... 168 B3
Whitecross EH49 ... 83 F3
Almond View EH47 ... 146 A1
Almond West Rd EH54 ... 148 A3
Almondbank Prim Sch
EH54 ... 148 A3
Almondbank Terr EH11 ... 122 C2
Almondell & Calder Wood
Ctry Pk EH52 ... 149 D4
Almondell Ct EH52 ... 117 F3
Almondell Rd EH52 ... 117 F3
Almondell Terr EH52 ... 117 F3
Almondhill Rd EH29 ... 89 D1
Almondside
Kirkliston EH29 ... 89 D1
Livingston EH54 ... 147 F1
Almondvale Ave EH54 ... 147 F1
Almondvale Bsns Pk
EH54 ... 147 E1
Almondvale Bvd EH54 ... 147 E1
Almondvale Cres EH54 ... 147 E1
Almondvale Ctr EH54 ... 147 E1
Almondvale Dr EH54 ... 147 F1
Almondvale E EH54 ... 147 F1
Almondvale N
Livingston EH54 ... 147 E1
Livingston EH54 ... 147 F1
Almondvale Parkway
EH54 ... 147 E1
Almondvale Pl EH54 ... 147 F1
Almondvale Rd EH54 ... 147 F1
Almondvale Rdbt EH54 ... 147 F1
Almondvale S EH54 ... 147 F1
Almondvale Stad
(Livingston FC) EH54 ... 147 E1
Almondvale Stadium Rd
EH54 ... 147 E1
Almondvale W EH54 ... 147 E1
Almondvale Way EH54 ... 147 E1
Almondview EH54 ... 147 F1
Alness Gr KY12 ... 28 C1
Alnwickhill Cres EH16 ... 154 C3
Alnwickhill Ct EH16 ... 154 C3
Alnwickhill Dr EH16 ... 154 C3
Alnwickhill Gdns EH16 ... 154 C3
Alnwickhill Gr EH16 ... 154 C3
Alnwickhill Loan EH16 ... 154 C3
Alnwickhill Pk EH16 ... 155 D3
Alnwickhill Rd EH16 ... 154 C3
Alnwickhill Terr EH16 ... 154 C3
Alnwickhill View EH16 ... 154 C3
Alpha St EH51 ... 64 B4
Alva Acad FK12 ... 5 D4
Alva Glen FK12 ... 5 D4
Alva Ind Est FK12 ... 5 E3
Alva Pl EH7 ... 94 A1
Alva Prim Sch FK12 ... 5 D3
Alva St EH2 ... 232 A3
Alyth Dr FK2 ... 60 A3
Amberley Path FK3 ... 61 F3
Ambrose Rise EH54 ... 148 A1
Amisfield Pk EH41 ... 132 B4
Amisfield Pl
Haddington EH41 ... 132 B4
Longniddry EH32 ... 98 C3
Amos Path EH20 ... 180 C4
Amulree Pl EH51 ... 63 E4
Ancrum Bank EH22 ... 156 C1
Ancrum Rd EH22 ... 156 C1
Anderson Ave
Armadale EH48 ... 143 F2
Crossford KY12 ... 28 A1
Newtongrange EH22 ... 183 D3
Anderson Cres FK1 ... 81 F3
Anderson Dr
Cowdenbeath KY4 ... 13 D1
Denny FK6 ... 36 C1
Falkirk FK2 ... 39 D1
Anderson Gdns FK2 ... 82 C3
Anderson Gn EH54 ... 114 C1
Anderson La
Kincardine FK10 ... 23 F2
Rosyth KY11 ... 46 B3
Anderson Park Rd
FK6 ... 36 C1
Anderson Pl
Edinburgh EH6 ... 93 F3
Stirling FK7 ... 7 D2

Anderson St
Bonnybridge FK4 ... 58 A3
Dysart KY1 ... 18 A4
Andersons Terr FK4 ... 57 D2
Andrew Ave EH48 ... 145 F3
Andrew Cres FK5 ... 38 B2
Andrew Ct EH26 ... 203 F4
Andrew Dodd's Ave
EH22 ... 183 F4
Andrew St KY5 ... 14 A3
Andrew Wood Ct EH6 ... 93 E3
Angle Park Terr EH11 ... 122 C3
Angres Ct EH22 ... 156 B4
Angus Rd ML8 ... 230 A1
Angus St EH51 ... 63 E3
Ann St EH4 ... 232 A4
Annabel Ct KY11 ... 47 E1
Annan Ct FK1 ... 60 B1
Annandale St EH7 ... 93 F1
Annandale Street La
EH7 ... 93 F1
Anne Dr Bridge of A FK9 ... 2 A3
Stenhousemuir FK5 ... 38 C2
Anne St Alloa FK10 ... 9 F4
Bathgate EH48 ... 145 F3
Penicuik EH26 ... 203 F4
Annet Rd FK6 ... 57 E3
Annfield Edinburgh EH6 ... 93 E3
Tranent EH33 ... 128 C3
Annfield Ct EH33 ... 129 E3
Annfield Dr FK7 ... 7 F2
Annfield Farm Rd KY11 ... 47 D4
Annfield Gdns FK8 ... 7 D3
Annfield St EH6 ... 93 E3
Anson Ave FK1 ... 59 F1
Antigua St [symbol] EH1 ... 93 F1
Antonine Ct EH31 ... 63 E3
Antonine Gdns FK4 ... 59 E3
Antonine Prim Sch FK4 ... 58 A2
Antonine St FK4 ... 59 E3
Appin Cres
Dunfermline KY12 ... 29 D2
Kircaldy KY2 ... 16 C4
Appin Gr FK2 ... 61 F2
Appin Terr
Edinburgh EH14 ... 122 B2
Shotts ML7 ... 192 A2
Appleton Parkway
EH54 ... 146 C3
Appleton Parkway Rdbt
EH54 ... 146 C3
Arboretum Ave EH4 ... 93 D1
Arboretum Pl EH3 ... 93 D1
Arboretum Rd EH3 ... 93 D2
Arbroath Cres FK9 ... 2 A2
Arbuthnot Rd EH20 ... 181 E4
Arbuthnot St FK1 ... 59 F3
Arcade FK8 ... 7 D4
Archers Ave FK7 ... 7 E1
Archibald Pl EH3 ... 232 C2
Archibald Russell Ct FK2 ... 61 F1
Ard Ct FK2 ... 60 C4
Ardeer Pl KY11 ... 29 E1
Arden St EH9 ... 123 E3
Ardgowan Pl ML7 ... 159 F1
Ardmillan Pl EH11 ... 122 C3
Ardmillan Terr EH11 ... 122 C3
Ardmore Dr FK2 ... 62 A1
Ardshiel Ave EH4 ... 91 E1
Ardvreck Pl FK2 ... 39 D2
Argyle Cres EH15 ... 125 E4
Argyle Park Terr EH9 ... 233 D1
Argyle Pl
Bonnyrigg and Lasswade
EH19 ... 181 F3
Edinburgh EH9 ... 123 E3
Argyle St EH6 ... 93 F3
Argyll Ave Falkirk FK2 ... 60 B3
Stirling FK8 ... 2 B1
Argyll Pl FK10 ... 10 B4
Argyll St FK10 ... 10 B4
Arkaig Dr KY12 ... 28 B1
Arkwright Ct EH39 ... 54 A4
Armadale Acad EH48 ... 143 F3
Armadale Prim Sch
EH48 ... 143 F3
Armadale Rd EH47 ... 170 A4
Armine Pl EH26 ... 204 A4
Armour Ave FK7 ... 20 B4
Arneil Pl FK2 ... 82 B4
Arnot St FK1 ... 60 B2
Arnothill FK1 ... 59 F2
Arnothill Bank [6] FK1 ... 60 A2
Arnothill Ct FK1 ... 59 F2
Arnothill Gdns FK1 ... 59 F2
Arnothill La FK1 ... 59 F2
Arnothill Mews FK1 ... 60 A2
Arnott Gdns EH14 ... 122 A1
Arnprior Rd EH23 ... 207 E4
Arns Gr FK10 ... 9 F4
Arnswell FK10 ... 5 E1
Arran EH6 ... 146 C3
Arran Cres KY2 ... 16 C3
Arran Ct Alloa FK10 ... 10 A3
Grangemouth FK3 ... 125 E4
Arran Terr FK1 ... 59 E3
Arras Gr EH26 ... 204 A4
Arrol Cres FK10 ... 10 B4
Arrol Pl EH30 ... 89 E4
Arrol Sq EH54 ... 146 C3
Arthur Pl KY4 ... 13 E2

Arthur St
Cowdenbeath KY4 13 E2
Dunfermline KY12 29 D3
Edinburgh EH6 93 F2
Arthur Street La EH6 93 F2
Arthur View Cres
EH22 156 A4
Arthur View Terr EH22 156 A4
Arthur's Dr FK5 38 C1
Artillery Pk EH41 101 D1
Ash Braes FK10 23 E2
Ash Gr Alloa FK10 10 B3
Bathgate EH48 145 F3
Blackburn EH47 171 E4
Carnock KY12 27 E3
Cowdenbeath KY4 13 D2
Dunfermline KY11 46 B4
Dunbar EH42 78 A1
Livingston EH54 148 A3
Stenhousemuir FK5 38 C1
Westquarter FK2 61 D1
Ash La EH20 180 C4
Ash Terr FK8 6 C3
Ashbank Ct EH48 144 C3
Ashbank Terr EH53 148 C2
Ashbrae Gdns FK7 7 D1
Ashburnham Gdns EH30 68 B1
Ashburnham Rd EH30 89 E4
Ashfield Ct EH42 78 C1
Ashfield Pl EH42 78 C1
Ashgrove Mayfield EH22 183 F4
Musselburgh EH21 126 C3
Ashgrove Pl EH21 126 C3
Ashgrove View EH21 126 C3
Ashley Ct EH49 84 C3
Ashley Dr EH11 122 C2
Ashley Gdns EH11 122 C2
Ashley Gr EH11 122 C2
Ashley Hall Gdns EH49 84 C3
Ashley Pl EH6 93 F2
Ashley Rd FK2 61 F2
Ashley St FK4 57 F3
Ashley Terr Alloa FK10 10 A4
Edinburgh EH11 122 C2
Ashton Gr EH16 124 A1
Ashville Terr EH6 94 A2
Asquith St KY1 17 D2
Assembly St EH6 94 A3
Assynt Bank EH26 204 A3
Astley Ainslie Hospl
EH9 123 E2
Atheling Gr EH30 89 E4
Athelstaneford Prim Sch
EH39 101 F4
Athol Cres FK2 61 D2
Athol Pl Bathgate EH48 145 D4
Dunfermline KY12 29 E2
Athol Terr EH48 145 D4
Atholl Cres EH3 232 A2
Atholl Crescent La
EH3 232 A2
Atholl Pl FK8 1 C1
Atholl Terr KY2 16 B4
Atrium Way FK4 58 A2
Attlee Cres EH22 183 F3
Auchengray Rd ML11 216 C1
Auchentyre Pl FK2 39 E2
Auchinbaird FK10 5 E1
Auchingane EH10 153 F3
Auchinleck Ct EH6 93 E3
Auchterderran Rd KY5 14 A4
Auchtertool Prim Sch
KY2 15 D1
Auction Mart EH41 101 D1
Audenhard Terr EH47 171 E1
Auld Brig Rd FK10 10 A3
Auld Orch EH19 182 B4
Auldcathie Pl EH52 87 F2
Auldgate EH29 89 D1
Auldhame Cotts EH39 55 F3
Auldhill Ave EH49 86 B2
Auldhill Cotts EH49 86 B2
Auldhill Cres EH49 86 B2
Auldhill Dr EH49 86 B2
Auldhill Entry EH49 86 B2
Auldhill Pl EH49 86 B2
Auldhill Rd EH49 86 B2
Auldhill Terr EH49 86 B2
Ava St KY1 17 D1
Avalon Gdns EH49 84 B4
Aven Dr FK2 60 C2
Avenue Pk Bridge of A FK9 1 C4
Mid Calder EH53 148 B2
Avenue Pk W EH53 148 B2
Avenue Rd
Cockenzie & Port Seton
EH32 97 E2
Dalkeith EH22 156 C1
Avenue The Bridge of A FK9 2 A4
Currie EH14 151 F4
Dalgety Bay KY11 47 F2
Falkirk FK2 39 E1
Gifford EH41 163 F2
Gorebridge EH23 183 D1
Lochgelly KY5 14 B4
Philpstoun EH49 86 B4
Whitburn EH47 170 A3
Avenue Villas EH4 92 C1
Averton ML11 215 D1
Avon Ct FK1 60 B1
Avon Dr EH49 84 B4
Avon Gr
Edinburgh EH4 91 D2
Penicuik EH26 204 A3
Avon Pk FK1 111 F3
Avon Pl Bo'ness EH51 63 F4
Edinburgh EH4 91 D2
Avon Rd Bathgate EH48 145 D4
Edinburgh EH4 91 D2
Grangemouth FK3 62 B4
Whitecross EH49 83 F3
Avon St Denny FK6 36 B2
Grangemouth FK3 40 A1
Avon Terr FK1 112 A3
Avonbank Ave FK3 61 F3
Avonbridge Prim Sch
FK1 112 A3
Avonbridge Rd FK1 110 A4
Avondale Cres EH48 143 F3
Avondale Dr EH48 143 F3
Avondale Pl EH3 93 D1
Avondale Rd FK2 62 A2
Avondhu Gdns FK3 61 F4
Avonlea Dr FK2 61 F2
Avonmill Rd EH49 84 B4
Avonmill View EH49 84 B4
Avonside Dr FK6 36 B3
Avontoun Cres EH49 84 A3
Avontoun Pk EH49 84 B3
Ayres Wynd EH32 96 C1
Aytoun Cres KY3 33 F1
Aytoun Gr KY12 28 C3

Baads Rd ML7 141 E1
Baberton Ave EH14 152 B3
Baberton Cres EH14 152 C3
Baberton Loan EH14 152 B3
Baberton Mains EH14 152 B4
Baberton Mains Ave
EH14 152 B4
Baberton Mains Bank
EH14 152 B4
Baberton Mains Brae
EH14 152 B4
Baberton Mains Cres
EH14 152 B4
Baberton Mains Ct
EH14 152 B4
Baberton Mains Dell
EH14 152 B4
Baberton Mains Dr
EH14 152 B4
Baberton Mains Gdns
EH14 152 B4
Baberton Mains Gn
EH14 152 B4
Baberton Mains Gr
EH14 152 B4
Baberton Mains Hill
EH14 152 B4
Baberton Mains Lea
EH14 152 B4
Baberton Mains Loan
EH14 152 C4
Baberton Mains Pk
EH14 152 B4
Baberton Mains Pl
EH14 152 B4
Baberton Mains Rise
EH14 152 B4
Baberton Mains Row
EH14 152 B4
Baberton Mains Terr
EH14 152 B4
Baberton Mains View
EH14 152 C4
Baberton Mains Way EH14 152 B4
Baberton Mains Wood
EH14 152 B4
Baberton Mains Wynd
EH14 152 B4
Baberton Pk EH14 152 B3
Bablins Wynd EH41 163 F2
Back Cswy KY12 42 B4
Back Dean EH4 122 C4
Back O' Hill Ind Est FK8 2 A1
Back O' Hill Rd FK8 2 A1
Back O' Yds KY11 47 D1
Back Rd Alva FK12 4 C4
Dunbar EH42 78 A1
Back St KY12 42 B4
Back Station Rd EH49 85 D4
Backdean Rd EH22 156 A4
Backlee EH16 155 D3
Backmarch Cres KY11 46 C2
Backmarch Rd KY11 46 C2
Backwood Ct FK10 10 C3
Badallan Pl EH47 193 F3
Badger Wood EH52 116 B1
Baileyfield Cres EH15 125 D4
Baileyfield Est EH15 125 D4
Baileyfield Rd
Edinburgh, Northfield
EH15 94 C1
Edinburgh, Portobello
EH15 125 D4
Bailie Gr EH15 125 D3
Bailie Path EH15 125 D3
Bailie Pl EH15 125 D3
Bailie Terr EH15 125 D3
Bailielands EH49 85 E4
Baillie St EH47 170 A4
Baillie Waugh Rd FK7 7 E2
Bain Sq EH54 147 E1
Bain St KY5 14 A4
Baingle Brae FK10 4 A2
Baingle Cres FK10 4 A2
Bainsford Prim Sch
FK2 60 A4
Baird Ave EH12 122 B3
Baird Dr Armadale EH48 143 F4
Edinburgh EH12 122 B3
Baird Gdns EH12 122 B3
Baird Gr EH12 122 B3
Baird Rd Armadale EH48 143 F4
Livingston EH54 147 D1
Ratho EH28 119 E2
Baird St FK1 59 E3
Baird Terr
Edinburgh EH12 122 B3
Haddington EH41 100 C1
Harthill ML7 168 B3
Baird's Way EH19 182 B3
Bairns Ford Ave FK2 60 A4
Bairns Ford Ct FK2 60 A4
Bairns Ford Dr FK2 60 A4
Bakehouse Cl EH8 233 E3
Baker St Bo'ness EH51 63 F3
Stirling FK8 7 D4
Balantyne Pl EH54 147 D2
Balbakie Rd ML7 168 C3
Balbardie Ave EH48 145 D4
Balbardie Cres EH48 145 D4
Balbardie Prim Sch
EH48 145 D4
Balbardie Rd EH48 145 D3
Balbirnie Pl EH12 122 C4
Balcarres Ct EH10 123 D1
Balcarres Pl EH21 126 B4
Balcarres Rd EH21 126 B4
Balcarres St EH10 123 D1
Balcastle Rd FK1 110 A3
Balderston Gdns EH16 124 A1
Balderstone's Wynd
EH39 54 B4
Baldridgeburn KY12 28 C3
Baldwin Cres KY2 17 D3
Balerno High Sch EH14 151 E1
Balfour Cres Larbert FK5 38 B1
Plean FK7 20 B2
Balfour Ct
Dunfermline KY12 29 E3
Edinburgh EH12 91 D1
Balfour Pl EH6 93 F2
Balfour St Alloa FK10 10 B4
Bannockburn FK7 7 E1
Bonnybridge FK4 57 F3
Edinburgh EH6 93 F2
Kirkcaldy KY2 17 D3
North Berwick EH39 54 B4
Stirling FK8 1 C1
Balfour Terr EH26 180 A1
Balfour's Sq EH33 128 B3
Balfron Loan EH4 91 E1
Balgone Barns Cotts
EH39 54 B1
Balgreen Ave EH12 122 A3
Balgreen Gdns EH12 122 A3
Balgreen Pk EH12 122 A3
Balgreen Prim Sch
EH11 122 B3
Balgreen Rd EH12 122 A3
Baliol St KY3 34 C1
Ballantyne Rd EH6 93 F3
Ballast Bank KY11 47 E1
Ballater Dr FK9 2 B2
Ballencrieff Mill EH48 144 C4
Ballencrieff Toll EH48 114 A1
Ballengeich Pass FK8 2 A1
Ballengeich Rd FK8 1 C1
Ballingry La KY5 14 A4
Ballingry St KY5 14 A4
Balloch Rd ML7 191 F3
Balm Well Ave EH16 155 D3
Balm Well Gr EH16 155 D3
Balm Well Pk EH16 155 D3
Balm Well Terr EH16 155 D3
Balmoral Dr Falkirk FK1 59 F2
Kircaldy KY2 16 B3
Balmoral Gdns
Brightons FK2 82 B4
Livingston EH54 173 E3
Balmoral Pl
Edinburgh EH3 93 D1
Stenhousemuir FK5 38 C2
Stirling FK8 7 D4
Balmoral Rd EH51 62 C3
Balmoral St FK1 59 F2
Balmuir Rd EH48 144 C4
Balmulzier Rd FK1 110 A4
Balnacraig KY12 28 A1
Balquhatstone Cres
FK1 110 A3
Balquhidderock FK7 7 E2
Balsusney Rd KY2 17 D3
Baltic St EH6 94 A3
Balure Cres FK7 8 B2
Balvaird Pl KY12 29 E3
Balwearie Cres KY2 17 D1
Balwearie Gdns KY2 16 C1
Balwearie Rd KY2 17 D1
Balwearie Sch KY2 17 D1
Banchory Cotts KY3 34 C3
Banchory Pl FK10 4 B2
Banchory Prim Sch FK10 4 B2
Bancroft Ave EH54 147 F2
Bandeath Ind Est FK7 9 D3
Bandeath Rd FK7 8 B2
Bandon Ave KY1 17 F4
Bangholm Ave EH5 93 D3
Bangholm Bower Ave
EH5 93 D3
Bangholm Gr EH5 93 E3
Bangholm Loan EH5 93 E3
Bangholm Pk EH5 93 D3
Bangholm Pl EH5 93 D3
Bangholm Rd EH5 93 D3
Bangholm Terr EH3 93 D2
Bangholm View EH5 93 E3
Bangly Brae EH41 100 A2
Bangor Rd EH6 93 F3
Bangour Village Hospl
EH52 116 A1
Bank Pl ML7 191 F2
Bank Rd East Linton EH40 103 F4
Harthill ML7 168 C3
Bank St Alloa FK10 10 A3
Edinburgh EH1 233 D3
Falkirk FK1 60 A3
Grangemouth FK3 40 A1
Inverkeithing KY11 47 E1
Kincardine FK10 23 E2
Kirkaldy KY1 17 F4
Lochgelly KY5 14 A4
Mid Calder EH53 148 B2
North Berwick EH39 54 A4
Penicuik EH26 203 F2
Slamannan FK1 110 A3
Stirling FK8 7 D4
Whitburn EH47 170 A4
Bankhead Ave EH11 121 E2
Bankhead Broadway
EH11 121 D2
Bankhead Cotts EH40 75 E3
Bankhead Cres FK4 57 E3
Bankhead Crossway N
EH11 121 D2
Bankhead Crossway S
EH11 121 E1
Bankhead Dr EH11 121 D2
Bankhead Gr EH30 68 B1
Bankhead Ind Est EH11 121 E2
Bankhead Medway
EH11 121 E2
Bankhead Pl EH11 121 E1
Bankhead Rd
Fishcross FK10 5 E2
Queensferry EH30 89 F4
Bankhead St EH11 121 E1
Bankhead Terr EH11 121 D1
Bankhead Way EH11 121 D1
Bankhill Ct FK3 61 E3
Bankpark Brae EH33 128 A4
Bankpark Cres EH33 128 A4
Bankpark Gr EH33 128 B4
Bankside FK2 60 B4
Bankside Ct FK6 36 C1
Bankside Ind Est FK2 60 B4
Bankton Brae EH54 173 F4
Bankton Ct
Livingston EH54 174 A4
Tranent EH33 128 B3
Bankton Dr EH54 173 F4
Bankton Gdns EH54 174 A4
Bankton Glade EH54 174 A4
Bankton Gn EH54 173 F4
Bankton Gr EH54 174 A4
Bankton Junc EH33 128 B4
Bankton Pk E EH54 148 A1
Bankton Pk W EH54 148 A1
Bankton Prim Sch
EH54 147 F1
Bankton Rd EH54 173 E4
Bankton Sq EH54 173 F4
Bankton Terr EH33 128 A4
Bankton Way EH54 173 F4
Bankton Wlk EH54 173 F4
Bannerman Ave KY11 47 E2
Bannerman St KY12 29 D3
Bannoch Brae KY12 29 E2
Bannock Rd FK7 8 B2
Bannockburn High Sch
FK7 7 E1
Bannockburn Hospl FK7 19 F4
Bannockburn Prim Sch
FK7 7 F1
Bannockburn Rd
Cowie FK7 20 B4
Stirling FK7 7 E2
Bannockburn Station Rd
FK7 8 A2
Bantaskin Prim Sch FK1 59 F2
Bantaskine Dr FK1 59 F2
Bantaskine Gdns FK1 59 F2
Bantaskine St FK1 59 F2
Banton Pl FK4 58 A2
Baptie Pl EH51 63 F3
Barassie Dr KY2 17 D4
Barbauchlaw Ave EH48 143 F3
Barbour Ave FK7 7 E2
Barbour Gr KY12 28 C3
Barclay Pl EH10 232 B1
Barclay Rd KY3 34 C2
Barclay St KY4 13 D2
Barclay Terr EH10 232 B1
Barclay Way EH54 147 F4
Barham Rd KY11 46 B1
Barkhill Rd EH49 84 C3
Barkin Ct FK1 60 A1
Barlaw Gdns EH48 144 A3
Barleyhill FK4 58 A3
Barleyknowe Cres
EH23 183 E1
Barleyknowe Gdns
EH23 183 E1
Barleyknowe La EH23 183 E1
Barleyknowe Pl EH23 183 E1
Barleyknowe Rd EH23 183 E1
Barleyknowe St EH23 183 E1
Barleyknowe Terr EH23 183 E1
Barn Park Cres EH14 152 C4
Barn Pk EH14 152 C4
Barn Rd FK8 7 D4
Barnbougle Ride EH30 90 B4
Barnego Rd FK6 36 B2
Barnes Gn EH54 147 E4
Barnet Cres KY1 17 D1
Barnhill Dr FK10 4 B1
Barnhill Pl KY11 48 B2
Barnhill Rd KY11 48 B2
Barns Ct EH47 170 C4
Barns Ness Terr EH42 139 D4
Barns Pk KY11 48 A1
Barnsdale Rd FK7 7 D2
Barnshot Rd EH13 153 D3
Barnton Ave EH4 91 E2
Barnton Ave W EH4 91 D2
Barnton Brae EH4 91 D2
Barnton Ct EH4 91 D2
Barnton Gdns EH4 91 F2
Barnton Gr EH4 91 D2
Barnton La FK1 60 A2
Barnton Loan EH4 91 F2
Barnton Park Ave EH4 91 E2
Barnton Park Cres EH4 91 E2
Barnton Park Dell EH4 91 E2
Barnton Park Dr EH4 91 E2
Barnton Park Gdns EH4 91 E2
Barnton Park Gr EH4 91 E2
Barnton Park Pl EH4 91 E2
Barnton Park View EH4 91 E2
Barnton Park Wood EH4 91 D1
Barnton Pk EH4 91 F2
Barnton St FK8 7 D4
Barntongate Ave EH4 91 D1
Barntongate Dr EH4 91 D1
Barntongate Terr EH4 91 D1
Barnwell Rd FK9 2 B2
Barons Hill Ave EH49 85 D4
Barons Hill Ct EH49 85 D4
Baronscourt Rd EH8 94 B1
Baronscourt Terr EH8 124 B4
Barony Ct EH51 63 F3
Barony Pl 6 EH3 93 E1
Barony St EH3 93 E1
Barony Terr EH12 121 E4
Barr Cres KY11 47 E1
Barra Pl FK5 39 D2
Barracks Rdbt EH54 146 C3
Barracks St EH32 97 E2
Barrie Ct EH54 148 B3
Barrie Pl
Dunfermline KY12 28 C3
Grangemouth FK3 61 E3
Barrie Rd FK5 38 C2
Barrie St KY12 28 C3
Barrie Terr EH48 145 E3
Barton Rd KY11 46 A1
Barton Terr EH47 193 F3
Bass Rock View EH39 55 D4
Bastion Wynd FK8 7 D4
Bath Pl EH15 95 D1
Bath Rd EH6 94 A3
Bath St EH15 125 D4
Bath Street La EH15 125 D4
Bathfield EH6 93 F3
Bathgate Acad EH48 145 F3
Bathgate Rd
Blackburn EH47 171 E4
East Whitburn EH47 170 C4
Bathgate Sta EH48 145 D3
Bathville Bsns Ctr EH48 144 A3
Baton Rd ML7 191 E3
Batterflats Gdns FK7 6 C3
Battery Rd
Grangemouth FK3 62 B4
North Queensferry KY11 68 B3
Battock Rd FK2 82 C4
Bavelaw Cres EH26 203 E3
Bavelaw Gdns EH14 151 E1
Bavelaw Rd EH14 151 E1
Baxter Cres FK6 36 B1
Baxter St FK7 8 B2
Baxter's Pl EH1 233 E4
Baxter's Wynd FK1 60 A2
Bayne Gdns EH49 84 A3
Bayne St FK8 2 A1
Bayswell Pk EH42 78 B2
Bayswell Rd EH42 78 B2
Beach La Edinburgh EH15 95 D1
Edinburgh EH15 125 D4
Musselburgh EH21 126 A4
Beach Rd Grangemouth FK9 41 D1
North Berwick EH39 54 A4
Beachmont Ct EH42 78 C1
Beachmont Pl EH42 78 C1
Beaconhurst Sch FK9 2 B3
Bean Row FK1 60 A2
Beancross Prim Sch FK3 61 E3
Beancross Rd FK3 61 E3
Beancross Rdbt FK3 61 D3
Bearcroft Gdns FK3 61 F4
Bearcroft Rd FK3 62 B4
Bearford Pl EH41 132 B4
Bearside Rd FK7 7 D2
Beath High Sch KY4 13 D2
Beath View KY11 29 F2
Beath View Rd KY4 13 D1
Beatlie Rd EH52 88 A2
Beatlie Sch EH52 88 A2
Beaton Ave FK7 7 E1
Beatty Ave FK8 2 A1
Beatty Cres KY1 17 E4
Beatty Ct KY1 17 E4
Beatty Pl KY12 29 E3
Beauchamp Gr EH16 155 D4
Beauchamp Rd EH16 155 D4
Beauclerc St FK12 5 D4
Beaufort Cres KY2 16 B3
Beaufort Dr FK2 39 D2
Beaufort Rd EH9 123 E2
Beauly Ct Falkirk FK1 60 B1
Grangemouth FK3 61 E2
Beauly Dr EH54 148 A2
Beauly Pl KY2 16 C4
Beaumont Dr FK2 39 D1
Beaverbank Pl EH7 93 E2

Beaverhall Rd EH7 ...... 93 E2
Beck Cres KY12 ...... 29 E3
Beda Pl FK7 ...... 8 B3
Bedford Ct Alloa FK10 ...... 10 A3
  Edinburgh **3** EH4 ...... 93 D1
Bedford Pl FK10 ...... 10 A3
Bedford St EH4 ...... 93 D1
Bedford Terr EH15 ...... 125 E4
Bedlormie Dr EH48 ...... 142 B1
Beech Ave Carrington EH23 ...... 206 C2
  Dalgety Bay KY11 ...... 48 C3
  Mid Calder EH53 ...... 144 B1
  Plean FK7 ...... 20 B2
Beech Cres Denny FK6 ...... 36 B2
  Larbert FK5 ...... 59 E4
Beech Gr Dunfermline KY11 ...... 46 B4
  Livingston EH54 ...... 148 A3
  Whitburn EH47 ...... 170 B3
Beech Gr Ave EH22 ...... 156 B1
Beech La KY12 ...... 2 A2
Beech Loan EH19 ...... 182 A3
Beech Pl Grangemouth FK3 ...... 61 E3
  Livingston EH54 ...... 147 E2
  Seafield EH47 ...... 146 A1
Beech Rd EH48 ...... 145 F3
Beech St EH42 ...... 78 A1
Beech Terr EH54 ...... 160 B3
Beech Way KY11 ...... 48 A3
Beechbank Cres EH53 ...... 148 C1
Beeches The
  Dalgety Bay KY11 ...... 48 B2
  Gullane EH31 ...... 52 A3
  Newtongrange EH22 ...... 183 D4
Beechgrove Rd EH22 ...... 183 F3
Beechmount Cres EH12 ...... 122 A4
Beechmount Ct ML7 ...... 192 A1
Beechmount Pk EH12 ...... 122 A3
Beechwood Alloa FK10 ...... 5 E1
  Crossford KY12 ...... 28 A1
  Linlithgow EH49 ...... 85 D3
Beechwood Gdns EH47 ...... 145 E1
Beechwood Loan EH47 ...... 117 D1
Beechwood Mains EH12 ...... 122 A4
Beechwood Pk
  Livingston EH54 ...... 146 C4
  Newtongrange EH22 ...... 183 D3
  Uphall Station EH54 ...... 117 D1
Beechwood Pl EH47 ...... 145 E1
Beechwood Rd
  Blackburn EH47 ...... 145 E1
  Haddington EH41 ...... 131 F4
Beechwood Terr EH6 ...... 94 A2
Beecraigs Ctry Pk EH49 ...... 85 D1
Beeslack High Sch EH26 ...... 204 A4
Begbie Pl EH54 ...... 147 D3
Begg Ave FK1 ...... 59 F2
Beldorney Pl KY12 ...... 28 A1
Belford Ct EH21 ...... 126 A3
Belford Ave EH4 ...... 92 C1
Belford Gdns EH4 ...... 92 C1
Belford Pk EH4 ...... 122 C4
Belford Rd EH4 ...... 122 C4
Belford Terr EH4 ...... 122 C4
Belfrange La EH3 ...... 232 C2
Belgrave Cres EH4 ...... 232 A3
  EH4 ...... 232 A4
Belgrave Gdns EH12 ...... 121 F4
Belgrave Mews **10** EH4 ...... 92 C1
Belgrave Pl EH4 ...... 232 A3
Belgrave Rd EH12 ...... 121 F3
Belhaven Hill (Boys Sch)
  EH42 ...... 78 A1
Belhaven Hospl EH42 ...... 78 A1
Belhaven Pl EH10 ...... 123 D1
Belhaven Rd EH42 ...... 78 B1
Belhaven Terr EH10 ...... 123 D1
Bell Ct FK3 ...... 40 C1
Bell Pl EH3 ...... 93 D1
Bell Rd KY11 ...... 46 C4
Bell Sq EH54 ...... 173 E3
Bell Stane EH30 ...... 68 A1
Bell's Mill Terr EH2 ...... 87 F1
Bell's Mills EH4 ...... 122 C3
Bell's Wynd FK1 ...... 60 A2
Bellamond Cres EH47 ...... 170 C4
Belleknowes Ind Est KY11 ...... 47 D2
Bellenden Gdns EH16 ...... 124 B1
Bellerophon Dr EH26 ...... 203 F2
Bellevue Edinburgh EH7 ...... 93 E1
  Maddiston FK2 ...... 82 C4
Bellevue Ave EH7 ...... 78 C1
Bellevue Cres EH3 ...... 93 E1
Bellevue Gdns EH7 ...... 93 E1
Bellevue Gr EH7 ...... 93 E1
Bellevue Pl EH7 ...... 93 E1
Bellevue Rd Alloa FK10 ...... 9 F3
  Edinburgh EH7 ...... 93 E2
Bellevue St Edinburgh EH7 ...... 93 E1
  Falkirk FK1 ...... 60 B2
Bellevue Terr EH7 ...... 93 E1
Bellfield Ave
  Dalkeith EH22 ...... 156 C1
  East Calder EH53 ...... 148 C1
  Musselburgh EH21 ...... 126 A3
Bellfield Cres KY1 ...... 18 A4
Bellfield La EH15 ...... 125 D4
Bellfield Rd Bannockburn FK7 ...... 7 F1
  Stirling FK8 ...... 7 D3
Bellfield Sq EH32 ...... 127 F4
Bellfield St EH15 ...... 125 D4
Bellfield View EH19 ...... 182 B4
Bellhouse Rd KY3 ...... 49 D4
Bellman Way KY11 ...... 48 A3
Bellman's Rd EH26 ...... 203 F3
Bellona Terr EH47 ...... 193 F3

Bells Brae EH4 ...... 232 A3
Bells Burn Ave EH49 ...... 85 E4
Bellsdyke Hospl FK5 ...... 38 B3
Bellsdyke Rd Falkirk FK2 ...... 39 E3
  Larbert FK5 ...... 38 B2
Bellsmains EH23 ...... 207 E3
Bellsmeadow Rd FK1 ...... 60 B2
Bellsquarry Prim Sch
  EH54 ...... 173 E4
Bellsquarry South Rd
  EH54 ...... 173 F3
Bellyeoman La KY12 ...... 29 E3
Bellyeoman Prim Sch
  KY12 ...... 29 E3
Bellyeoman Rd KY12 ...... 29 E3
Bellyford Rd EH33 ...... 128 A1
Belmont Ave
  Dennyloanhead FK4 ...... 57 E3
  Edinburgh EH12 ...... 122 A4
  Shieldhill FK1 ...... 81 F4
Belmont Cres EH12 ...... 122 A4
Belmont Dr ML7 ...... 192 A1
Belmont Gdns EH12 ...... 122 A4
Belmont Pk EH12 ...... 122 A4
Belmont Rd EH12 ...... 122 A4
Belmont St FK1 ...... 60 B2
Belmont Terr EH12 ...... 122 A4
Belmont View EH12 ...... 122 A4
Belstane Pk ML8 ...... 230 A2
Belstane Rd ML8 ...... 230 A2
Belsyde Ct EH49 ...... 84 B3
Belvedere Pk EH6 ...... 93 E3
Belvedere Rd EH48 ...... 144 C4
Belwood Cres EH26 ...... 180 A1
Belwood Rd EH26 ...... 179 F1
Ben Alder Pl KY2 ...... 16 C3
Ben Ledi Rd KY2 ...... 16 C3
Ben Lomond View KY12 ...... 27 D3
Ben Nevis Pl KY2 ...... 16 C3
Ben Sayers Pk EH39 ...... 54 C3
Benarty St KY2 ...... 16 C3
Bendachin Dr KY3 ...... 29 F3
Bendameer Rd KY3 ...... 33 E1
Benhar Prim Sch ML7 ...... 168 B3
Benhar Rd Harthill ML7 ...... 167 F1
  Shotts ML7 ...... 192 A3
Benjamin Dr EH21 ...... 126 B1
Bennett Wood Terr EH52 ...... 87 F2
Bennie Mus EH48 ...... 145 D3
Bennochy Ave KY2 ...... 17 D3
Bennochy Ct KY2 ...... 17 D3
Bennochy Gdns KY2 ...... 17 D3
Bennochy Rd KY2 ...... 16 C3
Bentheads FK7 ...... 19 F4
Benview FK7 ...... 7 E1
Benview Terr FK10 ...... 5 F2
Beresford Ave EH5 ...... 93 E3
Beresford Gdns EH5 ...... 93 E3
Beresford Pl EH5 ...... 93 D3
Beresford Rise EH54 ...... 148 A1
Berkeley St FK7 ...... 7 D2
Bernard Shaw St KY12 ...... 28 C3
Bernard St EH6 ...... 94 A3
Berry St KY5 ...... 14 A4
Berryhill Cres FK3 ...... 61 F3
Berryhill Pl ML7 ...... 192 A1
Berrylaw Pl KY12 ...... 28 C2
Berrylaw Rd KY12 ...... 28 B2
Bertram Pl ML7 ...... 191 E3
Bertram St Harthill ML7 ...... 168 B3
  Shotts ML7 ...... 191 F3
Bervie Dr EH54 ...... 148 A1
Berwick Pl Dysart KY1 ...... 18 A4
  Kirkaldy KY1 ...... 17 E3
Bethesda Gr FK2 ...... 82 C3
Beulah EH21 ...... 126 C3
Bevan Dr FK12 ...... 5 D4
Bevan Pl KY11 ...... 46 C2
Bevan Rd EH22 ...... 183 E3
Bevan-lee Ct EH22 ...... 157 D2
Beveridge Ave EH22 ...... 183 F3
Beveridge Cl EH22 ...... 183 F3
Beveridge Rd KY1 ...... 17 D4
Beveridge Sq EH54 ...... 147 F1
Beveridge St KY1 ...... 29 E1
Bickerton Terr EH47 ...... 170 A3
Bickram Cres KY1 ...... 26 B4
Biggar Rd Edinburgh EH13 ...... 154 A2
  Silverburn EH26 ...... 202 C3
Biggin Wa's KY1 ...... 17 F4
Bingham Ave EH15 ...... 124 C3
Bingham Broadway EH15 ...... 125 D3
Bingham Cres EH15 ...... 125 D3
Bingham Crossway EH15 ...... 124 C3
Bingham Dr EH15 ...... 125 D3
Bingham Medway EH15 ...... 124 C3
Bingham Pl EH15 ...... 124 C3
Bingham Way EH15 ...... 124 C3
Binnie Ave KY3 ...... 33 F1
Binnie Pl FK2 ...... 39 F1
Binning Rd KY11 ...... 110 A2
Binning Wood Rd EH42 ...... 75 F4
Binny Pk EH52 ...... 65 F1
Binny Pk EH52 ...... 116 C4
Birch Cres EH20 ...... 180 C4
Birch Ct Edinburgh EH4 ...... 91 D1
  Livingston EH54 ...... 147 F4
Birch Gr KY11 ...... 46 B4
Birchbank KY4 ...... 13 D1
Birchwood FK10 ...... 5 E1
Birk Hedges EH41 ...... 130 C3
Birkdale Dr EH52 ...... 116 C2
Birkdale Pk EH48 ...... 144 A3
Birkenshaw Way EH48 ...... 143 F3

Birkenside EH23 ...... 207 E3
Birkfield Loan ML8 ...... 230 B1
Birkfield Pl ML8 ...... 230 B1
Birkhill Clay Mine EH49 ...... 62 C1
Birkhill Cres EH51 ...... 63 F3
Birkhill Rd FK7 ...... 6 C3
Birkhill St EH51 ...... 63 F3
Birkhill Sta EH49 ...... 62 C2
Birnam Pk KY2 ...... 16 C4
Birnam Rd KY2 ...... 16 C4
Birnie Brae KY5 ...... 14 A4
Birnie St KY5 ...... 14 A4
Birniehill Ave EH48 ...... 144 C2
Birniehill Cres EH48 ...... 144 C2
Birniehill Rd EH48 ...... 144 C2
Birniehill Terr EH48 ...... 144 C2
Birniewell Rd FK1 ...... 110 A3
Birrell Dr KY11 ...... 29 E1
Birrell Street Wynd KY1 ...... 17 E3
Birrell's La KY1 ...... 17 F4
Birsley Rd EH33 ...... 128 B3
Bishops Pk EH15 ...... 148 B1
Black Craigs KY2 ...... 16 B4
Blackbarony Rd **1** EH16 ...... 124 A1
Blackburn Ave KY12 ...... 28 B3
Blackburn Dr KY4 ...... 13 D2
Blackburn Prim Sch EH47 ...... 145 E1
Blackburn Rd
  Addiewell EH55 ...... 171 F1
  Blackburn EH48 ...... 145 E2
Blackchapel Cl EH15 ...... 125 D2
Blackchapel Rd EH15 ...... 125 D2
Blackcot Ave EH22 ...... 183 E3
Blackcot Dr EH22 ...... 183 E3
Blackcot Pl EH22 ...... 183 E3
Blackcot Rd EH22 ...... 183 E3
Blacket Ave EH9 ...... 123 F3
Blacket Pl EH9 ...... 123 F3
Blackfaulds Ct EH47 ...... 193 F3
Blackfaulds Dr EH47 ...... 193 F3
Blackfaulds Pl EH47 ...... 193 F3
Blackford Ave EH9 ...... 123 E2
Blackford Bank EH9 ...... 123 E2
Blackford Gate EH9 ...... 123 E2
Blackford Glen Rd EH16 ...... 123 F1
Blackford Hill Gr EH9 ...... 123 E1
Blackford Hill Rise EH9 ...... 123 E1
Blackford Hill View EH9 ...... 123 E2
Blackfriars St EH1 ...... 233 E3
Blackhall Prim Sch EH4 ...... 92 A1
Blackhall St ML7 ...... 192 A2
Blackhill Rd EH48 ...... 142 C2
Blacklaw Prim Sch KY11 ...... 29 E1
Blacklaw Rd KY11 ...... 29 E1
Blackmount Terr FK2 ...... 82 C3
Blackmuir Pl FK10 ...... 4 B2
Blackness Castle EH49 ...... 65 E2
Blackness Prim Sch EH49 ...... 65 E2
Blackridge Prim Sch EH48 ...... 142 B2
Blackston Rd FK1 ...... 112 A3
Blackthorn Ct EH4 ...... 91 D1
Blackwood Cres EH9 ...... 123 F3
Blackwood Gn EH22 ...... 183 E2
Blaeberry Gdns EH4 ...... 91 D1
Blaeberryhill Rd EH47 ...... 170 B3
Blaefaulds Cres FK6 ...... 57 E4
Blair Ave EH51 ...... 63 F3
Blair Dr Dunfermline KY12 ...... 28 C3
  Kelty KY4 ...... 12 B4
Blairdardie Cres KY1 ...... 59 F2
Blairdenon Dr FK10 ...... 5 D1
Blairdenon Rd FK12 ...... 4 C3
Blairforkie Dr FK9 ...... 1 C4
Blairhall Prim Sch KY12 ...... 26 A4
Blairhill Ave KY2 ...... 82 B4
Blairmore Rd KY2 ...... 16 B4
Blairmuckhole
  and Forrestdyke Rd
  ML7 ...... 167 F4
Blairmuir Wlk KY12 ...... 26 C4
Blake St KY11 ...... 46 C2
Blamey Cres KY4 ...... 13 D1
Blantyre Terr EH10 ...... 123 D2
Blawearie Rd EH33 ...... 128 B3
Bleachfield Edinburgh EH6 ...... 93 E2
Blenheim Ct Carluke ML8 ...... 230 A1
  Penicuik EH26 ...... 204 A4
Blenheim Pl FK5 ...... 38 C3
Blindwell Brae EH41 ...... 133 F1
Blindwells FK12 ...... 4 C3
Blinkbonnie Terr FK1 ...... 110 A3
Blinkbonny Ave EH4 ...... 92 B1
Blinkbonny Cres EH4 ...... 92 B1
Blinkbonny Gdns EH4 ...... 92 B1
Blinkbonny Gr EH4 ...... 92 B1
Blinkbonny Gr W EH4 ...... 92 B1
Blinkbonny Rd Currie EH14 ...... 152 A3
  Falkirk FK1 ...... 59 F2
Blinkbonny Terr EH4 ...... 92 A1
Blinny Ct ML7 ...... 192 A1
Bloom Ct ML7 ...... 147 D2
Bloom Pl EH54 ...... 147 D2
Bloom Rdbt EH54 ...... 147 E2
Bloomfield Pl EH48 ...... 143 E3
Blyth Rd EH27 ...... 117 E2
Blyth St KY7 ...... 14 B3
Bo'mains Ind Est EH51 ...... 63 F3

Bo'mains Rd EH51 ...... 63 F3
Bo'ness Rd EH51 ...... 63 F3
Bo'ness & Kinneil Railway
  EH51 ...... 63 E4
Bo'ness Public Sch (Prim)
  EH51 ...... 63 F4
Bo'ness Rd
  Grangemouth FK3, EH51 ...... 62 A3
  Polmont FK2 ...... 62 A3
  Queensferry EH30 ...... 67 F1
Bo'ness Sta EH51 ...... 64 A4
Boat Gn EH3 ...... 93 E2
Bog Rd Laurieston FK2 ...... 60 C2
  Penicuik EH26 ...... 203 F3
  Whitburn EH47 ...... 170 A3
Bog Rdbt FK2 ...... 60 C2
Bog Road Ind Est FK2 ...... 60 C2
Bog The FK1 ...... 64 A4
Bogend Rd Bannockburn FK7 ...... 19 F4
  Larbert FK2 ...... 38 A4
Boghall Dr EH48 ...... 145 F3
Boghall Prim Sch EH48 ...... 145 F3
Boghall Rd EH48 ...... 145 F3
Boghead Cres EH48 ...... 144 C3
Bogies Wynd KY1 ...... 17 E3
Bogily Rd KY2 ...... 16 C2
Bogpark Rd EH21 ...... 126 A3
Bogsmill Rd EH14 ...... 122 A1
Bogwood Ct EH22 ...... 183 E4
Bogwood Dr KY12 ...... 28 A1
Bogwood Rd EH22 ...... 183 F3
Bohun Ct FK7 ...... 7 E2
Bolam Dr KY3 ...... 33 F1
Bolan Sq KY5 ...... 14 A4
Bon Accord Cres ML7 ...... 161 F2
Bonaly Ave EH13 ...... 153 D3
Bonaly Brae EH13 ...... 153 D3
Bonaly Cres EH13 ...... 153 D3
Bonaly Ctry Pk H.H.L.S 152 C1
Bonaly Dr EH13 ...... 153 D3
Bonaly Gdns EH13 ...... 153 D3
Bonaly Gr EH13 ...... 153 D3
Bonaly Prim Sch EH13 ...... 153 D3
Bonaly Prim Sch (Annexe)
  EH13 ...... 153 D3
Bonaly Rd EH13 ...... 153 D3
Bonaly Rise EH13 ...... 153 D3
Bonaly Steading EH13 ...... 153 D3
Bonaly Terr EH13 ...... 153 D3
Bonaly Wester EH13 ...... 153 D3
Bonar Pl EH6 ...... 93 E3
Bonhard Ct EH51 ...... 64 A3
Bonnar St EH12 ...... 29 D2
Bonnington EH27 ...... 150 A4
Bonnington Ave EH6 ...... 93 E3
Bonnington Gr EH6 ...... 93 E3
Bonnington Ind Est EH6 ...... 93 F2
Bonnington Prim Sch EH6 ...... 93 F2
Bonnington Rd
  Edinburgh EH6 ...... 93 E3
  Wilkieston EH27 ...... 150 A3
Bonnington Road La EH6 ...... 93 F2
Bonnington Terr EH6 ...... 93 E3
Bonnybank Ct EH23 ...... 207 E4
Bonnybank Rd EH23 ...... 207 E4
Bonnybridge Hospl FK4 ...... 58 B3
Bonnybridge Prim Sch
  FK4 ...... 58 A3
Bonnybridge Rd FK4 ...... 57 F3
Bonnyfield Rd FK4 ...... 57 F3
Bonnyhaugh EH6 ...... 93 F2
Bonnyhaugh La EH6 ...... 93 E2
Bonnyhill Rd Falkirk FK1 ...... 59 D2
  High Bonnybridge FK4 ...... 58 B2
Bonnyrigg Prim Sch EH19 ...... 182 B3
Bonnyton Pl KY11 ...... 29 F1
Bonnytoun Ave EH49 ...... 85 E4
Bonnytoun Terr EH49 ...... 85 E4
Bonnyview Gdns FK4 ...... 58 A4
Bonnywood Ave FK4 ...... 58 A4
Booth Pl FK1 ...... 46 B3
Booth Pl FK1 ...... 60 B2
Boothacre La EH6 ...... 94 B2
Boreland Pk KY11 ...... 47 E2
Boreland Rd Dysart KY1 ...... 18 A3
  Inverkeithing KY11 ...... 47 E2
Borestone Cres FK7 ...... 7 D1
Borestone Ct FK7 ...... 7 D1
Borestone Pl FK7 ...... 7 D1
Borestone Prim Sch FK7 ...... 7 D1
Boroughdales EH42 ...... 78 B1
Boroughloch EH8 ...... 233 E1
Boroughloch Sq EH8 ...... 233 E1
Boroughmuir High Sch
  EH10 ...... 123 D1
Boroughmuir Sec Sch (Annexe)
  EH11 ...... 122 C2
Borrowmeadow Rd FK7 ...... 7 F4
Borrowstoun Cres EH51 ...... 63 E3
Borrowstoun Pl EH51 ...... 63 E3
Borrowstoun Rd EH51 ...... 63 E4
Borthwick Castle PH EH23 ...... 207 D2
Borthwick Castle Rd
  EH23 ...... 207 F1
Borthwick Castle Terr
  EH23 ...... 207 E1
Borthwick Pl EH12 ...... 122 C4
Borthwick View EH23 ...... 208 A2
Boswall Ave EH5 ...... 93 D3
Boswall Cres EH5 ...... 93 D3
Boswall Gdns EH5 ...... 92 C3
Boswall Gn EH5 ...... 93 D3

Boswall Gr EH5 ...... 92 C3
Boswall Loan EH5 ...... 92 C3
Boswall Parkway EH5 ...... 92 C3
Boswall Pl EH5 ...... 92 C3
Boswall Quadrant EH5 ...... 92 C3
Boswall Rd EH5 ...... 93 D3
Boswall Sq EH5 ...... 92 C3
Boswall Terr EH5 ...... 92 C3
Boswell Dr Kinghorn KY3 ...... 35 D2
  Oakley KY12 ...... 26 C3
Boswell Rd KY5 ...... 14 A4
Botkenner Prim Sch FK2 ...... 39 F2
Botkennar Rd FK2 ...... 39 F2
Bothwell Gdns KY11 ...... 29 D1
Bothwell St
  Dunfermline KY11 ...... 29 D1
  Edinburgh EH7 ...... 94 A1
Boulevard Rdbt EH54 ...... 147 E1
Boundary Rd E EH14 ...... 151 F4
Boundary Rd N EH14 ...... 151 F4
Boundary St EH51 ...... 64 A4
Bouprie Rise KY11 ...... 48 A2
Bourtree Gr KY12 ...... 26 B4
Bow Butts KY12 ...... 29 D1
Bow St FK8 ...... 7 D4
Bowhill Terr EH3 ...... 93 D3
Bowhouse Dr KY1 ...... 35 D4
Bowhouse Gdns FK10 ...... 10 A3
Bowhouse Prim Sch FK1 ...... 61 E3
Bowhouse Rd Alloa FK10 ...... 10 A3
Bowhouse Sq FK3 ...... 61 E3
Bowhousebog ... ML7 ...... 191 D1
Bowhousebog or Liquo
  ML7 ...... 191 D1
Bowhousebog Rd ML7 ...... 191 D1
Bowling Green Rd
  Kirkliston EH29 ...... 89 D1
Bowling Green St KY4 ...... 13 E2
Bowling Green The FK6 ...... 93 F3
Bowmont Pl EH8 ...... 233 E1
Bowmont Terr EH42 ...... 78 C1
Bowmore Wlk ML7 ...... 192 A2
Bowyett EH48 ...... 113 F3
Boyd Pl KY5 ...... 14 A4
Boyd St Falkirk FK2 ...... 60 A3
Boyd's Entry EH1 ...... 233 E3
Boyd-Orr Dr EH26 ...... 203 D4
Brackenlees Rd FK2 ...... 40 A3
Brackensbrae EH52 ...... 117 D3
Bradbury St FK2 ...... 39 D1
Brae Heads Loan EH40 ...... 103 E3
Brae Pk EH4 ...... 91 D2
Brae Rd EH51 ...... 62 B3
Brae The Bannockburn FK7 ...... 7 E1
  Cambusbarron FK7 ...... 6 B3
  Penicuik EH26 ...... 180 B1
Braefoot Gr KY11 ...... 48 A1
Braefoot Rd EH55 ...... 171 F2
Braefoot Terr **2** EH16 ...... 124 A1
Braehead Alloa FK10 ...... 4 B1
  Alva FK12 ...... 5 D4
  Bo'ness EH51 ...... 63 F4
Braehead Ave
  Edinburgh EH4 ...... 91 D2
  Linlithgow EH49 ...... 84 C3
  Tullibody FK10 ...... 4 B1
Braehead Bank EH4 ...... 91 D2
Braehead Cres EH4 ...... 91 D2
Braehead Dr Edinburgh EH4 ...... 91 D2
  Linlithgow EH49 ...... 84 C3
Braehead Gr Bo'ness EH51 ...... 63 F4
  Edinburgh EH4 ...... 91 D2
Braehead Loan EH4 ...... 91 D2
Braehead Pk Edinburgh EH4 ...... 91 D2
  Linlithgow EH49 ...... 84 C3
Braehead Pl EH49 ...... 84 C3
Braehead Prim Sch FK7 ...... 7 E2
Braehead Rd
  Edinburgh EH4 ...... 91 D2
  Stirling FK7 ...... 7 E2
Braehead Rdbt EH54 ...... 147 E2
Braehead Row EH4 ...... 91 D2
Braehead Terr EH49 ...... 84 C3
Braekirk Ave EH27 ...... 149 E1
Braemar Cres
  Carluke ML8 ...... 230 A2
  Falkirk FK2 ...... 60 B3
Braemar Gdns
  Brightons FK2 ...... 82 B4
Braemar Pl FK5 ...... 39 D2
Braemount KY4 ...... 13 D1
Braepark Rd EH4 ...... 91 D2
Braes The Lochgelly KY5 ...... 14 A4
  Tullibody FK10 ...... 4 B2
Braeside Alloa FK10 ...... 10 A3
  Shieldhill FK1 ...... 81 F4
Braeside Cres FK2 ...... 82 C3
Braeside Gdns EH53 ...... 148 A1
Braeside La EH53 ...... 148 A2
Braeside Pl Laurieston FK2 ...... 61 D1
  Redding FK2 ...... 82 A4
  Reddingmuirhead FK2 ...... 82 A4
Braeside Rd
  Gorebridge EH37 ...... 207 E4
  Loanhead EH20 ...... 181 E4
Braeside Rd N EH23 ...... 207 E4
Braeside Rd S EH23 ...... 207 E4

Braeview
East Linton EH40 .... 103 E4
Laurieston FK2 .... 60 C2
Stenhousemuir FK5 .... 38 B1
Braewell Gdns EH49 .... 84 B4
Braid Ave EH10 .... 123 D1
Braid Cres EH10 .... 123 D1
Braid Farm Rd EH10 .... 123 D1
Braid Gn EH54 .... 147 E4
Braid Hills App EH10 .... 154 A4
Braid Hills Ave EH10 .... 123 D1
Braid Hills Cres EH10 .... 154 A4
Braid Hills Dr EH10 .... 154 B4
Braid Hills Rd EH10 .... 154 A4
Braid Mount EH10 .... 154 A4
Braid Mount Crest EH10 .... 154 A4
Braid Mount Rise EH10 .... 154 A4
Braid Mount View EH10 .... 154 A4
Braidburn Cres EH10 .... 123 D1
Braidburn Terr EH10 .... 123 D1
Braidlaw Pk EH26 .... 203 E3
Braigh Gdns KY12 .... 28 B3
Bramble Dr EH4 .... 91 D1
Bramdean Gr EH10 .... 154 A4
Bramdean Pl EH10 .... 154 A4
Bramdean Rise EH10 .... 154 A4
Bramdean View EH10 .... 154 A4
Brand Dr EH15 .... 125 D4
Brand Gdns EH15 .... 125 E4
Brandfield St EH3 .... 232 A1
Brandon St EH3 .... 93 E1
Brands Row EH3 .... 93 E2
Brands Row KY4 .... 30 C4
Brandy Riggs KY12 .... 27 E1
Brandy Wells KY12 .... 27 E1
Brandyhill FK10 .... 5 F2
Brankholm Brae KY11 .... 46 B2
Brankholm La KY11 .... 46 B3
Brankholm La KY11 .... 46 B1
Branning Ct KY1 .... 17 E3
Bransfill Pk FK10 .... 10 A4
Bransfill Rd FK10 .... 10 A4
Branston Wynd KY1 .... 35 D4
Bravo St EH51 .... 62 C3
Bread St EH3 .... 232 B2
Bread Street La EH3 .... 232 B2
Breadalbane Pl FK2 .... 61 F1
Breadalbane St EH6 .... 93 F2
Breakers Way KY11 .... 47 F1
Brechin Dr FK2 .... 62 A1
Breck Terr EH26 .... 204 A4
Breich Dale EH55 .... 194 B3
Breich Terr EH55 .... 194 C3
Brentham Ave FK8 .... 7 D3
Brentham Cres FK8 .... 7 D3
Breslin Terr ML7 .... 168 B3
Breton Ct FK1 .... 60 B2
Brewery Cl EH20 .... 68 A1
Brewery La EH47 .... 78 A1
Brewery Pk EH41 .... 132 A4
Brewlands Ave EH51 .... 63 E3
Brewster Pl EH36 .... 36 B1
Brewster Sq EH54 .... 173 E3
Briar Brae FK2 .... 62 A4
Briar Cotts EH47 .... 171 E1
Briar Pl KY11 .... 29 E2
Briarbank EH54 .... 147 E3
Briarbank Terr EH11 .... 122 C2
Briarcliff St KY1 .... 17 F2
Briardene FK2 .... 61 D2
Briarhill Ave KY11 .... 48 A2
Briars Rd FK10 .... 4 C1
Brickfield EH15 .... 95 D1
Brickworks Rd EH33 .... 128 A4
Bridge Cres FK6 .... 36 B1
Bridge End
East Whitburn EH47 .... 170 B4
Edinburgh EH16 .... 124 A2
Shotts ML7 .... 191 E3
Bridge End Cotts EH27 .... 150 B3
Bridge of Allan Prim Sch
FK9 .... 2 A3
Bridge of Allan Sta FK9 .... 1 C4
Bridge Pl Broxburn EH52 .... 117 F3
Denny FK6 .... 36 B1
Edinburgh [4] EH3 .... 93 D1
Shotts ML7 .... 192 A2
Bridge Rd Balerno EH14 .... 151 E1
Edinburgh EH13 .... 153 D3
Bridge St Bonnybridge FK4 .... 58 A3
Cowdenbeath KY4 .... 13 D2
Dunfermline KY12 .... 28 C2
East Linton EH40 .... 103 F4
Edinburgh EH15 .... 95 D1
Faulkhouse EH47 .... 193 F3
Haddington EH41 .... 132 B4
Kincardine FK10 .... 23 E2
Kirkaldy KY1 .... 17 D1
Musselburgh EH21 .... 126 B3
Newbridge EH28 .... 119 D3
Penicuik EH26 .... 203 F2
Tranent EH33 .... 128 B3
Bridge Street La EH15 .... 95 D1
Bridge Terr FK10 .... 10 A3
Bridge View KY11 .... 68 B3
Bridgecastle Cotts EH48 .... 112 C1
Bridgecastle Rd EH48 .... 144 C1
Bridgehaugh Rd FK9 .... 2 A1
Bridgehill FK1 .... 112 A3
Bridgend Ct EH48 .... 144 C3
Bridgend Pk EH48 .... 144 C3
Bridgend Pl EH47 .... 162 B2
Bridgend Prim Sch EH49 .... 86 B2
Bridgend Rd FK1 .... 112 A3
Bridgeness Cres EH51 .... 64 B4

Bridgeness La EH51 .... 64 B4
Bridgeness Rd EH51 .... 64 B4
Bridges The KY11 .... 48 A1
Bridgeside Ave EH47 .... 170 A3
Bridgeton Cotts EH48 .... 112 C1
Brierbush Cres EH33 .... 129 E3
Brierbush Rd EH33 .... 129 E3
Briery Bank EH41 .... 132 B4
Briery Bauks EH8 .... 233 E2
Brig-O-Doon Gr FK7 .... 20 C4
Bright's Cres EH9 .... 123 F2
Brighton Pl EH15 .... 125 D4
Brighton St EH1 .... 233 D2
Brisbane St EH54 .... 148 A3
Bristo Pl EH1 .... 233 D2
Bristo Sq EH8 .... 233 D2
Britwell Cres EH7 .... 94 B1
Brixwold Bank EH19 .... 182 B3
Brixwold Dr EH19 .... 182 B3
Brixwold Neuk EH19 .... 182 B3
Brixwold Pk EH19 .... 182 B3
Brixwold Rise EH19 .... 182 B3
Brixwold View EH19 .... 182 B3
Broad St Alloa FK10 .... 10 A3
Cowdenbeath KY4 .... 13 E1
Denny FK6 .... 36 C1
Stirling FK8 .... 7 D4
Broad Wynd Edinburgh EH6 .... 94 A3
Kirkaldy KY1 .... 17 E3
Broadgait EH31 .... 52 A2
Broadgait Ct EH31 .... 52 A2
Broadgait Gn EH31 .... 52 A2
Broadhurst Rd EH22 .... 183 E4
Broadleys Rd FK7 .... 7 E4
Broadleys Rdbt FK7 .... 7 E4
Brock Pl FK7 .... 7 D1
Brock St KY11 .... 68 A3
Brocks Way EH52 .... 118 A4
Brockville Pk (Falkirk FC)
FK1 .... 60 A3
Brockwood Ave EH26 .... 203 E3
Brodick Pl KY1 .... 59 E2
Brodick Rd KY2 .... 16 C4
Brodie Ave EH30 .... 54 B3
Brodie St FK2 .... 60 A4
Broich The FK12 .... 4 C4
Bronte Pl FK5 .... 39 D2
Brook St Alva FK12 .... 5 D3
Menstrie FK11 .... 3 F3
Brook Way EH52 .... 116 A1
Brooke La FK3 .... 61 E3
Brooke St FK3 .... 61 E3
Brookfield Pl FK12 .... 5 D3
Brookfield Terr EH25 .... 180 C3
Brookside FK2 .... 61 F1
Broom Cl FK7 .... 20 B3
Broom Gr KY11 .... 46 C4
Broom Pk E FK11 .... 4 A3
Broom Pk W FK11 .... 4 A3
Broom Rd Kircaldy KY2 .... 16 B4
Stirling FK7 .... 7 E2
Broom Wlk EH54 .... 148 A2
Broom Wynd ML7 .... 191 F3
Broomage Ave FK5 .... 38 A2
Broomage Cres FK5 .... 38 A2
Broomage Dr FK5 .... 38 A1
Broomage Pk FK5 .... 38 B1
Broombank Terr EH12 .... 121 E2
Broomburn Gr EH12 .... 121 F2
Broomfield Cres EH12 .... 121 E2
Broomfield Dr KY12 .... 29 D3
Broomfield Rd EH14 .... 13 E3
Broomfield Terr EH12 .... 121 F2
Broomhall Ave EH12 .... 121 E2
Broomhall Bank EH12 .... 121 E3
Broomhall Cres EH12 .... 121 E3
Broomhall Dr EH12 .... 121 E3
Broomhall Gdns EH12 .... 121 E3
Broomhall Loan EH12 .... 121 E3
Broomhall Pk EH12 .... 121 E3
Broomhall Rd EH12 .... 121 E2
Broomhall Terr EH12 .... 121 E3
Broomhead Dr KY12 .... 28 C3
Broomhead Pk KY12 .... 28 C3
Broomhill KY3 .... 50 C4
Broomhill Ave
Burntisland KY3 .... 33 F1
Larbert FK5 .... 38 A1
Penicuik EH26 .... 203 F2
Broomhill Dr EH22 .... 156 C1
Broomhill Pk EH22 .... 156 C1
Broomhill Pl Denny FK6 .... 36 B2
Stirling FK7 .... 6 C3
Broomhill Rd
Bonnybridge FK4 .... 58 A2
Penicuik EH26 .... 203 F2
Broomhill St ML7 .... 168 B3
Broomhouse Ave EH11 .... 121 E2
Broomhouse Bank EH11 .... 121 F2
Broomhouse Cres EH11 .... 121 F2
Broomhouse Ct EH11 .... 121 F2
Broomhouse Dr EH11 .... 121 E2
Broomhouse Gdns EH11 .... 121 E2
Broomhouse Gdns W EH11 .... 121 E2
Broomhouse Loan EH11 .... 121 F2
Broomhouse Medway
EH11 .... 121 F2
Broomhouse Mkt EH11 .... 121 F2
Broomhouse Path EH11 .... 121 E2
Broomhouse Pk EH11 .... 121 E2
Broomhouse Pl S EH11 .... 121 E2
Broomhouse Prim Sch
EH11 .... 121 F2

Broomhouse Rd EH11 .... 121 E2
Broomhouse Row EH11 .... 121 F2
Broomhouse Sq EH11 .... 121 F2
Broomhouse St N EH11 .... 121 F2
Broomhouse St S EH11 .... 121 F1
Broomhouse Terr EH11 .... 121 F2
Broomhouse Wlk EH11 .... 121 F2
Broomhouse Wynd EH11 .... 121 F2
Broomieknowe
Bonnyrigg and
Lasswade EH18 .... 182 A4
Dunfermline KY11 .... 29 E2
Tullibody FK10 .... 4 A3
Broomieknowe Gdns
EH19 .... 182 A4
Broomieknowe Pk EH19 .... 182 A4
Broomieknowe Dr FK10 .... 23 E3
Broomlea Cres EH12 .... 121 E3
Broompark Gdns
Denny FK6 .... 36 C1
East Calder EH53 .... 148 C2
Broompark Rd
East Calder EH53 .... 148 C2
Edinburgh EH12 .... 121 E3
Broompark View EH53 .... 148 C2
Broombridge Rd FK7 .... 7 E2
Broomside EH19 .... 16 B4
Broomside Pl FK5 .... 38 B1
Broomside Rd EH54 .... 146 C3
Broomside Terr EH12 .... 121 F2
Broomyknowe EH14 .... 152 C4
Broomyknowe Dr EH54 .... 146 C3
Brora Pl KY12 .... 28 B1
Brosdale Ct FK1 .... 60 A1
Brougham Pl EH3 .... 232 C1
Brougham St EH3 .... 232 B1
Broughton High Sch EH4 .... 92 C1
Broughton Market EH3 .... 93 E1
Broughton Place La EH1 .... 93 E1
Broughton Prim Sch EH7 .... 93 E2
Broughton Rd EH7 .... 93 E2
Broughton St EH1 .... 93 E1
Broughton Street La EH1 .... 93 E1
Brown Ave Alloa FK10 .... 4 C1
Stirling FK9 .... 2 A1
Brown St Armadale EH48 .... 143 F2
Edinburgh EH8 .... 233 E2
Falkirk FK1 .... 59 E3
Haddington EH41 .... 132 A4
Shotts ML7 .... 192 A2
Whitburn EH47 .... 170 A3
Brown's Cl EH8 .... 233 F3
Brown's Pl
East Linton EH40 .... 103 E4
Edinburgh EH1 .... 232 C2
Browning Farm Cotts
EH39 .... 74 B3
Broxburn Acad EH52 .... 117 E3
Broxburn Prim Sch EH52 .... 117 F3
Bruart Ave FK5 .... 38 C2
Bruce Cres Falkirk FK2 .... 39 D2
Plean FK7 .... 20 B2
Bruce Dr Fallin FK7 .... 8 B3
Stenhousemuir FK5 .... 38 C2
Bruce Gdns Brightons FK2 .... 82 B4
Dalkeith EH22 .... 157 D1
Bruce Gr EH30 .... 160 C3
Bruce Pl FK3 .... 61 F4
Bruce Rd Bathgate EH48 .... 146 F3
Grangemouth EH51 .... 62 C3
Bruce St Alloa FK10 .... 10 B4
Bannockburn FK7 .... 7 D1
Clackmannan FK10 .... 11 D2
Dunfermline KY12 .... 28 C2
Edinburgh EH10 .... 123 D1
Falkirk FK2 .... 60 B4
Kinghorn KY3 .... 35 D2
Plean FK7 .... 20 B2
Stirling FK8 .... 2 A1
Bruce Terr Cambusbarron FK7 .... 6 B3
Kinghorn KY3 .... 35 D2
Bruce View FK7 .... 7 D1
Brucefield Ave KY11 .... 29 D1
Brucefield Cres FK10 .... 11 D2
Brucefield Dr EH47 .... 170 A3
Brucefield Feus KY11 .... 29 D2
Brucefield Ind Est EH54 .... 173 E3
Brucefield Pk E EH54 .... 173 E3
Brucefield Pk N EH54 .... 173 E3
Brucefield Pk W EH54 .... 173 E3
Brucefield Terr KY4 .... 13 F3
Brucehaven Cres KY11 .... 45 F2
Brucehaven Rd KY11 .... 45 E2
Brunstane Bank EH15 .... 125 E3
Brunstane Cres EH15 .... 125 E3
Brunstane Gardens Mews
EH15 .... 125 E3
Brunstane Gdns
Edinburgh EH15 .... 125 E4
Penicuik EH26 .... 203 E3
Brunstane Prim Sch EH15 .... 125 E3
Brunstane Rd EH15 .... 125 E4
Brunstane Rd N EH15 .... 125 E4
Brunstane Rd S EH15 .... 125 E3
Brunswick Rd EH7 .... 93 F1
Brunswick St EH7 .... 93 F1
Brunswick Street La EH7 .... 93 F1
Brunswick Terr EH7 .... 93 F1
Brunt Gr EH42 .... 106 B4
Brunt La EH42 .... 106 B3
Brunt Pl EH42 .... 106 C4
Brunton Terr EH7 .... 93 F1
Brunton's Cl EH22 .... 157 D2
Bruntsfield Ave EH10 .... 123 D3

Bruntsfield Cres EH10 .... 123 D3
Bruntsfield Gdns EH10 .... 123 D3
Bruntsfield Pl EH10 .... 232 B1
Bruntsfield Prim Sch
EH10 .... 123 D3
Bruntsfield Terr EH10 .... 123 D3
Bryans Ave EH22 .... 183 F4
Bryans Prim Sch EH22 .... 183 F4
Bryans Rd EH22 .... 183 D3
Bryce Ave Edinburgh EH7 .... 94 C1
Falkirk FK2 .... 39 D1
Bryce Cres EH14 .... 152 A3
Bryce Gdns EH14 .... 152 A3
Bryce Gr EH7 .... 94 C1
Bryce Pl EH14 .... 152 A3
Bryce Rd EH14 .... 152 A3
Bryony The KY10 .... 4 A1
Bryson Rd EH11 .... 122 C2
Bryson St FK2 .... 60 A3
Bryson Street Ind Est FK2 .... 60 A3
Buccleuch Pl EH8 .... 156 C2
Buccleuch Pl EH8 .... 233 D1
Buccleuch St
Dalkeith EH22 .... 157 D2
Edinburgh EH8 .... 233 E1
Buccleuch Terr EH8 .... 233 E1
Buchan La EH55 .... 172 B1
Buchan Pl FK3 .... 61 E3
Buchan Rd Bathgate EH48 .... 144 C4
Broxburn EH52 .... 117 E3
Grangemouth EH51 .... 62 B3
Buchanan Cres EH54 .... 147 D3
Buchanan Ct Bo'ness EH51 .... 63 F3
Edinburgh EH7 .... 60 A4
Kirkaldy KY2 .... 17 D2
Buchanan Dr FK9 .... 2 A2
Buchanan Gdns FK2 .... 61 E1
Buchanan St
Dunfermline KY12 .... 29 D2
Edinburgh EH6 .... 93 F2
Buckie Rd EH22 .... 183 F3
Buckingham Terr EH4 .... 232 A4
Buckstane Pk EH10 .... 154 A3
Buckstone Ave EH10 .... 154 A3
Buckstone Bank EH10 .... 154 A3
Buckstone Circ EH10 .... 154 B3
Buckstone Cl EH10 .... 154 B3
Buckstone Cres EH10 .... 154 A4
Buckstone Crook EH10 .... 154 B3
Buckstone Ct EH10 .... 154 A3
Buckstone Dell EH10 .... 154 A4
Buckstone Dr EH10 .... 154 A4
Buckstone Gate EH10 .... 154 B3
Buckstone Gdns EH10 .... 154 A3
Buckstone Gn EH10 .... 154 B3
Buckstone Gr EH10 .... 154 A3
Buckstone Hill EH10 .... 154 B4
Buckstone Howe EH10 .... 154 B3
Buckstone Lea EH10 .... 154 B3
Buckstone Loan EH10 .... 154 B3
Buckstone Loan E EH10 .... 154 B3
Buckstone Neuk EH10 .... 154 B4
Buckstone Prim Sch
EH10 .... 154 B3
Buckstone Rd EH10 .... 154 A3
Buckstone Rise EH10 .... 154 B4
Buckstone Shaw EH10 .... 154 B3
Buckstone View EH10 .... 154 A4
Buckstone Way EH10 .... 154 A4
Buckstone Wood EH10 .... 154 A3
Buffies Brae KY12 .... 28 C2
Bughtknowes Dr EH48 .... 145 E4
Bughtlin Dr EH12 .... 91 D1
Bughtlin Gdns EH12 .... 121 D4
Bughtlin Gn EH12 .... 91 D1
Bughtlin Loan EH12 .... 121 D4
Bughtlin Mkt EH12 .... 121 D4
Bughtlin Pl EH12 .... 91 D1
Bughtlin Rd EH12 .... 91 D1
Buiyeon Rd EH30 .... 89 D4
Buller St KY5 .... 14 A4
Bullet Loan EH41 .... 132 B4
Bullock Chase FK6 .... 36 B1
Bungalow The FK5 .... 38 A1
Bunting Cres FK7 .... 20 C4
Burdiehouse Ave EH17 .... 155 D2
Burdiehouse Cres EH17 .... 155 D2
Burdiehouse Crossway
EH17 .... 155 D2
Burdiehouse Dr EH17 .... 155 D2
Burdiehouse Loan EH17 .... 155 D2
Burdiehouse Medway
EH17 .... 155 D2
Burdiehouse Pl EH17 .... 155 D2
Burdiehouse Prim Sch
EH17 .... 155 D2
Burdiehouse Sq EH17 .... 155 D2
Burdiehouse St EH17 .... 155 D2
Burdiehouse Terr EH17 .... 155 D2
Burgess Hill EH49 .... 86 D3
Burgess Rd EH30 .... 89 E4
Burgess St EH6 .... 94 A3
Burgh Mews FK10 .... 10 A3
Burgh Mills La EH49 .... 84 C3
Burgh Rd KY11 .... 13 E2
Burghlee Cres EH20 .... 181 E4
Burghlee Terr EH20 .... 181 E4
Burghmuir Ct EH49 .... 85 E4
Burghmuir Ind Est FK7 .... 7 D3
Burghtoft EH17 .... 155 F3
Burleigh Cres KY11 .... 47 E2

Burleigh Way FK10 .... 10 B3
Burlington St EH6 .... 93 F3
Burn Dr FK7 .... 7 F2
Burnbank Carnock KY12 .... 27 E4
Livingston EH54 .... 147 E3
Loanhead EH20 .... 181 D4
Burnbank Rd Falkirk FK2 .... 60 A4
Grangemouth KY11 .... 61 E3
Burnbrae Alloa FK10 .... 10 B4
Edinburgh EH12 .... 121 D4
Faulkhouse EH47 .... 193 F3
Burnbrae Gdns Alva FK12 .... 5 D3
Falkirk FK1 .... 60 A3
Burnbrae Pk KY10 .... 33 F2
Burnbrae Rd Falkirk FK1 .... 60 A3
Harthill ML7 .... 169 D3
Shotts ML7 .... 191 F2
Stoneyburn EH47 .... 171 D1
Burnbrae Terr EH47 .... 170 B3
Burndene Dr EH20 .... 155 D1
Burnee FK10 .... 5 F2
Burney Pl KY11 .... 46 C2
Burnfield EH54 .... 147 D1
Burnfield Pl FK2 .... 60 B4
Burnfoot Ct FK3 .... 61 E3
Burnfoot La [1] FK1 .... 60 A2
Burngrange Cotts EH55 .... 172 B1
Burngrange Ct EH55 .... 172 B1
Burngrange Gdns EH55 .... 172 A1
Burnhead Cres EH16 .... 155 D3
Burnhead Gr EH16 .... 155 D3
Burnhead La FK1 .... 60 B2
Burnhead Loan EH16 .... 155 D3
Burnhead Path E EH16 .... 155 D3
Burnhead Path W EH16 .... 155 D3
Burnhead Rd FK5 .... 38 B2
Burnhouse Dr
Dechmont EH52 .... 116 B1
Whitburn EH47 .... 169 F3
Burnhouse Ind Est EH47 .... 169 F3
Burnhouse Rd EH52 .... 116 B2
Burnhouse Sch EH47 .... 170 A3
Burnlea Dr EH47 .... 171 D1
Burnmill Pl EH47 .... 171 D1
Burns Ave Armadale EH48 .... 143 F3
Bathgate EH48 .... 145 D3
Burns Cres Harthill ML7 .... 168 C3
Laurieston FK2 .... 60 C2
Whitburn EH47 .... 170 A3
Burns Ct EH54 .... 148 B3
Burns Pl ML7 .... 191 D3
Burns St Dunfermline KY12 .... 28 C3
Edinburgh EH6 .... 94 A2
High Valleyfield KY12 .... 26 A1
Stirling FK8 .... 2 A1
Burns Terr Bathgate EH48 .... 145 D3
Cowie FK7 .... 20 B4
Burnside Dechmont EH52 .... 116 A1
Edinburgh EH12 .... 121 D4
Haddington EH41 .... 131 F4
Prestonpans EH32 .... 96 C1
Burnside Ave
Armadale EH48 .... 143 E2
Easthouses EH22 .... 183 E4
Kinghorn KY3 .... 34 C2
Polbeth EH55 .... 172 C3
Burnside Bsns Ctr KY11 .... 47 E2
Burnside Cres
Clackmannan FK10 .... 11 D3
Easthouses EH22 .... 183 E4
Faulkhouse EH47 .... 193 F3
Plean FK7 .... 20 B2
Rosyth KY11 .... 47 D3
Shotts ML7 .... 191 E3
Burnside Ct EH54 .... 134 B1
Burnside Gdns EH49 .... 83 F3
Burnside La EH55 .... 172 C3
Burnside Pk EH14 .... 151 E1
Burnside Pl Falkirk FK2 .... 39 D2
Rosyth KY11 .... 47 D2
Burnside Rd
Bathgate EH48 .... 144 C4
Gorebridge EH23 .... 183 E1
Menstrie FK11 .... 3 F3
Polbeth EH55 .... 172 C3
Redding FK2 .... 61 D1
Burnside Terr EH7 ....
Burnside View EH55 .... 171 E1
Burnsknowe EH54 .... 146 C3
Burntisland Prim Sch KY3 .... 33 E1
Burntisland Rd KY3 .... 34 C1
Burntisland Sta KY3 .... 50 C4
Burnvale Broxburn EH52 .... 118 A2
Livingston EH54 .... 147 F2
Burt Ave KY3 .... 34 C2
Burt Gr KY11 .... 29 F1
Burt St KY12 .... 29 D3
Bush St KY11 .... 126 A3
Bush Terr EH21 .... 126 A3
Bute EH54 .... 144 A2
Bute Cres Dunfermline KY11 .... 29 F2
Shotts ML7 .... 191 E3
Bute Pl FK3 .... 61 E3
Bute St FK3 .... 61 E3
Butler's Pl EH54 .... 147 D2
Butlerfield Ind Est EH19 .... 183 D2
Butterfly World EH18 .... 156 B2

Butts The EH41 .... 132 A4
Buxley Rd EH33 .... 128 A1
By-Pass Rd FK4 .... 57 F3
Byburn EH52 .... 116 C4
Byrehope Rd EH52 .... 117 D2
Byres The KY11 .... 46 B3
Byreside EH47 .... 146 A1
Byron Rd ML7 .... 191 D3

Cables Wynd EH6 .... 93 F3
Caddell's Row Cotts EH4 ...... 91 D3
Cadell Dr FK2 .... 39 D3
Cadell Pl EH32 .... 97 E2
Cadgers Loan FK7 .... 20 A1
Cadiz St EH6 .... 94 A3
Cadogan Rd EH16 .... 155 D4
Cadzow Ave EH51 .... 63 F3
Cadzow Cres EH51 .... 63 F4
Cadzow La EH51 .... 63 F4
Cadzow Pl EH7 .... 94 A1
Caerketton Ave EH25 ...... 180 C3
Caerlaverock Ct EH12 ...... 121 D4
Caesar Rd EH33 .... 128 B3
Caesar Way EH33 .... 128 B3
Caird's Row EH21 .... 126 A4
Cairn Gr KY12 .... 28 B1
Cairn's La EH51 .... 64 A4
Cairnbank Gdns EH26 ...... 203 F2
Cairnbank Rd EH26 .... 203 F2
Cairncubie Rd KY12 .... 29 E4
Cairneyhill Prim Sch KY12 .. 27 E1
Cairneyhill Rd KY12 .... 28 A1
Cairneymount Ave FK2 .... 83 D3
Cairneymount Rd ML8 ...... 230 A1
Cairngorm Cres KY12 ...... 16 C3
Cairngorm Pl EH16 .... 93 F3
Cairngorm Rd EH3 .... 93 F3
Cairnhill Ct ML8 .... 230 A1
Cairnie Pl EH47 .... 170 A3
Cairnmuir Rd EH12 .... 121 F4
Cairnoch Way FK7 .... 7 F1
Cairnoch Wlk FK6 .... 36 B1
Cairnpapple Henge & Cairn
  EH48 .... 114 B2
Cairnpark Sch EH14 .... 122 A1
Cairns Dr EH14 .... 177 D4
Cairns Gdns EH14 .... 177 D4
Cairns St E KY1 .... 17 F4
Cairns St W KY1 .... 17 E4
Cairns The
  Charlestown KY11 .... 45 D2
  Menstrie FK11 .... 4 A3
Cairntows Cl EH16 .... 124 B2
Cairnwell Pl
  Cairneyhill KY12 .... 27 E1
  Kircaldy KY2 .... 16 C4
Caithness Pl KY1 .... 17 F4
Caithness Pl Edinburgh EH5 .. 93 D3
  Kirkcaldy KY1 .... 17 F4
Caiyside EH10 .... 154 A2
Caiystane Ave EH10 ...... 154 A3
Caiystane Cres EH10 ..... 154 A3
Caiystane Dr EH10 .... 153 F3
Caiystane Gdns EH10 ..... 154 A3
Caiystane Hill EH10 ..... 154 A3
Caiystane Terr EH10 ..... 154 A3
Caiystane View EH10 ..... 154 A3
Calais View KY11 .... 29 F1
Calaisburn Pl KY11 ...... 29 F1
Calder Cres
  Armadale EH48 .... 144 A3
  Edinburgh EH11 .... 121 D1
Calder Ct Edinburgh EH11 .. 121 E1
  Stirling FK7 .... 7 E3
Calder Dr Edinburgh EH11 .. 121 E1
  Shotts ML7 .... 192 A2
Calder Gdns EH11 .... 121 E1
Calder Gr EH11 .... 121 E1
Calder House Rd EH53 ..... 148 A1
Calder Park Rd EH53 ...... 148 A1
Calder Pk EH11 .... 121 E1
Calder Pl Dalgety Bay KY11 .. 48 A2
  Edinburgh EH11 .... 121 E1
  Falkirk FK1 .... 60 B1
Calder Rd
  Edinburgh, East Hermiston
  EH14 .... 121 D1
  Edinburgh, Sighthill EH11 .. 121 E1
  Livingston EH54 .... 173 E3
Calder Rd Gdns EH11 ...... 122 A2
Calder View EH11 .... 121 E1
Calder's Lawn EH41 ...... 101 D1
Calderburn Rd EH55 ...... 173 D3
Caldercruix Rd FK1 ...... 110 A1
Calderhall Ave EH51 ...... 64 A4
Calderhall Cres EH53 ..... 148 C2
Calderhall Terr EH53 ..... 148 C2
Calderhead High Sch
  ML7 .... 191 F3
Calderhead Rd ML7 ...... 191 E4
Caledonia Rd Rosyth KY11 .. 46 A1
  Shotts ML7 .... 191 F3
Caledonia Way KY11 ...... 46 A2
Caledonian Cres EH11 .... 232 A1
Caledonian Ct FK2 ...... 39 D4
Caledonian Gdns FK10 ..... 9 E3
Caledonian Pl EH11 ...... 232 A1
Caledonian Rd Alloa FK10 .. 9 F3
  EH11 .... 232 A1
  Faulihouse EH47 .... 170 B3
Caledonian Terr EH47 .... 193 E3
Calgary Ave EH54 .... 147 F2
California Prim Sch FK1 .. 81 F3
California Rd FK1 .... 82 C3
California Terr FK1 ...... 81 F3
Callander Dr FK5 .... 59 E4
Callander Pl TD13 .... 140 C2

Callendar Ave FK1 .... 60 A1
Callendar Bsns Pk FK1 .... 60 C2
Callendar Bvd FK1 .... 60 C2
Callendar Pk FK1 .... 60 B2
Callendar Rd FK1 .... 60 B2
Callendar Riggs FK1 ...... 60 B2
Callendar Square Sh Ctr [5]
  FK1 .... 60 A2
Calliope Rd KY12 .... 46 A1
Calton Cres FK7 .... 7 D2
Calton Hill EH1 .... 233 E4
Calton Rd EH8 .... 233 E3
Caltrop Pl FK7 .... 7 F2
Calum Macdonald Ct KY11 .. 46 C2
Cambridge Ave EH6 ...... 93 F2
Cambridge Gdns EH6 ...... 93 F2
Cambridge St EH1 .... 232 B2
Cambusbarron Prim Sch
  FK7 .... 6 B3
Cambusnethan St [7] EH7 .. 94 A1
Camdean Cres KY11 ...... 46 B3
Camdean La KY11 .... 46 B3
Camdean Prim Sch KY11 .. 46 B2
Camelon Ed Ctr FK1 ...... 59 F3
Camelon Rd FK1 .... 59 F3
Camelon Sta FK1 .... 59 E3
Cameron Cres
  Bonnyrigg and Lasswade
  EH19 .... 181 F3
  Edinburgh EH16 .... 124 A2
Cameron Gr KY11 .... 47 D2
Cameron House Ave
  EH16 .... 124 A2
Cameron Knowe EH49 ...... 86 B3
Cameron March EH16 ...... 124 A2
Cameron Pk EH16 .... 124 A2
Cameron Pl KY2 .... 39 D1
Cameron Smaill Rd EH14 .. 151 F4
Cameron St KY12 .... 28 C2
Cameron Terr
  Edinburgh EH16 .... 124 A2
  Slamannan FK1 .... 110 A2
Cameron Toll EH16 ...... 124 A2
Cameron Toll Gdns EH16 .. 124 A2
Cameron Toll (Sh Ctr)
  EH16 .... 124 A2
Cameron Way EH54 ...... 147 F4
Cameronian Dr ML8 ...... 230 A1
Cameronian St FK8 ...... 7 D4
Camilla Gr KY11 .... 15 E1
Cammo Bank EH4 .... 91 D1
Cammo Brae EH4 .... 91 D1
Cammo Gdns EH4 .... 91 D1
Cammo Hill EH4 .... 90 C1
Cammo Parkway EH4 ...... 91 D1
Cammo Rd EH4 .... 91 D1
Cammo Wlk EH4 .... 90 C1
Camp Rd Crombie KY12 .... 44 B3
  Mayfield EH22 .... 183 F4
Camp Wood View EH22 .... 183 F3
Campbell Ave EH12 ...... 122 B4
Campbell Cres
  Laurieston FK2 .... 60 C2
  Lochgelly KY5 .... 14 A4
Campbell Ct
  Longniddry EH32 .... 98 B3
  Stirling FK7 .... 6 C2
Campbell Dr FK5 .... 38 A1
Campbell Park Cres EH13 .. 152 C3
Campbell Park Dr EH13 .. 152 C3
Campbell Rd
  Edinburgh EH12 .... 122 B4
  Longniddry EH32 .... 98 B3
Campbell St KY12 .... 29 D2
Camperdown Rd KY11 ...... 46 B1
Campfield St FK2 .... 60 A3
Campie La EH21 .... 126 A3
Campie Prim Sch EH21 .. 126 A3
Campie Rd EH21 .... 126 A3
Campie Terr FK2 .... 39 F1
Camps Rd KY12 .... 27 E3
Camps Rigg EH54 .... 147 D4
Campsie Cres KY2 .... 16 C4
Campsie Rd FK3 .... 61 F3
Campus Rdbt EH54 ...... 147 E1
Campview EH22 .... 156 A4
Campview Cres EH22 ..... 156 B4
Campview Gdns EH22 ..... 156 A4
Campview Gr EH22 .... 156 B4
Campview Rd EH19 .... 182 A3
Campview Terr EH22 ..... 156 A4
Camus Ave EH10 .... 154 A3
Camus Pk EH10 .... 154 A3
Camus Pl E EH10 .... 154 A3
Camus Pl W EH10 .... 154 A3
Camus Rd E EH10 .... 154 A3
Camus Rd W EH10 .... 154 A3
Canaan La EH10 .... 123 D2
Canal St
  Falkirk, Camelon FK1 .... 59 E3
  Falkirk, Grahamston FK2 .. 60 A4
Canal Wlk FK2 .... 61 E1
Canalyard Ind East FK1 .. 60 A1
Canavan Ct FK7 .... 7 D2
Canberra St EH54 .... 148 A3
Candie Cres EH30 .... 61 F3
Candie Rd FK3 .... 62 A4
Candimilne Ct ML8 ...... 230 A1
Candlemaker Row EH1 ..... 233 D2
Candlemaker's Cres
  EH17 .... 155 F3
Candlemaker's Pk EH17 ... 155 F3
Candleriggs FK10 .... 10 A3
Candleriggs Ct FK10 ...... 10 A3
Caneluk Ave ML8 .... 230 A1

Canmore Dr FK5 .... 38 C2
Canmore Gr KY12 .... 29 D3
Canmore St
  Dunfermline KY12 .... 29 D2
  Kinghorn KY3 .... 34 C1
  Queensferry EH30 .... 89 D4
Canmore Terr KY12 ...... 29 D2
Canmore Prim Sch KY11 .. 29 F1
Canning St EH3 .... 232 B2
Canning Street La EH3 .... 232 A2
Cannon Wynd EH6 .... 93 F3
Cannonmills Sch (Specl) .. 93 E2
Cannons Way FK2 .... 39 D1
Cannop Cres EH47 .... 170 C1
Canon La EH3 .... 93 E1
Canon Lynch Ct KY12 .... 28 C2
Canon St EH3 .... 93 E1
Canongate EH8 .... 233 E3
Canonmills EH3 .... 93 E2
Canthill Gdns ML7 ...... 191 D2
Cantlie Pl KY11 .... 46 C2
Cantsdam Rd KY4 .... 12 C4
Canty Gr EH22 .... 98 B2
Capelaw Rd EH13 .... 153 D3
Caplaw Way EH26 .... 203 E3
Caponflat Cres EH41 ..... 100 C1
Caponhall Ct EH33 ...... 128 B3
Caponhall Dr EH33 ...... 128 B3
Caponhall Rd EH33 ...... 128 B3
Cappers Ct EH48 .... 143 F2
Captain's Dr EH16 ...... 155 D3
Captain's Loan EH16 ..... 155 D3
Captain's Rd EH17 ...... 155 D3
Captain's Row EH16 ...... 155 D3
Caputhall Rd EH54 ...... 146 B3
Carberry Ct EH21 .... 157 F4
Carberry Mains Cotts
  EH21 .... 127 D1
Carberry Pl EH12 .... 122 C4
Carberry Rd EH21 .... 126 C2
Carbrook Dr FK7 .... 20 B2
Carbrook Pl FK3 .... 61 F3
Carcraig Pl KY11 .... 48 A2
Cardross Ave EH52 ...... 117 D3
Cardross Cres EH52 ..... 117 E3
Cardross Rd EH52 .... 116 B2
Cardrowan Rd FK7 ...... 20 B1
Carfrae Gdns EH4 .... 92 A1
Carfrae Gr EH4 .... 92 A1
Carfrae Pk EH4 .... 92 A1
Carfrae Rd EH4 .... 92 A1
Cargil Terr EH5 .... 93 D3
Cargilfield Sch EH4 ..... 91 D2
Carhowden Rd FK2 ...... 61 D2
Carlaverock Ave EH33 .... 128 B3
Carlaverock Cres EH33 ... 128 B3
Carlaverock Ct EH33 ..... 128 B3
Carlaverock Dr EH33 ..... 128 B3
Carlaverock Gr EH33 ..... 128 B3
Carlaverock Terr EH33 ... 128 C2
Carlaverock View EH33 ... 128 B3
Carlaverock Wlk EH33 .... 128 B3
Carledubs Ave EH52 ..... 117 D3
Carledubs Cres EH52 .... 117 D3
Carlie Ave FK9 .... 2 A3
Carlin Craig KY3 .... 34 C1
Carlin La ML8 .... 230 A1
Carlingnose Ct KY11 ..... 68 B3
Carlingnose Pk KY11 ..... 68 B3
Carlingnose Point KY11 .. 68 B3
Carlingnose View KY11 .... 68 B3
Carlingnose Way KY11 .... 68 B3
Carlops Ave EH26 .... 203 F3
Carlops Cres EH26 .... 203 F3
Carlops Rd EH26 .... 203 E2
Carlouk La ML8 .... 230 A1
Carlowrie Ave EH30 ...... 89 F4
Carlowrie Cres EH30 ..... 89 F4
Carlowrie Pl EH23 .... 207 E4
Carlton St EH4 .... 93 D1
Carlton Terr EH7 .... 93 E1
Carlton Terrace La EH7 .. 233 F4
Carlton Terrace Mews
  EH7 .... 233 F4
Carluke High Sch ML8 .... 230 A1
Carluke Prim Sch ML8 .... 230 A2
Carlyle Ct
  Haddington EH41 .... 132 A4
  Livingston EH54 .... 148 B3
Carlyle Gdns EH41 ...... 101 D1
Carlyle La KY12 .... 28 C3
Carlyle Pl Edinburgh EH7 .. 94 A1
  Musselburgh EH21 .... 126 B3
Carlyle Rd KY12 .... 28 C3
Carlyle St KY12 .... 28 C3
Carlyle Terr EH48 .... 145 E3
Carmel Ave EH29 .... 89 D1
Carmel Rd EH29 .... 89 D1
Carmelaws EH49 .... 85 D3
Carmelite Rd EH30 ...... 89 D4
Carmondean Centre Rd
  EH54 .... 147 D3
Carmondean Ctr EH54 .... 147 D3
Carmondean Prim Sch
  EH54 .... 147 D4
Carmuir ML11 .... 215 D1
Carmuirs Ave FK1 ...... 59 E3
Carmuirs Dr FK1 .... 59 E3
Carmuirs Prim Sch FK1 .. 59 E3
Carmuirs St FK1 .... 59 E3
Carnaughton Pl FK12 ..... 4 C3
Carnbee Ave EH16 ...... 155 E3
Carnbee Cres EH16 ..... 155 E3
Carnbee Dell EH16 ..... 155 E3
Carnbee End EH16 ...... 155 E3
Carnbee Pk EH16 .... 155 E3

Carnbee Pl KY12 .... 29 E2
Carnegie Ave KY12 ...... 46 C4
Carnegie Birthplace Mus
  KY12 .... 29 D2
Carnegie Campus (Bsns Pk)
  KY11 .... 46 C4
Carnegie Dr
  Dunfermline KY12 .... 29 D2
  Falkirk FK1 .... 59 E3
Carnegie Rd EH48 ...... 146 A3
Carnegie St EH8 .... 233 E2
Carneil Rd KY12 .... 27 E4
Carneil Terr KY12 ...... 27 E3
Carnethie St EH24 ...... 181 F1
Carnethy Ave
  Edinburgh EH13 .... 153 D3
  Penicuik EH26 .... 203 F3
Carnethy Cres 16 C4
Carnock Prim Sch KY12 .. 27 E4
Carnock Rd KY12 .... 28 B3
Carnock St
  Cowie FK7 .... 20 C4
  Edinburgh EH6 .... 94 A2
Carnwath Rd ML8 ...... 230 A1
Caroline Cres FK12 ...... 4 C3
Caroline Gdns
  Edinburgh EH12 .... 121 F4
  Mid Calder EH53 .... 148 A1
Caroline Park Ave EH5 ... 92 B3
Caroline Park Gr EH5 .... 92 B3
Caroline Pl EH12 ...... 121 F4
Caroline Terr EH12 ..... 121 E4
Carpet La EH6 .... 94 A3
Carradale Ave FK1 ...... 59 E2
Carribber Ave EH49 ...... 84 A3
Carriber Ct EH22 ...... 183 E4
Carrick Cres KY11 ...... 48 A2
Carrick Ct FK7 .... 7 E4
Carrick Dr KY11 .... 48 A2
Carrick Gdns EH54 ..... 173 E3
Carrick Knowe Ave EH12 .. 121 F3
Carrick Knowe Dr EH12 .. 121 F3
Carrick Knowe Gdns EH12 .. 121 F3
Carrick Knowe Gr EH12 .. 121 F3
Carrick Knowe Hill EH12 .. 121 F3
Carrick Knowe Loan EH12 .. 121 F3
Carrick Knowe Parkway
  EH12 .... 121 F3
Carrick Knowe Prim Sch
  EH12 .... 121 F3
Carrick Knowe Rd EH12 .. 121 F2
Carrick Knowe Terr EH12 .. 121 F3
Carrick Pl
  Falkirk, Roughlands FK2 .. 39 D2
  Falkirk, Tamfourhill FK1 .. 59 E2
Carriden Brae EH51 ...... 64 B3
Carriden Glade EH51 ..... 64 B4
Carrington Cres EH4 ..... 92 C2
Carrington Mains Cotts
  EH23 .... 206 B3
Carrington Rd EH4 ...... 92 C1
Carron End FK2 .... 39 D1
Carron La KY11 .... 29 F2
Carron Pl Edinburgh EH6 .. 94 A2
  Grangemouth FK3 .... 61 E2
  Kircaldy KY2 .... 7 D1
Carron Prim Sch FK2 .... 39 E1
Carron Rd FK2 .... 60 A4
Carron Terr FK2 .... 84 C4
Carron View FK2 .... 82 C4
Carron Wlk EH54 .... 148 A2
Carronbank Ave FK2 .... 39 D1
Carronbank Cres FK6 .... 39 D1
Carronbank Ct FK2 ...... 39 D1
Carronflats Rd FK3 ...... 61 F4
Carrongrove Ave FK2 .... 39 D1
Carrongrove Rd FK2 ..... 39 D1
Carronhall Ave FK2 ...... 39 E2
Carronshore Prim Sch
  FK2 .... 39 E2
Carronshore Rd FK2 ..... 39 E1
Carronside Pl FK6 ...... 36 B1
Carronside St FK2 ...... 60 A4
Carronvale Ave FK5 ...... 38 B1
Carronvale Rd FK5 ...... 38 B1
Carsaig Ct FK9 .... 2 A3
Carse Knowe EH49 ...... 85 E4
Carse Terr FK10 .... 9 F4
Carse View Airth FK2 ... 22 C2
  Bo'ness EH51 .... 63 E3
Carsebridge Rd FK10 .... 10 B4
Carsebridge Row FK10 ... 10 B4
Carseview Bannockburn FK7 .. 7 F1
  Tullibody FK10 .... 4 A1
Carson Pl KY11 .... 46 C3
Carswell Pl KY12 ...... 28 C3
Carswell Rd KY5 .... 14 A4
Cassel's La EH6 .... 93 F2
Casselbank St EH6 ...... 93 F2
Cassels La EH6 .... 93 F2
Cast The EH18 .... 181 E3
Castellau Cotts EH41 .... 78 B1
Castings Ave FK2 ...... 60 A4
Castings Ct
  Falkirk, Grahamston FK2 .. 60 A4
  Falkirk, Middlefield FK2 .. 60 A3
Castings Dr FK2 .... 60 A3
Castings Rd FK2 .... 60 A3
Castings The KY12 ...... 28 B3
Castlandhill Rd KY11 .... 47 D1
Castle Ave Airth FK2 .... 22 C2
  Cockenzie & Port Seton EH32 .. 97 F2
  Edinburgh EH12 .... 120 C4
  Falkirk FK2 .... 60 A3
  Gorebridge EH23 .... 207 E4
Castle Bsns Pk The FK8 .. 1 C1

Castle Cres Denny FK6 .... 36 B1
  East Calder EH53 .... 148 C1
  Falkirk FK2 .... 60 B4
  Torwood FK5 .... 37 F4
Castle Ct Falkirk FK2 .... 3 F3
  Menstrie FK11 .... 3 F3
Castle Dr Airth FK2 ...... 22 C2
  Dunfermline KY11 .... 46 C3
  Falkirk FK2 .... 60 B4
  Stenhousemuir FK5 ...... 38 C1
Castle Gate EH42 .... 78 B2
Castle Gogar EH12 ...... 120 B4
Castle Mains Pl EH39 .... 53 D3
Castle Moffat EH41 ..... 166 A4
Castle Pk EH39 .... 54 C3
Castle Pl Dunbar EH42 .... 78 B2
  Falkirk FK2 .... 60 B4
  Gorebridge EH23 .... 207 E4
Castle Rd
  Cockenzie & Port Seton EH32 .. 97 F2
  Falkirk FK2 .... 60 B4
  Menstrie FK11 .... 3 F3
  Rosyth KY11 .... 46 C1
  Stirling FK9 .... 2 B2
  Tranent EH33 .... 128 B3
  Winchburgh EH52 .... 88 A1
Castle Row KY12 .... 28 B3
Castle St Alloa FK10 ..... 10 A3
  Clackmannan FK10 ...... 11 D2
  Dunbar EH42 .... 78 B2
  Edinburgh EH2 .... 232 B3
Castle Terr
  Cockenzie & Port Seton
  EH32 .... 97 F2
  Denny FK6 .... 36 B1
  Edinburgh EH1 .... 232 B2
  Fallin FK7 .... 8 B2
  Gorebridge EH23 .... 207 E4
  Pencaitland EH34 ...... 160 B3
Castle Wlk EH32 .... 97 F2
Castle Wynd N EH1 ...... 232 C2
Castle Wynd S EH1 ...... 232 C2
Castleblair La KY12 ...... 28 C2
Castleblair Mews KY12 ... 28 C3
Castleblair Pk KY12 ..... 28 C3
Castlebrae Bsns Ctr
  EH16 .... 124 C2
Castlebrae Com Sch
  EH16 .... 124 C2
Castlegait EH42 .... 7 D4
Castlehill Bo'ness EH51 .. 63 E4
  Edinburgh EH1 .... 232 C3
Castlehill Ave FK1 ...... 110 A3
Castlelaurie St FK2 ...... 60 B4
Castlelaw Cres EH25 ..... 180 C3
Castlelaw Ct EH26 ...... 203 F3
Castlelaw Fort &
  Souterrain EH26 ...... 179 E2
Castlelaw Rd EH13 ...... 153 D3
Castlemains Pl EH39 ..... 53 E3
Castlemount Terr KY2 .... 16 B4
Cath Church of St Mary
  EH12 .... 232 A3
Cathcart Pl EH11 .... 122 C3
Cathedral La EH1 .... 233 D4
Catherine St FK7 .... 7 D4
Catherine Terr FK6 ...... 145 E1
Cathlaw La EH48 .... 114 A3
Cathrine Gr EH51 .... 64 A3
Catriona Terr EH26 ...... 180 A1
Cattle Market KY10 ...... 11 D3
Cauldhame Cres FK2 .... 6 B3
Causeway The
  Bridge of A FK9 .... 2 B3
  Edinburgh EH15 .... 124 B3
Causewayhead Rd FK9 .... 2 B2
Causewayside EH9 ...... 123 F3
Cavalry Park Dr EH15 ... 124 B3
Cawder Gdns FK4 .... 1 C4
Cawder Rd FK4 .... 1 C4
Cawdor Cres KY2 .... 16 C3
Cecil St FK7 .... 7 D3
Cedar Ave Kirkaldy KY1 .. 17 E4
  Stirling FK8 .... 6 C3
Cedar Cres
  Cowdenbeath KY4 .... 13 E3
  Westquarter FK2 .... 61 E3
  Whitburn EH47 .... 170 B3
Cedar Dr EH32 .... 97 D2
Cedar Gr
  Dunfermline KY11 .... 46 B4
  Stenhousemuir FK5 ..... 38 C1
Cedar Rd Dunbar EH42 ... 78 A1
  Grangemouth FK3 ...... 61 E4
Cedar Wynd ML7 .... 192 A3
Cedarbank EH54 .... 147 F3
Cedarbank Sch EH54 ..... 147 F3
Cedars The FK10 .... 4 A1
Cedric Rise EH54 .... 148 A1

Cemetery Rd Dalkeith EH22 156 C1
Fauldhouse EH47 .... 193 E3
Prestonpans EH32 .... 96 C1
Shotts ML7 .... 192 A2
Central Ave FK4 .... 61 E3
Central Bvd FK5 .... 38 A2
Central Dock Rd FK3 .... 40 C1
Central Dr FK5 .... 38 C2
Central Park Ave FK5 .... 38 A2
Central Park Bsns Pk FK5 .. 38 A2
Central Pk (Cowdenbeath FC)
KY4 .... 13 E2
Central Rd KY12 .... 44 B4
Central Ret Pk FK1 .... 60 B3
Central Way KY11 .... 48 B3
Centre Intc EH54 .... 148 A1
Chacefield St FK4 .... 58 A3
Chacefield Wood FK6 .... 57 F4
Chalmers Cres EH9 .... 123 E3
Chalmers Hospl EH3 .... 232 C2
Chalmers St EH54 .... 146 B3
Chalmers St
Dunfermline KY12 .... 28 C2
Edinburgh EH3 .... 232 C1
Chalmerston Rd FK9 .... 1 A2
Chalton Rd FK9 .... 2 A1
Chalybeate EH41 .... 131 F4
Chamberlield Rd KY12 .... 29 E3
Chamberlain Rd EH10 .... 123 D2
Chambers Dr FK2 .... 39 D1
Chambers St EH1 .... 233 D2
Chamfron Gdns FK7 .... 7 F2
Champigny Ct EH21 .... 126 C3
Chancelot Cres EH6 .... 93 E3
Chancelot Gr EH5 .... 93 E3
Chancelot Terr EH6 .... 93 E3
Chandler's Rise KY11 .... 47 F2
Chandler's Wlk KY11 .... 47 F2
Channel Brae EH42 .... 136 B4
Chapel Bank EH22 .... 158 B3
Chapel Cres FK2 .... 39 D2
Chapel Ct EH16 .... 124 C2
Chapel Dr FK5 .... 38 C2
Chapel Gr KY2 .... 16 B4
Chapel La Edinburgh EH6 .... 94 A3
Falkirk FK1 .... 60 A3
Chapel Level KY2 .... 16 C4
Chapel Loan EH25 .... 181 D2
Chapel Pl
High Valleyfield KY12 .... 26 A1
Inverkeithing KY11 .... 47 E2
Kirkcaldy KY1 .... 16 B4
North Queensferry KY11 .... 68 B3
Pathhead EH37 .... 185 D3
Chapel Rd KY2 .... 16 B4
Chapel St Cowdenbeath KY4 .. 13 E2
Dunfermline KY12 .... 28 C2
Edinburgh EH8 .... 233 E1
High Valleyfield KY12 .... 26 A1
Kincardine FK10 .... 23 F2
Lochgelly KY5 .... 14 A4
Chapel Villas KY1 .... 48 A1
Chapel Wynd EH1 .... 232 C2
Chapelfauld Gn KY12 .... 29 F2
Chapelhill
Clackmannan FK10 .... 11 D2
Dirleton EH39 .... 53 D2
Kirkcaldy KY2 .... 16 B4
Chapelhill St EH10 .... 23 E3
Chapelton Ave EH55 .... 172 C2
Chapelton Dr EH55 .... 172 C2
Chapelton Gdns EH55 .... 172 C2
Chapelton Pl EH55 .... 172 C2
Chapelton Terr EH55 .... 172 C2
Chapelwell Pl KY11 .... 29 F2
Charing Cross FK3 .... 40 B1
Charles Ave FK9 .... 2 A3
Charles Cres
Bathgate EH48 .... 145 F3
Carluke ML8 .... 230 A1
Charles Ct KY11 .... 45 F2
Charles Dr FK5 .... 59 E4
Charles La EH48 .... 145 F3
Charles Rodger Pl FK9 .... 2 A3
Charles St Alloa FK10 .... 9 F4
Edinburgh EH8 .... 29 D1
Penicuik EH26 .... 203 F4
Shotts ML7 .... 192 A2
Stirling FK8 .... 7 D3
Charles Street La EH8 .... 233 D2
Charles Way KY11 .... 45 F2
Charles Way S KY11 .... 45 F2
Charlesfield EH48 .... 145 F3
Charlesfield La EH54 .... 147 D1
Charlotte Dundas Ct FK3 .. 61 F3
Charlotte Hill Ct FK5 .... 38 A2
Charlotte La EH2 .... 232 B3
Charlotte Sq EH2 .... 232 B3
Charlotte St Brightons FK2 .. 82 A4
Kirkcaldy KY1 .... 17 D2
Shotts ML7 .... 192 A2
Charlton Gr EH25 .... 180 C2
Charter St FK7 .... 7 D2
Charterhall Gr EH9 .... 123 E2
Charterhall Rd EH9 .... 123 E1
Charteris Ct EH32 .... 98 B3
Charteris Pk EH32 .... 98 B3
Charteris Rd EH32 .... 98 B3
Chartershall Rd FK7 .... 7 D1
Chattan Ave FK2 .... 24 A2
Chattan Ind Est FK4 .... 58 B2
Cherry Ave EH48 .... 145 F3
Cherry La EH22 .... 183 F3
Cherry Pl KY4 .... 13 E2
Cherry Tree Ave EH14 .... 151 F2
Cherry Tree Cres EH14 .... 151 F2
Cherry Tree Gdns EH14 .... 151 E2
Cherry Tree Gr EH14 .... 151 E2
Cherry Tree Loan EH14 .... 151 F2
Cherry Tree Pk EH14 .... 151 F2
Cherry Tree View EH14 .... 151 F2
Cherrybank EH7 .... 29 E3
Cherryton Dr FK10 .... 11 D3
Chessel's Ct EH8 .... 233 E3
Chesser Ave EH14 .... 122 B2
Chesser Cres EH14 .... 122 B2
Chesser Gdns EH14 .... 122 A2
Chesser Gr EH14 .... 122 A2
Chesser Loan EH14 .... 122 A2
Chester Ct EH19 .... 182 A3
Chester Dr EH22 .... 183 E3
Chester Dr EH19 .... 182 A3
Chester St EH3 .... 232 A3
Chester View EH22 .... 183 E3
Chesters View EH19 .... 182 A3
Chestnut Ave Kirkcaldy KY1 .. 17 E4
Whitburn EH47 .... 170 B3
Chestnut Cres FK6 .... 36 B2
Chestnut Gr Bo'ness EH51 .. 63 E3
Bonnyrigg and Lasswade
EH19 .... 182 A3
Dunfermline KY11 .... 46 C4
Livingston EH54 .... 148 A3
Stenhousemuir FK5 .... 38 C2
Winchburgh EH52 .... 87 F1
Chestnut St EH5 .... 92 C4
Cheviot Pl FK3 .... 61 F3
Cheviot Rd KY2 .... 16 C4
Cheyne St EH4 .... 93 D1
Chief's Cl KY1 .... 17 E4
Chisholm Ave FK9 .... 2 A2
Chisholm Cres KY5 .... 14 A4
Chisholm Pl FK3 .... 61 D3
Chisholm St KY12 .... 29 E4
Chisholm Terr EH26 .... 203 F4
Christian Cres EH15 .... 125 D4
Christian Gr EH15 .... 125 D4
Christie Pl KY1 .... 17 E4
Christie St KY12 .... 29 D3
Christie Terr FK5 .... 38 C2
Christiemiller Ave EH7 .... 94 C1
Christiemiller Gr EH7 .... 94 C1
Christiemiller Pl EH7 .... 94 C1
Chuckie Pend EH3 .... 232 B2
Church Ct Kirkcaldy KY1 .... 17 E2
Philpstoun EH49 .... 86 B3
Church Gdns EH32 .... 98 C3
Church Gr Alloa FK10 .... 5 E1
Burntisland KY3 .... 33 E1
Church Hill EH10 .... 123 D2
Church Hill Pl EH10 .... 123 D2
Church La Denny FK6 .... 36 B2
Kirkcaldy KY1 .... 17 E2
Limekilns KY11 .... 45 E2
Church Pk EH48 .... 145 D3
Church Pl Armadale EH48 .. 144 A3
Bathgate EH48 .... 145 D4
Crossgates KY4 .... 30 C4
Falkirk FK2 .... 60 A3
Fauldhouse EH47 .... 193 F3
Longridge EH47 .... 170 B1
Church Rd Bo'ness EH51 .... 63 F4
Bonnyrigg and Lasswade
EH18 .... 155 F1
California FK1 .... 81 F3
North Berwick EH39 .... 54 B4
Church St Addiewell EH55 .. 171 E1
Alloa FK10 .... 10 A3
Broxburn EH52 .... 117 F3
Burntisland KY3 .... 33 E1
Cowdenbeath KY4 .... 13 E2
Dunbar EH42 .... 78 C1
Falkirk FK2 .... 39 E1
Haddington EH41 .... 132 A4
Harthill ML7 .... 168 B3
High Bonnybridge FK4 .... 58 B2
Inverkeithing KY11 .... 47 E2
Kingseat KY12 .... 12 A1
Kirkcaldy KY1 .... 45 E2
Limekilns KY11 .... 45 E2
Loanhead EH20 .... 181 E4
Lochgelly KY5 .... 14 A4
Stenhousemuir FK5 .... 38 C2
Tranent EH33 .... 128 B4
Church Street La EH33 .... 128 B4
Church Wlk Denny FK6 .... 36 C1
Kinghorn KY3 .... 35 D2
Church Wynd EH51 .... 63 F4
Churchill Dr EH10 .... 123 D2
Churchill Dr FK9 .... 2 A3
Churchill St KY1 .... 46 C2
Churchill St KY10 .... 50 A4
Churchill Way EH27 .... 149 F2
Churchway KY3 .... 98 C3
Cinderhall Pl EH33 .... 128 A1
Circle The EH22 .... 156 A4
Circus Gdns EH3 .... 232 B4
Circus La EH3 .... 93 D1
Circus Pl EH3 .... 232 B4
Citadel Pl EH6 .... 93 F3
Citadel St EH6 .... 93 F3
City Hospl EH14 .... 153 E4
City Mus EH6 .... 233 E4
City Of Edinburgh By-Pass
The Dalkeith EH22 .... 157 D4
Edinburgh EH10 .... 154 B2
Whitecraig EH21 .... 126 C4
Clackmae Gr EH16 .... 154 C4
Clackmae Rd EH16 .... 154 C4

Clackmannan Coll of F Ed
FK10 .... 10 A4
Clackmannan Prim Sch
FK10 .... 11 D2
Clackmannan Rd FK10 .... 10 B3
Clanranald Pl FK1 .... 59 F1
Clare Ct EH39 .... 54 A4
Clarebank Cres EH6 .... 94 A2
Claremont FK10 .... 9 F4
Claremont Bank EH7 .... 93 E2
Claremont Cres EH7 .... 93 E2
Claremont Ct EH7 .... 93 E2
Claremont Dr FK9 .... 2 B4
Claremont Gdns EH6 .... 94 B2
Claremont Gr EH7 .... 93 E2
Claremont Ind Est FK10 .. 10 A3
Claremont Pk EH6 .... 94 A2
Claremont Prim Sch FK10 .. 10 A3
Claremont Rd EH6 .... 94 A2
Claremont St EH6 .... 57 F3
Clarence St EH3 .... 93 D1
Clarendon Cres
Edinburgh EH4 .... 232 A4
Linlithgow EH49 .... 85 D3
Clarendon Pl FK8 .... 7 D4
Clarendon Rd
Linlithgow EH49 .... 85 D3
Stirling FK8 .... 7 D4
Claret Rd
Grangemouth, Bowhouse
FK3 .... 61 F3
Grangemouth, Oil Refinery
FK3 .... 62 B4
Clarinda Ave FK1 .... 59 D3
Clarinda Gdns EH22 .... 157 E2
Clarinda Terr EH16 .... 124 B1
Clark Ave EH5 .... 93 E3
Clark Bldgs EH35 .... 159 F4
Clark Pl Edinburgh EH5 .. 93 D3
Kirkcaldy KY2 .... 16 B3
Clark Rd Edinburgh EH5 .. 93 D3
Inverkeithing KY11 .... 47 D1
Clark St FK7 .... 7 D1
Clarkson Rd EH52 .... 117 E3
Claverhouse Dr EH16 .... 155 D4
Claycrofts Pl FK7 .... 7 F1
Clayhills Gr EH14 .... 151 D1
Clayhills Pk EH14 .... 151 D1
Clayknowes Ave EH21 .... 126 A3
Clayknowes Cres EH21 .... 126 A3
Clayknowes Ct EH21 .... 126 A3
Clayknowes Dr EH21 .... 125 F3
Clayknowes Pl EH21 .... 126 A3
Clayknowes Way EH21 .... 126 A3
Claymore Dr FK7 .... 7 E2
Clearburn Cres EH16 .... 124 A2
Clearburn Gdns EH16 .... 124 A2
Clearburn Rd
Edinburgh EH16 .... 124 A2
Gorebridge EH23 .... 183 D1
Cleaves The FK10 .... 4 A1
Cleekim Dr EH15 .... 125 D2
Cleekim Rd EH15 .... 125 D2
Cleghorn Dr EH52 .... 117 D3
Cleikiminrig EH15 .... 125 D2
Cleish Gdns KY2 .... 16 C3
Cleish Pl KY1 .... 29 E1
Cleland St EH47 .... 170 A4
Clement Rise EH54 .... 148 A1
Clerics Hill EH29 .... 89 D1
Clerk Gr KY11 .... 29 E1
Clerk St Edinburgh EH8 .. 233 E1
Loanhead EH20 .... 181 E4
Clerkington Rd EH41 .... 131 F4
Clerkington Wlk EH41 .... 131 F4
Clermiston Ave EH4 .... 91 E1
Clermiston Cres EH4 .... 91 E1
Clermiston Gdns EH4 .... 91 E1
Clermiston Gn EH4 .... 91 E1
Clermiston Gr EH4 .... 91 E1
Clermiston Hill EH4 .... 91 E1
Clermiston Loan EH4 .... 91 E1
Clermiston Medway EH4 .. 91 E1
Clermiston Pk EH4 .... 91 E1
Clermiston Pl EH4 .... 91 E1
Clermiston Prim Sch EH4 .. 91 F1
Clermiston Rd N EH4 .... 91 F1
Clermiston View EH4 .... 91 F1
Clerwood Bank EH12 .... 121 E4
Clerwood Gdns EH12 .... 121 E4
Clerwood Gr EH12 .... 121 E4
Clerwood Loan EH12 .... 121 E4
Clerwood Pk EH12 .... 121 E4
Clerwood Pl EH12 .... 121 E4
Clerwood Row EH12 .... 121 E4
Clerwood Terr EH12 .... 121 E4
Clerwood View EH12 .... 121 E4
Clerwood Way EH12 .... 121 E4
Cleuch Ave FK10 .... 4 A1
Cleuch Dr FK10 .... 4 A1
Cleuch Rd EH52 .... 207 F1
Cleuchbrae EH55 .... 172 B2
Cleveland Dr KY11 .... 47 D1
Clifford Rd
North Berwick EH39 .... 54 B3
Stirling FK8 .... 7 D3
Clifton Hall Sch EH28 .. 118 B1
Clifton Rd EH28 .... 118 C1
Clifton Trad Est EH28 .. 118 A2
Clifton View EH52 .... 118 A3
Climpy Ho EH52 .... 118 A3
Climpy Rd ML11 .... 219 D3
Clinkum Bank KY12 .... 26 B2
Clinton Rd EH9 .... 123 D2

Clive St ML7 .... 191 F3
Clockluine Rd KY11 .... 47 F3
Clockmill La EH7, EH8 .... 94 A1
Close The KY11 .... 46 B1
Clova Dr EH54 .... 173 F3
Clovenstone Dr EH14 .... 152 C4
Clovenstone Gdns EH14 .... 152 C4
Clovenstone Pk EH14 .... 152 C4
Clovenstone Prim Sch
EH14 .... 152 C4
Clovenstone Rd EH14 .... 152 C4
Clover Pl EH51 .... 63 F3
Cloverbank EH54 .... 147 F3
Cloverstone Rbdt EH14 .... 152 C4
Cloves The FK11 .... 4 A3
Cluanie Ave ML7 .... 191 F3
Cluffiatt EH30 .... 67 F1
Cluffiatt Brae EH30 .... 67 F1
Clune Rd KY12 .... 27 F4
Clune St KY11 .... 29 F2
Cluny Ave EH10 .... 123 D1
Cluny Dr Edinburgh EH10 .. 123 D1
Stenhousemuir FK5 .... 38 C2
Cluny Gdns EH10 .... 123 E1
Cluny Pl EH10 .... 123 E2
Cluny Terr EH10 .... 123 D1
Clyde Cres Dunfermline KY11 29 F1
Larbert FK5 .... 38 A2
Clyde Dr Livingston EH54 .. 148 A2
Shotts ML7 .... 192 A2
Clyde St Edinburgh EH1 .. 233 D4
Falkirk FK1 .... 59 F3
Grangemouth FK3 .... 40 A1
Clydesdale St EH51 .... 63 F3
Clydevale Pl EH54 .... 117 D1
Coal Neuk EH33 .... 128 B3
Coal Rd KY12 .... 28 C2
Coal Wynd Bannockburn FK7 .. 7 E1
Kirkcaldy KY1 .... 17 E2
Coalgate EH10 .... 10 A3
Coalgate Ave EH33 .... 128 C4
Coalgate Rd EH33 .... 128 C4
Coalhill EH6 .... 93 F3
Coalpots Way FK10 .... 5 F2
Coates Cres EH3 .... 99 F2
Coates Cres EH3 .... 232 A3
Coates Gdns EH12 .... 122 C4
Coatfield La EH6 .... 94 A3
Cobblebrae Cres FK2 .... 39 D1
Cobden Cres EH9 .... 123 F2
Cobden Rd EH9 .... 123 F2
Cobden St Alva FK12 .... 5 D4
Alva, The Boll FK12 .... 5 D4
Coblecrook Gdns FK12 .. 4 C3
Coblecrook La FK12 .... 4 C3
Coblecrook Pl FK12 .... 4 C3
Coburg St EH6 .... 93 F3
Cochran Pl EH7 .... 93 E1
Cochran Terr EH7 .... 93 E1
Cochrane Ave Falkirk FK2 .. 60 A2
Inverkeithing KY11 .... 47 E1
Cochrane Cres FK12 .... 4 C4
Cochrane Pl EH6 .... 94 A2
Cochrane Rd KY11 .... 46 A1
Cochrane Sq EH54 .... 173 D2
Cochrane St
Bathgate EH48 .... 145 D4
Falkirk FK1 .... 60 A2
Cochrane Way KY11 .... 48 A3
Cochrane Wlk KY11 .... 29 F2
Cochranes The FK10 .... 5 D4
Cochrie Pl FK10 .... 4 B1
Cochrina Pl EH24 .... 181 E1
Cockburn Cres
Balerno EH14 .... 177 D4
Whitecross EH49 .... 84 A3
Cockburn Ct EH35 .... 159 F4
Cockburn Dr EH35 .... 159 E3
Cockburn Sq EH37 .... 185 D3
Cockburn St
Edinburgh EH1 .... 233 D3
Falkirk FK1 .... 60 A2
Cockburnhill Rd EH14 .. 177 D4
Cockburnspath Sch TD13 . 140 C2
Cockenzie Prim Sch EH32 .. 97 E2
Cockshaw St KY4 .... 13 E1
Cockles Brae EH41 .... 132 C2
Cockmilane Brae EH41 .. 132 B3
Cockpen Ave EH19 .... 182 A3
Cockpen Cres EH19 .... 182 A3
Cockpen Dr EH19 .... 182 A3
Cockpen Pl EH19 .... 182 A3
Cockpen Rd EH19 .... 182 A3
Cockpen Terr EH19 .... 182 A3
Cockpen View EH19 .... 182 A3
Coillesdene Ave EH15 .. 125 E4
Coillesdene Cres EH15 .. 125 E4
Coillesdene Dr EH15 .... 125 E4
Coillesdene Gdns EH15 .. 125 E4
Coillesdene Gr EH15 .... 125 E4
Coillesdene Loan EH15 .. 125 E4
Coillesdene Terr EH15 .. 125 E4
Coire Loan ML7 .... 192 A2
Coldingham Pl KY12 .... 29 E2
Colduie Circ KY11 .... 62 A1
Colegate Rd EH7 .... 208 B4
Coles Pl KY4 .... 31 D3
Colinshiel Ave EH48 .... 144 C4
Colinshiel St EH48 .... 144 C4
Colinshiel View EH48 .... 143 F4
Colinton Mains Cres EH13 153 F3

Clerwood Way EH12 .... 121 E4
Colinton Mains Dr EH13 .. 153 E4
Colinton Mains Gdns
EH13 .... 153 E4
Colinton Mains Gn EH13 .. 153 E4
Colinton Mains Gr EH13 .. 153 E4
Colinton Mains Loan
EH13 .... 153 E4
Colinton Mains Pl EH13 .. 153 E4
Colinton Mains Rd EH13 .. 153 E3
Colinton Mains Terr EH13 . 153 E4
Colinton Prim Sch EH13 .. 153 E4
Colinton Rd EH10, EH13 .. 122 C2
Coll Pl FK3 .... 61 E3
College Cres FK2 .... 60 B4
College Wynd EH1 .... 233 D2
Colliers Rd FK2 .... 8 B2
Collingwood Ct FK1 .... 59 F3
Collins Dr KY11 .... 45 F3
Collins Pl EH3 .... 93 D1
Colliston Rd KY12 .... 29 E3
Collyland Rd FK10 .... 5 E2
Colmestone Gate EH10 .. 154 A3
Colonsay Ave FK2 .... 61 E1
Colonsay Terr FK1 .... 60 A1
Colquhoun St FK7 .... 7 E3
Colquhoun Terr FK7 .... 7 E3
Colsnaur FK11 .... 4 A3
Coltbridge Ave EH12 .... 122 B4
Coltbridge Gdns EH12 .... 122 B4
Coltbridge Millside EH12 . 122 C4
Coltbridge Terr EH12 .... 122 B4
Coltbridge Vale EH12 .... 122 C4
Coltnes Ave ML7 .... 212 A4
Colton Ct KY12 .... 28 C2
Columba Ave EH4 .... 92 A1
Columba Rd EH4 .... 92 A1
Columbia Ave EH54 .... 147 F2
Colvin St EH42 .... 78 C1
Combfoot Cotts EH53 .... 148 B2
Comely Green Cres [10]
EH7 .... 94 A1
Comely Green Pl [9] EH7 .. 94 A1
Comely Bank EH4 .... 93 D1
Comely Bank Gr EH4 .... 92 C1
Comely Bank Pl EH4 .... 93 D1
Comely Bank Place Mews [7]
EH4 .... 93 D1
Comely Bank Rd EH4 .... 92 C1
Comely Bank Row EH4 .... 93 D1
Comely Bank St EH4 .... 92 C1
Comely Bank Terr [1] EH4 .. 93 D1
Comely Park La KY12 .... 29 D2
Comely Park Prim Sch
KY11 .... 60 A2
Comely Park Terr [15] EH7 .. 60 A2
Comely Pk Dunfermline KY12 29 D2
Maddiston FK2 .... 82 C4
Comiston Dr EH10 .... 60 A2
Comiston Gdns EH10 .... 123 D1
Comiston Gr EH10 .... 123 D1
Comiston Pl EH10 .... 123 D1
Comiston Prim Sch EH13 .. 153 F3
Comiston Rd EH10 .... 154 A4
Comiston Rise EH10 .... 154 A4
Comiston Springs Ave
EH10 .... 154 A4
Comiston Terr EH10 .... 123 D1
Comiston View EH10 .... 154 A4
Commercial Prim Sch
KY11 .... 29 E2
Commercial Rd KY11 .... 47 E1
Commercial School La
KY12 .... 29 D2
Commercial St
Edinburgh EH6 .... 93 F3
Kirkcaldy KY1 .... 17 E3
Commissioner St EH51 .... 64 A4
Commodores Wlk KY11 .. 46 B1
Compass Sch EH41 .... 131 F4
Compressor House Rd FK2 . 62 B3
Compton Rd FK3 .... 61 E3
Comrie Terr EH51 .... 64 A3
Concorde Way KY11 .... 47 E2
Coneyhill Rd FK9 .... 2 A4
Coneypark FK6 .... 6 C3
Conifer Rd EH22 .... 183 F4
Coningsby Pl FK10 .... 93 E3
Connaught Pl EH6 .... 93 E3
Conner Ave FK2 .... 60 A4
Considine Gdns [3] EH8 .. 94 B1
Considine Terr [2] EH8 .. 94 B1
Constable Rd FK7 .... 94 A3
Constitution Pl EH6 .... 94 A3
Constitution St EH6 .... 94 A3
Conway Ct FK1 .... 59 F2
Cook Ct KY5 .... 14 A4
Cook Cres EH22 .... 183 E3
Cook Pl KY1 .... 18 A4
Cook St KY5 .... 14 A4
Cooper's La FK10 .... 23 F2
Cope La EH32 .... 97 E2
Copeland Cres KY4 .... 13 D1
Copland Pl FK12 .... 4 C4
Copper Beech Wynd KY12 .. 27 E1
Corbett Pl KY11 .... 29 F1
Corbiehall EH51 .... 63 F4
Corbiehill Ave EH4 .... 92 A2
Corbiehill Cres EH4 .... 92 A2
Corbiehill Gdns EH4 .... 92 A2
Corbiehill Gr EH4 .... 92 A2
Corbiehill Pk EH4 .... 92 A2
Corbiehill Pl EH4 .... 92 A2
Corbiehill Rd EH4 .... 91 F2
Corbiehill Terr EH4 .... 92 A2
Corbieshot EH15 .... 125 D3
Corbiewood Dr FK7 .... 19 F4

Cordiner's Land EH1 .... 232 C2
Corentin Ct FK1 .... 60 B2
Cormillin Pl KY12 .... 26 A1
Corn Exchange Rd FK8 ...... 7 D4
Cornbank-St James'
  Prim Sch EH26 .... 203 E3
Cornfield Rd EH54 .... 147 D2
Cornhill Cres FK7 .... 7 D2
Cornhill Terr EH6 .... 94 A2
Cornton Bsns Pk FK9 ...... 2 A2
Cornton Cres FK9 .... 2 A3
Cornton Prim Sch FK9 ...... 2 A2
Cornton Rd FK9 .... 2 A2
Cornwall St EH1 .... 232 B2
Cornwallis Pl EH3 .... 93 E1
Coronation Pl
  Mayfield EH22 .... 183 E4
  Skinflats FK2 .... 39 F2
Corpach Dr KY12 .... 28 C1
Corporation St FK1 .... 60 B2
Corrennie Dr EH10 .... 123 D1
Corrennie Gdns EH10 ... 123 D1
Corrie Ave FK5 .... 38 C2
Corrie Ct EH22 .... 183 D2
Corrie Pl FK1 .... 59 E2
Corruna Ct ML8 .... 230 A1
Corslet Cres EH14 .... 152 A3
Corslet Pl EH14 .... 152 A3
Corslet Rd EH14 .... 152 A3
Corston Pk EH54 .... 148 A2
Corstorphine Bank Ave
  .... 121 E4
Corstorphine Bank Dr
  EH12 .... 121 E4
Corstorphine Bank Terr
  EH12 .... 121 E4
Corstorphine High St
  EH12 .... 121 E3
Corstorphine Hill Ave
  EH12 .... 121 F4
Corstorphine Hill Cres
  EH12 .... 121 F4
Corstorphine Hill Gdns
  EH12 .... 121 F4
Corstorphine Hill Rd
  EH12 .... 121 F4
Corstorphine Hospl EH12 121 F3
Corstorphine House Ave
  EH12 .... 121 F3
Corstorphine Park Gdns
  EH12 .... 121 F3
Corstorphine Prim Sch
  EH12 .... 121 E3
Corstorphine Rd EH12 ... 122 A4
Cortachy Ave FK5 .... 39 D2
Cortleferry Dr EH22 ...... 156 C1
Cortleferry Gr EH22 .... 156 C1
Cortleferry Pk EH22 .... 156 C1
Cortleferry Terr EH22 .... 156 C1
Corunna Pl EH6 .... 93 F3
Corunna Terr EH26 .... 204 A4
Cossars Wynd EH42 .... 78 B1
Cotburn Cres KY3 .... 33 F1
Cotlands Ave EH32 .... 98 B2
Cotlands Pk EH32 .... 98 B2
Cotlaws EH29 .... 89 D1
Cottage Cres FK1 .... 59 F3
Cottage Gn EH4 .... 91 D2
Cottage Homes EH13 ... 153 D4
Cottage La EH21 .... 126 C3
Cottage Pk FK4 .... 92 A1
Cotton La FK4 .... 61 D2
Cotts The EH49 .... 86 C2
Coulport Pl KY12 .... 28 C1
Council Houses
  Athelstaneford EH39 .. 101 F4
  Bolton EH41 .... 162 C4
  Drem EH39 .... 73 D2
  Gifford EH41 .... 133 E3
Countess Ave EH42 .... 78 B1
Countess Cres EH42 .... 78 B1
Countess Rd EH42 .... 78 B1
County Hospl FK10 .... 10 A4
County Houses KY4 .... 31 D3
County Rd KY4 .... 96 C1
County Sq EH22 .... 96 C1
Couper Ave EH39 .... 54 B3
Couper Gr KY11 .... 29 F1
Couper St EH6 .... 93 F3
Court St EH41 .... 132 A4
Courthill FK12 .... 5 D4
Cousin's La KY12 .... 28 C2
Cousland Cres EH41 ...... 146 A1
Cousland Dr EH22 .... 158 B3
Cousland Rd EH54 .... 147 F3
Cousland Terr EH41 ...... 146 A1
Couston Dr KY11 .... 48 A2
Couston Pl KY11 .... 48 A2
Couston Rd KY11 .... 48 A2
Couston St KY12 .... 29 D2
Cove Cres ML7 .... 191 F3
Covenanter Rd ML7 ...... 168 B2
Covenanters La EH30 ..... 68 A1
Coville Pl EH3 .... 93 D1
Cow Wynd FK1 .... 60 A2
Cowan Rd EH11 .... 122 C2
Cowan St Bathgate EH48 145 F3
  Bonnybridge FK4 .... 58 A3
Cowan Terr EH26 .... 204 A4
Cowan's Cl EH8 .... 233 E1
Cowane St FK8 .... 7 D4
Cowden Cres EH22 .... 157 E2
Cowden Gr EH22 .... 157 E2
Cowden La EH22 .... 157 E2
Cowden Pk EH22 .... 157 E2
Cowden Terr EH22 .... 157 E2
Cowden View EH22 .... 157 E2

Cowdenbeath Prim Sch
  KY4 .... 13 E2
Cowdenbeath Rd KY3 ...... 33 F1
Cowdenbeath Sta KY4 ..... 13 E2
Cowdenhill Rd EH51 .... 64 A4
Cowgate EH1 .... 233 D2
Cowgatehead EH1 .... 233 D2
Cowie Prim Sch FK7 .... 20 B4
Cowie Rd FK7 .... 20 A4
Cowiehall Rd FK7 .... 20 B4
Cowpits Ford Rd EH21 ... 126 B2
Cowpits Rd EH21 .... 126 B1
Coxfield EH11 .... 122 B2
Coxithill Rd FK7 .... 7 D2
Craig Ave Haddington EH41 101 D1
  Whitburn EH47 .... 169 F3
Craig Cres KY9 .... 2 B2
Craig Ct Bridge of A FK9 ... 2 A3
  Burntisland KY3 .... 33 E1
Craig Leith Rd FK7 .... 7 E3
Craig St Blackridge EH48 ... 142 C2
  Rosyth KY11 .... 47 D2
Craigbank Alloa FK10 .... 5 E1
  Crossford KY12 .... 28 B1
Craigbank Prim Sch FK10 ... 5 E1
Craigbank Rd FK1 .... 112 A3
Craigbeath Ct KY4 .... 13 D3
Craigburn Ct FK1 .... 59 F1
Craigcrook Ave EH4 .... 92 A1
Craigcrook Gdns EH4 ...... 92 A1
Craigcrook Gr EH4 .... 92 A1
Craigcrook Pk EH4 .... 92 A1
Craigcrook Pl 5 EH4 .... 92 B1
Craigcrook Rd EH4 .... 91 F1
Craigcrook Sq EH4 .... 92 A1
Craigcrook Terr 8 EH4 ..... 92 B1
Craigdimas Gr KY11 .... 48 A1
Craigearn Ave KY2 .... 16 A4
Craigend Dr FK2 .... 83 D3
Craigend Pk EH16 .... 124 B1
Craigend Rd FK7 .... 7 D2
Craigentinny Ave EH7 ..... 94 C1
Craigentinny Ave N EH6 ... 94 B2
Craigentinny Cres EH7 ... 94 C1
Craigentinny Gr EH7 .... 94 C1
Craigentinny Pl EH7 .... 94 C1
Craigentinny Prim Sch
  EH7 .... 94 B1
Craigentinny Rd EH7 ...... 94 B1
Craigford Dr FK7 .... 7 E1
Craigforth Cres FK8 .... 6 C3
Craighall Ave EH6 .... 93 E3
Craighall Bank EH6 .... 93 E3
Craighall Cres EH6 .... 93 E3
Craighall Gdns EH6 .... 93 E3
Craighall Rd EH6 .... 93 E3
Craighall St FK8 .... 1 C1
Craighall Terr
  Edinburgh EH6 .... 93 E3
  Musselburgh EH21 ...... 126 C3
Craighill Gdns EH10 .... 122 C1
Craighill View EH46 .... 142 C2
Craigholm La KY3 .... 33 F1
Craighorn FK11 .... 4 A3
Craighorn Dr FK11 .... 59 F1
Craighorn Rd FK12 .... 4 C3
Craighouse Gdns EH10 ... 122 C1
Craighouse Gdns EH10 ... 122 C1
Craighouse Pk EH10 .... 122 C1
Craighouse Rd EH10 .... 122 C1
Craighouse Terr EH10 ..... 122 C1
Craigie Ct KY5 .... 38 A1
Craigiebield Cres EH26 ... 203 F2
Craigielaw Farm Cotts
  EH32 .... 71 D2
Craigievar Ave KY2 .... 39 D2
Craigievar Gdns KY2 .... 16 C3
Craigievar Sq EH12 .... 121 D4
Craigievar Wynd EH12 ... 121 D4
Craiginn Ct EH48 .... 142 B2
Craiginn Terr EH48 .... 142 B2
Craigknochie Terr KY3 .... 33 F1
Craiglaw EH52 .... 116 B1
Craiglea Ct EH48 .... 142 B2
Craiglea Dr EH10 .... 123 D1
Craiglea Pl EH10 .... 122 C1
Craigleith FK10 .... 5 F2
Craigleith Ave Falkirk FK1 59 F1
  North Berwick EH39 ...... 54 B3
Craigleith Ave N EH4 ...... 122 B4
Craigleith Ave S EH4 ...... 122 B4
Craigleith Bank EH4 .... 92 B1
Craigleith Cres EH4 .... 92 B1
Craigleith Dr EH4 .... 92 B1
Craigleith Gdns EH4 .... 92 B1
Craigleith Gr EH4 .... 92 B1
Craigleith Hill EH4 .... 92 B1
Craigleith Hill Ave EH4 ... 92 B1
Craigleith Hill Cres EH4 ... 92 B1
Craigleith Hill Gdns EH4 ... 92 B1
Craigleith Hill Gn EH4 .... 92 B1
Craigleith Hill Gr EH4 ..... 92 B1
Craigleith Hill Loan EH4 ... 92 B1
Craigleith Hill Pk EH4 ..... 92 B1
Craigleith Hill Row EH4 ... 92 B1
Craigleith Rd Edinburgh EH4 92 C1
  Grangemouth FK3 .... 61 E3
Craigleith Ret Pk EH4 ..... 92 B2
Craigleith Rise EH4 .... 122 B4
Craigleith View EH4 .... 122 B4
Craiglockhart Ave EH14 ... 122 B1
Craiglockhart Bank EH14 122 B1
Craiglockhart Cres EH14 122 B2
Craiglockhart Dell Rd
  .... 122 B1
Craiglockhart Dr N EH14 122 B1
Craiglockhart Dr S EH14 122 B1
Craiglockhart Gdns EH14 122 B1

Craiglockhart Gr EH14 .... 153 E4
Craiglockhart Pk EH14 ... 122 B1
Craiglockhart Pl EH14 .... 122 B1
Craiglockhart Pl EH14 .... 122 B1
Craiglockhart Prim Sch
  EH11 .... 122 C2
Craiglockhart Quadrant
  EH14 .... 122 B1
Craiglockhart Rd EH14 ... 122 B1
Craiglockhart Rd N
  EH14 .... 122 B1
Craiglockhart Sports Ctr
  EH14 .... 122 C2
Craiglockhart Terr EH14 122 C2
Craiglockhart View EH14 122 B1
Craigluscar Dr KY12 .... 28 A4
Craigluscar Rd KY12 ...... 28 A4
Craigmillar Castle EH16 ... 124 B1
Craigmillar Castle Ave
  EH16 .... 124 C2
Craigmillar Castle Gdns
  EH16 .... 124 B2
Craigmillar Castle Gr
  EH16 .... 124 B2
Craigmillar Castle Loan
  EH16 .... 124 C2
Craigmillar Castle Rd
  EH16 .... 124 B1
Craigmillar Castle Terr
  EH16 .... 124 B1
Craigmillar Pk EH16 .... 124 A2
Craigmillar Pl FK5 .... 38 C2
Craigmillar Prim Sch
  EH16 .... 124 C2
Craigmount Gdns EH12 ... 26 C1
Craigmount KY2 .... 16 A4
Craigmount App EH12 .... 121 E4
Craigmount Ave EH12 .... 121 E4
Craigmount Ave N EH12 ... 91 D1
Craigmount Bank EH4 .... 91 D1
Craigmount Bank W EH4 ... 91 D1
Craigmount Brae EH12 ... 91 D1
Craigmount Cres EH12 ... 121 E4
Craigmount Ct EH4 .... 91 D1
Craigmount Dr EH12 ...... 121 E4
Craigmount Gdns EH12 ... 121 E4
Craigmount Gn EH12 ..... 121 E4
Craigmount Gr EH12 ...... 121 D4
Craigmount Gr N EH12 ... 121 D4
Craigmount Hill EH4 ...... 91 D1
Craigmount Loan EH12 ... 121 E4
Craigmount Pk EH12 ...... 121 E4
Craigmount Pl EH12 .... 121 E4
Craigmount Sec Sch
  EH12 .... 121 D4
Craigmount Terr EH12 ... 121 D4
Craigmount View EH12 ... 121 D4
Craigmount Way EH12 ... 91 E1
Craigmuir Prim Sch EH4 ... 92 B3
Craigmyle St KY12 .... 29 E3
Craigomus Cres EH14 ..... 9 D1
Craigour Ave EH17 .... 155 E4
Craigour Cres EH17 .... 155 E4
Craigour Dr EH17 .... 155 E4
Craigour Gdns EH17 ...... 155 E4
Craigour Gn EH17 .... 155 E4
Craigour Gr EH17 .... 155 E4
Craigour Loan EH17 ...... 155 E4
Craigour Pl EH17 .... 155 E4
Craigour Terr EH17 .... 155 E4
Craigpark EH48 .... 113 F3
Craigpark Ave EH28 ...... 119 E1
Craigpark Cres EH28 ..... 119 E1
Craigridge Pl KY11 .... 48 B3
Craigrie Terr EH42 .... 184 B3
Craigrigg Cotts EH48 .... 112 C2
Craigroyston Com
  High Sch EH4 .... 92 A2
Craigs Ave EH12 .... 121 E3
Craigs Bank EH12 .... 121 E3
Craigs Chalet Pk EH49 ... 84 A2
Craigs Cres EH12 .... 121 E4
Craigs Ct EH48 .... 113 F3
Craigs Dr EH12 .... 121 E4
Craigs Gdns EH12 .... 121 E4
Craigs Gr EH12 .... 121 E4
Craigs Loan EH12 .... 121 E4
Craigs Pk EH12 .... 121 D4
Craigs Rd EH12 .... 121 D4
Craigs Terr EH22 .... 82 C4
Craigseaton EH52 .... 117 D3
Craigshill East Rd EH54 ... 148 A3
Craigshill Rd EH54 .... 148 A3
Craigshill West Rd EH54 ... 148 A3
Craigston Dr KY12 .... 29 E3
Craigswood EH54 .... 148 A3
Craigton Cres FK12 .... 4 C3
Craigton Pl EH52 .... 87 F1
Craigton Pl KY12 .... 13 E1
Craigview Alloa FK10 .... 5 E1
  Bo'ness EH51 .... 64 B4
Craigward FK10 .... 10 A3
Craigwell Path KY11 .... 44 B4
Crame Terr EH22 .... 156 C1
Cramond Ave EH4 .... 91 E3
Cramond Brae EH4 .... 91 D3
Cramond Brig Toll EH4 ... 90 C2
Cramond Cres EH4 .... 91 D3
Cramond Ct EH4 .... 91 D3
Cramond Gdns
  Edinburgh EH4 .... 91 D3
  Kirkcaldy KY2 .... 16 C4
Cramond Glebe Gdns
  EH4 .... 91 E3
Cramond Glebe Rd EH4 ... 91 E3
Cramond Glebe Terr EH4 ... 91 E3
Cramond Gn EH4 .... 91 D3
Cramond Pk EH4 .... 91 D3

Cramond Pl
  Dalgety Bay KY11 .... 48 B2
  Edinburgh EH4 .... 91 E3
Cramond Prim Sch EH4 ... 91 D3
Cramond Rd N EH4 .... 91 E3
Cramond Rd S EH4 .... 91 D2
Cramond Regis EH4 .... 91 D2
Cramond Terr EH4 .... 91 D3
Cramond Vale EH4 .... 91 D3
Cramond Village EH4 ..... 91 D4
Cranshaws Dr FK2 .... 61 E1
Cranston Dr EH22 .... 158 B3
Cranston Prim Sch EH37 184 C3
Cranston St Edinburgh EH8 233 E3
  Penicuik EH26 .... 203 F3
Crarae Ave EH4 .... 122 B4
Crathes Ave FK5 .... 39 D2
Crathes Gdns EH54 ...... 173 F3
Crathie Dr FK6 .... 36 B2
Craufurdland EH4 .... 90 C3
Crawfield Ave EH51 .... 63 F3
Crawfield La EH51 .... 63 F3
Crawfield Rd EH51 .... 63 F2
Crawford Dr FK2 .... 82 A4
Crawford Pl KY12 .... 29 E4
Crawford Sq FK2 .... 82 B2
Crawfurd Rd EH16 .... 124 A2
Crawlees Cres EH22 ...... 183 D4
Craws Knowe ML11 ...... 215 D1
Creel Ct EH39 .... 54 B4
Creran Dr FK7 .... 57 E3
Crescent The
  Edinburgh EH10 .... 123 D1
  Gowkshill EH23 .... 183 E2
  Rosyth KY11 .... 46 A1
Creteil Ct KY1 .... 60 B2
Creteil Pl FK3 .... 61 E4
Crewe Bank EH5 .... 92 C3
Crewe Cres EH5 .... 92 C3
Crewe Gr EH5 .... 92 C3
Crewe Loan EH5 .... 92 B3
Crewe Pl EH5 .... 92 B3
Crewe Rd N EH5 .... 92 B3
Crewe Rd S EH4 .... 92 C2
Crewe Rd W EH5 .... 92 B3
Crewe Road Gdns EH5 ... 92 B3
Crewe Terr EH5 .... 92 C3
Crewe Toll EH4 .... 92 B2
Crichton Ave EH43 .... 185 D3
Crichton Castle EH37 .... 208 C4
Crichton Dr
  Grangemouth FK3 .... 61 F4
  Pathhead EH37 .... 185 D3
Crichton Rd EH37 .... 185 D3
Crichton St EH8 .... 233 D2
Crichton Terr EH37 .... 185 D3
Cricket Pl KY12 .... 61 E1
Crighton Pl EH6 .... 93 F2
Crimond Pl FK1 .... 81 F4
Cringate Gdns FK7 .... 7 F1
Crockett Gdns EH26 ...... 203 E3
Croft An Righ KY3 .... 35 D2
Croft Pl EH54 .... 147 E3
Croft St Dalkeith EH22 ... 157 D2
  Penicuik EH26 .... 203 F2
Croft's Rd FK10 .... 4 A1
Croft-An-Righ EH8 .... 233 F4
Crofters Gate FK7 .... 7 D4
Crofters Way EH47 .... 170 C3
Croftfoot Dr EH47 .... 194 A3
Croftfoot Pl FK6 .... 36 B2
Crofthead Ct FK8 .... 2 A1
Crofthead Ctr EH54 ...... 173 E4
Crofthead Intc EH54 ..... 173 F4
Crofthead Rd Stirling FK8 ... 2 A1
Crofthead St EH47 .... 171 D1
Croftmalloch Prim Sch
  EH47 .... 170 A3
Crofts Rd TD13 .... 140 C1
Crofts The EH42 .... 104 C1
Croftsacre TD13 .... 140 C1
Croftshaw Rd FK10 .... 5 D4
Croftside Ct FK3 .... 61 F3
Cromarty Pl KY1 .... 17 F4
Crombie Prim Sch KY12 ... 44 B4
Cromwell Pl EH6 .... 60 B2
Cromwell Pl EH6 .... 93 F3
Cromwell Rd
  Burntisland KY3 .... 33 F1
  Falkirk FK1 .... 60 B2
  North Berwick EH39 ...... 54 A4
  Rosyth KY11 .... 46 C3
Cromwell Rd W FK1 .... 60 B2
Crookston Ct EH21 .... 126 C2
Crookston Rd EH21 .... 126 C2
Crophill FK10 .... 5 E1
Crosford Prim Sch KY12 ... 28 B2
Cross Brae FK1 .... 81 E3
Cross Loan EH35 .... 159 F4
Cross Row KY11 .... 45 D2
Cross St Dysart KY1 .... 18 A4
  Tillicoultry FK13 .... 6 A3
Cross The Linlithgow EH49 ... 85 D4
  Lochgelly KY5 .... 14 A4
Cross Way KY11 .... 48 B2
Cross Wynd KY12 .... 29 D2
Crossen La ML8 .... 230 A1
Crossgatehead Rd FK2 ... 82 B4
Crossgates Prim Sch KY4 ... 30 C3
Crossgreen Dr EH52 ..... 117 D3
Crossgreen Pl EH52 ...... 117 D3
Crosshill Dr
  Bathgate EH48 .... 145 E3
  Bo'ness EH51 .... 63 F3
Crossroads Pl KY11 .... 46 C2
Crosswood Ave EH14 ... 177 D4
Crosswood Cres EH14 ... 177 D4

Crosswood Terr EH55 .... 217 F2
Crowhill Rd KY11 .... 48 B2
Crown Gdns FK10 .... 9 F4
Crown Pl EH6 .... 93 F2
Crown St EH6 .... 93 F2
Crownest Loan FK5 .... 38 C1
Cruachan Ave FK5 .... 2 A2
Cruachan Ct Falkirk FK1 ... 60 B2
  Penicuik EH26 .... 204 A3
Cruachan Pl FK3 .... 61 F3
Cruckburn Wynd FK7 .... 6 C2
Cruicks Rd KY11 .... 68 B4
Cruickshank Dr FK1 .... 63 E1
Cruikshank's Ct FK6 .... 36 C1
Crum Cres FK7 .... 7 E1
Crusader Dr EH25 .... 180 C2
Crusader Rise EH54 ...... 148 A1
Crystal Works EH26 ...... 203 F3
Cuddy La EH10 .... 123 D2
Cuddyhouse Rd KY12 ..... 12 B2
Cuffabouts EH51 .... 64 B4
Cuguen Pl EH18 .... 156 A1
Cuiken Ave EH26 .... 203 F3
Cuiken Bank EH26 .... 203 E3
Cuiken Prim Sch EH26 ... 203 E3
Cuiken Terr EH26 .... 203 F3
Cuikenburn EH26 .... 203 F4
Cuil Gr FK7 .... 28 B3
Cuillin Ct FK1 .... 60 B1
Cuillin Pl FK3 .... 61 F3
Cullalo Cres KY3 .... 49 E4
Cullalo Ct KY3 .... 48 B2
Cullalo Nature Reserve
  KY3 .... 32 A2
Cullaloe View KY4 .... 13 E1
Cullaloe Ct KY4 .... 16 C4
Cullen Sq FK5 .... 146 B3
Culloch Rd FK1 .... 110 A3
Culmore Pl FK1 .... 60 C1
Culross Abbey KY12 .... 25 E1
Culross Palace KY12 .... 42 B4
Culross Prim Sch KY12 .... 42 B4
Cultenhove Cres
  Grangemouth FK3 .... 61 F3
  Stirling FK7 .... 6 C2
Cultenhove Pl FK7 .... 7 D2
Cultenhove Rd FK7 .... 7 D2
Cultins Rd EH11 .... 121 D2
Cultrig Dr FK47 .... 170 A3
Culvain Pl FK1 .... 60 B1
Culzean Cres KY2 .... 16 B4
Culzean Pl FK5 .... 38 C2
Cumberland St EH3 .... 93 E1
Cumbernauld Rd FK4 ..... 57 D2
Cumbrae Ct EH22 .... 17 D4
Cumbrae Dr FK1 .... 59 F2
Cumbrae Terr KY2 .... 17 D4
Cumin Pl EH9 .... 123 F2
Cumlodden Ave EH12 ... 122 B4
Cumnor Cres EH16 .... 124 A1
Cunnigar Gdns EH53 .... 148 B2
Cunnigar Hill View EH53 ... 148 B2
Cunningham Cres EH52 ... 117 E3
Cunningham Ct
  Longniddry EH32 .... 98 B2
  North Berwick EH39 ...... 54 A3
Cunningham Dr ML7 .... 168 B3
Cunningham Gdns FK2 ... 60 C3
Cunningham Rd
  Rosyth KY11 .... 46 B1
  Stenhousemuir FK5 ...... 39 D2
  Stirling FK7 .... 7 D4
Cunningham St FK3 .... 61 E3
Curling Knowe KY4 .... 31 D3
Curling Pk KY4 .... 30 C3
Curran Cres EH52 .... 117 F3
Currie High Sch EH14 ... 151 F2
Curriehill Castle Dr EH14 ... 151 E2
Curriehill Prim Sch EH14 ... 152 A2
Curriehill Rd EH14 .... 151 F3
Curriehill Sta EH14 .... 151 F3
Currieside Ave ML7 ...... 191 F2
Currieside Pl ML7 .... 191 E2
Currievale Dr EH14 .... 151 E2
Currievale Park Gr EH14 ... 151 F2
Currievale Pk EH14 .... 151 F2
Cushenquarter Dr FK7 ... 20 B2
Custom House Sq EH42 ... 78 C2
Custonhall Pl FK6 .... 36 B1
Cuthill Cres EH47 .... 171 E1
Cuthill Terr EH47 .... 171 E1
Cuttyfield Pl FK2 .... 39 E2
Cypress Gr KY11 .... 46 B4

D'arcy Cres EH22 .... 183 F4
D'arcy Rd EH22 .... 183 F3
D'arcy Terr EH22 .... 183 F4
Daiches Braes EH15 ...... 125 E3
Dairy Cotts EH39 .... 53 D1
Dairy Prim Sch EH11 ..... 122 C3
Daisy Terr EH11 .... 122 C2
Dalachy Cotts KY3 .... 32 C1
Dalbeath Cres KY4 .... 13 D1
Dalbeath Gdns KY4 .... 12 C1
Dalcross Way KY12 .... 29 E3
Dalderse Ave FK2 .... 60 A3
Dalgety Ave EH7 .... 94 A1
Dalgety Bay Prim Sch
  KY11 .... 48 A2
Dalgety Bay Sta KY11 ..... 48 A2
Dalgety Gdns KY11 .... 48 B3
Dalgety House View KY11 ... 48 B3
Dalgety Rd EH7 .... 94 A1
Dalgety St EH7 .... 94 A1
Dalgleish Ct FK8 .... 7 D4

Dalgrain Rd FK3 .... 40 A1
Dalhousie Ave EH19 .... 182 A3
Dalhousie Ave W EH19 ..... 182 A3
Dalhousie Dr EH19 .... 182 A3
Dalhousie Gdns EH19 ...... 182 A4
Dalhousie Rd EH22 .... 156 C1
Dalhousie Rd E EH19 .... 182 A3
Dalhousie Rd W EH19 ...... 182 A3
Dalhousie Terr EH10 .... 123 D1
Dalkeith High Sch EH22 ... 157 D2
Dalkeith Rd EH16 .... 233 F1
Dalkeith St EH15 .... 125 E4
Dallas Ave KY3 .... 33 F1
Dallas Dr KY2 .... 16 C4
Dalling Rd EH48 .... 144 C3
Dalmahoy Cres EH14 .... 151 E2
Dalmahoy Rd EH28 .... 119 E1
Dalmeny Dr EH30 .... 69 E1
Dalmeny Prim Sch EH30 .... 89 F4
Dalmeny Rd EH6 .... 93 E3
Dalmeny St EH6 .... 93 F2
Dalmeny Sta EH30 .... 89 E4
Dalmeny View KY11 .... 48 B2
Dalmore Dr FK12 .... 4 C3
Dalmorglen Pk FK7 .... 6 C2
Dalratho Rd FK3 .... 61 F4
Dalry Pl EH11 .... 232 A2
Dalry Rd EH11 .... 122 C4
Dalrymple Cres
  Edinburgh EH9 .... 123 F2
  Musselburgh EH21 .... 126 A3
Dalrymple Gdns EH22 ...... 158 B3
Dalrymple Loan EH21 ...... 126 B3
Dalton Ct EH22 .... 183 F3
Dalum Ct EH20 .... 181 D4
Dalum Dr EH20 .... 181 D4
Dalum Gr EH20 .... 181 D4
Dalum Loan EH20 .... 181 D4
Dalziel Ct EH47 .... 171 E1
Dalziel Pl EH7 .... 94 A1
**Damhead
  Holdings Scheme** EH10 .. 154 B1
Damside EH4 .... 232 A3
Danderhall Cres EH22 ...... 156 A4
Danderhall Prim Sch
  EH22 .... 156 A4
Dania Ct EH11 .... 121 F2
Daniel Pl KY11 .... 46 B3
**Daniel Stewart's
  & Melville Coll** EH4 .... 92 C1
Danube St EH4 .... 232 A4
Dargai Pl EH12 .... 117 D3
Darian La EH51 .... 63 F4
Darmeid Pl ML7 .... 212 A4
Darnaway St EH3 .... 232 B4
Darrach Dr FK6 .... 93 D3
Darney Terr KY3 .... 34 C1
Darnley St FK8 .... 7 D4
Darrach Dr FK6 .... 36 A3
Darwin St EH54 .... 148 A3
Davaar Ave EH54 .... 2 C4
Davaar Pl FK1 .... 59 E2
Davenport Pl KY11 .... 46 C2
David Henderson Ct KY12 .. 29 D2
David Millar Pl EH22 .... 28 C3
David Scott Ave EH22 ...... 183 F4
David St Dunfermline KY12 .. 29 D3
  Kirkaldy KY1 .... 17 D2
  Lochgelly KY5 .... 14 A4
David The First St KY3 .... 34 C1
David's Loan FK2 .... 39 E1
Davids Mains Prim Sch
  EH4 .... 91 F2
Davidson Gdns EH4 .... 92 A2
Davidson La ML8 .... 230 A1
Davidson Pk EH4 .... 92 C2
Davidson Rd EH4 .... 92 C2
Davidson St FK7 .... 7 E1
Davidson Terr EH41 .... 100 C1
Davidson Way EH54 .... 147 F4
Davie St EH8 .... 233 E2
Daviot Rd KY12 .... 29 F3
Dawson Ave Alloa FK10 ...... 9 F4
  Livingston EH54 .... 147 F3
Dawson Park Sch FK2 .... 39 D1
Dawson Pl EH51 .... 63 F3
Dawson St FK2 .... 60 A4
De Quincey Path EH18 .... 181 F3
De Quincey Rd EH18 .... 181 F3
Deacons Ct EH49 .... 85 D3
Dean Bank La EH3 .... 93 D1
Dean Cres FK8 .... 2 B1
Dean Ct EH32 .... 98 B2
Dean Gn KY12 .... 28 A1
Dean Gr KY12 .... 28 A1
Dean Park Cres EH4 .... 232 A4
Dean Park Mews EH4 .... 93 D1
Dean Park Prim Sch
  EH14 .... 151 E1
Dean Park Sch EH14 .... 151 E1
Dean Path EH4 .... 92 C1
Dean Pk Gowkhall KY12 ...... 27 F4
  Longniddry EH32 .... 98 B2
  Newtongrange EH22 .... 183 D3
Dean Pl EH22 .... 183 D3
Dean Park St EH4 .... 93 D1
Dean Pl Penicuik EH26 ..... 203 E3
  Seafield EH47 .... 146 A1
Dean Rd Bo'ness EH51 .... 63 F3
  Kirkaldy KY2 .... 17 D2
  Longniddry EH32 .... 98 B2
  Penicuik FH26 .... 203 F3
Dean Ridge KY12 .... 27 F4
Dean St Edinburgh EH4 ...... 93 D1
  Whitburn EH47 .... 170 A4

Dean Terr EH4 .... 232 A4
Dean The EH40 .... 75 F1
Deanburn EH26 .... 203 F4
Deanburn Gr EH51 .... 63 E3
Deanburn Pk EH49 .... 84 C3
Deanburn Prim Sch EH51 .. 63 E3
Deanburn Rd EH49 .... 84 C3
Deanburn Wlk EH51 .... 63 E3
Deanery CE EH7 .... 94 B1
Deanfield Cres EH51 .... 63 F4
Deanfield Dr EH51 .... 63 F3
Deanfield Pl EH51 .... 63 F3
Deanfield Rd EH51 .... 63 F3
Deanfield Terr EH51 .... 63 F3
Deangate Gdns EH51 .... 63 E3
Deanpark St EH4 .... 93 D1
Deanpark Ave EH14 .... 151 E1
Deanpark Bank EH14 .... 151 E1
Deanpark Brae EH14 .... 151 E1
Deanpark Cres EH14 .... 151 E1
Deanpark Ct EH14 .... 151 D1
Deanpark Gdns EH14 .... 151 E1
Deanpark Gr EH14 .... 151 E1
Deanpark Pl EH14 .... 151 E1
Deans Com High Sch
  EH54 .... 147 D4
Deans Ind Est EH54 .... 146 B4
Deans North Rd EH54 ...... 146 C4
Deans Prim Sch EH54 .... 146 C3
Deans Rd EH54 .... 146 B3
Deans Rdbt EH54 .... 146 B3
Deans Service Units EH54 . 146 C3
Deans South EH54 .... 146 C3
Deanswood Pk EH54 .... 146 C3
Deantown Ave EH21 .... 157 F4
Deantown Dr EH21 .... 126 C1
Deantown Path EH21 .... 126 C1
Deas Rd Inverkeithing KY11 .. 47 D1
  Shotts ML7 .... 191 E3
Dechmont Inf Sch EH22 ... 116 A1
Dechmont Rd EH12 .... 121 D3
Dechmont Rdbt EH52 .... 116 B1
Dedridge East Ind Est
  EH54 .... 148 A1
Dedridge East Rd EH54 .... 148 A1
Dedridge North Rd EH54 .. 147 F1
Dedridge Prim Sch EH54 .. 148 A1
Dedridge West Rd EH54 ... 173 F4
Dee Dr EH54 .... 148 A3
Dee Pl EH54 .... 148 A3
Dee St ML7 .... 191 E3
Deep Sea World KY11 .... 68 B3
Deer Park Bsns Campus
  EH54 .... 116 B1
Deer Park Dr EH54 .... 116 B1
Deer Park Prim Sch EH54 .. 116 B1
Deer Park Rd Abercorn EH30 .. 66 C1
  Dechmont EH54 .... 116 B1
Deerhill EH52 .... 116 B1
Deerpark EH10 .... 5 F1
Deerpark Prim Sch EH10 ..... 5 F1
Deeside Dr ML8 .... 230 A2
Delisle St EH42 .... 78 B1
Dell Ave EH48 .... 143 F3
Dell Rd EH13 .... 153 D4
Delph Rd FK10 .... 4 A3
Delphwood Cres FK10 .... 4 B1
Delta Ave EH21 .... 127 D3
Delta Cres EH21 .... 127 D3
Delta Dr EH21 .... 127 D3
Delta Gdns EH21 .... 127 D3
Delta Pl EH21 .... 126 B2
Delta Rd EH21 .... 127 D3
Delta View EH21 .... 127 D3
Dempster Pl KY12 .... 28 C2
Den La ML7 .... 191 E3
Den Rd KY2, KY1 .... 17 E3
Denburn Pl KY2 .... 17 E3
Denburn Rd KY2 .... 17 E4
Denend Cres KY2 .... 17 D3
Denham Green Ave EH5 ...... 93 D3
Denham Green Pl EH5 .... 93 D3
Denham Green Terr EH5 ...... 93 D3
Denholm Ave EH21 .... 125 F2
Denholm Gr EH48 .... 143 F4
Denholm Rd EH21 .... 125 F3
Denholm Way EH21 .... 125 F3
Denny High Sch FK6 .... 57 F2
Denny Prim Sch FK6 .... 36 B1
Denny Rd Bankhead FK4 ...... 57 F3
  Larbert FK5 .... 38 A1
Denovan Rd FK6 .... 36 C2
Dequincey Wlk EH33 .... 128 B3
Derby St EH6 .... 93 E3
Derwent Dr FK8 .... 6 C3
Derwent Ave FK1 .... 59 F2
Devon Ct EH20 .... 4 A1
Devon Dr FK10 .... 4 C2
Devon Pl Edinburgh EH12 .. 122 C4
  Fallin FK10 .... 4 A1
Devon Rd EH10 .... 10 B3
Devon St EH3 .... 40 A1
Devon Terr KY11 .... 29 F1
Devon Village FK10 .... 5 F2
Devonbank FK10 .... 5 F2
Devonway FK10 .... 11 D3
Dewar Ave FK10 .... 9 F3
Dewar Pl EH3 .... 232 A2
Dewar Place La EH3 .... 232 A2
Dewar Sq EH54 .... 146 B3
Dewar St Dunfermline KY12 .. 28 C2
  Lochgelly KY5 .... 14 A4
Dewshill Cotts ML7 .... 167 D2
Dick Cres KY3 .... 33 F1
Dick Gdns EH47 .... 160 C3
Dick Pl Edinburgh EH9 ...... 123 E2
  Rosyth KY11 .... 46 C3
  Stoneyburn EH47 .... 171 E1
Dick St KY12 .... 29 E3

Dick Terr EH26 .... 203 F3
Dickburn Cres FK4 .... 57 F3
Dickies Wells FK2 .... 5 E4
Dickson Cr KY5 .... 14 A4
Dickson St
  Dunfermline KY12 .... 29 D1
  Edinburgh EH6 .... 93 F2
  West Calder EH55 .... 172 B1
Dicksons Gr EH19 .... 182 A4
Dinmont Dr EH16 .... 124 A1
Dirleton Ave EH39 .... 54 A4
Dirleton Castle EH39 .... 53 D2
Dirleton Gdns FK10 .... 9 E3
Dirleton La EH10 .... 9 F3
Dirleton Prim Sch EH39 ...... 53 D3
Dirleton Rd Dirleton EH39 ... 53 D3
  North Berwick EH39 .... 53 D3
Distillery La EH11 .... 122 C4
Diverswell FK10 .... 5 E1
Dixon Terr EH47 .... 170 A3
Dobbie Ave FK5 .... 38 B1
Dobbie's Rd EH19 .... 182 A4
Dobson's Pl EH41 .... 131 F4
Dobson's View EH41 .... 131 F4
Dobson's Wlk EH41 .... 131 F4
Dochart Cres FK2 .... 61 F1
Dochart Dr EH14 .... 91 E1
Dochart Path FK3 .... 61 E3
Dochart Pl KY1 .... 60 B1
Dock Pl EH6 .... 93 F3
Dock Rd KY3 .... 40 B1
Dock St Bo'ness EH51 .... 64 A4
  Edinburgh EH6 .... 93 F3
  Falkirk FK2 .... 39 E1
Doctor's Row KY1 .... 17 F4
Dog Well Wynd EH49 .... 85 D4
Dollar Ave FK2 .... 60 A4
Dollar Cres EH4 .... 16 B4
Dollar Ct KY12 .... 28 C3
Dollar Gdns FK2 .... 60 A4
Dollar Gr KY3 .... 33 F1
Dollar Ind Est KY1 .... 60 A3
Dollar Rd KY3 .... 33 F1
Dolphin Ave EH14 .... 151 F2
Dolphin Gdns E EH14 .... 151 F2
Dolphin Gdns W EH14 ...... 151 F2
Dolphin Rd EH14 .... 151 F2
Don Dr EH54 .... 148 A3
Don Rd KY11 .... 29 F1
Don St FK3 .... 40 A1
Donald St KY12 .... 29 E3
Donaldson Ct FK10 .... 23 F2
Donaldson Pl FK7 .... 6 B3
**Donaldson's Sch
  for the Deaf** EH12 .... 122 C4
  Edinburgh, Calton EH12 .. 122 C4
  Edinburgh, Stockbridge EH4 93 D1
Donibristle Gdns KY11 .... 48 A1
Donibristle Ind Pk KY11 ...... 48 A1
Donibristle Prim Sch
  KY11 .... 48 A1
Doo Dells La KY3 .... 34 C1
Doo'cot Brae FK10 .... 10 A4
Doocot Brae EH51 .... 64 A4
Doon Ave EH42 .... 78 B1
Doon Wlk EH54 .... 148 A3
Dora Ct KY4 .... 13 E3
Dornie Wynd ML7 .... 192 A2
Dorrator Rd FK1 .... 59 F3
Dorset Pl EH11 .... 123 D3
Double Dykes EH21 .... 126 B2
Double Hedges Pk EH16 ... 124 A1
Double Hedges Rd EH16 ... 124 A1
Double Row KY11 .... 45 D2
Dougall Ct EH22 .... 183 E3
Dougall Pl EH22 .... 183 E3
Dougall Rd EH22 .... 183 E3
Douglas Ave Brightons FK2 . 82 B4
  Crossford KY12 .... 28 A1
  Grangemouth FK3 .... 61 F3
  Linlithgow EH49 .... 84 C3
Douglas Cres
  Bonnyrigg and Lasswade
  EH19 .... 182 A4
  Edinburgh EH12 .... 122 C4
  Longniddry EH32 .... 98 C3
Douglas Gardens Mews
  EH4 .... 122 C4
Douglas's Sch EH54 .... 146 C4
Douglas Gdns EH4 .... 122 C4
Douglas Pl Bo'ness EH51 .... 63 F3
  Kirkaldy KY1 .... 18 A4
  Linlithgow EH49 .... 84 C3
  Stenhousemuir FK5 .... 38 C2
Douglas Rd Bo'ness EH51 .... 63 F3
  Longniddry EH32 .... 98 C3
  Rosyth KY11 .... 46 B1
Douglas St Bannockburn FK7 .. 7 F1
  Dunfermline KY12 .... 29 D2
  Kirkaldy KY1 .... 17 D2
Douglas Terr
  Edinburgh EH11 .... 63 F3
  Stirling FK7 .... 2 A1
Douglas Terr
  Stirling FK7 .... 6 C1
Douglaswynd EH52 .... 117 D3
Doune Cres FK5 .... 39 D2
Doune Pk KY11 .... 48 A2
Doune Terr EH3 .... 232 B4
Dovecot Brae EH54 .... 128 B4
Dovecot Gr EH14 .... 122 A1
Dovecot Loan EH14 .... 122 A1
Dovecot Pk Aberdour KY3 ... 49 D3
  Edinburgh EH14 .... 153 D4
  Linlithgow EH49 .... 85 E4
  Pencaitland EH34 .... 160 C3
Dovecot Pl FK10 .... 4 A2

Dovecot Rd
  Edinburgh EH12 .... 121 E3
  Tullibody KY2 .... 4 C2
  Westquarter FK2 .... 61 D1
Dovecot Way EH34 .... 160 C4
Dovecote Pl EH54 .... 147 E2
Dovehill FK10 .... 10 A4
Dovan Pl FK7 .... 6 A3
Dower Cres EH51 .... 64 A4
Dowie's Mill La EH4 .... 90 C2
Downfield KY4 .... 13 E3
Downfield Pl EH11 .... 122 C3
Downie Gr EH12 .... 121 F3
Downie Pl EH21 .... 126 B3
Downing Ct EH25 .... 183 F2
Downing Point KY11 .... 48 A1
Downs Cres KY4 .... 13 D2
Dreghorn Ave EH13 .... 153 F3
Dreghorn Dr EH13 .... 153 F3
Dreghorn Gdns EH13 .... 153 F3
Dreghorn Gr EH13 .... 153 F3
Dreghorn Junc EH10 .... 153 F3
Dreghorn Link EH10 .... 153 F3
Dreghorn Loan EH13 .... 153 D3
Dreghorn Pl EH13 .... 153 F3
Drem Farm Cotts EH39 ...... 73 D2
Drem Sta EH39 .... 73 D1
Drip Rd FK9 .... 1 C1
Dronachy Rd KY2 .... 16 C2
Drossie Rd FK1 .... 60 A2
Drove Loan FK6 .... 57 F3
Drove Loan Cres FK6 .... 57 F4
Droverhall Ave KY4 .... 31 D3
Droverhall Pl KY4 .... 31 D3
Drovers Rd EH52 .... 118 A3
Drum Ave EH17 .... 155 F3
Drum Brae Ave EH12 .... 121 E4
Drum Brae Cres EH4 .... 91 E1
Drum Brae Dr EH4 .... 91 E1
Drum Brae Gdns EH12 ...... 121 E4
Drum Brae Gr EH4 .... 91 E1
Drum Brae N EH4 .... 91 D1
Drum Brae Neuk EH12 ...... 121 E4
Drum Brae Park App
  EH12 .... 121 E4
Drum Brae Pk EH12 .... 121 E4
Drum Brae Pl EH12 .... 121 E4
Drum Brae S EH12 .... 121 E4
Drum Brae Terr EH4 .... 91 E1
Drum Brae Wlk EH4 .... 91 D1
Drum Cotts EH17 .... 155 F3
Drum Cres EH17 .... 155 F3
Drum Pl
  East Whitburn EH47 .... 170 C4
  Edinburgh EH17 .... 155 F3
Drum Rd Bo'ness EH51 .... 64 B3
  Dunfermline KY11 .... 29 F3
Drum St EH17 .... 155 F3
Drum Terr EH7 .... 94 A1
Drum View Ave EH22 .... 156 A4
Drumacre Rd EH51 .... 64 A3
Drumbowie Prim Sch
  FK6 .... 82 B1
Drumbrae Prim Sch EH4 .. 121 E4
Drumclair Ave FK1 .... 110 A3
Drumcross Rd EH48 .... 145 D4
Drumdryan St EH3 .... 232 B1
Drumlanrig Pl FK5 .... 38 C2
Drummohr Ave EH21 .... 126 C1
Drummohr Gdns EH21 ..... 127 D3
Drummond Com High Sch
  EH7 .... 93 E1
Drummond La FK8 .... 7 D3
Drummond Pk FK3 .... 61 E4
Drummond Pl
  Blackridge EH48 .... 142 B2
  Bonnybridge FK4 .... 58 A4
  Dunfermline KY12 .... 29 E3
  Edinburgh EH3 .... 93 E1
  Falkirk FK1 .... 59 F2
  Grangemouth FK3 .... 61 E4
  Stirling FK8 .... 7 D3
Drummond Place La FK8 ..... 7 D3
Drummond Sq
  Livingston EH54 .... 173 E3
  Lochgelly KY5 .... 14 A4
Drummond St EH8 .... 233 E2
Drummore Dr EH32 .... 127 F4
Drummormie Rd KY12 .... 27 E1
Drumpark Ave FK3 .... 61 F3
Drumpark St FK7 .... 7 D2
Drumsheugh Gdns EH3 ... 232 A3
Drumshoreland Ave
  EH53 .... 144 A4
Drumshoreland Cres
  EH53 .... 148 A4
Drumshoreland Pl EH53 ... 148 A4
Drumshoreland Rd EH53 .. 148 A4
Drumside Terr EH51 .... 64 A4
Drumview Gdns EH53 .... 64 A3
Dryburgh Ave FK6 .... 36 B1
Dryburgh Rd FK3 .... 61 F3
Dryburgh Way FK2 .... 61 F3
Dryden Ave EH20 .... 181 D4
Dryden Cres EH20 .... 181 D4
Dryden Gdns EH7 .... 93 F2
Dryden Glen EH20 .... 180 C4
Dryden Gr EH25 .... 181 D2
Dryden Pl EH9 .... 233 F1
Dryden Rd EH20 .... 180 C4
Dryden Terr Edinburgh EH7 .. 93 F2
  Loanhead EH20 .... 181 D4
Dryden View EH20 .... 180 C4
Drylaw Ave EH4 .... 92 B1
Drylaw Cres EH4 .... 92 A1

Drylaw Gdns
  East Linton EH40 .... 103 E4
  Edinburgh EH4 .... 92 A2
Drylaw Gn EH4 .... 92 A1
Drylaw Gr EH4 .... 92 A1
Drylaw House Gdn EH4 .... 92 A2
Drylaw House Paddock
  EH4 .... 92 A2
Drylaw Terr EH40 .... 103 E4
Drylawhill EH40 .... 75 E1
Dryle St KY4 .... 13 D2
Drysdale Ave EH47 .... 170 A4
Drysdale St FK10 .... 10 A3
Duart Cres EH4 .... 91 E1
Dublin Meuse EH3 .... 93 E1
Dublin St EH1 .... 233 D4
Dublin Street La N EH1 ...... 93 E1
Dublin Street La S EH3 ...... 233 D4
Duddingston Cres EH52 ..... 88 A4
Duddingston Gdns S EH15 124 C3
Duddingston Gr E EH15 .... 124 C3
Duddingston Gr W EH15 ... 124 C3
Duddingston Loan EH15 ... 124 C3
Duddingston Mills EH8 ..... 124 C4
Duddingston Pk EH15 .... 125 D4
Duddingston Pk S EH15 .... 125 D3
Duddingston Prim Sch
  EH15 .... 124 C4
Duddingston Rd EH15 ...... 124 C4
Duddingston Rd W EH15 .. 124 B3
Duddingston Rise EH15 .... 124 C3
Duddingston Row EH15 .... 124 C3
Duddingston Sq E EH15 .... 124 C4
Duddingston Sq W EH15 ... 124 C3
Duddingston Yds EH15 ..... 125 D3
Duddingston Terr EH52 ...... 88 A4
Duddingston Gdns N EH15 124 C3
Dudgeon Pl KY12 .... 89 D1
Dudley Ave EH6 .... 93 E3
Dudley Ave S H6 .... 93 F3
Dudley Bank EH6 .... 93 E3
Dudley Cres EH6 .... 93 E3
Dudley Gdns EH6 .... 93 E3
Dudley Gr EH6 .... 93 E3
Dudley Terr EH6 .... 93 E3
Duff Cres FK8 .... 1 C1
Duff St EH11 .... 122 C3
Duff St La EH11 .... 122 C3
Duffy Pl KY11 .... 46 C2
Dugald Stewart Ave EH54 . 148 A1
Duglas Rise EH54 .... 148 A1
Duke Pl EH6 .... 94 A3
Duke St Alva FK12 .... 5 D4
  Bannockburn FK7 .... 7 E1
  Clackmannan FK10 .... 11 D2
  Dalkeith EH22 .... 157 D2
  Denny FK6 .... 36 B1
  Dunbar EH42 .... 78 A1
  Edinburgh EH6 .... 94 A2
  Grangemouth FK3 .... 61 E4
  Rosewell EH24 .... 181 E1
  West Barns EH42 .... 77 F1
Duke's Wlk EH8 .... 94 A1
Dumbarton Rd FK8 .... 6 C4
Dumbeg Pk EH14 .... 152 B4
Dumbiedykes Rd EH8 .... 233 F2
Dumbryden Dr EH14 .... 121 F1
Dumbryden Gdns EH14 .... 121 F1
Dumbryden Gr EH14 .... 121 F1
Dumbryden Prim Sch
  EH14 .... 121 F1
Dumbryden Rd EH14 .... 121 F1
Dumyat Ave FK12 .... 5 D4
Dumyat Dr FK1 .... 59 F2
Dumyat Rd Alva FK12 .... 4 C3
  Menstrie FK11 .... 3 F3
  Stirling FK9 .... 2 B2
Dumyat St FK10 .... 4 C1
Dunard Gdn EH9 .... 123 E2
Dunbar Cres FK5 .... 38 C2
Dunbar Gate FK6 .... 36 C2
Dunbar Gram Sch EH42 ...... 78 A1
Dunbar Pl KY1 .... 16 C3
Dunbar Prim Sch EH42 .... 78 B1
Dunbar Rd
  Edinburgh EH41 .... 101 D3
  North Berwick EH39 .... 54 C3
Dunbar St EH3 .... 232 B1
Dunbar Sta EH42 .... 78 C1
Duncairn Ave FK4 .... 57 F2
Duncan Ave FK2 .... 39 D2
Duncan Cres KY11 .... 29 F1
Duncan Gdns EH33 .... 126 A3
Duncan Gn EH54 .... 147 D4
Duncan Pl EH6 .... 94 A2
Duncan St Bonnybridge FK4 . 57 F3
  Edinburgh EH9 .... 123 F2
  Kirkaldy KY2 .... 17 D2
Duncanson Ave FK10 .... 10 A4
Duncanson Dr KY3 .... 33 F1
Duncan Inn Ind Est FK6 ...... 36 C1
Duncarron Pl FK6 .... 36 C1
Duncur Rd EH41 .... 52 B2
Dundaff Ct FK6 .... 36 B1
Dundas Ave
  North Berwick EH39 .... 54 B3
  Queensferry EH30 .... 89 E4
Dundas Cotts EH52 .... 87 F4
Dundas Cres
  Clackmannan FK10 .... 11 D2
  Dalkeith EH22 .... 156 C1
  Laurieston FK2 .... 61 D2

Dundas Gdns EH23 .... 183 D1
Dundas Gr EH22 .... 156 C1
Dundas Pk EH19 .... 182 B4
Dundas Pl EH29 .... 89 D1
Dundas Rd Dalkeith EH22 ... 156 C1
Laurieston EH42 .... 61 D2
North Berwick EH39 .... 54 B3
Rosyth KY11 .... 67 E4
Stirling FK9 .... 2 A2
Dundas St Bathgate EH48 ... 145 D4
Bo'ness EH51 .... 63 F4
Bonnyrigg and Lasswade
EH19 .... 182 B4
Edinburgh EH3 .... 93 E1
Grangemouth FK3 .... 61 E3
Lochgelly KY5 .... 14 A4
Townhill KY12 .... 29 E4
Dundee Ct FK2 .... 60 A4
Dundee Pl FK2 .... 60 A4
Dundee St EH11 .... 232 A1
Dundee Terr EH11 .... 122 C3
Dundonald Rd KY11 .... 46 B2
Dundonald St EH3 .... 93 E1
Dundrennan Cotts EH16 ... 124 B1
Dunearn Bank KY3 .... 33 E1
Dunearn Dr KY2 .... 16 C3
Dunearn Sch KY2 .... 16 C4
Dunedin St EH7 .... 93 E2
Dunfermline Abbey KY12 ... 28 C2
Dunfermline Bsns Ctr
KY11 .... 29 D1
Dunfermline Bsns Pk
KY11 .... 46 B3
Dunfermline High Sch
KY11 .... 29 D1
Dunfermline Mus KY12 ... 29 D2
Dunfermline Rd
Crossgates KY4 .... 30 C3
Limekilns KY11 .... 45 F2
Dunfermline Sta KY12 ... 29 D2
Dunfermline Wynd KY11 ... 47 D1
Dunglass Church TD13 ... 140 B2
Dunimarle St KY12 .... 26 A1
Dunipace Cres KY12 .... 29 F3
Dunipace Prim Sch FK6 ... 36 B2
Dunkeld Pl FK2 .... 39 E1
Dunlin Brae EH54 .... 147 E3
Dunlop Sq EH54 .... 146 B3
Dunlop Terr EH26 .... 204 A3
Dunmar Cres FK10 .... 4 C1
Dunmar Dr FK10 .... 4 C1
Dunn Cres KY11 .... 29 F2
Dunn Pl EH52 .... 87 F1
Dunn St EH52 .... 117 D3
Dunn Terr ML7 .... 168 C3
Dunnet Way FK52 .... 118 A3
Dunnikier Prim Sch KY2 ... 17 D3
Dunnikier Rd KY1 .... 17 E3
Dunnikier Way KY1 .... 17 E4
Dunning Pl KY1 .... 39 E1
Dunnottar Dr FK5 .... 38 C2
Dunnottar Pl KY2 .... 16 C2
Dunollie Ct EH12 .... 121 D4
Dunollie Gdns EH41 .... 132 B4
Dunpender Dr EH41 .... 100 C1
Dunpender Rd EH40 .... 103 E4
Dunrobin Ave FK5 .... 38 C3
Dunrobin Pl EH3 .... 93 D1
Dunrobin Rd KY2 .... 16 C2
Duns Rd EH41 .... 163 F3
Dunsire St KY1 .... 17 F4
Dunsmuir Ct EH12 .... 121 E3
Dunster Rd FK2 .... 2 B2
Dunure Cres FK4 .... 58 A3
Dunure Pl KY2 .... 16 C2
Dunure St FK4 .... 58 A3
Dunvegan Ave Kirkcaldy KY2 . 16 B3
Stenhousemuir FK5 .... 38 B2
Dunvegan Ct Alloa FK10 ... 10 A3
Crossford KY12 .... 28 A1
Edinburgh EH4 .... 91 D2
Dunvegan Dr Falkirk FK2 ... 39 E1
Stirling FK9 .... 2 A2
Dunvegan Gdns EH54 .... 173 F3
Dunvegan Pl
Bonnyrigg FK4 .... 57 F3
Polmont FK2 .... 62 A1
Dura Rd ML7 .... 212 B3
Durar Dr EH4 .... 91 E1
Durham Gr
Bathgate EH48 .... 144 C3
Edinburgh EH15 .... 124 C4
Durham Bank EH19 .... 182 B3
Durham Dr Bathgate EH48 . 144 C3
Edinburgh EH15 .... 125 D3
Durham Gdns N EH15 .... 125 D4
Durham Gdns S EH15 .... 125 D3
Durham Gr
Edinburgh EH15 .... 124 C4
Newmills KY12 .... 26 B1
Durham Place E EH15 ... 125 D4
Durham Pl La EH15 .... 125 D4
Durham Pl W EH15 .... 124 C4
Durham Rd EH15 .... 125 D4
Durham Sq EH15 .... 125 D4
Durham Terr
Edinburgh EH15 .... 124 C4
Newmills KY12 .... 26 B1
Durie's Pk KY5 .... 50 B4
Durie Pl KY12 .... 29 F2
Durie's Pk EH33 .... 128 A1
Durward Rise EH54 .... 148 A1
Durwood Gr EH16 .... 124 A1
Dyfrig St ML7 .... 191 F3
Dyke Brow ML7 .... 169 D3

Dyke Rd ML7 .... 169 D2
Dykehead Prim Sch ML7 ... 191 F3
Dykes Rd EH26 .... 203 F4
Dykeside Rd EH48 .... 144 C4
Dymond Gr KY1 .... 46 C4
Dysart Prim Sch KY1 .... 18 A4
Dysart Rd KY1 .... 17 F3

Eagle Brae EH54 .... 147 E2
Eagle Rock EH4 .... 91 D4
Earl Grey St EH3 .... 232 B2
Earl Haig Gdns EH5 .... 93 D3
Earl Of Mar Ct FK10 .... 10 A3
Earl's Gate Rdbt FK3 .... 61 D4
Earl's Rd FK3 .... 61 D4
Earls Ct FK10 .... 10 A3
Earls Pl EH47 .... 193 F3
Earlsburn Ave FK7 .... 7 D2
Earlshill Dr FK7 .... 7 D1
Earlston EH32 .... 94 A1
Earn Ct Alloa FK10 .... 10 B3
Earn Gr KY11 .... 46 B3
Earn Gr KY12 .... 57 E3
Earn Pl FK6 .... 57 E3
Earn Rd KY1 .... 17 E4
Earn Terr ML7 .... 191 F3
East Adam St EH8 .... 233 E2
East Albert Rd KY1 .... 17 E3
East Ave Blairhall KY12 ... 26 A4
Dunfermline KY11 .... 46 C4
East Baldridge Dr KY12 ... 28 C3
East Barnton Ave EH4 ... 173 F4
East Barnton Ave EH4 .... 91 F2
East Barnton Gdns EH4 ... 91 F2
East Bay KY11 .... 68 B3
East Boreland Pl FK6 .... 36 C1
East Bridge St FK1 .... 60 B2
East Brighton Cres EH15 . 125 D4
East Broomhill Rd KY3 ... 50 C4
East Caiystane Pl EH10 ... 154 A3
East Caiystane Rd EH10 ... 154 A3
East Calder Prim Sch
EH53 .... 148 C2
East Campbell Ct EH32 ... 98 B3
East Castle Rd EH10 .... 123 D2
East Castle St EH10 .... 10 A3
East Champanyie EH9 ... 123 F2
East Clapperfield EH16 ... 124 A1
East Claremont St EH7 ... 93 E2
East Comiston EH10 .... 154 A3
East Craigs Prim Sch
EH12 .... 121 D4
East Craigs Rigg EH12 ... 121 D4
East Croft EH28 .... 119 F1
East Cromwell St EH6 ... 93 F3
East Ct
Edinburgh, Greendykes
EH16 .... 124 C2
Edinburgh, Ravelston 7 EH4 . 92 B1
East End EH55 .... 38 B1
East End Rd EH52 .... 172 B2
East End Park
(Dunfermline Athletic FC)
KY12 .... 29 E2
East Farm Of Gilmerton
EH17 .... 155 F3
East Fenton Farm Cotts
EH39 .... 73 E4
East Fergus Pl KY1 .... 17 D2
East Fettes Ave EH4 .... 92 C2
East Fountainbridge EH3 . 232 B2
East Garleton Cotts EH39 . 100 C3
East Glen Ave EH54 .... 146 C3
East Harbour Rd KY11 ... 45 D2
East Hermitage Pl EH6 ... 94 A2
East Leven St KY3 .... 50 C4
East Lillypot EH5 .... 93 D3
East Link Rd EH9 .... 2 A1
East Links Rd Dunbar EH42 . 78 C1
Gullane EH31 .... 52 A1
East Linton Prim Sch EH40 103 E4
East Linton Station Ind Est
EH40 .... 103 F4
East Loan EH32 .... 97 D1
East London St EH7 .... 93 E1
East Lorimer Pl EH32 .... 97 E2
East Main St
Armadale EH48 .... 144 A3
Blackburn EH47 .... 171 E4
Broxburn EH52 .... 117 F3
Harthill ML7 .... 168 C3
Uphall EH52 .... 117 D2
Whitburn EH47 .... 170 A4
East Mains FK11 .... 4 A3
East Mains Ind Est EH52 . 118 A3
East March St KY1 .... 17 F4
East Market St EH8 .... 233 E3
East Mayfield EH9 .... 123 F2
East Montgomery Pl 4
EH7 .... 93 F1
East Murrayfield FK7 .... 7 F1
East Newington Pl EH9 ... 123 F3
East Norton Pl 3 EH7 .... 93 F1
East Parkgrove EH52 .... 117 D3
East Parkside EH16 .... 233 F1
East Pier St KY1 .... 63 F4
East Plean Prim Sch FK7 . 20 B2
East Port KY1 .... 29 D2
East Port Ave EH42 .... 158 B2
East Preston St EH8 .... 233 F1
East Preston Street La 6
EH8 .... 123 F3
East Quality St KY1 .... 18 A4
East Queensway EH26 ... 203 F3
East Rd Grangemouth FK2 . 62 B3
North Berwick EH39 .... 54 B4
East Restalrig Terr EH6 ... 94 A2

East Savile Rd EH16 .... 123 F2
East Sciennes St 8 EH9 ... 123 F3
East Scotland Street La 2
EH3 .... 93 E1
East Seaside EH32 .... 96 C1
East Silvermills La EH3 ... 93 D1
East Stirling St KY12 .... 5 D4
East Suffolk Rd EH16 .... 124 A2
East Telferton EH7 .... 94 C1
East Terr EH30 .... 68 B1
East Toll KY3 .... 33 F1
East Trinity Rd EH5 .... 93 E3
East Vennel FK10 .... 10 A3
East Vows Wlk KY1 .... 35 D4
East Way KY11 .... 48 B3
East Werberside EH4 .... 92 C2
East Whitefield KY12 .... 29 F3
Eastburn Dr FK1 .... 60 A2
Eastcroft Dr FK2 .... 62 A1
Eastcroft St FK5 .... 38 A1
Easter Bankton EH54 .... 174 A4
Easter Belmont Rd EH12 ... 122 A3
Easter Carmairs Prim Sch
FK1 .... 59 D3
Easter Cornton Rd EH14 ... 18 A4
Easter Currie Cres EH14 ... 152 A3
Easter Currie Ct EH14 .... 152 A2
Easter Currie Pl EH14 .... 152 A2
Easter Currie Terr EH14 ... 152 A2
Easter Drylaw Ave EH4 ... 92 B2
Easter Drylaw Bank EH4 ... 92 B2
Easter Drylaw Dr EH4 .... 92 B2
Easter Drylaw Gdns EH4 ... 92 B2
Easter Drylaw Gr EH4 .... 92 B2
Easter Drylaw Loan EH4 ... 92 B2
Easter Drylaw Pl EH4 .... 92 B2
Easter Drylaw View EH4 ... 92 B2
Easter Drylaw Way EH4 ... 92 B2
Easter Ferrygate Pk EH39 . 53 F4
Easter Haugh EH13 .... 153 E4
Easter Hermitage EH6 ... 94 A2
Easter Livilands EH7 .... 7 E2
Easter Park Dr EH4 .... 91 F2
Easter Rd Broxburn EH52 . 117 F3
Edinburgh EH6 .... 94 A2
Shotts ML7 .... 191 E3
Easter Road Stad
(Hibernian FC) EH7 .... 94 A1
Easter Steil EH10 .... 122 C1
Easter Warriston EH7 .... 93 E3
Easterfield Ct EH54 .... 147 E2
Eastern Ind Est EH15 .... 125 E2
Easterton Cres FK7 .... 20 C4
Easterton Dr FK7 .... 20 C4
Easterton Gr FK7 .... 20 C4
Easterton Gdns EH48 ... 143 F3
Eastertoun Prim Sch
EH48 .... 143 F3
Eastfield EH15 .... 125 D4
Eastfield Dr EH26 .... 203 F3
Eastfield Farm Rd EH26 ... 203 F4
Eastfield Gdns EH15 .... 125 E4
Eastfield Ind Est EH26 ... 203 F3
Eastfield Park Rd EH26 ... 203 F3
Eastfield Pl EH15 .... 125 E4
Eastfield Carluke ML8 ... 230 A1
Eastfield EH28 .... 120 A4
Faulkhouse EH47 .... 193 F4
North Berwick EH39 .... 54 B3
Eastfield View EH47 .... 193 F4
Easthouses Ct EH22 .... 174 C1
Easthouses Ind Est
EH22 .... 183 E4
Easthouses Way EH22 ... 157 E1
Easthouses Rd
Dalkeith EH22 .... 157 E1
Easthouses EH22 .... 183 E4
Easton Ct FK8 .... 2 A1
Easton Dr FK1 .... 81 E4
Easton Rd EH48 .... 144 C4
Eastwood Pk
Faulkhouse EH47 .... 193 F4
Livingston EH54 .... 147 D4
Ebenezer Pl FK1 .... 81 F3
Eccles Ct FK7 .... 7 D2
Ecclesmachan Rd EH52 ... 116 C3
Echline EH30 .... 89 D2
Echline Ave EH30 .... 88 C4
Echline Dr EH30 .... 88 C4
Echline Farm Cotts EH30 . 88 B3
Echline Gdns EH30 .... 67 F1
Echline Gn EH30 .... 67 F1
Echline Gr EH30 .... 68 A1
Echline Pk EH30 .... 68 A1
Echline Prim Sch EH30 ... 68 A1
Echline Rigg EH30 .... 68 A1
Echline Steadings EH30 ... 88 C4
Echline Terr EH30 .... 88 C4
Echline View EH30 .... 88 C4
Echobank KY11 .... 47 D1
Eden Dr EH54 .... 148 A2
Eden La EH10 .... 123 D2
Eden Rd Alloa FK10 .... 9 F4
Dunfermline KY11 .... 46 B3
Edenhall Bank EH21 ... 126 C3
Edenhall Cres EH21 .... 126 C3
Edenhall Hospl EH21 ... 126 C3
Edenhall Rd EH21 .... 126 C3
Edgefield Ind Est EH20 ... 155 E1
Edgefield Pl EH20 .... 181 E4
Edgefield Rd EH20 .... 155 E1
Edgehead Rd EH37 .... 184 B4
Edina Pl EH7 .... 94 A1
Edina St EH7 .... 93 F1
Edinburgh Acad EH3 .... 93 D1
Edinburgh Acad
(Prep Sch) The EH3 .... 93 D2
Edinburgh Castle EH1 ... 232 C3

Edinburgh Fort Ret Pk
EH15 .... 125 D2
Edinburgh Pk
Edinburgh EH12 .... 120 C3
Edinburgh EH12 .... 121 D2
Edinburgh Rd
Bathgate EH48 .... 145 E3
Cockenzie & Port Seton EH32 . 97 D2
Dalkeith EH22 .... 157 D2
Harthill ML7 .... 168 B3
Linlithgow EH49 .... 85 D2
Musselburgh EH21 .... 126 A3
Newbridge EH28 .... 119 D3
Penicuik EH26 .... 204 A4
Tranent EH33 .... 128 A3
West Barns EH42 .... 77 F1
West Linton EH46 .... 220 A1
Edinburgh West Off Pk
EH12 .... 121 D2
Edinburgh Coll of Art
EH3 .... 232 C2
Edinburgh Rd EH48 .... 145 E3
Edington Cottage Hospl
EH39 .... 54 B4
Edington Pl KY1 .... 18 A4
Edmonstone Ave EH54 ... 156 A4
Edmonstone Dr EH22 ... 156 A4
Edmonstone Rd EH22 ... 156 A4
Edmonstone Terr EH22 ... 156 A4
Edmonton Ave EH54 .... 147 F2
Edward Ave
Stenhousemuir FK5 .... 38 C2
Stirling FK8 .... 2 B1
Edward Rd FK7 .... 39 F2
Edward Rd FK8 .... 2 B1
Edward St Dunfermline KY12 . 29 D3
Kirkcaldy KY2 .... 17 D4
Eglington Pl KY11 .... 47 E1
Eglinton Gr EH12 .... 28 C3
Eglinton Cres EH12 .... 122 C4
Eighth St EH27 .... 183 D3
Eildon St EH3 .... 93 E2
Eildon Terr EH3 .... 93 E2
Eilean La KY12 .... 26 C1
Elam Terr EH51 .... 63 F4
Elbe St EH6 .... 94 A3
Elcho Ct EH32 .... 98 C3
Elcho Pl EH32 .... 97 E2
Elcho Rd EH52 .... 96 C3
Elcho Terr Aberlady EH32 . 71 E2
Edinburgh EH15 .... 125 E4
Longniddry EH32 .... 98 C3
Elder Pl KY11 .... 46 C3
Elder St Dunbar EH42 .... 78 A1
Edinburgh EH1 .... 233 D4
Tranent EH33 .... 128 B4
Elder St E EH1 .... 233 D4
Elderslie Dr FK2 .... 82 A4
Eldin Ind Est EH20 .... 155 E1
Eldindean Pl EH19 .... 182 A4
Eldindean Rd EH19 .... 182 B4
Eldindean Terr EH19 .... 182 B4
Eldrick Ave EH47 .... 193 F3
Eldrick Cres EH47 .... 193 E3
Eldrick La EH47 .... 193 F3
Eldrick View EH47 .... 193 F3
Electra Pl EH15 .... 95 D1
Elgin Ct KY12 .... 29 D1
Elgin Dr FK7 .... 7 D2
Elgin Pl FK1 .... 60 B2
Elgin Rd KY4 .... 13 E2
Elgin St Dunfermline KY12 . 29 D1
Edinburgh EH7 .... 93 F1
Kirkcaldy KY2 .... 17 D3
Elgin St N EH7 .... 93 F1
Elgin Terr EH7 .... 93 F1
Eliburn North Intc EH54 ... 147 D3
Eliburn Rd EH54 .... 147 D2
Eliburn South Rd EH54 ... 147 E2
Elie Ave EH54 .... 146 C3
Elim Dr FK1 .... 80 B3
Elizabeth Ave
Grangemouth FK3 .... 61 F4
Larbert FK5 .... 38 B1
Elizabeth Cres FK1 .... 59 D3
Elizabeth Dr EH48 .... 145 F3
Elizabeth Gdns EH47 ... 145 F3
Elizabeth St Dunfermline KY12 . 29 E1
Stirling FK8 .... 7 D3
Elizafield EH6 .... 93 F2
Ellaleen Gr KY12 .... 28 A1
Ellangowan Terr EH16 ... 124 B1
Ellen St EH47 .... 170 A4
Ellen's Glen Loan EH17 ... 155 E4
Ellen's Glen Rd EH17 ... 155 E4
Ellersly Rd EH12 .... 122 B4
Elliot Gdns EH14 .... 153 E4
Elliot Pk EH14 .... 153 E4
Elliot Pl EH14 .... 153 E4
Elliot Rd EH14 .... 153 E4
Elliot St EH7 .... 93 F1
Elliot Terr EH14 .... 153 E4
Elliothill St KY11 .... 29 D1
Ellis Pl EH52 .... 117 D2
Elliston Pl KY12 .... 29 E3
Ellon Rd KY7 .... 34 C4
Elm Gr Alloa FK10 .... 10 B3
Blackburn EH47 .... 171 E4
Dunfermline KY11 .... 46 B4
Larbert FK5 .... 38 B2
Livingston EH54 .... 148 A3
Elm Pk EH47 .... 171 F4
Elm Pl Edinburgh EH6 .... 94 A2
Kirkcaldy KY2 .... 17 D2
Mayfield EH22 .... 183 E3

Elm Rd EH48 .... 145 F3
Elm Row
Bonnyrigg and Lasswade
EH18 .... 156 A1
Edinburgh EH7 .... 93 F1
Elm Sq EH47 .... 170 B3
Elm St Dunbar EH42 .... 78 A1
Stirling FK8 .... 1 C1
Elmbank EH11 .... 4 A3
Elmbank Cres FK4 .... 57 E3
Elmbank Rd FK7 .... 7 D2
Elmbank St FK3 .... 61 E3
Elmfield Ct EH22 .... 157 D2
Elmfield Pl EH22 .... 157 D2
Elmfield Rd EH22 .... 157 D2
Elms The EH10 .... 153 F4
Elmwood Pk EH54 .... 146 C4
Elmwood Rd ML7 .... 192 A1
Elmwood Terr EH6 .... 94 A2
Elphinstone Cres EH22 ... 22 C2
Elphinstone Prim Sch
EH33 .... 128 A1
Elphinstone Rd EH33 ... 128 A3
Elphinstone Sq EH54 ... 146 B3
Elphinstone St EH10 ... 23 F2
Elphinstone Wlk EH33 ... 128 B3
Eltringham Gdns EH14 ... 122 B2
Eltringham Gr EH14 .... 122 B2
Eltringham Terr EH14 ... 122 B2
Emily Ct EH23 .... 183 E1
Emily Pl EH23 .... 183 E1
Empire St EH47 .... 170 A4
Endrick Dr FK6 .... 57 F3
Endrick Pl FK7 .... 7 D2
Engelen Dr FK10 .... 10 A3
Engine La EH48 .... 145 D3
Engine Pl EH48 .... 145 D3
Engine Rd Gorebridge EH23 183 D1
Loanhead EH20 .... 181 E4
Engineering Training Sch
KY2 .... 17 D2
Ennis Pk EH55 .... 172 C3
Eppiestane Rd EH47 ... 170 B3
Epworth Gdns FK2 .... 82 A4
Erbach Ave FK2 .... 61 D2
Ercall Rd FK2 .... 82 C4
Erica Gr KY11 .... 46 C4
Ericht Pl ML7 .... 191 F3
Eriskay Ct FK1 .... 60 B1
Errgath Rd EH51 .... 64 A1
Erskine Brae KY12 .... 25 E1
Erskine Hill FK2 .... 61 F1
Erskine Loan EH31 .... 52 A2
Erskine Pl
Clackmannan FK10 .... 10 C3
Mid Calder EH53 .... 148 B3
Erskine Rd Broxburn EH52 . 117 E3
Gullane EH31 .... 52 A2
Erskine Sq KY11 .... 29 E1
Erskine St Alloa FK10 .... 10 A4
Alva FK12 .... 5 D4
Lochgelly KY5 .... 14 A4
Erskine Way
Livingston EH54 .... 147 E4
Shotts ML7 .... 191 F2
Erskine Wynd KY12 .... 27 D4
Esk Dr EH54 .... 148 A3
Esk Glades EH22 .... 157 D2
Esk Pl EH22 .... 156 C2
Eskbank Rd
Bonnyrigg and Lasswade
EH19 .... 182 B4
Dalkeith EH22 .... 156 C1
Eskbank Road Rdbt EH22 . 156 B1
Eskbank Terr EH22 .... 156 C1
Eskdaill Ct EH22 .... 157 D2
Eskdaill St EH22 .... 157 D2
Eskdale Ct EH19 .... 182 A4
Eskdale Dr EH19 .... 182 B4
Eskdale Mews EH21 ... 126 B3
Eskdale Terr EH19 .... 182 A4
Eskfield Gr EH22 .... 156 B1
Eskgrove Dr EH22 .... 180 C3
Eskhill EH26 .... 203 F3
Eskmill Ind Est EH26 ... 204 A3
Eskmill Rd EH26 .... 204 A3
Eskside E EH21 .... 126 B3
Eskside W EH21 .... 126 B3
Eskvale Cres EH26 .... 204 A3
Eskvale Dr EH26 .... 204 A3
Eskview Ave EH21 .... 126 A3
Eskview Cres EH21 .... 126 A3
Eskview Gr Dalkeith EH22 . 156 C2
Musselburgh EH21 .... 126 A3
Eskview Rd Mayfield EH22 . 183 E3
Musselburgh EH21 .... 126 A3
Eskview Terr EH21 .... 126 A3
Eskview Villas EH22 .... 156 C1
Esplanade Edinburgh EH1 . 232 C3
Kirkcaldy KY1 .... 17 E1
Esplanade Terr EH15 ... 125 E4
Essendean Pl EH4 .... 91 E1
Essendean Terr EH4 .... 91 E1
Essex Brae EH4 .... 91 D2
Essex Pk EH4 .... 91 D2
Essex Rd EH4 .... 91 D2
Esslemont Rd EH16 .... 124 A1
Ethel Terr EH10 .... 123 D1
Etive Pl Dalgety Bay KY11 . 48 A1
Grangemouth FK2 .... 61 F2
Etive Way Polmont FK2 ... 61 E1
Shotts ML7 .... 192 A2

Etive Wlk EH54 ... 148 A2
Etna Ct FK2 ... 60 B4
Etna Rd FK7 ... 60 B4
Eton Terr EH4 ... 232 A4
Ettrick Cres KY11 ... 48 A2
Ettrick Ct Falkirk FK1 ... 60 B1
 Grangemouth FK3 ... 61 F3
Ettrick Dr EH14 ... 148 A3
Ettrick Dr EH10 ... 123 D3
Ettrick Rd EH10 ... 122 C2
Ettrickdale Pl EH3 ... 93 D2
Eva Pl EH9 ... 123 F1
Evans Gdns EH19 ... 182 B4
Evans St FK5 ... 38 A2
Evelyn Terr EH26 ... 180 B1
Everard Rise EH44 ... 148 A1
Evershed Ct KY11 ... 29 F1
Evershed Dr KY11 ... 29 F1
Ewart Ave EH48 ... 144 A3
Ewart Gr EH51 ... 63 F3
Ewerland EH4 ... 91 D2
Ewing Ave FK2 ... 60 A4
Ewing Ct FK7 ... 7 E2
Ewing Dr FK2 ... 60 A4
Ewing Pl FK2 ... 60 A4
Ewing St Cowdenbeath KY4 ... 13 D1
 Lochgelly KY5 ... 14 A3
 Penicuik EH26 ... 203 F4
Excise La FK10 ... 23 F2
Excise St FK10 ... 23 F2
Exmouth St EH54 ... 148 A3
Eyre Cres EH3 ... 93 E1
Eyre Pl EH3 ... 93 E1
Eyre Terr EH3 ... 93 E1

Fa'side Ave EH33 ... 128 B3
Fa'side Ave N EH21 ... 127 D2
Fa'side Ave S EH21 ... 127 D2
Fa'side Avenue Ct EH21 ... 127 D2
Fa'side Bldgs EH21 ... 127 D2
Fa'side Cres Tranent EH33 ... 128 B3
 Wallyford EH21 ... 127 D2
Fa'side Dr EH21 ... 127 D2
Fa'side Gdns EH21 ... 127 D2
Fa'side Rd EH33 ... 128 B3
Fa'side Terr EH21 ... 127 D2
Fa'side View EH33 ... 128 B3
Factory Rd Bathgate EH48 ... 144 C2
 Cowdenbeath KY4 ... 13 E2
 Kirkaldy KY1 ... 17 E3
Fair Isle Prim Sch KY2 ... 16 C4
Fair Isle Rd KY2 ... 16 C4
Fair Pl KY11 ... 47 D2
Fair-a-Far EH4 ... 91 D3
Fair-a-Far Cotts EH4 ... 91 D3
Fair-a-Far Shot EH4 ... 91 D3
Fairbairn Rd EH54 ... 147 E2
Fairbrae EH11 ... 121 F2
Fairfax Ct KY3 ... 33 F1
Fairfield Alloa FK10 ... 5 E1
 Livingston EH54 ... 147 E4
Fairfield Ave FK4 ... 58 A3
Fairfield Pl FK2 ... 60 B3
Fairfield Sch FK10 ... 5 D1
Fairford Gdns EH16 ... 124 A1
Fairgreen Pl FK7 ... 19 F4
Fairhaven Terr EH42 ... 82 A4
Fairhill Rd FK7 ... 7 D1
Fairinsfield EH52 ... 117 D3
Fairley Ct KY12 ... 27 E1
Fairlie Dr FK1 ... 59 E3
Fairlie Gdns FK1 ... 59 E3
Fairlie St FK1 ... 59 E3
Fairmile Ave EH10 ... 154 A3
Fairmont Pk EH47 ... 169 F3
Fairmount Dr FK10 ... 5 D1
Fairspark Terr EH51 ... 63 E3
Fairview Rd EH28 ... 119 F4
Fairview Terr FK2 ... 82 A4
Fairway EH41 ... 131 F4
Fairway The KY1 ... 17 F4
Fairways KY12 ... 29 D3
Fairways Ave FK2 ... 82 C3
Fairways Pl FK4 ... 58 A4
Fairy Fa' Cres KY4 ... 30 C3
Fairyburn Rd FK10 ... 9 F4
Fairykirk Rd KY11 ... 47 D2
Faith Mission Coll The EH17 ... 155 E3
Falahill Cotts EH38 ... 228 A2
Falcon Ave EH10 ... 123 D2
Falcon Brae EH54 ... 147 E3
Falcon Ct EH10 ... 123 D2
Falcon Dr FK5 ... 38 A2
Falcon Gdns EH10 ... 123 D2
Falcon Rd EH10 ... 123 D2
Falcon Rd W EH10 ... 123 D2
Falconer Ct FK7 ... 7 E2
Falconer Rise EH54 ... 147 F1
Falcons The EH31 ... 52 A2
Falkirk Coll of F & H Ed Flexible Learning Ctr FK2 ... 60 C3
Falkirk & District Royal Infmy FK1 ... 60 A2
Falkirk High Sch FK1 ... 59 F2
Falkirk High Sta FK1 ... 60 A2
Falkirk Rd Bannockburn FK7 ... 19 F4
 Bonnybridge FK4 ... 58 B3
 Falkirk, Glen Village FK1 ... 60 A1
 Falkirk, Westfield FK1 ... 60 C3
 Grangemouth FK3 ... 61 D4
 Larbert FK5 ... 59 E4
 Linlithgow EH49 ... 84 C4
Falkland Gdns EH12 ... 91 F1

Falkland Pl FK5 ... 38 C2
Falla Hill Prim Sch EH47 ... 193 E3
Fallas Pl EH47 ... 193 E3
Fallin Prim Sch FK7 ... 8 B3
Fallodon Cres KY2 ... 17 D2
Falside Cres EH48 ... 144 C3
Falside Dr EH48 ... 144 C3
Falside Terr EH48 ... 144 C3
Faraday Pl EH55 ... 171 F1
Farm Ave EH18 ... 181 F3
Farm Cotts
 Pencaitland EH34 ... 160 B3
 Wallyford EH21 ... 127 E3
Farm Rd Cowdenbeath KY4 ... 13 D2
 Cowie FK7 ... 20 B4
 Crombie KY12 ... 44 B3
 Falkirk FK7 ... 8 B3
 Roslin EH25 ... 204 C3
Farm Row KY12 ... 30 A3
Farm St FK2 ... 39 D1
Farmer's Bldgs EH37 ... 185 D3
Farne Ct KY2 ... 16 C4
Farnell Way KY12 ... 27 E2
Farquhar Sq EH48 ... 142 B2
Farquhar Terr EH30 ... 68 A1
Farquharson Way KY11 ... 59 F1
Farrer Gr EH7 ... 94 C1
Farrer Terr EH7 ... 94 C1
Farret Terr EH47 ... 171 E4
Fartervot Royal Hospl for Sick Children EH4 ... 123 E2
Fauldburn EH12 ... 91 D1
Fauldburn Pk EH12 ... 91 D1
Fauldhouse Rd EH47 ... 170 A1
Fauldhouse Sta EH47 ... 193 E3
Featherhall Ave EH12 ... 121 E3
Featherhall Cres EH12 ... 121 E3
Featherhall Cres N EH12 ... 121 E3
Featherhall Cres S EH12 ... 121 E3
Featherhall Gr EH12 ... 121 E3
Featherhall Pl EH12 ... 121 E3
Featherhall Rd EH12 ... 121 E3
Featherhall Terr EH12 ... 121 E3
Fell's Rd EH55 ... 172 C3
Fells Road Ind Est EH55 ... 147 D4
Fendoch Rd FK3 ... 61 F4
Fenton St FK10 ... 10 A4
Fentoun Gait EH31 ... 52 B1
Fere Gait FK10 ... 23 F2
Fergus Ave EH14 ... 147 F2
Fergus Pl KY11 ... 29 E1
Fergus Wynd KY1 ... 17 D1
Ferguson Ct EH22 ... 126 B2
Ferguson Dr Denny FK6 ... 36 B1
 Falkirk FK2 ... 39 D3
 Musselburgh EH21 ... 126 A2
Ferguson Gdns EH21 ... 126 B2
Ferguson Gn EH21 ... 126 A2
Ferguson Gr FK4 ... 58 A3
Ferguson Pl KY3 ... 33 F1
Ferguson Rd ... 1 C1
Ferguson View EH21 ... 126 A2
Ferguson Way
 Livingston EH54 ... 147 E4
 Newtongrange EH22 ... 183 D2
Ferguson Rd EH52 ... 117 F3
Fern Lea Gr KY2 ... 39 E2
Fernbank EH54 ... 147 F3
Fernie Pl KY12 ... 28 C3
Ferniehill Ave EH17 ... 155 F3
Ferniehill Dr EH17 ... 155 F3
Ferniehill Gdns EH17 ... 155 F4
Ferniehill Gr EH17 ... 155 F4
Ferniehill Pl EH17 ... 155 F4
Ferniehill Rd EH17 ... 155 F3
Ferniehill Sq EH17 ... 155 F3
Ferniehill St EH17 ... 155 F3
Ferniehill Terr EH17 ... 155 F3
Fernielaw Ave
 Edinburgh EH13 ... 152 C2
 Edinburgh, Bonaly EH13 ... 153 D3
Fernieside Ave EH17 ... 155 F4
Fernieside Cres EH17 ... 155 F4
Fernieside Dr EH17 ... 155 F4
Fernieside Gdns EH17 ... 155 F4
Fernieside Gr EH17 ... 155 F4
Fernieside Prim Sch EH17 ... 155 F4
Fernlea EH52 ... 116 C3
Ferrard Rd KY2 ... 17 D2
Ferrier Cres EH48 ... 144 A3
Ferris Way KY11 ... 48 A2
Ferry La KY11 ... 68 A3
Ferry Muir Gait EH30 ... 89 D4
Ferry Orch FK9 ... 2 B1
Ferry Rd Edinburgh EH4, EH5 ... 92 B2
 South Alloa FK7 ... 9 F2
 Stirling FK9 ... 2 A1
Ferry Road Ave EH4 ... 92 B2
Ferry Road Dr EH4 ... 92 B3
Ferry Road Gdns EH4 ... 92 B2
Ferry Road Gr EH4 ... 92 B2
Ferry Toll Pl KY11 ... 46 C1
Ferry Toll Rd KY11 ... 46 C1
Ferrybarns Ct KY11 ... 68 A3
Ferryburn Gn EH30 ... 89 E4
Ferryfield EH5 ... 93 D2
Ferrygate Cotts EH39 ... 53 E3
Ferryhill Prim Sch EH4 ... 92 B2
Ferryhill Rd KY11 ... 68 B4
Ferrymuir La EH30 ... 89 D4
Ferrymuir Rd EH30 ... 89 D4
Fetteresk Cotts EH26 ... 203 F2
Fettes Ave EH4 ... 92 C1
Fettes Coll EH4 ... 92 C2
Fettes Rise EH4 ... 92 C2

Fettes Row EH3 ... 93 E1
Fiddich Dr EH14 ... 173 F3
Fidra Ave EH39 ... 53 D3
Fidra Ct EH39 ... 53 F4
Fidra Rd EH39 ... 54 A4
Fife Coll of F & H Ed EH1 ... 17 D2
Fife Coll Priory Campus KY1 ... 17 E3
Fife Pl KY11 ... 46 A1
Fifth St EH22 ... 183 D3
Figgate Bank EH15 ... 95 D1
Figgate La EH15 ... 95 D1
Figgate St EH15 ... 95 D1
Fillyside Ave EH7 ... 94 C1
Fillyside Rd EH7 ... 94 C2
Fillyside Terr EH7 ... 94 C2
Finches The EH31 ... 52 A2
Findhorn Pl Edinburgh EH9 ... 123 F2
 Falkirk FK1 ... 60 B1
 Kircaldy KY2 ... 16 C4
Findlay Ave EH7 ... 94 B2
Findlay Cotts EH7 ... 94 B2
Findlay Cres KY11 ... 46 C2
Findlay Gdns EH7 ... 94 B2
Findlay Gr EH7 ... 94 B2
Findlay Medway EH7 ... 94 B2
Findlay St KY11 ... 46 C2
Fingal Pl EH9 ... 233 D1
Fingzies Pl EH6 ... 94 A2
Finistere Ave FK1 ... 60 A2
Finlaggan Ct EH12 ... 121 D4
Finlarig Ct FK5 ... 38 C2
Finlay Ave EH53 ... 148 C2
Finlay Pl EH22 ... 183 F3
Fintry Rd FK3 ... 61 E3
Fir Gr Dunfermline KY11 ... 46 C4
 Livingston EH54 ... 148 A3
 Westquarter FK2 ... 61 D1
Fir La FK5 ... 38 B1
Firbank Gr EH53 ... 148 C2
Firpark Terr FK7 ... 6 B3
Firr Hill High Sch EH14 ... 153 F4
Firrhill Cres EH13 ... 153 F4
Firrhill Dr EH13 ... 153 F4
Firrhill Loan EH13 ... 153 F4
Firs Cres FK7 ... 7 E1
Firs Entry FK7 ... 7 E1
Firs Pk (East Stirlingshire FC)
Firs Rd FK10 ... 4 B1
Firs St FK2 ... 60 B3
Firs The Bannockburn FK7 ... 7 E1
 Dalgety Bay KY11 ... 48 A1
First Gait EH14 ... 151 F4
First St EH22 ... 183 D2
Firth Cres EH26 ... 180 B1
Firth Rd Auchendinny EH26 ... 180 B1
 Livingston EH54 ... 147 F4
 Roslin EH25 ... 204 C3
Firwood Dr EH51 ... 63 E2
Fishcross Prim Sch FK10 ... 5 E2
Fishergate Rd EH32 ... 97 F2
Fisherrow Ind Est EH21 ... 126 A3
Fishers' Rd EH51 ... 63 E2
Fishers Rd EH32 ... 97 E2
Fishers Wynd EH21 ... 126 A3
Fishmarket Sq EH6 ... 93 E4
Fishwives' Cswy EH7, EH15 ... 94 C1
Fitzgerald Pl EH48 ... 113 F3
Fitzroy Sq KY1 ... 18 A4
Fitzroy St KY1 ... 18 A4
Five Gates EH42 ... 76 A3
Flare Rd FK2 ... 62 A3
Flax Mill Rd ML7 ... 168 C3
Fleets Gr EH33 ... 128 B2
Fleets Ind Est EH33 ... 128 B2
Fleets Rd EH33 ... 128 B3
Fleets View EH33 ... 128 B2
Fleming Dr FK5 ... 39 D2
Fleming Gdns FK1 ... 59 F3
Fleming Pl EH48 ... 142 C2
Fleming Rd EH48 ... 141 F3
Fleming Way KY3 ... 33 F1
Flemington Gdns EH47 ... 169 F3
Flesh Wynd KY1 ... 17 E3
Fleshmarket Cl EH1 ... 233 D3
Fletcher Gr EH26 ... 203 F4
Flint Cres FK7 ... 20 B4
Floors Pl KY2 ... 16 B3
Floors Terr EH42 ... 78 B1
Florabank Rd EH41 ... 101 D1
Flower Pl KY4 ... 12 C4
Fod St KY11 ... 30 A3
Fodbank View KY11 ... 29 F2
Foot Pl KY11 ... 46 C2
Foote St KY5 ... 14 A3
Forbes Cres FK5 ... 38 B1
Forbes Ct FK7 ... 60 C3
Forbes Rd Edinburgh EH10 ... 123 D3
 Falkirk FK1 ... 60 B1
 Rosyth KY11 ... 46 B1
Forbes St Alloa FK10 ... 9 F3
 Edinburgh EH8 ... 233 E1
Forbeslea Gdns KY12 ... 27 F4
Ford Rd Bonnybridge FK4 ... 58 A3
 Haddington EH41 ... 132 B4
Ford View KY12 ... 27 E1
Ford's Rd EH11 ... 122 A2
Fordell Bank KY11 ... 48 B2
Fordell Gdns KY3 ... 16 B3
Fordell Way KY11 ... 47 E1
Forebraes KY10 ... 10 A4
Foredale Terr EH51 ... 64 B4
Forest Kirk ML8 ... 230 A1
Forest Pl KY12 ... 28 B4
Forest Rd EH42 ... 62 A1
Forest View FK2 ... 29 E4

Forestbank EH54 ... 147 F3
Forester Gr FK10 ... 4 C1
Forester High Sch EH12 ... 121 E2
Forester's Lea Cres KY12 ... 29 F2
Forester's View EH33 ... 128 B3
Forfar Pl FK2 ... 62 A1
Forgie Cres FK2 ... 83 D3
Forgien Cres FK9 ... 2 A3
Forgien Rd FK9 ... 2 A3
Forker Ave KY11 ... 46 B2
Forkneuk Rd EH52 ... 116 C2
Forkneuk Steadings EH52 ... 116 C3
Forman Gr KY11 ... 29 F1
Forres Dr KY2 ... 16 B4
Forres St EH3 ... 232 B4
Forrest Hill EH1 ... 233 D2
Forrest Pl ML7 ... 168 C3
Forrest Rd Edinburgh EH1 ... 233 D2
 Forrestfield ML6 ... 141 D1
 Salsburgh ML7 ... 167 D3
 Stirling FK8 ... 2 A1
Forrest St ML7 ... 191 F3
Forrest Wlk EH52 ... 116 C2
Forrester Ct KY5 ... 14 A4
Forrester Park Ave EH12 ... 121 E2
Forrester Park Dr EH12 ... 121 E2
Forrester Park Gdns EH12 ... 121 E2
Forrester Park Gn EH12 ... 121 E2
Forrester Park Gr EH12 ... 121 E2
Forrester Park Loan EH12 ... 121 E2
Forrester Park Rd EH12 ... 121 E2
Forrester Pl FK2 ... 22 B2
Forrester Rd Armadale EH48 ... 143 F4
 Edinburgh EH12 ... 121 E2
Forrestfield Rd ML6 ... 141 D3
Fort Ho EH6 ... 93 F3
Fort St EH6 ... 93 F3
Forth Ave Kirkaldy KY2 ... 17 D2
 Larbert FK5 ... 38 A2
Forth Ave Ind Est KY2 ... 17 D2
Forth Cres Alloa FK10 ... 10 B3
 Dalgety Bay KY11 ... 48 A2
 High Valleyfield KY12 ... 26 A1
 Stirling FK8 ... 7 E4
Forth Ct
 Cockenzie & Port Seton EH32 ... 97 F2
 Dalgety Bay KY11 ... 48 A2
 Dunfermline KY12 ... 29 D1
 Stirling FK8 ... 2 A1
Forth Dr EH54 ... 148 A3
Forth Gdns
 Cockenzie & Port Seton EH32 ... 97 F2
 Oakley KY12 ... 26 C4
Forth Gr EH32 ... 97 F2
Forth Ind Est EH5 ... 92 C4
Forth Park Dr KY2 ... 17 D3
Forth Park Gdns KY2 ... 17 D3
Forth Park Maternity Hospl KY2 ... 17 D3
Forth Pl Bridge of A FK9 ... 2 A3
 Queensferry EH30 ... 89 F4
 Burntisland KY3 ... 50 C4
 Queensferry EH30 ... 46 C3
Forth Prim Sch ML11 ... 215 D1
Forth Rd KY11 ... 46 A1
Forth Reach KY11 ... 47 F1
Forth St Cambus FK10 ... 9 D4
 Dunfermline KY12 ... 29 D1
 Edinburgh EH1 ... 93 E1
 Fallin FK7 ... 8 B2
 Grangemouth FK3 ... 61 E4
 Kincardine FK10 ... 23 E2
 Stirling FK8 ... 7 D4
Forth Street La EH39 ... 54 B4
Forth Terr EH30 ... 89 E4
Forth View
 Dalgety Bay KY11 ... 48 A2
 Inverkeithing KY11 ... 47 D1
 Kincardine FK10 ... 23 F2
 Kirknewton EH27 ... 149 F2
 Stirling FK8 ... 2 A1
 West Barns EH42 ... 77 F1
Forth View Ave EH14 ... 148 C1
Forth View Cotts KY12 ... 26 A1
Forth View Cres
 Currie EH14 ... 151 F2
 Danderhall EH22 ... 156 A4
Forth View Ind Est KY12 ... 26 A1
Forth View Rd EH14 ... 151 F2
Forth Wynd EH32 ... 97 F2
Forthbank Ind Est FK10 ... 10 A2
Forthbank Rd KY12 ... 25 F1
Forthbank (Stirling Albion FC) FK2 ... 7 F4
Forthside Terr KY11 ... 68 B3
Forthvale FK11 ... 4 A3
Forthview FK7 ... 7 F1
Forthview Ave EH21 ... 127 D2
Forthview Cres
 Bo'ness EH51 ... 63 F3
 Musselburgh EH21 ... 127 D3
 Redding FK1, FK2 ... 61 F1
Forthview Ct EH21 ... 127 D3
Forthview Gdns FK2 ... 82 A4
Forthview Rd
 Edinburgh EH4 ... 92 B1
 Longniddry EH32 ... 98 C3
Forthview Terr
 Edinburgh EH4 ... 92 A1
 Reddingmuirhead FK2 ... 82 A4
 Wallyford EH21 ... 127 D2
Forties Rd KY12 ... 44 C3
Fortingall Cres FK2 ... 62 A1
Fortissat Ave ML7 ... 191 E3
Fortissat Rd ML7 ... 167 D1

Fortuna Ct FK1 ... 60 B2
Forster Gr FK10 ... 4 C1
Forvie Pl KY11 ... 48 A2
Foulden Pl KY12 ... 29 E2
Foulford Pl KY4 ... 13 D2
Foulford Prim Sch KY4 ... 13 D3
Foulford Rd KY4 ... 13 D2
Foulford St KY4 ... 13 E2
Foulshiels Rd EH47 ... 171 E1
Fountain Cl EH1 ... 233 E2
Foundry La EH20 ... 155 E1
Foundry Loan FK5 ... 38 A1
Foundry Rd
 Bonnybridge FK4 ... 58 A3
 Shieldhill ... 191 F2
Foundry St
 Dunfermline KY12 ... 29 D2
Fountain Pl EH20 ... 181 E4
Fountain Rd FK9 ... 2 A2
Fountainbridge EH3 ... 232 A1
Fountainhall Rd EH9 ... 123 F2
Fountainhead Rd EH48 ... 145 D4
Fountainpark Cres EH51 ... 64 B4
Fourth Gait EH14 ... 151 F4
Fourth St EH22 ... 183 D3
Fowler Cres
 Loanhead EH20 ... 181 E4
 Maddiston FK2 ... 83 D3
Fowler Pl FK2 ... 61 F2
Fowler St EH33 ... 128 B4
Fowler Terr EH11 ... 122 C3
Fowlers Ct EH32 ... 96 C1
Fox Covert Ave EH12 ... 91 F1
Fox Covert Gr EH12 ... 91 F1
Fox Covert RC Prim Schs EH12 ... 91 F1
Fox Spring Cres EH10 ... 154 A4
Fox Spring Rise EH10 ... 154 A4
Fox St EH6 ... 94 A3
Foxknowe Pl EH54 ... 147 D2
Franchi Dr FK5 ... 38 C3
Francis Ct KY5 ... 28 B3
Francis St KY5 ... 14 A4
Frankfield Cres KY11 ... 48 B2
Frankfield Pl KY11 ... 48 B2
Frankfield Rd KY11 ... 48 B2
Fraser Ave Edinburgh EH5 ... 93 D3
 Inverkeithing KY11 ... 47 E1
Fraser Cres EH5 ... 93 D3
Fraser Dr KY5 ... 14 A4
Fraser Gdns EH5 ... 93 D3
Fraser Gr EH5 ... 93 D3
Fraser Pl Dysart KY1 ... 18 A4
 Grangemouth FK3 ... 61 E3
 Stirling FK9 ... 2 A2
Fraser Rd EH54 ... 146 C1
Frederick Cres KY11 ... 29 D1
Frederick St EH2 ... 232 C4
Freeland Ave EH52 ... 117 D3
Freelands Rd
 Edinburgh EH28 ... 120 A2
 Ratho EH28 ... 119 F2
Freeport Village EH55 ... 172 A2
Fremantle St EH54 ... 148 A3
Freskyn Pl EH52 ... 118 A3
Frew Ct KY11 ... 29 E1
Friar's Croft EH42 ... 78 B1
Friars Brae EH49 ... 85 D3
Friars Loan EH49 ... 85 D3
Friars St FK8 ... 7 D4
Friars Way EH49 ... 85 D3
Friarton Gdns EH26 ... 203 E3
Friendship Gdns FK2 ... 39 E2
Frobisher Ave FK1 ... 59 F2
Frogston Ave EH10 ... 154 A3
Frogston Brae EH17 ... 154 C2
Frogston Gdns EH10 ... 154 B3
Frogston Gr EH10 ... 154 B3
Frogston Rd E EH17 ... 154 C3
Frogston Rd W EH10 ... 154 B2
Frogston Terr EH10 ... 154 B3
Fullerton Dr FK2 ... 61 F2
Fulmar Brae EH54 ... 147 E3
Fulmar Way KY11 ... 48 A2
Furcheons Pk EH8 ... 124 C4
Furnace La EH51 ... 64 B4
Furnace Pl KY4 ... 13 F3
Furniss Ave KY11 ... 46 B3
Fyne La ML7 ... 191 F3

Gaberston Ave FK10 ... 10 B4
Gagarin Way KY4 ... 13 F4
Gair Cres ML8 ... 230 A2
Gair Rd ML8 ... 230 A3
Gair Wynd ML7 ... 192 A2
Gairdoch Dr FK2 ... 39 E2
Gairdoch St FK2 ... 60 A4
Gairloch Cres FK2 ... 22 B2
Gala Gn EH42 ... 78 A1
Galabraes Cres EH48 ... 145 E4
Galachlawshot EH10 ... 154 B3
Galachlawside EH10 ... 154 B3
Galadale EH22 ... 183 D3
Galadale Cres EH22 ... 183 D3
Galadale Dr EH22 ... 183 D3
Gallacher Pl KY4 ... 13 F3
Gallagher Gn EH54 ... 147 E4
Gallamuir Dr FK7 ... 20 B2
Gallamuir Rd FK7 ... 20 B3
Galloolee The EH13 ... 153 E3
Gallow View EH52 ... 88 A4
Galloway Ct FK1 ... 60 A3
Galloway St FK1 ... 60 A3
Gallows Loan KY12 ... 25 E1
Galmeilen EH52 ... 117 E3
Galt Ave EH21 ... 127 D3
Galt Cres EH21 ... 127 D3
Galt Dr EH21 ... 127 D3

Galt Rd EH21 .... 127 D3
Galt Terr EH21 .... 127 D3
Gambeson Cres FK7 .... 7 E2
Gamekeeper's Loan EH4 .... 91 D3
Gamekeeper's Pk EH4 .... 91 D3
Gamekeeper's Rd EH4 .... 91 D3
Garbett Rd EH54 .... 147 E1
Garden City EH47 .... 171 D1
Garden Pl Cairneyhill KY12 ...... 29 E4
Garden Pl Cairneyhill KY12 ...... 27 E1
Clackmannan FK10 .... 11 D2
Livingston EH54 .... 147 E2
Townhill KY12 .... 29 E4
Garden St FK1 .... 60 B3
Garden Terr
Clackmannan FK10 .... 11 D2
Edinburgh EH4 .... 91 F2
Falkirk FK1 .... 60 B3
Westquarter FK2 .... 61 D1
Gardener Rd EH42 .... 78 B1
Gardener St EH42 .... 78 B2
Gardener's Wlk EH26 .... 203 E3
Gardeners' La KY12 .... 29 D2
Gardeners' St KY12 .... 29 D2
Gardenhead FK2 .... 61 F1
Gardens The Aberlady EH32 .. 71 E3
Dirleton EH39 .... 53 D3
Gardiner Cres EH32 .... 97 D1
Gardiner Gr EH4 .... 92 A1
Gardiner Pl
Cowdenbeath KY4 .... 13 D1
Newtongrange EH22 .... 183 D3
Gardiner Rd
Cowdenbeath KY4 .... 13 E1
Edinburgh EH4 .... 92 A1
Prestonpans EH32 .... 97 D1
Gardiner St KY5 .... 14 A4
Gardiner Terr
Edinburgh EH4 .... 92 A1
Tranent EH33 .... 128 A4
Gardner Cres EH3 .... 169 F3
Gardner Terr EH11 .... 171 D1
Gardner's Cres EH3 .... 232 B2
Gardners La EH48 .... 145 D3
Gardum Gdns KY7 .... 81 E4
Gardrum Pl FK2 .... 82 C4
Gareloch Way EH47 .... 170 B4
Garleton Ct EH31 .... 52 A1
Garleton Dr EH41 .... 100 C1
Garngrew Rd FK4 .... 57 D2
Garrison EH1 .... 60 A3
Garry Pl Falkirk FK1 .... 60 B1
Grangemouth FK3 .... 61 F3
Garry St KY5 .... 14 A4
Garry Wlk ML7 .... 191 F3
Garry Wlk EH48 .... 148 A2
Garscube Terr EH12 .... 122 B4
Gartclush Gdns FK7 .... 19 F4
Gartcows Ave FK1 .... 60 A2
Gartcows Cres FK1 .... 60 A2
Gartcows Dr FK1 .... 60 A2
Gartcows Gdns FK1 .... 59 F2
Gartcows Pl FK1 .... 60 A2
Gartcows Rd FK1 .... 60 A2
Garten Dr ML7 .... 192 A2
Garthill Gdns FK1 .... 60 A2
Garthill La FK1 .... 60 A2
Gartmorn Rd FK10 .... 5 E1
Garvald La FK6 .... 36 B1
Garvald Rd FK6 .... 57 E4
Garvally Cres FK10 .... 10 A4
Garvock Bank KY11 .... 29 F2
Garvock Hill KY12 .... 29 E2
Garvock Terr KY12 .... 29 E2
Gas Wynd KY1 .... 17 D1
Gasworks La
North Berwick EH39 .... 53 F3
Whitburn EH47 .... 170 A4
Gateside Ave
Bonnybridge FK4 .... 58 B3
Haddington EH41 .... 100 B1
Gateside Ct KY4 .... 13 D2
Gateside Ind Est KY4 .... 13 D2
Gateside Rd
Haddington EH41 .... 131 E4
Kirkliston EH29 .... 89 D1
Stirling FK7 .... 7 D3
Whitburn EH47 .... 169 F3
Gauger's Bush EH42 .... 76 A4
Gauze Pl EH51 .... 64 A3
Gauze Rd EH51 .... 64 A3
Gavin Pl EH54 .... 147 D3
Gavins Rd FK10 .... 4 C1
Gayfield Cl 8 EH1 .... 93 F1
Gayfield Place La EH1 .... 93 F1
Gayfield Sq EH1 .... 93 F1
Gayfield St EH1 .... 93 F1
Gayfield Street La 7 EH1 .. 93 F1
Gaynor Ave EH20 .... 181 D4
Gean Rd FK10 .... 9 F4
Gellatly Rd KY11 .... 29 E1
Gelnorchy Terr EH9 .... 123 F2
George Ave EH20 .... 181 D4
George Cres
Loanhead EH20 .... 181 D4
Ormiston EH35 .... 159 E4
George Dr EH20 .... 181 E4
George Heriot's Sch EH3 .. 232 C2
George IV Bridge EH1 .... 233 D2
George Sq EH8 .... 233 D1
George Square La EH8 .... 233 D1
George St Alva FK12 .... 5 D3
Armadale EH48 .... 143 F3
Bathgate EH48 .... 145 D3
Bo'ness EH51 .... 63 F3
Cowdenbeath KY4 .... 13 D2
Dunfermline KY11 .... 29 D1
Edinburgh EH2 .... 232 C3

George St continued
Falkirk FK1 .... 60 A3
Grangemouth FK3 .... 61 F4
Kincardine FK10 .... 23 F2
Kirkaldy KY1 .... 17 D2
Larbert FK5 .... 38 B2
Laurieston FK2 .... 60 C2
Ormiston EH35 .... 159 F4
George Terr EH20 .... 181 D4
George Watson's Coll
EH10 .... 122 C2
George Watson's Coll
Lower Prim Sch EH10 .. 122 C2
George Watson's Coll
Upper Prim Sch EH10 .. 122 C2
George Way EH33 .... 128 B3
George Wlk EH33 .... 128 B3
Gerald Terr FK5 .... 38 C2
Gib Gr KY11 .... 29 F1
Gibbdun Pl FK6 .... 57 F4
Gibbs Entry EH8 .... 233 E2
Gibbshill Pl FK7 .... 168 B3
Gibraltar Ct EH22 .... 157 D2
Gibraltar Gdns EH22 .... 157 D2
Gibraltar Rd EH22 .... 157 D2
Gibraltar Terr EH22 .... 157 D2
Gibson Dr EH22 .... 157 E2
Gibson St EH7 .... 93 F2
Gibson Terr EH11 .... 232 A1
Gibsongray St FK2 .... 60 A4
Gideon Ct EH48 .... 145 D4
Gideon St EH48 .... 145 D4
Gifford Pk EH8 .... 233 E1
Gifford Rd EH41 .... 132 B4
Giffordgate EH41 .... 132 A4
Gilbertstoun EH15 .... 125 E3
Gilbertstoun Brig EH15 ...... 125 E3
Gilbertstoun Loan EH15 .. 125 E3
Gilbertstoun Pl EH15 .... 125 E3
Gilbertstoun Wynd EH15 .. 125 E3
Gilbert Ave EH39 .... 54 B3
Gilchrist Cres EH47 .... 170 A1
Gilchrist Dr FK1 .... 59 F2
Giles St EH6 .... 93 F3
Gilfillan Pl FK2 .... 39 E1
Gilfillan Rd KY11 .... 29 F2
Gill Pk FK6 .... 36 A3
Gill Way KY11 .... 46 B3
Gillespie Cres EH10 .... 232 B1
Gillespie Gr KY11 .... 29 F2
Gillespie Pl Bannockburn FK7 .. 7 D1
Edinburgh EH11 .... 232 B1
Gillespie Rd EH13 .... 152 C2
Gillespie St EH3 .... 232 B1
Gillespie Terr FK7 .... 20 B1
Gillie Ct KY11 .... 29 E1
Gillies Dr FK7 .... 7 E2
Gillies Hill FK7 .... 6 A3
Gillsland Rd EH10 .... 122 C2
Gilmerton Dykes Ave EH17 155 E3
Gilmerton Dykes Cres
EH17 .... 155 E3
Gilmerton Dykes Dr EH17 .. 155 E3
Gilmerton Dykes Gr EH17 .. 155 E3
Gilmerton Dykes Loan
EH17 .... 155 E3
Gilmerton Dykes Pl EH17 .. 155 E3
Gilmerton Dykes Rd EH17 .. 155 E3
Gilmerton Dykes St EH17 .. 155 E3
Gilmerton Dykes Terr
EH17 .... 155 E3
Gilmerton Dykes View
EH17 .... 155 E3
Gilmerton Pl EH17 .... 155 E3
Gilmerton Prim Sch EH17 .. 155 E3
Gilmerton Rd EH16, EH17 .. 155 E4
Gilmerton Road Rdbt
EH22 .... 156 B2
Gilmerton Station Rd
EH17 .... 155 F2
Gilmore Pk EH3 .... 232 A1
Gilmore Pl EH3 .... 123 D3
Gilmour Rd EH16 .... 123 F2
Gilmour St
Cowdenbeath KY4 .... 13 E3
Edinburgh EH8 .... 233 E2
Gilsay Ct FK1 .... 60 B1
Gilston Cres FK2 .... 62 A1
Gladney Sq KY1 .... 17 D1
Gladsmuir ML11 .... 215 D1
Gladsmuir Junc EH33 .... 130 A4
Gladstone Pl
Dunfermline KY12 .... 29 D3
Edinburgh EH6 .... 94 A2
Stirling FK8 .... 7 D3
Gladstone Terr EH9 .... 123 F3
Glaive Ave FK7 .... 7 E2
Glamis Gdns
Dalgety Bay KY11 .... 48 A2
Polmont FK2 .... 61 F1
Glamis Pl KY11 .... 48 A2
Glamis Rd Kinghorn KY3 ...... 34 C2
Kircaldy KY1 .... 16 B4
Glamis Terr KY3 .... 34 C2
Glasclune Ct EH39 .... 54 B4
Glasclune Gdns EH39 .... 54 B4
Glasgow Rd
Bannockburn FK7 .... 19 E4
Bathgate EH48 .... 144 C3
Denny FK6 .... 36 C1
Edinburgh EH12 .... 121 D3
Falkirk FK1 .... 59 E3
Longcroft FK4 .... 57 E2
Ratho Station EH28 .... 119 E3
Stirling FK7 .... 7 D1

Glaskhill Terr EH26 .... 203 F3
Glass Cres EH52 .... 87 F1
Glass Pl EH52 .... 87 F1
Glass Rd EH52 .... 87 F1
Glassel Park Rd EH32 .... 98 B2
Glasshouse Loan FK10 .... 10 A3
Glasswork St KY1 .... 17 D2
Glebe Ave Stirling FK8 .... 7 D4
Uphall EH52 .... 117 D2
Glebe Cres Alva FK12 .... 5 D4
Athelstaneford EH39 .... 101 F4
Stirling FK8 .... 7 D4
Glebe Ct EH47 .... 193 E3
Glebe Gdns
Edinburgh EH12 .... 121 E3
Prestonpans EH32 .... 96 C1
Glebe Gr EH12 .... 121 E3
Glebe Pk Inverkeithing KY11 .. 47 D1
Kirkaldy KY1 .... 17 E3
Glebe Pl
Bonnyrigg and Lasswade
EH18 .... 155 F1
Burntisland KY3 .... 33 F1
Kinghorn KY3 .... 34 C2
Glebe Rd Bathgate EH48 .. 145 E3
Edinburgh EH12 .... 121 E3
Kincardine FK10 .... 23 F3
Uphall EH52 .... 117 D2
West Calder EH55 .... 172 B1
Whitburn EH47 .... 170 A3
Glebe St Dalkeith EH22 .... 157 D2
Denny FK6 .... 36 C1
Falkirk FK1 .... 60 A3
Glebe Terr Alloa FK10 .... 4 C3
Edinburgh EH12 .... 121 E3
Haddington EH41 .... 101 D1
Inverkeithing KY11 .... 47 D1
Uphall EH52 .... 117 D2
Glebe The Aberdour KY3 .... 49 E4
Alva FK12 .... 5 D4
Clackmannan FK10 .... 11 D2
East Linton EH40 .... 103 F4
East Saltoun EH34 .... 161 E4
Edinburgh EH4 .... 91 D3
Kirkliston EH29 .... 89 D1
Linlithgow EH49 .... 85 D3
Pencaitland EH34 .... 160 C4
West Calder EH55 .... 172 B1
Gledhill Ave EH51 .... 64 B3
Glen Albyn Dr KY2 .... 16 A4
Glen Artney Gr KY11 .... 29 E1
Glen Avon Pl FK2 .... 82 C4
Glen Beasdale Ct KY11 .... 29 E1
Glen Brae FK1 .... 60 A2
Glen Bridge Pl KY12 .... 28 C2
Glen Bruar Pl KY2 .... 16 A4
Glen Clova Cres KY12 .... 27 E1
Glen Cres Falkirk FK1 .... 60 A1
Livingston EH54 .... 146 C3
Glen Ct EH54 .... 146 B3
Glen Fruin Gr KY11 .... 29 E1
Glen Isla Gr KY11 .... 29 E1
Glen Isla Rd KY2 .... 16 B4
Glen Lyon Ct FK2 .... 62 A1
Glen Moriston Dr KY12 .... 27 E1
Glen Nevis Dr KY11 .... 29 E1
Glen Ogle Ct FK2 .... 62 A1
Glen Pl EH26 .... 203 F3
Glen Rd Armadale EH48 ...... 143 F3
Bathgate EH48 .... 145 D4
Livingston EH54 .... 146 C3
Plean FK7 .... 20 B1
Shotts ML7 .... 191 F2
Torwood FK7 .... 37 E4
Glen St EH3 .... 233 D2
Glen Terr Denny FK6 .... 36 C2
Livingston EH54 .... 146 C3
Glen Tye Rd FK7 .... 7 F2
Glen View Bo'ness EH51 .... 63 E2
Dennyloanhead FK4 .... 57 E3
Glen View Cres EH23 .... 207 E4
Glen View Ct EH23 .... 207 E4
Glen View Rd EH23 .... 207 E4
Glen Way EH48 .... 145 D4
Glenafeoch Rd ML8 .... 230 A1
Glenallan Dr EH16 .... 124 A1
Glenallan Loan EH16 .... 124 A1
Glenalmond EH47 .... 170 B3
Glenalmond Ct
Broxburn EH52 .... 117 D3
Whitburn EH47 .... 170 B3
Glenalmond Terr EH48 .... 145 D4
Glenard View EH1 .... 64 B3
Glenavon Dr KY12 .... 27 E1
Glenavon Terr EH48 .... 145 D4
Glenbank EH1 .... 60 A1
Glenbervie Ave FK5 .... 38 A2
Glenbervie Cres FK5 .... 38 A2
Glenbervie Dr FK5 .... 38 A2
Glenbervie Gr KY11 .... 29 E1
Glenbervie Rd FK3 .... 61 F4
Glenbridge Ct KY12 .... 28 C2
Glenbrook EH14 .... 176 C4
Glenburn Gdns EH47 .... 170 B3
Glenburn Pl KY4 .... 13 E1
Glenburn Rd Falkirk FK1 .... 60 B1
North Berwick EH39 .... 54 B3
Glencairn Cres EH12 .... 122 C4
Glencairn St Falkirk FK1 .... 59 D3
Glencoe Rd Carluke ML8 ...... 230 A1
Stirling FK8 .... 2 A1
Glencorse Pk EH26 .... 204 B4
Glencorse Prim Sch EH26 180 A1

Glencoul Ave KY11 .... 48 A2
Glencross Gdns EH26 .... 203 D3
Glendenning Dr EH29 .... 89 D1
Glendevon Ave EH12 .... 122 A3
Glendevon Dr FK1 .... 1 C1
Glendevon Gdns EH12 .... 122 A3
Glendevon Gr EH12 .... 122 A3
Glendevon Pk
Edinburgh EH12 .... 122 A3
Winchburgh EH52 .... 87 F1
Glendevon Pl EH12 .... 122 A3
Glendevon Rd EH12 .... 122 A3
Glendevon Terr EH12 .... 122 A3
Glendinning Cres EH16 ...... 155 D4
Glendinning Dr EH29 .... 88 C1
Glendinning Pl EH29 .... 88 C1
Glendinning Rd EH29 .... 88 C1
Gleneagles Ct EH47 .... 170 B3
Gleneagles Way EH54 .... 146 C3
Glenesk Cres EH52 .... 156 C2
Glenfield Carnock KY12 .... 27 E1
Livingston EH54 .... 147 D2
Glenfield Ave KY11 .... 13 E3
Glenfield Cres KY4 .... 13 E3
Glenfield Ct KY4 .... 13 E3
Glenfield Gdns KY4 .... 13 E3
Glenfield Ind Est KY4 .... 13 E3
Glenfield Rd KY4 .... 13 E3
Glenfinlas St EH3 .... 232 B3
Glenfuir Rd FK1 .... 59 E3
Glenfuir St FK1 .... 59 E3
Glengairn Wlk KY11 .... 29 E1
Glengarry Cres FK1 .... 59 F1
Glengyle Terr EH3 .... 232 C1
Glenisla Gardens La EH9 .. 123 E2
Glenisla Gdns EH9 .... 123 E2
Glenkinchie Distillery
EH34 .... 160 C1
Glenlee Ave EH8 .... 94 C2
Glenlockhart Bank EH14 .. 122 B1
Glenlockhart Rd EH10 .... 122 C1
Glenlockhart Valley EH14 .. 122 B1
Glenmavis Cres ML8 .... 230 A1
Glenmavis Ct ML8 .... 230 A1
Glenmavis Dr EH48 .... 145 D4
Glenmore EH47 .... 170 B3
Glenmore Dr FK4 .... 57 F4
Glenmore St EH3 .... 233 E3
Glenochil Pk FK10 .... 4 C2
Glenochil Rd FK10 .... 60 A2
Glenochil Terr FK10 .... 4 C2
Glenogle Ct EH3 .... 93 D1
Glenogle Pl 1 EH3 .... 93 D1
Glenogle Rd EH3 .... 93 D1
Glenogle Terr EH3 .... 93 D1
Glenorchy Rd EH39 .... 54 A3
Glenpark Rd FK3 .... 61 F4
Glensburgh Rd KY11 .... 29 E1
Glenside Ct
Armadale EH48 .... 143 F3
Grangemouth FK3 .... 143 F3
Glenside Gdns EH48 .... 143 F3
Glentye Gdns FK1 .... 59 F1
Glenure Loan EH4 .... 91 E1
Glenvarloch Cres EH16 ...... 155 D4
Glenview Denny FK6 .... 36 A2
Menstrie FK11 .... 4 A3
Penicuik EH26 .... 203 F3
Glenview Cres EH47 .... 171 D1
Glenview Dr FK1 .... 59 F1
Glenview Rd EH47 .... 171 D1
Glenwinnel Rd FK12 .... 4 C4
Glenwood Dr EH48 .... 58 A1
Glenyards Rd FK4 .... 58 A3
Gloag Pl EH55 .... 172 B2
Globe Rd KY11 .... 46 B1
Gloucester La EH3 .... 232 B4
Gloucester Pl EH3 .... 232 B4
Gloucester Sq EH3 .... 232 B4
Gloucester St EH3 .... 232 B4
Glover's Ct KY3 .... 35 D2
Glowrorum Dr FK6 .... 57 F4
Glynwed Ct FK2 .... 60 A4
Godfrey Ave FK6 .... 36 B1
Godfrey Cres FK5 .... 38 B1
Goff Ave EH7 .... 94 C1
Gogar Loan KY9 .... 3 E3
Gogar Pl FK7 .... 7 E1
Gogar Rdbt EH12 .... 120 C3
Gogar Station Rd EH12 ...... 120 B1
Gogarbank Farm EH12 .... 120 B3
Gogarburn Hospl EH12 .... 120 B3
Gogarloch Haugh EH12 ...... 121 D3
Gogarloch Muir EH12 .... 121 D3
Gogarloch Rd EH12 .... 121 D3
Gogarloch Syke EH12 .... 121 D3
Gogarstone Rd EH28 .... 120 A3
Goldenacre Terr EH3 .... 93 D2
Goldenstones Ave EH42 .. 78 C1
Goldpark Pl EH54 .... 147 D2
Golf Course Rd
Bonnyrigg and Lasswade
EH19 .... 182 A4
Cowdenbeath KY4 .... 13 E3
Linlithgow EH49 .... 84 B3
Goil Ct EH54 .... 147 E1
Golf Dr EH52 .... 99 F2
Golf House Rd EH42 .... 78 C1
Goltdrum St KY12 .... 28 C1
Goodall Cres EH22 .... 116 A1
Goodall Pl EH22 .... 116 A1
Goodall's Pl EH54 .... 132 B4
Goodman Pl FK2 .... 82 C4
Goose Green Ave EH21 ...... 126 B4
Goose Green Cres EH21 ..... 126 B4

Goose Green Pl EH21 .... 126 B4
Goose Green Rd
Gullane EH31 .... 52 A1
Musselburgh EH21 .... 126 B4
Goosecroft Rd FK8 .... 7 D4
Gordon Ave
Bathgate EH48 .... 145 D3
Bonnyrigg and Lasswade
EH19 .... 181 F3
Gordon Cres Bridge of A FK9 .. 2 A2
Stirling FK8 .... 1 C1
Gordon Ct EH52 .... 117 F3
Gordon Dr FK10 .... 10 A4
Gordon Loan EH12 .... 121 F4
Gordon Pl FK1 .... 59 F3
Gordon Rd
Edinburgh EH12 .... 121 F4
Rosyth KY11 .... 46 A1
Gordon Terr
Dunfermline KY11 .... 29 D1
Edinburgh EH16 .... 124 A1
Gordon Way EH54 .... 147 E4
Gore Ave EH23 .... 207 E4
Gorebridge Prim Sch
EH23 .... 207 E4
Goremire Rd ML8 .... 230 A1
Gorgie Park Cl EH14 .... 122 B2
Gorgie Park Rd EH14 .... 122 B2
Gorgie Rd EH11 .... 122 B2
Gorrie St Denny FK6 .... 36 B1
Dunfermline KY11 .... 29 E1
Gorsebank EH54 .... 147 F3
Gort Pl FK3 .... 61 E3
Gorton Loan EH24 .... 181 E1
Gorton Pl EH24 .... 181 E1
Gorton Rd EH24 .... 181 E1
Goschen Pl EH51 .... 63 E2
Goschen Terr EH52 .... 117 D3
Gosford Ho KY10 .... 71 D1
Gosford Pl EH6 .... 93 E3
Gosford Rd
Cockenzie & Port Seton EH32 .. 97 E2
Longniddry EH32 .... 16 B4
Gote La EH30 .... 68 A1
Gourlaw Cotts EH24 .... 205 D4
Gourlay St KY2 .... 17 D2
Gourlaybank EH41 .... 101 D1
Gowan Ave FK1 .... 60 A3
Gowan Rd FK1 .... 60 A3
Gowanbank EH47 .... 193 F3
Gowanbrae Ct FK4 .... 29 E2
Gowanbrae Pl FK4 .... 29 E2
Gowanbrae Terr KY12 .... 29 E2
Gowanhill Gdns FK8 .... 1 C1
Gowandale Dr FK1 .... 110 A3
Grace St KY5 .... 14 B4
Gracefield Ct EH54 .... 126 A3
Gracemount Ave EH16 ...... 155 D4
Gracemount Dr EH16 .... 155 D3
Gracemount High Sch
EH16 .... 155 D3
Gracemount Pl EH16 .... 155 D3
Gracemount Prim Sch
EH16 .... 155 D3
Gracemount Rd EH16 .... 155 D3
Gracemount Sq EH16 .... 155 D3
Gracie Cres FK2 .... 8 B2
Gracie's Wynd EH48 .... 144 A3
Gradlon Pl FK1 .... 60 A2
Graeme High Sch FK1 .... 60 B2
Graeme Pl FK1 .... 59 F1
Graham Ave Larbert FK5 ...... 38 A2
Stirling FK9 .... 2 B2
Graham Cres EH51 .... 64 A4
Graham Ct EH47 .... 171 F4
Graham St Bridge of A FK9 .... 2 A2
Graham Terr FK2 .... 22 B2
Graham Way EH54 .... 147 E4
Graham's Rd FK6,FK2 .... 204 B4
Graham's Rd FK2 .... 60 B3
Grahamsdyke Ave EH51 .... 64 A4
Grahamsdyke La EH51 .... 58 A2
Grahamsdyke La EH51 .... 64 A4
Grahamsdyke Rd
Bo'ness EH51 .... 64 B3
Bathgate EH48 .... 58 A2
Grahamsdyke St FK2 .... 61 D2
Grahamsdyke Terr EH51 .... 64 A4
Grahamston Sta FK1 .... 60 B3
Graiglaw Pl EH52 .... 116 B1
Graigleith View FK10 .... 4 B2
Grainger St KY5 .... 14 A4
Grampian Cres FK3 .... 61 F3
Grampian Ct KY11 .... 46 C1
Grampian Gdns KY11 .... 16 C3
Grampian Pl KY11 .... 29 E2
Grampian Rd KY11 .... 46 C1
Grampian Rd Rosyth KY11 .... 46 C1
Stirling FK7 .... 6 C3
Grampion Ct EH54 .... 147 F1
Granary Rd FK2 .... 62 A1
Granary Sq FK2 .... 60 A4
Granby Ave EH54 .... 147 F2
Granby Rd EH16 .... 123 F2
Grandfield EH6 .... 93 E3
Grandville EH6 .... 93 E3

Grange Ave FK2 .... 60 B3
Grange Cotts KY3 .... 34 C3
Grange Cres EH9 .... 123 E2
Grange Cres EH32 .... 96 C1
Grange Cres W EH32 .... 127 F4
Grange Ct
  ⑤ Edinburgh EH9 .... 123 F3
  North Berwick EH39 .... 54 B3
Grange Dr
  Dunfermline KY11 .... 46 B4
  Falkirk FK2 .... 60 B3
Grange Gdns FK9 .... 2 B4
Grange Gr EH32 .... 96 C1
Grange Knowe EH49 .... 85 E4
Grange La FK3 .... 40 B1
Grange Loan Bo'ness EH51 .... 64 A4
  Edinburgh EH9 .... 123 E2
Grange Loan Gdns EH9 .... 123 E2
Grange Pk KY11 .... 46 B4
Grange Pl Grangemouth FK3 .... 61 E1
  Redding FK2 .... 61 E1
Grange Rd Alloa FK10 .... 9 F3
  Bridge of A FK9 .... 2 B3
  Broxburn EH52 .... 117 F2
  Burntisland KY3 .... 33 E1
  Dunfermline KY11 .... 46 B3
  Edinburgh EH9 .... 123 E3
  Livingston EH54 .... 148 A4
  North Berwick EH39 .... 54 A3
  Polmont FK2, FK3 .... 61 E2
  Prestonpans EH32 .... 96 C1
Grange Sch EH51 .... 64 A4
Grange Terr Bo'ness EH51 ..... 64 A4
  Edinburgh EH9 .... 123 E2
Grange The FK2 .... 82 C4
Grange View EH54 .... 85 E4
Grange Wynd KY11 .... 46 B4
Grangeburn Rd FK3 .... 40 C1
Grangemouth High Sch
  FK3 .... 61 F3
Grangemouth Rd FK2 .... 60 C3
Grangepans EH51 .... 64 A4
Grangeview FK5 .... 38 C1
Grannies Park Ind Est
  EH22 .... 157 D2
Grant Ave EH13 .... 153 D3
Grant Pl KY9 .... 2 A2
Grant St Alloa FK10 .... 9 F3
  West Calder EH55 .... 172 B2
Granton Cres EH5 .... 92 C3
Granton Gdns EH5 .... 92 C3
Granton Gr EH5 .... 92 C3
Granton Mains Ave EH4 .... 92 B3
Granton Mains Bank EH4 ...... 92 B3
Granton Mains Brae EH4 .... 92 B3
Granton Mains E EH4 .... 92 B3
Granton Mains E EH4 .... 92 B3
Granton Mains Gait EH4 .... 92 B3
Granton Mains Vale EH4 .... 92 B3
Granton Mains Wynd EH4 ...... 92 B3
Granton Medway EH5 .... 92 C3
Granton Park Ave EH5 .... 92 C4
Granton Pl EH5 .... 92 C3
Granton Prim Sch EH5 .... 92 C3
Granton Rd EH5 .... 93 D3
Granton Sq EH5 .... 92 C4
Granton Terr EH5 .... 92 C3
Granton View
  Dalgety Bay KY11 .... 47 F1
  Edinburgh EH5 .... 92 C3
Grants Bank KY12 .... 29 D2
Grantully Pl EH9 .... 123 F2
Granville Terr EH10 .... 123 D3
Granville Way KY11 .... 46 C2
Grassmarket EH1 .... 232 C2
Gray Buchanan Ct FK2 .... 61 E1
Gray Pk KY4 .... 13 E3
Gray Pl KY11 .... 47 E2
Gray St ML7 .... 192 A2
Gray's Ct EH8 .... 233 E2
Gray's Loan EH10 .... 122 C2
Graysmill Sch EH14 .... 122 B1
Graystale Rd FK7 .... 7 F1
Graystonelee Rd ML7 .... 191 E3
Great Cannon Bank EH15 ...... 95 D1
Great Carleton Pl EH16 .... 125 D2
Great Carleton Sq EH16 .... 125 D2
Great Junction St EH6 .... 93 F3
Great King St EH3 .... 93 E1
Great Michael Cl EH6 .... 93 E4
Great Michael Rd KY11 .... 46 A1
Great Michael Rise EH6 .... 93 E3
Great Michael Sq EH6 .... 93 E4
Great Stuart St EH3 .... 232 A3
Green Apron Pk EH54 .... 54 A3
Green La
  Bonnyrigg and Lasswade
    EH18 .... 181 F4
  Grangemouth FK3 .... 61 F4
Green St Edinburgh EH7 .... 93 E1
  Townhill KY12 .... 29 E4
Green The Alva FK12 .... 5 D4
  Bathgate EH48 .... 145 E4
  Edinburgh EH4 .... 91 F2
  Pencaitland EH34 .... 160 C3
  West Barns EH42 .... 77 F1
Green Tree La EH51 .... 63 E3
Greenacre EH14 .... 152 C4
Greenacre Ct FK7 .... 7 F1
Greenacre Pl FK7 .... 7 F1
Greenbank Ave EH10 .... 123 D1
Greenbank Cres EH10 .... 154 A4
Greenbank Dr
  Cowdenbeath KY4 .... 13 D1
  Edinburgh EH10 .... 123 D1

Greenbank Gdns EH10 .... 153 F4
Greenbank Gr EH10 .... 153 F4
Greenbank La EH10 .... 122 C1
Greenbank Loan EH10 .... 122 C1
Greenbank Pl EH10 .... 153 F4
Greenbank Pl
  Edinburgh EH10 .... 123 D1
  Falkirk FK1 .... 59 E2
Greenbank Rd
  Edinburgh EH10 .... 122 C1
  Falkirk FK1 .... 59 E2
Greenbank Rise EH10 .... 153 F4
Greenbank Row EH10 .... 153 F4
Greenbank Terr EH10 .... 123 D1
Greenburn Rd EH47 .... 193 F3
Greencraig Ave FK1 .... 81 E3
Greendykes Ave EH16 .... 124 C2
Greendykes Dr EH16 .... 124 C2
Greendykes Gdns EH16 .... 124 C2
Greendykes Ind Est EH52 ..... 117 E3
Greendykes Loan ⑦
  EH16 .... 124 C2
Greendykes Prim Sch
  EH16 .... 124 C2
Greendykes Rd
  Broxburn EH52 .... 117 F3
  Edinburgh EH16 .... 124 C1
Greendykes Steadings
  EH52 .... 117 F4
Greendykes Terr EH16 .... 124 C2
Greenend Dr EH17 .... 155 E4
Greenend Gdns EH17 .... 155 E4
Greenend Gr EH17 .... 155 E4
Greenfield Cres EH14 .... 177 E4
Greenfield Rd EH14 .... 177 E4
Greenfield St Alloa FK10 .... 10 A4
  Bonnybridge FK4 .... 58 A3
Greenhall Rd EH23 .... 183 E1
Greenhead FK12 .... 5 D3
Greenheads Rd EH39 .... 54 C3
Greenhill Ct
  Bonnybridge FK4 .... 58 A1
  Edinburgh EH10 .... 123 D3
  Fauldhouse EH47 .... 193 F3
Greenhill Gdns EH10 .... 123 D2
Greenhill Pk
  Edinburgh EH10 .... 123 D2
  Penicuik EH26 .... 203 E3
Greenhill Pl EH10 .... 123 D2
Greenhill Rd
  Blackridge EH48 .... 142 C2
  Bonnybridge FK4 .... 58 A2
Greenhill Terr EH10 .... 123 D3
Greenhill Terr FK2 .... 82 C4
Greenhithe Terr FK2 .... 82 C4
Greenhorn's Well Ave FK1 ..... 59 F2
Greenhorn's Well Cres
  FK1 .... 59 F2
Greenhorn's Well Dr FK1 ...... 59 F2
Greenlaw Gr EH26 .... 180 A1
Greenlaw Hedge EH13 .... 153 F4
Greenlaw Rig EH13 .... 153 F4
Greenloanings KY2 .... 16 B4
Greenmantle Loan ⑨
  EH16 .... 124 A1
Greenmount KY4 .... 13 D1
Greenmount Dr
  Burntisland KY3 .... 33 F1
  Shieldhill FK1 .... 81 E3
Greenmount Rd N KY3 .... 33 F1
Greenmount Rd S KY3 .... 34 A1
Greenpark Dr FK2 .... 82 C4
Greenrigg Cotts ML7 .... 169 D3
Greenrigg Prim Sch ML7 .... 168 C3
Greens The FK2 .... 82 C3
Greenside EH48 .... 113 F3
Greenside La EH1 .... 233 E4
Greenside Pl
  Edinburgh EH1 .... 233 E4
  Rosewell EH24 .... 181 E1
Greenside Row EH1 .... 233 E4
Greenside St FK10 .... 10 A3
Greenvale Dr FK2 .... 82 C4
Greenville Ct FK1 .... 59 F2
Greenwell St EH47 .... 193 F3
Greenwell Terr EH32 .... 82 C4
Greenwells Dr FK2 .... 82 C4
Greenwood Ave FK8 .... 7 D4
Greenwood Pk EH54 .... 147 E3
Greenwood St ML7 .... 191 F3
Gregory Rd EH54 .... 173 D4
Greig Cres EH48 .... 144 A3
Greig Pl KY5 .... 14 A4
Greig Rd KY1 .... 46 A1
Grendon Ct FK8 .... 7 D3
Grendon Gdns FK8 .... 7 D3
Grey Craigs KY12 .... 27 E1
Grey School Cnr EH32 .... 96 C1
Greyfriar's Wlk KY11 .... 47 E2
Greyfriars EH1 .... 233 D2
Greyfriars Bobby Meml
  EH1 .... 233 D2
Greygoran FK10 .... 5 E1
Grierson Ave EH5 .... 93 D3
Grierson Cres
  Cambusbarron FK7 .... 6 B3
  Edinburgh EH5 .... 93 D3
Grierson Gdns EH5 .... 93 D3
Grierson Rd EH5 .... 92 C3
Grierson Sq EH5 .... 93 D3
Grierson Villas EH5 .... 93 D3
Grieve Ct EH26 .... 203 F4
Grieve St Dunfermline KY12 ... 28 C2
  Kirkcaldy KY2 .... 17 D3
Griffith Dr EH47 .... 162 A1
Griffiths St FK1 .... 60 A2
Grigor Ave EH4 .... 92 B2
Grigor Dr EH4 .... 92 B2
Grigor Gdns EH4 .... 92 C2

Grigor Terr EH4 .... 92 B2
Grindlay St EH3 .... 232 B2
Grindlay Street Ct EH3 .... 232 B2
Groathill Ave EH4 .... 92 B1
Groathill Gdns E ② EH4 .... 92 B1
Groathill Gdns W ① EH4 ...... 92 B1
Groathill Rd N EH4 .... 92 B2
Groathill Rd S EH4 .... 92 B1
Grodwell Dr FK12 .... 4 C4
Grosvenor Gdns EH12 .... 122 C4
Grosvenor St EH12 .... 232 A2
Grove Cres FK2 .... 39 D1
Grove End EH18 .... 182 A4
Grove St Denny FK6 .... 36 B1
  Edinburgh EH3 .... 232 A2
  Musselburgh EH21 .... 126 B3
Grove The EH21 .... 126 C3
Grundie's Well Rd EH17 .... 155 F3
Guardians Wood EH12 .... 122 B4
Guardwell Cres EH17 .... 155 E4
Guildhall St KY12 .... 29 D2
Guildie Howes Rd EH23 .... 207 F1
Guildiehaugh Rdbt EH48 ...... 145 E3
Guildry Gr KY12 .... 29 F2
Gullan's Cl EH1 .... 233 E3
Gullane Prim Sch EH31 .... 52 A1
Gunn Rd FK3 .... 61 E3
Gunner Rd FK3 .... 62 A4
Guthrie St EH1 .... 233 D2
Guttergates Rd KY11 .... 30 A3
Gyle Ave EH12 .... 120 C3
Gyle Park Gdns EH12 .... 121 D3
Gyle Rdbt EH12 .... 120 C3
Gyle Sh Ctr EH12 .... 121 D3
Gylemuir Prim Sch EH12 ...... 121 E3
Gylemuir Rd EH12 .... 121 E3
Gylers Rd EH39 .... 53 D3

Haddington Inf Sch
  EH41 .... 132 A4
Haddington Pl EH7 .... 93 F1
Haddington Rd
  East Linton EH40 .... 103 E4
  Musselburgh EH21 .... 127 D3
  North Berwick EH39 .... 54 B3
  Tranent EH33 .... 128 C3
Haddington Station
  Ind Est EH41 .... 131 F4
Haddon's Ct EH8 .... 233 E2
Haddow Gr KY3 .... 50 B4
Hadfast Rd EH22 .... 158 B3
Hadrian Way EH51 .... 64 A3
Haig Ave Kirkaldy KY1 .... 17 E4
  Dunfermline KY12 .... 28 C2
Haig St EH3 .... 61 E3
Hailes App EH13 .... 153 D4
Hailes Ave EH13 .... 153 D4
Hailes Bank EH13 .... 153 D4
Hailes Castle EH41 .... 103 D2
Hailes Cres EH13 .... 153 D4
Hailes Gdns EH13 .... 153 D4
Hailes Gr EH13 .... 153 D4
Hailes Loan EH41 .... 103 D2
Hailes Pk EH13 .... 153 D4
Hailes Pl EH29 .... 89 E2
Hailes St EH3 .... 232 B1
Hailes Terr EH13 .... 153 D4
Hailesland Gdns EH14 .... 121 F1
Hailesland Gr EH14 .... 121 F1
Hailesland Pk EH14 .... 121 F1
Hailesland Pl EH14 .... 121 F1
Hailesland Prim Sch
  EH14 .... 152 C4
Hailesland Rd EH14 .... 121 F1
Hailstonegreen ML11 .... 215 D1
Hailstones Cres EH48 .... 143 F3
Hainburn Pk EH10 .... 153 F3
Haining Gr FK2 .... 83 D3
Haining Pl
  Grangemouth FK3 .... 61 F4
  Livingston EH54 .... 147 D3
Haining Rd EH49 .... 83 F3
Haining Terr EH49 .... 83 F3
Hakness Cres EH33 .... 128 B3
Halbeath Dr KY11 .... 29 F3
Halbeath Pl KY11 .... 29 F3
Halbeath Rd
  Dunfermline KY11 .... 29 F3
  Halbeath KY11 .... 30 A3
Halbeath Ret Pk KY11 .... 30 A3
Halberts Cres FK7 .... 7 D1
Haldane Ave Bridge of A FK9 .. 2 A3
  Haddington EH41 .... 100 C1
Haldane Gr KY12 .... 26 B4
Haldane Sq EH54 .... 173 E3
Halkettshall KY1 .... 48 A1
Halkett Cres KY11 .... 29 E1
Hall Cres EH31 .... 52 A1
Hall Dr KY5 .... 14 A4
Hall Rd EH52 .... 117 F3
Hall Row KY11 .... 45 D2
Hall St Cowdenbeath KY4 .... 13 E2
  Lochgelly KY5 .... 14 B4
Hallcraigs EH27 .... 149 F2
Hallcroft Cl EH28 .... 119 E1
Hallcroft Cres EH28 .... 119 E1
Hallcroft Gdns EH28 .... 119 E1
Hallcroft Grn EH28 .... 119 E1
Hallcroft Neuk EH28 .... 119 E1
Hallcroft Pk EH28 .... 119 E1
Hallcroft Rise EH28 .... 119 E1
Hallglen Pk EH4 .... 60 A1
Hallglen Rd FK1 .... 60 A1
Hallglen Terr EH41 .... 60 A1
Hallhead Rd EH16 .... 123 F1
Hallhill EH42 .... 106 B4

Halliburton Terr EH39 .... 53 D2
Hallows The KY1 .... 17 F4
Hallpark FK10 .... 10 B4
Hallyards Rd
  Newbridge EH29 .... 119 D4
  Ratho Station EH28 .... 119 E3
Halmyre St EH6 .... 94 A2
Halyard Rise KY11 .... 47 F1
Halyard Terr KY2 .... 15 D1
Hamburgh Pl EH6 .... 93 F3
Hamilton Ave
  Linlithgow EH49 .... 84 C3
  Stenhousemuir FK5 .... 38 C2
Hamilton Cres
  Gullane EH31 .... 52 A1
  Maddiston FK2 .... 82 C3
  Newtongrange EH22 .... 183 D3
Hamilton Dr
  Edinburgh EH15 .... 124 C4
  Falkirk FK1 .... 60 A2
  Stirling FK9 .... 2 B2
Hamilton Dr W EH15 .... 124 C4
Hamilton Gdns EH15 .... 124 C4
Hamilton Gr EH15 .... 124 C4
Hamilton La
  Bathgate EH48 .... 144 C4
  Bo'ness EH51 .... 64 A4
Hamilton Pk
  Edinburgh EH15 .... 124 C4
  Linlithgow EH49 .... 84 C3
  Rosyth KY11 .... 46 C2
Hamilton Rd
  Bathgate EH48 .... 144 C4
  Grangemouth FK3 .... 61 F3
  Gullane EH31 .... 52 A1
  Larbert FK2 .... 38 B3
  North Berwick EH39 .... 54 A4
  Stirling FK9 .... 2 B2
Hamilton St Falkirk FK1 .... 59 E3
  Lochgelly KY5 .... 14 A3
Hamilton Terr
  Edinburgh EH15 .... 125 D4
  High Valleyfield KY12 .... 26 A1
  Inverkeithing KY11 .... 47 D2
Hamilton Wynd EH6 .... 93 F3
Hammermen's Entry EH8 ...... 233 E3
Handax ML11 .... 215 D1
Nancy's Way EH51 .... 64 A4
Hanover Ct Broxburn EH52 .... 117 F3
  Livingston EH54 .... 147 D2
Hanover Grange EH2 .... 61 E4
Hanover St EH2 .... 232 C4
Harbour Dr KY11 .... 47 F2
Harbour Pl EH15 .... 95 D1
  Inverkeithing KY11 .... 47 E2
Harbour Rd Bo'ness EH51 ...... 64 B4
  Edinburgh EH15 .... 95 D1
  Kinghorn KY3 .... 35 D1
  Musselburgh EH21 .... 126 A3
Harburn Ave EH54 .... 146 C3
Harburn Ave W EH54 .... 146 C4
Harburn Cres EH55 .... 172 C2
Harburn Gdns EH55 .... 172 C2
Harburn La EH55 .... 172 C2
Harburn Rd EH55 .... 172 C2
Harcourt Rd KY2 .... 17 D3
Hardengreen Bsns Ctr
  EH22 .... 156 C1
Hardengreen Ind Est
  EH22 .... 156 C1
Hardengreen Junc EH22 .... 182 C4
Hardgate EH41 .... 101 D1
Hardgate Ct EH41 .... 101 D1
Hardhill Dr EH48 .... 144 C3
Hardhill Pl EH48 .... 144 A3
Hardhill Rd EH48 .... 144 C3
Hardhill Terr EH48 .... 144 C3
Hardie Cres FK7 .... 8 B2
Hardie Ct FK7 .... 7 D2
Hardie Rd EH54 .... 146 B4
Hardie Terr EH40 .... 103 E4
Hardwell Cl EH8 .... 233 E2
Hardy Gdns EH48 .... 145 F3
Hareburn Ave FK1 .... 112 A3
Harelaw Rd EH13 .... 153 D3
Hares Cl EH32 .... 97 E2
Harestanes Rd EH48 .... 143 F2
Harewood Cres EH16 .... 124 C2
Harewood Dr EH16 .... 124 C2
Harewood Rd EH16 .... 124 C2
Harkenburn Gdns EH26 .... 203 E3
Harlaw Gr EH26 .... 203 E3
Harlaw Hill EH32 .... 96 C1
Harlaw March EH14 .... 177 E4
Harlaw Rd Balerno EH14 .... 177 F4
  Currie EH14 .... 152 A1
Harlawhill Gdns EH32 .... 97 D1
Harley Ct FK2 .... 82 C4
Harley St KY11 .... 47 D2
Harlington Pl FK2 .... 82 C4
Harlow Ave FK2 .... 61 E1
Harmeny Sch EH14 .... 177 E4
Harness Ct EH20 .... 181 E4
Harpenside Cres EH39 .... 53 E3
Harper's Brae EH26 .... 204 A3
Harperdean Terr EH41 .... 100 C1
Harriebrae Pk KY12 .... 28 C2
Harriet St KY1 .... 17 E4
Harris Dr KY7 .... 16 C4
Harris Pl Dunfermline KY11 .... 29 F1
  Grangemouth FK3 .... 61 E3
Harrismith Pl EH7 .... 94 A1

Harrison Gdns EH11 .... 122 C2
Harrison La EH11 .... 122 C3
Harrison Pl
  Edinburgh EH11 .... 122 C2
  Falkirk FK1 .... 59 F3
Harrison Rd EH11 .... 122 C3
Harrysmuir Cres EH53 .... 148 A4
Harrysmuir N EH53 .... 148 A4
Harrysmuir Prim Sch EH53 .. 147 F3
Harrysmuir Rd EH53 .... 148 A4
Harrysmuir S EH53 .... 148 A4
Harrysmuir Terr EH53 .... 148 A4
Hart St EH1 .... 93 E1
Hart Street La EH1 .... 93 E1
Hart Wynd FK7 .... 7 F1
Hartfield Terr ML7 .... 212 A4
Harthill Rd
  Blackridge EH48 .... 142 B1
  Fauldhouse EH47 .... 193 E3
Hartington Gdns EH10 .... 123 D3
Hartington Pl EH10 .... 123 D3
Hartley Pl FK3 .... 61 D3
Hartshill Prim Sch ML7 .... 168 C3
Hartwood Gdns ML7 .... 191 D1
Hartwood Rd Shotts ML7 ...... 191 D1
  West Calder EH55 .... 172 B1
Hartwoodhill Hospl ML7 .... 191 D3
Harvest Dr EH28 .... 119 D3
Harvest Rd EH28 .... 119 D3
Harvesters Way EH14 .... 152 B4
Harvey Ave FK2 .... 61 F1
Harvey Wynd FK8 .... 2 A1
Harvieston Villas EH23 .... 207 E4
Hatfield Pl ⑧ EH48 .... 145 D4
Hatton Pl EH9 .... 123 E3
Haugh Gdns FK2 .... 39 D1
Haugh Park EH14 .... 122 A1
Haugh Rd Burntisland KY3 .... 50 B4
  Stirling FK9 .... 2 A1
Haugh St Edinburgh EH4 .... 93 D1
  Falkirk FK2 .... 39 D1
Haven The KY11 .... 47 F1
Haven's Edge KY11 .... 45 F2
Hawes Brae EH30 .... 68 B1
Hawk Brae EH54 .... 147 F3
Hawkcraig Rd KY3 .... 49 E4
Hawkhead Cres EH16 .... 155 D4
Hawkhead Gr EH16 .... 155 D4
Hawkhill EH7 .... 94 A2
Hawkhill Ave EH7 .... 94 A2
Hawkhill Ct EH7 .... 94 A2
Hawkhill Rd Alloa FK10 .... 10 B3
  Kincardine FK10 .... 23 E3
Hawkins Terr EH26 .... 204 A4
Hawksmuir KY1 .... 17 E3
Hawkwood Terr ML11 .... 215 D1
Hawley Rd FK1 .... 60 B2
Hawthorn Bank
  Carnock KY12 .... 27 E3
  Queensferry EH30 .... 68 A1
  Seafield EH47 .... 172 A4
Hawthorn Cres
  Easthouses EH22 .... 183 E4
  Failin FK7 .... 8 B2
  Hill of B KY4 .... 12 C1
  Stirling FK8 .... 1 C1
Hawthorn Dr Denny FK6 .... 36 B2
  Falkirk FK1 .... 59 F2
  Failin FK7 .... 8 B2
  Harthill ML7 .... 168 C3
  Shotts ML7 .... 192 B2
Hawthorn Gdns EH20 .... 155 F3
Hawthorn Pl
  Edinburgh EH17 .... 155 F3
  Ormiston EH35 .... 159 E4
  Uphall EH52 .... 116 C2
Hawthorn Rd EH32 .... 97 D2
Hawthorn St FK3 .... 61 E3
Hawthorn Terr EH32 .... 97 D2
Hawthornbank La EH4 .... 232 A3
Hawthornbank Pl EH6 .... 93 E3
Hawthornbank Rd EH11 .... 100 C1
Hawthornden Terr EH6 .... 93 F3
Hawthornden Ave EH19 .... 182 A4
Hawthornden Gdns EH19 ...... 182 A4
Hawthornden Prim Sch
  EH19 .... 181 F3
Hawthorne Pl FK5 .... 38 B1
Hawthorne Terr The EH31 ..... 52 A2
Hawthornvale EH6 .... 93 E3
Hay Ave EH16 .... 124 C2
Hay Dr EH16 .... 125 D2
Hay Gr KY11 .... 29 F1
Hay Pl EH16 .... 124 C2
Hay Rd EH16 .... 124 C2
Hay Terr EH16 .... 124 C2
Hayfield Edinburgh EH12 ...... 121 D4
  Falkirk FK2 .... 60 B4
Hayfield Ind Est KY7 .... 17 D4
Hayfield Pl KY7 .... 17 E4
Hayfield Rd Falkirk FK2 .... 60 B4
  Kirkaldy KY1 .... 17 E4
Hayfield Terr FK6 .... 57 F4
Haygate Ave FK2 .... 82 C4
Haymarket EH12 .... 232 A2
Haymarket Sta EH12 .... 232 A2
Haymarket Terr EH12 .... 122 C4
Haypark Bsns Ctr FK2 .... 61 F1
Haypark Rd FK6 .... 57 E4
Hayworth Ave FK2 .... 61 D2
Hazel Ave KY2 .... 17 D3
Hazel Cres FK6 .... 36 B2
Hazel Ct EH42 .... 78 A1
Hazel Dr EH19 .... 182 A3
Hazel Gr Dunfermline KY11 ... 46 C4
  Falkirk FK2 .... 60 B4
  Livingston EH54 .... 148 A3
  Shotts ML7 .... 192 A2

Hazel La EH20 .... 180 C4
Hazel Rd FK3 .... 61 E3
Hazelbank Gdns FK8 .... 2 A1
Hazelbank Terr EH11 ...... 122 C2
Hazeldean Ave EH51 .... 63 E3
Hazeldean Terr EH16 ...... 122 A1
Hazelhurst FK2 .... 82 C4
Hazelwood Gr FK16 .... 124 B1
Head of Muir Prim Sch
  FK6 .... 57 E3
Headlesscross Rd ML7 .... 192 C1
Headrig Rd EH20 .... 71 E2
Headrigg Row EH16 .... 124 A1
Headwell Ave KY12 .... 29 D3
Headwell Rd KY12 .... 29 D3
Heaney Ave EH53 .... 148 A4
Heath Rd KY11 .... 46 C4
Heather Ave FK1 .... 81 E3
Heather Gr
  Dunfermline KY11 .... 46 C4
  Maddiston FK2 .... 83 D3
Heather Pk EH47 .... 146 A4
Heather Rise EH54 .... 147 E3
Heatherdale Gdns FK6 ...... 57 F4
Heathervale Wlk EH48 .... 144 A3
Heatherwood Pk EH53 .... 146 A4
Heathery The KY11 .... 46 C4
Hedge Row EH20 .... 180 C4
Hedges The FK1 .... 59 F3
Heggie's Wynd KY1 .... 17 D1
Heights Rd EH48 .... 142 B2
Helen Pl KY11 .... 48 B3
Helmsdale Pk KY12 .... 28 C1
Henderland Rd EH12 ...... 122 B4
Henderson Ave FK10 .... 10 A4
Henderson Cres EH52 ..... 117 D3
Henderson Ct EH53 .... 148 C2
Henderson Gdns
  Edinburgh EH6 .... 93 F3
  Tranent EH33 .... 128 B3
Henderson Pl Alva FK12 ..... 5 D4
  Broxburn EH52 .... 117 D3
  Edinburgh EH3 .... 93 E1
Henderson Place La EH3 .... 93 D1
Henderson Row EH3 .... 93 D1
Henderson St
  Bridge of A FK9 .... 2 A4
  Edinburgh EH6 .... 93 F3
  Kingseat KY12 .... 12 A1
  Lochgelly KY5 .... 14 A4
Henderson Terr EH11 ...... 122 C3
Hendry Cres KY2 .... 17 D3
Hendry Rd KY2 .... 17 D3
Hendry St FK2 .... 60 A4
Hendry's Wynd KY1 .... 17 D1
Hennings The FK10 .... 5 E1
Henry Ross Pl EH30 .... 68 A1
Henry St Alva FK12 .... 5 D3
  Bo'ness EH51 .... 64 A3
  Grangemouth FK3 .... 61 F4
Henryson Rd KY11 .... 29 F2
Hens Nest Rd EH47 .... 170 C3
Hens Nest Road Crofts
  EH47 .... 170 C2
Hepburn Dr EH22 .... 157 E1
Hepburn Rd EH41 .... 101 D1
Herald Rise EH54 .... 147 F1
Herbertshire St FK6 .... 36 C1
Hercus Loan EH21 .... 126 A3
Herd Gn EH14 .... 147 D4
Herd Terr EH20 .... 181 D4
Herdmanflatt EH41 .... 101 D1
Herdmanflatt Hospl
  EH41 .... 101 D1
Hershshill Ave FK1 .... 81 E3
Heriot Bridge EH1 .... 232 C2
Heriot Gdns KY3 .... 33 F1
Heriot Hill Terr EH7 .... 93 E2
Heriot Pl EH3 .... 232 C2
Heriot Row EH3 .... 232 B4
Heriot St KY11 .... 47 E1
Heriot Way EH38 .... 228 B1
Heriot-Watt Univ EH14 ... 151 F4
Heritage Dr FK2 .... 39 D2
Hermand Cres EH11 .... 122 A2
Hermand St EH11 .... 122 B2
Hermand Terr EH11 .... 122 B2
Hermiston Gait Ret Pk
  EH11 .... 121 D2
Hermiston House Rd
  EH14 .... 120 C1
Hermiston June EH11 ...... 121 D1
Hermitage Dr EH10 .... 123 D1
Hermitage Gdns EH10 .... 123 D1
Hermitage Park Gr FK6 ..... 94 A2
Hermitage Park Prim Sch
  EH6 .... 94 A2
Hermitage Pk EH6 .... 94 A2
Hermitage Pk S EH6 .... 94 A2
Hermitage Pl EH6 .... 94 A2
Hermitage Rd FK9 .... 2 C3
Hermitage Terr EH10 ...... 123 D1
Hermits Croft EH8 .... 233 F1
Heron Ind Complex EH54 . 146 B4
Hervey St FK10 .... 10 A4
Heugh Brae EH39 .... 54 C3
Heugh Rd EH39 .... 54 C3
Heugh St FK1 .... 60 A2
Heugh The EH33 .... 128 B4
Hewitt Pl KY3 .... 49 E4
Heyford Pl FK7 .... 6 B3
Higginson Loan EH22 ...... 183 F3
High Academy Gr EH48 ... 143 F3
High Academy St EH48 ... 143 F3
High Beveridgewell KY12 .. 28 C3
High Brae EH48 .... 113 F3
High Buckstone EH10 ..... 154 B3

High Meadow ML8 .... 230 B1
High Mill Rd ML8 .... 230 A1
High Park Rise EH26 .... 203 F2
High Port EH4 .... 85 D4
High Rd Maddiston FK2 ...... 83 D3
  Roslin EH25 .... 204 C3
  Spott EH42 .... 106 B2
High Riggs EH3 .... 232 B2
High School Wynd EH1 ... 233 E2
High School Yds EH1 ...... 233 E2
High St Aberdour KY3 .... 49 D4
  Aberlady EH32 .... 71 E2
  Airth FK2 .... 22 B2
  Alloa FK10 .... 10 A3
  Bathgate EH48 .... 145 D4
  Bonnybridge FK4 .... 58 A3
  Bonnyrigg and Lasswade
    EH18 .... 156 A1
  Bonnyrigg and Lasswade
    EH19 .... 182 A4
  Burntisland KY3 .... 50 C4
  Clackmannan FK10 .... 10 C2
  Cockenzie & Port Seton EH32 . 97 E2
  Cowdenbeath KY4 .... 13 E2
  Dalkeith EH22 .... 157 D2
  Dunbar EH42 .... 78 B1
  Dunbar, Belhaven EH42 ... 78 A1
  Dunfermline KY12 .... 29 D1
  Dysart KY1 .... 18 A4
  East Linton EH40 .... 103 E4
  Edinburgh EH1 .... 233 D3
  Falkirk FK1 .... 60 A2
  Gifford EH41 .... 163 F2
  Haddington EH41 .... 132 A4
  Inverkeithing KY11 .... 47 D1
  Kincardine FK10 .... 23 F2
  Kinghorn KY3 .... 34 C1
  Kirkcaldy KY1 .... 17 E2
  Kirkliston EH29 .... 89 D1
  Linlithgow EH49 .... 85 D4
  Loanhead EH20 .... 181 E4
  Lochgelly KY5 .... 14 A4
  Musselburgh EH21 .... 126 B3
  North Berwick EH39 .... 54 B4
  Ormiston EH35 .... 159 F4
  Penicuik EH26 .... 203 F2
  Prestonpans EH32 .... 96 C1
  Queensferry EH30 .... 68 B1
  Shotts ML7 .... 191 F2
  Slamannan FK1 .... 110 A4
  Tranent EH33 .... 128 B3
High Station Rd FK1 .... 60 A2
High View Gr FK1 .... 81 E3
Highfield Livingston EH54 . 147 D2
  North Berwick EH39 .... 54 A2
Highfield Ave EH44 .... 84 C4
Highfield Cres EH44 .... 84 C4
Highfield Rd EH39 .... 54 A3
Highland Dr FK5 .... 38 B2
Highland Dykes Cres FK4 .. 58 A3
Highland Dykes Dr FK4 ..... 58 A3
Highlea Circ EH14 .... 177 D4
Highlea Gr EH14 .... 177 D4
Hill Cres EH48 .... 145 D4
Hill Gr KY12 .... 26 B4
Hill House Rd FK6 .... 57 F4
Hill of Beath Prim Sch
  KY4 .... 12 C1
Hill Pk FK10 .... 10 A4
Hill Pl Alloa FK10 .... 10 A4
  Edinburgh EH8 .... 233 E2
  Kirkcaldy KY1 .... 17 E2
  Mayfield EH22 .... 183 F3
  Shotts ML7 .... 191 F3
Hill Rd Gullane EH31 .... 51 F1
  Harthill ML7 .... 168 B3
  Pathhead EH37 .... 185 D3
Hill Sq EH8 .... 233 E2
Hill St Alloa FK10 .... 10 A4
  Cowdenbeath KY4 .... 13 E2
  Dunfermline KY12 .... 29 D2
  Dysart KY1 .... 18 A4
  Edinburgh EH2 .... 232 C4
  Inverkeithing KY11 .... 47 D1
  Kirkcaldy KY1 .... 17 D2
  Stirling FK7 .... 7 D2
Hill Street La N EH2 .... 232 C4
Hill Street La S EH2 .... 232 C4
Hill View EH26 .... 204 A3
Hillary Rd FK1 .... 38 C1
Hilldale KY11 .... 47 D2
Hillcoat Loan EH15 .... 95 D1
Hillcrest Pl EH15 .... 95 D1
Hillcrest Bo'ness EH51 ...... 63 F3
  Cowdenbeath KY4 .... 13 D2
Hillcrest Ave KY2 .... 16 C3
Hillcrest Dr FK10 .... 10 B3
Hillcrest Pk FK6 .... 57 E4
Hillcrest Rd FK1 .... 59 E4
Hillend Ind Pk KY11 .... 48 B3
Hillend Rd KY11 .... 47 E2
Hillfoot Terr ML8 .... 230 A2
Hillfoots Rd FK9 .... 2 C2
Hillhead EH39 .... 182 A4
Hillhead Ave ML8 .... 230 A1
Hillhead Dr FK1 .... 59 F4
Hillhouse Ave EH48 .... 144 C4
Hillhouse Cres EH27 .... 149 F2
Hillhouse Rd EH4 .... 92 A1
Hillhouse Terr EH27 .... 149 F2
Hillhouseridge Rd ML7 ... 191 E3
Hillock Ave FK2 .... 61 F4
Hillpark Ave EH4 .... 91 F2
Hillpark Brae EH4 .... 91 F1
Hillpark Cres Bannockburn FK7 . 7 E1
  Edinburgh EH4 .... 91 F1

Hillpark Ct EH4 .... 91 F2
Hillpark Dr Bannockburn FK7 . 7 E1
  Edinburgh EH4 .... 91 F1
Hillpark Gdns EH4 .... 91 F1
Hillpark Gn EH4 .... 91 F1
Hillpark Gr EH4 .... 91 F1
Hillpark Loan EH4 .... 92 A1
Hillpark Rd EH4 .... 91 F1
Hillpark Terr EH4 .... 91 F1
Hillpark Way EH4 .... 92 A1
Hillpark Wood EH4 .... 92 A1
Hillside EH23 .... 5 E1
Hillside Ave KY11 .... 48 A2
Hillside Camp Rd KY11 .... 46 C1
Hillside Cres N EH23 ...... 207 E4
Hillside Cres S EH23 .... 207 E4
Hillside Dr EH48 .... 142 B2
Hillside Pl Blackridge EH48 . 142 B2
  Longridge EH47 .... 170 B1
Hillside Rd EH30 .... 90 B2
Hillside Sch KY3 .... 49 E4
Hillside St EH7 .... 93 F1
Hillside Terr Alloa FK10 ..... 10 A4
  Craigiehall EH30 .... 90 B3
  Westquarter FK2 .... 61 D2
Hillview Cowdenbeath KY4 . 13 D2
  Edinburgh EH4 .... 92 A1
  Fauldhouse EH47 .... 193 F3
  Oakley KY12 .... 26 C4
Hillview Ave EH52 .... 117 F3
Hillview Cotts EH28 .... 119 E1
Hillview Cres
  Crossgates KY4 .... 30 C3
  Edinburgh EH12 .... 121 E4
Hillview Dr Bridge of A FK9 .. 2 A3
  Edinburgh EH12 .... 121 E4
Hillview La EH54 .... 173 F2
Hillview Pl Broxburn EH52 . 117 F3
  Crossgates KY4 .... 30 C3
  Fallin FK7 .... 8 B2
Hillview Rd Brightons FK2 .. 82 B4
  Edinburgh EH12 .... 121 E4
  High Bonnybridge FK4 ...... 58 B2
  Larbert FK5 .... 38 B2
  Ormiston EH35 .... 159 F4
Hillview Terr Alloa FK10 ..... 10 B3
  Edinburgh EH12 .... 121 E4
Hillwood Ave EH28 .... 119 C3
Hillwood Cres EH28 .... 119 E3
Hillwood Prim Sch EH28 . 119 E3
Hillwood Rd EH28 .... 119 E3
Hillwood Rise EH28 .... 119 E3
Hillwood Terr
  Ratho Station EH28 .... 119 E3
  Rosyth KY11 .... 47 D2
Hilton FK7 .... 20 C4
Hilton Cres EH10 .... 10 B4
Hilton Cres EH16 .... 132 A4
Hilton Rd Alloa FK10 .... 10 B4
  Cairneyhill KY12 .... 27 F1
  Rosyth KY11 .... 46 B1
Hilton Terr FK7 .... 8 B2
Hilton View KY4 .... 13 F3
Hinkar Way FK2 .... 24 C4
Hirst Ct FK7 .... 8 B2
Hirst Gdns ML7 .... 191 E3
Hirst Rd ML7 .... 167 E2
Hirstrigg Cotts ML7 .... 167 D2
Hoban Sq EH52 .... 117 F3
Hobart St EH54 .... 148 A3
Hodge St FK1 .... 60 A2
Hogarth Ave EH23 .... 183 E1
Hoggan Cres KY11 .... 29 E1
Hoghill Ct EH53 .... 148 C2
Hoghill Pl EH53 .... 148 C2
Holborn Pl KY11 .... 46 C3
Holbourne Pl FK11 .... 4 A4
Holden Way KY11 .... 48 A3
Holly Ave FK5 .... 38 C2
Holly Bank EH54 .... 183 F4
Holly Cres KY11 .... 46 C4
Holly Pl KY1 .... 17 E4
Holly Terr EH19 .... 182 A3
Holly Wlk EH20 .... 180 C4
Hollybank Pl EH53 .... 148 C1
Hollybank Terr EH11 .... 122 C2
Holmes Farm La EH52 .... 117 D3
Holmes Holdings EH52 ... 117 E2
Holmes Rd EH52 .... 117 D2
Holmlea Ave FK2 .... 82 B4
Holton Cres KY11 .... 5 E1
Holton Sq KY11 .... 5 E1
Holy Cross Prim Sch
  EH6 .... 93 F2
Holy Family RC Prim Sch
  EH52 .... 87 F1
Holy Rood RC Sec Sch
  EH15 .... 124 B3
Holy Trinity Episcopal Prim Sch
  FK8 .... 7 D4
Holygate Pl EH52 .... 117 F3
Holyrood Bsns Pk EH16 .. 124 B2
Holyrood Park Rd EH16 .. 233 F1
Holyrood Pl
  Dunfermline KY12 .... 29 D2
  Stenhousemuir FK5 .... 38 C2
Holyrood Rd EH8 .... 233 E3
Home Farm Cotts EH52 .... 87 F3
Home Pk KY3 .... 49 F4
Home St EH3 .... 232 B1
Homesteads The FK8 .... 6 C2
Honeybank Cres ML8 ...... 230 A2
Honeyman Ct EH44 .... 143 F4
Hookney Terr FK6 .... 36 B1
Hope Cotts EH51 .... 64 B3
Hope La EH15 .... 125 D4

Hope Park Cres
  Edinburgh EH8 .... 233 E1
  Haddington EH41 .... 101 D1
Hope Park Gdns EH48 ..... 144 C3
Hope Park Sq EH8 .... 233 E1
Hope Park Terr EH8 .... 233 E1
Hope Pk EH41 .... 101 D1
Hope Pl EH21 .... 124 C3
Hope St Bo'ness EH51 .... 63 F4
  Carluke ML8 .... 230 A1
  Cowdenbeath KY4 .... 13 F3
  Edinburgh EH2 .... 232 B3
  Falkirk FK1 .... 60 A3
  Inverkeithing KY11 .... 47 D1
  Queensferry EH30 .... 89 D4
  Stirling FK8 .... 1 C1
Hope Street La EH2 .... 232 B3
Hope Terr EH9 .... 123 E2
Hopefield Dr EH47 .... 171 E4
Hopefield Pk EH19 .... 182 A3
Hopefield Pl
  Blackburn EH47 .... 171 E4
  Bonnyrigg and Lasswade
    EH19 .... 182 A3
Hopefield Prim Sch EH19 . 182 A3
Hopefield Rd EH47 .... 171 E4
Hopefield Terr
  Bonnyrigg and Lasswade
    EH19 .... 182 A3
Hopetoun Cres
  Bonnyrigg and Lasswade
    EH19 .... 182 A4
  Edinburgh EH7 .... 93 E1
Hopetoun Dr
  Bridge of A FK9 .... 2 A4
  Haddington EH41 .... 100 C1
Hopetoun Ho EH30 .... 66 C2
Hopetoun La EH48 .... 145 D3
Hopetoun Mews EH41 .... 101 D1
Hopetoun Mon EH39 ...... 100 C3
Hopetoun Pl KY2 .... 16 B3
Hopetoun Rd
  Queensferry EH30 .... 68 A1
  Rosyth KY11 .... 46 B1
Hopetoun St
  Bathgate EH48 .... 145 D3
  Edinburgh EH7 .... 93 F2
Hopetoun Terr
  Gullane EH31 .... 52 A2
  Ormiston EH35 .... 159 F4
Hopetoun View KY11 .... 48 B2
Hopeward Ct KY11 .... 48 B2
Hopeward Mews KY11 ...... 48 B1
Hoprig Pk T013 .... 140 C1
Hoprig Rd T013 .... 140 C1
Hornbeam Cres FK2 .... 61 D2
Horne Terr EH11 .... 232 A1
Horsburgh Bank EH14 .... 151 E2
Horsburgh Gdns EH14 .... 151 E2
Horsburgh Gr EH14 .... 151 E2
Horse Wynd EH8 .... 233 F3
Hoseason Gdns EH4 .... 91 F2
Hosie Rigg EH15 .... 125 D3
Hospital Hill KY11 .... 29 D1
Hospital Intc EH54 .... 147 F4
Hospital Rd EH41 .... 100 C1
Hot Pot Wynd KY1 .... 18 A3
Houldsworth Cres ML7 ... 212 A4
Houldsworth St KY11 .... 26 A4
House O' Muir Rd ML7 .... 167 D2
House O'Hill Ave EH4 .... 92 A2
House O'Hill Brae EH4 ...... 92 A2
House O'Hill Gdns EH4 ..... 92 A2
House O'Hill Gn EH4 .... 92 A2
House O'Hill Gr EH4 .... 92 A2
House O'Hill Pl EH4 .... 92 A2
House O'Hill Rd EH4 .... 92 A2
House O'Hill Row EH4 .... 92 A2
House O'Hill Terr EH4 .... 92 A2
Houston Ct KY12 .... 29 E1
Houston Rd
  Livingston EH54 .... 147 D3
  Uphall Station EH54 .... 117 D1
Houstoun Gdns EH52 ...... 116 C2
Houstoun Ind Est
  Dechmont EH54 .... 146 C4
  Livingston EH54 .... 147 F4
Houstoun Intc EH54 .... 147 F3
Houstoun Rd EH54 .... 147 F3
Houston NW EH54 .... 146 C3
Howard Cres KY11 .... 29 E1
Howard Pl Dysart KY1 .... 18 A4
  Edinburgh EH3 .... 93 E2
Howard St Edinburgh EH3 . 93 E2
  Falkirk FK1 .... 59 F3
Howburn Cres ML7 .... 168 B3
Howburn Rd ML7 .... 168 B3
Howden East Rd EH54 .... 147 F2
Howden Hall Cres EH16 .. 154 C3
Howden Hall Ct EH16 ..... 154 C3
Howden Hall Dr EH16 ..... 154 C3
Howden Hall Gdns EH16 . 155 D3
Howden Hall Loan EH16 . 154 C3
Howden Hall Pk EH16 ..... 154 C3
Howden Hall Rd EH16 .... 155 D3
Howden Hall Way EH16 .. 155 D3
Howden South Rd EH54 .. 147 F1
Howden St EH8 .... 233 E1
Howden St Andrew's
  RC Prim Sch EH54 .... 147 F2
Howden West Rd EH54 ... 147 F2
Howe Pk EH10 .... 153 F3
Howe St EH3 .... 232 C4
Howetown FK10 .... 5 E2
Howgate Prim Sch EH26 . 204 A1

Howgate Sh Ctr 7 FK1 ...... 60 A2
Howie's Pl FK1 .... 59 D2
Howieson Ave EH51 .... 63 F3
Howieson Gn EH52 .... 116 C2
Howlands Rd FK7 .... 7 D2
Howley Ave EH54 .... 147 F2
Hudson Rd KY11 .... 46 C2
Hugh Ave KY5 .... 14 A4
Hugh Miller Pl EH3 .... 93 D1
Hugh Pl KY5 .... 14 A4
Hugh Russell Pl EH30 ...... 89 D4
Hughes Cres EH22 .... 183 F3
Humbie Prim Sch EH36 ... 187 D1
Hume Cres FK9 .... 2 A3
Hume Ct FK9 .... 2 A3
Hummel Rd EH31 .... 51 F1
Hungerage Sq EH33 .... 128 C3
Hunt Cl EH22 .... 157 D2
Hunt Pl KY12 .... 28 A1
Huntburn Ave EH49 .... 85 E4
Hunter Ave EH20 .... 181 E4
Hunter Ct EH20 .... 181 E4
Hunter Gdns
  Bonnybridge FK4 .... 58 A3
  Broxburn EH52 .... 118 A3
  Denny FK6 .... 36 B1
Hunter Gr Bathgate EH48 . 145 F3
  Whitburn EH47 .... 161 F4
Hunter Hospl KY1 .... 17 D2
Hunter Pl Dunfermline KY12 . 28 C3
  Kirkaldy KY1 .... 17 D2
  Shotts ML7 .... 191 F3
  Stenhousemuir FK5 .... 39 D2
Hunter Sq Edinburgh EH1 . 233 D3
  Gorebridge EH23 .... 207 E4
Hunter St Kirkaldy KY1 ..... 17 D2
  Shotts ML7 .... 191 E3
Hunter Terr
  Bonnyrigg and Lasswade
    EH19 .... 182 A4
  Loanhead EH20 .... 181 E4
Hunter's Cl EH1 .... 232 C2
Hunter's La EH47 .... 170 A3
Hunter's Tryst Prim Sch
  EH13 .... 153 F4
Hunterfield Ct EH23 .... 207 E4
Hunterfield Pk EH23 .... 183 E1
Hunterfield Rd EH23 ...... 207 E4
Hunterfield Terr EH23 ..... 183 D1
Hunters Hill EH26 .... 203 E3
Huntingdon Pl EH7 .... 93 F1
Huntlaw Rd EH34 .... 160 C3
Huntly Cres FK8 .... 1 C1
Huntly House Mus EH8 ... 233 E3
Huntly Cres KY2 .... 16 B4
Huntly St EH3 .... 93 E2
Huntly Terr ML7 .... 192 C2
Huron Ave EH54 .... 147 F2
Hursted Ave EH22 .... 183 E4
Hurworth St FK1 .... 59 F2
Husband Pl KY11 .... 29 F1
Hutchison Ave EH14 .... 122 B2
Hutchison Cotts EH14 .... 122 B2
Hutchison Crossway EH14 . 122 B2
Hutchison Gdns EH14 .... 122 B2
Hutchison Loan EH14 ..... 122 B2
Hutchison Medway EH14 . 122 B2
Hutchison Pk EH14 .... 122 B2
Hutchison Pl EH14 .... 122 B2
Hutchison Rd EH14 .... 122 B2
Hutchison Terr EH14 ...... 122 B2
Hutchison View EH14 ..... 122 B2
Hutton Pk FK10 .... 10 B4
Hutton Rd EH54 .... 173 E3
Hyndshaw Rd ML8 .... 230 A2
Hyvot Ave EH17 .... 155 F3
Hyvot Bank Ave EH17 ..... 155 F3
Hyvot Ct EH17 .... 155 E3
Hyvot Gdns EH17 .... 155 F3
Hyvot Gn EH17 .... 155 E3
Hyvot Gr EH17 .... 155 F3
Hyvot Loan EH17 .... 155 E3
Hyvot Pk EH17 .... 155 F3
Hyvot Terr EH17 .... 155 F3
Hyvot View EH17 .... 155 F3

Ibris Pl EH39 .... 54 A4
Icehouse Brae FK2 .... 61 D2
Implement Rd EH42 .... 77 F1
Inchbank EH4 .... 91 E2
Inchcolm Ave FK3 .... 61 F3
Inchcolm Dr KY11 .... 68 A3
Inchcolm Pl KY11 .... 29 F1
Inchcolm Terr EH30 .... 89 D4
Inchcorse Pl EH48 .... 145 E1
Inchcross EH48 .... 144 C2
Inchcross Ind Est EH48 ... 144 C2
Inches The KY1 .... 18 A3
Inchgarvie Cres KY11 .... 29 F2
Inchgarvie Pk EH30 .... 68 A1
Inchgarvie Rd KY2 .... 16 C4
Inchkeith Ave EH30 .... 89 E4
Inchkeith Ct EH7 .... 93 F2
Inchkeith Dr KY11 .... 29 F2
Inchkeith Pl FK1 .... 60 A1
Inchmickery Ave KY11 ...... 48 B3
Inchmickery Rd KY11 .... 48 B3

Inchmuir Rd EH48 .... 145 D1
Inchna FK11 .... 4 A3
Inchview EH32 .... 96 C1
Inchview Cres EH21 ...... 127 E3
Inchview Gdns KY11 ...... 48 A2
Inchview N EH32 .... 96 C1
Inchview Prim Sch EH4 ... 92 B2
Inchview Rd EH21 .... 127 E3
Inchview Terr EH7 ...... 94 C1
Inchyra Rd FK3 .... 61 F3
India Pl EH3 .... 232 B4
India St EH3 .... 232 B4
Industrial Rd EH42 ...... 94 A2
Industry La EH1 .... 93 F3
Infirmary St EH1 .... 233 E2
Ingleston Ave FK6 ...... 36 B3
Inglewood FK10 .... 9 F4
Inglewood Pl EH16 ...... 155 D4
Inglewood Rd EH10 ..... 9 F4
Inglewood St EH54 ..... 147 F3
Inglis Ave EH32 .... 97 E2
Inglis Cres KY3 .... 34 C2
Inglis Ct EH11 .... 232 C2
Inglis Dr FK2 .... 39 E1
Inglis Farm EH32 ...... 97 E2
Inglis Green Rd EH14 ... 122 A1
Inglis Pl FK2 .... 82 C4
Inglis St KY12 .... 29 D2
Ingram Pl FK2 .... 82 C3
Inkerman Ct EH26 ...... 204 A4
Inn Pl EH54 .... 147 D1
Innerpeffray Dr FK2 .... 39 D2
Innerwick Prim Sch EH42 .. 108 A1
Institution St KY1 ..... 17 F4
Inver Ct FK2 .... 39 E1
Inverallan Ct FK9 ..... 1 C4
Inverallan Dr FK9 ..... 1 C4
Inverallan Rd FK9 ..... 1 C4
Inveralmond
 Com High Sch EH54 ... 147 E3
Inveralmond Dr EH54 ... 91 D3
Inveralmond Gdns EH4 ... 91 D3
Inveralmond Gr EH4 .... 91 D3
Inverary Dr FK5 .... 38 C3
Inveravon Rd EH30 ..... 155 D1
Inveravon Rdbt EH51 .... 62 B3
Inveravon Terr EH21 .... 126 B3
Inveresk Brae EH21 .... 126 B3
Inveresk Ind Est EH21 ... 126 B3
Inveresk Mills Ind Pk EH21 .. 126 A3
Inveresk Rd EH21 ...... 126 B3
Inveresk Village Rd EH21 .. 126 B2
Inverkeithing High Sch KY11 .. 47 E2
Inverkeithing Mus KY11 .. 47 D1
Inverkeithing Prim Sch KY11 .. 47 D2
Inverkeithing Rd
 Aberdour KY3 .... 49 D4
 Crossgates KY4 ...... 30 C3
Inverkeithing Sta KY11 .. 47 E2
Inverkip Dr ML7 ...... 191 F3
Inverleith Ave EH3 ..... 93 D2
Inverleith Ave S EH3 .... 93 D2
Inverleith Gr EH3 ..... 92 C2
Inverleith Pl EH3 ..... 93 D2
Inverleith Place La EH3 .. 93 D2
Inverleith Row EH3 .... 93 D2
Inverleith Terr EH3 .... 93 D2
Inverleith Terrace La EH3 . 93 E2
Invertiel Rd KY1 ...... 35 D4
Invertiel Terr KY1 ..... 17 D1
Inzievar Prim Sch KY12 .. 26 C4
Inzievar Terr KY12 .... 27 D3
Iona Pl FK1 .... 60 A1
Iona Rd KY1 .... 29 F2
Iona St EH6 .... 93 F2
Ireland Ave EH47 ..... 169 F3
Irene Terr FK1 .... 82 C1
Ironmills Rd EH22 ..... 156 B2
Irvine Cres EH48 ..... 144 C3
Irvine Pl FK8 .... 7 D4
Irving Ct FK1 .... 59 F3
Islands Cres FK1 ..... 60 A1
Islay Ct FK3 .... 61 E3
Islay Rd KY11 ...... 29 F3
Ivanhoe Cres EH16 .... 124 A1
Ivanhoe Pl FK8 ...... 2 A1
Ivanhoe Rise EH54 .... 148 A1
Ivy Gr KY11 .... 46 C4
Ivy La KY1 .... 18 A4
Ivy Terr EH11 ...... 122 C3
Ivybank Ct FK2 ..... 61 D1
Izatt Ave KY11 ..... 29 D1
Izatt St FK10 ...... 10 A4
Izatt Terr FK10 .... 11 D2

Jacklin Gn EH54 ...... 147 D4
Jackson Ave EH3 ..... 61 E4
Jackson Pl EH54 ..... 147 E2
Jackson St EH26 ..... 203 F3
Jacob Pl FK1 .... 60 A2
Jail Wynd FK8 ...... 7 D4
Jamaica Mews EH3 .... 232 B4
Jamaica St EH3 ..... 232 B4
Jamaica St W EH3 .... 232 B4
Jamaica Street North La EH3 .. 232 B4
Jamaica Street South La EH3 .. 232 B4
James Croft Dr FK1 ... 59 F1
James Ct KY4 ...... 13 E1
James Gillespie's High Sch EH9 .. 123 E3
James Gillespie's High Sch Annexe EH3 .. 232 B1
James Gillespie's Prim Sch EH3 .. 123 E3
James Gr KY1 ...... 17 D1
James Hog Cres KY12 .. 26 C3
James Lean Ave EH22 .. 157 D2
James Leary Way EH19 .. 182 B4
James' Park La KY3 ... 33 F1
James' Pk KY3 ..... 33 F1
James Smith Ave FK2 .. 82 C3
James St Alva FK12 ... 5 D3
 Armadale EH48 ..... 143 F3
 Bannockburn FK7 .... 7 E1
 Cowdenbeath KY4 .... 13 E1
 Dunfermline KY12 ... 29 D2
 Edinburgh EH15 .... 125 E4
 Falkirk FK2 ...... 60 A3
 Haggs FK4 ...... 57 D2
 Laurieston FK2 .... 60 B4
 Musselburgh EH21 ... 126 B3
 Stenhousemuir FK5 .. 38 B1
 Stirling FK8 ..... 2 A1
James Street La EH15 .. 125 E4
James Watt Ave EH51 .. 64 A4
James Wilson Dr FK2 .. 83 D3
James Young
 High Sch The EH54 .. 147 F1
Jameson Pl EH6 .... 93 F2
Jamieson Ave Bo'ness EH51 .. 63 F3
Jamieson Gdns ML7 ... 191 F3
Jane St EH6 ...... 93 F2
Janefield EH17 .... 155 D2
Jarnac Ct EH22 .... 157 D2
Jarvey St EH48 .... 145 D4
Jarvie Pl FK2 .... 60 A4
Jasper Ave FK2 ... 61 D2
Jawbanes Rd KY2 ... 35 D4
Jean Armour Ave ⑥ EH16 .. 124 A1
Jean Armour Dr EH22 .. 157 E1
Jeffrey Ave EH4 ... 92 A1
Jeffrey Bank EH51 .. 63 F4
Jeffrey St EH1 .... 233 E3
Jeffrey Terr FK2 ... 61 F1
Jellyholm Rd FK10 .. 10 C4
Jennie Rennie's Rd KY11 .. 29 F1
Jessfield Pl EH51 .. 63 F3
Jessfield Terr EH6 .. 93 F3
Jewel & Esk Valley Coll
 Dalkeith EH22 .... 156 C1
 Edinburgh EH15 ... 125 E3
Jewel The EH15 ... 125 D3
Jock's Hill Cres EH49 .. 84 C4
John Bernard Way EH23 .. 207 E3
John Brown Ct EH41 .. 132 A4
John Cres EH13 .... 128 B3
John Davidson Dr FK6 .. 36 B2
John Humble St EH22 .. 183 F3
John Knox Pl EH26 ... 203 F3
John Knox Rd EH32 ... 98 C3
John Mason Ct EH30 .. 89 E4
John Muir City Pk EH42 .. 77 E2
John Murray Dr FK9 .. 2 A4
John Row Pl EH20 ... 27 D4
John Rushforth Pl FK8 .. 1 C1
John Smith Way ML7 .. 191 E3
John St Dunfermline KY11 .. 29 D1
 Edinburgh EH15 ... 125 E4
 Falkirk FK2 ..... 60 A4
 Haggs FK4 ..... 57 D2
 Kincardine FK10 ... 23 E2
 Kirkcaldy KY2 .... 17 D1
 Penicuik EH26 .... 203 F3
 Stirling FK8 .... 7 D4
John Street La
 Penicuik EH26 .... 203 F3
John Street La EH15 .. 125 E4
John Street La W EH15 .. 125 E4
John Stuart Gait KY12 .. 26 C3
John Woods Pl KY4 ... 30 C4
John's La EH6 .... 94 A3
John's Pl EH6 .... 94 A3
Johnnie Cope's Rd EH33 .. 128 A4
Johnsburn Gn EH14 ... 151 D1
Johnsburn Haugh EH14 .. 151 D1
Johnsburn Pk EH14 ... 177 D4
Johnsburn Rd EH14 ... 151 D1
Johnston Ave
 Stenhousemuir FK5 .. 38 C2
 Stirling FK8 .... 2 A2
 Uphall EH52 .... 116 C2
Johnston Cres
 Dunfermline KY11 .. 29 D1
 Lochgelly KY5 ... 14 A4
Johnston Ct EH52 ... 116 C2
Johnston Pk
 Cowdenbeath KY4 .. 13 E3
 Inverkeithing KY11 . 47 D1
Johnston Pl Denny FK6 .. 36 B1
 Penicuik EH26 .... 203 F4
Johnston St FK7 ... 7 E1
Johnston Terr
 Cockenzie & Port Seton EH32 .. 97 E2
 Edinburgh EH1 ... 232 C2
Johnstone La ML8 ... 230 A1
Johnstone St Alva FK12 .. 5 D3
 Menstrie FK11 ... 3 F3
Jones Ave FK5 .... 59 D4
Joppa Gdns EH15 ... 125 E4
Joppa Gr EH15 .... 125 E4
Joppa Pk EH15 .... 125 E4
Joppa Rd EH15 .... 125 E4
Joppa Terr EH15 ... 125 E4
Jordan La EH10 ... 123 D2
Joseph Scott Gdns EH52 .. 117 F2
Jubilee Ave EH54 .. 146 C3
Jubilee Cres EH47 .. 183 E3
Jubilee Dr KY11 ... 46 A1
Jubilee Rd Denny FK6 .. 36 C2
 Newbridge HE12 ... 119 F4
 Whitburn EH47 ... 170 A3
Junction Pl EH6 ... 93 F3
Junction Rd KY1 ... 17 E4
Juner Pl EH23 .... 183 E1
Juniper Ave EH14 .. 152 B3
Juniper Gdns EH14 .. 152 B3
Juniper Gr
 Dunfermline KY11 .. 46 B4
 Edinburgh EH14 ... 152 B3
 Livingston EH54 .. 148 A3
Juniper Green Prim Sch EH14 .. 152 B3
Juniper Park Rd EH14 .. 152 B3
Juniper Pl EH14 ... 152 B3
Juniper Terr EH14 .. 152 B3
Juniperlee EH14 ... 152 B3
Jura EH54 ...... 146 C3
Jura Pl FK3 ..... 61 E3
Justinhaugh Dr EH49 .. 84 B4

Kaemuir Ct EH48 .... 112 C3
Kaim Cres EH54 .... 145 E3
Kaimes Ave EH27 ... 149 F2
Kaimes Cres EH27 .. 149 F2
Kaimes Gdns EH27 .. 149 F2
Kaimes Gr EH27 ... 149 F2
Kaimes Pl EH27 ... 149 F2
Kaimes Rd EH12 ... 121 F4
Kaimes View EH22 .. 155 E3
Kaimes View EH12 .. 156 A4
Kaims Brae EH54 ... 147 E1
Kaims Ct EH54 .... 147 D1
Kaims Gdns EH54 ... 147 E1
Kaims Gr EH54 .... 147 E1
Kaims Pl EH54 .... 147 E1
Kames Pl EH27 .... 29 E3
Kames Rd ML7 .... 191 F3
Katesmill Rd EH14 .. 153 D4
Katherine St
 Kirkcaldy KY2 .... 17 D3
 Livingston EH54 .. 148 A3
Katrine Cres KY2 .. 16 C4
Katrine Ct EH54 ... 10 B3
Katrine Dr KY12 .. 28 C1
Katrine Pl FK6 ... 57 E3
Katrine Rd Shotts ML7 .. 191 F3
 Whitburn EH47 ... 170 B4
Kay Gdns EH27 ... 97 E2
Keavil Pl KY12 ... 28 C1
Kedslie Pl EH16 ... 154 C4
Kedslie Rd EH16 .. 154 C4
Keir Ave FK8 .... 2 A4
Keir Gdns FK9 ... 2 A4
Keir Hardie Ave FK2 .. 61 D2
Keir Hardie Dr EH22 .. 183 F3
Keir Hardie Rd FK12 .. 5 D4
Keir St Bridge of A FK9 .. 2 A4
 Cowdenbeath KY4 .. 13 D3
 Edinburgh EH3 ... 232 C2
Keirsbeath Ct KY12 .. 12 A1
Keith Ave FK7 ... 7 E2
Keith Cres EH4 .. 92 A1
Keith Gdns EH52 .. 117 E3
Keith Pl Dunfermline KY12 .. 29 E2
 Inverkeithing KY11 . 47 E2
Keith Rd KY11 ... 46 B1
Keith Row EH4 .. 92 B1
Keith St FK10 ... 23 F2
Keith Terr EH4 .. 92 A1
Kekewich Ave EH7 .. 94 C1
Kellie Pl FK10 ... 10 A4
Kelliebank EH10 .. 9 F3
Kelly Dr FK6 ... 36 C2
Kelly's La ML8 .. 230 A1
Kellywood Cres FK10 .. 23 E2
Kelso Dr ML8 ... 230 B1
Kelso Pl KY2 ... 17 D3
Kelso St EH52 ... 117 D3
Kelty Ave EH51 .. 64 A4
Kelvin Dr ML7 .. 192 A2
Kelvin Sq EH54 .. 148 A4
Kelvin St EH43 .. 40 A1
Kemp Pl EH3 ... 93 D1
Kemper Ave FK1 .. 59 F2
Kempston Pl EH30 .. 89 E4
Kendieshill Ave FK2 .. 83 D3
Kenilworth Dr
 Edinburgh EH16 .. 155 D4
 Laurieston FK2 .. 60 C2
Kenilworth La EH13 .. 61 E3
Kenilworth Pl FK9 .. 2 A4
Kenilworth Rise EH54 .. 147 F1
Kenilworth St EH51 .. 61 E3
Kenmore Ave
 Livingston EH54 .. 146 C3
 Polmont FK2 .... 62 A1
Kenmore Terr KY12 .. 29 E3
Kenmuir St FK1 .. 59 D3
Kenmure Ave EH8 .. 124 B4
Kenmure Pl
 Dunfermline KY12 .. 29 E3
 Stenhousemuir FK5 .. 38 C2
Kennard Rd FK2 .. 82 B4
Kennard St Falkirk FK2 .. 60 A4
 Lochgelly KY5 .. 14 A4
Kennedie Pk EH53 .. 148 B2

Kennedy Cres
 Dunfermline KY12 .. 29 D3
 Kirkcaldy KY2 ... 17 F3
 Tranent EH33 ... 128 B4
Kenningknowes Rd FK7 .. 6 C3
Kennington Ave EH20 .. 181 D4
Kennington Terr EH20 .. 181 D4
Kent Rd Alloa FK10 .. 9 F4
 Stirling FK7 ... 7 D3
Kent St KY12 ... 28 B3
Kentigern Mall EH26 .. 203 F3
Keppel Rd EH19 .. 54 A3
Keppock Pl FK1 .. 59 F1
Kepscaith Cres EH47 .. 170 A3
Kepscaith Gr EH47 .. 170 A3
Kepscaith Rd EH47 .. 170 A3
Kerr Ave EH22 ... 156 C1
Kerr Cres FK4 ... 57 D2
Kerr Pl Denny FK6 .. 36 B1
 Dunfermline KY11 .. 29 F1
Kerr Rd EH33 ... 128 B3
Kerr St 93 D1
Kerr's Wynd EH21 .. 126 B3
Kerrisk Dr KY11 .. 29 F1
Kerse Gdns FK2 .. 60 C3
Kerse Green Rd FK10 .. 10 C3
Kerse Pk FK4 ... 57 D2
Kerse Pl FK1 ... 60 B3
Kerse Rd Grangemouth FK3 .. 61 E4
 Stirling FK7 ... 7 E3
Kersebonny Rd FK8 .. 6 B4
Kersie Rd FK7 ... 20 A3
Kersie Terr FK7 .. 9 F2
Kersiebank Ave FK3 .. 61 F3
Kestrel Brae EH54 .. 147 E3
Kestrel Dr FK7 ... 82 C4
Kettil'stoun Cres EH49 .. 84 B3
Kettil'stoun Gr EH49 .. 84 B3
Kettil'stoun Mains EH49 .. 84 B3
Kettilstoun Rd EH49 .. 84 B4
Keverkae EH10 ... 9 F3
Kevock Rd EH18 .. 155 E1
Kidd St KY1 .... 17 E4
Kidbagie St FK10 .. 23 E2
Kilbean Dr FK1 .. 59 F1
Kilbirnie Terr FK6 .. 36 B2
Kilbrennan Dr FK1 .. 59 E1
Kilburn Rd KY11 .. 28 A2
Kilchrist Pl FK1 .. 59 E1
Kilchurn Ct EH12 .. 121 D4
Kilcruik Rd KY3 .. 34 C2
Kildean Hospl FK8 .. 1 C1
Kildean Sch FK8 .. 1 C1
Kildonan Pk KY12 .. 28 C1
Kildrummy Ave FK5 .. 38 C2
Kilduthie Pl FK10 .. 23 F3
Kilfinan Rd ML7 .. 191 E3
Kilgour Ave EH17 .. 17 E4
Kilgraston Rd EH9 .. 123 E2
Killin Ct KY12 ... 28 C1
Killin Dr FK2 ... 62 A1
Kilochan Way KY12 .. 29 E3
Kilmartin Way KY12 .. 29 E3
Kilmaurs Rd EH16 .. 124 A2
Kilmaurs Terr EH16 .. 124 A2
Kilmory Ct FK1 .. 59 E2
Kilmory Gdns ML8 .. 230 A2
Kilmun Rd KY2 .. 16 B4
Kilmundy Dr KY3 .. 33 E1
Kilncraigs Ct FK10 .. 10 A4
Kilncraigs Rd FK10 .. 10 B3
Kilncroft Side EH14 .. 122 A1
Kilne Pl EH54 ... 147 D2
Kilns Pl FK2 ... 60 B3
Kilns Rd FK1 ... 60 A3
Kilpair St EH41 .. 132 A4
Kilpunt Gdns EH52 .. 118 A3
Kilpunt Rdbt EH52 .. 118 A3
Kilpunt View FK10 .. 118 A3
Kilrie Cotts KY2 .. 33 F4
Kilrymont Rd KY11 .. 211 D1
Kilspindie Ct EH32 .. 71 E2
Kilsyth Rd FK4 .. 57 D2
Kilwinning Pl EH21 .. 126 B3
Kilwinning St EH21 .. 126 B3
Kilwinning Terr EH21 .. 126 B3
Kinacres Gr EH51 .. 64 B4
Kincairne Ct FK10 .. 23 F2
Kincardine Rd FK2 .. 39 E2
Kincraig Pl KY12 .. 28 C1
Kinellan Gdns EH12 .. 122 B4
Kinellan Rd EH12 .. 122 A4
King Cres EH55 ... 172 B2
King Edwards Way EH47 .. 89 D1
King James IV Rd KY11 .. 46 B1
King Malcolm Cl EH10 .. 154 B3
King O' Muirs Ave FK10 .. 4 C2
King O' Muirs Dr FK10 .. 4 C2
King St Armadale EH48 .. 144 A3
 Bathgate EH48 ... 145 D3
 Cowdenbeath KY4 .. 13 E2
 Edinburgh EH6 ... 93 F3
 Falkirk FK2 .... 60 B3
 Inverkeithing KY11 .. 47 E1
 Kirkcaldy KY1 ... 17 E4
 Musselburgh EH21 .. 126 B3
 Shotts ML7 .... 191 F2
 St Andrews KY16 .. 211 D4
 Stirling FK8 ... 7 D4
King's Ave EH55 .. 98 B2
King's Court EH22 .. 89 B2
King's Cramond EH4 .. 91 D2
King's Cres Carluke ML8 .. 231 A1
 Edinburgh EH22 .. 89 B2
King's Dr KY3 ... 34 C2
King's Gate EH52 .. 98 B2
King's Knoll Gdns EH39 .. 54 B3
King's Mdw EH16 .. 124 A2

King's Meadow Prim Sch EH41 .. 132 A4
King's Park Prim Sch EH22 .. 157 D1
King's Park Rd FK8 .. 7 D4
King's Pk EH32 ... 98 B3
King's Pl KY11 ... 46 C2
King's Rd Edinburgh EH15 .. 95 D1
 Longniddry EH32 .. 98 B3
 Rosyth KY11 ... 46 C3
 Tranent EH33 ... 128 B3
King's Rd EH47 ... 170 A3
King's Stables La EH1 .. 232 C2
King's Stables Rd EH1 .. 232 C2
King's Terr EH15 .. 94 C1
Kingfisher Brae EH54 .. 147 E3
Kinghorn Pl EH6 .. 93 E3
Kinghorn Prim Sch KY3 .. 34 C1
Kinghorn Rd Burntisland KY3 .. 34 A1
 Kirkcaldy KY1, KY2 .. 35 D4
Kinghorn Sta KY3 .. 34 C2
Kinglass Ave EH51 .. 64 A4
Kinglass Ct EH51 .. 64 A3
Kinglass Dr EH51 .. 64 A3
Kinglass Pk EH51 .. 64 A3
Kings Bldgs
 (Univ of Edinburgh) EH9 .. 123 E1
Kings Ct Alloa FK10 .. 10 A4
 ⑧ Falkirk FK1 .... 60 A2
 Stenhousemuir FK5 .. 38 B1
Kings Haugh EH16 .. 124 B2
Kings Park Hospl FK7 .. 6 C3
Kings Rd FK3 ... 61 F4
Kingsburgh Ct EH40 .. 103 E4
Kingsburgh Gdns EH40 .. 103 E4
Kingsburgh Rd EH12 .. 122 B4
Kingseat Ave FK3 .. 61 E3
Kingseat Pl FK1 .. 59 F2
Kingseat Rd
 Dunfermline KY12 .. 29 E3
 Halbeath KY11, KY12 .. 30 A3
Kingsfield EH49 .. 85 E4
Kingsinch Sch EH16 .. 124 A1
Kingsknowe Ave EH14 .. 122 A1
Kingsknowe Cres EH14 .. 122 A1
Kingsknowe Ct EH14 .. 121 F1
Kingsknowe Dr EH14 .. 122 A1
Kingsknowe Gdns EH14 .. 153 D4
Kingsknowe Gr EH14 .. 153 D4
Kingsknowe Pk EH14 .. 153 D4
Kingsknowe Pl EH14 .. 121 F1
Kingsknowe Rd N EH14 .. 122 A1
Kingsknowe Rd S EH14 .. 122 A1
Kingsknowe Sta EH14 .. 122 A1
Kingsknowe Terr EH14 .. 122 A1
Kingslaw Ct EH33 .. 128 B2
Kingslaw Farm Cotts EH33 .. 128 C3
Kingsley Ave KY5 .. 38 C2
Kingsport Ave FK4 .. 147 F2
Kingstables La FK8 .. 7 D4
Kingsthorne Pk FK54 .. 116 C1
Kingston Ave EH16 .. 124 B1
Kingston Cotts EH39 .. 53 F1
Kingswell Pk FK10 .. 10 B4
Kinninmonth St KY1 .. 17 D1
Kinlelth Ind Est EH14 .. 152 A2
Kinloch Pl FK3 .. 61 E3
Kinloch Rd KY12 .. 26 A1
Kinnaird Ave FK2 .. 39 D2
Kinnaird Dr FK5 .. 38 C2
Kinnaird Pk EH15 .. 125 E2
Kinnaird Pl Dunfermline KY12 .. 29 E3
 Kirkcaldy KY2 ... 16 B2
Kinnear Rd EH3 .. 93 D2
Kinneddar Dr EH51 .. 63 E3
Kinneil Dr EH51 .. 63 E3
Kinneil Prim Sch EH51 .. 63 E3
Kinneil Rd EH51 .. 63 E4
Kinninmonth St KY1 .. 17 D1
Kinnis Ct EH39 .. 29 F1
Kinnonmonth Ave KY3 .. 33 E1
Kintyre Pl FK1 .. 59 E2
Kippielaw Dr EH22 .. 157 E1
Kippielaw Gdns EH22 .. 157 E1
Kippielaw Medway EH22 .. 157 E1
Kippielaw Pk EH22 .. 183 E4
Kippielaw Rd EH22 .. 157 E1
Kippielaw Wlk EH22 .. 157 E1
Kippithill EH36 .. 187 E4
Kirk Ave FK5 .. 38 C1
Kirk Brae Edinburgh EH16 .. 155 D4
 Innerwick EH42 .. 108 A1
 Kincardine FK10 .. 23 F3
 Longridge EH47 .. 171 F1
Kirk Cramond EH4 .. 91 E3
Kirk La EH54 .. 147 D1
Kirk Loan EH12 .. 121 F3
Kirk Pk Dunbar EH42 .. 78 B1
 Edinburgh EH16 .. 155 D4
Kirk Ports EH39 .. 54 B4
Kirk Rd Aberlady EH32 .. 71 E2
 Bathgate EH48 .. 145 D3
 Shotts ML7 .. 191 F2
Kirk St Cockenzie & Port Seton EH32 .. 97 E2
 Edinburgh EH6 .. 93 F2
 Kincardine FK10 .. 23 F2
 Prestonpans EH32 .. 96 C1
Kirk View EH41 .. 132 B4
Kirk Wynd
 Clackmannan FK10 .. 11 D3
 ⑧ Falkirk FK1 .. 60 A2
 Kirkcaldy KY1 .. 17 E2
 Stirling FK7 .. 7 D2
Kirkcaldy High Sch KY1 .. 17 D4

Kirkcaldy Mus & Art Gallery KY1 .... 17 D2
Kirkbank Rd KY3 .... 33 F1
Kirkbrae FK10 .... 10 C2
Kirkbride Terr FK7 .... 20 B2
Kirkburn FK1 .... 110 A4
Kirkcaldy Rd
  Burntisland KY3 .... 33 F1
  Kinghorn KY3 .... 35 D2
Kirkcaldy Sta KY1 .... 17 D2
Kirkfield E EH54 .... 147 D2
Kirkfield View EH54 .... 147 E2
Kirkfield W EH54 .... 147 D2
Kirkflat EH52 .... 117 D3
Kirkford Ct KY4 .... 13 D2
Kirkgate Alloa FK10 .... 5 E1
  Burntisland KY3 .... 50 C4
  Currie EH14 .... 152 A2
  Dunfermline KY12 .... 28 C2
  Edinburgh EH16 .... 155 D4
  Inverkeithing KY11 .... 47 D2
  Linlithgow EH49 .... 85 D4
  West Calder EH55 .... 172 B2
Kirkhall Pl FK6 .... 36 C1
Kirkhill Ct Broxburn EH52 .... 117 E3
  Fauldhouse EH47 .... 193 F3
Kirkhill Dr EH16 .... 124 A2
Kirkhill Gdns
  Edinburgh EH16 .... 124 A3
  Penicuik EH26 .... 203 F3
Kirkhill Pk EH52 .... 117 E3
Kirkhill Prim Sch EH52 .... 117 D3
Kirkhill Rd Broxburn EH52 .... 117 E3
  Edinburgh EH16 .... 124 A2
  Penicuik EH26 .... 203 F3
Kirkhill Terr
  Broxburn EH52 .... 117 E3
  Edinburgh EH16 .... 124 A3
  Gorebridge EH23 .... 183 D1
Kirkhill Way EH26 .... 203 F3
Kirkland Dr FK6 .... 36 A1
Kirklands Dunfermline KY12 .... 29 D1
  Edinburgh EH12 .... 121 E2
  Penicuik EH26 .... 203 F3
Kirklands Park Cres EH29 .... 88 C1
Kirklands Park Gdns EH29 .... 88 C1
Kirklands Park Gr EH29 .... 88 C1
Kirklands Park Gr EH29 .... 88 C1
Kirkliston Prim Sch
  EH29 .... 89 D1
Kirkliston Rd EH30 .... 89 D4
Kirknewton Prim Sch
  EH27 .... 149 E2
Kirknewton Sta EH27 .... 149 E2
Kirkslap FK6 .... 36 C1
Kirkstyle Gdns EH29 .... 89 D1
Kirkton Ave EH48 .... 145 E3
Kirkton Bank EH26 .... 203 D3
Kirkton Bsns Pk EH54 .... 147 D2
Kirkton N EH54 .... 147 D2
Kirkton Pl Cowdenbeath KY4 .... 13 D3
  Falkirk FK2 .... 39 E2
Kirkton Rd KY3 .... 33 F1
Kirkton South Rd EH54 .... 147 E1
Kirkway FK2 .... 22 B2
Kirkwood Ave FK2 .... 6 C1
Kirkwood Cres KY12 .... 28 A1
Kisimul Ct EH12 .... 121 D2
Kitchener Cres EH32 .... 98 C3
Kittle Yds EH9 .... 123 F2
Knaphill KY11 .... 46 C4
Knights Way FK6 .... 36 B1
Knightsbridge Rd
  Livingston EH54 .... 147 E4
  Uphall EH52 .... 116 B1
Knightslaw Pl EH26 .... 203 E3
Knightsridge Cres EH54 .... 116 B1
Knightsridge East Rd
  EH54 .... 147 E4
Knightsridge Prim Sch
  EH54 .... 147 D4
Knightsridge Rdbt EH54 .... 116 B1
Knightsridge West Rd
  EH54 .... 147 D4
Knockenhair Rd EH42 .... 78 A1
Knockhill Cl KY5 .... 14 A4
Knockhouse Gdns KY12 .... 28 A1
Knockhouse Rd KY12 .... 28 A1
Knoll Croft Rd ML7 .... 192 A2
Knowe Park Rd EH47 .... 171 D1
Knowe The Alloa FK10 .... 5 E1
  Dalgety Bay KY11 .... 4 A2
Knowefaulds Rd FK10 .... 4 A2
Knowehead Rd FK2 .... 61 E1
Knowepark Ct EH47 .... 171 D1
Knowes Rd EH41 .... 131 F4
Knowetop EH54 .... 173 E4
Knowetop EH25 .... 180 C2
Knowhead Rd KY12 .... 28 A1
Knox Acad EH41 .... 132 A4
Knox Pl EH41 .... 132 A4
Komarom Pl EH22 .... 157 E2
Kyle Ave FK7 .... 20 C4
Kyle Pl EH7 .... 233 F4
Kyles The KY1 .... 17 F3

La Porte Prec FK3 .... 61 E4
Labrador Ave EH54 .... 147 F2
Laburnum Ct KY1 .... 17 E4
Laburnum Gr
  Burntisland KY3 .... 33 F1
  Stirling FK8 .... 6 C3
Laburnum Pk EH22 .... 183 F3
Laburnum Rd
  Dunfermline KY11 .... 29 E1
  Whitburn EH47 .... 170 B3
Lade Braes KY11 .... 48 A2
Lade Ct EH49 .... 84 C4

Lade Dr FK5 .... 59 E4
Lade Gn KY11 .... 48 A2
Lade Mill FK7 .... 7 E1
Lade Rd FK4 .... 58 A3
Ladehead EH6 .... 93 E2
Ladeside Ave EH47 .... 171 E4
Ladeside Cres FK5 .... 38 C1
Ladeside Dr EH47 .... 171 E4
Ladeside Gdns EH47 .... 171 D4
Ladeside Prim Sch FK5 .... 59 E4
Ladeside Rd EH47 .... 171 E4
Lademeadow EH12 .... 121 F3
Lady Brae EH23 .... 207 E4
Lady Brae Pl EH23 .... 207 F4
Lady Ct EH47 .... 170 B4
Lady Helen Cotts KY5 .... 15 D4
Lady Helen St KY1 .... 17 D1
Lady Jane Gdns EH39 .... 54 B3
Lady Jane Rd EH39 .... 54 B3
Lady Lawson St EH3 .... 232 C2
Lady Menzies Pl 8 EH7 .... 94 A1
Lady Nairn Ave KY1 .... 17 F3
Lady Nairne Cres EH8 .... 124 B4
Lady Nairne Gr EH8 .... 124 B4
Lady Nairne Loan EH8 .... 124 B4
Lady Nairne Pl EH8 .... 124 B4
Lady Nairne Rd KY12 .... 28 C3
Lady Pl EH54 .... 147 D3
Lady Rd EH16 .... 124 A2
Lady Road Pl EH22 .... 183 D3
Lady Victoria Bsns Ctr
  EH22 .... 183 D2
Lady Wood Pl EH54 .... 147 D3
Lady Wynd EH1 .... 232 C2
Ladyburn Pl KY3 .... 35 D2
Ladycroft EH14 .... 151 E1
Ladygate Ct FK2 .... 39 D2
Ladysmill FK2 .... 60 B3
Ladysmill Ct KY12 .... 29 D1
Ladysmill Ind Est FK1 .... 60 B3
Ladysneuk Rd FK9 .... 2 B1
Ladywell EH12 .... 121 E3
Ladywell Ave EH12 .... 121 E3
Ladywell Ct
  Edinburgh EH12 .... 121 E3
  Larbert FK5 .... 38 A2
Ladywell Dr FK10 .... 4 A2
Ladywell E Cres EH54 .... 147 E3
Ladywell East Rd EH54 .... 147 F3
Ladywell Gdns EH12 .... 121 E3
Ladywell Gr FK10 .... 11 D2
Ladywell Prim Sch FK1 .... 60 A4
Ladywell Rd EH12 .... 121 E3
Ladywell View EH51 .... 63 E3
Ladywell Way EH21 .... 126 B3
Ladywell West Rd EH54 .... 147 E3
Ladywood FK10 .... 11 E2
Ladywood Prim Sch
  EH54 .... 204 A4
Lagan Rd ML8 .... 230 A1
Laggan Ave ML7 .... 192 A2
Laggan Path ML7 .... 179 F3
Laichfield EH14 .... 122 A2
Laichpark Pl EH14 .... 122 A2
Laichpark Rd EH14 .... 122 A2
Laing Gdns EH52 .... 117 E3
Laing Terr Edinburgh EH15 .... 125 E4
  Penicuik EH26 .... 203 F4
Laird Terr EH19 .... 182 B3
Laird's Entry EH37 .... 185 E2
Lakeside Rd KY2 .... 16 C2
Lamb's Cl EH8 .... 233 E1
Lamb's Pend EH26 .... 203 E3
Lambert Dr KY12 .... 29 E2
Lambert Terr FK10 .... 10 B4
Lamberton Ave FK7 .... 7 E2
Lambie St EH34 .... 160 C3
Lambie St EH47 .... 170 A4
Lamer St EH42 .... 78 B1
Lamington Rd EH13 .... 130 B4
Lammerlaws Rd KY3 .... 50 C4
Lammermoor Gdns
  EH33 .... 128 A3
Lammermoor Terr
  Edinburgh EH16 .... 124 B1
  Tranent EH33 .... 128 A3
Lammermuir Cres
  Dunbar EH42 .... 78 B1
  Haddington EH41 .... 132 B4
Lammermuir Ct EH31 .... 52 A1
Lammermuir Pl KY2 .... 16 C3
Lammerview
  Gladsmuir EH33 .... 130 B4
  Tranent EH33 .... 128 B3
Lamond View KY5 .... 38 B1
Lamont Cres FK7 .... 8 B3
Lamont Way EH54 .... 147 E4
Lampacre Rd EH12 .... 121 F3
Lanark Ave EH14 .... 147 D3
Lanark Rd
  Edinburgh, Kingsknowe
  EH14 .... 122 A1
  Edinburgh, Westerhailes
  EH13 .... 152 C3
Landale Gdns KY3 .... 33 F1
Landale Pl KY3 .... 33 F1
Landale St KY5 .... 14 A4
Lane The EH21 .... 126 C1
Lang Loan EH17 .... 155 E2
Langfauld Gdns EH48 .... 144 C3
Langhill Pl FK6 .... 36 B1
Langlaw Prim Sch EH22 .... 183 E4
Langlaw Rd EH22 .... 183 E4
Langlees Prim Sch FK2 .... 60 A4
Langlees St FK2 .... 39 E1
Langriggs EH41 .... 132 A4

Langside EH40 .... 103 E4
Langside Cres EH55 .... 173 D3
Langside Dr EH48 .... 142 A2
Langside Gdns EH55 .... 173 D3
Langton Ave EH53 .... 148 C2
Langton Gdns EH53 .... 148 C2
Langton Rd
  East Calder EH53 .... 148 C2
  Edinburgh EH9 .... 123 F2
  Westquarter FK2 .... 61 D2
Langton View EH53 .... 148 C2
Lanrigg Ave EH47 .... 193 F4
Lanrigg Rd EH47 .... 193 F4
Lansbury Ct EH22 .... 157 D2
Lansbury St KY1 .... 17 F4
Lansdowne Cres
  Edinburgh EH12 .... 232 A2
  Kincardine EH10 .... 23 F2
  Shotts ML7 .... 192 A2
Lapicide Pl EH6 .... 93 F3
Larbert Ave EH54 .... 147 D4
Larbert High Sch FK5 .... 38 C1
Larbert High Sch (Annexe)
  FK5 .... 38 C1
Larbert Pl FK4 .... 58 A3
Larbert Sta FK5 .... 38 B1
Larbert Village Prim Sch
  FK5 .... 38 A1
Larbourfield EH11 .... 121 E1
Larch Cres EH22 .... 183 F3
Larch Dr EH47 .... 170 B3
Larch Gr Dunfermline KY11 .... 46 B4
  Stenhousemuir FK5 .... 38 C2
Larch St FK3 .... 61 E3
Larchbank EH54 .... 147 F3
Larches The FK10 .... 10 A4
Larchfield EH14 .... 151 E1
Larchfield Ave ML7 .... 192 A1
Larchfield Neuk EH14 .... 151 E1
Largo Pl EH6 .... 93 F3
Larkfield Dr EH22 .... 156 C1
Larkfield Rd EH22 .... 156 C1
Lasswade Bank EH17 .... 155 E3
Lasswade Gr EH17 .... 155 E3
Lasswade High Sch EH19 .... 182 B4
Lasswade Prim Sch EH19 .... 182 B4
Lasswade Rd
  Bonnyrigg and Lasswade
  EH18 .... 156 A1
  Dalkeith EH22 .... 156 C1
  Edinburgh EH16, EH17 .... 155 E3
  Loanhead EH20 .... 181 E4
Latch EH13 .... 153 E4
Latch Rd EH42 .... 78 C1
Latch The KY12 .... 27 E1
Lathallan Dr FK2 .... 61 F1
Lauder Gdns KY11 .... 30 A3
Lauder Loan EH9 .... 123 F2
Lauder Lodge EH22 .... 157 D2
Lauder Pl EH8 .... 233 F4
Lauder Rd Dalkeith EH22 .... 157 E1
  Edinburgh EH9 .... 123 E2
Lauderdale Cres EH42 .... 78 B1
Lauderdale St EH9 .... 123 E3
Laurel Bank EH22 .... 157 E1
Laurel Bank Pl EH22 .... 183 F3
Laurel Bank Rd EH22 .... 183 F3
Laurel Cres KY1 .... 17 D4
Laurel Ct FK1 .... 59 E3
Laurel Gr Bonnybridge FK4 .... 57 F2
  Westquarter FK2 .... 61 D1
Laurel Pl FK4 .... 57 F2
Laurel Rd KY11 .... 46 B1
Laurel Terr EH11 .... 122 C3
Laurelbank Ave FK4 .... 58 A2
Laurelbank EH53 .... 148 C1
Laurelhill Gdns FK8 .... 6 C3
Laurelhill Pl FK8 .... 7 D3
Laurieston Prim Sch FK2 .... 61 D2
Laurie St EH6 .... 94 A3
Lauriston Castle EH4 .... 91 F3
Lauriston Dr KY12 .... 29 E3
Lauriston Farm Rd EH4 .... 91 F2
Lauriston Gdns EH3 .... 232 C1
Lauriston Pk EH3 .... 232 C1
Lauriston St EH3 .... 232 C2
Lauriston Terr EH3 .... 232 C2
Laurmont Ct FK2 .... 61 D2
Laverock Dr EH26 .... 203 E3
Laverock Pk EH49 .... 85 D3
Laverockbank Ave EH5 .... 93 E3
Laverockbank Cres EH5 .... 93 E3
Laverockbank Gdns EH5 .... 93 E3
Laverockbank Gr EH5 .... 93 E3
Laverockbank Rd EH5 .... 93 E3
Laverockbank Terr EH5 .... 93 E3
Laverockdale Cres EH13 .... 153 D3
Laverockdale Loan EH13 .... 153 D3
Laverockdale Pk EH13 .... 153 D3
Law Pl EH15 .... 95 D1
Law Rd Dunfermline KY11 .... 29 D1
  North Berwick EH39 .... 54 B4
Lawers Cres FK2 .... 62 A1
Lawers Pl FK3 .... 61 F3
Lawers Sq EH26 .... 204 A4
Lawfield Rd EH22 .... 183 E4
Lawhead Cotts EH46 .... 220 B3
Lawhead Pl EH26 .... 203 E3
Lawmarket EH1 .... 233 D3
Lawrence St EH41 .... 131 F4
Lawrie Dr EH26 .... 203 F4
Lawson Cres EH30 .... 89 E4

Lawson Gdns KY1 .... 17 F4
Lawson Pl Dunbar EH42 .... 78 B1
  Maddiston EH42 .... 83 D3
Lawson St KY1 .... 5 F2
Laxford Cres KY11 .... 48 A2
Leadburn Ave KY12 .... 29 D4
Leadervale Rd EH16 .... 154 C4
Leadervale Terr EH16 .... 154 C4
Leadside Cres KY12 .... 29 D4
Leamington Pl EH10 .... 232 B1
Leamington Rd EH3 .... 232 A1
Leamington Terr EH10 .... 123 D3
Learmonth Ave EH4 .... 92 C1
Learmonth Cres
  Edinburgh EH4 .... 92 C1
  West Calder EH55 .... 172 B2
Learmonth Ct EH4 .... 92 C1
Learmonth
  Gardens News ☰ EH4 .... 93 D1
Learmonth Gdns ☰ EH4 .... 92 C1
Learmonth Gr EH4 .... 92 C1
Learmonth Pk ☰ EH4 .... 92 C1
Learmonth Pl EH4 .... 232 A4
Learmonth St FK1 .... 60 A2
Learmonth Terr EH4 .... 92 C1
Learmonth Terrace La
  EH4 .... 232 A4
Ledi Ave FK10 .... 4 A2
Ledi Pl EH26 .... 81 F4
Ledi Terr EH26 .... 204 A4
Ledi View FK9 .... 2 A2
Ledmore Pl FK1 .... 60 C1
Lee Cres EH15 .... 125 D4
Leighton Cres EH22 .... 183 E4
Leighton St KY12 .... 26 A1
Leith Acad EH6 .... 94 A2
Leith Ave KY3 .... 33 F1
Leith Pl FK5 .... 57 E4
Leith Prim Sch EH6 .... 93 F3
Leith St EH1 .... 233 D4
Leith Walk Prim Sch EH7 .... 93 F1
Leith Wlk EH6, EH7 .... 93 F2
Lempockwells Rd EH34 .... 160 C3
Lendrick Ave FK1 .... 59 F1
Lennel Ave EH12 .... 122 B4
Lenniemuir EH12 .... 90 A1
Lennox Ave FK7 .... 7 D2
Lennox Gdns EH49 .... 84 B4
Lennox Milne Ct EH41 .... 132 A4
Lennox Rd EH41 .... 132 B4
Lennox Row EH5 .... 93 D3
Lennox St EH4 .... 232 A4
Lennox Street La EH4 .... 232 A4
Lennox Terr FK1 .... 61 F3
Lennoxlove Acredales
  EH41 .... 132 A4
Leny Pl KY12 .... 28 C3
Lenzie Ave EH54 .... 147 D3
Leopold Pl 6 EH7 .... 93 F1
Leslie Pl EH4 .... 93 D1
Leslie Rd KY11 .... 47 F2
Leslie St KY1 .... 35 D4
Lestrange Terr FK12 .... 5 D4
Letham Ave EH53 .... 148 A4
Letham Cotts EH42 .... 39 E4
Letham Cres EH53 .... 148 A4
Letham Dr EH41 .... 131 F4
Letham Gait KY11 .... 47 F2
Letham Gdns EH53 .... 148 A4
Letham Gr EH53 .... 148 A4
Letham Hill Ave KY11 .... 47 F2
Letham Hill Way KY11 .... 47 F2
Letham Pk Dunbar EH42 .... 78 B1
Letham Pl Dunbar EH42 .... 78 B1
  Pumpherston EH53 .... 148 A4
Letham Prim Sch EH54 .... 78 B1
  Livingston EH54 .... 148 A4
Letham Rise KY11 .... 47 F2
Letham Terr EH53 .... 148 A4
Letham Terrs 22 B1
  North Berwick EH39 .... 54 A4
Leuchatsbeath Dr KY4 .... 13 D3
Leven Cl EH3 .... 232 B1
Leven Ct FK10 .... 10 B3
Leven Ct ML7 .... 191 F3
Leven St Edinburgh EH3 .... 232 B1
  Falkirk FK2 .... 60 A4
Leven Terr EH3 .... 232 C1
Leven Wlk EH54 .... 147 E2
Leven Wlk EH54 .... 147 E2
Leving Pl EH54 .... 147 E2
Lewis Ct Alloa FK10 .... 10 A3
Lewis Rd FK2 .... 61 E1
Lewisvale Ave EH21 .... 126 C3
Lewisvale Ct EH21 .... 126 C3
Leyden Pk EH19 .... 182 A4
Leyden Pl EH19 .... 182 A4
Leys Park Rd KY12 .... 29 D2
Liberton Brae EH16 .... 155 D4
Liberton Dr EH16 .... 154 C4
Liberton Gdns EH16 .... 155 D4
Liberton High Sch EH17 .... 155 E4
Liberton Hospl EH16 .... 155 D4
Liberton Pl EH16 .... 155 D4
Liberton Prim Sch EH16 .... 154 A1
Liberton Rd EH16 .... 124 A1
Liddesdale Pl EH3 .... 93 D1
Liddle Dr EH51 .... 64 A2
Lidgate Shot EH28 .... 119 F1
Liggar's Pl KY12 .... 28 C3
Liggat Pl EH52 .... 117 F3
Liggat Syke Pl EH52 .... 118 A3

Lighton Terr EH47 .... 171 D1
Lilac Ave EH22 .... 183 F3
Lilac Cres KY1 .... 17 E4
Lilac Gr KY11 .... 46 B4
Lillies La EH41 .... 163 F3
Lily Terr EH11 .... 122 C3
Lilybank Ct FK10 .... 5 E1
Lilyhill Terr EH8 .... 94 B1
Lime Ave EH30 .... 66 C1
Lime Gr Dunfermline KY11 .... 29 F1
  Larbert FK5 .... 38 B1
  Mayfield EH22 .... 183 F2
  North Berwick EH39 .... 54 C3
  Polmont FK2 .... 61 F1
Lime Pl EH19 .... 182 A3
Lime Rd FK1 .... 59 D2
Lime St EH6 .... 93 F3
Limebank Pk EH53 .... 148 C1
Limefield EH47 .... 155 F3
Limefield Ave EH55 .... 173 D3
Limefield Cres EH48 .... 145 F3
Limefield Gdns EH55 .... 173 D3
Limefield Rd
  Bathgate EH48 .... 145 E4
  West Calder EH55 .... 173 D3
Limekilns EH34 .... 161 D3
Limekilns Gr EH53 .... 148 C1
Limekilns Prim Sch KY11 .... 45 F2
Limekilns Rd KY12 .... 28 C1
Limerigg Prim Sch FK1 .... 110 B1
Limes The EH10 .... 123 D2
Limetree Wlk EH47 .... 76 B3
Limeylands Cres EH35 .... 159 E4
Limeylands Rd EH35 .... 159 E4
Lina St KY2 .... 17 D3
Linburn Gr KY11 .... 29 F2
Linburn Pk EH27 .... 150 A3
Linburn Pl KY11 .... 29 F2
Linburn Rd KY11 .... 29 F2
Lindean Pl EH6 .... 94 A2
Lindean Terr EH27 .... 149 F3
Linden Ave Denny FK6 .... 36 B2
  Stirling FK7 .... 7 E3
Linden Gr EH54 .... 148 A3
Lindores Dr Kirkcaldy KY2 .... 16 C4
  Tranent EH33 .... 128 B3
Lindsay Dr FK9 .... 2 A2
Lindsay Pl Edinburgh EH6 .... 93 F3
  Lochgelly KY5 .... 14 A4
Lindsay Rd EH6 .... 93 F3
Lindsay Sq EH54 .... 146 B3
Lindsay St EH6 .... 93 F3
Lindsay's Wynd KY12 .... 26 C3
Lingerwood Farm Cotts
  EH22 .... 183 D2
Lingerwood Rd EH22 .... 183 D2
Lingerwood Wlk EH22 .... 183 D2
Linhouse Dr EH53 .... 148 C2
Linhouse Rd EH53 .... 148 C2
Link Rd KY11 .... 47 F2
Linkfield Ct EH21 .... 126 C3
Linkfield Rd EH21 .... 126 C3
Links Ave EH21 .... 126 A4
Links Ct Bo'ness EH51 .... 64 A4
  Cockenzie & Port Seton EH32 .... 97 E2
Links Dr KY12 .... 28 A1
Links Gardens La EH6 .... 94 A3
Links Gdns EH6 .... 94 A3
Links Pl Bo'ness EH51 .... 64 A4
  Burntisland KY3 .... 50 C4
  Cockenzie & Port Seton
  EH32 .... 97 F2
Links Rd Bo'ness EH51 .... 64 A4
  Cockenzie & Port Seton
  EH32 .... 97 F2
  Longniddry EH32 .... 98 C3
  North Berwick EH39 .... 54 A4
Links View
  Cockenzie & Port Seton
  EH32 .... 97 F2
  Musselburgh EH21 .... 126 B4
Links Wlk EH32 .... 97 F2
Linlithgow Acad EH49 .... 84 C3
Linlithgow Canal Mus
  EH49 .... 85 D3
Linlithgow Palace EH49 .... 85 C2
Linlithgow Pl FK5 .... 38 C2
Linlithgow Prim Sch
  West Port Annexe EH49 .... 84 C3
Linlithgow Sta EH49 .... 85 D4
Linlithgow Story (Mus) The
  EH49 .... 85 D3
Linlithgow Terr EH35 .... 159 F4
Linmill Rd FK1 .... 112 A3
Linn Mill EH30 .... 67 F2
Linn Pl EH52 .... 115 F3
Linnet Way EH52 .... 114 C2
Linsay Macdonald Ct KY12 .... 29 E2
Lint Riggs FK1 .... 60 A3
Linton Pl KY11 .... 46 C2
Linty La EH26 .... 203 E3
Linview La EH54 .... 173 F2
Lion Well Wynd EH49 .... 84 C4
Lionthorn Rd FK1 .... 59 F1
Lipney FK11 .... 4 A3

Lismore Ave
4 Edinburgh EH8 .... 94 B1
Kirkcaldy KY2 .... 16 C4
Lismore Cres EH4 .... 94 B1
Lismore Ct FK1 .... 60 A1
Lismore Pl KY2 .... 16 C4
Lismore Prim Sch EH15 .. 124 C3
Lister Cl FK9 .... 2 A3
Lister Rd EH54 .... 147 D1
Listloaning Pl EH49 .... 84 B4
Listloaning Rd EH49 .... 84 B4
Liston Dr EH29 .... 89 D1
Liston Pl EH29 .... 89 D1
Liston Rd EH29 .... 89 D1
Little Acre EH22 .... 183 E4
Little Carriden EH51 .... 64 B3
Little Cswy KY12 .... 42 B4
Little Denny Rd FK6 .... 36 B1
Little Footworn KY12 .... 44 C3
Little France Mills EH16 .. 124 B1
Little King St EH1 .... 233 D4
Little Rd EH16 .... 155 D4
Little Sandhaven KY12 .... 42 B4
Livery St EH48 .... 145 D4
Livesay Rd KY11 .... 46 B1
Livesey Terr EH26 .... 204 A4
Lvilands Ct FK8 .... 7 D3
Lvilands Gate FK8 .... 7 D3
Lvilands La FK8 .... 7 D3
Livingston Mill EH54 .... 147 D1
Livingston North Sta
EH54 .... 147 D3
Livingston Rd EH54 .... 147 F3
Livingston South Sta
EH54 .... 174 A4
Livingstone Cres FK2 .... 60 C3
Livingstone Dr
Bo'ness EH51 .... 63 E3
Burntisland KY3 .... 33 F1
Laurieston FK2 .... 61 D1
Livingstone E Rdbt EH54 .. 116 B1
Livingstone La KY3 .... 49 E4
Livingstone Pl EH9 .... 123 E3
Livingstone Quadrant
ML7 .... 168 B2
Livingstone St EH55 .... 171 F1
Livingstone Terr FK1 .... 61 D1
Lixmount Ave EH5 .... 93 E3
Lixmount Gdns EH5 .... 93 E3
Lizzie Brice's Rdbt EH54 .. 148 A1
Llynallan Rd ML7 .... 168 A3
Loan Pl ML7 .... 168 C3
Loan The Bo'ness EH51 .... 63 E3
Loanhead EH20 .... 181 D4
Pathhead EH37 .... 184 B4
Queensferry EH30 .... 68 A4
Torpichen EH48 .... 113 F3
Loanburn EH26 .... 203 F3
Loanburn Ave EH26 .... 203 F3
Loanfoot Cres EH52 .... 117 D3
Loanfoot Gdns FK7 .... 20 B2
Loanfoot Rd EH52 .... 117 D2
Loanhead Ave
Bankhead FK4 .... 57 E3
Grangemouth FK3 .... 61 F3
Loanhead Hospl EH20 ..... 181 E4
Loanhead Pl KY2 .... 17 D3
Loanhead Prim Sch EH20 . 181 E4
Loanhead Prim Sch
(Annexe) EH20 .... 181 E4
Loanhead Rd EH20 .... 155 D1
Loaning Cres EH7 .... 94 B1
Loaning Rd EH7 .... 94 B1
Loaninghill Pk EH52 .... 117 D2
Loaninghill Rd EH52 .... 117 D2
Loch Awe Way EH47 .... 170 B4
Loch Earn Way EH47 .... 170 B4
Loch Fyne Way EH47 .... 170 B4
Loch Linnhe Ct EH47 .... 170 B4
Loch Maree Way EH47 .... 170 B4
Loch Pl EH30 .... 68 A1
Loch Rd Edinburgh EH4 .... 92 A1
Queensferry EH30 .... 68 A1
Tranent EH33 .... 128 B3
Loch Sq EH33 .... 128 B3
Loch St KY12 .... 29 E4
Loch Trool Way EH47 .... 170 B4
Lochaber Cres ML7 .... 192 A2
Lochaber Dr FK5 .... 38 C2
Lochbank EH54 .... 147 F3
Lochbrae FK10 .... 5 E1
Lochbridge Rd EH39 .... 54 B3
Lochend Ave Dunbar EH42 .. 78 C1
Edinburgh EH7 .... 94 A2
Lochend Castle Barns EH7 . 94 A1
Lochend Cl EH8 .... 233 F3
Lochend Cres Dunbar EH42 . 78 B1
Edinburgh EH7 .... 94 B1
Lochend Dr EH7 .... 94 A1
Lochend Gdns EH7 .... 94 A1
Lochend Gr EH7 .... 94 A1
Lochend Ind Est EH28 ..... 119 D3
Lochend Pk EH7 .... 94 A2
Lochend Quadrant EH7 .... 94 A1
Lochend Rd Dunbar EH42 .. 78 C1
Edinburgh EH6 .... 94 A2
Ratho Station EH28 .... 119 D4
Lochend Rd N EH21 .... 126 A3
Lochend Rd S
Edinburgh EH7 .... 94 A1
Musselburgh EH21 .... 126 A3
Lochend Sq EH7 .... 94 A1
Lochgelly Ind Pk KY5 .... 14 B4
Lochgelly North
Specl Sch (Prim) KY5 .... 14 A4

Lochgelly Rd KY4 .... 13 E3
Lochgelly South Prim Sch
KY5 .... 14 A4
Lochgelly West Prim Sch
KY5 .... 14 A4
Lochgreen Hospl FK1 .... 59 F1
Lochgreen Rd FK1 .... 59 F1
Lochhead Ave FK6 .... 36 C1
Lochhill Cotts EH32 .... 99 F4
Lochies Rd Burntisland KY3 . 34 A1
Clackmannan FK10 .... 10 C3
Lochinvar Pl FK4 .... 58 B2
Lochinvar Rd KY11 .... 46 B1
Lochlands Ind Est FK5 .... 59 D4
Lochmaben Dr FK5 .... 38 C2
Lochpark Pl FK6 .... 36 C1
Lochridge Pl FK6 .... 36 B1
Lochrin Pl EH3 .... 232 B1
Lochshot Pl EH54 .... 147 D2
Lochside Ave EH12 .... 120 C2
Lochside Cres
Edinburgh EH12 .... 120 C2
Redding KY2 .... 61 D1
Lochside Ct EH12 .... 121 D2
Lochside Dr EH12 .... 121 D2
Lochside Rd FK1 .... 110 B1
Lock Rd KY11 .... 52 A4
Lock Sixteen FK1 .... 59 E3
Lockerby Cotts EH16 .... 155 E3
Lockerby Cres EH16 .... 155 E3
Lockerby Gr EH16 .... 155 E3
Lockhart Terr EH25 .... 180 C2
Lockharton Ave EH10 .... 122 C1
Lockharton Cres EH10 ..... 122 C1
Lockharton Gdns EH14 .... 122 C2
Lodge Dr FK5 .... 38 C1
Lodge St EH41 .... 130 A4
Logan St EH3 .... 93 E1
Logan Way EH54 .... 147 E4
Loganlea Ave EH7 .... 94 B1
Loganlea Cres EH55 .... 171 E1
Loganlea Dr EH7 .... 94 B1
Loganlea Gdns EH7 .... 94 B1
Loganlea Loan EH7 .... 94 B1
Loganlea Pl EH7 .... 94 B1
Loganlea Rd
Addiewell EH55 .... 171 E1
Edinburgh EH7 .... 94 B1
Loganlea Terr
Addiewell EH55 .... 171 E1
Edinburgh EH7 .... 94 B1
Logie Dr FK5 .... 38 A2
Logie Green Gdns EH7 .... 93 E2
Logie Green Loan EH7 .... 93 E2
Logie Green Rd EH7 .... 93 E2
Logie La EH7 .... 2 B4
Logie Mill EH7 .... 93 E2
Logie Pl KY12 .... 28 B3
Logie Rd FK9 .... 2 B2
Lomond Cres
Dunfermline KY11 .... 29 F1
Stenhousemuir FK5 .... 38 C2
Stirling FK9 .... 2 A2
Whitburn EH47 .... 161 D4
Lomond Ct FK10 .... 10 B2
Lomond Dr Bannockburn FK7 . 7 F1
Falkirk FK2 .... 39 E1
Lomond Gdns KY2 .... 16 C3
Lomond Rd Edinburgh EH5 . 93 D3
Grangemouth FK3 .... 61 F3
Shotts ML7 .... 191 F3
Lomond St FK10 .... 4 C1
Lomond Vale EH26 .... 204 A4
Lomond View EH48 .... 112 C2
Lomond Way FK6 .... 57 E3
Lomond Wlk EH20 .... 155 D1
London Rd Dalkeith EH22 .. 157 D2
Edinburgh EH7 .... 94 A1
London St EH3 .... 93 E1
London Street Prim Sch
EH7 .... 93 E1
Loney Cres FK6 .... 57 F4
Long Byres EH52 .... 117 F3
Long Craig Rd KY1 .... 35 D4
Long Craigs EH32 .... 97 F2
Long Craigs Terr KY3 .... 35 D2
Long Cram EH41 .... 131 F4
Long Crook EH30 .... 89 D4
Long Dalmahoy Rd EH27 .. 150 B2
Long Row Halbeath KY12 .... 30 A4
Menstrie FK11 .... 4 A4
Longannet Cotts FK10 .... 24 A1
Longbraes Gdns KY2 .... 16 B3
Longcroft Gdns EH49 .... 84 C4
Longdales Ave FK2 .... 60 A4
Longdales Ct FK2 .... 60 A4
Longdales Pl FK2 .... 60 A4
Longdales Rd FK2 .... 60 A4
Longdyke Pl FK2 .... 39 E2
Longdykes Rd EH32 .... 97 D1
Longford ML11 .... 215 D1
Longformacus Rd EH16 ... 155 D4
Longhill Gdns KY11 .... 48 A2
Longniddry Prim Sch
EH32 .... 98 C3
Longniddry Sta EH32 .... 98 C3
Longpark EH49 .... 147 D2
Longridge Prim Sch
EH47 .... 170 B1
Longridge Rd EH47 .... 170 A3
Longstone Ave
East Linton EH40 .... 103 E4
Edinburgh EH14 .... 122 A1
Longstone Cres EH14 ...... 122 A1
Longstone Gdns EH14 ..... 121 F2
Longstone Pk EH14 .... 122 A1
Longstone Rd EH14 .... 122 A1

Longstone Prim Sch
EH14 .... 122 A1
Longstone Rd EH14 .... 122 A1
Longstone St EH14 .... 122 A1
Lonsdale Cres KY3 .... 33 F1
Lonsdale Terr EH3 .... 232 C1
Lookaboutye Brae FK10 ..... 11 D2
Lord President Rd EH39 .... 54 A4
Lord President St EH39 ..... 54 A4
Loretto Ct EH21 .... 126 A2
Loretto RC Prim Sch
EH21 .... 126 B3
Loretto Sch EH21 .... 126 B3
Lorimar PH FK2 .... 39 E1
Lorne Gdns FK2 .... 60 C2
Lorne Gr EH20 .... 155 D1
Lorne Pl EH6 .... 93 F2
Lorne Prim Sch EH6 .... 93 F2
Lorne Rd FK5 .... 38 B1
Lorne Sq Edinburgh EH6 ...... 93 F2
North Berwick EH39 .... 54 B4
Lorne St Edinburgh EH6 .... 93 F2
Kirkcaldy KY1 .... 17 F4
Lornshill Acad FK10 .... 9 C1
Lornshill Cres KY10 .... 9 F4
Losshill FK11 .... 4 A3
Lothian Bank EH22 .... 156 C1
Lothian Coll of Nursing &
Midwifery EH3 .... 232 C2
Lothian Cres Bo'ness EH51 . 64 A3
Stirling FK9 .... 2 A2
Lothian Ct KY11 .... 47 E1
Lothian Dr EH22 .... 183 E4
Lothian Rd Dalkeith EH22 .. 157 D2
Edinburgh EH1 .... 232 B2
Lothian St Bathgate EH48 . 145 D4
Bo'ness EH51 .... 64 A4
Bonnyrigg and Lasswade
EH19 .... 182 B4
Burntisland KY3 .... 50 C4
Dalkeith EH22 .... 157 D2
Edinburgh EH1 .... 123 D4
Rosewell EH24 .... 181 E1
Lothian Terr Kirkcaldy KY2 .. 17 D1
Newtongrange EH22 .... 183 D2
Lothian View KY11 .... 47 D1
Loudon's Wlk FK6 .... 36 C2
Loudoun EH48 .... 142 B2
Loughborough Rd KY1 .... 17 F4
Loughrigg KY11 .... 47 D2
Louisa Sq EH24 .... 181 E1
Louise St KY11 .... 29 E1
Lovedale Ave EH14 .... 151 D1
Lovedale Cres EH14 .... 151 D1
Lovedale Gdns EH14 .... 151 D1
Lovedale Gr EH14 .... 151 D1
Lovedale Rd EH14 .... 151 D1
Lovells Glen EH49 .... 84 B4
Lovers La EH30 .... 89 E4
Lovers Loan Alva FK12 .... 5 D4
Dunfermline KY12 .... 28 C1
Low Brae EH48 .... 113 F3
Low Causewayside
Culross KY12 .... 42 B4
Newmills KY12 .... 26 B1
Low Cswy Culross KY12 .... 25 F1
Torryburn KY12 .... 26 C1
Low Doors The EH7 .... 149 F1
Low Port Prim Sch EH49 ... 85 D4
Lower Alderston Rd
EH41 .... 100 C1
Lower Bathville EH48 .... 144 A3
Lower Bridge St FK8 .... 2 A1
Lower Broomieknowe
EH18 .... 182 A4
Lower Castlehill FK8 .... 2 A1
Lower Gilmore Pl EH3 ...... 232 A1
Lower Granton Rd EH5 ...... 93 D3
Lower Joppa EH15 .... 125 E4
Lower London Rd EH7 .... 94 A1
Lower Valleyfield View
EH26 .... 203 F2
Lowlandman's Rd KY12 ..... 45 E2
Lowlands Crofts EH55 ...... 196 B2
Lowrie Ave EH26 .... 203 E3
Lowry Pl KY11 .... 46 C2
Ludgate FK10 .... 4 A3
Luffness Ct EH32 .... 71 E2
Luffness Mains Cotts
EH39 .... 72 A2
Lugton Brae EH52 .... 156 C2
Lugton Sch EH22 .... 156 C2
Lumley Ct FK1 .... 61 E4
Lumley Pl FK3 .... 61 E4
Lumley St FK3 .... 61 E4
Lumphinnans
Prim & Com Sch KY4 .... 13 E3
Lumphinnans Rd KY5 .... 14 A4
Lumsdaine Dr KY11 .... 48 A1
Lumsden Ct
Broxburn EH52 .... 117 E3
Ratho EH28 .... 119 E1
Lundin Rd KY12 .... 28 A2
Lussielaw Rd EH9 .... 123 F2
Lutton Court Bsns Ctr
EH8 .... 233 E1
Lutton Pl EH8 .... 233 E1
Luvain Gdns EH48 .... 142 B2
Lyall Cres FK1 .... 61 F1
Lyars Rd EH32 .... 98 B1
Lyarthall EH52 .... 117 E3
Lychgate Rd FK10 .... 4 A1
Lydgait EH41 .... 101 D1
Lydgait Gdns EH41 .... 101 D1

Lyefield Pl EH54 .... 147 D2
Lygon Rd EH16 .... 123 F1
Lyle Gn EH54 .... 147 D4
Lynburn Sch KY11 .... 29 F1
Lyne Gr KY12 .... 28 B1
Lyne St EH7 .... 94 A1
Lynedoch Pl EH3 .... 204 A4
Lynebank
(Psychiatric) Hospl KY11 .. 30 A3
Lynedoch PH EH3 .... 80 A3
Lynedoch Pl EH3 .... 232 A3
Lynedoch Place La EH3 .... 232 A3
Lyness Ct FK2 .... 61 F1
Lynn Lea Ave EH41 .... 132 B4
Lyon Cres FK9 .... 2 A3
Lyon Ct EH51 .... 63 E3
Lyon Dr EH54 .... 173 F3

Mac Cormick Terr EH26 ... 203 F4
Macadam Pl FK1 .... 59 E3
Macarthur Cres FK2 .... 82 C3
Macbeth Moir Rd EH21 .... 127 D3
Macbeth Rd KY11 .... 29 F2
Macdonald Ave EH48 .... 143 F3
Macdonald Dr FK7 .... 7 D2
Macdonald Pl KY3 .... 34 A1
Macdonald Sq KY11 .... 46 A1
Macdonald Rd EH9 .... 123 F2
Macduff Cres KY3 .... 34 C1
Mace Ct FK7 .... 7 E2
Macfarlane Cres FK1 .... 60 A3
Macfarlane Pl EH52 .... 116 C2
Machrie Ct FK1 .... 59 E2
Macindoe Cres KY1 .... 17 E4
Macintosh Pl FK1 .... 60 A3
Macintosh Rd EH54 .... 146 C1
Mackenzie Cres KY5 .... 14 B4
Mackenzie Pl
Edinburgh EH3 .... 232 B4
Falkirk FK1 .... 60 A1
Mackenzie Terr FK3 .... 61 E3
Mackie Pl KY11 .... 29 F1
Maclachlan Ave FK6 .... 36 C1
Maclardy Ct EH52 .... 116 C2
Maclaren Terr FK2 .... 39 D1
Maclean Cres KY12 .... 5 E4
Maclean Pl FK7 .... 7 E2
Maclean Terr EH48 .... 142 B2
Macmerry Ind Est EH33 .. 129 F3
Macmerry Prim Sch
EH33 .... 129 E3
Macmillan Rd EH54 .... 147 E1
Macnair Ave EH39 .... 54 B3
Macpherson Pl FK1 .... 59 E2
Mactaggart Loan EH22 .... 183 D2
Madderfield Mews EH49 .... 85 D4
Maddiston Prim Sch FK2 .... 82 C3
Maddiston Rd FK2 .... 82 C4
Madeira Pl EH6 .... 93 F3
Madeira St EH6 .... 93 F3
Madill Pl FK5 .... 38 C2
Maesterton Pl EH22 .... 183 D2
Mag's Bank EH41 .... 133 D1
Magdala Cres EH12 .... 122 C4
Magdala Mews EH12 .... 122 C4
Magdalene Ave EH15 .... 125 D3
Magdalene Ct EH15 .... 125 D3
Magdalene Dr EH15 .... 125 D3
Magdalene Gdns EH15 ..... 125 D3
Magdalene Loan EH15 ..... 125 D3
Magdalene Medway EH15 . 125 D3
Magdalene Pl EH15 .... 125 D3
Maggie Wood's Loan FK1 .. 59 F3
Magnus Rd FK1 .... 62 B3
Maidencraig Cres EH4 .... 92 B2
Maidencraig Gr EH4 .... 92 B1
Maidenpark Pl EH51 .... 63 F3
Maidlands EH49 .... 85 E4
Main Point EH3 .... 232 C2
Main Rd Charlestown KY11 .. 45 D2
Crombie KY12 .... 45 D4
Grangemouth FK3 .... 62 A4
Macmerry EH33 .... 129 E3
Main St Aberdour KY3 .... 49 E4
Airth FK2 .... 22 B2
Alloa FK10 .... 10 B3
Auchtertool KY2 .... 15 D1
Avonbridge FK1 .... 112 A3
Balerno EH14 .... 151 E1
Bannockburn FK7 .... 7 E1
Bathgate EH48 .... 145 D4
Blackridge EH48 .... 142 B2
Bo'ness EH51 .... 64 A4
Bonnybridge FK4 .... 58 A3
Brighton's FK2 .... 82 B4
Cairneyhill KY12 .... 27 E1
California FK1 .... 81 E3
Cambus FK10 .... 9 D4
Carnock KY12 .... 27 E4
Carrington EH23 .... 206 B3
Clackmannan FK10 .... 11 D2
Comrie EH22 .... 26 B4
Cowdenbeath, Hill of Beath
KY4 .... 13 D1
Cowdenbeath, Lumphinnans
KY4 .... 13 F3
Cowie FK7 .... 20 B4
Crossford KY12 .... 28 B1
Crosshill KY5 .... 14 A2
Dalmeny EH29, EH30 .... 89 F4
Dechmont EH52 .... 116 B3
East Calder EH53 .... 148 C2
East Saltoun EH34 .... 166 B2
East Whitburn EH47 .... 170 B4
Edinburgh EH4 .... 93 E4
East 91 F2
Elphinstone EH33 .... 128 A1

Main St continued
Falkirk FK1 .... 59 F3
Falkirk, Bainsford FK2 .... 60 A4
Falkirk, Carronshore FK2 ... 39 E2
Falkirk FK1 .... 59 F3
Fauldhouse EH47 .... 193 E3
Forth ML11 .... 215 D1
Gifford EH41 .... 163 F3
Gorebridge EH23 .... 207 E4
Gullane EH31 .... 52 A1
Halbeath KY11 .... 30 A4
High Valleyfield KY12 .... 25 F1
Kirkliston EH29, EH30 .... 89 D1
Kirknewton EH53, EH27 ... 149 F1
Larbert FK5 .... 38 B1
Limekilns KY11 .... 45 E2
Livingston EH49 .... 84 B4
Livingston, Deans EH54 .... 146 C3
Lochgelly KY5 .... 14 A4
Longniddry EH32 .... 98 C3
Longridge EH47 .... 170 B1
Mid Calder EH53 .... 148 B2
Newton EH52 .... 88 A4
Newtongrange EH22 .... 183 D3
North Queensferry KY11 .... 68 B3
Ormiston EH35 .... 159 F4
Pathhead EH37 .... 185 D3
Pathhead, Dewartown EH37 . 184 B3
Philpstoun EH49 .... 86 B4
Plean FK7 .... 20 B2
Polmont FK2 .... 61 F1
Ratho EH28 .... 119 E1
Redding FK2 .... 61 E1
Roslin EH25 .... 181 D2
Shieldhill FK1 .... 81 E3
Shotts ML7 .... 192 A2
Slamannan FK1 .... 110 A4
Stenhousemuir FK5 .... 38 C1
Stirling, Cambusbarron FK7 . 6 B3
Stirling, St Ninians FK7 .... 7 D2
Stoneyburn EH47 .... 171 D1
Torphichen EH48 .... 26 B1
Townhill KY12 .... 29 E4
Tullibody FK10 .... 4 A1
West Calder EH55 .... 172 B2
Westfield EH48 .... 112 C3
Winchburgh EH52 .... 87 F2
Main St E EH11 .... 123 E4
Main St S Hillend KY11 .... 47 F2
East 3 F3
Mains Of Craigmillar
EH16 .... 124 B1
Mains Rd Harthill ML7 ...... 168 C3
Linlithgow EH49 .... 84 C3
Maitland Ave
Bannockburn FK7 .... 7 E1
Musselburgh EH21 .... 126 A3
Maitland Cres FK7 .... 7 E1
Maitland Hog La EH29 .... 89 D1
Maitland Park Rd EH21 .... 126 A3
Maitland Rd
Kirkliston EH29 .... 89 D1
Rosyth KY11 .... 67 D4
Maitland St
Dunfermline KY12 .... 28 C2
Musselburgh EH21 .... 126 A3
Majors Loan FK1 .... 60 A2
Majors Pl FK1 .... 60 A2
Malbet Pk EH16 .... 155 D4
Malcolm Ct EH48 .... 144 C3
Malcolm Dr FK5 .... 38 C2
Malcolm St KY11 .... 29 D1
Mall Ave EH21 .... 126 B3
Mall The EH54 .... 148 A3
Mallard Brae EH54 .... 147 E3
Mallens Brae EH48 .... 114 A3
Malleny Millgate EH14 .... 177 E4
Mallny Ave EH14 .... 151 E1
Malplaquet Ct ML8 .... 230 A1
Malta Gn EH4 .... 93 D1
Malta Terr EH4 .... 93 D1
Maltings The
Auchtertool KY2 .... 15 D1
Linlithgow EH49 .... 84 B3
Mamre Dr FK1 .... 81 F3
Man O' War Way EH51 .... 64 A4
Mandel Rigg FK2 .... 82 C3
Mandela Ave FK2 .... 60 B4
Manderston St EH6 .... 93 F2
Mandora Ct ML8 .... 230 A1
Manitoba Ave FK10 .... 11 D2
Mannan Dr FK10 .... 11 D2
Mannering Pl EH16 .... 155 D4
Mannfield Ave FK4 .... 57 F2
Manor Cres FK10 .... 4 A1
Manor Gdns EH41 .... 3 D2
Manor Loan FK11 .... 4 A2
Manor Pl EH3 .... 232 A3
Manor Powis Cotts FK11 ...... 3 D2
Manse St FK1 .... 60 A2
Manor Wynd FK7 .... 83 D3
Manse Ave
Dechmont EH48 .... 143 F3
Whitburn EH47 .... 170 A3
Manse Cres FK7 .... 7 D2
Manse Ct EH53 .... 148 C2
Manse Gr EH47 .... 171 E1
Manse La Auchtertool KY3 .. 33 F1
Cockenzie & Port Seton
EH32 .... 97 E2
Musselburgh EH21 .... 126 B3
Manse Pl Bannockburn FK7 .. 7 E1
Bathgate EH48 .... 145 F3
Falkirk FK1 .... 60 A2
Inverkeithing KY11 .... 47 D1
Slamannan FK1 .... 110 A4

Manse Rd Carrington EH23 .. 206 B3
Crossgates KY4 30 C4
Dirleton EH39 53 D3
Edinburgh EH12 121 E3
Forth ML11 215 D1
Inverkeithing KY11 47 D1
Kincardine FK10 23 F3
Kinghorn KY3 34 C2
Kirkliston EH29 89 D1
Linlithgow EH49 85 D3
Roslin EH25 181 D2
Shotts ML7 192 A2
Torphichen EH48 113 F3
Whitburn EH47 170 A3
Manse St Aberdour KY3 49 E4
Edinburgh EH12 121 E3
Manse View
Armadale EH48 143 F3
Innerwick EH42 107 F1
Mansefield
Athelstaneford EH39 101 F4
East Calder EH53 148 C2
Mansefield Ct
2 Bathgate EH48 145 D4
Livingston EH54 147 E2
Mansefield Gr EH48 145 D3
Mansefield St EH48 145 D4
Mansewood Cres EH47 170 A3
Mansfield Ave Alloa FK10 5 E1
Musselburgh EH21 126 B3
Newtongrange EH22 183 D3
Mansfield Ct EH21 126 B3
Mansfield Pl
Edinburgh EH3 93 E1
Musselburgh EH21 126 B3
Newtongrange EH22 183 D3
Mansfield Rd
Balerno EH14 177 E4
Musselburgh EH21 126 B3
Newtongrange EH22 183 D3
Mansionhouse Rd
Edinburgh EH9 123 E3
Falkirk FK1 59 E3
Manson Sq EH54 146 B3
Manuel Terr EH49 83 F3
Maple Ave FK5 38 C2
Maple Ct FK10 10 A3
Maple Gr EH54 148 A3
Maple Pl FK6 36 B2
Maple St KY2 17 D4
Mar Pl Alloa FK10 5 E1
Stirling FK8 7 D4
Mar St FK10 10 A3
Mar Terr FK10 11 D2
Maranatha Cres FK2 82 B4
March Gr EH4 92 A1
March Pines EH4 91 F1
March Rd EH4 92 A1
Marchbank Dr EH14 177 E4
Marchbank Gdns EH14 177 E4
Marchbank Gr EH14 177 E4
Marchbank Pl EH14 177 E4
Marchbank Way EH14 151 E1
Marchburn Dr EH26 203 E3
Marches Dr EH48 144 A3
Marches The
Armadale EH48 144 A3
Stirling FK8 7 D4
Marchfield Gr EH4 92 A2
Marchfield Park La EH4 91 F2
Marchfield Pk EH4 91 F2
Marchfield Terr EH4 92 A2
Marchglen FK13 5 F3
Marchhall Cres EH16 124 A3
Marchhall Pl EH16 124 A3
Marchhall Rd EH16 124 A3
Marchlands Ave EH51 64 A4
Marchlands La EH51 64 A4
Marchmont Ave FK2 61 F1
Marchmont Cres EH9 123 E3
Marchmont Ct FK2 61 F1
Marchmont Rd EH9 123 E3
Marchmont St EH9 123 E3
Marchside Ct FK10 5 E1
Marchwood Ave EH48 145 E3
Marchwood Cres EH48 145 E3
Marchwood Ct EH33 128 A1
Mardale Cres EH10 123 D2
Maree Ct FK10 10 B3
Maree Pl Crossford KY12 28 A1
Kircaldy KY2 16 C4
Maree Wlk EH54 148 A2
Margaret Ave
Bathgate EH48 145 F3
Haggs FK4 57 D2
Margaret Ct FK6 36 C1
Margaret Dr FK4 58 A3
Margaret Rd FK7 7 E1
Margaret Terr FK5 38 C2
Maria St KY1 17 E3
Marina Rd EH48 145 F3
Marine Dr EH4, EH5 92 A3
Marine Espl EH6 94 B3
Marine Par EH39 54 B4
Marine Rd Dunbar EH42 78 B2
Gullane EH31 52 A2
Marine Terr EH31 52 A2
Mariner Ave FK1 59 D3
Mariner Dr FK1 59 D3
Mariner Gdns FK1 59 E3
Mariner Rd FK1 59 E3
Mariner St FK1 59 D3
Mariners St KY2 17 D3
Mariners Wlk KY11 47 F2
Marion St KY1 17 D1
Marionville Ave EH7 94 B1
Marionville Cres EH7 94 B1
Marionville Dr EH7 94 B1
Marionville Gr EH7 94 B1
Marionville Pk EH7 94 A1
Marionville Rd EH7 94 A1
Marischal Dr EH16 124 C2
Marischal Pl 6 EH4 92 B1
Maritime La EH6 94 A3
Maritime St EH6 94 A3
Marjoribanks St EH48 145 D3
Market Ct EH41 101 D1
Market La EH49 85 D4
Market Pl
North Berwick EH39 54 B4
Whitburn EH47 170 A4
Market St Bo'ness EH51 63 F4
Dunfermline KY12 29 D2
Edinburgh EH1 233 D3
Haddington EH41 132 A4
Mid Calder EH53 148 B2
Musselburgh EH21 126 A3
Marketgate EH35 159 F4
Markfield Rd KY11 48 B2
Markle Steading EH40 103 D4
Marlborough Dr FK9 2 B2
Marlborough St EH15 125 D4
Marly Gn EH39 54 A3
Marly Rise EH39 54 A3
Marmion Ave EH25 180 C2
Marmion Cres
Edinburgh EH16 124 A1
North Berwick EH39 54 A4
Marmion Rd
Bathgate EH48 145 D4
Grangemouth FK3 61 E3
North Berwick EH39 54 A4
Marmion St FK2 60 A4
Marquis Dr FK10 11 D2
Marrfield Rd EH54 117 D1
Marrfield Terr EH54 117 D1
Marschal Ct FK7 7 E2
Marshall Pl KY11 29 D1
Marshall Rd EH29 89 D1
Marshall St
Cockenzie & Port Seton EH32 . 97 D2
Cowdenbeath KY4 13 E2
Edinburgh EH8 233 D2
Grangemouth FK3 61 E4
Marshall's Ct EH1 233 E4
Marshill FK10 10 A3
Martin Brae EH54 147 E3
Martin Gr EH19 182 B4
Martin Pl EH22 156 C1
Mary Erskine
Sch for Girls The EH4 92 A1
Mary Erskine & Stewart's
Melville Jun Sch The EH4 .. 92 C1
Mary Pl Clackmannan FK10 11 D3
Dunfermline KY11 29 D1
Mary Sq FK2 61 D2
Mary St FK2 60 C2
Mary Stevenson Dr FK10 10 A4
Mary Street Rdbt FK2 60 C2
Mary's Pl EH4 93 D1
Maryburn Rd EH22 183 E4
Maryfield 2 EH7 93 F1
Maryfield Pk EH53 148 B1
Maryfield Pl
Bonnyrigg and Lasswade
EH19 182 B4
2 Edinburgh EH7 94 A1
Falkirk FK1 59 D2
Maryflats Pl FK3 61 F4
Maryhall St KY1 17 E3
Marywell KY1 17 E3
Masefield Way EH12 90 A1
Mason Pl EH18 181 F3
Masserene Rd KY2 16 C3
Masterton Rd KY11 47 D4
Mather Terr FK2 60 C2
Mathers Ave EH47 169 F3
Mathieson Pl KY11 29 F1
Matthew St KY2 17 D3
Maukeshill Ct EH54 147 E1
Maulsford Ave EH22 156 A4
Maurice Ave FK7 7 E2
Maurice Pl EH9 123 E1
Mauricewood Ave EH26 203 F4
Mauricewood Bank EH26 203 F4
Mauricewood Gr EH26 203 F4
Mauricewood Pk EH26 203 F4
Mauricewood Prim Sch
EH26 204 A4
Mauricewood Rd EH26 203 F4
Mauricewood Rise EH26 203 F4
Mavisbank EH20 181 E4
Mavisbank Ave FK1 81 E3
Mavisbank Pl EH18 181 F3
Maxton Cres FK12 5 E4
Maxton Ct EH22 157 D2
Maxton Pl KY11 46 C2
Maxwell Cres KY4 13 D1
Maxwell Pl FK8 7 D4
Maxwell Rd EH39 53 D2
Maxwell Sq EH54 173 E3
Maxwell St EH10 123 D2
May Terr EH39 54 A4
Maybank Villas EH12 121 E4
Mayburn Ave EH20 155 D1
Mayburn Bank EH20 181 D4
Mayburn Cres EH20 155 D1
Mayburn Ct EH20 181 D4
Mayburn Dr EH20 155 D1
Mayburn Gr EH20 181 D4
Mayburn Hill EH20 181 D4
Mayburn Loan EH20 155 D1
Mayburn Terr EH20 155 D1
Mayburn Vale EH20 181 D4
Mayburn Wlk EH20 181 D4
Maybury Rd EH12 121 D4
Mayfield Ave EH21 126 A2
Mayfield Cres
Clackmannan FK10 11 D3
Loanhead EH20 181 E4
Musselburgh EH21 126 A2
Mayfield Ct Armadale EH48 . 143 F2
Loanhead EH20 181 E4
Stirling FK7 7 D2
Mayfield Dr
Armadale EH48 143 F3
Longcroft FK4 57 D2
Mayfield Gdns EH9 123 F2
Mayfield Gdns La EH9 123 F2
Mayfield Ind Est EH22 183 E3
Mayfield Mews FK1 59 F2
Mayfield Pk EH21 126 A2
Mayfield Pl Mayfield EH22 183 E3
Musselburgh EH21 126 A2
Mayfield Prim Sch EH22 183 E3
Mayfield Rd
Easthouses EH22 183 E4
Edinburgh EH9 123 F2
Redding FK2 61 E1
Mayfield St FK7 7 D2
Mayfield Terr EH9 123 F2
Mayflower St KY12 29 E4
Maygate KY12 29 D2
Mayne Ave FK9 2 A3
Mayshade Rd EH20 155 D1
Mayville Bank EH21 127 D3
Mayville Gdns EH5 93 E3
Mayville Gdns E EH5 93 E3
Mayville Pk EH42 78 B2
McAdam Sq EH54 173 E3
McAlley Ct FK9 1 C4
McAllister Ct FK7 7 E1
McCall Gdns EH40 103 E4
McCallum Ct EH48 143 F4
McCann Ave EH52 117 D3
McCathie Dr EH22 183 D3
McClelland Cres KY11 29 D1
McDiarmid Gr EH22 183 D2
McDonald Pl EH7 93 F2
McDonald Rd EH7 93 F2
McDonald St EH7 93 F2
McDouall Stewart Mus
KY1 18 A4
McDouall Stuart Pl KY1 18 A4
McGinley Way EH49 84 B3
McGregor Ave KY5 14 A4
McGrigor Rd Rosyth KY11 46 B1
Stirling FK7 7 D2
McIntosh Ct EH52 117 E3
McKane Pl KY12 28 C1
McKay Dr KY11 29 F1
McKell Ct FK1 60 A2
McKenzie St KY1 17 F4
McKinlay Cres FK10 10 B4
McKinlay Terr EH20 181 D4
McKinnon Dr EH22 183 F3
McKinnon Rd EH47 193 F4
McLachlan Ave FK7 7 D1
McLachlan St FK5 38 B1
McLaren Ave EH49 84 A3
McLaren Ct FK5 38 B1
McLaren Rd EH9 124 A2
McLaren Terr FK7 7 D2
McLauchlan Rise KY3 49 D4
McLauchlan View ML7 168 C3
McLean Pl
Bonnyrigg and Lasswade
EH18 181 F3
Gorebridge EH23 207 E4
McLean Sch KY12 28 C3
McLean Wlk EH22 183 D2
McLeod Cres EH32 96 C1
McLeod St Broxburn EH52 117 F3
Edinburgh EH11 122 C3
McMartin Ct EH47 170 B4
McNeil Cres EH48 144 A3
McNeil Path EH33 128 B3
McNeil Way EH33 128 B3
McNeil Wlk EH33 128 B3
McNeill Ave EH20 181 D4
McNeill Pl EH20 181 D4
McNeill St EH11 232 A1
McNeill Terr EH20 181 D4
McPhail Sq EH33 128 B3
McPherson Dr FK8 2 A1
McQuade St EH19 182 B4
McRae Cres KY3 33 F1
McTaggart Ave FK6 36 C1
McVean Pl FK4 57 D2
Meadow Cres EH47 193 F3
Meadow Ct
Burntisland KY3 33 F1
Carluke ML8 230 B1
Meadow Dr EH47 171 D1
Meadow Gn FK10 5 D1
Meadow La EH8 233 D1
Meadow Pk FK12 5 D3
Meadow Pl Bilston EH25 180 C3
Dunfermline KY11 29 F2
Edinburgh EH9 232 C1
Stirling FK8 2 B1
Stoneyburn EH47 171 D1
Meadow Place Rd EH12 121 E3
Meadow Rd Currie EH14 151 F4
Stoneyburn EH47 171 D1
Meadow St FK1 60 B2
Meadowbank
Edinburgh EH8 94 A1
Livingston EH54 147 F3
Ormiston EH35 159 F3
Meadowbank Ave 13 EH8 94 A1
Meadowbank Cres
Edinburgh EH8 94 A1
Ormiston EH35 159 E4
Meadowbank Rd
Kirknewton EH27 149 F2
Ormiston EH35 159 F4
Meadowbank Sports Ctr
EH7 94 A1
Meadowbank St FK2 61 E1
Meadowbank View EH27 149 F2
Meadowend KY12 28 B1
Meadowfield
Burntisland KY3 33 F1
Cowdenbeath KY4 13 E3
Dalgety Bay KY11 48 A2
Meadowfield Ave EH8 124 C4
Meadowfield Ct EH8 124 B4
Meadowfield Dr EH8 124 B4
Meadowfield Gdns EH8 124 B3
Meadowfield Ind Est KY3 33 F1
Meadowfield Rd EH12 120 C4
Meadowfield Terr EH8 124 B3
Meadowforth Rd FK7 7 E4
Meadowhead Ave EH55 171 F1
Meadowhead Cres EH55 171 F1
Meadowhead Gdns EH55 171 F1
Meadowhead Gr EH55 171 F1
Meadowhead Loan EH55 171 F1
Meadowhead Pl EH55 171 E1
Meadowhead Terr EH55 171 E1
Meadowhouse Rd EH12 121 F3
Meadowland Rd FK9 2 A3
Meadowpark EH41 132 A4
Meadowpark Rd EH48 144 C3
Meadowside EH33 128 C3
Meadowspot EH10 122 C1
Meadowview KY12 28 A1
Mearenside EH12 121 D4
Medwyn Pl FK10 9 F3
Meeks Rd FK2 60 A3
Meeting House Dr EH33 128 B3
Meggat Pl EH26 204 A4
Meggetland Terr EH14 122 C2
Meikle Rd EH54 147 F1
Melbourne Pl EH39 54 B4
Melbourne Rd
Broxburn EH52 117 F3
North Berwick EH39 54 B4
Melbourne St EH54 148 A3
Meldrum Cres KY3 33 E1
Meldrum Ct KY11 29 F1
Meldrum Prim Sch EH54 146 C4
Meldrum Rd KY2 17 D3
Melford Ave ML7 192 A2
Melfort Dr FK7 7 D2
Melgund Pl KY5 14 A4
Melgund Terr EH7 93 E1
Mellerstain Rd KY2 16 B3
Mellock Gdns FK1 59 F1
Mellor Ct KY11 46 C2
Melrose Cres KY2 17 E3
Melrose Dr FK3 61 F3
Melrose Pl 10 FK1 60 A2
Melville Cotts EH18 156 B2
Melville Cres EH3 232 A3
Melville Dr EH9 233 D1
Melville Dykes Rd EH18 156 B1
Melville Gate EH22 156 B2
Melville Gate Rd EH22 156 C2
Melville Gdns KY3 50 B4
Melville Pl Bridge of A FK9 2 A4
Kircaldy KY2 16 B3
Melville Rd EH22 156 C1
Melville St Edinburgh EH3 232 A3
Falkirk FK1 60 A3
Lochgelly KY5 14 A4
Melville Street La EH3 232 A3
Melville Terr
Dalkeith EH22 156 C1
Edinburgh EH9 233 E1
Stirling FK8 7 D3
Melville View EH18 182 A4
Menstrie Castle FK11 3 F3
Menstrie Pl FK11 4 A3
Menstrie Prim Sch FK11 4 A3
Menteith Ct FK10 10 B3
Menteith Dr KY11 29 F1
Menteith Rd FK9 2 A2
Mentone Ave EH15 95 D1
Mentone Gdns EH9 123 F2
Mentone Terr EH9 123 F2
Menzies Cres KY2 16 C3
Menzies Dr FK8 2 A1
Menzies Rd EH48 145 D3
Mercat Pl FK10 11 D2
Mercat The KY1 17 E2
Mercer Pl KY11 29 F2
Mercer St FK10 23 F2
Merchant St EH1 233 D2
Merchiston Ave
Edinburgh EH10 123 D3
Falkirk FK2 60 A4
Merchiston Bank Ave
EH10 123 D2
Merchiston Bank Gdns
EH10 123 D2
Merchiston Castle Sch
EH14 153 D4
Merchiston Cres EH10 123 D2
Merchiston Gdns
Edinburgh EH10 122 C2
Falkirk FK2 60 A3
Merchiston Gr EH11 122 C2
Merchiston Ind Est FK2 60 B4
Merchiston Mews EH10 123 D3
Merchiston Pk EH10 123 D3
Merchiston Pl EH10 123 D3
Merchiston Rd
Falkirk, Grahamston FK2 60 A3
Falkirk, Mungal FK2 60 A4
Merchiston Terr FK2 60 A4
Meredith Dr FK5 38 C2
Merker Terr EH49 84 C3
Merkland Cres KY11 48 A2
Merkland Dr FK1 60 C1
Merlin Way KY11 48 B3
Merlyon Way EH26 203 E4
Merrick Rd FK3 61 F3
Merrick Way FK3 61 F3
Merryfield Ave EH33 129 E3
Mertoun Pl EH11 122 C3
Merville Cres FK1 81 F3
Merville Terr FK1 81 F3
Methven Dr KY12 29 D3
Methven Pl KY1 17 D1
Methven Rd KY1 17 D1
Methven Terr EH18 181 F3
Meuse La EH2 233 D3
Michaelson Sq EH54 147 E1
Mid Beveridgewell KY12 28 C3
Mid Brae KY12 28 C3
Mid Cswy KY12 42 B4
Mid Gogarloch Syke
EH12 121 D3
Mid Liberton EH16 124 A1
Mid New Cultins EH11 121 D1
Mid Rd KY3 34 C2
Mid Road Ind Est EH32 127 F4
Mid St Bathgate EH48 145 D3
Kirkaldy KY1 17 E3
Livingston EH54 146 C3
Lochgelly KY5 14 A4
Mid Steil EH10 122 C1
Midcalder Prim Sch EH53 . 148 B1
Middle Meadow Wlk EH8 . 233 D1
Middle Street La FK3 40 B1
Middlebank St KY11 46 C3
Middleby St EH9 123 F2
Middlefield EH7 93 F2
Middlefield Ind Ctr FK2 60 B4
Middlefield Ind Est FK2 60 C4
Middlefield Rd FK2 60 B3
Middleknowe EH14 152 B4
Middlemass Ct FK2 60 A3
Middlemuir Rd FK7 7 E3
Middlepark EH14 152 B4
Middleshot EH14 152 B4
Middleshot Rd EH31 52 A2
Middleshot Sq EH32 97 D1
Middleton FK11 4 A3
Middleton Ave EH52 117 D2
Middleton Rd EH52 117 D2
Middlewood Pk EH54 146 C4
Midhope Pl EH52 88 A1
Midmar Ave EH10 123 E1
Midmar Dr EH10 123 E1
Midmar Gdns EH10 123 D1
Midthorn Cres FK2 60 C3
Midtown FK11 3 F3
Milburn Cres EH48 143 E3
Milesmark Ct KY12 28 B3
Milesmark Prim Sch KY12 .. 28 B3
Mill Farm Rd KY3 49 D4
Mill Hill FK7 6 B3
Mill La Edinburgh EH6 93 F3
Kincardine FK10 23 F2
Mill Lade EH49 84 C4
Mill Rd Alloa FK10 10 A3
Armadale EH48 143 F3
Bathgate EH48 145 D4
Blackburn EH47 171 E4
Cambusbarron FK7 6 B3
Clackmannan FK10 11 D3
Dunfermline KY11 29 D1
Falkirk FK2 39 D2
Harthill ML7 168 C3
Linlithgow EH49 84 B4
Stenton EH42 104 B1
Mill Rdbt EH54 147 D2
Mill Road Ind Est EH49 84 B4
Mill St Alloa FK10 10 A3
Dunfermline KY12 28 C2
Kirkcaldy KY1 17 D1
Mill Wynd
East Linton EH40 103 F4
Haddington EH41 132 A4
Prestonpans EH32 96 C1
Millar Cres EH10 123 D2
Millar Pl Edinburgh EH10 123 D2
High Bonnybridge FK4 58 A2
Stenhousemuir FK2 39 D3
Stirling FK8 2 B1
Millar Place La EH10 123 D2
Millar Rd EH33 128 B3
Millars Wynd FK10 5 E1
Millbank EH14 151 E1
Millbank Gr EH23 207 E4
Millbank Pl EH52 116 C2
Millbank Sq EH47 170 A4
Millbank Terr FK2 82 C4
Millbrae EH53 148 B3
Millbrae Wynd EH14 122 A1
Millbrook Pl FK11 3 F3
Millburn Rd
Bathgate EH48 144 C3
Westfield EH48 112 C3
Millburn St FK2 60 B3
Milldean Gr KY12 29 E3
Miller Ave KY12 28 A1
Miller Cres EH51 64 B3
Miller Pk FK2 61 F1
Miller Pl Airth FK2 22 C2
Harthill ML7 168 C3
Miller Rd Dunfermline KY12 .. 28 C3
Grangemouth EH51 62 C3
Miller Row EH4 232 A3

Miller St Carluke ML8 .... 230 A1
Harthill ML7 .... 168 C3
Kirkcaldy KY1 .... 17 F4
Millerfield EH49 .... 84 B4
Millerfield Pl EH9 .... 123 E3
Millerhill Rd Dalkeith EH22 . 125 C1
Danderhall EH22 .... 156 B4
Millfield Haddington EH41 ... 132 A4
Livingston EH54 .... 147 D1
Millfield Dr FK2 .... 61 E1
Millflats St FK2 .... 39 C1
Millgate EH52 .... 87 F1
Millhall Rd FK7 .... 7 E4
Millhall La EH48 .... 145 D4
Millhill EH21 .... 126 B3
Millhill La EH21 .... 126 B3
Millhill St KY11 .... 126 B3
Millhill Wynd EH21 .... 126 B3
Millie St KY1 .... 17 E3
Millway EH34 .... 161 D3
Miln-acre EH6 .... 93 E2
Milne Cres KY4 .... 13 E2
Milne Rd KY11 .... 46 C1
Milnepark Rd FK7 .... 19 F4
Milton Brae FK7 .... 7 D1
Milton Cl FK6 .... 36 B2
Milton Cres
  Bannockburn FK7 .... 7 E1
  Edinburgh EH15 .... 125 D3
Milton Dr EH15 .... 125 E4
Milton Gdns EH7 .... 7 D1
Milton Gdns N EH15 .... 125 D3
Milton Gdns S EH15 .... 125 D3
Milton Glen EH15 .... 125 F4
Milton Gn KY12 .... 29 D1
Milton Gr Bannockburn FK7 .... 7 E1
  Edinburgh EH15 .... 125 E3
Milton Link EH15 .... 125 E3
Milton Pl FK6 .... 36 B2
Milton Rd Bannockburn FK7 ... 7 E1
  Edinburgh EH15 .... 125 D3
  Kirkcaldy KY1 .... 17 D1
Milton Rd E EH15 .... 125 E4
Milton Rd W EH15 .... 124 C3
Milton Row FK6 .... 36 C2
Milton St EH8 .... 94 A1
Milton Terr
  Bannockburn FK7 .... 7 D1
  Edinburgh EH15 .... 125 F4
Minard Rd ML7 .... 191 E3
Mine Rd FK9 .... 2 A4
Miner's Terr EH21 .... 127 D3
Mingle Pl EH51 .... 64 A3
Minstrel Ct EH25 .... 181 D2
Minthill Pl ML7 .... 168 B3
Minto Ct KY1 .... 5 D3
Minto Gdns KY12 .... 5 D3
Minto Pl KY2 .... 16 C2
Minto St Edinburgh EH9 ...... 123 F3
  Lochgelly KY5 .... 14 A4
Mission La ⑨ FK1 .... 60 A2
Mitchell Cres Alloa FK10 .... 4 A4
  Cowdenbeath KY4 .... 13 D1
Mitchell Pl Falkirk FK1 .... 59 F1
  Kirkcaldy KY1 .... 17 E3
Mitchell Rd KY1 .... 46 B1
Mitchell St Dalkeith EH22 ... 156 C2
  Edinburgh EH6 .... 94 A3
  Kirkcaldy KY1 .... 17 E3
Mitchell Way EH33 .... 128 B4
Mitchell Wlk KY11 .... 46 C2
Mitchellhall Brae EH41 ...... 132 C3
Moat Dr EH14 .... 122 B2
Moat Pl EH14 .... 122 B2
Moat St EH14 .... 122 B2
Moat Terr EH14 .... 122 B2
Moat View EH25 .... 180 C2
Mochrum Dr KY12 .... 45 A4
Modan Rd FK7 .... 7 D2
Moffat Ave
  Bonnyrigg and Lasswade
  EH19 .... 182 A3
  Falkirk FK2 .... 39 E2
Moffat Crest KY5 .... 14 A4
Moffat Rd EH35 .... 159 E3
Moidart Rd EH47 .... 170 B4
Moir Ave EH21 .... 127 D3
Moir Cres EH21 .... 127 D3
Moir Ct KY4 .... 12 C4
Moir Dr EH21 .... 127 D3
Moir Pl EH21 .... 127 D3
Moir St FK10 .... 10 A4
Moir Terr EH21 .... 127 D3
Moira Pk EH7 .... 94 C1
Moira Terr EH7 .... 94 C1
Moira Terrace La EH7 .... 94 C1
Mollison Ave ML7 .... 168 C3
Monar Ct KY11 .... 45 A4
Monastery St KY12 .... 29 D2
Moncks Rd FK1 .... 60 B2
Moncrieff Terr EH9 .... 123 F3
Moncrieff Way EH54 .... 147 E4
Moncur St KY12 .... 29 E4
Monkbarns Gdns EH16 .... 155 C4
Monkland Rd EH48 .... 144 C3
Monkmains Rd EH41 .... 132 B4
Monkrigg Pl EH41 .... 132 B4
Monksrig Rd EH26 .... 203 E3
Monkswood Rd EH22 .... 183 D2
Monktonhall Pl EH21 .... 126 A2
Monktonhall Terr EH21 ..... 126 A2
Monkwood Ct EH9 .... 123 E2
Monmouth Terr EH3 .... 93 D2
Montagu Terr EH3 .... 93 D2
Montague St EH8 .... 233 E1

Monteith Wlk ML7 .... 191 F3
Montfort Pl FK1 .... 60 A2
Montgomery Cres FK2 .... 39 D1
Montgomery Dr FK2 .... 39 D1
Montgomery St
  Edinburgh EH7 .... 93 F1
  Falkirk FK2 .... 60 C3
  Grangemouth FK3 .... 61 E3
  Kirkcaldy KY2 .... 17 D3
Montgomery Street La
  Edinburgh EH7 .... 93 F1
Montgomery Way FK9 .... 2 A2
Montgomery Well FK2 .... 39 D1
Montpelier EH10 .... 123 D3
Montpelier Pk EH10 .... 123 D3
Montpelier Terr EH10 .... 123 D3
Montrose Rd Polmont FK2 .... 62 A1
  Stirling FK9 .... 2 B2
Montrose Terr EH7 .... 233 F4
Montrose Way FK4 .... 57 E3
Moodie St KY12 .... 29 D2
Moor Rd Fala EH37 .... 210 B3
  Pathhead EH37 .... 185 E2
  Pencaitland EH35 .... 186 A3
Moore House Sch EH48 ...... 145 F3
Mooreland Gdns EH55 .... 171 E1
Moorelands EH55 .... 171 E1
Moorfield Cotts EH22 .... 156 B4
Moorfoot Ct EH19 .... 182 A4
Moorfoot Pl
  Bonnyrigg and Lasswade
  EH19 .... 182 A3
  Penicuik EH26 .... 203 F3
Moorfoot View
  Bilston EH26 .... 180 C3
  Bonnyrigg and Lasswade
  EH19 .... 182 A3
  Gorebridge EH23 .... 207 E4
Moorings The KY11 .... 47 F1
Moorside St M8 .... 230 A1
Morar Dr FK3 .... 61 E3
Morar Pl FK3 .... 61 E3
Morar St EH54 .... 28 A1
Morar Way ML7 .... 192 A2
Moray Ct Auchtertool KY2 ... 15 D1
  Dalgety Bay KY11 .... 48 A2
Moray Dr EH49 .... 84 C3
Moray House Coll
  Halls of Residence
  EH8 .... 124 A2
Moray House Coll of Ed
  Edinburgh, Canongate EH8 . 233 E3
  Edinburgh, Cramond EH4 ..... 91 E3
Moray Park Terr EH7 .... 94 B1
Moray Pk KY11 .... 48 A2
Moray Pl Edinburgh EH3 ..... 232 B4
  Grangemouth FK3 .... 61 F4
  Linlithgow EH49 .... 84 C3
Moray Prim Sch FK3 .... 61 F4
Moray Way N KY11 .... 48 B2
Moray Way S KY11 .... 48 A1
Morayvale KY3 .... 49 E4
Moredun Dykes Rd ML7 ..... 155 E3
Moredun Park Ct EH17 ...... 155 E4
Moredun Park Dr EH17 ...... 155 E4
Moredun Park Gdns
  EH17 .... 155 E4
Moredun Park Gn EH17 ..... 155 F4
Moredun Park Gr EH17 ...... 155 F4
Moredun Park Loan
  EH17 .... 155 E4
Moredun Park Rd EH17 ..... 155 F4
Moredun Park St EH17 ...... 155 F4
Moredun Park View
  EH17 .... 155 F4
Moredun Park Way EH17 ... 155 E3
Moredun Park Wlk EH17 .... 155 F4
Moredun Prim Sch EH17 .... 155 E4
Moredunvale Bank EH17 .... 155 E4
Moredunvale Gn EH17 .... 155 E4
Moredunvale Gr EH17 .... 155 E4
Moredunvale Loan EH17 .... 155 E4
Moredunvale Pl EH17 .... 155 E4
Moredunvale Rd EH17 .... 155 E4
Moredunvale View EH17 .... 155 E4
Moredunvale Way EH17 ..... 155 E4
Morgan Ct FK7 .... 7 E2
Morgan Gdns EH30 .... 68 A1
Moriston Ct FK3 .... 61 F2
Moriston Dr EH54 .... 173 F3
Morley Cres FK7 .... 7 D2
Morlich Cres KY11 .... 48 A1
Morlich Gr KY11 .... 48 A1
Morlich Pk KY11 .... 48 A1
Morlich Pl KY11 .... 48 A1
Morlich Rd KY11 .... 48 A1
Morlich Wlk EH54 .... 148 A2
Mornay Way ML7 .... 191 E3
Morningside Ct EH10 .... 123 D1
Morningside Dr EH10 .... 123 D1
Morningside Gdns EH10 ..... 122 C1
Morningside Gr EH10 .... 122 C1
Morningside Pk EH10 .... 123 D2
Morningside Rd EH10 .... 123 D2
Morningside Terr EH10 ...... 123 D2
Morris Ct KY11 .... 47 E1
Morris Rd EH23 .... 183 E3
Morris Sq EH54 .... 147 F1
Morris Terr FK8 .... 7 D4
Morrison Ave
  Bonnyrigg EH4 .... 57 F3
  Tranent EH33 .... 128 C3
Morrison Circ EH3 .... 232 A2
Morrison Cres EH3 .... 232 A2

Morrison Dr
  Bannockburn FK7 .... 7 E1
  Dunfermline KY11 .... 46 C4
Morrison Link EH3 .... 232 A2
Morrison St EH3 .... 232 A2
Morrison Way EH54 .... 147 E4
Mortimer Ct KY11 .... 48 A1
Morton St EH15 .... 125 E4
Mortonhall Gate EH16 ...... 154 C3
Mortonhall Park Ave
  EH17 .... 154 C3
Mortonhall Park Bank
  EH17 .... 155 D3
Mortonhall Park Cres
  EH17 .... 155 D3
Mortonhall Park Dr
  EH17 .... 155 D3
Mortonhall Park Gdns
  EH17 .... 154 C3
Mortonhall Park Gr
  EH17 .... 154 C3
Mortonhall Park Pl
  EH17 .... 155 D3
Mortonhall Park Terr
  EH17 .... 155 D3
Mortonhall Park View
  EH17 .... 154 C3
Mortonhall Park Way
  EH17 .... 154 C3
Mortonhall Rd EH9 .... 123 E2
Morven Ct FK1 .... 60 B1
Morven Dr FK2 .... 61 E1
Morven Gr KY2 .... 16 C4
Morven Pl KY11 .... 48 A2
Morven St EH4 .... 91 E1
Morvenside EH14 .... 152 B4
Morvenside Cl EH14 .... 152 B4
Moss Intc EH54 .... 147 E3
Moss Rd FK7 .... 8 B2
Moss Way KY11 .... 48 A3
Moss-side Rd KY4 .... 13 D2
Mossband La ML7 .... 191 F3
Mossbank
  Cowdenbeath KY4 .... 13 D1
  Livingston EH54 .... 147 F3
  Rosyth KY11 .... 46 C3
Mossburn Ave ML7 .... 168 B3
Mosscastle Rd FK1 .... 110 A4
Mossend Ct EH17 .... 155 D3
Mossend Terr EH17 .... 155 D3
Mossgiel Ave Cowie FK7 ...... 20 B4
  Stirling FK8 .... 2 A1
Mossgiel Cotts EH54 .... 146 B4
Mossgiel St FK1 .... 59 D3
Mossgiel Terr FK2 .... 61 D2
Mossgiel Wlk ⑬ EH16 ...... 124 A1
Mosshall Ind Est EH47 ...... 171 D4
Mosshat EH55 .... 216 C2
Mosshouse FK7 .... 6 C2
Mosside Dr EH47 .... 145 F3
Mosside Gr EH47 .... 171 E4
Mosside Terr EH47 .... 145 E1
Moston Terr EH9 .... 123 F2
Motion St KY5 .... 14 A4
Moubray Gr EH30 .... 89 E4
Moubray Rd KY11 .... 48 B3
Moulin Way KY12 .... 29 F3
Mound Pl EH1 .... 232 C3
Mound The EH2 .... 232 C3
Mount Grange EH9 .... 123 E2
Mount Hooly Cres KY11 ..... 68 B3
Mount Hope EH9 .... 2 B4
Mount Lodge Pl EH15 .... 125 D4
Mount Oliphant FK7 .... 20 B4
Mount Pleasant EH48 .... 143 F3
Mount Vernon Rd EH16 .... 155 D4
Mount William FK10 .... 5 F1
Mountbatten Pl KY11 .... 46 C2
Mountbatten St FK3 .... 61 E3
Mountcastle Bank EH8 ...... 124 C4
Mountcastle Cres EH8 .... 124 C4
Mountcastle Dr N EH15 ..... 124 C3
Mountcastle Dr S EH15 ...... 124 C3
Mountcastle Gdns EH8 ...... 124 C4
Mountcastle Gn EH8 .... 94 C1
Mountcastle Gr EH8 .... 124 C4
Mountcastle Loan EH8 .... 124 C4
Mountcastle Pk EH8 .... 94 C1
Mountcastle Pl ② EH8 .... 94 C1
Mountcastle Terr EH8 .... 94 C1
Mountfair Gdns EH33 .... 129 E3
Mountfair Pl EH33 .... 129 E3
Mountnooly Loan EH10 ..... 154 B3
Mountjoy Terr EH21 .... 126 B4
Mowbray Ct FK7 .... 7 E2
Mowbray Gdns KY4 .... 30 C3
Mowbray Rise EH54 .... 147 F1
Muckle Hill Pk KY11 .... 47 D1
Mucklets Ave EH21 .... 126 A2
Mucklets Cres EH21 .... 126 A2
Mucklets Ct EH21 .... 126 A2
Mucklets Dr EH21 .... 126 A2
Mucklets Pl EH21 .... 125 F2
Mucklets Rd EH21 .... 126 A2
Mudale Ct FK1 .... 60 B1
Mugdrum Ct EH52 .... 116 C2
Muir Ct KY4 .... 30 C3
Muir Rd Bathgate EH48 ..... 144 C4
  Livingston EH54 .... 148 A3
  Townhill KY12 .... 29 E1
Muir St FK5 .... 38 B1
Muir Wood Cres EH14 .... 152 A3
Muir Wood Dr EH14 .... 152 A3
Muir Wood Gr EH14 .... 152 A3
Muir Wood Pl EH14 .... 152 A3
Muir Wood Rd EH14 .... 152 A3
Muiralehouse Rd FK7 .... 19 F4

Muiravonside Cntry Pk
  EH49 .... 83 F2
Muirdyke Ave FK2 .... 39 E2
Muiredge & Jersey Rd
  ML7 .... 191 D4
Muirend Ave EH14 .... 152 C4
Muirend Ct EH55 .... 64 A3
Muirend Rd ML7 .... 7 D3
Muirepark Ct EH51 .... 64 A3
Muirfield Cres EH31 .... 52 A1
Muirfield Dr Gullane EH31 .. 52 A1
  Uphall EH52 .... 116 C2
Muirfield Gdns EH20 .... 181 E4
Muirfield Pk EH31 .... 52 A2
Muirfield Rd FK5 .... 38 C1
Muirfield Steading EH31 ..... 52 A1
Muirfield Terr EH31 .... 52 A1
Muirfield Way EH14 .... 146 C3
Muirhall Pl FK5 .... 38 B2
Muirhall Rd FK5 .... 38 B2
Muirhead Ave FK2 .... 60 A4
Muirhead Pl M Harthill ML7 . 168 B2
  Penicuik EH26 .... 203 F3
Muirhead Rd FK5 .... 38 C2
Muirhouse Ave EH4 .... 92 A2
Muirhouse Bank EH4 .... 92 A2
Muirhouse Cl EH4 .... 92 A2
Muirhouse Cres EH4 .... 92 A3
Muirhouse Dr EH4 .... 92 A3
Muirhouse Gdns EH4 .... 92 A3
Muirhouse Gn EH4 .... 92 A2
Muirhouse Gr EH4 .... 92 A3
Muirhouse Loan EH4 .... 92 A2
Muirhouse Medway EH4 ..... 92 A3
Muirhouse Parkway EH4 ..... 92 A2
Muirhouse Pk EH4 .... 92 A2
Muirhouse Pl E EH4 .... 92 A2
Muirhouse Pl W EH4 .... 92 A2
Muirhouse Prim Sch EH4 .... 92 A2
Muirhouse Terr EH4 .... 92 A2
Muirhouse View EH4 .... 92 A3
Muirhouse Way EH4 .... 92 A2
Muirlaun ML11 .... 215 D1
Muirpark EH22 .... 156 C1
Muirpark Ct EH33 .... 128 C3
Muirpark Dr Shieldhill FK1 ... 81 E3
  Tranent EH33 .... 128 C3
Muirpark Gdns
  Tranent EH33 .... 128 C3
  Tullibody FK10 .... 4 C2
Muirpark Gr EH33 .... 128 C3
Muirpark Pl EH33 .... 128 C3
Muirpark Rd EH33 .... 128 C3
Muirpark Terr EH33 .... 128 C3
Muirpark Wynd EH33 .... 128 C3
Muirside Ct KY12 .... 27 E1
Muirside Dr EH33 .... 128 C3
Muirside Gr KY12 .... 27 E1
Muirside La KY12 .... 44 B4
Muirside Rd FK10 .... 4 A2
Muirton Rd FK7 .... 7 E3
Muirton Rdbt FK7 .... 7 E3
Muirton Way KY11 .... 48 A3
Mulberry Dr FK1 .... 81 E3
Mulberry Terr FK10 .... 5 D4
Muldron Terr ML7 .... 192 A1
Mull Ct Alloa FK10 .... 10 A3
  Grangemouth FK3 .... 61 E3
Mumrills Rd FK2 .... 61 E2
Mungal Ct FK2 .... 60 A4
Mungalend FK2 .... 60 A4
Mungalhead Rd FK2 .... 60 A4
Mungle St EH55 .... 172 B2
Munnoch Way FK1 .... 2 A2
Munro Dr EH13 .... 153 D3
Munro Gdns FK2 .... 60 A2
Munro Pl EH10 .... 9 E3
Munro Rd FK9 .... 2 A3
Munro St Kirkcaldy KY1 ...... 17 D1
  Stenhousemuir FK5 .... 38 C2
Munro Way EH54 .... 147 E4
Murano Pl EH7 .... 93 F1
Murderdean Rd EH22 .... 183 E2
Murdoch Terr EH11 .... 232 A1
Murdostoun Cres ML7 .... 168 C2
Murieston Cres EH11 .... 122 C3
Murieston Crescent La
  EH11 .... 122 C3
Murieston Ct EH54 .... 174 A3
Murieston Dr EH54 .... 174 A3
Murieston East Rd EH54 .... 174 A4
Murieston Gdns EH54 .... 174 A3
Murieston Gn EH54 .... 173 F3
Murieston La EH11 .... 122 C3
Murieston Pk EH54 .... 173 F3
Murieston Pl EH11 .... 122 C3
Murieston Rd
  Edinburgh EH11 .... 122 C3
  Livingston EH54 .... 173 F3
Murieston Terr EH11 .... 122 C3
Murieston Vale EH54 .... 173 F3
Murieston Valley EH54 .... 174 A3
Murieston West Rd EH54 ... 173 F4
Murieston Wlk EH54 .... 173 F3
Murieston Wood EH54 .... 173 F3
Murieston Rd
  Edinburgh EH11 .... 122 C3
  Livingston EH54 .... 173 F3
Murnin Ct FK2 .... 58 A2
Murnin Rd FK4 .... 57 F2
Murnin Road Ind Est FK4 .... 58 A2
Murray Cotts EH12 .... 121 E3
Murray Cres EH2 .... 203 E4
Murray PI Cambusbarron FK7 . 6 C3
  Stirling FK8 .... 7 D4
Murray Rd KY11 .... 46 B1
Murray Way EH54 .... 147 E4
Murray Wlk KY11 .... 29 F2

Murrayburn App EH14 .... 121 E1
Murrayburn Dr EH14 .... 121 E1
Murrayburn Gate EH14 ..... 152 B4
Murrayburn Gdns EH14 ..... 121 F1
Murrayburn Gn EH14 .... 121 F1
Murrayburn Junc EH14 ...... 152 B4
Murrayburn Pk EH14 .... 121 F1
Murrayburn Pl EH14 .... 121 E1
Murrayburn Prim Sch
  EH14 .... 121 F1
Murrayburn Rd EH14 .... 121 E1
Murrayfield Ave EH12 .... 122 B4
Murrayfield Dr
  Blackburn EH47 .... 171 E4
  Edinburgh EH12 .... 122 B4
Murrayfield Gdns EH12 ...... 122 B4
Murrayfield Hospl EH12 .... 122 A4
Murrayfield Pl
  Bannockburn FK7 .... 7 E1
  Edinburgh EH12 .... 122 B4
Murrayfield Prim Sch
  EH12 .... 121 F1
Murrayfield Rd EH12 .... 122 B4
Murrayfield Rugby Gd
  EH12 .... 122 B3
Murrayfield Terr
  Bannockburn FK7 .... 7 E1
  Blackburn EH47 .... 171 E4
Murrays Brae The EH17 ..... 155 E2
Murrays The EH17 .... 155 E2
Murraysgate Cres EH47 ..... 169 F3
Murraysgate Ind Est
  EH47 .... 169 F3
Murrayshall Rd FK7 .... 7 D2
Murrel Rd KY3 .... 49 E4
Murrel Terr KY3 .... 49 E4
Mus of Childhood EH1 .... 233 E3
Mus of Flight EH39 .... 74 B1
Music Hall La KY12 .... 29 D2
Musselburgh Burgry
  Prim Sch EH21 .... 126 B3
Musselburgh Gram Sch
  EH21 .... 126 B3
Musselburgh Rd
  Dalkeith EH22 .... 157 D2
Musselburgh Sta EH21 ...... 126 A2
Myers Ct KY12 .... 28 A3
Mylne Pl FK2 .... 39 D1
Mylneburn Gdns KY11 .... 45 E2
Myothill Rd FK6 .... 57 E4
Myre Cres KY3 .... 35 D2
Myre Dale EH10 .... 182 B3
Myreside Ct EH10 .... 122 C1
Myreside Rd EH10 .... 122 C2
Myreton KY11 .... 4 A3
Myreton Dr FK7 .... 19 F4
Myreton Rd FK3 .... 61 E3
Myreton Way FK1 .... 59 F2
Myretoungate FK12 .... 4 C3
Myrtle Cres
  Bilston EH25 .... 180 C3
  Kirkcaldy KY2 .... 16 C3
Myrtle Gr EH22 .... 183 E4
Myrtle Terr EH11 .... 122 C3

Nailer Rd Falkirk FK1 .... 59 F3
  Stirling FK7 .... 7 D1
Nairn Ct FK1 .... 60 B1
Nairn Rd FK2 .... 60 A4
Nairn St KY1 .... 17 E3
Naismith Ct FK3 .... 40 C1
Namayo Ave FK2 .... 60 A4
Namur Rd EH26 .... 204 A4
Nantwich Dr EH7 .... 94 B2
Napier Ave EH48 .... 145 E3
Napier Cres FK2 .... 60 A4
Napier Pl FK2 .... 60 A4
Napier Rd
  Edinburgh EH10 .... 123 D2
  Rosyth KY11 .... 46 B1
Napier Sq EH54 .... 148 A4
Napier St KY1 .... 17 F4
Napier Univ
  Edinburgh EH10 .... 122 C1
  Edinburgh, Craiglockhart
  EH11 .... 122 B1
  Edinburgh, Sighthill EH11 .. 121 E1
Napier Univ
  (Craiglockhart Campus)
  EH10 .... 122 C1
Nasmyth Ct EH54 .... 148 A3
Nasmyth Rd KY11 .... 46 A1
Nasmyth Sq EH54 .... 148 A3
Natal Pl KY4 .... 13 E2
National Gallery EH2 .... 232 C3
National Liby of Scotland
  EH1 .... 233 D3
National Portrait Gallery
  EH2 .... 233 D4
Navar Ct ML7 .... 192 A2
Nebit The FK12 .... 4 C3
Neidpath Ct
  Edinburgh EH12 .... 121 D4
  Longniddry EH32 .... 98 C3
Neidpath Dr FK5 .... 38 C2
Neidpath Pl KY12 .... 29 E1
Neilson Park Rd EH41 .... 131 D4
Neilson Sq EH54 .... 146 B3
Neilsons La EH54 .... 60 A2
Neilston Cres EH54 .... 155 D4
Neilston Rd EH54 .... 147 E2
Nelson Ave EH54 .... 147 E2
Nelson Gdns FK3 .... 40 C1
Nelson Pl FK7 .... 7 E3
Nelson Rd EH51 .... 62 C3

Nelson St Edinburgh EH3 ..... 232 C4
Grangemouth FK3 ..... 61 E4
Kirkcaldy KY2 ..... 17 D3
Rosyth KY11 ..... 46 C3
Ness The KY12 ..... 26 C1
Nether Craigour EH17 ..... 124 B1
Nether Currie Cres EH14 ..... 152 A3
Nether Currie PI EH14 ..... 152 A3
Nether Currie Prim Sch
EH14 ..... 152 A3
Nether Currie Rd EH14 ..... 152 A3
Nether Dechmont Cotts
EH54 ..... 147 D4
Nether St Dysart KY1 ..... 18 A4
Kirkcaldy KY1 ..... 17 E3
Netherbank EH16 ..... 154 C3
Netherbank View EH16 ..... 154 C3
Netherbeath Rd KY4 ..... 30 C4
Netherby Rd KY4 ..... 22 B2
Edinburgh EH5 ..... 93 D3
Netherfield Rd FK2 ..... 61 E1
Nethergate KY3 ..... 35 D1
Nethergate The FK12 ..... 4 C3
Netherlaw EH39 ..... 54 B3
Nethermains Prim Sch
FK6 ..... 36 B1
Nethermains Rd FK6 ..... 36 B1
Nethershot Rd EH32 ..... 97 D1
Netherton Gr EH47 ..... 170 A2
Netherton PI EH47 ..... 170 A2
Netherton St ML7 ..... 168 B3
Nethertown Broad St
KY12 ..... 29 D1
Netherwood Pk EH54 ..... 147 D4
Nethhill Dr EH54 ..... 116 C1
Nettlehill Rd
Livingston EH54 ..... 147 F4
Uphall Station EH54 ..... 147 F4
Neucks The FK1 ..... 111 D3
Nevis Cres FK10 ..... 10 A4
Nevis Dr EH54 ..... 173 F3
Nevis Gdns EH26 ..... 204 A4
Nevis PI Falkirk FK1 ..... 60 B1
Grangemouth FK3 ..... 61 F3
Shotts ML7 ..... 147 E2
New Arthur PI EH8 ..... 233 E2
New Broompark EH5 ..... 92 C4
New Broughton 5 EH3 ..... 93 E1
New Carron Rd FK5 ..... 39 D2
New Coll EH1 ..... 232 C3
New Hallglen Rd FK1 ..... 60 B1
New Halls Rd EH30 ..... 68 B1
New Holygate EH17 ..... 117 E3
New Houses EH39 ..... 74 B2
New Hunterfield EH23 ..... 183 D1
New John's PI EH8 ..... 233 E1
New La EH6 ..... 93 E3
New Line Rd FK7 ..... 19 D4
New Liston Rd EH29 ..... 89 D1
New Market Rd EH14 ..... 122 B2
New Mart Rd EH14 ..... 122 A2
New Meadowspott
EH22 ..... 157 D1
New Orchardfield EH6 ..... 93 F2
New Rd FK7 ..... 7 E1
New Row Dunfermline KY12 ..... 29 D2
East Fortune EH39 ..... 24 A2
Kincardine FK10 ..... 24 A2
Tranent EH33 ..... 128 B3
New Skinners CI EH1 ..... 233 E3
New St Bridge of A FK9 ..... 1 C4
Cockenzie & Port Seton
EH32 ..... 97 E2
Edinburgh EH8 ..... 233 E3
Musselburgh EH21 ..... 126 A3
Prestonpans EH32 ..... 96 C1
Slamannan FK1 ..... 110 A4
Tranent EH33 ..... 128 B4
New Star Bank EH22 ..... 183 D3
New Swanston EH10 ..... 153 F3
New Tower PI EH15 ..... 95 D1
New Well Wynd EH49 ..... 84 C3
Newbattle Abbey Cres
EH22 ..... 182 C4
Newbattle Gdns EH22 ..... 157 D1
Newbattle High Sch
EH22 ..... 183 E4
Newbattle Terr EH10 ..... 123 D2
Newbiggin Cres FK10 ..... 4 B1
Newbiggin Rd FK3 ..... 61 F3
Newbigging
Auchtertool KY2 ..... 15 E1
Musselburgh EH21 ..... 126 B3
Newbigging Terr KY2 ..... 15 E1
Newbridge Ind Est EH28 ..... 118 C3
Newbridge Rdbt EH28 ..... 119 D3
Newburn PI KY12 ..... 29 E2
Newbyres Ave EH23 ..... 183 E1
Newbyres Cres EH23 ..... 207 E4
Newbyres Gdns EH23 ..... 207 E4
Newcarron Ct FK2 ..... 60 A4
Newcraighall Bsns Pk
EH15 ..... 125 D2
Newcraighall Dr EH21 ..... 125 E2
Newcraighall Prim Sch
EH21 ..... 125 F2
Newcraighall Rd EH15 ..... 125 D2
Newhailes Ave EH21 ..... 126 A3
Newhailes Cres EH21 ..... 126 A3
Newhailes Rd EH15 ..... 125 F3
Newhaven PI EH6 ..... 93 E4
Newhaven Rd EH6 ..... 93 E3
Newhouse 7 D3
Newhouse Ave EH42 ..... 78 C1
Newhouse Bsns Pk FK3 ..... 61 E4
Newhouse Dr FK1 ..... 59 F1
Newhouse PI 78 C1
Newhouse Rd FK3 ..... 61 E4

Newhouses Rd EH52 ..... 118 A2
Newington Rd EH9 ..... 123 F3
Newland Ave EH48 ..... 145 D3
Newlands Pk
Dunfermline KY12 ..... 29 D3
Edinburgh EH9 ..... 123 F2
Newlands PI EH10 ..... 4 B2
Newlands Rd
Bannockburn FK7 ..... 19 E4
Brightons FK2 ..... 82 B4
Grangemouth FK3 ..... 61 E3
Newliston Dr KY2 ..... 16 B4
Newmains Farm La EH29 ..... 89 D1
Newmains Rd EH29 ..... 89 D1
Newmarket FK7 ..... 7 F2
Newmarket Ctr FK1 ..... 60 A3
Newmarket St FK1 ..... 60 A3
Newmill & Canthill Rd
ML7 ..... 191 D3
Newmills FK10 ..... 4 A2
Newmills Ave EH14 ..... 151 E2
Newmills Cres EH14 ..... 151 E2
Newmills Gr EH14 ..... 151 E2
Newmills Rd Currie EH14 ..... 151 E2
Dalkeith EH22 ..... 157 D2
Newmills Terr EH22 ..... 157 D2
Newpark Cres FK7 ..... 7 D1
Newpark Rd
Livingston EH54 ..... 173 E3
Stirling FK7 ..... 7 D1
Newpark Rdbt EH54 ..... 173 E4
Newraith St EH17 ..... 155 F3
Newton Ave FK2 ..... 40 A2
Newton Church Rd EH22 ..... 156 B4
Newton Cres KY11 ..... 47 D2
Newton PI KY11 ..... 46 C2
Newton Port EH41 ..... 101 D1
Newton Rd FK3 ..... 40 A1
Newton St
Easthouses EH22 ..... 183 E4
Edinburgh EH11 ..... 122 C3
Newtongrange Prim Sch
EH22 ..... 183 D3
Newtonloan St Andrew's
Prim Sch EH23 ..... 183 D2
Newtonshaw FK10 ..... 5 E1
Newtown FK10 ..... 63 F3
Newtown St EH51 ..... 63 F3
Newyearfield Bsns Pk
EH54 ..... 147 E3
Newyearfield Rdbt EH54 ..... 147 E3
Nicholson Way EH54 ..... 147 E4
Nicklaus Gn EH54 ..... 147 D4
Nicol PI EH52 ..... 117 E3
Nicol Rd EH52 ..... 117 E3
Nicol St KY1 ..... 17 D2
Nicolson Sq EH8 ..... 233 E2
Nicolson St EH8 ..... 233 E2
Nicolton Ave EH2 ..... 82 C4
Nicolton Rd EH2 ..... 62 A1
Niddrie Farm Gr EH16 ..... 124 C2
Niddrie House Ave 6
EH16 ..... 124 C2
Niddrie House Dr EH16 ..... 125 D2
Niddrie House Gdns
EH16 ..... 124 C2
Niddrie House Pk EH16 ..... 124 C2
Niddrie House Sq EH16 ..... 124 C2
Niddrie Mains Ct EH16 ..... 125 D2
Niddrie Mains Dr EH16 ..... 124 C2
Niddrie Mains Rd EH16 ..... 124 C2
Niddrie Mains Terr EH16 ..... 124 C2
Niddrie Marischal Cres
EH16 ..... 124 C2
Niddrie Marischal Dr 4
EH16 ..... 124 C2
Niddrie Marischal Gdns 2
EH16 ..... 124 C2
Niddrie Marischal Gn 5
EH16 ..... 124 C2
Niddrie Marischal Gr
EH16 ..... 125 D2
Niddrie Marischal Loan 3
EH16 ..... 124 C2
Niddrie Marischal PI
EH16 ..... 124 C2
Niddrie Marischal Rd
EH16 ..... 125 D2
Niddrie Marischal St 1
EH16 ..... 124 C2
Niddrie Mill Ave EH15 ..... 125 D2
Niddrie Mill Cres EH15 ..... 125 D3
Niddrie Mill Dr EH15 ..... 125 D2
Niddrie Mill Gr EH15 ..... 125 D2
Niddrie Mill PI EH15 ..... 125 D2
Niddrie Mill Prim Sch
EH15 ..... 125 D2
Niddrie Mill Terr EH15 ..... 125 D2
Niddry Rd EH22 ..... 87 F1
Niddry St EH1 ..... 233 D3
Niddry St S EH1 ..... 233 E2
Niddry View EH52 ..... 87 F1
Nidrie Cotts EH15 ..... 125 E2
Nielson Ct EH47 ..... 171 D4
Nigel Loan EH16 ..... 155 D3
Niven Rd KY11 ..... 47 E2
Niven's Knowe Rd EH10 ..... 180 C4
Nivensknowe Pk EH20 ..... 180 C4

No 7 Pit Rd KY4 ..... 13 E2
Nobel PI EH25 ..... 180 C2
Nobel View FK2 ..... 82 A4
Noble PI EH6 ..... 94 A2
Norman Rise EH54 ..... 147 F1
Normand Brae KY1 ..... 18 A4
Normand Rd KY1 ..... 18 A4
North Approach Rd FK10 ..... 23 F2
North Ave FK2 ..... 83 D4
North Bank Rd EH22 ..... 127 F4
North Bank St EH1 ..... 233 D3
North Berwick High Sch
EH39 ..... 54 B3
North Bridge EH1 ..... 233 D3
North Bridge St
Bathgate EH48 ..... 145 D3
Grangemouth FK3 ..... 40 B1
North Bughtlin Bank EH12 ..... 91 D1
North Bughtlin Brae EH12 ..... 91 D1
North Bughtlin Neuk
EH12 ..... 91 D1
North Bughtlin PI EH12 ..... 91 D1
North Bughtlin Rd EH12 ..... 91 D1
North Bughtlin Gr EH12 ..... 91 D1
North Bughtlinrig EH12 ..... 91 D1
North Bughtlinside EH12 ..... 91 D1
North Cairntow EH16 ..... 124 B3
North Castle St Alloa FK10 ..... 10 A3
Edinburgh EH2 ..... 232 B4
North Charlotte St EH2 ..... 232 B3
North Clyde Street La
EH1 ..... 233 D4
North Cres
Dunfermline KY11 ..... 46 C4
Prestonpans EH32 ..... 97 D1
North East Circus PI 10
EH3 ..... 93 D1
North East Cumberland
Street La EH3 ..... 93 E1
North East Thistle
Street La EH2 ..... 233 D4
North Esk Lodge
(Loretto Jun Sch) EH21 ..... 126 B3
North Esk Rd KY11 ..... 46 C4
North Fort St EH6 ..... 93 F3
North Gate EH48 ..... 113 F3
North Grange Ave EH32 ..... 96 C1
North Grange Gr EH32 ..... 96 C1
North Grange Rd EH32 ..... 96 C1
North Greendykes Rd
EH52 ..... 116 B1
North Greens EH15 ..... 125 D3
North Gyle Ave EH12 ..... 121 D3
North Gyle Dr EH12 ..... 121 D4
North Gyle Farm Ct
EH12 ..... 121 D3
North Gyle Farm La
EH12 ..... 121 D3
North Gyle Gr EH12 ..... 121 D3
North Gyle Loan EH12 ..... 121 D4
North Gyle Pk EH12 ..... 121 D4
North Gyle Rd EH12 ..... 121 D4
North Gyle Terr EH12 ..... 121 D3
North High St EH21 ..... 126 A3
North Hillhousefield EH6 ..... 93 F3
North Junction St EH6 ..... 93 F3
North Larches KY11 ..... 29 F2
North Leith Sands EH6 ..... 93 F4
North Loanhead KY11 ..... 45 F2
North Lorimer PI EH32 ..... 97 D2
North Main St FK2 ..... 39 E2
North Meggetland EH14 ..... 122 C2
North Overgate KY3 ..... 34 C2
North Park Terr EH4 ..... 93 D1
North Peffer PI EH16 ..... 124 B2
North Prim Sch KY2 ..... 17 D3
North Queensferry Sta
KY11 ..... 68 A4
North Rd Dunbar EH42 ..... 78 B2
Fauldhouse EH47 ..... 193 F4
Inverkeithing KY11 ..... 47 E2
North Reeves PI EH47 ..... 170 A3
North Roundall KY11 ..... 45 F2
North Row KY11 ..... 45 D2
North Seton Pk EH32 ..... 97 E2
North Shore Rd KY11 ..... 40 C1
North St Alloa FK10 ..... 10 A4
Armadale EH48 ..... 143 F3
Bo'ness FK51 ..... 64 A3
Clackmannan FK10 ..... 11 D2
Dunbar EH42 ..... 78 A1
Falkirk FK2 ..... 60 A4
Lochgelly KY5 ..... 14 A4
Ratho EH28 ..... 119 E1
Stirling FK8 ..... 2 A1
North St Andrew La EH2 ..... 233 D4
North St Andrew St EH2 ..... 233 D4
North St David St EH2 ..... 233 D4
North View Burntisland KY3 ..... 50 C4
West Calder EH55 ..... 172 B2
North Way KY11 ..... 48 B3
North Werber Pk EH4 ..... 92 C2
North Werber PI EH4 ..... 92 C2
North West Circus PI
EH3 ..... 93 D1
North West Cumberland
Street La EH3 ..... 93 E1
North West Thistle
Street La
EH2 ..... 232 C4
North Wood Rd FK10 ..... 4 B1
North Wynd EH22 ..... 157 D2
Northbank Ct EH51 ..... 64 A3
Northbank Dr EH51 ..... 64 A3
Northbank Pk EH51 ..... 63 F3
Northbank Rd KY12 ..... 27 E1
Northend KY7 ..... 6 B3

Northfield
Cowdenbeath KY4 ..... 13 E3
Tranent EH33 ..... 128 C3
Northfield Ave
Edinburgh EH8 ..... 124 B4
Shotts ML7 ..... 192 A1
Northfield Broadway
EH8 ..... 124 C4
Northfield Cir EH8 ..... 124 C4
Northfield Cotts EH55 ..... 172 B2
Northfield Cres
Longridge EH47 ..... 170 B1
Edinburgh EH8 ..... 124 C4
Northfield Ct EH32 ..... 127 F4
Northfield Dr EH8 ..... 124 C4
Northfield E EH33 ..... 128 C3
Northfield Farm Ave
EH8 ..... 124 C4
Northfield Farm Rd EH8 ..... 124 C4
Northfield Gdns
Clackmannan FK10 ..... 11 D2
Edinburgh EH8 ..... 124 C4
Prestonpans EH32 ..... 127 F4
Northfield Gr EH8 ..... 124 C4
Northfield Mdws EH47 ..... 170 B1
Northfield Park Gr EH8 ..... 124 C4
Northfield Pk EH8 ..... 124 C4
Northfield Rd Denny FK6 ..... 36 B2
Edinburgh EH8 ..... 124 C4
Northfield Sq EH8 ..... 124 C4
Northfield Terr
Edinburgh EH8 ..... 124 B4
Longridge EH47 ..... 170 B1
Northflat PI ML8 ..... 230 A1
Northlawn Ct EH4 ..... 91 F2
Northlawn Terr EH4 ..... 91 F2
Northrig Cotts EH41 ..... 133 D4
Northumberland
Place La EH3 ..... 232 C4
Northumberland St EH3 ..... 232 C4
Northumberland Street
North East La EH3 ..... 93 E1
Northumberland Street
North West La EH3 ..... 232 C4
Northumberland Street
South East La EH3 ..... 232 C4
Northumberland Street
South West La EH3 ..... 232 C4
Northwood Pk EH4 ..... 146 C4
Norton Pk EH7 ..... 94 A1
Norton PI KY11 ..... 29 F1
Norton St FK12 ..... 5 A2
Norval PI KY11 ..... 46 C2
Norwood Ave Alloa FK10 ..... 9 F4
Bonnybridge FK4 ..... 58 A4
Whitburn EH47 ..... 170 A3
Norwood Cres FK10 ..... 9 F4
Norwood Ct
Bonnybridge FK4 ..... 58 A4
Whitburn EH47 ..... 170 A3
Norwood Gr EH47 ..... 170 A3
Norwood PI EH47 ..... 58 A4
Norwood Rd FK10 ..... 9 F4
Novar Cres KY1 ..... 17 D1
Nungate Rd EH39 ..... 54 A4
Nunraw Abbey EH41 ..... 134 C1
Nursery Rd FK1 ..... 59 F2

Ochilmount FK7 ..... 7 F1
Ochiltree Cres EH53 ..... 148 A1
Ochiltree Ct EH53 ..... 148 A1
Ochiltree Dr EH53 ..... 148 A1
Ochiltree Gdns EH16 ..... 124 B1
Ochiltree Terr FK1 ..... 59 D3
Ochilview Alva FK12 ..... 5 D4
Cowdenbeath KY4 ..... 13 F3
Cowie FK7 ..... 20 C3
Ochilview Dr KY12 ..... 26 A1
Ochilview Pk
(Stenhousemuir FC)
FK5 ..... 38 B2
Ochilview PI EH51 ..... 63 F3
Ochilview Rd EH51 ..... 63 F3
Ochilview Terr EH51 ..... 63 F3
Ochville Terr FK10 ..... 5 E2
Octavia St KY2 ..... 17 D3
Ogilface Cres EH48 ..... 142 B1
Ogilvie PI FK9 ..... 2 A3
Ogilvie Rd FK9 ..... 2 A3
Ogilvie Terr EH11 ..... 122 C2
Ogilvie Way EH54 ..... 147 E4
Ogilvy Cres EH47 ..... 193 F3
Old Abbey Rd EH39 ..... 54 A4
Old Bellsdyke Rd FK5 ..... 38 C2
Old Bridge St FK10 ..... 10 A3
Old Broughton 4 EH3 ..... 93 E1
Old Burdiehouse Rd
EH17 ..... 155 D2
Old Church La EH15 ..... 124 B3
Old Craighall Junc EH21 ..... 126 A1
Old Craighall Rd EH22 ..... 156 C4
Old Dalkeith Rd EH22 ..... 156 B3
Old Dean Rd EH22 ..... 98 B2
Old Denny Rd FK5 ..... 38 A2
Old Drove Rd
Cambusbarron FK7 ..... 6 B3
West Linton EH46 ..... 219 D2
Old Eastfield St ML7 ..... 168 B3
Old Edinburgh Rd EH22 ..... 156 C2
Old Farm Ave EH13 ..... 153 D4
Old Farm PI EH13 ..... 153 D4
Old Fishmarket CI EH1 ..... 233 D3
Old Forge Gr EH22 ..... 26 C4
Old Hillview PI KY4 ..... 30 C3
Old Kirk PI KY12 ..... 29 E2
Old Kirk Rd
Dunfermline KY12 ..... 29 E2
Edinburgh EH12 ..... 121 F4
North Queensferry KY11 ..... 68 B3
Old Linbun Rd KY11 ..... 29 F2
Old Liston Rd EH28 ..... 119 D3
Old Mill Ct EH47 ..... 170 C4
Old Mill Ctyd The KY11 ..... 29 D1
Old Mill La
Edinburgh EH16 ..... 124 A1
Gifford EH41 ..... 163 F3
Oakley KY12 ..... 26 C3
Old Mill Rd
Broxburn EH52 ..... 117 F3
Shotts ML7 ..... 191 D1
Old Newmills Rd EH14 ..... 151 E2
Old Orch The KY11 ..... 45 E2
Old Perth Rd KY4 ..... 13 D2
Old Redding Rd FK2 ..... 60 C2
Old Refinery Rd FK3 ..... 62 A4
Old School Ct FK10 ..... 4 A1
Old Star Rd EH22 ..... 183 D3
Old Tolbooth Wynd EH8 ..... 233 E3
Old Town Bannockburn FK7 ..... 7 E1
Broxburn EH52 ..... 117 F3
Oldwalls PI EH4 ..... 62 B4
Oldwalls Rd FK3 ..... 62 B4
Olive Bank Rd EH21 ..... 126 A3
Olivebank Rd EH21 ..... 126 A3
Olympia Arc KY1 ..... 17 D2
Onich PI ML7 ..... 192 A2
Onslow St EH54 ..... 148 A3
Orchard Bank EH4 ..... 92 C1
Orchard Brae EH4 ..... 92 C1
Orchard Brae Ave EH4 ..... 92 C1
Orchard Brae Gdns EH4 ..... 92 C1
Orchard Brae Gdns W 1
EH4 ..... 92 C1
Orchard Brae W EH4 ..... 92 C1
Orchard Cres
Edinburgh EH4 ..... 92 B1
Prestonpans EH32 ..... 96 C1
Orchard Ct
East Linton EH40 ..... 103 F4
Kinghorn KY3 ..... 35 D2
Longniddry EH32 ..... 98 B2
Orchard Dr EH4 ..... 92 B1
Orchard Gdns KY3 ..... 35 D2
Orchard Gr Edinburgh EH4 ..... 92 C1
Haddington EH41 ..... 101 D1
Kincardine FK10 ..... 23 F2
Polmont FK2 ..... 61 F1
Orchard House Hospl FK8 ..... 2 A1
Orchard La
Dunfermline KY11 ..... 29 E1
Dysart KY1 ..... 18 A4
Edinburgh EH4 ..... 92 C1
Livingston EH54 ..... 147 D3
Orchard Rd Bridge of A FK9 ..... 2 B4
Edinburgh EH4 ..... 92 B1
Grangemouth FK3 ..... 61 E4
Kinghorn KY3 ..... 34 C2
Orchard Rd S EH4 ..... 92 B1
Orchard Sq KY11 ..... 45 E2

Orchard St Falkirk FK1 ..... 60 A3
Grangemouth FK3 ..... 61 E4
Orchard Terr
Clackmannan FK10 ..... 11 E1
Edinburgh EH4 ..... 92 C1
Kinghorn KY3 ..... 34 C2
Torryburn KY12 ..... 26 C1
Orchard The
Brightons FK2 ..... 82 B4
Crossford KY12 ..... 28 A1
Ormiston EH35 ..... 159 F4
Tranent EH33 ..... 128 B4
Tullibody FK10 ..... 4 A1
Orchard Toll EH4 ..... 92 C1
Orchard View EH22 ..... 156 C1
Orchardcroft FK8 ..... 7 D4
Orchardfield EH40 ..... 103 E4
Orchardfield Ave EH12 ..... 121 E3
Orchardfield Terr EH27 ..... 150 A3
Orchardhead Loan EH16 ..... 155 D4
Orchardhead Rd EH16 ..... 155 D4
Ordnance Rd KY12 ..... 44 B4
Oriel Cres KY2 ..... 17 D2
Oriel Rd KY2 ..... 16 C3
Orkney Ct FK10 ..... 10 A3
Orkney Pl Falkirk FK1 ..... 60 A1
Kirkcaldy KY1 ..... 17 F4
Orlit Cotts EH39 ..... 74 B2
Ormelie Terr EH15 ..... 125 E4
Ormidale Terr EH12 ..... 122 B4
Ormiston Ave EH33 ..... 128 C3
Ormiston Cres E EH33 ..... 128 C3
Ormiston Cres W EH33 ..... 128 C3
Ormiston Dr Alloa FK10 ..... 4 C1
East Calder EH53 ..... 149 D2
Ormiston Pk KY12 ..... 29 E3
Ormiston Pl EH22 ..... 96 C1
Ormiston Prim Sch EH35 ..... 159 F4
Ormiston Rd EH33 ..... 128 B3
Orr Terr ML7 ..... 168 B2
Orrin Gr KY11 ..... 48 A2
Orrock Dr KY3 ..... 33 F1
Orrok Pk EH16 ..... 124 A1
Orwell Pl
Dunfermline KY12 ..... 29 E2
Edinburgh EH11 ..... 122 C3
Orwell Prim Sch EH10 ..... 122 C3
Orwell Terr EH11 ..... 122 C3
Osborne Ct EH32 ..... 97 E2
Osborne Dr FK10 ..... 23 F2
Osborne Gdns FK1 ..... 59 F2
Osborne Terr
Cockenzie & Port Seton
 EH32 ..... 97 E2
Edinburgh EH12 ..... 122 C4
Ossian Dr EH54 ..... 173 F3
Oswald Ave FK3 ..... 61 F4
Oswald Ct EH9 ..... 123 E2
Oswald Rd EH9 ..... 123 E2
Oswald St ML7 ..... 60 A2
Oswald Terr EH12 ..... 121 E3
Oswalds Wynd KY1 ..... 17 E2
Otterburn Pk EH14 ..... 153 D4
Otterston Gr KY11 ..... 48 A2
Otterston Pl KY12 ..... 29 E3
Oudenarde Ct ML8 ..... 230 A1
Our Lady of Lourdes
 RC Prim Sch EH47 ..... 171 E4
Our Lady's RC Prim Sch
 EH47 ..... 171 D1
Overhaven KY11 ..... 45 F2
Overton Cres Denny FK6 ..... 36 B1
East Calder EH53 ..... 149 D2
Redding FK2 ..... 61 D1
Overton Mains KY1 ..... 17 F4
Overton Rd
Grangemouth, Bowhouse
 FK3 ..... 61 E3
Grangemouth, Oil Refinery
 FK3 ..... 62 A4
Kirkcaldy KY1 ..... 17 F4
Owen sq EH54 ..... 147 F1
Oxcars Dr KY11 ..... 48 A2
Oxcraig St EH5 ..... 92 C4
Oxenfoord Ave EH37 ..... 185 D3
Oxenfoord Dr EH37 ..... 185 D3
Oxford St EH8 ..... 233 F1
Oxford Terr EH4 ..... 232 A4
Oxgang Rd FK3 ..... 61 F4
Oxgangs Ave EH13 ..... 153 F4
Oxgangs Bank EH13 ..... 153 F3
Oxgangs Brae EH13 ..... 153 F3
Oxgangs Broadway EH13 ..... 153 F3
Oxgangs Cres EH13 ..... 153 F3
Oxgangs Dr EH13 ..... 153 F4
Oxgangs Farm Ave EH13 ..... 153 F3
Oxgangs Farm Dr EH13 ..... 153 F3
Oxgangs Farm Gdns
 EH13 ..... 153 F3
Oxgangs Farm Gr EH13 ..... 153 F3
Oxgangs Farm Loan
 EH13 ..... 153 F3
Oxgangs Farm Terr EH13 ..... 153 F3
Oxgangs Gdns EH13 ..... 153 F3
Oxgangs Gn EH13 ..... 153 F4
Oxgangs Gr EH13 ..... 153 F4
Oxgangs Hill EH13 ..... 153 F4
Oxgangs Loan EH13 ..... 153 F4
Oxgangs Medway EH13 ..... 153 F3
Oxgangs Path EH13 ..... 153 F3
Oxgangs Pk EH13 ..... 153 F3
Oxgangs Pl EH13 ..... 153 F4
Oxgangs Prim Sch EH13 ..... 153 F4

Oxgangs Rd EH10 ..... 154 A3
Oxgangs Rd N EH13 ..... 153 F4
Oxgangs Rise EH13 ..... 153 F4
Oxgangs Row EH13 ..... 153 F3
Oxgangs St EH13 ..... 153 F3
Oxgangs Terr EH13 ..... 153 F3

Paddock The Gullane EH31 ..... 52 A1
Musselburgh EH21 ..... 126 B4
North Berwick EH39 ..... 54 B3
Paddockholm The EH12 ..... 121 F3
Page St KY5 ..... 14 A4
Paisley Ave EH8 ..... 124 B4
Paisley Cres EH8 ..... 124 B4
Paisley Dr EH8 ..... 124 B4
Paisley Gdns EH8 ..... 124 B4
Paisley Gr EH8 ..... 124 B4
Paisley Terr EH8 ..... 124 B4
Palmer Pl EH14 ..... 151 F2
Palmer Rd EH14 ..... 151 F2
Palmer Rise EH54 ..... 147 F1
Palmerston Pl EH12 ..... 232 A3
Palmerston Place La
 EH12 ..... 232 A2
Palmerston Rd EH9 ..... 123 E3
Pan Ha' KY11 ..... 18 A3
Panbrae Rd EH51 ..... 63 F4
Pankhurst Loan EH22 ..... 157 E2
Panmure Pl EH3 ..... 232 C1
Pannie Rd KY1 ..... 17 E4
Panstead St FK1 ..... 61 F4
Panton Gn EH54 ..... 147 D4
Papana Cotts EH41 ..... 134 B1
Papple Farm Cotts EH41 ..... 134 B3
Paradise La FK10 ..... 23 F2
Paradykes Ave EH20 ..... 181 D4
Paradykes Prim Sch EH20 ..... 181 D4
Pardovan Cres EH49 ..... 86 B4
Pardovan Pl KY1 ..... 59 F3
Pariothall 9 EH3 ..... 93 D1
Paris Ave FK6 ..... 36 C1
Paris St EH3 ..... 61 F4
Park Ave Bankhead FK4 ..... 57 F3
Bilston EH25 ..... 180 B3
Brightons FK2 ..... 82 B4
Bonnybridge FK4 ..... 58 A2
Cowdenbeath KY4 ..... 13 E2
Dunbar EH42 ..... 78 B1
Dunfermline KY12 ..... 29 D2
Gorebridge EH23 ..... 125 D4
Gorebridge EH23 ..... 183 E1
Laurieston FK2 ..... 60 C2
Loanhead EH20 ..... 181 D4
Musselburgh EH21 ..... 125 D4
Stenhousemuir FK5 ..... 38 B1
Stirling FK8 ..... 7 D3
Park Cres Alloa FK10 ..... 5 E1
Bannockburn FK7 ..... 7 E1
Bonnyrigg and Lasswade
 EH19 ..... 182 A4
Easthouses EH22 ..... 183 E4
Edinburgh EH16 ..... 155 D4
Falkirk FK2 ..... 39 D1
Gifford EH41 ..... 163 F3
Loanhead EH20 ..... 181 D4
Westquarter FK2 ..... 61 D2
Park Ct Broxburn EH52 ..... 117 D3
Musselburgh EH21 ..... 126 C3
Park Dr Bannockburn FK7 ..... 7 E1
Brightons FK2 ..... 82 B4
Stenhousemuir FK5 ..... 38 B1
West Calder EH55 ..... 173 D3
Park Gdns Bannockburn FK7 ..... 7 E1
Edinburgh EH16 ..... 155 D4
Musselburgh EH21 ..... 126 C3
Park Gr Broxburn EH52 ..... 117 D3
Edinburgh EH16 ..... 155 D4
Park Grove Pl EH21 ..... 126 C3
Park Grove Terr EH21 ..... 126 C3
Park Hill EH23 ..... 183 D1
Park La Aberdour KY3 ..... 49 D4
Bo'ness EH51 ..... 64 A4
Edinburgh EH15 ..... 125 D4
Haddington EH41 ..... 131 F4
Musselburgh EH21 ..... 126 C3
Stirling FK8 ..... 7 D4
Park Lea KY11 ..... 47 D3
Park Pl Alloa FK10 ..... 10 B4
Clackmannan KY10 ..... 11 D2
Dunfermline KY12 ..... 29 D2
Edinburgh EH6 ..... 93 E3
Hill of B KY4 ..... 36 C4
Kinghorn KY3 ..... 34 C1
Kirkcaldy KY1 ..... 17 D2
Livingston EH54 ..... 147 D3
Stirling FK7 ..... 6 C3
Park Prim Sch FK10 ..... 10 A3
Park Rd Blackridge EH48 ..... 142 C2
Bonnyrigg and Lasswade
 EH19 ..... 182 A4
Broxburn EH52 ..... 117 F3
Cockenzie & Port Seton
 EH32 ..... 97 E2
Cowdenbeath KY4 ..... 13 D2
Dalkeith EH22 ..... 156 C1
Edinburgh EH6 ..... 93 E3
Falkirk FK2 ..... 39 D1
Gifford EH41 ..... 163 F3
Gorebridge EH23 ..... 183 E1
Grangemouth FK3 ..... 61 E4
Harthill ML7 ..... 169 D3
Kirkcaldy KY1 ..... 17 F4
Menstrie FK11 ..... 4 A3
Newtongrange EH22 ..... 181 D3
Ormiston EH35 ..... 159 E3
Rosyth KY11 ..... 46 C3
Shotts ML7 ..... 191 E3

Park Rd W KY11 ..... 46 B3
Park Road Prim Sch KY11 ..... 47 D2
Park St Alva FK12 ..... 5 D4
Cowdenbeath KY4 ..... 13 E2
Cowie FK7 ..... 20 C4
Falkirk FK1 ..... 60 A3
High Bonnybridge FK4 ..... 58 B2
Lochgelly KY5 ..... 14 A4
Park Terr Brightons FK2 ..... 82 B4
Broxburn EH52 ..... 117 D3
Kirknewton EH27 ..... 149 F1
Newcraighall EH21 ..... 125 F2
Stirling FK8 ..... 2 A3
Tullibody FK10 ..... 4 A1
Park View Brightons FK2 ..... 82 C4
Broxburn EH52 ..... 117 D3
Fauldhouse EH47 ..... 193 F4
Kirkcaldy KY2 ..... 16 C3
Loanhead EH20 ..... 181 D4
Musselburgh EH21 ..... 126 C3
Pencaitland EH34 ..... 160 C4
Prestonpans EH32 ..... 97 D1
Stoneyburn EH47 ..... 171 E1
Westfield EH48 ..... 112 C2
Whitburn EH47 ..... 170 A4
Park View E EH32 ..... 97 E2
Park View S KY11 ..... 47 D1
Park View W EH32 ..... 97 E2
Park-View EH32 ..... 98 C3
Parkandarroch Cres
 ML8 ..... 230 A1
Parkdyke FK7 ..... 6 C3
Parkend Cres FK1 ..... 59 E3
Parker Ave FK7 ..... 94 C1
Parker Rd FK7 ..... 94 C1
Parker St FK7 ..... 94 C1
Parkfoot Ct FK1 ..... 60 A2
Parkgate Alva FK12 ..... 4 C3
Rosyth KY11 ..... 46 C2
Parkgrove Ave EH4 ..... 91 E1
Parkgrove Bank EH4 ..... 91 E1
Parkgrove Cres EH4 ..... 91 E1
Parkgrove Dr EH4 ..... 91 E1
Parkgrove Gn EH4 ..... 91 E1
Parkgrove Loan EH4 ..... 91 E1
Parkgrove Neuk EH4 ..... 91 E1
Parkgrove Path EH4 ..... 91 E1
Parkgrove Pl EH4 ..... 91 E1
Parkgrove Rd EH4 ..... 91 E1
Parkgrove Row EH4 ..... 91 E1
Parkgrove Terr EH4 ..... 91 E1
Parkgrove View EH4 ..... 91 E1
Parkhall Dr FK2 ..... 83 D3
Parkhead Ave EH11 ..... 121 F1
Parkhead Cotts EH55 ..... 172 C1
Parkhead Cres
 Edinburgh EH11 ..... 121 F1
 West Calder EH55 ..... 172 C2
Parkhead Ct EH10 ..... 10 B4
Parkhead Dr EH11 ..... 121 F1
Parkhead Gdns
 Edinburgh EH11 ..... 121 F1
 West Calder EH55 ..... 172 C2
Parkhead Gr EH11 ..... 121 F1
Parkhead Loan EH11 ..... 121 F1
Parkhead Pk EH22 ..... 183 E4
Parkhead Pl
 Easthouses EH22 ..... 183 E4
 Edinburgh EH11 ..... 121 F1
Parkhead Prim Sch
 EH55 ..... 172 C2
Parkhead Rd Alloa FK10 ..... 10 B4
Falkirk FK1 ..... 60 A1
Linlithgow EH49 ..... 84 C4
Parkhead St EH11 ..... 121 F1
Parkhead Terr EH11 ..... 121 F1
Parkhead View EH11 ..... 121 F1
Parkland Gr Comrie KY12 ..... 26 B4
Stoneyburn EH47 ..... 170 C1
Parklands Cres KY11 ..... 48 A2
Parkneuk Rd KY12 ..... 28 B3
Parkside EH28 ..... 119 D3
Parkside Ct Dalkeith EH22 ..... 157 D2
Plean FK7 ..... 20 B4
Parkside Pl EH22 ..... 157 D2
Parkside Rd ML7 ..... 191 E2
Parkside Sq KY11 ..... 47 D2
Parkside St
 Edinburgh EH8 ..... 233 F1
 Rosyth KY11 ..... 46 C2
Parkside Terr EH16 ..... 233 F1
Parkvale Pl EH6 ..... 94 A2
Parkview Ave FK1 ..... 59 F1
Parkway KY11 ..... 10 A4
Parkwood Cres EH12 ..... 117 F2
Parkwood Gdns EH52 ..... 117 E3
Parliament Sq EH1 ..... 233 D3
Parliament St EH6 ..... 93 F3
Parrotshot EH15 ..... 125 D3
Parsonage The EH21 ..... 126 B3
Parsons Green Prim Sch
 EH8 ..... 124 B4
Parsons Green Terr 1
 EH8 ..... 94 B1
Parsonspool
 Bonnyrigg and Lasswade
 EH19 ..... 182 B3
Dunbar EH42 ..... 78 B1
Paterson Dr FK1 ..... 81 E3
Paterson Pl Bonnybridge
 FK4 ..... 58 B3
Paterson Way KY11 ..... 29 D1
Paterson's Ct EH52 ..... 117 F3
Path Brae EH29 ..... 89 D1

Path The Bannockburn FK7 ..... 7 E1
Kirkcaldy KY1 ..... 17 E3
Pathead Prim Sch KY1 ..... 17 D1
Pathfoot Ave FK9 ..... 2 B4
Pathfoot Dr FK9 ..... 2 B4
Pathfoot Rd FK9 ..... 2 B4
Pathhead Ct KY12 ..... 17 E3
Pathhead Prim Sch
 EH37 ..... 185 D2
Patie's Rd EH14 ..... 153 E4
Paton St Alloa FK10 ..... 10 A4
Dunfermline KY12 ..... 29 E3
Patrick Dr FK1 ..... 81 F4
Patterson La KY4 ..... 13 E2
Patterson Pl KY2 ..... 17 D3
Patterson St KY2 ..... 17 D3
Pattison St EH6 ..... 94 A3
Pattle Ct EH39 ..... 54 A4
Paul Dr FK2 ..... 22 C2
Paul Pl KY4 ..... 13 E2
Paul St KY5 ..... 14 A3
Pavilion View EH10 ..... 97 D1
Paxstone Cres ML7 ..... 168 C3
Paxstone Dr ML7 ..... 168 C3
Paxton Cres KY5 ..... 14 A4
Paxton Pl KY1 ..... 14 A4
Peachdales EH41 ..... 131 F4
Peacock Ct EH6 ..... 93 D3
Peacocktail Cl EH15 ..... 125 D2
Pearce Ave EH12 ..... 121 E4
Pearce Gr EH12 ..... 121 E4
Pearce Rd EH12 ..... 121 E4
Pearson Ave FK4 ..... 57 E3
Pearson Pl FK4 ..... 57 E3
Peathill Rd FK4 ..... 58 A3
Peatville Gdns EH14 ..... 122 A1
Peatville Terr EH14 ..... 122 A1
Peddie Pl FK3 ..... 61 E4
Peden St ML7 ..... 168 B3
Peebles Rd EH26 ..... 203 F2
Peebles St KY1 ..... 35 D4
Peel Pentland Ctr
 EH20 ..... 155 D1
Peel Prim Sch EH54 ..... 147 E2
Peel Rdbt EH54 ..... 147 E2
Peel Terr EH9 ..... 123 F2
Peffer Bank EH16 ..... 124 B2
Peffer Ind Est EH16 ..... 124 B2
Peffer Pl EH16 ..... 124 B2
Peffer St EH16 ..... 124 B2
Peffer's Pl EH41 ..... 132 A4
Peffermill Ind Est EH16 ..... 124 B2
Peffermill Prim Sch
 EH16 ..... 124 B2
Peffermill Rd EH16 ..... 124 B2
Peggy's Mill Rd EH4 ..... 91 D2
Peirson Rd KY11 ..... 29 F2
Pelstream Ave FK7 ..... 7 D2
Pembroke Pl EH12 ..... 122 C4
Pembroke St FK5 ..... 38 B2
Pencaitland Prim Sch
 EH34 ..... 160 C3
Pencraig Brae EH40 ..... 103 E3
Penders La FK1 ..... 60 A3
Pendreich Ave EH19 ..... 182 B4
Pendreich Dr EH19 ..... 182 B4
Pendreich Gr EH19 ..... 182 B4
Pendreich Terr EH19 ..... 182 B4
Pendreich View EH19 ..... 182 B4
Pendreich Way FK9 ..... 2 C2
Penicuik High Sch EH26 ..... 203 F3
Penicuik Rd EH25 ..... 180 C2
Pennelton Pl EH51 ..... 63 F3
Pennyschool Pl FK10 ..... 11 D2
Pennywell Ct EH4 ..... 92 A3
Pennywell Gdns EH4 ..... 92 A3
Pennywell Gr EH4 ..... 92 A3
Pennywell Medway EH4 ..... 92 A3
Pennywell Pl EH4 ..... 92 A3
Pennywell Rd EH4 ..... 92 A3
Pennywell Villas EH4 ..... 92 A3
Pentland Ave
 Bathgate EH48 ..... 145 F3
 Currie EH14 ..... 151 F2
 Edinburgh EH13 ..... 153 D4
 Newton grange EH23 ..... 183 D2
 Penicuik EH26 ..... 203 F3
Pentland Cres
 Edinburgh EH10 ..... 154 A4
 Rosewell EH24 ..... 181 E2
Pentland Ct Bilston EH25 ..... 180 C2
 Dalgety Bay KY11 ..... 48 B2
Pentland Dr
 Edinburgh EH10 ..... 153 F3
 Whitburn EH47 ..... 170 B3
Pentland Gait Off Pk
 EH11 ..... 121 D1
Pentland Hills
 Regional Pk EH14, EH26 ..... 201 E4
Pentland Ind Est EH20 ..... 181 D4
Pentland Pk
 Livingston EH54 ..... 148 A2
 Loanhead EH20 ..... 180 C2
Pentland Pl Currie EH14 ..... 151 F2
 Kirkcaldy KY2 ..... 16 C3
Pentland Rd
 Bonnyrigg and Lasswade
 EH19 ..... 182 A4
 Edinburgh EH13 ..... 153 D4
 Edinburgh, Old Pentland
 EH10 ..... 154 B1
Pentland Rise KY11 ..... 48 B3
Pentland Terr
 Dunfermline KY11 ..... 29 F1
 Edinburgh EH10 ..... 154 A4
 High Valleyfield KY12 ..... 26 A1
Penicuik EH26 ..... 203 F3

Pentland View Currie EH14 ..... 151 F2
Dalkeith EH22 ..... 157 E1
Edinburgh EH16 ..... 154 A3
Uphall EH52 ..... 117 D3
Pentland View Cres
 EH25 ..... 180 C2
Pentland View Ct EH14 ..... 147 D3
Pentland View Dr EH25 ..... 180 C2
Pentland View Rd
 Kirkliston EH29 ..... 89 D1
 Roslin EH25 ..... 180 C2
Pentland View Terr EH25 ..... 180 C2
Pentland Way FK3 ..... 61 F3
Pentland Wlk EH10 ..... 170 B3
Pentlands Gdns EH10 ..... 154 A4
Peppercraig Quarry
 EH41 ..... 100 C1
Percival St KY7 ..... 17 D3
Perdieus Mount KY12 ..... 29 D1
Perdrixknowe EH14 ..... 122 B1
Perth Rd KY4 ..... 13 E3
Perth St EH3 ..... 93 D1
Petershill Gdns EH48 ..... 145 E4
Peterswell Brae FK7 ..... 7 E1
Pettigrew's Cl EH22 ..... 157 D2
Pettycur Bay KY3 ..... 34 C1
Pettycur Rd KY3 ..... 34 C1
Peveril Rise EH54 ..... 173 F4
Peveril Terr EH16 ..... 155 D4
Phantassie Sq EH40 ..... 103 F4
Philip Ave Bathgate EH48 ..... 145 F3
 Linlithgow EH49 ..... 84 C4
Philip Dr FK5 ..... 38 B1
Philip Pl EH26 ..... 203 F4
Philip St FK7 ..... 60 A4
Philpingstone La EH51 ..... 64 B4
Philpingstone Rd EH51 ..... 64 B4
Phoenix La KY12 ..... 28 C2
Picardy Pl EH1 ..... 233 D4
Pier Pl EH6 ..... 93 E4
Pier Rd EH5 ..... 64 B4
Pierhead Bldgs KY11 ..... 68 B3
Piersfield Gr EH8 ..... 94 B1
Piersfield Pl EH8 ..... 94 B1
Piersfield Terr EH8 ..... 94 B1
Piershill La 7 EH8 ..... 94 B1
Piershill Pl 8 EH8 ..... 94 B1
Piershill Sq E EH8 ..... 124 B4
Piershill Sq W EH8 ..... 94 B1
Piershill Terr 9 EH8 ..... 94 B1
Pike Rd FK7 ..... 7 E2
Pilgrims Hill EH49 ..... 85 E4
Pilkham Ct KY4 ..... 13 E2
Pilmuir St KY12 ..... 29 D3
Pilrig Gdns EH6 ..... 93 F2
Pilrig House Cl EH6 ..... 93 F2
Pilrig St EH6 ..... 93 F2
Pilton Ave EH5 ..... 92 C3
Pilton Cres EH5 ..... 92 C3
Pilton Dr EH5 ..... 92 C3
Pilton Dr N EH5 ..... 92 C3
Pilton Loan EH5 ..... 92 C3
Pilton Pk EH5 ..... 92 C3
Pilton Pl EH5 ..... 92 C3
Pine Gn EH51 ..... 63 E2
Pine Gr Alva FK10 ..... 10 B3
 Dunfermline KY11 ..... 29 E1
 Livingston EH54 ..... 148 A3
 Westquarter FK2 ..... 61 D1
Pine St EH42 ..... 78 A1
Pine Wlk FK5 ..... 38 A3
Pineapple The FK2 ..... 23 E1
Pinebank EH54 ..... 147 F3
Pines The EH31 ..... 52 A2
Pinewood Dr KY11 ..... 48 A2
Pinewood Pk EH54 ..... 146 C4
Pinewood Pl KY11 ..... 183 F3
Pinewood Rd EH22 ..... 183 F3
Pinewood Sch EH47 ..... 171 F4
Pinewood View EH22 ..... 183 F3
Pinkerton Pl KY11 ..... 46 C3
Pinkhill EH12 ..... 122 A3
Pinkie Ave EH21 ..... 126 C3
Pinkie Dr EH21 ..... 126 C3
Pinkie Hill Cres EH21 ..... 126 C3
Pinkie Pl EH21 ..... 126 C3
Pinkie Rd EH21 ..... 126 C3
Pinkie St Peter's Prim Sch
 EH21 ..... 126 C3
Pinkie Terr EH21 ..... 126 C3
Pinkie Wlk EH33 ..... 128 B3
Pinnel Pl KY11 ..... 48 A3
Pipe La EH15 ..... 95 D1
Pipe St EH15 ..... 95 D1
Piper Cres KY3 ..... 33 E1
Pirig Cotts EH6 ..... 93 F2
Pirleyhill Dr FK1 ..... 60 A1
Pirleyhill Gdns FK1 ..... 60 A1
Pirnhall Rd FK7 ..... 19 E2
Pirniefield Bank EH6 ..... 94 B2
Pirniefield Gdns EH6 ..... 94 B2
Pirniefield Gr EH6 ..... 94 B2
Pirniefield Pl EH6 ..... 94 B2
Pirniefield Terr EH6 ..... 94 B2
Pirnhall Prim Sch EH4 ..... 92 B3
Pirnie St KY6 ..... 93 F2
Pitbauchlie Bank KY11 ..... 29 E1
Pitcairn St KY11 ..... 29 F1
Pitcorthie Dr KY11 ..... 29 E1
Pitcorthie Prim Sch KY11 ..... 29 F1
Pitcorthie Rd KY11 ..... 29 E1
Pitdinnie Pl KY12 ..... 27 E1
Pitdinnie Rd KY12 ..... 27 E1
Pitfairn Rd FK10 ..... 5 F2

Pitfirane Pk KY12 — 28 A1
Pitfour Pl KY2 — 16 B4
Pitlochry Pl 4 EH7 — 94 A1
Pitreavie Bsns Pk KY11 — 46 B4
Pitreavie Cres KY11 — 46 B4
Pitreavie Ct KY11 — 46 B3
Pitreavie Dr KY11 — 46 B3
Pitreavie Prim Sch KY11 — 46 B4
Pitsligo Rd EH10 — 123 D2
Pitt St EH6 — 93 F3
Pitt Terr FK8 — 7 D3
Pittencrieff Ct EH21 — 126 C3
Pittencrieff House Mus KY12 — 28 C2
Pittencrieff Prim Sch KY12 — 28 C2
Pittencrieff St KY12 — 28 C2
Pittville St EH15 — 125 E4
Pittville Street La EH15 — 125 D4
Place Charente EH22 — 157 E1
Plane Gr KY11 — 46 C4
Plane St EH42 — 78 A1
Plantation St KY5 — 14 A4
Player Gn EH54 — 147 D4
Players Rd FK7 — 7 E4
Plean Ctry Pk FK7 — 20 A1
Pleasance Edinburgh EH8 — 233 E2
   Falkirk FK1 — 60 A2
Pleasance Brae KY12 — 27 F1
Pleasance Ct
   15 EH — 60 A3
   Halbeath KY12 — 30 A4
Pleasance Gdns FK1 — 60 A3
Pleasance Rd
   Dunfermline KY12 — 29 F3
   Falkirk FK2 — 60 A3
   Halbeath KY12 — 30 A4
Pleasance Row ML11 — 215 D2
Pleasance The EH32 — 71 E2
Plewlandcroft EH30 — 68 A1
Plewlands Ave EH10 — 122 C1
Plewlands Gdns EH10 — 122 C1
Plewlands Pl EH30 — 68 A1
Plewlands Terr EH10 — 122 C1
Pleydell Pl EH16 — 155 D4
Plough La EH33 — 128 B3
Plover Brae EH54 — 147 E3
Poachers Gn FK10 — 11 D3
Poingarry Rd EH39 — 54 A4
Polbeth Ave EH55 — 172 C3
Polbeth Cres EH55 — 172 C3
Polbeth Gdns EH55 — 172 C3
Polbeth Ind Est EH55 — 172 C3
Polbeth Pl EH55 — 172 C3
Polbeth Rd EH55 — 172 C3
Polbeth West Calder Ind Est EH55 — 172 C3
Poldrate EH41 — 132 A4
Polkemmet Ctry Pk EH47 — 169 E4
Polkemmet Dr ML7 — 169 D3
Polkemmet La ML7 — 168 C3
Polkemmet Prim Sch EH47 — 170 A3
Polkemmet Rd
   Harthill ML7 — 168 C3
   Whitburn EH47 — 169 F3
Pollock Halls of Residence (Univ of Edinburgh) EH16 — 124 A3
Pollock Wlk KY12 — 28 C3
Polmaise Ave FK7 — 7 D2
Polmaise Cres FK7 — 8 B3
Polmaise Ct FK7 — 7 D2
Polmaise Rd
   Cambusbarron FK7 — 6 C2
   Stirling FK7 — 6 C3
Polmont House Gdns FK2 — 61 F1
Polmont Pk FK2 — 61 F2
Polmont Rd FK2 — 61 D2
Polmont Sta FK2 — 61 F1
Polson Gdns EH33 — 128 A3
Polton Avenue Rd EH19 — 182 A3
Polton Bank EH18 — 181 F3
Polton Bank Terr EH18 — 181 F3
Polton Cotts EH19 — 181 E3
Polton Ct EH19 — 182 A4
Polton Gdns EH18 — 182 A4
Polton Pl EH19 — 182 A4
Polton Rd
   Bonnyrigg and Lasswade,
   Loanhead EH20, EH18 — 181 E4
Polton Rd W EH18 — 181 F3
Polton St EH19 — 182 A3
Polton Terr EH18 — 182 A4
Polwarth Ave FK2 — 62 A3
Polwarth Cres
   Edinburgh EH11 — 123 D3
   Prestonpans EH32 — 97 D1
Polwarth Gdns EH11 — 122 C3
Polwarth Gr EH11 — 122 C3
Polwarth Pk EH11 — 122 C3
Polwarth Pl EH11 — 122 C3
Polwarth Terr
   Edinburgh EH11 — 122 C2
   Prestonpans EH32 — 97 D1
Polworth Pl KY4 — 13 E2
Pomathorn Bank EH26 — 203 F2
Pomathorn Rd EH26 — 203 F2
Pompee Rd FK10 — 5 D1
Ponton St EH3 — 232 B1
Poolewe Dr FK2 — 61 E1
Poplar Cres KY2 — 17 D4
Poplar Gr
   Dunfermline KY11 — 46 C4
   Livingston EH54 — 148 A3

Poplar La EH6 — 94 A3
Poplar St Dunbar EH42 — 78 A1
   Grangemouth FK3 — 61 E4
   Mayfield EH22 — 183 F3
Poplar Terr EH19 — 182 A3
Poplars The FK10 — 4 A1
Port Buchan EH52 — 117 E3
Port Edgar Water Sports Ctr EH30 — 67 F1
Port Hamilton EH3 — 232 B2
Port St Clackmannan FK10 — 11 D2
   Inverkeithing KY11 — 47 E1
   Stirling FK8 — 2 A2
Portal Rd FK3 — 61 E3
Portdownie FK1 — 59 E3
Porteous' Pend EH1 — 232 C2
Porterfield KY12 — 26 C4
Porterfield Rd EH4 — 92 C3
Portgower Pl EH4 — 93 D1
Portland Pl Edinburgh EH6 — 93 F3
   Fauldhouse EH47 — 193 E3
Portland St EH6 — 93 F3
Portobello High Sch EH15 — 124 C4
Portobello Rd EH8 — 94 C1
Portree Cres FK7 — 62 A1
Portsburgh Sq EH1 — 232 C2
Post Office La KY3 — 68 B3
Posthill FK10 — 5 E1
Potter Pl FK7 — 39 F2
Potterrow EH8 — 233 D2
Potters Path EH33 — 128 B3
Pottery St KY1 — 17 F4
Pottery The
   Edinburgh EH15 — 95 D1
   Prestonpans EH32 — 96 C1
Pottis Rd FK7 — 7 E2
Pottishaw Pl EH48 — 145 E1
Povert Rd EH19, EH23 — 182 C1
Powdermill Brae EH23 — 207 E3
Powdrake Rd FK3 — 61 F4
Pratt St KY1 — 17 D1
President Kennedy Dr FK2 — 20 B2
Preston Ave
   Linlithgow EH49 — 84 C3
   Prestonpans EH32 — 97 D1
Preston Cres
   Inverkeithing KY11 — 47 E1
   Linlithgow EH49 — 84 C3
   Prestonpans EH32 — 97 D1
Preston Cross Cotts EH32 — 97 D1
Preston Ct
   Linlithgow EH49 — 84 C3
   Prestonpans EH32 — 127 F4
Preston Lodge High Sch EH32 — 97 D1
Preston Mill EH40 — 103 F4
Preston Pk EH49 — 84 C3
Preston Pl EH37 — 185 D2
Preston Rd
   East Linton EH40 — 103 F4
   Linlithgow EH49 — 84 C3
   Prestonpans EH32 — 97 D1
Preston St
   High Valleyfield KY12 — 26 A1
   Rosewell EH24 — 181 E1
Preston Street Prim Sch EH8 — 233 F1
Preston Terr
   Inverkeithing KY11 — 47 E1
   Linlithgow EH49 — 84 C3
   Prestonpans EH32 — 97 D1
Preston Tower EH32 — 97 D1
Prestonfield Ave EH16 — 124 A2
Prestonfield Bank EH16 — 124 A2
Prestonfield Cres EH16 — 124 A2
Prestonfield Gdns EH16 — 124 A2
Prestonfield Prim Sch EH16 — 124 A2
Prestonfield Rd EH16 — 124 A2
Prestonfield Terr EH16 — 124 A2
Prestongrange Rd EH32 — 127 F4
Prestongrange Terr EH32 — 96 C1
Prestonhall Cres EH24 — 181 E1
Prestonhall Rd EH24 — 181 E1
Prestonkirk Gdns EH40 — 103 F4
Prestonpans Prim Sch
   Prestonpans, Cuthill EH32 — 96 C1
   Prestonpans, Preston — 128 A4
Prestonpans Sta EH32 — 128 A4
Pretoria Pl
   Cowdenbeath KY4 — 13 D2
   Polmont FK2 — 61 F1
Pretoria Rd FK5 — 38 A1
Priest Bank EH41 — 134 B1
Priestfield Ave EH16 — 124 A2
Priestfield Cres EH16 — 124 A2
Priestfield Gdns EH16 — 124 A2
Priestfield Gr EH16 — 124 A3
Priestfield Rd EH16 — 124 A3
Priestfield Rd N EH16 — 124 A3
Prime Gilt Box St KY2 — 17 D3
Primmer Pl KY4 — 13 E2
Primrose Ave
   Grangemouth FK3 — 61 D3
   Rosyth KY11 — 46 B3
Primrose Bank Rd EH5 — 93 D3
Primrose Cres EH22 — 157 E1
Primrose Ct
   Broxburn EH52 — 117 F3
   Rosyth KY11 — 46 B3
Primrose Dr EH30 — 90 B2
Primrose Gdns
   Carrington EH23 — 206 B3
   Queensferry EH30 — 89 E4

Primrose La
   Cowdenbeath KY4 — 13 E3
   Kincardine FK10 — 23 F2
   Rosyth KY11 — 46 B3
Primrose Pl Alloa FK10 — 10 A3
   Livingston EH54 — 147 D3
Primrose Rd Alloa FK10 — 10 A4
Primrose St Alloa FK10 — 10 A4
   Bonnybridge FK4 — 58 A3
   Edinburgh EH6 — 94 A2
Primrose Terr
   Dalkeith EH22 — 157 E1
   Edinburgh EH11 — 122 C3
   Falkirk FK2 — 60 B3
Prince Regent St EH6 — 93 F3
Princes St California EH1 — 81 F3
   Edinburgh EH2 — 232 C3
   Falkirk FK1 — 60 A3
   Grangemouth FK3 — 61 F4
   Stirling FK8 — 7 D4
Princess Margaret Rose Hospl (Orthopaedic) EH10 — 154 B3
Princess Mary Pl EH41 — 101 D1
Princess Mary Rd EH41 — 101 D1
Princess St FK4 — 58 A3
Priors Grange EH48 — 113 F3
Priorscroft EH48 — 113 F3
Priory Gr EH30 — 89 D4
Priory Rd EH48 — 113 F3
Priory Rd Linlithgow EH49 — 84 C2
   Whitecross EH49 — 83 F3
Priory Sq FK10 — 23 F2
Priory Wlk EH41 — 132 B4
Priory Wynd EH39 — 54 A4
Promenade
   Edinburgh EH15 — 95 D1
   Limekilns KY11 — 45 E2
   Musselburgh EH21 — 126 A4
Prora Cotts EH39 — 73 E2
Prospect Bank Cres EH6 — 94 B2
Prospect Bank Gdns EH6 — 94 A2
Prospect Bank Gr EH6 — 94 B2
Prospect Bank Pl EH6 — 94 B2
Prospect Bank Rd EH6 — 94 B2
Prospect Bank Sch EH6 — 94 A2
Prospect Bank Terr EH6 — 94 B2
Prospect St
   Cowdenbeath KY4 — 13 D2
   Falkirk FK1 — 59 F3
Prospecthill Rd FK1 — 60 A1
Providence Brae EH51 — 63 F4
Provost Haugh Ave FK12 — 5 E4
Provost Milne Gr EH30 — 89 E4
Provost Rd Bo'ness EH51 — 63 E3
   Linlithgow EH49 — 85 D4
Pryde Ave EH19 — 182 A4
Pryde Terr EH19 — 182 A4
Puir Wife's Brae EH48 — 145 E3
Pullar Ave FK9 — 2 A3
Pullar Ct FK9 — 2 A3
Pumpherston Prim Sch EH53 — 148 A4
Pumpherston Rd EH54, EH53 — 148 B3
Pyothall Rd EH52 — 117 E3
Pypers Wynd EH32 — 96 C1

Quadrant EH32 — 54 B4
Quadrant La EH26 — 54 B4
Quadrant The EH26 — 203 F3
Quakerfield FK7 — 7 F1
Quality St Dysart KY1 — 18 A4
   Edinburgh EH4 — 91 F2
   North Berwick EH39 — 54 B4
Quality Street Junc EH4 — 91 F2
Quality Street La EH4 — 91 F2
Quarrywood Ct EH54 — 147 E2
Quarrolhall Cres FK2 — 39 D2
Quarry Brae Brightons FK2 — 82 C4
   Kirkcaldy KY1 — 17 F4
Quarry Cl EH48 — 233 E1
Quarry Cotts EH15 — 125 D2
Quarry Ct KY4 — 13 D2
Quarry Howe EH14 — 151 E1
Quarry Knowe EH14 — 19 F4
Quarry Pl Alloa FK10 — 10 B4
   Shotts ML7 — 191 D3
Quarry Rd
   Cambusbarron FK7 — 6 B3
   Fauldhouse EH47 — 193 F3
   Shotts ML7 — 191 E3
Quarry St ML7 — 191 E3
Quarrybank EH14 — 152 B4
Quarrybank Cl EH14 — 152 B4
Quarrybank Ct EH14 — 152 B4
Quarrybank End EH14 — 152 B4
Quarryfoot Gdns EH19 — 182 B4
Quarryfoot Gn EH19 — 182 B4
Quarryford Dr EH19 — 182 A4
Quarryford Farm Cotts EH41 — 190 C4
Quarryknowes The EH51 — 63 F3
Quarryside Ct KY12 — 28 B3
Quarryview EH14 — 152 B4
Quayside St EH6 — 93 F3
Quebec Ave EH54 — 147 F2
Queen Anne Dr EH28 — 119 D3
Queen Anne High Sch KY11 — 29 E3
Queen Anne Pk EH28 — 119 D3
Queen Anne St KY11 — 29 D3
Queen Charlotte La EH6 — 94 A3
Queen Charlotte St EH6 — 94 A3
Queen Margaret Cl EH10 — 154 B3
Queen Margaret Coll EH12 — 121 E4
Queen Margaret Coll (Leith Campus) EH6 — 94 A2

Queen Margaret Dr EH30 — 89 E4
Queen Margaret Fauld KY12 — 29 F3
Queen Margaret Hospl KY12 — 29 F3
Queen Margaret St KY3 — 34 C1
Queen Margaret's Pl KY11 — 68 B3
Queen St Alloa FK10 — 10 A4
   Alva FK12 — 5 D4
   Bannockburn FK7 — 7 E1
   Edinburgh EH2 — 232 C4
   Falkirk FK1 — 60 B3
   Fallin FK7 — 8 B2
   Grangemouth FK3 — 61 F4
   Inverkeithing KY11 — 47 D1
   Stirling FK8 — 2 A1
Queen Street Gdns E EH3 — 232 C4
Queen Street Gdns W EH3 — 232 C4
Queen's Ave
   Bridge of A FK9 — 2 A3
   Edinburgh EH4 — 92 A1
Queen's Ave S EH4 — 92 A1
Queen's Bay Cres EH15 — 125 E4
Queen's Bldgs KY11 — 46 C3
Queen's Cres
   Carluke ML8 — 230 A1
   Edinburgh EH9 — 123 F2
   Falkirk FK1 — 59 F3
Queen's Ct FK9 — 1 C4
Queen's Dr EH8 — 233 F2
Queen's Dr Larbert FK5 — 38 B1
   Pencaitland EH34 — 160 C3
Queen's Gdns EH4 — 92 B1
Queen's La FK9 — 2 A3
Queen's Park Ave EH8 — 94 A1
Queen's Park Ct EH8 — 124 B4
Queen's Rd EH12 — 78 C1
Queen's Rd
   Broxburn EH52 — 117 F2
   Dunbar EH42 — 78 C1
   Edinburgh EH4 — 92 B1
   Stirling FK8 — 6 C4
Queen's St FK1 — 81 F3
Queen's Wlk EH16 — 124 C2
Queens Ave
   Broxburn EH52 — 117 F2
   Haddington EH41 — 100 C1
Queens Cres FK3 — 34 C1
Queens Cres FK5 — 38 B2
Queens Dr Denny FK6 — 36 C2
   Falkirk FK1 — 59 F3
Queens Gdns EH53 — 148 C2
Queens Terr EH53 — 148 C2
Queens Way KY11 — 46 A1
Queensferry High Sch EH30 — 89 E4
Queensferry Mus EH30 — 68 B1
Queensferry Rd
   Dunfermline KY11 — 46 A1
   Edinburgh, Braepark EH4 — 91 D2
   Edinburgh, Orchard Brae — 92 B1
   Kirkliston EH29 — 89 A1
   Rosyth KY11 — 46 C3
Queensferry St EH2 — 232 A3
Queensferry Street La EH2 — 232 B3
Quench Rd FK2 — 62 A3
Quentin Rise EH54 — 147 F1
Quidenham Ct EH19 — 54 A3
Quilts The EH6 — 93 F3
Quilts Wynd EH6 — 93 F3
Quoiters Ct EH47 — 171 E4

R L Stevenson's Birthplace & Mus EH3 — 93 E2
Race Rd EH48 — 144 C4
Rae Ct FK2 — 39 E2
Rae St Cowdenbeath KY4 — 13 E1
   Stenhousemuir FK5 — 38 B2
Rae's Ct EH16 — 155 D3
Raeburn Cres
   Kirkcaldy KY2 — 17 D2
   Whitburn EH47 — 170 A3
Raeburn Mews EH4 — 93 D1
Raeburn Pl EH4 — 93 D1
Raeburn Rigg EH54 — 147 D3
Raeburn St EH4 — 93 D1
Raes Gdns EH19 — 182 B4
Rainhill Ave FK2 — 82 C3
Raith Ave KY4 — 13 D2
Raith Cres KY2 — 17 D2
Raith Dr KY2 — 17 D2
Raith Gdns KY2 — 16 C2
Raleigh Ct FK1 — 59 F3
Ramage Rd ML8 — 230 A1
Ramillies Ct Carluke ML8 — 230 A1
   Penicuik EH26 — 204 A4
Ramsay Ave FK2 — 61 D3
Ramsay Cotts EH19 — 182 C2
Ramsay Cres
   Bathgate EH48 — 145 E3
   Burntisland KY3 — 33 F1
   Mayfield EH22 — 183 F2
Ramsay Ct EH54 — 148 B3
Ramsay La
   Kincardine FK10 — 23 F2
   Limekilns KY11 — 45 E2
Ramsay Pl Edinburgh EH15 — 95 D1
   Stirling FK8 — 2 B1
Ramsay Rd KY1 — 17 D1

Ramsay Terr EH18 — 181 F3
Ramsay Wlk EH22 — 183 F3
Ramsey Ct FK10 — 23 F2
Ramsey Gdn EH1 — 232 C3
Ramsey La EH1 — 232 C3
Ramsey Pl Penicuik EH26 — 203 E3
   Rosyth KY11 — 46 C2
Ramsey Tullis Ave FK10 — 4 B1
Ramsey Tullis Dr FK10 — 4 B1
Randolph Cliff EH3 — 232 A3
Randolph Cres
   Bannockburn FK7 — 7 E1
   Brightons FK2 — 82 B4
   Edinburgh EH3 — 232 A3
Randolph Ct FK8 — 7 D3
Randolph Gdns FK6 — 36 B1
Randolph Ind Est KY1 — 18 A4
Randolph La EH3 — 232 B3
Randolph Pl
   Bannockburn FK7 — 7 E1
   Edinburgh EH3 — 232 B3
   Kirkcaldy KY1 — 18 A4
Randolph Rd FK8 — 7 D3
Randolph St
   Cowdenbeath KY4 — 13 E2
   Dunfermline KY12 — 29 D2
Randolph Terr FK7 — 7 D2
Randyford Rd FK2 — 60 B3
Randyford St FK2 — 60 C3
Range Rd FK2 — 62 B4
Rankeillor St EH8 — 233 E1
Rankin Ave EH9 — 123 F1
Rankin Dr EH9 — 123 F1
Rankin Rd EH9 — 123 F2
Rankine Ave EH54 — 148 B3
Rankine Cl FK10 — 10 B3
Rannoch Dr
   Crossford KY12 — 28 A1
   Whitburn EH47 — 170 B4
Rannoch Gr EH4 — 91 E1
Rannoch Pl Edinburgh EH4 — 91 E1
   Shieldhill FK1 — 81 F4
   Shotts ML7 — 191 F3
   Stenhousemuir FK5 — 38 C2
Rannoch Rd
   Edinburgh EH4 — 91 E1
   Grangemouth FK3 — 61 E2
   Kirkcaldy KY2 — 16 C4
   Rosyth KY11 — 46 C1
   Whitburn EH47 — 170 B4
Rannoch Terr EH4 — 91 E1
Rannoch Wlk
   Livingston EH54 — 148 A3
   Whitburn EH47 — 170 B4
Ransome Gdns EH4 — 91 E1
Raploch Prim Sch FK8 — 1 C1
Raploch Rd FK8 — 1 C1
Rashiecleugh Rd EH54 — 194 C3
Rashiehill FK1 — 110 A3
Rashiehill Terr EH55 — 194 C3
Rashinhill ML11 — 215 D1
Rashierig EH52 — 117 D3
Rashierigg Pl EH47 — 171 E3
Ratcliffe Terr EH9 — 123 F2
Rathbone Pl EH15 — 95 D1
Ratho Park Rd EH28 — 119 F1
Ratho Pl KY11 — 29 E2
Ratho Prim Sch EH28 — 119 E1
Rattray Gdns EH47 — 171 F4
Rattray St FK2 — 64 A4
Rattray Terr KY5 — 14 A4
Ravelrig Hill EH14 — 151 D1
Ravelrig Pk EH14 — 151 D1
Ravelrig Rd EH14 — 151 D1
Ravelston Dykes EH12 — 122 B4
Ravelston Dykes La EH4 — 122 A4
Ravelston Dykes Rd EH4 — 122 A4
Ravelston Gdn EH4 — 122 B4
Ravelston Hts EH4 — 92 B1
Ravelston House Gr 9 EH4 — 92 B1
Ravelston House Loan 8 EH4 — 92 B1
Ravelston House Pk EH4 — 92 B1
Ravelston House Rd EH4 — 92 B1
Ravelston Pk EH4 — 122 C4
Ravelston Rise EH4 — 122 B4
Ravelston Terr EH4 — 92 C1
Ravelsykes Rd EH26 — 203 E3
Ravendean Gdns EH26 — 203 E3
Ravensby Ct KY12 — 17 E3
Ravenscraig Park Nature Trail KY1 — 17 F3
Ravenscraig St KY1 — 17 F3
Ravenscroft Gdns EH17 — 155 F3
Ravenscroft Pl EH17 — 155 F3
Ravenscroft St EH17 — 155 F3
Ravenshaugh Cres EH21 — 127 D3
Ravenshaugh Rd EH21 — 127 D4
Ravenswood Ave EH16 — 124 B1
Ravenswood Rise EH54 — 173 F3
Rectory La KY1 — 18 A4
Red Craigs KY2 — 16 B4
Red Fox Cres EH26 — 180 A1
Red Row KY11 — 45 E2
Redbrae Ave EH51 — 64 A3
Redbrae Rd FK1 — 59 E3
Redbraes Gr EH7 — 93 E2
Redbraes Pl EH7 — 93 E2
Redburn Rd
   Blackridge EH48 — 142 A1
   Prestonpans EH32 — 96 C1
Redburn Rd N EH32 — 96 C1
Redburn Wynd KY1 — 17 E2
Redcraig Rd EH53 — 148 C1

Redcroft Pl EH47 .... 171 D1
Redcroft St EH22 .... 156 A4
Redcroft Terr EH47 .... 171 D1
Redding Ind Est FK2 .... 61 D1
Redding Rd Brightons FK2 .... 82 B4
Redding FK2 .... 61 D1
Reddingmuirhead Rd
FK2 .... 61 D1
Reddoch Rd FK2 .... 62 A2
Redford Ave EH13 .... 153 E3
Redford Bank EH13 .... 153 E3
Redford Cres EH13 .... 153 E3
Redford Dr EH13 .... 153 E3
Redford Gdns EH13 .... 153 E3
Redford Gr EH13 .... 153 E3
Redford Loan EH13 .... 153 E3
Redford Neuk EH13 .... 153 E3
Redford Pl EH13 .... 153 E3
Redford Rd EH13 .... 153 E3
Redford Terr EH13 .... 153 E3
Redford Wlk EH13 .... 153 E3
Redgauntlet Terr EH16 ...... 124 B1
Redhall Ave EH14 .... 122 A1
Redhall Bank Rd EH14 ...... 122 A1
Redhall Cres EH14 .... 122 A1
Redhall Dr EH14 .... 122 A1
Redhall Gdns EH14 .... 122 A1
Redhall Gr EH14 .... 122 A1
Redhall House Dr
EH14 .... 122 A1
Redhall Pl EH14 .... 122 A1
Redhall Rd EH14 .... 122 A1
Redhall View EH14 .... 122 A1
Redhaws Rd ML7 .... 192 A2
Redheugh Loan EH23 .... 183 E1
Redheughs Ave EH12 .... 121 D2
Redheughs Rigg EH12 ...... 121 D2
Redholm Pk EH39 .... 54 C3
Redhouse Cotts EH49 .... 86 C2
Redhouse Ct EH47 .... 171 F4
Redhouse Pl EH47 .... 145 E1
Redhouse Rd EH47 .... 172 A4
Redlands Ct EH47 .... 170 C4
Redlands Rd FK10 .... 4 A2
Redmill Cotts EH47 .... 170 C4
Redmill Ct EH47 .... 170 C4
Redmill View EH47 .... 170 C4
Redmire Cres ML7 .... 212 A4
Redpath Dr FK2 .... 39 D2
Redwell Pl FK10 .... 9 F4
Redwing Brae EH54 .... 147 E3
Redwood Gr EH22 .... 182 C3
Redwood Wlk EH22 .... 183 D3
Reed Dr EH22 .... 183 D4
Reedlands Dr FK6 .... 57 E4
Regal Gr ML7 .... 191 F2
Regent Pl EH7 .... 94 A1
Regent Rd EH7, EH8 .... 233 E4
Regent Sq EH49 .... 85 D4
Regent St
Edinburgh EH15 .... 125 D4
Kincardine FK10 .... 23 F2
Regent Street La EH15 ...... 125 D4
Regent Terr EH7 .... 233 F4
Regent Terrace Mews
EH7 .... 233 F4
Regents Way KY11 .... 48 A2
Regis Ct EH4 .... 91 D2
Register Pl EH2 .... 233 D4
Register St EH51 .... 63 F4
Reid Ave KY4 .... 30 C3
Reid St
Dunfermline KY12 .... 29 D2
Lochgelly KY5 .... 14 A4
Reid Terr EH3 .... 93 D1
Reid's Cl EH8 .... 233 F3
Reilly Gdns FK4 .... 58 A2
Reilly Rd FK4 .... 58 A2
Relugas Gdns EH9 .... 123 F2
Relugas Pl EH9 .... 123 F2
Relugas Rd EH9 .... 123 F2
Rendall Gdns EH52 .... 117 F3
Rennie Pl EH40 .... 103 E4
Rennie Sq EH54 .... 173 E3
Rennie St FK1 .... 60 A3
Rennie's Isle EH6 .... 93 F3
Research Ave N
Currie EH14 .... 151 F4
Edinburgh EH14 .... 120 C1
Research Ave S EH14 ...... 151 F4
Restalrig Ave EH7 .... 94 B1
Restalrig Cir EH7 .... 94 B2
Restalrig Cres EH7 .... 94 B2
Restalrig Dr EH7 .... 94 B1
Restalrig Gdns EH7 .... 94 B1
Restalrig Pk EH7 .... 94 A2
Restalrig Rd EH6 .... 94 A2
Restalrig Rd S EH7 .... 94 B1
Restalrig Sq EH7 .... 94 B2
Restalrig Terr EH6 .... 94 A2
Reveston La EH47 .... 170 A3
Reveston Way EH49 .... 84 A3
Rhodders Gr FK12 .... 5 D4
Rhodes St KY11 .... 29 D1
Riccarton Ave EH14 .... 152 A3
Riccarton Cres EH14 ...... 152 A2
Riccarton Dr EH14 .... 152 A3
Riccarton Gr EH14 .... 152 A3
Riccarton Mains Rd
EH14 .... 152 A3
Riccarton Prim Sch
EH14 .... 151 F2
Riccarton Rd EH14 .... 84 C3
Richmond Dr FK2 .... 82 B4
Richmond La EH8 .... 233 E2

Richmond Pl
Edinburgh EH8 .... 233 E2
Lochgelly KY5 .... 14 A4
Richmond Terr
Bo'ness EH51 .... 63 F4
Edinburgh EH11 .... 232 A2
Riddochhill Cres EH47 ...... 171 E4
Riddochhill Ct EH47 .... 171 D4
Riddochhill Dr EH47 .... 171 E4
Riddochhill Rd EH47 .... 171 E4
Riddochhill View EH47 ...... 171 D4
Ridge Way KY11 .... 48 A3
Riding Pk EH4 .... 91 D2
Ridley Dr KY11 .... 46 C2
Riego St FK3 .... 232 B2
Rifle Rd FK3 .... 62 B4
Rigg Pl EH42 .... 78 B1
Rig St EH42 .... 71 E2
Riggs View KY12 .... 27 E1
Rigley Terr EH32 .... 127 F4
Rillbank Cres EH9 .... 233 D1
Rillbank Terr EH9 .... 123 E3
Rimmon Cres ML7 .... 191 F3
Ring Rd FK10 .... 10 A4
Ringwood Pl EH16 .... 155 D4
Rintoul Ave KY12 .... 26 A4
Rintoul Pl Blairhall KY12 .... 26 A4
Edinburgh EH3 .... 93 D1
Riselaw Cres EH10 .... 154 A4
Riselaw Pl EH10 .... 154 A4
Riselaw Rd EH10 .... 154 A4
Riselaw Terr EH10 .... 154 A4
Ritchie Pl Bo'ness EH51 .... 64 A3
Edinburgh EH11 .... 122 C3
Grangemouth FK3 .... 61 E3
Rivaldsgreen Cres EH49 .... 85 D3
River St FK2 .... 39 D1
River View KY11 .... 48 A1
River Wlk EH4 .... 91 D2
Riverbank View FK8 .... 7 E4
Riversdale Cres EH12 ...... 122 B4
Riversdale Gr EH12 .... 122 B4
Riversdale Rd EH12 .... 122 B4
Riverside Edinburgh EH4 .... 91 E4
Newbridge EH28 .... 118 C3
Riverside Ct EH54 .... 147 E2
Riverside Dr
Haddington EH41 .... 101 D1
Stirling FK8 .... 2 B1
Riverside Gdns EH21 ...... 126 A3
Riverside Pl EH41 .... 101 E1
Riverside Prim Sch
Livingston EH54 .... 148 A2
Stirling FK8 .... 2 A1
Riverside Rd
Craigiehall EH30 .... 90 C2
Grangemouth FK2 .... 62 A3
Riverside Terr FK10 .... 23 F2
Riverside View FK10 ...... 10 A2
Road 10 FK3 .... 62 B3
Road 11 FK3 .... 62 B3
Road 13 FK3 .... 62 B3
Road 24 FK3 .... 62 A3
Road 25 FK3 .... 62 A3
Road 27 FK3 .... 62 A3
Road 28 FK3 .... 62 A3
Road 29 FK3 .... 62 A3
Road 30b FK3 .... 62 A3
Road 30c FK3 .... 62 A3
Road 31 FK3 .... 62 A3
Road 32 FK3 .... 62 A3
Road 33 FK2, FK3 .... 62 A3
Road 4 FK3 .... 62 B3
Road 4a FK3 .... 62 B3
Road 4b FK3 .... 62 B3
Road 6 FK3 .... 62 B3
Road 7 FK3 .... 62 B3
Road 9 FK3 .... 62 B3
Roanhead Terr FK10 ...... 23 F2
Roanshead Rd EH22 .... 183 E4
Robb's Loan EH14 .... 122 B2
Robb's Loan Gr EH14 ...... 122 B2
Robert Bruce Ct FK5 .... 38 A1
Robert Burns Dr EH16 .... 124 A1
Robert Burns Mews
EH22 .... 157 E2
Robert Dick Ct FK10 ...... 4 B1
Robert Hardie Ct FK5 ...... 38 B1
Robert Knox Ave FK10 ...... 4 B1
Robert Smilie Ave EH22 .... 183 F3
Robert Smith Ct KY4 ...... 13 F3
Robert St ML7 .... 191 F2
Roberts Ave FK2 .... 61 E1
Roberts St KY1 .... 17 F4
Robertson Ave
Bathgate EH48 .... 144 C3
Bonnybridge FK4 .... 58 A3
Edinburgh EH11 .... 122 B3
Prestonpans EH32 .... 97 D1
Tranent EH33 .... 128 B3
Robertson Bank EH23 ...... 207 E1
Robertson Ct FK48 .... 143 F2
Robertson Dr EH33 .... 128 B4
Robertson Pl FK7 .... 7 D2
Robertson Rd KY12 .... 29 E3
Robertson Way EH54 ...... 147 E4
Robertson's Cl
Dalkeith EH22 .... 157 D2
Edinburgh EH1 .... 233 E2
Robertsons Bank EH7 ...... 207 E4
Robins Neuk EH33 .... 129 E3
Rocheid Pk EH4 .... 92 C2
Rochester Terr EH10 ...... 123 D2
Rocks Rd KY11 .... 45 D2

Rockville Gr EH49 .... 85 D3
Rockville Terr EH19 .... 182 A4
Roddinglaw Rd EH12 ...... 120 B2
Rodel Dr FK2 .... 61 F1
Rodney Pl EH7 .... 93 E1
Rodney St Edinburgh EH7 .. 93 E1
Grangemouth FK3 .... 61 E3
Roebuck Pl EH51 .... 63 E3
Rolland St KY12 .... 29 D2
Roman Camp EH47 .... 185 D2
Roman Camp Cotts
EH52 .... 117 E1
Roman Camp Way
EH37 .... 185 D2
Roman Dr FK1 .... 59 E3
Roman Rd
Bonnybridge FK4 .... 58 A2
Inverkeithing KY11 .... 47 D1
Roman Way EH51 .... 63 E3
Romero Pl EH16 .... 123 F3
Romyn Rd KY11 .... 46 B1
Roomlin Gdns KY1 .... 17 F4
Roosevelt Rd EH27 .... 149 F2
Rope Wlk EH32 .... 96 C1
Ropeway KY11 .... 46 A1
Rosabelle Rd EH25 .... 180 C2
Rosabelle St KY1 .... 17 F4
Rose Ave EH19 .... 182 B3
Rose Cotts EH19 .... 182 B3
Rose Cres KY12 .... 29 D2
Rose Ct EH44 .... 91 F2
Rose Gdns
Bonnyrigg and Lasswade
EH19 .... 182 B3
Cairneyhill KY12 .... 27 E1
Rose Gr EH19 .... 182 B3
Rose La Lochgelly KY5 ...... 14 A4
Queensferry EH30 .... 68 A1
Torryburn KY12 .... 26 C1
Rose Pk PK5 .... 93 D3
Rose Pl EH19 .... 182 B3
Rose St Alloa FK10 .... 4 C1
Bonnybridge FK4 .... 58 A3
Burntisland KY3 .... 50 C4
Cowdenbeath KY4 .... 13 E2
Dunfermline KY12 .... 29 D2
Edinburgh EH2 .... 232 C3
Rose Street North La
EH2 .... 232 C3
Rose Street South La
EH2 .... 232 C3
Rose Terr
Bonnyrigg and Lasswade
EH19 .... 182 B3
Denny FK6 .... 36 B1
Stenhousemuir FK5 .... 38 C2
Rose Way EH19 .... 182 B3
Rosebank Alloa FK10 ...... 5 E1
Cowdenbeath KY4 .... 13 E2
Dunfermline KY11 .... 29 E1
Rosebank Ave FK1 .... 59 F3
Rosebank Cotts EH3 ...... 232 A2
Rosebank Gdns
Alloa FK10 .... 10 B4
Dunfermline KY12 .... 28 B3
Edinburgh EH5 .... 93 D3
Kincardine FK10 .... 23 F2
Rosebank Gr EH5 .... 93 D3
Rosebank Rd EH5 .... 93 D3
Rosebank Rdbt EH54 ...... 173 D4
Roseberry Ct EH30 .... 89 E4
Roseberry Pl EH54 .... 147 D3
Rosebery Ave EH30 .... 89 E4
Rosebery Cres
Bathgate EH48 .... 145 D3
Edinburgh EH12 .... 122 C4
Gorebridge EH23 .... 207 E3
Rosebery Crescent La
EH12 .... 122 C4
Rosebery Ct
Dalgety Bay KY11 .... 47 F1
Kirkcaldy KY1 .... 17 D3
Rosebery Gr KY11 .... 47 F1
Rosebery Pl
Dalgety Bay KY11 .... 47 F1
Stirling FK8 .... 2 A1
Rosebery Terr KY1 .... 17 D3
Rosebery View KY11 ...... 47 F1
Roseburn Ave EH12 ...... 122 B4
Roseburn Cliff EH12 ...... 122 C4
Roseburn Cres EH12 ...... 122 B4
Roseburn Dr EH12 .... 122 B4
Roseburn Gdns EH12 ...... 122 B4
Roseburn Maltings
EH12 .... 122 C4
Roseburn Pl EH12 .... 122 B4
Roseburn Prim Sch
EH12 .... 122 B3
Roseburn St EH12 .... 122 B3
Roseburn Terr EH12 ...... 122 C4
Rosebush Cres KY11 ...... 29 D2
Rosedale Ct FK4 .... 205 E4
Rosefield Ave EH15 .... 125 D4
Rosefield Avenue La EH15 . 125 D4
Rosefield La EH15 .... 125 D4

Rosefield Pl EH15 .... 125 D4
Rosefield St EH15 .... 125 D4
Rosehall Pl FK41 .... 131 F4
Rosehall Rd ML7 .... 191 E2
Rosehall Terr FK1 .... 60 A2
Rosehall Wlk EH41 .... 131 F4
Rosehill Cres KY4 .... 13 D2
Rosehill Pl EH48 .... 147 D2
Rosehill Terr EH30 .... 89 E4
Roseland PK Bo'ness FK2 .. 82 C4
Roselea Dr FK2 .... 82 C4
Rosemead Terr FK1 .... 81 F3
Rosemill Ct KY12 .... 26 B1
Rosemount Ave KY2 ...... 17 D4
Rosemount Bldgs EH3 ...... 232 A2
Rosemount Ct EH48 ...... 145 D3
Rosemount Dr EH52 ...... 116 C2
Roseneath Pl EH9 .... 123 E3
Roseneath St EH9 .... 123 E3
Roseneath Terr EH9 ...... 123 E3
Rosevale Pl EH6 .... 94 A2
Rosevale Terr EH6 .... 94 A2
Roseville Gdns EH5 .... 93 E3
Rosewell Prim Sch
EH24 .... 181 F1
Rosewell Rd EH19 .... 181 F2
Roslin Glen Ctry Pk
EH25 .... 180 C1
Roslin Prim Sch EH25 .... 180 C2
Roslin Prim Sch (Annexe)
EH25 .... 180 B3
Ross Ave KY11 .... 48 A1
Ross Cres Falkirk FK1 ...... 59 E3
Tranent EH33 .... 128 B3
Ross Ct FK2 .... 7 D2
Ross Gdns Edinburgh EH9 . 123 F2
Kirkcaldy KY1 .... 17 D4
Ross High Sch EH33 ...... 128 B3
Ross La KY12 .... 28 C2
Ross Pl Edinburgh EH9 .... 123 F2
Ross Rd Kinghorn KY3 ...... 34 C1
Newtongrange EH22 ...... 183 D3
Ross St EH16 .... 123 F1
Ross St KY12 .... 29 D3
Rossend Terr KY3 .... 50 B4
Rossie Pl EH7 .... 94 A1
Rossland Pl KY3 .... 34 C1
Rosslyn Cres EH6 .... 93 F2
Rosslyn St KY1 .... 17 F4
Rosslyn Terr EH6 .... 93 F2
Rossmylee Hospl EH25 .... 204 C3
Rossness Dr KY3 .... 34 C1
Rossvail Sch FK1 .... 59 E3
Rosyth Europarc
North Queensferry KY11 .. 68 A4
Rosyth KY11 .... 46 B1
Rosyth Sta KY11 .... 46 C3
Rothes Dr EH54 .... 173 F3
Rothesay Mews EH3 ...... 122 C4
Rothesay Pl
Edinburgh EH3 .... 232 A3
Musselburgh EH21 .... 126 B3
Rothesay Terr EH3 .... 232 A3
Roughburn Rd FK9 .... 2 A3
Roughlands Cres FK2 ...... 39 D2
Roughlands Dr FK2 .... 39 D2
Roull Dr EH12 .... 121 E3
Roull Pl EH12 .... 121 F3
Roull Rd EH12 .... 121 E3
Round The KY2 .... 29 E2
Roundel The FK2 .... 60 B4
Roundelwood FK10 .... 5 D1
Roundhouse FK2 .... 20 B4
Rowallan Ct EH12 .... 121 D4
Rowallan Dr FK7 .... 7 F3
Rowan Cres Falkirk FK1 .... 59 D2
Shotts ML7 .... 192 A2
Rowan Ct FK7 .... 7 F1
Rowan Dr EH47 .... 145 F1
Rowan Gdns EH19 .... 182 A3
Rowan Gr
Dunfermline KY11 .... 29 E1
Livingston EH54 .... 148 A3
Rowan La EH47 .... 145 E1
Rowan St Blackburn EH47 . 145 E1
Dunbar EH42 .... 78 A1
Rowan Terr
Blackburn EH47 .... 171 E4
Cowdenbeath KY4 .... 13 E2
Rowan Tree Ave EH14 .... 151 F2
Rowan Tree Gr EH14 ...... 151 F2
Rowanhill Cl EH32 .... 97 E2
Rowanhill Dr EH32 .... 97 E2
Rowanhill Pk EH32 .... 97 E2
Rowanhill Way EH32 ...... 97 E2
Rowans The Alloa FK10 .... 5 E1
Gullane EH31 .... 52 A2
Rowantree Rd EH22 ...... 183 F4
Roxburgh Pl
Edinburgh EH8 .... 233 E2
Stenhousemuir FK5 .... 38 C3
Roxburgh St
Edinburgh EH8 .... 233 E2
Grangemouth FK3 .... 61 F4
Roxburghe Pk EH42 ...... 78 C1
Roxburghe Terr EH42 ...... 78 C1
Roy Dr EH54 .... 173 E3
Royal Blind Sch EH16 .... 123 F2
Royal Botanic Garden
EH3 .... 93 D2
Royal Cir EH3 .... 93 D1
Royal Coll of Physicians
EH2 .... 232 C4
Royal Cres EH3 .... 93 E1
Royal Dr EH54 .... 203 E4
Royal (Dick)
Veterinary Coll EH8 ...... 233 e1
Royal Edinburgh Hospl
EH10 .... 123 D2

Royal Gdns FK8 .... 7 D4
Royal High Prim Sch
EH8 .... 124 B4
Royal High Sch The EH4 .. 91 E2
Royal Hospl
for Sick Children EH9 .... 123 E3
Royal Infirmary
of Edinburgh EH3 .... 233 D2
Royal Mile Prim Sch
EH8 .... 233 F3
Royal Mus of Scotland
EH1 .... 233 D2
Royal Observatory EH9 .... 123 E1
Royal Park Terr EH8 ...... 94 A1
Royal Scot Way KY12 ...... 29 D3
Royal Scottish Acad
EH2 .... 232 C3
Royal Scottish
National Hospl The
FK5 .... 37 F2
Royal Terr
Edinburgh EH7 .... 233 E4
Linlithgow EH49 .... 84 C3
Royal Victoria Hospl EH4 .. 92 B1
Royal Yacht Britannia
EH6 .... 93 F4
Royston Mains Ave EH5 .. 92 C3
Royston Mains Cl EH5 .... 92 C3
Royston Mains Cres EH5 .. 92 C3
Royston Mains Gdns EH5 . 92 C3
Royston Mains Gr EH5 .... 92 C3
Royston Mains Pl EH5 .... 92 B3
Royston Mains Rd EH5 .... 92 C3
Royston Mains St EH5 .... 92 B3
Royston Prim Sch EH5 .... 92 C3
Royston Rdbt EH54 ...... 146 C4
Royston Terr EH3 .... 93 D2
Rudolf Steiner Sch
EH10 .... 122 C2
Rulley View FK6 .... 36 B2
Rullion Green Ave EH26 .. 203 E4
Rullion Green Cres EH26 . 203 E4
Rullion Green Gr EH26 .... 203 E4
Rullion Rd EH26 .... 203 E3
Rumblingwell KY12 ...... 28 B3
Rumlie The FK1 .... 110 A3
Run The EH51 .... 64 B4
Rushbank EH54 .... 147 F3
Ruskie Rd FK9 .... 2 A2
Ruskin Pl EH22 .... 183 F3
Russel Ct KY5 .... 14 A4
Russel St KY3 .... 60 A3
Russell Ave EH48 .... 143 F2
Russell Ct KY11 .... 29 E1
Russell Gdns EH12 ...... 122 C4
Russell Gr KY3 .... 33 F1
Russell Pl Kirkcaldy KY1 .... 17 E3
Oakley KY12 .... 26 C4
Russell Rd
Cowdenbeath KY4 .... 13 D2
Lochgelly KY5 .... 14 A4
Russell St
Bridge of A FK9 .... 2 A4
Kirkcaldy KY1 .... 17 F4
Rutherford Dr EH16 ...... 124 A1
Rutherford Sq EH54 ...... 173 E3
Ruthven Rd EH39 .... 53 D2
Rutland Court La EH3 .... 232 B2
Rutland Sq EH1 .... 232 B3
Rutland St EH1 .... 232 B3
Ryebank EH54 .... 147 F3
Ryehill Ave EH6 .... 94 A2
Ryehill Gdns EH6 .... 94 A2
Ryehill Gr EH6 .... 94 A2
Ryehill Pl EH6 .... 94 A2
Ryehill Terr EH6 .... 94 A2
Rymalton KY1 .... 17 E3

Sacred Heart RC Prim Sch
Grangemouth FK3 .... 61 F3
Penicuik EH26 .... 203 F3
Saddletree Loan EH16 .... 124 B1
Sailors' Wlk KY3 .... 50 B4
Sainford Cres FK2 .... 39 D1
Sainthill Ct EH39 .... 54 A4
St Aidan's Rd EH9 .... 123 F2
St Andrew Pl EH6 .... 94 A2
St Andrew Sq EH2 .... 233 D4
St Andrew St
Dalkeith EH22 .... 157 D2
Dunfermline KY11 .... 29 E1
North Berwick EH39 ...... 54 B4
St Andrew's Ct FK5 ...... 38 A2
St Andrew's Dr Airth FK2 .. 22 A4
Armadale EH48 .... 143 F4
Uphall EH52 .... 116 C2
St Andrew's High Sch
KY2 .... 17 E4
St Andrew's Prim Sch
FK1 .... 60 B2
St Andrew's St EH54 ...... 146 C3
St Andrew's [?] FK1 ...... 60 A2
St Ann's Ave EH18 .... 181 F3
St Ann's Path EH18 ...... 181 F3
St Anne's Cres FK7 ...... 7 F1
St Anne's Ct EH22 .... 183 D3
St Anthony La EH6 .... 93 F3
St Anthony Pl EH6 .... 93 F3
St Anthony St EH6 .... 93 F3
St Anthony's RC Prim Sch
EH6 .... 143 F2
St Augustine's High Sch
EH12 .... 121 E2
St Baldred's Cres EH39 .... 54 B4
St Baldred's Rd EH39 ...... 54 B4

St Bernadette's
RC Prim Sch FK10 .... 4 A1
St Bernard's Cres EH4 ...... 93 D1
St Bernard's Row 5 EH4 .... 93 D1
St Bride's RC Prim Sch
KY4 .... 13 E2
St Bridget's Church KY11 .. 48 B2
St Bridgets Brae KY11 .... 48 B2
St Brycedale Ave KY1 .... 17 D2
St Brycedale Rd KY1 .... 17 D2
St Catherine FK2 .... 82 C4
St Catherine's Gdns
EH12 .... 122 A3
St Catherine's Pl EH9 ...... 123 F3
St Catherine's RC
Prim Sch EH16 .... 155 D3
St Catherine's Wynd
KY12 .... 28 C2
St Catherines Cres ML7 .. 191 F3
St Clair Ave EH6 .... 94 A2
St Clair Cres EH25 .... 181 D2
St Clair Pl EH6 .... 94 A2
St Clair Rd EH6 .... 94 A2
St Clair St Edinburgh EH6 . 94 A2
Kirkcaldy KY1 .... 17 F4
St Clair Terr EH11 .... 122 C1
St Clement's Cres EH21 .. 127 D2
St Clement's Gdns N
EH21 .... 127 D2
St Clement's Gdns S
EH21 .... 127 D2
St Clement's Terr EH21 ... 127 D2
St Colm's Abbey KY3 .... 49 D1
St Colm's Ed Ctr & Coll
EH16 .... 93 D2
St Colme Ave KY3 .... 49 D3
St Colme Cres KY3 .... 49 D4
St Colme Dr KY11 .... 48 B3
St Colme Rd KY11 .... 48 B2
St Colme St EH3 .... 232 B4
St Columba's High Sch
EH11 .... 29 F2
St Columba's RC
Prim Sch EH46 .... 145 F3
St Crispin's Pl FK1 .... 60 A2
St Crispin's Sch EH16 .... 123 F2
St Cuthbert's RC Prim Sch
EH14 .... 122 B2
St David's Bsns Pk KY11 ... 48 A2
St David's Ct
Dalgety Bay KY11 .... 48 A2
Larbert FK5 .... 38 A1
St David's Pl EH3 .... 232 A2
St David's RC High Sch
EH22 .... 157 D1
St David's RC Prim Sch
Dalkeith EH22 .... 157 E1
Edinburgh EH4 .... 92 B2
St David's Terr EH3 .... 232 A2
St Davids EH22 .... 183 D3
St Davids Dr KY11 .... 48 A2
St Denis & Cranley Sch
EH10 .... 122 C2
St Fillan's Terr EH10 ...... 123 D1
St Fillans Cres KY3 .... 49 E4
St Fillans Gr KY3 .... 49 E4
St Fillans Pl KY2 .... 16 B4
St Fillans Rd KY2 .... 16 B4
St Francis' RC Prim Sch
FK2 .... 60 A3
St Francis's RC Prim Sch
EH16 .... 124 C2
St Gabriel's RC Prim Sch
EH32 .... 96 C1
St Gabriel's RC Prim Sch
EH32 .... 127 F4
St George's Ct FK5 .... 38 A1
St George's Sch EH12 ... 122 C4
St Georges Sch for girls
EH12 .... 122 B4
St Germains Terr EH33 .. 129 E3
St Giles' Cath EH1 .... 233 D3
St Giles Sq FK1 .... 59 D3
St Giles St EH1 .... 233 D3
St Giles Way FK1 .... 59 D3
St Helen's Pl EH48 .... 143 F3
St James Ctr EH1 .... 233 D4
St James' Orch FK9 .... 2 B1
St James' Pl EH1 .... 233 D4
St James Pl KY3 .... 35 D1
St James Sq EH1 .... 233 D4
St James's Gdns EH26 ... 203 F2
St James's View FK10 .... 203 F2
St Joesph's Hospl EH24 .. 205 F4
St John Ogilvie
RC Prim Sch EH54 .... 146 C3
St John St
Edinburgh EH8 .... 233 E3
Spott EH42 .... 106 B2
Stirling FK8 .... 7 D4
St John the Baptist RC Sch
EH47 .... 193 F3
St John Vianney Prim Sch
EH16 .... 124 A1
St John's Ave
Edinburgh EH12 .... 121 F3
Falkirk FK2 .... 60 B3
Linlithgow EH49 .... 84 C3
St John's Cres EH12 .... 121 F3
St John's Ct KY11 .... 47 E2
St John's Dr EH12 .... 121 F3
St John's Gate FK6 .... 36 B1
St John's Gdns Denny FK6 .. 36 B1
Edinburgh EH12 .... 121 F3
St John's Hill EH8 .... 233 E2
St John's Hospl EH54 ..... 147 E2
St John's Pl KY12 .... 29 E2

St John's Pl EH48 .... 113 F3
St John's Prim Sch
Edinburgh EH15 .... 125 D4
Rosyth KY11 .... 46 C2
St John's Rd
Broxburn EH52 .... 117 F2
Edinburgh EH12 .... 121 F3
St John's Terr EH12 .... 121 F3
St John's Way EH51 .... 63 F3
St Joseph's Cotts EH33 .. 128 B4
St Joseph's Prim Sch
Bonnyrbridge FK4 .... 58 A2
Edinburgh EH11 .... 121 F2
St Joseph's RC Prim Sch
EH49 .... 84 C3
St Joseph's Sch EH32 .... 128 B4
St Joseph's Spcl Sch
EH14 .... 181 F1
St Josephs RC Prim Sch
EH47 .... 169 F3
St Katharine's Brae
EH16 .... 155 D3
St Katharine's Cres
EH16 .... 155 D3
St Katharine's Loan
EH16 .... 155 D3
St Kenneth's RC Prim Sch
EH54 .... 147 E4
St Kentigern Rd EH26 .... 203 E3
St Kentigerns Acad
EH47 .... 171 D4
St Kilda Cres KY2 .... 16 C4
St Laurence Cres FK1 .... 110 A3
St Lawrence St KY11 .... 29 E1
St Leonard's EH8 .... 123 F3
St Leonard's Bank EH8 .. 233 F1
St Leonard's Crag EH8 .. 233 F1
St Leonard's Ct KY3 .... 35 D2
St Leonard's Hill EH8 ..... 233 E1
St Leonard's Lane EH8 .. 233 E1
St Leonard's Pl
Dunfermline KY11 .... 29 D1
Kinghorn KY3 .... 34 C2
St Leonard's Street
EH8 .... 233 E1
St Leonard's St
Dunfermline KY11 .... 29 D1
Edinburgh EH8 .... 233 E1
St Lukes Prim Sch EH22 .. 183 E3
St Magdalene's EH49 .... 85 D4
St Margaret St KY12 .... 29 D2
St Margaret's Cres FK2 .... 61 F1
St Margaret's Dr EH48 ... 143 F3
St Margaret's Pl EH9 ..... 123 E2
St Margaret's Prep Sch
EH16 .... 124 A2
St Margaret's RC Prim Sch
KY11 .... 29 E2
St Margaret's RC Prim Sch
FK2 .... 61 E1
St Margaret's RC Acad
EH54 .... 147 E2
St Margaret's RC Prim Sch
Cowie FK7 .... 20 B4
Loanhead EH20 .... 155 E1
Queensferry EH30 .... 68 B1
St Margaret's Rd
Edinburgh EH9 .... 123 D2
North Berwick EH39 .... 54 B4
St Margaret's Sch EH16 .. 124 A2
St Margaret's Special
Sen Coll EH16 .... 124 A2
St Margarets Ct EH39 .... 54 B4
St Margarets Dr KY12 .... 29 D2
St Marie's Prim Sch KY7 ... 17 E4
St Mark's La EH15 .... 125 D4
St Mark's Pl EH15 .... 125 D4
St Mark's RC Prim Sch
EH14 .... 153 F4
St Martin's Ct EH41 .... 132 B4
St Martin's Gate EH41 ... 132 A4
St Martin's Pl EH41 .... 132 B4
St Martin's RC Prim Sch
EH33 .... 128 B3
St Mary's (Leith)
RC Prim Sch EH6 .... 94 A3
St Mary's Music Sch
EH12 .... 122 C4
St Mary's Pl
Edinburgh EH15 .... 125 E4
Kirkcaldy KY1 .... 17 D3
St Mary's Place La EH15 .. 125 E4
St Mary's RC Cath EH1 ... 233 D4
St Mary's RC Prim Sch
Bannockburn FK7 .... 7 E1
Bathgate EH48 .... 145 D3
Bo'ness EH51 .... 64 A4
Bonnyrigg and Lasswade
EH19 .... 93 E1
Polbeth EH55 .... 172 C3
Stirling FK8 .... 1 C1
St Mary's RC Sch EH41 .. 132 A4
St Mary's St EH1 .... 233 E3
St Marys Wynd FK8 .... 7 D4
St Marys Pl FK8 .... 61 F4
St Matthew's RC Prim Sch
EH47 .... 7 E1
St Michael's Ave EH21 ... 126 B3
St Michael's Hospl EH49 .. 85 D3
St Michael's Wynd EH49 .. 85 D4
St Michaels La EH49 .... 85 D4
St Modan's High Sch FK7 .. 7 E2
St Modans Ct EH41 .... 132 B4
St Mungo's High Sch FK2 .. 60 A3
St Mungo's Prim Sch
FK10 .... 10 B3

St Mungo's View EH26 ... 203 F3
St Mungo's Wynd FK10 ... 10 A3
St Nicholas Prim Sch
EH52 .... 117 E2
St Nicholas (Spcl Sch)
EH32 .... 96 C1
St Ninian's Ave EH49 .... 84 C4
St Ninian's Dr EH12 .... 121 E4
St Ninian's RC Prim Sch
Edinburgh EH7 .... 94 B1
Livingston EH54 .... 148 A1
St Ninian's Rd
Edinburgh EH12 .... 121 E4
Linlithgow EH49 .... 84 C4
St Ninian's Row EH1 ...... 233 D4
St Ninian's Terr EH10 .... 122 C1
St Ninians Terr EH49 .... 84 C4
St Ninians Prim Sch FK7 .. 7 D2
St Ninians Rd
Cambusbarron FK7 .... 6 C3
Stirling FK8 .... 7 D3
St Ninians Row EH1 .... 93 E1
St Ninians Way
Blackness EH49 .... 65 F2
Musselburgh EH21 .... 127 D3
St Patrick Sq EH8 .... 233 E1
St Patrick St EH8 .... 233 E1
St Patrick's RC Prim Sch
EH6 .... 36 C2
St Patrick's Sq EH8 .... 233 E1
St Patrick's RC Prim Sch
ML7 .... 191 F2
St Paul's Dr EH48 .... 144 A3
St Paul's RC Prim Sch
EH13 .... 148 C2
St Peter's EH3 .... 232 C1
St Peter's RC Sch EH10 .. 123 D2
St Ronan's Terr EH10 .... 123 D1
St Serf's Pl FK10 .... 4 A2
St Serf's Rd
High Valleyfield KY12 .... 26 A1
Tullibody FK10 .... 4 A2
St Serf's Rd EH12 .... 122 C4
St Serf's Sch EH12 .... 122 C4
St Serf's Wlk FK10 .... 4 A2
St Serfs Gr FK10 .... 11 D2
St Stephen Pl EH3 .... 93 D1
St Stephen St EH3 .... 93 D1
St Teresa Pl EH10 .... 122 C2
St Thomas of Aquins
RC High Sch EH9 .... 232 C1
St Thomas Rd EH9 .... 123 F2
St Thomas's Pl FK7 .... 6 C3
St Thomas's Well FK7 .... 6 C3
St Valery Dr FK7 .... 7 D2
St Vincent St EH3 .... 93 D1
Salamanca Cres EH26 ... 204 A4
Salamander Pl EH6 .... 94 A3
Salamander St EH6 .... 94 A3
Salen Loan ML7 .... 192 A2
Salisbury Pl EH9 .... 123 F3
Salisbury Rd EH16 .... 123 F3
Salisbury St KY7 .... 17 E4
Salisbury View EH32 .... 183 E3
Salmon Dr FK1 .... 59 F1
Salmon Inn Rd FK2 .... 61 E1
Salmond Pl EH7 .... 94 A1
Salt Preston Pl EH32 .... 96 C1
Saltcoats Dr FK3 .... 61 F4
Saltcoats Gdns EH32 ...... 173 F3
Saltcoats Rd
Grangemouth FK3 .... 62 A4
Gullane EH31 .... 52 A1
Salter's Rd Dalkeith EH22 . 157 E3
Wallyford EH21 .... 127 D2
Salters'Gr EH21 .... 157 E2
Salters' Rd Dalkeith EH22 . 157 E2
Pathhead EH37 .... 186 A1
Salters' Terr EH22 .... 157 E2
Saltire Gdns EH39 .... 101 F4
Saltoun Prim Sch EH41 .. 161 F3
Saltpans KY11 .... 45 D2
Salvage Rd KY11 .... 46 B1
Salvesen Cres EH4 .... 92 A3
Salvesen Gdns EH4 .... 92 A3
Salvesen Terr EH4 .... 92 A3
Samoa Terr EH26 .... 204 A4
Sand Port EH6 .... 94 A3
Sandport Trad Est EH6 ..... 93 F3
Sandeman Ct FK10 .... 23 F2
Sanderson Terr KY2 .... 15 D1
Sanderson's Gr EH33 ..... 128 B4
Sandersons Wynd EH33 .. 128 B4
Sandford Gdns EH15 ...... 125 D4
Sandiland Dr EH53 .... 148 A1
Sandilands KY11 .... 45 E2
Sandport Pl EH6 .... 93 F3
Sandport St EH6 .... 93 F3
Sands The EH41 .... 132 A4
Sandy Loan Gullane EH31 .. 52 A1
Lauriston FK2 .... 61 D2
Sandy Rd KY3 .... 32 B3
Sandyford Ave EH49 .... 84 A3
Sandyhill Ave ML7 .... 192 A2
Sandyloan Cres FK2 .... 61 D2
Sandyvale Pl ML7 .... 192 A2
Sang Pl KY1 .... 17 D3
Sang Rd KY1 .... 17 D3
Sarazen Ct EH54 .... 147 D4
Sarazen Gn EH54 .... 147 D4
Sauchenbush Rd KY2 .... 16 C3
Sauchie Ct FK7 .... 7 F1
Sauchie Hospl FK10 .... 10 B4
Sauchie St FK7 .... 7 D2
Sauchiebank FK11 .... 4 A3
Saughbank EH22 .... 117 D3
Saughs The EH22 .... 183 D2
Saughton Ave EH11 .... 122 B2

Saughton Cres EH12 ...... 122 A3
Saughton Gdns EH12 ..... 122 A3
Saughton Gr EH12 .... 122 A3
Saughton Loan EH12 ...... 122 A3
Saughton Mains Ave
EH11 .... 121 F2
Saughton Mains Bank
EH11 .... 122 A2
Saughton Mains Dr
EH11 .... 121 F2
Saughton Mains Gdns
EH11 .... 121 F2
Saughton Mains Gr
EH11 .... 122 A2
Saughton Mains Loan
EH11 .... 121 F2
Saughton Mains Pk EH11 . 121 F2
Saughton Mains Pl EH11 . 121 F2
Saughton Mains St EH11 . 122 A2
Saughton Mains Terr
EH11 .... 121 F2
Saughton Pk EH12 .... 122 A3
Saughton Rd EH11 .... 121 F2
Saughton Rd N EH12 ...... 121 F3
Saughtonhall Ave EH12 .. 122 B3
Saughtonhall Ave W
EH12 .... 122 B3
Saughtonhall Cir EH12 ... 122 B3
Saughtonhall Cres EH12 . 122 A3
Saughtonhall Dr EH12 .... 122 A3
Saughtonhall Gdns EH12 . 122 B3
Saughtonhall Gr EH12 .... 122 B3
Saughtonhall Pl EH12 ..... 122 B3
Saughtonhall Terr EH12 .. 122 B3
Saunders St
Edinburgh EH3 .... 232 B4
Kirkcaldy KY1 .... 17 D1
Savile Pl EH9 .... 123 F2
Savile Terr EH9 .... 123 F2
Sawers Ave FK6 .... 36 B1
Saxe Coburg Pl EH3 .... 93 D1
Saxe Coburg St EH3 .... 93 D1
Scarlett Pk EH21 .... 127 D3
Schaw Ct FK10 .... 5 E1
Schaw Rd EH32 .... 97 D1
Schawpark Ave FK10 .... 5 E1
Schiltron Way FK7 .... 7 E2
Scholars' Brae KY3 .... 50 C4
School Brae Bo'ness EH51 .. 63 F4
Bonnyrigg and Lasswade
EH18 .... 156 A1
Dysart KY1 .... 18 A4
Edinburgh EH4 .... 91 D3
West Barns EH42 .... 105 F4
School Gn
Bonnyrigg and Lasswade
EH18 .... 156 A1
Longniddry EH32 .... 98 C3
School La Bathgate EH48 . 145 D3
Cockenzie & Port Seton
EH32 .... 97 E2
Menstrie FK11 .... 4 A4
Mid Calder EH53 .... 148 B2
Shotts ML7 .... 212 A4
School Pl EH52 .... 116 B2
School Rd Aberlady EH32 ... 71 E2
East Linton EH40 .... 103 F4
Laurieston FK2 .... 61 D2
Redding FK2 .... 170 B1
North Berwick EH39 .... 54 B4
Reddinge EH47 .... 61 D2
Tullibody FK10 .... 4 A1
School Row KY12 .... 28 B3
School St
Cowdenbeath KY4 .... 13 E2
Shotts ML7 .... 212 A4
School Wlk FK5 .... 38 B2
School Wynd KY1 .... 17 D1
Schoolyard Ct EH25 .... 181 D2
Sciennes EH9 .... 123 F3
Sciennes Hill Pl 1 EH9 .... 123 F3
Sciennes House Pl 2
EH9 .... 123 F3
Sciennes Prim Sch EH9 .. 123 E3
Sciennes Rd EH9 .... 123 E3
Sclanderstunn Rd FK6 ...... 57 E4
Scobie Pl KY12 .... 29 E2
Scollon Ave EH19 .... 182 B4
Scone Gdns EH8 .... 94 B1
Scotch Whisky
Heritage Ctr The EH1 ...... 123 E4
Scotia Pl FK2 .... 60 B3
Scotland Dr KY12 .... 29 F2
Scotland St EH3 .... 93 E1
Scotlands Cl EH51 .... 63 F4
Scotmill Way KY11 .... 47 F2
Scots Mill Pl KY11 .... 47 F2
Scotstoun Ave EH30 .... 89 E4
Scotstoun Gn EH30 .... 89 D4
Scotstoun Gr EH30 .... 89 D4
Scotstoun Rd FK7 .... 20 C4
Scott Ave FK1 .... 61 F1
Scott Cres FK10 .... 10 A3
Scott Ct EH54 .... 148 B3
Scott Pl EH47 .... 193 F3
Scott Rd EH26 .... 203 F4
Scott Terr Bannockburn KY12 . 28 C3
Grangemouth FK3 .... 61 E3
Kirkcaldy KY1 .... 17 D1
Stirling FK8 .... 2 A1
Scott St EH41 .... 132 A4
Scottish Ag Mus EH28 .... 119 F3
Scottish Ag
Science Agency EH12 ...... 121 D4
Scottish Mining Mus Lady
Victoria Colliery EH22 ..... 183 D2

Scottish Nat Gall of Mod Art
EH4 .... 122 C4
Scottish Pol Coll FK10 .... 23 F3
Scottish Prison Service
Coll FK2 .... 82 B4
Sea Wynd FK1 .... 71 E3
Seabegs Cres FK4 .... 58 A2
Seabegs Pl FK4 .... 58 A2
Seabegs Rd FK4 .... 57 F2
Seacliff EH39 .... 56 A3
Seacot EH6 .... 94 B2
Seafield Ave EH6 .... 94 B2
Seafield Cres EH42 .... 52 C1
Seafield Pl EH51 .... 59 F1
Seafield Inf Sch EH54 .... 146 C3
Seafield Moor Rd EH25 .. 180 B3
Seafield Rd
Dalgety Bay KY11 .... 48 A1
Edinburgh EH6 .... 94 B2
Seafield Rd E Bilston EH25 . 180 C3
Blackburn EH47 .... 171 F4
Edinburgh EH6 .... 94 B2
Kirkcaldy KY1 .... 35 C4
Seafield Rd E EH15 .... 94 C2
Seafield Rows EH47 .... 146 A1
Seafield St EH6 .... 94 B2
Seafield View
Kinghorn KY3 .... 35 D2
Kirkcaldy KY1 .... 35 C4
Seafield Way EH15 .... 94 C2
Seaforth Dr EH4 .... 92 B1
Seaforth Pl Burntisland KY3 . 50 C4
Kirkcaldy KY1 .... 17 F4
Stirling FK8 .... 7 D4
Seaforth Rd FK2 .... 39 E1
Seaforth Terr
Bonnyrigg and Lasswade
EH19 .... 181 F3
3 Edinburgh EH4 .... 92 B1
Sealcar St EH5 .... 92 C4
Sealock Ct FK3 .... 61 F4
Sealstrand KY11 .... 48 B2
Seaport St EH6 .... 94 A3
Seaside Pl KY3 .... 49 E4
Seaton Pl FK1 .... 60 B2
Seaview Cres EH15 .... 125 F4
Seaview Pl FK3 .... 63 F4
Seaview Terr EH15 .... 125 F4
Seco Pl KY4 .... 13 E2
Second Gait EH54 .... 151 F4
Second St EH22 .... 183 D2
Sedgebank EH54 .... 147 F3
Seggarsdean Ct EH41 ..... 132 B4
Seggarsdean Pk EH41 ..... 132 B4
Seggarsdean Terr EH41 .. 132 B4
Selkirk Ave KY4 .... 13 E2
Selkirk Rd KY11 .... 67 D4
Selm Pk EH54 .... 148 A2
Selvage St KY11 .... 47 D2
Selvage St KY11 .... 47 D2
Semple St EH3 .... 232 B2
Seton Chapel EH32 .... 97 F2
Seton Ct
Cockenzie & Port Seton
EH32 .... 97 E2
Tranent EH33 .... 128 B3
Seton Dr FK7 .... 7 E2
Seton Mains EH32 .... 98 A2
Seton Pl
Cockenzie & Port Seton
EH32 .... 97 E2
Dalgety Bay KY11 .... 48 B3
Edinburgh EH9 .... 123 F3
Kirkcaldy KY2 .... 16 B4
Seton Rd EH32 .... 98 C3
Seton Terr EH51 .... 64 A4
Seton View EH32 .... 97 F2
Seton Wynd EH32 .... 97 F2
Seventh St EH22 .... 183 D3
Shadepark Cres EH22 ..... 157 D2
Shadepark Dr EH22 .... 157 D2
Shadepark Gdns EH22 .... 157 D2
Shaftesbury Pk EH11 ...... 122 C2
Shaftesbury St EH11 .... 122 C2
Shafto Pl EH51 .... 10 A4
Shamrock St KY4 .... 29 D3
Shandon Cres EH11 .... 122 C2
Shandon Pl EH11 .... 122 C2
Shandon Rd EH11 .... 122 C2
Shandon St EH11 .... 122 C2
Shandon Terr EH11 .... 122 C2
Shandwick Pl EH2 .... 232 A3
Shanks Ave FK6 .... 57 F4
Shanks Rd EH47 .... 170 A4
Shanks Terr EH47 .... 93 F1
Shaw's Sq EH1 .... 93 F1
Shaw's St EH7 .... 93 F2
Shaw's Terr EH7 .... 93 F2
Shaw St EH26 .... 180 A1
Shawbridge EH47 .... 162 C1
Sheephousehill EH47 ...... 193 F3
Shepardlands Gr KY12 ..... 26 B4
Shepherd Cres KY3 .... 50 B4
Sherbrooke Rd KY11 .... 46 B2
Sheriff Bank EH6 .... 93 F3
Sheriff Brae EH6 .... 93 F3

Sheriff Pk EH6 .... 93 F3
Sheriffhall Junc EH22 .... 156 B3
Sheriffmuir Rd FK9 .... 2 B4
Sheriffmuirlands FK9 ...... 2 B2
Sheriffs Pk EH49 .... 85 F4
Sherriff Hall Cotts EH39 .. 74 C4
Sherriff La FK5 .... 38 C2
Sherwood Ave EH19 ...... 182 B3
Sherwood Cres EH19 ..... 182 B3
Sherwood Ct EH19 .... 182 B3
Sherwood Dr EH19 .... 182 B3
Sherwood Gr EH19 .... 182 B3
Sherwood End Est EH19 .. 182 B4
Sherwood Loan EH19 .... 182 B3
Sherwood Pk EH19 ...... 182 B3
Sherwood Pl EH19 ...... 182 B3
Sherwood Terr EH19 .... 182 B3
Sherwood View EH19 ... 182 B3
Sherwood Way EH19 .... 182 B3
Sherwood Wlk EH19 .... 182 B3
Shetland Ct FK10 .... 10 A3
Shetland Pl K1 .... 17 F4
Shiel Ct FK2 .... 62 C4
Shiel Gdns Falkirk FK2 ... 39 E1
Shotts ML7 .... 192 A2
Shiel Wlk EH54 .... 148 A3
Shieldhill Prim Sch FK1 .. 81 E3
Shields Ct EH52 .... 117 F3
Shields Rd KY11 .... 29 F2
Shieling The KY12 .... 27 F1
Shillinghill FK10 .... 10 A3
Shinwell Pl KY11 .... 46 C2
Shiphaugh Pl FK8 .... 2 B1
Shiree Way K10 .... 9 F3
Shirra's Brae Rd FK2 ..... 7 E2
Shoestanes Rd EH38 .... 228 B1
Shoestanes Terr EH38 ... 228 A1
Shore EH6 .... 94 A3
Shore Pl EH6 .... 94 A3
Shore Rd Aberdour KY3 ... 49 E4
Airth FK2 .... 22 B2
Dysart KY1 .... 18 A3
Queensferry EH30 .... 68 A1
Shore The 7 D4
Shore St EH42 .... 78 C2
Shore The FK10 .... 10 A3
Shorthope St EH21 ..... 126 B3
Shotts Rd
Fauldhouse EH47 .... 193 E2
Harthill ML7 .... 167 F1
Shotts Sta ML7 .... 191 F2
Shottsburn Rd ML7 ..... 167 D2
Shottskirk Rd ML7 ...... 167 E3
Shrub Mount EH15 ...... 95 D1
Shrub Place La EH7 ...... 93 F1
Sibbald Pl EH54 .... 147 D3
Sibbalds Brae EH48 .... 144 B3
Sidegate EH41 .... 132 A4
Sidehead Rd ML7 ...... 168 C3
Sidlaw Pl KY2 .... 16 C3
Sidlaw St KY2 .... 16 C3
Sienna Gdns EH9 .... 123 F3
Sighthill Ave EH11 ..... 121 F1
Sighthill Bank EH11 .... 121 E1
Sighthill Cres EH11 .... 121 E1
Sighthill Ct EH11 ...... 121 E1
Sighthill Dr EH11 ...... 121 E1
Sighthill Gdns EH11 ... 121 E1
Sighthill Gn EH11 ...... 121 F1
Sighthill Ind Est EH11 . 121 D2
Sighthill Loan EH11 ... 121 E1
Sighthill Neuk EH11 ... 121 E1
Sighthill Pk EH11 ...... 121 E1
Sighthill Prim Sch EH11 . 121 E1
Sighthill Rd EH11 ...... 121 E1
Sighthill Rise EH11 .... 121 E1
Sighthill St EH11 ...... 121 E1
Sighthill Terr EH11 .... 121 E1
Sighthill View EH11 ... 121 E1
Sighthill Wynd EH11 .. 121 E1
Silk Ho H1 .... 60 A3
Silver St Dunbar EH42 ... 78 B1
Kincardine FK10 .... 23 F2
Silverbarton Terr KY3 ... 33 E1
Silverburn Dr EH26 ... 203 D3
Silverdale Rd FK2 .... 82 C4
Silverknowes Ave EH4 ... 91 F2
Silverknowes Bank EH4 . 91 F2
Silverknowes Brae EH4 . 92 A2
Silverknowes Cres EH4 . 91 F2
Silverknowes Ct EH4 ... 91 F2
Silverknowes Dell EH4 . 91 F2
Silverknowes Dr EH4 ... 91 F2
Silverknowes Eastway
EH4 .... 91 F2
Silverknowes Gdns EH4 . 92 A2
Silverknowes Gn EH4 ... 92 A2
Silverknowes Gr EH4 ... 91 F3
Silverknowes Hill EH4 . 91 F2
Silverknowes Loan EH4 . 91 F2
Silverknowes Midway
EH4 .... 92 A2
Silverknowes Neuk EH4 . 92 A2
Silverknowes Parkway
EH4 .... 91 F3
Silverknowes Pl EH4 ... 91 F3
Silverknowes Prim Sch
EH4 .... 92 A3
Silverknowes Rd EH4 ... 91 F3
Silverknowes Rd E EH4 . 92 A2
Silverknowes Rd S EH4 . 91 F2
Silverknowes Southway
EH4 .... 92 A2

Silverknowes Terr EH4 ... 91 F2
Silverknowes View EH4 .. 92 A2
Simon Sq EH8 .... 233 E2
Simpson Cres EH48 ..... 145 E3
Simpson Dr FK2 .... 83 D3
Simpson Parkway EH52 . 147 D1
Simpson Rd EH52 ...... 118 A3
Simpson St FK1 .... 59 F3
Simpson Wlk KY11 ...... 46 C1
Sinclair Cres FK6 .... 36 B1
Sinclair Ct Aberlady EH32 . 71 E2
Bannockburn FK7 .... 7 F1
Sinclair Dr
Cowdenbeath KY4 .... 13 D1
Fallin FK7 .... 8 B2
Sinclair Gdns KY12 ..... 29 D2
Sinclair Pl FK2 .... 39 D1
Sinclair Way EH54 ..... 147 E3
Sinclairtown Prim Sch
KY1 .... 17 F4
Sir George Bruce Rd
KY12 .... 26 C4
Sir Harry Lauder Rd EH15 125 D4
Sir James Black Gait KY5 . 14 A4
Sir Walter Scott Pend
EH6 .... 96 C1
Sir Walter Scott's Mon
EH2 .... 233 D3
Sir William Fraser Homes
EH13 .... 153 D4
Sir William Wallace Ct
FK5 .... 38 A2
Sivewright Ct FK10 ..... 23 F2
Sixth St EH22 .... 183 D3
Skaithmuir Ave FK2 .... 39 D2
Skaithmuir Cres FK2 ... 39 D2
Skelmorlie Pl FK5 ...... 38 C2
Skeltie Muir Ave EH19 . 182 A3
Skeltiemuir Ct EH19 ... 182 A3
Skeltiemuir Gr EH19 ... 182 A3
Skene St FK4 .... 58 A3
Skibo Ct KY12 .... 29 D2
Skibo Pl KY2 .... 16 B3
Skye Ct FK3 .... 61 E3
Skye Dr FK3 .... 61 F1
Skye Rd KY11 .... 29 F1
Skylaw Terr ML11 ..... 215 D1
Skythorn Way FK1 ...... 59 F1
Slaeside EH14 .... 151 E1
Slamannan Prim Sch
FK1 .... 110 A4
Slamannan Rd
Avonbridge FK1 .... 112 A3
Falkirk FK1 .... 60 A1
Slamannan FK1 .... 110 A1
Slateford Rd EH14 ..... 122 B2
Slateford Sta EH14 .... 122 B2
Sleigh Dr EH7 .... 94 B1
Sleigh Gdns EH7 .... 94 B1
Sligo St KY12 .... 26 C4
Sloan St EH6 .... 93 F2
Small St KY5 .... 14 A3
Smallburn Pl FK3 .... 61 F3
Smeaton Gdns KY2 ..... 17 E3
Smeaton Gr EH21 ...... 126 B2
Smeaton Ind Site KY1 .. 17 E4
Smeaton Rd KY1 .... 17 E3
Smiddy Wynd FK12 .... 5 D3
Smikleyknowes La EH30 . 54 A3
Smith Art Gallery & Mus
FK8 .... 7 D4
Smith Ave KY4 .... 13 D2
Smith Pl FK6 .... 36 B1
Smith St FK2 .... 60 A4
Smith's Pl EH6 .... 93 F2
Smith's Terr KY1 .... 17 E3
Smithfield Loan FK10 .. 9 F3
Smithfield St EH11 .... 122 B3
Smithy Brae EH27 .... 149 F1
Smithy Green Ave EH22 . 156 A4
Smithy Row EH34 ...... 74 A2
Snab Brae EH51 .... 63 E3
Snab La EH51 .... 63 E4
Snowden Sch Ltd FK8 ... 7 D4
Snowdon Pl FK8 .... 7 D3
Snowdon Place La FK7 .. 7 D3
Society La EH55 .... 172 B2
Society Pl EH55 .... 172 B2
Society Rd EH30 .... 67 F1
Solway Dr FK6 .... 36 B1
Somerset Pl EH6 .... 94 A2
Somerville Rd KY11 .... 46 B1
Somerville Sq KY3 ..... 50 C4
Somerville St KY3 ..... 50 C4
Sommers Pk EH53 .... 148 B1
Somnerville Gdns EH30 . 89 E4
Somnerfield Ave EH41 . 131 F4
Somnerfield Cres EH41 . 131 F4
Somnerfield Ct EH41 .. 131 F4
Somnerfield Gr EH41 .. 131 F4
Somnerfield Pk EH41 .. 131 F4
Souillac Dr FK6 .... 36 B1
South Acres KY12 ...... 27 E1
South Approach Rd FK2 . 23 D1
South Bantaskine Dr FK1 . 60 A2
South Bantaskine Rd FK1 . 60 A2
South Barnton Ave FK1 . 91 F2
South Beechwood EH12 . 122 A3
South Brae FK2 .... 83 D3
South Bridge EH1 ..... 233 D3
South Bridge St
Bathgate EH48 .... 145 D3
Grangemouth FK3 .... 40 B1
South Broomage Ave FK5 . 38 B1
South Charlotte St EH2 . 232 B3

South Clerk St EH8 .... 233 E1
South College St EH8 . 233 D2
South Craigs Rd FK2 ... 82 C4
South Cres EH32 .... 97 D1
South Dewar St KY12 .. 28 C2
South Doors EH32 ...... 97 E2
South Dr KY11 .... 46 C3
South East Circus Pl
EH3 .... 232 B4
South East Cumberland
Street La EH3 .... 93 E1
South East Thistle
Street La EH3 .... 232 C4
South Elixa Pl EH8 .... 124 B4
South Ettrick Rd EH10 . 122 C2
South Fergus Pl KY1 ... 17 D2
South Fort St EH6 ...... 93 F3
South Gait EH33 .... 53 F4
South Gayfield La EH1 .. 93 F1
South Gillsland Rd EH10 . 122 C2
South Grange Ave FK2 . 127 F4
South Gray St EH9 .... 123 F2
South Gray's Cl EH1 .. 233 E3
South Green Dr FK2 ... 22 C2
South Groathill Ave EH4 . 92 B1
South Gyle Access EH12 . 121 E2
South Gyle Broadway
EH12 .... 121 D2
South Gyle Cres EH12 . 121 D2
South Gyle Crescent La
EH12 .... 121 D2
South Gyle Gdns EH12 . 121 E2
South Gyle Ind Est EH12 . 121 D2
South Gyle Loan EH12 . 121 D3
South Gyle Mains EH12 . 121 D3
South Gyle Pk EH12 ... 121 D3
South Gyle Rd EH12 ... 121 D3
South Gyle Sta EH12 .. 121 D2
South Gyle Wynd EH12 . 121 E2
South Hamilton Rd EH39 . 54 A4
South Hill St KY3 ...... 50 C4
South Hirst Rd ML7 ... 167 E2
South Knowe KY4 ..... 30 C2
South Larch Rd KY11 .. 29 F2
South Lauder Rd EH9 .. 123 F2
South Laverockbank Ave
EH5 .... 93 E4
South Learmonth Ave [7]
EH4 .... 92 C1
South Loch Pk EH48 .. 145 D3
South Lodge Ave EH53 . 148 B1
South Lorimer Pl EH32 . 97 E2
South Lorne Pl EH6 ... 93 F2
South Lumley St FK3 .. 61 E4
South Marshall St FK3 . 61 E4
South Maybury EH12 .. 121 D3
South Mellis Pk EH8 .. 124 C4
South Melville La FK1 .. 60 A3
South Mid St EH48 .... 145 D3
South Morningside
Prim Sch EH10 .... 123 D1
South Morton St EH15 . 125 E4
South Oswald Rd EH9 . 123 E2
South Overgate KY1 ... 35 D2
South Oxford St EH8 .. 123 F3
South Philpingstone La
EH51 .... 64 B4
South Pilmuir Rd FK10 . 11 D2
South Pk Armadale EH48 . 143 F2
Edinburgh EH6 .... 93 E4
South Pleasance Ave FK1 . 60 A2
South Queensferry
Prim Sch EH30 .... 68 B1
South Rd
Charlestown KY11 ...... 45 D2
Kirkcaldy KY1 .... 34 C2
South Scotstoun EH30 . 89 E4
South Seton Pk EH32 .. 97 E2
South Shore Rd FK3 ... 41 D1
South Sloan St EH6 ... 93 F2
South St Andrew St EH2 . 233 D4
South St David St EH2 . 233 D3
South Steil EH10 ...... 122 C1
South Trinity Rd EH5 .. 93 D3
South View
Burntisland KY3 .... 50 C4
Stenhousemuir FK5 ..... 38 B1
South Village EH53 ... 148 B3
South West Cumberland
Street La EH3 .... 93 E1
South West Thistle
Street La EH2 .... 232 C4
Southbank EH14 .... 91 F2
Southcroft FK12 .... 4 C3
Southerton Cres KY2 .. 16 C2
Southerton Gdns KY2 . 16 C2
Southerton Rd KY2 .... 16 C2
Southfield KY4 .... 13 E3
Southfield Ave ML7 ... 192 A2
Southfield Bank EH15 . 124 C3
Southfield Cres
Shotts ML7 .... 192 A2
Stirling FK8 .... 7 D3
Southfield Dr FK1 ..... 110 A3

Southfield Farm Gr
EH15 .... 124 C4
Southfield Gdns E EH15 . 124 C3
Southfield Gdns W EH15 . 124 C3
Southfield Hospl EH17 . 155 E4
Southfield Load EH15 .. 124 C3
Southfield Loan EH15 . 124 C3
Southfield Pl EH15 ... 125 D4
Southfield Rd
Cousland EH22 .... 158 B3
Shotts ML7 .... 192 A2
Southfield Rd E EH15 . 124 C3
Southfield Rd W EH15 . 124 C3
Southfield Sq EH15 ... 124 C3
Southfield Terr EH15 .. 124 C3
Southhouse Ave EH17 . 155 D3
Southhouse Broadway
EH17 .... 155 D2
Southhouse Cres EH17 . 155 E2
Southhouse Gdns EH17 . 155 D2
Southhouse Gr EH17 .. 155 D2
Southhouse Loan EH17 . 155 D3
Southhouse Medway
EH17 .... 155 D3
Southhouse Rd EH17 . 155 D3
Southhouse Sq EH17 . 155 D3
Southhouse Terr EH17 . 155 E3
Southlawn Ct EH4 ..... 91 F2
Spa Pl EH15 .... 95 D1
Spalding Cres EH22 ... 157 D2
Speedwell Ave EH22 .. 156 A4
Spence Ave KY3 .... 33 F1
Spence St
Bonnybridge FK4 .... 58 A3
Edinburgh EH16 ...... 123 F3
Spencer Pl Edinburgh EH5 . 93 D2
Kirkcaldy KY1 .... 17 F4
Spencerfield Rd KY11 .. 47 E1
Spencerfield Steadings
KY11 .... 47 F2
Spens La KY11 .... 47 F2
Spey Ct Grangemouth FK3 . 61 E3
Stirling FK7 .... 7 E3
Spey Dr EH54 .... 148 A2
Spey St EH7 .... 93 F2
Spey Street La EH7 .... 93 F2
Spey Terr EH7 .... 93 F2
Spier's Pl EH6 .... 93 F3
Spinkhill FK2 .... 60 C1
Spinnaker Way KY11 .. 47 F1
Spinner's Ct EH7 ...... 27 E1
Spinney The KY11 .... 155 E3
Spinneys The KY1 ..... 48 B2
Spittal Hill FK9 .... 2 B2
Spittal St Edinburgh EH3 . 232 B2
Stirling FK8 .... 7 D3
Spittalfield Cres KY11 .. 47 E1
Spittalfield Rd KY11 .. 47 E1
Spott Ave EH42 .... 106 B2
Spott Loan EH42 ..... 106 B2
Spott Rd EH42 .... 78 C1
Spottiswoode Gdns
EH53 .... 148 B1
Spottiswoode Rd EH9 . 123 E3
Spottiswoode St EH9 . 123 E3
Sprig Way ML7 .... 168 C3
Spring Gdns EH8 ...... 94 A1
Springbank Gdns FK2 . 60 B3
Springbank Rd
Shotts ML7 .... 191 E3
Stirling FK7 .... 7 E3
Springbank Terr KY12 . 29 F2
Springfield Edinburgh EH6 . 93 F2
West Barns EH42 ..... 105 F4
Springfield Cres
North Berwick EH39 .... 54 A4
Queensferry EH30 ..... 67 F1
Springfield Ct EH49 ... 85 E4
Springfield Dr FK1 ..... 59 F1
Springfield Gdns EH39 . 54 A4
Springfield La EH30 ... 67 F1
Springfield Pl
Gorebridge EH23 ...... 207 E4
Queensferry EH30 ..... 67 F1
Roslin EH25 .... 181 D2
Springfield Prim Sch
EH49 .... 85 E4
Springfield Rd Alloa FK10 . 10 B4
Denny FK6 .... 36 C1
Linlithgow EH49 .... 85 E4
Penicuik EH26 .... 222 C3
Queensferry EH30 ..... 67 F1
Stirling FK7 .... 7 E3
Springfield St EH6 .... 93 F2
Springfield Terr
Queensferry EH30 ..... 67 F1
West Barns EH42 ..... 105 F4
Springfield View EH30 . 68 A1
Springhead Rd ML7 ... 212 A4
Springhill Brae KY4 .... 30 C3
Springhill & Leadloch Rd
ML7 .... 192 C1
Springhill Rd ML7 .... 192 A2
Springhill View ML7 .. 192 A2
Springkerse Ind Est FK7 . 7 E3
Springkerse Rd FK7 .... 7 E3
Springkerse Rdbt FK7 . 7 E3
Sprinty Ave EH35 .... 159 E4
Sprinty Dr EH35 ...... 159 E4
Sprotwell Terr FK10 .. 5 E1
Spruce Dr EH47 ...... 170 B3

Spruce Gr
Dunfermline KY11 ..... 46 B3
Livingston EH54 ...... 148 A3
Spylaw Ave EH13 ..... 152 C4
Spylaw Bank Rd EH13 . 153 D4
Spylaw Pk EH13 ...... 152 C4
Spylaw Rd EH10 ...... 122 C2
Spylaw St EH13 ...... 153 D4
Square The
Cockburnspath TD13 .. 140 C2
Danderhall EH22 ...... 156 A4
East Linton EH40 ..... 103 F4
Fallin FK7 .... 8 B2
Gifford EH41 .... 163 F3
Kirkliston EH29 .... 89 D1
Newtongrange EH22 . 206 C3
Penicuik EH26 .... 203 F2
Scott EH42 .... 106 B2
Torphichen EH48 ..... 113 F3
Sraehouse Wynd ML8 . 230 A1
Stable La EH10 .... 123 D2
Stable Rd ML7 .... 159 E4
Stables Rd KY11 ...... 46 B1
Staffa EH54 .... 146 C3
Staffa Pl FK1 .... 60 A1
Stafford St EH3 ...... 232 A3
Stair Pk Edinburgh EH12 . 122 A4
Tranent EH33 .... 128 A4
Standalane FK10 .... 23 F2
Standhill Ct EH48 .... 144 C2
Standing Stone Wlk KY11 . 29 F1
Standingstane Rd EH30 . 89 F3
Stane Brae FK2 .... 192 A2
Stane Prim Sch ML7 . 192 A2
Stane Rd ML7 .... 192 A1
Stanedykehead EH16 . 154 C3
Stanhope Pl EH12 .... 122 C4
Stanhope St EH12 .... 122 C4
Stanistone Rd ML5 .. 230 A1
Stankards Rd EH52 .. 116 C2
Stanley Ave EH25 ... 180 C3
Stanley Dr Bridge of A FK9 . 2 A4
Harthill ML7 .... 167 D3
Stanley Gdns FK2 ..... 62 D3
Stanley Pl Edinburgh EH7 . 94 A1
Ormiston EH35 ...... 159 F4
Stanley Rd Edinburgh EH6 . 93 E3
Harthill ML7 .... 169 D3
Stanley St EH15 ...... 125 D4
Stanley Terr KY12 .... 27 D3
Stanton Ave FK2 ...... 9 F3
Stanwell St EH6 .... 93 F2
Stapeley Ave EH7 .... 94 C1
Starbank Rd EH5 ..... 93 D3
Stark Ave FK1 .... 59 E3
Stark's Brae EH51 .... 64 A4
Stark's Park
(Raith Rovers FC) KY1 . 17 D1
Starlaw Ave EH48 ... 145 F3
Starlaw Bsns Pk EH54 . 146 B2
Starlaw Cres EH48 .. 145 F3
Starlaw Gdns EH48 .. 145 F3
Starlaw Rd EH54, EH47 . 146 B2
Starlaw Terr EH48 ... 145 F3
Starlaw West Rdbt
EH47 .... 146 A2
Starlaw Wlk EH48 ... 145 F3
Starryshaw Rd ML7 . 191 F3
Station Ave EH41 .... 131 F4
Station Brae
Edinburgh EH15 ...... 125 D4
Kinghorn KY3 .... 34 C1
Station Ct Addiewell EH55 . 171 F1
Haddington EH41 .... 131 F4
North Berwick EH39 .. 54 A4
Station Hill EH39 .... 54 A4
Station Loan EH14 .. 151 E2
Station Pl KY3 .... 49 E4
Station Rd
Addiewell EH55 ...... 171 F1
Armadale EH48 ..... 143 F2
Bannockburn FK7 ..... 7 F1
Blackridge EH48 .... 142 B1
Bridge of A FK9 .... 1 C4
Brightons FK2 .... 83 E1
Broxburn EH52 ...... 117 F3
Cambus FK10 .... 4 A1
Cowdenbeath KY4 .... 13 E2
Cowie FK7 .... 20 B4
Dalkeith EH22 .... 156 C1
Dirleton EH39 .... 53 E2
Dunbar EH42 .... 78 C1
Dysart KY1 .... 18 A4
East Linton EH40 ... 103 F4
Edinburgh EH12 .... 121 F3
Gifford EH41 .... 163 F3
Gorebridge EH23 ... 207 E4
Grangemouth FK3 .... 40 B1
Guillane EH31 .... 52 A1
Kincardine FK10 ..... 23 E2
Kirkcaldy KY2, KY1 .. 17 D1
Kirkliston EH29 .... 89 D1
Kirknewton EH27 .... 85 D4
Loanhead EH20 ..... 181 E4
Lochgelly KY5 .... 14 A2
Musselburgh EH21 . 126 B3
Newtongrange EH22 . 206 C3
North Berwick EH39 .. 54 A4
Oakley KY12 .... 26 C3
Prestonpans EH32 ... 128 A4
Queensferry EH30 .... 68 B1
Ratho Station EH28 . 119 E3
Roslin EH25 .... 181 D2
Shotts ML7 .... 191 F2
Slamannan FK1 ...... 110 A3
Stirling FK8 .... 7 D4
Uphall EH52 .... 116 C2

Station Rd continued
Uphall Station EH54 117 D1
Whitecross EH49 83 F3
Station Row FK1 110 A3
Station Terr EH29 89 D1
Staunton Rise EH54 173 E4
Stead's Pl EH6 93 F2
Steading The EH32 98 B1
Steadings The EH49 84 A4
Steel Gr KY12 26 B4
Steel's Pl EH10 123 D2
Steele Ave EH22 183 F3
Steelyard The EH48 145 D3
Steeple Cres KY11 48 A2
Steil Gr EH33 128 B3
Steils The EH10 122 C1
Stein Sq FK7 7 F1
Stein's Pl KY4 13 E2
Stenhouse Ave EH11 122 A2
Stenhouse Ave W EH11 122 A2
Stenhouse Cotts EH11 122 A2
Stenhouse Cres EH11 122 A2
Stenhouse Cross EH11 122 A2
Stenhouse Dr
Burntisland KY3 33 E1
Edinburgh EH11 122 A2
Stenhouse Gdns EH11 122 A2
Stenhouse Gdns N EH11 122 A2
Stenhouse Gr EH11 122 A2
Stenhouse Mill Cres EH11 122 A2
Stenhouse Mill La EH11 122 A2
Stenhouse Mill Wynd
EH11 122 A2
Stenhouse Pl E EH11 122 A2
Stenhouse Pl W EH11 122 A2
Stenhouse Prim Sch
EH11 122 A2
Stenhouse Rd
Edinburgh EH11 122 A2
Stenhousemuir FK5 38 C1
Stenhouse St KY4 13 D2
Stenhouse St E EH11 122 A2
Stenhouse St W EH11 121 F2
Stenhouse Terr EH11 122 A2
Stenhousemuir Prim Sch
FK5 38 B2
Stennis Gdns EH17 155 E4
Stenton Loan EH42 135 F4
Stenton Prim Sch EH42 104 C1
Stenton Rd EH42 105 F4
Stephen Pl KY5 14 A4
Stephen's Dr KY11 47 E2
Steps St FK5 38 C2
Steuart Rd FK9 1 C4
Stevenlaw's Cl EH1 233 D3
Stevenson Ave EH11 122 B3
Stevenson Coll of F Ed
EH11 121 E2
Stevenson Ct Bridge of A FK9 2 A3
Livingston EH54 148 B3
Longniddry EH32 98 B2
Stevenson Dr EH11 122 A2
Stevenson Gr EH11 122 B3
Stevenson La EH22 183 D2
Stevenson Pk EH32 98 B2
Stevenson Pl EH18 181 E3
Stevenson Rd
Edinburgh EH11 122 B3
Penicuik EH26 204 A4
Stevenson St FK3 61 E3
Stevenson Terr
Bathgate EH48 145 E3
Edinburgh EH11 122 B3
Stevenson Way EH32 98 B2
Stewart Ave Bo'ness EH51 63 F4
Currie EH14 151 F2
Linlithgow EH49 84 C3
Stewart Clark Ave EH30 89 E4
Stewart Cres Currie EH14 151 F2
Lochgelly KY5 14 A4
Stewart Dr EH47 169 F4
Stewart Gdns EH14 151 F2
Stewart Gr
Danderhall EH22 156 A4
Harthill ML7 168 C3
Stewart Pk EH22 158 B3
Stewart Pl Currie EH14 151 F2
Kirkliston EH29 89 D1
Stewart Rd Currie EH14 151 F2
Falkirk FK2 60 B3
Stewart Sq FK8 2 A1
Stewart St
Bonnybridge FK4 57 F3
Cambusbarron FK7 6 B3
Dysart KY1 18 A4
Townhill KY12 29 E4
West Calder EH55 172 B1
Stewart Terr
Edinburgh EH11 122 C3
Queensferry EH30 68 A1
Stewart Way EH54 147 E3
Stewartfield EH6 93 E2
Stewartfield Cres EH52 117 F3
Stewartfield Rd EH52 117 F3
Stirling Castle FK8 1 C1
Stirling Ent Pk FK7 7 E4
Stirling F Ed Ctr FK7 7 E3
Stirling High Sch FK8 7 D3
Stirling Pl FK7 20 B2
Stirling Rd Alloa FK10 9 F4
Alva FK12 4 C4
Edinburgh EH5 93 D3
Falkirk FK1 59 E4
Fallin FK7 8 B2
Larbert FK5 37 F3
Torwood FK5 37 F3
Tullibody FK10 4 A2
Stirling Royal Infmy FK8 7 D3
Stirling St Alva FK12 5 D4
Denny FK6 36 B2
Stirling Sta FK8 7 D4
Stobhill Prim Sch EH23 207 E4
Stobhill Rd EH23 183 D2
Stobie Pl KY12 26 C4
Stobs Pl KY2 16 B4
Stockbridge Prim Sch
EH3 93 D1
Stone Ave EH22 183 E3
Stone Cres EH22 183 E3
Stone Pl EH22 183 E3
Stonebank EH54 147 F3
Stonedyke Cres ML8 230 A2
Stonedyke Rd ML8 230 A2
Stoneheap Crofts EH47 194 C4
Stonelaws Cotts EH40 75 D3
Stoneybank Ave EH21 126 A2
Stoneybank Cres EH21 126 A2
Stoneybank Ct EH21 126 A3
Stoneybank Dr EH21 126 A3
Stoneybank Gdns EH21 126 A3
Stoneybank Gdns N
EH21 126 A3
Stoneybank Gdns S
EH21 126 A3
Stoneybank Gr EH21 126 A2
Stoneybank Pl EH21 126 A2
Stoneybank Rd EH21 126 A2
Stoneybank Terr EH21 126 A2
Stoneyburn Prim Sch
EH47 171 E2
Stoneyflatts EH30 89 D4
Stoneyflatts Cres EH30 89 D4
Stoneyflatts Pk EH30 89 D4
Stoneyhill Ave EH21 126 A3
Stoneyhill Cres EH21 126 A3
Stoneyhill Ct EH21 126 A3
Stoneyhill Dr EH21 126 A3
Stoneyhill Farm Rd
EH21 126 A3
Stoneyhill Gr EH21 126 A3
Stoneyhill Pl EH21 126 A3
Stoneyhill Rd EH21 126 A3
Stoneyhill Rise EH21 126 A3
Stoneyhill Steading
EH21 126 A3
Stoneyhill Terr EH21 126 A3
Stoneyhill Wynd EH21 126 A3
Stoneywood Pk FK6 36 A1
Stony Brae FK10 24 B1
Stony Croft Rd EH30 68 B1
Stories Pk EH40 103 F4
Strachan Gdns EH4 92 A1
Strachan Rd EH4 92 A1
Strachan St FK1 59 F2
Straiton Mains EH20 155 D1
Straiton Pk EH20 155 D1
Straiton Pl EH15 125 D4
Straiton Rd
Loanhead EH20 180 C4
Straiton EH20 155 D1
Strang's Pl FK1 81 F3
Strathallan Ct FK9 2 A3
Strathallan Dr KY2 16 C3
Strathallan Rd FK9 2 A3
Strathalmond Ct EH4 90 C2
Strathalmond Gn EH4 90 C2
Strathalmond Pk EH4 90 C2
Strathalmond Rd EH4 90 C2
Strathavon Terr EH48 112 C3
Strathbeg Dr KY11 47 F2
Strathbrock Pl
Broxburn EH52 117 F3
Uphall EH52 116 C2
Strathearn Pl EH9 123 D2
Strathearn Rd
Edinburgh EH9 123 E2
Kirkcaldy KY1 17 F4
North Berwick EH39 53 F4
Strathesk Gr EH26 204 A3
Strathesk Pl EH26 204 A3
Strathfillan Rd EH9 123 E2
Strathkinnes Rd KY2 17 D2
Strathlachlan Ave ML8 230 A1
Strathlogie EH48 112 C3
Strathmiglo Pl FK5 38 C2
Strathmore Cres FK9 2 A2
Strathmore Dr
Dunfermline KY12 29 E3
Stirling FK9 2 A2
Strathmore St KY3 34 C2
Strathyre Dr EH47 171 E1
Strawberry Bank
Dalkeith EH22 156 C1
Linlithgow EH49 85 D3
Streets Pl KY12 29 E4
Stripehead FK10 10 A3
Striven Dr FK2 39 E1
Striven Pl KY2 16 C4
Stromness Gdns EH54 173 E3
Strowan Rd FK3 61 F4
Strowan Sq FK3 61 F4
Struan Dr KY11 47 D2
Struan Pl KY11 47 D2
Strude Howe FK12 5 D4
Strude Mill FK12 5 D4
Strude St FK12 5 D4
Stuart Cres EH12 121 D4
Stuart Ct EH12 121 D4
Stuart Gn EH12 121 D4
Stuart Gr FK3 61 D3
Stuart Pk EH12 121 D4
Stuart Pl KY4 13 E3
Stuart Rd KY11 46 B1
Stuart Sq EH12 121 D4
Stuart Terr EH48 145 D3
Stuart Wynd EH12 121 D4
Succoth Ave EH12 122 B4
Succoth Ct EH12 122 B4
Succoth Gdns EH12 122 B4
Succoth Pk EH12 122 B4
Succoth Pl EH12 122 B4
Suffolk Rd EH16 123 F2
Suilven Hts FK2 61 D2
Summer Bank EH3 93 E1
Summer Pl EH3 93 E2
Summerfield Gdns EH6 94 A2
Summerfield Pk EH42 78 A1
Summerfield Pl EH6 94 A2
Summerfield Rd EH42 78 B1
Summerford FK1 59 E2
Summerford Gdns FK1 59 E2
Summerford Rd FK1 59 E2
Summerhall EH8 233 E1
Summerhall Cres EH9 233 E1
Summerhall Pl EH9 233 E1
Summerhall Sq EH9 233 E1
Summerlee EH32 96 C1
Summerside Pl EH6 93 E3
Summerside St EH6 93 E3
Summertrees Ct EH16 124 A1
Summerville Ct EH54 148 A4
Suna Path ML7 192 A2
Sunart Pl FK3 61 E3
Sunbury Mews EH4 122 C4
Sunbury Pl EH4 122 C4
Sunningdale La KY12 28 B3
Sunnybank ML7 191 F3
Sunnybank Pl 12 EH7 94 A1
Sunnybank Rd FK7 7 D2
Sunnybrae ML11 215 D1
Sunnydale Dr EH48 142 C2
Sunnydale Rd EH48 142 C2
Sunnylaw Pl FK1 59 F2
Sunnylaw Rd FK9 2 A4
Sunnyside Edinburgh EH7 94 A1
Stirling FK7 7 D2
Stoneyburn EH47 171 D1
Sunnyside Ave EH48 145 E4
Sunnyside Ct FK10 10 A4
Sunnyside Pl KY5 14 A3
Sunnyside Prim Sch FK10 10 A4
Sunnyside Rd Alloa FK10 10 A4
Brightons FK2 82 B4
Falkirk FK1 59 F3
Sunnyside St FK1 59 F3
Surcoat Loan FK7 7 F2
Sutherland Ave Alloa FK10 10 B4
Stirling FK8 2 B1
Sutherland Cres EH48 145 D3
Sutherland Dr FK6 57 E4
Sutherland Pl KY1 17 F4
Sutherland St EH12 122 C4
Sutherland Way EH54 147 E3
Suttie Way FK9 1 C4
Suttieslea Cres EH22 183 E3
Suttieslea Dr EH22 183 E3
Suttieslea Pl EH22 183 E3
Suttieslea Rd EH22 183 E3
Suttieslea Wlk EH22 183 E3
Sutton Park Cres FK5 38 C2
Sutton Pl FK2 60 B3
Swallow Craig KY11 48 A1
Swallowdrum Rd KY12 28 B3
Swan Cres EH23 207 E4
Swan Pl FK3 61 E3
Swan Rd Kirkcaldy KY1 17 D2
Tranent EH33 128 B3
Swan Spring Ave EH10 154 A4
Swanfield EH6 93 F3
Swanston Ave EH10 154 A3
Swanston Cres EH10 154 A3
Swanston Dr EH10 154 A2
Swanston Gdns EH10 154 A3
Swanston Gn EH10 154 A3
Swanston Gr EH10 154 A2
Swanston Loan EH10 154 A3
Swanston Muir EH10 153 F3
Swanston Pk EH10 154 A3
Swanston Pl EH10 154 A3
Swanston Rd EH10 154 A2
Swanston Row EH10 154 A3
Swanston Terr EH10 154 A3
Swanston View EH10 154 A3
Swanston Way EH10 154 A3
Swinburne Dr FK10 5 D1
Swintons Pl KY4 12 C1
Sword's Way FK2 39 D1
Sycamore Ave
Bo'ness EH51 63 E3
Cockenzie & Port Seton
EH32 97 E2
Kirkcaldy KY1 17 E4
Sycamore Cres KY4 13 E3
Sycamore Dr EH47 170 B3
Sycamore Gdns EH12 121 F3
Sycamore Gr
Dunfermline KY11 46 B4
Winchburgh EH52 87 F1
Sycamore Pl FK8 6 C3
Sycamore Rd EH22 183 F3
Sycamore Wlk EH47 171 E4
Sycamores The FK10 4 A1
Sydney Pk EH7 94 C1
Sydney Pl EH7 94 C1
Sydney St EH54 148 A3
Sydney Terr EH7 94 C1
Sylvan Gr EH51 63 E3
Sylvan Pl EH9 123 E3
Sylvan Way EH48 144 C3
Syme Pl KY11 46 B3
Symington Pl FK2 39 D2

Ta-Verne La KY11 29 E1
Tailend Ind Pk EH54 146 B2
Tailend Rdbt EH54 146 B2
Tait Dr Larbert FK5 59 E4
Penicuik EH26 203 F3
Tait St EH22 157 D2
Talbot St FK3 61 E4
Talisman Pl EH16 124 A1
Talman Gdns FK2 61 F2
Tam O'Shanter Dr FK7 20 B4
Tamfourhill Ave FK1 59 E2
Tamfourhill Ind Est FK1 59 E2
Tamfourhill Rd FK1 59 E2
Tanera Ct FK1 60 A1
Tanhouse Brae KY12 42 B4
Tanners Rd FK1 60 A2
Tannery La FK8 2 A1
Tantallon Castle EH39 55 F4
Tantallon Dr FK2 39 D2
Tantallon Gdns EH54 173 F4
Tantallon Pl EH9 123 E3
Tantallon Rd EH39 54 C3
Tantallon Terr EH39 54 C4
Tapitlaw Gr KY12 26 B4
Tappoch Pl FK5 38 A2
Taransay Dr FK2 61 F1
Tarbert Pl FK2 61 F1
Tarbert Terr FK10 23 F2
Tarbet Pl ML8 230 A1
Tarbrax Path ML7 192 A2
Tarbrax Rd EH55 217 F1
Tarduff Dr FK2 83 D3
Tarduff Pl FK6 36 A1
Targate Rd KY12 28 B3
Targe Wynd FK7 7 F2
Target Rd FK3 62 B4
Tartraven Pl EH52 118 A3
Tarvit St EH3 232 C1
Tashieburn Rd ML11 215 F1
Tavern Cotts KY4 30 C4
Taxi Way KY11 48 B3
Tay Ct FK10 10 B3
Tay Pl ML7 191 F3
Tay St Edinburgh EH11 122 C3
Falkirk FK2 39 E1
Grangemouth FK3 40 A1
Tay Terr KY11 29 F1
Tay Wlk EH54 148 A2
Taylor Ave KY4 13 E2
Taylor Ct FK3 40 C1
Taylor Gdns EH6 93 F3
Taylor Gn EH54 147 E4
Taylor Pl EH22 157 E1
Taylor Rd EH47 169 F3
Taylor's Rd FK5 38 B1
Taymouth Rd FK2 62 A1
Tedder St FK3 61 E3
Telferton EH7 94 C1
Telford Coll EH4 92 C2
Telford Coll
Lochend Annexe EH6 94 A2
Telford Coll North Campus
EH5 92 C3
Telford Ct FK7 7 E1
Telford Dr EH4 92 B2
Telford Gdns EH4 92 B2
Telford Pl Edinburgh EH4 92 B2
Linlithgow EH49 84 B4
Telford Rd EH4 92 B2
Telford Sq Falkirk FK1 59 F3
Livingston EH54 147 F4
Telford View EH49 84 B3
Telny Pl KY3 49 E4
Templar La EH31 52 A1
Templar Pl EH31 52 A1
Templar Rise EH54 173 E4
Templar's Cramond EH4 91 D2
Templars Cres KY3 34 C2
Temple Ave EH48 144 A3
Temple Denny Rd FK6 36 B1
Temple Park Cres EH11 122 C3
Temple Pk EH23 206 B1
Temple Prim Sch EH23 206 B1
Templedean Pk EH41 101 D1
Templehall Ave KY2 16 C4
Templeland Gr EH12 121 E4
Templeland Rd EH12 121 E4
Ten Acres FK10 5 D1
Tenacres Pl FK3 61 F3
Tenacres Rd FK3 62 A4
Tenant's March EH55 172 B2
Tennant St EH6 93 F2
Tennent Pk EH53 148 B1
Tenth St EH22 183 D3
Tern Brae EH54 147 E3
Terrace St KY1 18 A4
Terrace The EH21 126 C1
Terragies EH26 203 E3
Terrars Croft EH8 233 F1
Terris St KY4 13 E2
Teviot Gr EH26 203 F4
Teviot Pl EH1 233 D2
Teviot St FK1 59 F2
Teviotdale Pl EH3 93 D1
Thane Pl KY11 29 F1
Thimblehall Dr KY12 29 E2
Thimblehall Pl KY12 29 E2
Thimblehall Rd KY12 29 F2
Third Gait EH14 151 F4
Third St EH22 183 D3
Thirlestane EH51 64 A4
Thirlestane La EH9 123 E2
Thirlestane Pl EH51 64 A4
Thirlestane Rd EH9 123 E3
Thistle Ave Denny FK6 36 B2
Grangemouth FK3 61 D3
Thistle Ind Est
Broxburn EH52 118 A3
Cowdenbeath KY4 13 F2
Stirling FK7 7 E3
Thistle Pl EH11 232 A1
Thistle St Alloa FK10 10 B3
Burntisland KY3 50 C4
Cowdenbeath KY4 13 E2
Dunfermline KY12 29 D3
Edinburgh EH2 232 C4
Falkirk FK2 60 B3
Kirkcaldy KY1 17 E2
Thompson Pl FK1 110 A2
Thomson Cres
Cockenzie & Port Seton
EH32 97 E2
Currie EH14 152 A3
Falkirk FK1 59 F2
Thomson Ct EH52 116 C2
Thomson Dr EH14 152 B3
Thomson Gn EH54 147 D4
Thomson Gr Currie EH14 152 A3
Uphall EH52 116 C2
Thomson Pl
Cambusbarron FK7 6 B3
Rosyth KY11 46 C2
Thomson Rd EH14 152 A3
Thomson Terr ML7 191 E3
Thorburn Gr EH13 153 E3
Thorburn Rd EH13 153 D3
Thorn Gr KY11 46 C4
Thorn Tree Pl KY12 26 C3
Thornbridge Gdns FK2 60 C2
Thornbridge Rd FK2 60 C3
Thornbridge Sq FK2 60 C3
Thorndale Gdns FK4 57 D1
Thorndene Ct FK1 59 F1
Thorne Ct EH39 54 A4
Thorne Rd FK10 4 C1
Thornhill Dr KY2 17 D3
Thornhill Rd Falkirk FK2 60 B3
Kirkcaldy KY2 17 E3
Thornton Ave FK4 58 A3
Thornton Pl EH47 193 E3
Thornton Rd EH24 181 E1
Thorntree Cres EH32 97 D1
Thorntree St EH6 94 A2
Thorntreeside EH6 94 A2
Thornville Terr EH6 94 A2
Thorny Bank EH22 157 E2
Thornybank Ind Est
EH22 157 E2
Thornybauk EH3 232 B1
Thornyhall EH22 157 E2
Threipmuir Ave EH14 177 E4
Threipmuir Gdns EH14 177 E4
Threipmuir Pl EH14 177 E4
Thrums The FK2 61 D2
Thurston Pl EH54 147 E3
Timber Bush EH6 94 A3
Timmeryetts EH52 117 E3
Timmons Pk KY5 14 A4
Timmons Pl FK6 36 B1
Tinian Cres KY12 26 B1
Tinto Dr FK3 61 F3
Tinto Pl Dunfermline KY11 29 F1
Edinburgh EH6 93 F2
Tipperlinn Rd EH10 123 D2
Tippet Knowes Ct EH52 87 F2
Tippet Knowes Pk EH52 87 F2
Tippet Knowes Rd EH52 87 F1
Tippethill Hospl EH48 144 A1
Tiree Cres FK2 61 E1
Tiree Pl Falkirk FK1 60 A1
Kirkcaldy KY2 16 C4
Titania FK10 10 A4
Todd Sq EH54 116 C1
Toddshill Rd EH29 89 D1
Tolbooth St
3 Falkirk FK1 60 A2
Kirkcaldy KY1 17 E2
Tolbooth Wynd EH6 94 A3
Toll Rd FK10 23 F2
Toll Rdbt EH54 146 C2
Toll View TD13 140 C2
Tollcross EH3 232 B1
Tollcross Prim Sch
EH3 232 B1
Tollgate KY11 29 D1
Tolmount Dr KY12 29 E2
Tolsta Cres FK2 61 F1
Tophill Entry FK1 59 F3
Toravon Dr FK2 83 D3
Torbain KY2 16 B4
Torbain Prim Sch KY2 16 B4
Torbain Rd KY2 16 A3
Torbane Ave EH47 170 C4
Torbane Dr EH47 170 C4
Torbeith Gdns KY4 12 C1
Torbothie Rd ML7 192 A2
Torbrex Farm Rd FK7 7 D2
Torbrex La FK7 7 D3
Torbrex Rd FK7 6 C2
Torburn Ave FK7 20 B2
Torduff Rd EH13 153 D2
Torlea Pl FK5 38 A2
Torness Power Sta
Visitor Ctr EH42 108 C2
Toronto Ave EH54 147 F2
Toronto Prim Sch
EH54 147 F2
Torosay Ave FK2 82 C3
Torphichen Ave EH53 148 A1
Torphichen Pl EH3 232 A2
Torphichen Preceptory
EH48 113 F3
Torphichen Prim Sch
EH48 113 F3
Torphichen Rd EH48 145 D4

Torphichen St
Bathgate EH48 .... 145 D4
Edinburgh EH3 .... 232 A2
Torphin Bank EH13 .... 152 C3
Torphin Rd EH13 .... 152 C3
Torrance Pk EH4 .... 91 E1
Torridon Ave FK2 .... 39 E1
Torridon Ct FK10 .... 10 B3
Torridon Dr KY11 .... 46 C1
Torridon La KY11 .... 46 C1
Torridon Pl Kirkcaldy KY2 .... 16 C4
Rosyth KY11 .... 46 C1
Torridon Rd EH47 .... 170 B4
Torridon Wlk EH54 .... 148 A2
Torrin Loan ML7 .... 192 A2
Torry Dr FK12 .... 4 C4
Torryburn Prim Sch KY12 .... 26 C1
Torsonce Rd KY22 .... 156 C1
Torvean Pl KY11 .... 29 E1
Torwood Ave
Grangemouth FK3 .... 61 F3
Larbert FK5 .... 38 A1
Torwood Pl KY12 .... 29 E3
Torwood Sch FK5 .... 37 F3
Touch Prim Sch KY11 .... 29 F2
Touch Pk FK7 .... 6 A3
Touch Wards KY12 .... 29 F2
Touchhill Cres FK7 .... 20 B2
Tory Rd KY11 .... 46 B1
Toward Ct EH12 .... 121 D4
Tower Gdns EH51 .... 64 B4
Tower Pl
Clackmannan FK10 .... 10 C3
Edinburgh EH6 .... 94 A3
Tower St Alloa FK10 .... 10 A4
Edinburgh EH6 .... 94 A3
Tower Terr KY11 .... 17 F4
Tower View FK10 .... 5 F1
Towerbank Prim Sch
EH15 .... 95 D1
Towers Ct FK2 .... 60 A3
Towers Pl FK9 .... 2 B2
Town Burn FK7 .... 6 C2
Town House St FK6 .... 36 C1
Townhall St KY11 .... 47 E1
Townhead Dysart KY1 .... 18 A4
Kinghorn KY3 .... 34 C2
Townhead Gdns EH47 .... 170 B3
Townhill Ctry Pk KY12 .... 29 E4
Townhill Prim Sch KY12 .... 29 E4
Townhill Rd KY12 .... 29 D3
Townsend Cres KY1 .... 17 E2
Townsend Pl KY1 .... 17 E2
Trafalgar La EH6 .... 93 F3
Trafalgar St EH6 .... 93 F3
Tranent Inf Sch EH33 .... 128 B4
Tranent Prim Sch EH33 .... 128 B4
Tranent Rd EH33 .... 128 A1
Transy Gr KY12 .... 29 E2
Transy Pl KY12 .... 29 E2
Traprain Cres EH48 .... 144 C4
Traprain Terr
Haddington EH41 .... 101 D1
Loanhead EH20 .... 181 E4
Traquair Pk E EH12 .... 121 F3
Traquair Pk W EH12 .... 121 F3
Trelawney Terr EH54 .... 204 A4
Tremayne Pl KY12 .... 28 C3
Trench Knowe EH10 .... 154 A3
Trenchard Pl KY12 .... 28 C3
Tressilian Gdns EH16 .... 124 A1
Trevelyan Cres EH34 .... 160 C3
Trevelyan Pl EH34 .... 160 C3
Trinity Acad EH6 .... 93 E3
Trinity Cres EH5 .... 93 D3
Trinity Ct EH5 .... 93 D3
Trinity Gr EH5 .... 93 D3
Trinity Prim Sch EH6 .... 93 E3
Trinity Rd EH5 .... 93 D3
Tron Ct FK10 .... 4 A1
Tron Sq EH1 .... 233 D3
Trondheim Parkway KY11 .... 47 E3
Trondheim Pl KY11 .... 29 F1
Trongate KY3 .... 35 C2
Troup Ct FK3 .... 61 E4
Tryst Pk EH10 .... 153 F3
Tryst Rd FK5 .... 38 B2
Tudor Ct FK2 .... 61 E1
Tuke St KY12 .... 29 D3
Tulliallan Castle FK10 .... 23 E3
Tulliallan Pl KY12 .... 39 D2
Tulliallan Prim Sch FK10 .... 23 F2
Tulliallan Terr FK10 .... 23 F2
Tullibody Rd FK10 .... 4 C1
Tulligarth Pk FK10 .... 10 A4
Tulloch Ct KY4 .... 13 E3
Tulloch Rd ML7 .... 192 A2
Tulloch St KY4 .... 16 B4
Tummel Pl
Grangemouth FK3 .... 61 F2
Stenhousemuir FK5 .... 38 C2
Turnbull Gr KY11 .... 29 F1
Turnbull Way EH54 .... 147 E3
Turner Ave EH14 .... 151 E2
Turner Pk EH14 .... 151 E2
Turner St EH48 .... 145 D4
Turnhigh Rd EH47 .... 170 A2
Turnhouse Farm Rd EH12 .... 90 B1
Turnhouse Rd EH12 .... 120 B4
Turret Ct FK10 .... 10 B3
Turret Dr FK12 .... 62 A1
Turret Gdns EH32 .... 127 E1
Turret Rd FK3 .... 61 E3
Turriff Pl KY12 .... 16 C4

Twain Ave FK5 .... 39 D2
Tweed Dr EH54 .... 148 A3
Tweed St Dunfermline KY11 .... 29 F1
Grangemouth FK3 .... 40 A1
Tweeddale Cres EH41 .... 163 F3
Tweeddale Ave EH41 .... 163 F3
Tweeddale Ct EH1 .... 233 E3
Tweeddale Dr KY11 .... 29 F1
Tweeddale Gr EH41 .... 163 F2
Tyhmebank EH54 .... 147 F3
Tyler's Acre Ave EH12 .... 121 F3
Tyler's Acre Gdns EH12 .... 121 F3
Tyler's Acre Rd EH12 .... 121 F3
Tyndrum Pl KY2 .... 16 C4
Tyne Ct East Linton EH40 .... 103 F4
Haddington EH41 .... 132 A4
Tynebank Rd EH41 .... 132 A4
Tynecastle High Sch
EH11 .... 122 C3
Tynecastle La EH11 .... 122 C3
**Tynecastle Pk (Heart of
Midlothian FC)** EH11 .... 122 C3
Tynecastle Terr EH11 .... 122 C3
Tynemount Ave EH35 .... 159 E3
Tynemount Rd EH35 .... 159 E4
Tyneview EH35 .... 159 F4
Tyrwhitt Pl KY11 .... 46 C2
Tytler Gdns EH8 .... 94 A1

Ugston Cotts EH41 .... 100 B1
Ulg Way ML7 .... 192 A2
Ulster Cres EH8 .... 124 B4
Ulster Dr EH8 .... 124 B4
Ulster Gdns EH8 .... 124 B4
Ulster Gr EH8 .... 124 B4
Ulster Terr EH8 .... 124 B4
Underwood Cotts FK7 .... 6 B3
Underwood Rd FK7 .... 6 B3
Union Dr EH47 .... 170 A3
Union Pk EH19 .... 182 A3
Union Pl Brightons FK2 .... 61 E1
Edinburgh EH1 .... 233 E4
Larbert FK5 .... 38 A1
Union Rd Bathgate EH48 .... 145 D3
Broxburn EH52 .... 117 E3
Falkirk FK1 .... 59 E3
Grangemouth FK3 .... 40 B1
Linlithgow EH49 .... 84 C3
Whitburn EH47 .... 170 A3
Union St Alloa FK10 .... 10 A3
Bo'ness EH51 .... 64 A4
Bridge of A FK9 .... 2 A4
Burntisland KY3 .... 50 C4
Cowdenbeath KY4 .... 13 E2
Edinburgh EH1 .... 93 F1
Falkirk FK2 .... 60 A4
Kirkcaldy KY5 .... 17 F4
Lochgelly KY5 .... 14 A4
Shotts ML7 .... 191 E3
Stenhousemuir FK5 .... 2 A1
Stirling FK8 .... 2 A1
Unity Pk ML7 .... 191 E2
**Univ of Dundee Sch of
Nursing & Midwifery
Fife Campus** KY12 .... 17 D2
Univ of Edinburgh EH 233 D2
**Univ of Stirling
(Dept of Nursing &
Midwifery, Forth Valley
Campus)** FK1 .... 60 C4
Universal Rd FK2 .... 60 C4
University of Stirling FK9 .... 2 B3
University Rd W FK9 .... 2 B3
Uphall Prim Sch EH52 .... 116 C2
Uphall Station Inf Sch
EH54 .... 117 D1
Uphall Station Rd EH53 .... 148 A4
Uphall Station Sta EH54 .... 117 D1
Upper Bathville EH48 .... 143 F2
Upper Bow EH1 .... 233 D3
Upper Bridge St FK8 .... 2 A1
Upper Broomieknowe
EH18 .... 182 A4
Upper Castlehill EH 7 D4
Upper Coltbridge Terr
EH12 .... 122 C4
Upper Craigour EH17 .... 155 F4
Upper Craigour Way
EH17 .... 124 B1
Upper Craigs FK8 .... 7 D4
Upper Cramond Ct EH4 .... 91 E4
Upper Dean Terr EH4 .... 232 A4
Upper Gilmore Pl EH3 .... 232 B1
Upper Gilmore Terr EH3 .... 232 B1
Upper Gray St EH9 .... 123 F3
Upper Grove Pl EH3 .... 232 A1
Upper Millhill St KY12 .... 29 D2
Upper Newmarket St FK1 .... 60 A4
Upper Wellheads KY11 .... 45 F2
Ure Cres EH4 .... 58 A3
Ure Ct FK2 .... 61 E4
Urquhart Cres KY12 .... 28 C2
Urquhart Ct KY12 .... 28 C2
Urquhart Farm Cotts KY12 .... 28 B1

Vale Dr FK9 .... 1 C3
Vale Pl FK6 .... 36 C2
Valeview FK5 .... 38 B1
Valley Field View EH26 .... 203 F2
Valley Gdns KY2 .... 16 C3
Valley Gdns S KY2 .... 16 C3
Valley Prim Sch KY2 .... 16 C3
Valley View KY2 .... 16 C3
Valleyfield Ave KY12 .... 26 A1
Valleyfield Pl
Cowdenbeath KY4 .... 13 E3
Stirling FK7 .... 7 E3

Valleyfield Rd EH26 .... 203 F2
Valleyfield St EH3 .... 232 C1
Valleyfield Woodland Pk
KY12 .... 26 A1
Valleyview Dr FK2 .... 60 A4
Valleyview Pl FK2 .... 60 A4
Vancouver Ave EH54 .... 147 F2
Vandeleur Ave FK4 .... 94 C1
Vandeleur Gr EH7 .... 94 C1
Vandeleur Pl EH7 .... 94 C1
Vardon Rd EH13 .... 52 A2
Vaucluse Pl EH26 .... 203 F2
Veere Pk KY12 .... 25 F1
Veitch's Sq EH4 .... 93 D1
Vellore Rd FK2 .... 83 D3
Venachar Pl KY12 .... 28 A1
Vennachar St ML7 .... 191 F3
Vennel The Denny FK6 .... 36 C1
Dunbar EH42 .... 78 C1
Linlithgow EH49 .... 85 D4
Ventnor Pl EH9 .... 124 A2
Ventnor Terr EH9 .... 123 F2
Venturefair Ave KY12 .... 29 D3
Veronica Cres KY1 .... 17 E4
Vetch Pk EH11 .... 101 D1
Vexhim Pk EH15 .... 125 D3
Vicar St FK1 .... 60 A3
Viceroy St KY2 .... 17 D3
Victor Park Terr EH12 .... 121 D4
Victoria Gdns
Kirkcaldy KY1 .... 17 D2
Newtongrange EH22 .... 182 C3
Victoria Hospl KY1 .... 17 D4
Victoria Pk
Fauldhouse EH47 .... 193 F4
Haddington EH41 .... 101 D1
Victoria Pl Bo'ness EH51 .... 64 A4
Brightons FK2 .... 61 E1
Dunbar EH42 .... 78 B2
Stirling FK8 .... 7 D4
Victoria Prim Sch
Edinburgh EH6 .... 93 E4
Bo'ness EH51 .... 64 B3
Victoria Rd Falkirk FK2 .... 60 B3
Fauldhouse EH47 .... 193 F4
Grangemouth FK3 .... 61 F4
Haddington EH41 .... 132 A4
Harthill ML7 .... 168 C3
Kirkcaldy KY1 .... 17 E3
Larbert FK5 .... 38 A1
Newtongrange EH22 .... 182 C3
North Berwick EH39 .... 54 B4
Stirling FK8 .... 7 D4
Victoria Sq FK8 .... 7 D4
Victoria St Alloa FK10 .... 10 A4
Dunbar EH42 .... 78 B2
Dunfermline KY12 .... 29 E1
Dysart KY1 .... 18 A4
Edinburgh EH1 .... 233 D3
Harthill ML7 .... 168 C3
Livingston EH54 .... 148 A2
Rosewell EH24 .... 181 E1
Victoria Terr
Dunfermline KY12 .... 29 D3
Edinburgh EH1 .... 233 D2
Haddington EH41 .... 132 A4
Menstrie FK11 .... 4 A1
Musselburgh EH21 .... 126 C3
Viewbank Dr EH19 .... 182 B4
Viewbank Rd EH19 .... 182 B4
Viewbank View EH19 .... 182 B4
Viewcraig Gdns EH8 .... 233 E2
Viewcraig St EH8 .... 233 E2
Viewfield EH19 .... 182 B4
Viewfield Ave EH19 .... 182 B4
Viewfield Rd
Edinburgh EH14 .... 152 C4
Tarbrax EH55 .... 217 D2
Viewfield St Harthill ML7 .... 168 C3
Stirling FK7 .... 7 D4
Viewfield Terr
Cowdenbeath KY4 .... 13 F3
Dunfermline KY12 .... 29 D3
Viewforth Bo'ness EH51 .... 64 A4
Edinburgh EH10 .... 123 D3
Dunbar EH42 .... 78 B2
North Berwick EH39 .... 54 B4
Viewforth Ave KY1 .... 17 F4
Viewforth Dr FK2 .... 61 D2
Viewforth Gdns
Edinburgh EH10 .... 123 D3
Kirkcaldy KY1 .... 17 F4
Tranent EH33 .... 128 B3
Viewforth Pl EH30 .... 89 D4
Viewforth Rd EH30 .... 89 D4
Viewforth Sq EH10 .... 123 D3
Viewforth St KY1 .... 17 F4
Viewforth Terr
Edinburgh EH10 .... 123 D3
Kirkcaldy KY1 .... 17 F4
Tranent EH33 .... 128 B3
Viewpark Gdns EH19 .... 182 A4
Villa Bank EH7 .... 36 C1
Villa Rd EH30 .... 68 A1
Village La EH54 .... 147 D2
Vinefields EH34 .... 160 C3
Violet Terr EH11 .... 122 C3
Vivian Terr EH4 .... 92 A2
Vogrie Cres S EH23 .... 207 E4
Vogrie Estate Ctry Pk
EH23 .... 207 E3
Vogrie Pl EH23 .... 207 E4
Vogrie Rd EH23 .... 207 E4
Voil Rd FK9 .... 2 A2
Volunteer's Gn KY1 .... 17 E2

Vorlich Cres EH26 .... 204 A4
Vorlich Dr FK1 .... 81 F4
Vorlich Pl KY11 .... 2 A2

Waddell St FK2 .... 39 E1
Wadingburn La EH18 .... 155 F1
Wadingburn Rd EH18 .... 181 F4
Waggon Rd Bo'ness EH51 .... 63 F4
Brightons FK2 .... 82 B4
Crossford KY11 .... 45 E4
Falkirk FK1 .... 60 A4
Wakefield Ave EH7 .... 94 C1
Walden Dr EH41 .... 163 F3
Walden Pl EH41 .... 163 F2
Walden Terr EH41 .... 163 F2
Walk The Alloa FK10 .... 10 A3
Dysart KY1 .... 18 A4
Walker Dr
Dennyloanhead FK4 .... 57 E3
Queensferry EH30 .... 68 A1
Walker Pl
Bonnyrigg and Lasswade
EH18 .... 181 F3
Dunfermline KY11 .... 29 E1
Walker Rd EH47 .... 193 E3
Walker St
Cowdenbeath KY4 .... 13 D2
Edinburgh EH3 .... 23 F2
Kincardine FK10 .... 23 F2
Kirkcaldy KY2 .... 17 D3
Lochgelly KY5 .... 14 A3
Walker Terr EH40 .... 103 E4
Walkers Ct EH14 .... 121 F1
Walkers Rig EH14 .... 121 F1
Walkers Wynd EH14 .... 121 F1
Wall Gdns FK1 .... 59 E3
Wall St KY1 .... 59 E3
Wallace Cres Brightons FK2 .... 82 B4
Denny FK6 .... 36 B1
Plean FK7 .... 20 B2
Roslin EH25 .... 181 D2
Wallace Ct
Grangemouth FK3 .... 61 E4
Stirling FK8 .... 2 A1
Wallace Gdns FK9 .... 2 B2
Wallace High Sch FK9 .... 2 A2
Wallace Mill Gdns EH53 .... 148 B2
Wallace Mon FK9 .... 2 C2
Wallace Pl
Cambusbarron FK7 .... 6 B3
Falkirk FK1 .... 60 B3
Fallin FK7 .... 8 B2
Tranent EH33 .... 128 B4
Wallace Rd EH48 .... 145 E3
Wallace Rd Alloa FK10 .... 10 B4
Bannockburn FK7 .... 7 F1
Dunfermline KY12 .... 29 E1
Grangemouth FK3 .... 61 E4
Wallace St
Cowdenbeath KY4 .... 13 E2
Falkirk FK2 .... 60 A3
Penicuik EH26 .... 203 F3
Wallace View
Shieldhill FK1 .... 81 E4
Tullibody FK10 .... 4 B2
Wallace Wlk EH47 .... 171 D1
Wallacelea FK2 .... 82 C4
Wallacestone Brae FK2 .... 82 A4
Wallacestone Prim Sch
FK2 .... 82 B4
Walls Pl KY11 .... 29 F1
Wallsend Ct KY12 .... 28 B3
Wallstale Rd FK7 .... 7 D2
Wallyford Ind Est EH21 .... 127 D2
Wallyford Prim Sch
EH21 .... 127 D3
Wallyford Sta EH21 .... 127 D3
Walmer Dr KY12 .... 29 D2
Walter Dr KY11 .... 46 B3
Walter Hay Ct KY11 .... 46 C2
Walter Scott Ave EH16 .... 124 A1
Wanless Ct EH 126 B3
Ward Ave FK2 .... 61 E1
Ward St FK10 .... 10 A3
Warden's Cl EH1 .... 123 E4
Wardie Ave EH5 .... 93 D3
Wardie Cres EH5 .... 93 D3
Wardie Dell EH5 .... 93 D3
Wardie House La EH5 .... 93 D3
Wardie Prim Sch EH5 .... 93 D3
Wardie Rd EH5 .... 93 D3
Wardie Sq EH5 .... 93 D3
Wardieburn Dr EH5 .... 92 C3
Wardieburn Pl E EH5 .... 92 C3
Wardieburn Pl N EH5 .... 92 C3
Wardieburn Pl S EH5 .... 92 C3
Wardieburn Pl W EH5 .... 92 C3
Wardieburn Rd EH5 .... 92 C3
Wardieburn St E EH5 .... 92 C3
Wardieburn St W EH5 .... 92 C3
Wardieburn Terr EH5 .... 92 C3
Wardiefield EH5 .... 93 D3
Wardlaw Cres
Oakley KY12 .... 26 C4
Wardlaw Pl
Edinburgh EH11 .... 122 C3
Wardlaw St
Cowdenbeath KY4 .... 13 E2
Wardlaw Terr EH11 .... 122 C3
Wardlaw Way KY12 .... 26 C4

Wardrop Cres EH48 .... 143 F2
Ware Rd Dirleton EH39 .... 53 E2
North Berwick EH39 .... 54 A4
Warrender Cres EH42 .... 78 C1
Warrender Ct EH39 .... 54 A3
Warrender Park Cres
EH9 .... 123 E2
Warrender Park Rd EH9 .... 123 E2
Warrender Park Terr
EH9 .... 123 E3
Warriston Ave EH3 .... 93 E2
Warriston Cres EH3 .... 93 E2
Warriston Dr EH3 .... 93 D2
Warriston Gdns EH3 .... 93 E2
Warriston Gr EH3 .... 93 D2
Warriston Rd EH3, EH7 .... 93 E2
Warriston Terr EH3 .... 93 D2
Washington La EH11 .... 122 C3
Water St EH6 .... 94 A3
Water Yett EH49 .... 84 C4
Waterfall Wlk EH22 .... 157 D1
Waterlands Gdns ML8 .... 230 A2
Waterloo Bank EH26 .... 203 F2
Waterloo Pl
Edinburgh EH1 .... 233 D3
Elphinstone EH33 .... 128 A1
Waters' Cl EH6 .... 94 A3
Waterside EH41 .... 132 A4
Watertoun Rd EH9 .... 123 F2
Watling Ave FK1 .... 59 E3
Watling Dr FK1 .... 59 E3
Watling Gdns FK1 .... 59 E3
Watling St FK1 .... 59 E3
Watson Cres EH11 .... 122 C3
Watson St
Cowdenbeath KY4 .... 13 E2
Falkirk FK2 .... 60 A3
Watt Ave EH48 .... 144 A3
Watt Gdns FK1 .... 59 E3
Watt Gr EH22 .... 183 E3
Watt Pk EH22 .... 183 D2
Watt Rd KY11 .... 46 A1
Watt St KY1 .... 18 A4
Watters Cres KY5 .... 14 B3
Wauchope Ave EH16 .... 124 C2
Wauchope Cres EH16 .... 124 C2
Wauchope Pl EH16 .... 124 C2
Wauchope Rd EH16 .... 124 C2
Wauchope Sq EH16 .... 124 C2
Wauchope Terr EH16 .... 124 C2
Waugh Path EH19 .... 182 B4
Waughton Cotts EH40 .... 74 C3
Waulkmill Dr EH26 .... 204 A3
Waulkmill Loan EH14 .... 121 E2
Waulkmill Rd EH26 .... 204 A3
Waulkmill View EH26 .... 203 F3
Wavell St KY1 .... 61 E3
Waverley Bridge EH1 .... 233 D3
Waverley Cres
Bonnyrigg and Lasswade
EH19 .... 182 B4
Grangemouth FK3 .... 61 E3
High Bonnybridge FK4 .... 58 A2
Livingston EH54 .... 147 D3
Waverley Ct EH19 .... 182 B4
Waverley Dr EH19 .... 182 B4
Waverley Park Terr EH8 .... 94 A1
Waverley Pk
Bonnyrigg and Lasswade
EH18 .... 182 B4
Edinburgh EH8 .... 94 A1
Mayfield EH22 .... 183 E3
Redding FK2 .... 61 D1
Waverley Rd
Bonnyrigg and Lasswade
EH18 .... 182 B4
Dalkeith EH22 .... 156 C1
Stenhousemuir FK5 .... 38 B1
Waverley St
Bathgate EH48 .... 145 D4
Falkirk FK2 .... 60 A4
Mayfield EH22 .... 183 E3
Waverley St Ind Units
EH22 .... 183 D3
Waverley Terr
Bonnyrigg and Lasswade
EH19 .... 182 B4
Mayfield EH22 .... 183 E3
Wayfarers Dr KY11 .... 47 F2
Wayfarers Pl KY11 .... 47 F2
Weaver Pl EH48 .... 145 D4
Weaver Row FK7 .... 7 D2
Weaver's Knowe Cres
EH14 .... 151 F3
Weavers Ct EH47 .... 170 A3
Weavers La EH47 .... 170 A3
Weavers Wlk KY11 .... 29 E1
Webster Ave FK2 .... 39 D2
Webster Ct EH52 .... 117 F3
Webster Pl KY11 .... 46 B3
Wedderburn Cres KY11 .... 29 F1
Wedderburn Pl KY11 .... 29 F1
Wedderburn Rd KY12 .... 28 B3
Wedderburn St KY12 .... 28 B3
Wedderburn Terr EH39 .... 54 B4
Wee Brae EH18 .... 156 A1
Wee Row KY5 .... 60 A3
Weir Ave KY4 .... 13 D1

Veir Cres EH22 ..... 156 C1
Veir Dr FK7 ..... 8 B2
Veir St Falkirk FK1 ..... 60 B3
Stirling FK8 ..... 1 C1
Well Rd Bridge of A FK9 ..... 2 A4
Lochgelly KY5 ..... 14 A4
Well Wynd EH33 ..... 128 B3
Wellflats Rd EH29 ..... 89 D1
Wellgate Dr FK9 ..... 2 B4
Wellgreen Pl FK8 ..... 7 D3
Wellhead Cl EH30 ..... 89 D4
Wellington Pl EH6 ..... 94 A3
Wellington Sch EH26 ..... 222 C3
Wellington St EH7 ..... 93 F1
Wellmyre FK10 ..... 11 D2
Wellpark EH52 ..... 116 C4
Wellpark Cres FK7 ..... 6 C2
Wellpark Terr FK4 ..... 58 A3
Wellside EH41 ..... 131 F4
Wellside Pl FK1 ..... 60 A3
Welsh Gdns FK9 ..... 2 A4
Welsh Rd EH47 ..... 169 F3
Wemyss Ct KY11 ..... 46 C3
Wemyss Gdns EH21 ..... 127 E3
Wemyss Pl
Cockenzie & Port Seton
EH32 ..... 97 E2
Edinburgh EH3 ..... 232 B4
Haddington EH41 ..... 132 A4
Wemyss Place Mews
EH3 ..... 232 B4
Wemyss Rd EH32 ..... 98 C3
Wemyss St
Cowdenbeath KY4 ..... 13 E2
Rosyth KY11 ..... 46 C3
Wemyss Terr EH32 ..... 98 C3
Wemyssfield KY11 ..... 17 D2
Werberdale Mews EH4 ..... 92 C2
Wes Twindygoul Gdns
EH3 ..... 128 B3
Wesley Pl FK7 ..... 82 A4
West Adam St CI18 ..... 233 E2
West Albert Rd FK1 ..... 17 D2
West Annandale St EH7 ..... 93 E2
West Approach Rd
EH3 EH11 ..... 232 A2
West Baldridge Rd KY12 ..... 28 C3
West Bankton EH54 ..... 173 F4
West Barns Prim Sch
EH42 ..... 77 F1
West Bay Rd EH39 ..... 54 A4
West Benhar Rd ML7 ..... 168 A2
West Boreland Rd FK6 ..... 36 B1
West Bow EH1 ..... 233 D2
West Bowling Green St
EH6 ..... 93 F3
West Bridge St FK1 ..... 60 A3
West Brighton Cres
EH15 ..... 125 D4
West Broomhill Rd KY3 ..... 50 C4
West Bryson Rd EH11 ..... 122 C3
West Burnside EH52 ..... 114 C3
West Cairn Cres EH26 ..... 203 F3
West Caiystane Rd EH10 ..... 154 A3
West Calder High Sch
EH55 ..... 173 D3
West Calder Sta EH55 ..... 172 B4
West Carmuirs Loan FK5 ..... 58 C3
West Carnethy Ave
EH13 ..... 153 E4
West Castle Rd EH10 ..... 123 D3
West Catherine Pl EH12 ..... 122 C4
West Cherrybank EH6 ..... 93 E3
West Church Dr FK3 ..... 40 A1
West Clifton Farm Cotts
EH55 ..... 149 E4
West Coates EH12 ..... 122 B4
West Colinton Ho EH13 ..... 153 D3
West College St EH1 ..... 233 D2
West Craigs Ave EH12 ..... 120 C3
West Craigs Cres EH12 ..... 120 C4
West Cres EH34 ..... 161 F2
West Croft EH28 ..... 119 F1
West Cromwell St EH6 ..... 93 F3
West Crosscauseway
EH8 ..... 233 E1
West Ct
Edinburgh, Niddrie Mains
EH16 ..... 124 C2
Edinburgh, Ravelston EH4 ..... 92 B1
West Dr Dunfermline KY12 ..... 29 D2
Larbert FK5 ..... 38 B1
West End EH55 ..... 172 B1
West End Gdns FK10 ..... 10 A3
West End Pl EH11 ..... 122 C3
West Fenton Cotts EH32 ..... 72 C4
West Fergus Pl KY11 ..... 17 D2
West Ferryfield EH5 ..... 92 C2
West Fountain Pl EH11 ..... 122 C3
West Gate Rd FK3 ..... 62 A4
West Glen Ave FK6 ..... 146 C3
West Gorgie Pk EH14 ..... 122 B2
West Gorgie Pl EH14 ..... 122 B2
West Grange Gdns EH9 ..... 123 E2
West Granton Rd EH5 ..... 92 B3
West Harbour Rd
Charlestown KY11 ..... 45 D2
Cockenzie & Port Seton
EH32 ..... 97 D4
Edinburgh EH5 ..... 92 C4
West Harwood Crofts
EH55 ..... 196 B3
West Holmes Gdns
EH21 ..... 126 C2
West James St KY11 ..... 5 A3
West Johnstone St FK12 ..... 5 D3
West La KY4 ..... 13 D1
West Leven St KY3 ..... 50 C4

West Link Rd KY9 ..... 2 B3
West Links Rd EH31 ..... 51 F1
West Loan EH32 ..... 96 C1
West Loan Ct EH32 ..... 127 F4
West Lodge Gdns FK10 ..... 9 F2
West Lorimer Pl EH32 ..... 97 D2
West Lothian Coll of F Ed
EH48 ..... 145 E3
West Main St
Armadale EH48 ..... 143 F3
Blackburn EH47 ..... 171 E4
Broxburn EH52 ..... 117 E3
Harthill ML7 ..... 168 C3
Uphall EH52 ..... 116 C2
Whitburn EH47 ..... 169 F3
West Mains Ind Est FK3 ..... 61 A4
West Mains Rd EH9 ..... 123 F1
West Mains St EH32 ..... 71 E2
West Maitland St EH12 ..... 232 A2
West March St KY1 ..... 17 E4
West Mayfield EH9 ..... 123 F2
West Mill La EH4 ..... 232 A3
West Mill Rd EH13 ..... 152 C3
West Montgomery Pl [S]
EH7 ..... 93 F1
West Muir Rd EH55 ..... 172 B1
West Murrayfield FK7 ..... 7 E1
West Nethertown St
KY12 ..... 29 D1
West Newington Pl EH9 ..... 123 F3
West Nicolson St EH8 ..... 233 E2
West Norton Pl EH7 ..... 233 F4
West Park Gr FK5 ..... 117 D3
West Park Pl EH11 ..... 122 C3
West Pilton Ave EH4 ..... 92 B2
West Pilton Bank EH4 ..... 92 B3
West Pilton Cres EH4 ..... 92 A3
West Pilton Crossway
EH4 ..... 92 B3
West Pilton Dr EH4 ..... 92 B3
West Pilton Gdns EH4 ..... 92 B3
West Pilton Gn EH4 ..... 92 B3
West Pilton Lea EH4 ..... 92 B3
West Pilton Loan EH4 ..... 92 B3
West Pilton March EH4 ..... 92 B3
West Pilton Pk EH4 ..... 92 B3
West Pilton Pl EH4 ..... 92 B3
West Pilton Rd EH4 ..... 92 B3
West Pilton Rise EH4 ..... 92 B3
West Pilton St EH4 ..... 92 B3
West Pilton Terr EH4 ..... 92 B3
West Pilton View EH4 ..... 92 B2
West Pk Carnock KY12 ..... 27 F2
Lochgelly KY5 ..... 14 A4
West Port Dunbar EH42 ..... 78 B1
Dysart KY1 ..... 18 A4
Edinburgh EH1 ..... 232 C2
Linlithgow EH49 ..... 84 C4
West Port Pl EH49 ..... 84 C3
West Powburn EH9 ..... 123 F2
West Preston St EH8 ..... 123 F3
West Prim Sch KY1 ..... 17 D1
West Quality St KY1 ..... 18 A4
West Rd Charlestown KY11 ..... 45 D2
Haddington EH41 ..... 131 F4
West Register St EH2 ..... 233 D4
West Register Street La
EH2 ..... 233 D4
West Relugas Rd EH9 ..... 123 E2
West Richmond St EH8 ..... 233 E2
West Savile Rd EH16 ..... 123 F2
West Savile Terr EH9 ..... 123 F2
West Scotland Street La [1]
EH3 ..... 93 E1
West Seaside EH32 ..... 96 C1
West Shore Rd EH5 ..... 92 B4
West Shore Road Trad Est
EH5 ..... 92 B4
West Silvermills La EH3 ..... 93 D1
West Sq EH11 ..... 46 C3
West St EH26 ..... 220 C2
West Stirling St FK12 ..... 4 C4
West Telferton EH7 ..... 94 C1
West Tollcross EH3 ..... 232 B1
West Torbain KY2 ..... 16 B4
West Vennel FK10 ..... 10 A3
West Way KY11 ..... 48 A3
West Werberside EH4 ..... 92 C2
West Windygoul EH33 ..... 128 A3
West Windygoul Gdns
EH33 ..... 128 A2
West Winnelstrae EH5 ..... 92 C2
West Woods EH4 ..... 92 C2
West Wynd KY1 ..... 17 E3
Westbank Ct EH33 ..... 129 E3
Westbank Gdns EH33 ..... 129 E3
Westbank Loan EH15 ..... 95 D1
Westbank Pl EH15 ..... 95 D1
Westbank Rd EH15 ..... 95 D1
Westbank St EH15 ..... 95 D1
Westbank Terr EH33 ..... 129 E3
Westburn Ave
Cowdenbeath KY4 ..... 13 D1
Edinburgh EH14 ..... 152 A4
Falkirk FK1 ..... 59 F2
Westburn Gdns EH14 ..... 152 A4
Westburn Gr EH14 ..... 152 A4
Westburn Middlefield
EH14 ..... 152 B4
Westburn Pk EH14 ..... 152 A4
Westburn Prim Sch
EH14 ..... 121 C1
Westcliffe Ct FK3 ..... 61 F3
Westcraigs Pk EH48 ..... 142 B2
Westcraigs Rd
Blackridge EH48 ..... 142 B2
Harthill ML7 ..... 168 C3

Westend Pl EH39 ..... 54 A4
Wester Bankton EH54 ..... 174 A4
Wester Bogie Rd KY2 ..... 16 A4
Wester Broom Ave EH12 ..... 121 E3
Wester Broom Dr EH12 ..... 121 E3
Wester Broom Gdns
EH12 ..... 121 E3
Wester Broom Gr EH12 ..... 121 E3
Wester Broom Pl EH12 ..... 121 E3
Wester Broom Terr EH12 ..... 121 E3
Wester Coates Ave EH12 ..... 122 C4
Wester Coates Gdns
EH12 ..... 122 C4
Wester Coates Pl EH12 ..... 122 C4
Wester Coates Rd EH12 ..... 122 C4
Wester Coates Terr EH12 ..... 122 C4
Wester Drylaw Ave EH4 ..... 92 A2
Wester Drylaw Dr EH4 ..... 92 A2
Wester Drylaw Pk EH4 ..... 92 B2
Wester Drylaw Pl EH4 ..... 92 A2
Wester Drylaw Row EH4 ..... 92 B1
Wester Hailes Pk EH14 ..... 152 B4
Wester Hailes Rd EH14 ..... 152 B4
Wester Hailes Sta EH14 ..... 152 B4
Wester Row EH14 ..... 120 C1
Wester Steil EH10 ..... 122 C1
Westerdunes Pk EH39 ..... 53 E4
Westergate Rd FK1 ..... 60 A1
Westerlands Dr FK8 ..... 7 D3
Westerlea Ct FK9 ..... 2 A3
Westerlea Dr FK9 ..... 2 A3
Westerlea (Sch for
Spastic Children) EH12 ..... 122 B4
Westermains EH48 ..... 143 F3
Western Ave Crossford KY12 ..... 28 A1
Falkirk FK2 ..... 60 A3
Western Gdns EH12 ..... 122 B4
Western General Hospl
EH4 ..... 92 B2
Western Pl EH12 ..... 122 B4
Western Terr EH12 ..... 122 B4
Westerton Dr 20 B4
Westerton Dr FK9 ..... 2 A4
Westerton Rd
Broxburn EH52 ..... 118 A3
Grangemouth FK3 ..... 61 F4
Westerton Terr FK2 ..... 39 E2
Westfield EH14 ..... 24 A2
Westfield Ave EH11 ..... 122 B3
Westfield Ct EH42 ..... 78 B3
Westfield Dr EH22 ..... 156 C1
Westfield Dr EH22 ..... 156 C1
Westfield Gr
Crossgates KY4 ..... 30 C3
Dalkeith EH22 ..... 156 C1
Westfield Pk EH22 ..... 156 C1
Westfield Pl EH11 ..... 36 C1
Westfield Prim Sch EH48 ..... 112 C2
Westfield Rd EH11 ..... 122 B3
Westfield Rdbt FK2 ..... 60 C3
Westfield St EH11 ..... 157 D2
Westfield St
Edinburgh EH11 ..... 122 B3
Falkirk FK2 ..... 60 C3
Westgarth Ave EH13 ..... 153 D3
Westgate Dunbar EH42 ..... 78 B2
Mid Calder EH53 ..... 148 A2
North Berwick EH39 ..... 54 A4
Westhall Cres KY12 ..... 27 E1
Westhall Gdns
Edinburgh EH10 ..... 123 D3
Uphall EH52 ..... 117 D2
Westhall Rd EH52 ..... 117 F2
Westhouse Ave EH22 ..... 183 F3
Westhouse Dr EH22 ..... 183 F3
Westhouse St EH22 ..... 183 F3
Westhouses Rd EH22 ..... 183 F3
Westmill Rd EH10 ..... 182 A4
Westmill Wynd EH18 ..... 182 A4
Westminster Pl FK5 ..... 38 C2
Westpoint EH42 ..... 78 B1
Westquarter Ave FK2 ..... 61 D1
Westquarter Prim Sch
FK2 ..... 61 D1
Westray Terr FK1 ..... 60 B1
Westside Plaza Sh Ctr
EH14 ..... 152 B4
Westview EH49 ..... 84 B4
Westview Cres FK10 ..... 4 B1
Westwater St KY5 ..... 14 A4
Westwood Ave EH17 ..... 17 F4
Westwood Pk EH54 ..... 146 C4
Westwood View EH17 ..... 29 F2
Westwood View EH15 ..... 94 C4
Wharry Rd FK12 ..... 4 C4
Wheatfield Gr EH20 ..... 181 D4
Wheatfield Loan EH20 ..... 155 D1
Wheatfield Pl EH11 ..... 122 B3
Wheatfield Rd EH11 ..... 122 B3
Wheatfield St EH11 ..... 122 C3
Wheatfield Terr EH11 ..... 122 B3
Wheatfield Wlk EH20 ..... 181 D4
Wheatlands Ave FK4 ..... 58 A3
Wheatlands Pl FK4 ..... 58 A3
Whim Rd EH31 ..... 51 F1
Whin Park Ind Est EH22 ..... 97 D2
Whin Pk EH32 ..... 97 D2
Whinbank EH54 ..... 147 F3
Whinhill EH15 ..... 124 B3
Whinneyknowe KY11 ..... 68 B3
Whinniehill Terr KY12 ..... 27 E3
Whinny Hill Cres KY11 ..... 47 D1
Whinnyburn Pl KY11 ..... 46 B3
Whinrig EH52 ..... 117 E3
Whins of Milton Sch FK7 ..... 7 D1
Whins Rd EH15 ..... 95 D1
Whins Rd Alloa FK10 ..... 10 B4
Stirling FK7 ..... 7 D1
Whinwell Rd FK8 ..... 2 A1

Whirlbut Cres KY11 ..... 29 D1
Whirlbut St KY11 ..... 29 D1
Whitburn Acad EH47 ..... 170 B4
Whitburn Rd
Bathgate EH48 ..... 144 C2
Livingston EH54 ..... 147 E2
Whitdale Prim Sch EH47 ..... 170 B3
White Castle EH14 ..... 166 B3
White Hart St EH42 ..... 157 D2
White Horse Cl EH8 ..... 233 F3
White Pk EH11 ..... 122 C3
White St EH47 ..... 170 A3
White's Cl EH22 ..... 157 D2
Whitecraig Ave EH21 ..... 126 C1
Whitecraig Cres EH21 ..... 126 C1
Whitecraig Gdns EH21 ..... 126 C1
Whitecraig Gdns E EH21 ..... 126 C1
Whitecraig Prim Sch
EH21 ..... 126 C1
Whitecraig Rd EH21 ..... 126 C1
Whitecross Prim Sch
EH49 ..... 83 F3
Whitedalehead Rd EH47 ..... 170 B3
Whitedales EH10 ..... 154 B3
Whitefield Neuk KY12 ..... 29 F3
Whitefield Rd KY12 ..... 29 F3
Whitegates Pl FK1 ..... 59 E2
Whitehall Rd EH30 ..... 89 E4
Whitehill Ave EH21 ..... 126 A2
Whitehill Dr
Blackburn EH47 ..... 171 E4
Dalkeith EH22 ..... 157 E1
Whitehill Farm Rd EH21 ..... 126 A2
Whitehill Gdns EH21 ..... 126 A2
Whitehill Gr EH22 ..... 157 E1
Whitehill Ind Est EH48 ..... 145 E1
Whitehill Pl
Rosewell EH24 ..... 181 E1
Stirling FK8 ..... 7 D3
Whitehill Rd
Blackburn EH47 ..... 145 E1
Edinburgh EH21 ..... 125 E2
Whitehill St EH21 ..... 125 F2
Whitehill View EH47 ..... 171 E4
Whitehouse Loan EH9 ..... 123 E3
Whitehouse Rd
Edinburgh EH4 ..... 91 D2
Stirling FK7 ..... 7 E4
Whitelaw Cres KY11 ..... 29 E1
Whitelaw Dr EH48 ..... 145 F3
Whitelaw Pl KY11 ..... 29 E1
Whitelaw Rd KY11 ..... 29 E1
Whitelaw St EH48 ..... 142 B1
Whitelea Cres EH14 ..... 177 E4
Whitelea Rd EH14 ..... 177 E4
Whiteloch Rd EH33 ..... 129 E3
Whitemoss Rd EH27 ..... 149 F1
Whitemyre Ct KY11 ..... 28 B3
Whitequarries Ind Est
EH52 ..... 88 B1
Whites Quay KY11 ..... 47 F1
Whiteside EH48 ..... 144 C3
Whiteside Ind Est EH48 ..... 144 C2
Whitesideloan FK2 ..... 82 C4
Whitestone Pl EH48 ..... 145 E1
Whitingford EH6 ..... 93 E3
Whitson Cres EH11 ..... 122 A3
Whitson Gr EH11 ..... 122 A3
Whitson Pl E EH11 ..... 122 A3
Whitson Pl W EH11 ..... 122 A3
Whitson Rd EH11 ..... 122 A3
Whitson Terr EH11 ..... 122 A3
Whitson Way EH11 ..... 122 A3
Whitson Wlk EH11 ..... 122 A3
Whitten La EH49 ..... 84 C4
Whittinghame Dr EH41 ..... 132 A4
Whittinghame Dr EH41 ..... 132 B4
Wholeflats Rd FK2 ..... 61 F2
Wholequarter Ave FK2 ..... 61 E1
Whyte Pl [3] EH7 ..... 94 A1
Whyte St Harthill ML7 ..... 168 C3
Loanhead EH20 ..... 181 D4
Whyte Wlk KY11 ..... 29 F2
Whytehouse Ave KY1 ..... 17 E4
Whyteman's Brae KY1 ..... 17 E4
Whytemans Brae Hospl
KY1 ..... 17 D4
Whytescauseway KY1 ..... 17 E4
Wilderness Rdbt EH54 ..... 173 E3
Wilderness The FK2 ..... 22 B2
Wildridge Way KY5 ..... 14 A4
Wilfred Terr [6] EH6 ..... 94 A1
Wilkieston Rd EH28 ..... 119 E1
William Black Pl EH30 ..... 89 E4
William Booth Pl FK7 ..... 7 D2
William Jameson Pl EH15 ..... 95 D1
William St
Dunfermline KY12 ..... 29 D2
Edinburgh EH3 ..... 232 A3
Kirkcaldy KY1 ..... 17 D1
William Street La NE EH3 ..... 232 A3
William Street La NW EH3 ..... 232 A3
William Street La SW EH3 ..... 232 A3
William Younger Ctr
(Mus) EH8 ..... 233 F3
Williamfield Ave FK7 ..... 7 D2
Williamfield Sq [2] EH15 ..... 125 D4
Williamson Ave FK2 ..... 39 F3
Williamson Pl FK2 ..... 60 B4
Williamson St EH6 ..... 93 E3
Williamston Intc EH54 ..... 148 A1
Williamston Prim Sch

Willow Dr KY1 ..... 17 D4
Willow Gr Dunfermline KY11 ..... 46 C4
Livingston EH54 ..... 148 A3
Willow Pk EH47 ..... 193 F3
Willow Rd EH22 ..... 183 F3
Willow Tree Pl EH14 ..... 151 E2
Willowbank EH54 ..... 147 F3
Willowbank Row EH6 ..... 93 E3
Willowbrae EH2 ..... 82 B4
Willowbrae Ave EH8 ..... 124 B4
Willowbrae Gdns EH8 ..... 124 B4
Willowbrae Rd EH8 ..... 124 B4
Willowdean EH49 ..... 86 B2
Willowpark (Specl Sch)
EH11 ..... 122 B3
Willows The
Cairneyhill KY12 ..... 27 E1
Tullibody FK10 ..... 4 A1
Wilson Ave Dalkeith EH22 ..... 157 E2
Denny FK6 ..... 36 B1
Falkirk FK1 ..... 59 E3
Kirkcaldy KY2 ..... 17 D3
Polmont FK2 ..... 61 F1
Prestonpans EH32 ..... 96 C1
Wilson Dr Bannockburn FK7 ..... 7 E1
Falkirk FK1 ..... 59 E3
Wilson Gdns FK1 ..... 59 E3
Wilson Rd Falkirk FK1 ..... 58 B2
Wilson St Falkirk FK1 ..... 59 E3
Gorebridge EH23 ..... 183 E1
Livingston EH54 ..... 146 C2
Shotts ML7 ..... 212 A4
Wilson St Blairhall KY12 ..... 26 A4
Cowdenbeath KY4 ..... 13 E2
Grangemouth FK3 ..... 61 E3
Penicuik EH26 ..... 203 F3
Townhill KY12 ..... 29 E4
Wilson Terr
Broxburn EH52 ..... 117 D3
Stoneyburn EH47 ..... 171 D1
Wilson Way KY11 ..... 46 B1
Wilson Wlk EH33 ..... 128 C3
Wilson's Cl KY12 ..... 29 D2
Wilson's Pk EH15 ..... 95 D1
Wilsontown Rd ML11 ..... 215 F1
Wilton Rd Carluke ML8 ..... 230 A1
Edinburgh EH16 ..... 123 F2
Winchburgh Cotts EH52 ..... 87 F1
Winchburgh Prim Sch
EH52 ..... 87 F1
Winchester Ave EH4 ..... 36 C2
Windlebrook KY11 ..... 47 D4
Windmill Knowe KY4 ..... 30 C3
Windmill La EH8 ..... 233 E1
Windmill Pl KY1 ..... 18 A4
Windmill Rd KY1 ..... 17 F4
Windmill St EH8 ..... 233 D1
Windsor Ave FK1 ..... 59 F2
Windsor Cres Falkirk FK1 ..... 59 F2
Haddington FK2 ..... 83 D3
Penicuik EH26 ..... 204 A3
Windsor Dr Denny FK6 ..... 36 B2
Falkirk FK1 ..... 59 F2
Penicuik EH26 ..... 204 A3
Windsor Gdns Alloa FK10 ..... 9 F4
Falkirk FK1 ..... 59 F2
Musselburgh EH21 ..... 126 C3
Windsor Park Dr EH21 ..... 126 C3
Windsor Park Pl EH21 ..... 126 C3
Windsor Park Terr EH21 ..... 126 C3
Windsor Pl
Edinburgh EH15 ..... 125 D4
Shotts ML7 ..... 191 F3
Windsor Rd Falkirk FK1 ..... 59 F2
Penicuik EH26 ..... 204 A3
Windsor Sq EH26 ..... 204 A3
Windsor St Edinburgh EH7 ..... 93 F1
Menstrie FK11 ..... 5 D3
Shotts ML7 ..... 191 F3
Windsor Street La EH7 ..... 93 F1
Windsor Terr EH26 ..... 204 A3
Windygate KY2 ..... 16 C1
Windygates Rd EH39 ..... 54 A3
Windygoul Cres EH33 ..... 128 C3
Windyhill Ave FK10 ..... 4 B2
Windyknowe Pk EH48 ..... 144 C3
Windyknowe Prim Sch
EH48 ..... 144 B3
Wingate Cres EH42 ..... 78 B1
Winifred Cres KY2 ..... 17 D3
Winifred St KY2 ..... 17 D3
Winterfield Mains EH42 ..... 78 A1
Winterfield Pl EH42 ..... 78 A1
Winton Cl
New Winton EH33 ..... 129 D2
Tranent EH33 ..... 128 C2
Winton Dr EH10 ..... 154 B2
Winton Gdns EH10 ..... 154 B2
Winton Gr Edinburgh EH10 ..... 154 B2
Tranent EH33 ..... 128 C2
Winton Loan
Edinburgh EH10 ..... 154 B2
Tranent EH33 ..... 128 C2
Winton Pk
Cockenzie & Port Seton
EH32 ..... 97 E2
Edinburgh EH10 ..... 154 A2
Winton Pl EH33 ..... 128 B3

Winton Terr
Edinburgh EH10 .... **154** A3
New Winton EH33 .... **129** D2
Winton Way EH33 .... **128** B2
Wishart Ave
Bonnyrigg and Lasswade
EH19 .... **182** B4
North Berwick EH39 .... **54** B3
Wishart Dr FK7 .... **7** E2
Wishart Pl
Dalkeith EH22 .... **156** C1
Kirkcaldy KY1 .... **17** F3
Wishaw Terr EH7 .... **94** A2
Wisp Gn EH15 .... **125** D2
Wisp The EH15 .... **125** D2
Witchbrae KY12 .... **29** D2
Wolfe Rd FK1 .... **60** B2
Wolrige Rd EH16 .... **155** D4
Wolseley Cres EH8 .... **94** B1
Wolseley Pl EH8 .... **94** B1
Wolsey Ave EH19 .... **182** B3
Wood Avens FK10 .... **4** B1
Wood Dr EH47 .... **169** F3
Wood Lea FK10 .... **23** F3
Wood Pl Livingston EH54 ... **147** E2
Rosyth KY11 .... **46** C3
Wood Rd KY11 .... **46** B1
Wood St FK3 .... **61** E4
Wood's Ct EH19 .... **182** A4
Woodbank KY4 .... **13** D1
Woodbank Gr KY12 .... **26** B4
Woodbine Terr EH6 .... **94** A2
Woodburn Ave
Dalkeith EH22 .... **157** E1
Redding FK2 .... **61** D1
Woodburn Bank EH22 ...... **157** E2
Woodburn Cres
Bonnybridge FK4 .... **57** F2
Oakley KY12 .... **26** C4
Redding FK2 .... **61** D1
Woodburn Dr
Alloa FK10 .... **4** C1
Dalkeith EH22 .... **157** D2

Woodburn Gdns
Dalkeith EH22 .... **157** E2
Falkirk FK2 .... **60** C3
Woodburn Gr EH22 .... **157** E1
Woodburn Loan EH22 .... **157** E2
Woodburn Medway EH22 ... **157** E2
Woodburn Pk EH22 .... **157** E2
Woodburn Pl EH22 .... **157** E2
Woodburn Prim Sch
EH22 .... **157** E2
Woodburn Rd
Dalkeith EH22 .... **157** E2
Falkirk FK2 .... **60** B3
Woodburn St
Dalkeith EH22 .... **157** E2
Falkirk FK2 .... **60** C3
Woodburn Terr
Dalkeith EH22 .... **157** E2
Edinburgh EH10 .... **123** D2
Woodburn View EH22 .... **157** E2
Woodburn Way FK12 .... **5** D3
Woodbush EH42 .... **78** C1
Woodbush Brae EH42 .... **78** C1
Woodbush Ct EH42 .... **78** C1
Woodbush Pl EH42 .... **78** C1
Woodend Ind Est KY4 ...... **13** D1
Woodend Pk EH25 .... **180** C2
Woodend Pl KY4 .... **13** D1
Woodend Rd ML8 .... **230** A1
Woodend Wlk EH48 .... **143** F3
Woodfield Ave EH13 .... **152** C3
Woodfield Pk
Bilston EH25 .... **180** B3
Edinburgh EH13 .... **152** C3
Woodhall Ave EH14 .... **152** B3
Woodhall Bank EH13 .... **152** C3
Woodhall Dr EH14 .... **152** B3
Woodhall Gr EH13 .... **152** C3
Woodhall Millbrae EH14 ... **152** C3
Woodhall Pl EH34 .... **160** C3
Woodhall Rd EH34 .... **160** B3
Woodhall Terr EH14 .... **152** B3
Woodhead Farm Rd KY12 ... **25** F1
Woodhead Gr EH48 .... **143** E3
Woodhead Pl EH48 .... **144** C3
Woodhead St KY12 .... **26** A1

Woodhill Ct FK3 .... **61** E3
Woodhill Gr KY12 .... **28** A1
Woodhill Rd EH48 .... **142** A2
Woodland Way FK6 .... **57** E4
Woodlands FK10 .... **5** F1
Woodlands Bank KY11 ...... **48** A2
Woodlands Cotts EH48 ..... **144** A3
Woodlands Cres FK1 .... **60** A2
Woodlands Dr
Bo'ness EH51 .... **63** E3
Brightons FK2 .... **82** C4
Crossford KY12 .... **28** A1
Woodlands Gr
Armadale EH48 .... **144** A3
Edinburgh EH15 .... **124** C3
Townhill KY12 .... **29** E4
Woodlands High Sch FK1 ... **60** A2
Woodlands Pk EH54 .... **146** C4
Woodlands Rd KY2 .... **16** B3
Woodlands Terr KY12 .... **26** A4
Woodlands The KY11 .... **46** C3
Woodlea Gdns FK10 .... **5** D1
Woodlea Pk FK10 .... **10** A4
Woodmill Cres KY11 .... **29** E2
Woodmill High Sch KY11 ... **29** F2
Woodmill Pl KY11 .... **29** F2
Woodmill Rd KY11 .... **29** E2
Woodmill St KY11 .... **29** D2
Woodmill Terr KY11 .... **29** D2
Woodmuir Pl EH55 .... **194** C3
Woodmuir Prim Sch
EH55 .... **194** C3
Woodmuir Rd
Breich EH55 .... **194** C3
Whitburn EH47 .... **170** B3
Woodrow EH23 .... **183** E1
Woodside KY4 .... **13** E2
Woodside Ave KY11 .... **46** C3
Woodside Ct
Cambusbarron FK7 .... **6** B3
Falkirk FK1 .... **60** A2
Woodside Dr EH26 .... **203** F3
Woodside Gdns
Brightons FK2 .... **82** C4
Musselburgh EH21 .... **126** C3
Woodside Gr FK5 .... **59** E4

Woodside Pl
Bridgend EH49 .... **86** B2
Fallin FK7 .... **8** B2
Woodside Rd Alloa FK10 ... **4** C1
Forrestfield ML6 .... **141** D2
Stirling FK8 .... **2** A2
Tullibody FK10 .... **4** A1
Woodside St KY11 .... **46** C3
Woodside Terr
Bridgend EH49 .... **86** B2
Clackmannan FK10 .... **10** C2
Edinburgh EH15 .... **125** E4
Falkirk FK1 .... **60** A2
Tarbrax EH55 .... **217** F2
Woodstock Pl EH16 .... **124** A1
Woodville Ct EH52 .... **117** E2
Woodville Terr EH6 .... **94** A2
Wooer St 4 FK1 .... **60** A2
Woolfords Cotts EH55 ...... **217** D4
Woolmet Cres EH22 .... **156** A4
Wordie Rd FK7 .... **6** C2
Wotherspoon Cres EH48 ... **143** F3
Wotherspoon Dr EH51 ...... **63** E3
Wright Pl Kirkcaldy KY1 ..... **17** E4
Lochgelly KY5 .... **14** A4
Wright St FK2 .... **60** A3
Writers Ct EH42 .... **78** B2
Wynd The Alva FK12 .... **5** D4
Dalgety Bay KY11 .... **48** B2
Gifford EH41 .... **163** F3
Ormiston EH35 .... **159** F4
Wyndford Ave EH52 .... **117** D3
Wyndford Pl EH52 .... **117** D3
Wyvern Pk EH9 .... **123** E2
Wyvis Pk EH26 .... **204** A4
Wyvis Pl ML7 .... **192** A2

Yardheads EH6 .... **93** F3
Yardley Pl FK12 .... **39** D1
Yarrow St EH26 .... **204** A4
Yarrow Pl FK3 .... **61** F3
Yeaman La EH11 .... **122** C3
Yeaman Pl EH11 .... **122** C3
Yester Pl EH41 .... **100** C1
Yester Prim Sch EH41 ...... **163** F2
Yetholm Pk KY12 .... **28** C1

Yetts The FK7 .... **6** B?
Yew Gr EH54 .... **148** A?
Yew Terr FK2 .... **61** D?
Yewlands Cres EH16 .... **155** D?
Yewlands Gdns EH16 .... **155** D?
Yieldshields Rd ML8 .... **231** E?
York Arc FK3 .... **40** B?
York Dr FK2 .... **60** B?
York La Edinburgh EH1 ...... **233** D?
Grangemouth FK3 .... **40** B?
York Pl Dunfermline KY12 ... **29** E?
Edinburgh EH1 .... **233** D?
Kirkcaldy KY1 .... **17** F?
York Rd Edinburgh EH5 ..... **93** E?
North Berwick EH39 .... **54** A?
York Sq FK3 .... **40** B?
York St FK2 .... **60** B?
Young Ave EH33 .... **128** B?
Young Cres EH48 .... **144** C?
Young Ct KY4 .... **13** E?
Young Sq EH54 .... **173** E?
Young St Edinburgh EH2 ... **232** B?
West Calder EH55 .... **172** B?
Young Street La N EH2 ..... **232** B?
Young Street La S EH2 ..... **232** B?
Young Terr KY4 .... **13** D2
Young's Terr KY1 .... **17** E?
Youngs Rd EH52 .... **118** A?
Yule Pl EH47 .... **145** E?
Yule Terr EH47 .... **171** E4

Zealandia Rd KY11 .... **46** A1
Zetland Dr
Grangemouth FK3 .... **61** D?
Laurieston FK2 .... **61** D2
Zetland Pl Edinburgh EH5 ... **93** D?
Lochgelly KY5 .... **14** A?
Skinflats FK2 .... **39** E?
Zetland St FK10 .... **11** D2
Zetland Terr FK2 .... **61** F1
Zoo (Royal Zoological Society of Scotland)
EH12 .... **121** F4

The Street Atlases are available from all good bookshops or by mail order direct from the publisher. Orders can be made in the following ways. **By phone** Ring our special Credit Card Hotline on **01933 443863** during office hours (9am to 5pm) or leave a message on the answering machine, quoting your full credit card number plus expiry date and your full name and address. **By post or fax** Fill out the order form below (you may photocopy it) and post it to: **Philip's Direct, 27 Sanders Road, Wellingborough, Northants NN8 4NL** or fax it to: **01933 443849**. Before placing an order by post, by fax or on the answering machine, please telephone to check availability and prices.

STREET ATLASES ORDER FORM

COLOUR LOCAL ATLASES

	PAPERBACK	
	Quantity @ £3.50 each	£ Total
CANNOCK, LICHFIELD, RUGELEY	☐ 0 540 07625 2	➤
DERBY AND BELPER	☐ 0 540 07608 2	➤
NORTHWICH, WINSFORD, MIDDLEWICH	☐ 0 540 07589 2	➤
PEAK DISTRICT TOWNS	☐ 0 540 07609 0	➤
STAFFORD, STONE, UTTOXETER	☐ 0 540 07626 0	➤
WARRINGTON, WIDNES, RUNCORN	☐ 0 540 07588 4	➤

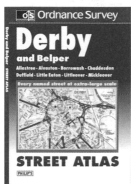

COLOUR REGIONAL ATLASES

	HARDBACK	SPIRAL	POCKET	
	Quantity @ £10.99 each	Quantity @ £8.99 each	Quantity @ £6.75 each	£ Total
BERKSHIRE	☐ 0 540 06170 0	☐ 0 540 06172 7	☐ 0 540 06173 5	➤
	Quantity @ £10.99 each	Quantity @ £8.99 each	Quantity @ £4.99 each	£ Total
MERSEYSIDE	☐ 0 540 06480 7	☐ 0 540 06481 5	☐ 0 540 06482 3	➤
	Quantity @ £12.99 each	Quantity @ £9.99 each	Quantity @ £4.99 each	£ Total
DURHAM	☐ 0 540 06365 7	☐ 0 540 06366 5	☐ 0 540 06367 3	➤
EAST KENT	☐ 0 540 07483 7	☐ 0 540 07276 1	☐ 0 540 07287 7	➤
WEST KENT	☐ 0 540 07366 0	☐ 0 540 07367 9	☐ 0 540 07369 5	➤
EAST SUSSEX	☐ 0 540 07306 7	☐ 0 540 07307 5	☐ 0 540 07312 1	➤
WEST SUSSEX	☐ 0 540 07319 9	☐ 0 540 07323 7	☐ 0 540 07327 X	➤
	Quantity @ £12.99 each	Quantity @ £9.99 each	Quantity @ £5.50 each	£ Total
GREATER MANCHESTER	☐ 0 540 06485 8	☐ 0 540 06486 6	☐ 0 540 06487 4	➤
TYNE AND WEAR	☐ 0 540 06370 3	☐ 0 540 06371 1	☐ 0 540 06372 X	➤
	Quantity @ £12.99 each	Quantity @ £9.99 each	Quantity @ £5.99 each	£ Total
BIRMINGHAM & WEST MIDLANDS	☐ 0 540 07603 1	☐ 0 540 07604 X	☐ 0 540 07605 8	➤
BUCKINGHAMSHIRE	☐ 0 540 07466 7	☐ 0 540 07467 5	☐ 0 540 07468 3	➤
CHESHIRE	☐ 0 540 07507 8	☐ 0 540 07508 6	☐ 0 540 07509 4	➤
DERBYSHIRE	☐ 0 540 07531 0	☐ 0 540 07532 9	☐ 0 540 07533 7	➤
EDINBURGH & East Central Scotland	☐ 0 540 07653 8	☐ 0 540 07654 6	☐ 0 540 07656 2	➤

PHILIP'S

STREET ATLASES
ORDER FORM

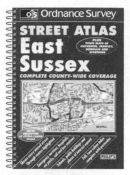

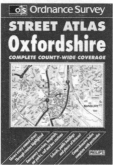

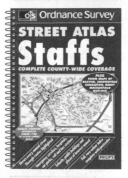

PHILIP'S

COLOUR REGIONAL ATLASES

	HARDBACK	SPIRAL	POCKET	
	Quantity @ £12.99 each	Quantity @ £9.99 each	Quantity @ £5.99 each	£ Total
GLASGOW & West Central Scotland	☐ 0 540 07648 1	☐ 0 540 07649 X	☐ 0 540 07651 1	➤
NORTH HAMPSHIRE	☐ 0 540 07471 3	☐ 0 540 07472 1	☐ 0 540 07473 X	➤
SOUTH HAMPSHIRE	☐ 0 540 07476 4	☐ 0 540 07477 2	☐ 0 540 07478 0	➤
HERTFORDSHIRE	☐ 0 540 06174 3	☐ 0 540 06175 1	☐ 0 540 06176 X	➤
OXFORDSHIRE	☐ 0 540 07512 4	☐ 0 540 07513 2	☐ 0 540 07514 0	➤
SURREY	☐ 0 540 06435 1	☐ 0 540 06436 X	☐ 0 540 06438 6	➤
WARWICKSHIRE	☐ 0 540 07560 4	☐ 0 540 07561 2	☐ 0 540 07562 0	➤
SOUTH YORKSHIRE	☐ 0 540 06330 4	☐ 0 540 06331 2	☐ 0 540 06332 0	➤
WEST YORKSHIRE	☐ 0 540 06329 0	☐ 0 540 06327 4	☐ 0 540 06328 2	➤
	Quantity @ £14.99 each	Quantity @ £9.99 each	Quantity @ £5.99 each	£ Total
LANCASHIRE	☐ 0 540 06440 8	☐ 0 540 06441 6	☐ 0 540 06443 2	➤
NOTTINGHAMSHIRE	☐ 0 540 07541 8	☐ 0 540 075426 6	☐ 0 540 07543 4	➤
STAFFORDSHIRE	☐ 0 540 07549 3	☐ 0 540 07550 7	☐ 0 540 07551 5	➤

BLACK AND WHITE REGIONAL ATLASES

	HARDBACK	SOFTBACK	POCKET	
	Quantity @ £11.99 each	Quantity @ £8.99 each	Quantity @ £3.99 each	£ Total
BRISTOL AND AVON	☐ 0 540 06140 9	☐ 0 540 06141 7	☐ 0 540 06142 5	➤
	Quantity @ £12.99 each	Quantity @ £9.99 each	Quantity @ £4.99 each	£ Total
CARDIFF, SWANSEA & GLAMORGAN	☐ 0 540 06186 7	☐ 0 540 06187 5	☐ 0 540 06207 3	➤
EAST ESSEX	☐ 0 540 05848 3	☐ 0 540 05866 1	☐ 0 540 05850 5	➤
WEST ESSEX	☐ 0 540 05849 1	☐ 0 540 05867 X	☐ 0 540 05851 3	➤

Post to: Philip's Direct,
27 Sanders Road, Wellingborough,
Northants NN8 4NL

◆ Free postage and packing

◆ All available titles will normally be dispatched within 5 working days of receipt of order but please allow up to 28 days for delivery

☐ Please tick this box if you do not wish your name to be used by other carefully selected organisations that may wish to send you information about other products and services

Registered Office: Michelin House, 81 Fulham Road, London SW3 6RB

Registered in England number: 3597451

I enclose a cheque / postal order, for a **total** of

made payable to *Octopus Publishing Group Ltd,* or please debit my

☐ Access ☐ American Express ☐ Visa ☐ Diners

Account no   account by ☐

☐☐☐☐ ☐☐☐☐ ☐☐☐☐ ☐☐☐☐

Expiry date ☐☐ ☐☐

Signature...

Name..

Address..

....

....POSTCODE